A Complement Work of Present
Acupunture and Moxibustion

Acupoints & Meridians

Editors—in—Chief **Liu Gongwang**

Translator—in—chief **Cao Liya**

Translation Revisor **Liu Gongwang**

HUAXIA PUBLISHING HOUSE

《Acupoints and Meridians》

Editor-in-Chief
  Liu Gongwang   Akira Hyodo

Associate Editors-in-Chief
  Jiang Geli   Jiao Mao   Hu Minghai
  Liu Yi   Feng Xuerui   Shang Xiukui

Editors
  Han Lijun   Wang Jing   Zhang Yanjun
  Li Qinghe   Fang Ling   Liang Chunyu
  Han Yu   Liu Yi   Zhu Xiaotang
  Wei Linhai   Fu Junru   Li Chang

Translator-in-Chief
  Cao Liya

Associate Translators-in-Chief
  Liu Changlin   Wang Wei   Zhang Biao
  Chu Lirong   Tan Chunming   Xu Li

Translators
  Miao Rong   Meng Fanjie   Yuan Keming
  Li Jie   Liu Weiwei   Han Juan
  Zhang Ru   Wang Jianjun   Wang Xiuyun
  Meng Xiangwen   Hu Suhui   Su Guixin

English Editor
  Aaron Cote   Tracey Cote   Dara Lia Cuarlas
  Paul Ling   Vouza Aspasia   Tilikidis Alexandros

Translation Revisor
  Liu Gongwang

Supervisors
  Shuji Goto   Dai Ximeng   Donald P. Lauda

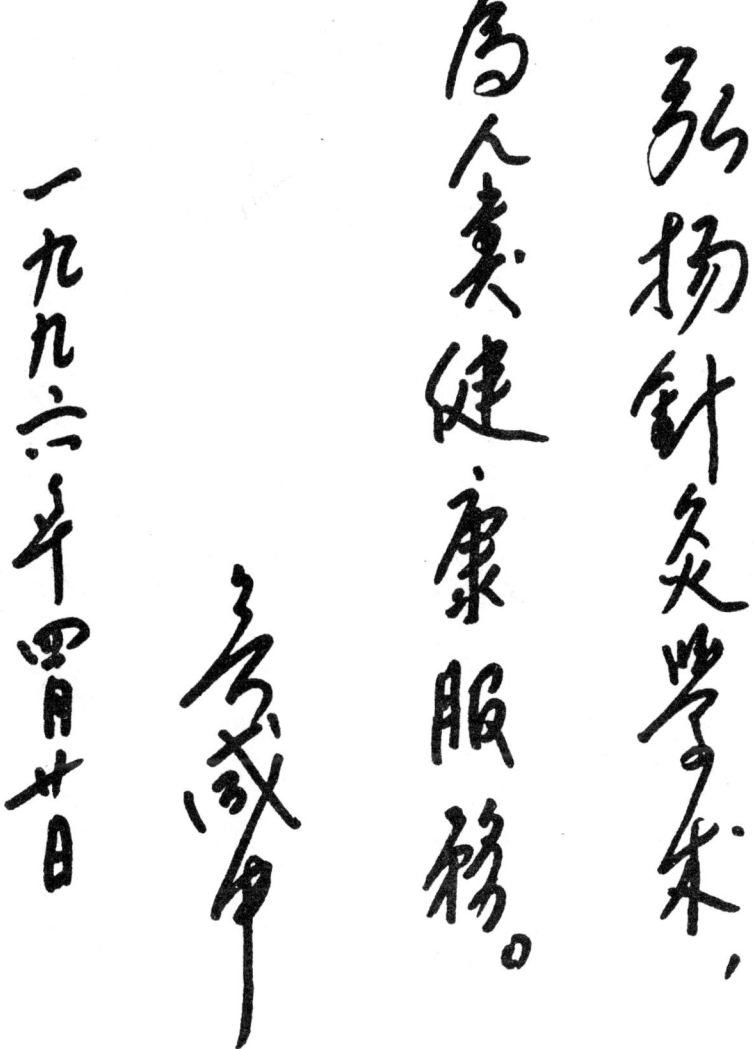

Promote and develop the academic learning of acupuncture and moxibustion and give service to the health of humanity!

Wu Xianzhong
April 20, 1996

(Inscription by Prof. Wu Xianzhong, academician of Academy of Engineering of China, Chairman of the Chinese Association of the Integration of Traditional and Western Medicine)

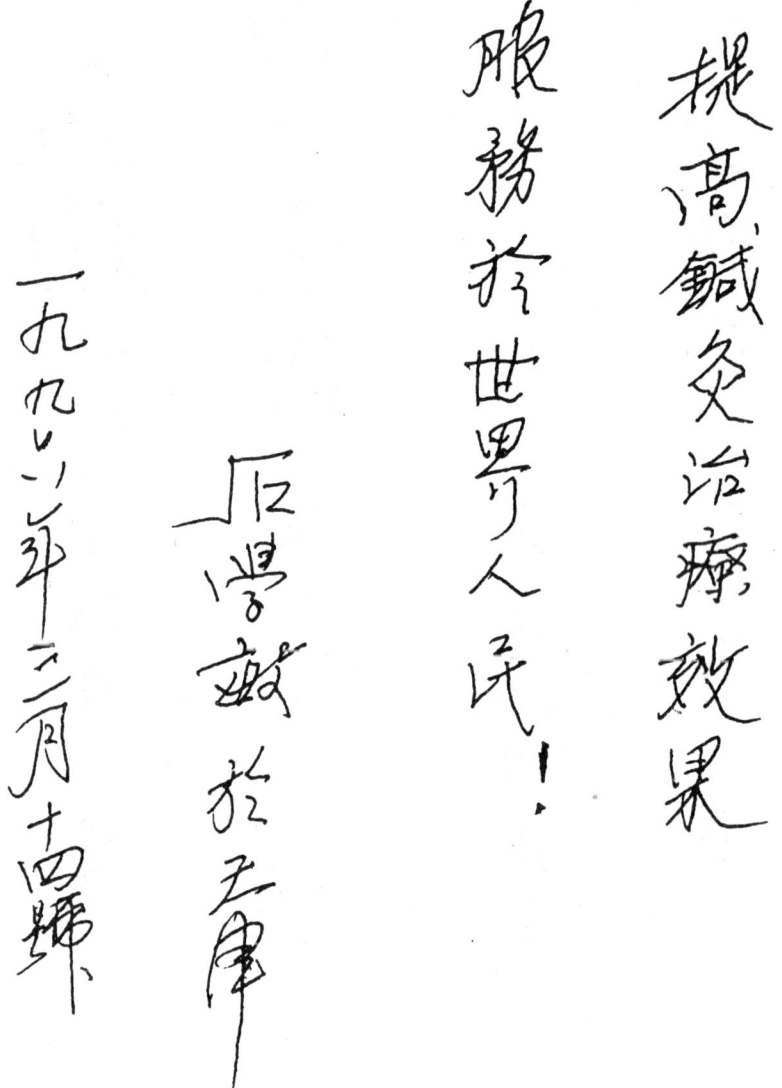

Enhance the curative effect of acupuncture-moxibustion therapy and serve the people of the world!

Shi Xuemin
March 14, 1996

(Inscription by Prof. Shi Xuemin, Member of the Council of China Acupuncture Association, President of the First Hospital Affiliated to Tianjin College of TCM)

Preface

Fundamentals of Acupuncture & Moxibustion and *Clinical Acupuncture & Moxibustion* were published in 1993 and 1996 respectively. Being granted a favor from readers both at home and abroad, the two books have been received an extensive favorable comment, and awarded the 2nd and the 1st prize of publication of Tianjin, China.

Today, the *Acupoints and Meridians* is being put into publication. It serves as a link connecting the two books mentioned above, thereby forms a series which presents a whole system from its theories, meridians and acupoints to the clinical treatment.

Meridians and Acupoints are some lines and points discovered by the ancient people and supposed to connect the body surface with the internal organs. This theory is still guiding the clinical treatment of T. C. M at the present time.

In recent years, further research has been made on meridians and acupoints in respects of biology, chemistry and physics. Yet, we still fail to find out a unique tissue and form of their existence.

I believe the theories of T. C. M on meridians and acupoints will serve as a permanent guidance in clinical treatment of T. C. M.

This book is a complete work which merges together the documents of the ancient and present, including plentyful information. According to Chinese National Standard, location and localization of 361 points and 48 extra points are clearly explained in the book. For each point, detailed introduction is given, such as "Name Explanation", "Indication", "Mechanism of Action" and "Regional Anatomy" etc. Some commonly used points are given further explanation based on the present-day research.

This book is characterized in its close combination with clinical practice, brevity in language, clear presentation and exquisity in both pictures and literary compositions.

In the course of translation, the help of Dr. Aaron Cote and Dr. Dara Lia Cuarlas etc are sought to make revision so that the errors in the versions were corrected to ensure the accuracy of the English translation.

At the time of publication, I am greatly indebted to Dr. Shuji Goto, the President of Goto College of Medical Arts and Sciences, Tokyo, Japan, for his help in completing this book.

Liu Gongwang
1997. 10. 10

CONTENTS

Chapter One　　General Introduction to the System of Meridians, Collaterals and Acupoints　1
　Ⅰ. **Discovery and Development of the Meridians, Collaterals and Acupoints**　2
　Ⅱ. **Classification and Nomenclature of the System of Meridians, Collaterals and Acupoints**　4
　Ⅲ. **Locations of the Meridians, Collaterals and Acupoints**　6
　　1. Locations of the Meridians and Colaterals　6
　　　1) Distribution on the Head　6
　　　2) Distribution in the Neck　7
　　　3) Distribution on the Back and at the Lumbar Region　7
　　　4) Distribution in the Thoracic and Abdominal Regions　7
　　　5) Distribution in the Upper Limbs　8
　　　6) Distribution in the Lower Limbs　9
　　2. Methods of Locating Acupoints　11
　　　1) Anatomical Landmarks　11
　　　2) Proportional Measurement　13
　　　3) Finger Measurement　13
　Ⅳ. **The Therapeutic Properties of the Meridians, Collaterals and Acupoints**　16
　　1. The Therapeutic Properties of the Meridians and Collaterals　16
　　2. The Therapeutic Properties of Acupoints　30
　　　1) The Local and Adjacent Therapeutic Properties of Acupoints　30
　　　2) The Remote Therapeutic Properties of Acupoints　30
　　　3) The Special Therapeutic Properties of Acupoints　30

Chapter Two　　The Eight Extra Meridians　42
　Ⅰ. **System of the Du Meridian**　42
　　1. Distribution of the Du Meridian and Its Collaterals　42
　　　1) Course of the Du Meridian　42
　　　2) Course of the Large Collaterals　42
　　　3) The Acupoints　42
　　2. Symptoms and Signs of Disorders of the Du Meridian and Its Large Collaterals　43
　　　1) Symptoms and Signs of the Disorders of the Du Meridian　43
　　　2) Symptoms and Signs of the Disorders of the Large Collaterals　43

II. **System of the Ren Meridian** 44
  1. Distribution of the Ren Meridian and Its Collaterals 44
    1) Course of the Ren Meridian 44
    2) Course of the Collaterals 44
  2. Symptoms and Signs of the Disorders of the Ren Meridian and Its Collaterals 45
    1) Symptoms and Signs of the Disorders of the Ren Meridian 45
    2) Symptoms and Signs of the Disorders of the Collaterals 45

Chapter Three The Three Yin Meridians of Hand 51

III. **System of the Lung Meridian of Hand Taiyin** 51
  1. Distribution of the Lung Meridian of Hand Taiyin 51
    1) Course of the Meridian 51
    2) Course of the Collaterals 51
    3) Divergent Meridian 52
    4) Muscle Region 52
    5) Cutaneous Region 53
    6) Acupoints 53
  2. Symptoms and Signs of the Disorders of the Lung Meridian of Hand Taiyin 54
    1) Symtoms and Sighs of the Disovders of the Meridian 54
    2) Symptoms and Signs of the Disorders of the Collaterals 55
    3) Symptoms and Signs of the Disorders of the Muscle Region 55

IV. **System of the Pericardium Meridian of Hand Jueyin** 56
  1. Distribution of the Pericardium Meridian of Hand Jueyin 56
    1) Course of the Meridian 56
    2) Course of the Collaterals 57
    3) Divergent Meridian 57
    4) Muscle Region 58
    5) Cutaneous Region 59
    6) Acupoints 59
  2. Symptoms and Signs of the Disorders of the Pericardium Meridian of Hand Jueyin 60
    1) Symptoms and Signs of the Disorders of the Meridian 60
    2) Symptoms and Signs of the Disorders of the Collaterals 60
    3) Symptoms and Signs of the Disorders of the Muscle Region 60

V. **System of the Heart Meridian of Hand Shaoyin** 60
  1. Distribution of the Heart Meridian of Hand Shaoyin 60
    1) Course of the Meridian 60
    2) Course of the Collaterals 61
    3) Divergent Meridian 62
    4) Muscle Region 62
    5) Cutaneous Region 63
    6) Acupoints 63
  2. Symptoms and Signs of the Disorders of the Heart Meridian of Hand Shaoyin 64
    1) Symptoms and Signs of the Disorders of the Meridian 64

2)Symptoms and Signs of the Disorders of the Collaterals　64
3)Symptoms and Signs of the Disorders of the Muscle Region　64

Chapter Four　　The Three Yang Meridians of Hand　65

VI. System of the Large Intestine Meridian of Hand Yangming　65
1. Distribution of the Large Intestine Meridian of Hand Yangming　65
   1)Course of the Meridian　65
   2)Course of the Collaterals　66
   3)Divergent Meridian　67
   4)Muscle Region　67
   5)Cutaneous Region　68
   6)Acupoints　68
2. Symptoms and Signs of the Disorders of the Large Intestine Meridian of Hand Yangming　68
   1)Symptoms and Signs of the Disorders of the Meridian　68
   2)Symptoms and Signs of the Disorders of the Collaterals　68
   3)Symptoms and Signs of the Disorders of the Muscle Region　68

VII. System of the Sanjiao Meridian of Hand Shaoyang　69
1. Distribution of the Sanjiao Meridian of Hand Shaoyang　69
   1)Course of the Meridian　69
   2)Course of the Collaterals　69
   3)Divergent Meridian　70
   4)Muscle Region　71
   5)Cutaneous Region　71
   6)Acupoints　72
2. Symptoms and Signs of Sanjiao Meridian of Hand Shaoyang　72
   1)Symptoms and Signs of the Disorders of the Meridian　72
   2)Symptoms and Signs of the Disorders of the Collaterals　72
   3)Symptoms and Signs of the Disorders of the Muscle Region　72

VIII. System of The Small Intestine Meridian of Hand Taiyang　73
1. Distribution of the Small Intestine Meridian of Hand Taiyang　73
   1)Course of the Meridian　73
   2)Course of the Collaterals　73
   3)Divergent Meridian　73
   4)Muscle Region　73
   5)Cutaneous Region　74
   6)Acupoints　75
2. Symptoms and Signs of the Small Intestine Meridian of Hand Taiyang　76
   1)Symptoms and Signs of the Disorders of the Meridian　76
   2)Symptoms and Signs of the Disorders of the Collaterals　76
   3)Symptoms and Signs of the Disorders of the Muscle Region　76

Chapter Five　　The Three Yin Meridians of Foot　77

IX. System of the Spleen Meridian of Foot Taiyin 77
1. Distribution of the Spleen Meridian of Foot Taiyin 77
    1) Course of the Meridian 77
    2) Course of the Collaterals 77
    3) Divergent Meridian 78
    4) Muscle Region 79
    5) Cutaneous Region 80
    6) Acupoints 81
2. Symptoms and Signs of the Disorders of the Spleen Meridian of Foot Taiyin 81
    1) Symptoms and Signs of the Disorders of the Meridian 81
    2) Symptoms and Signs of the Disorders of the Collaterals 81
    3) Symptoms and Signs of the Disorders of the Muscle Region 81

X. System of the Liver Meridian of Foot Jueyin 82
1. Distribution of the Liver Meridian of Foot Jueyin 82
    1) Course of the Meridian 82
    2) Course of the Collaterals 82
    3) Divergent Meridian 83
    4) Muscle Region 84
    5) Cutaneous Region 85
    6) Acupoints 85
2. Symptoms and Signs of the Disorders of the Liver Meridian of Foot Jueyin 85
    1) Symptoms and Signs of the Disorders of the Meridian 85
    2) Symptoms and Signs of the Disorders of the Collaterals 85
    3) Symptoms and Signs of the Disorders of the Muscle Region 85

XI. System of the Kidney Meridian of Foot Shaoyin 86
1. Distribution of the Kidney Meridian of Foot Shaoyin 86
    1) Course of the Meridian 86
    2) Course of the Collaterals 87
    3) Divergent Meridian 88
    4) Muscle Region 89
    5) Cutaneous Region 90
    6) Acupoints 90
2. Symptoms and Signs of the Disorders of the Kidney Meridian of Foot Shaoyin 90
    1) Symptoms and Signs of the Disorders of the Meridian 90
    2) Symptoms and Signs of the Disorders of the Collaterals 90
    3) Symptoms and Signs of the Disorders of the Muscle Region 90

Chapter Six   The Three Yang Meridians of Foot 92
XII. System of the Stomach Meridian of Foot Yangming 92
1. Distribution of the Stomach Meridian of Foot Yangming 92
    1) Course of the Meridian 92
    2) Course of the Collaterals 92
    3) Divergent Meridian 95

4)Muscle Region　95
　　　5)Cutaneous Region　95
　　　6)Acupoints　95
　2. Symptoms and Signs of the Disorders of the Stomach Meridian of Foot Yangming　95
　　　1)Symptoms and Signs of the Disorders of the Meridian　95
　　　2)Symptoms and Signs of the Disorders of the Collaterals　96
　　　3)Symptoms and Signs of the Disorders of the Muscle Region　96

XIII. System of the Gallbladder Meridian of Foot Shaoyang　97
　1. Distribution of the Gallbladder Meridian of Foot Shaoyang　97
　　　1)Course of the Meridian　97
　　　2)Course of the Collaterals　97
　　　3)Divergent Meridian　97
　　　4)Muscle Region　98
　　　5)Cutaneous Region　100
　　　6)Acupoints　100
　2. Symptoms and Signs of the Disorders of the Gallbladder Meridian of Foot Shaoyang　100
　　　1)Symptoms and Signs of the Disorders of the Meridian　100
　　　2)Symptoms and Signs of the Disorders of the Collaterals　100
　　　3)Symptoms and Signs of the Disorders of the Muscle Region　100

XIV. System of the Bladder Meridian of Foot Taiyang　101
　1. Distribution of the Bladder Meridian of Foot Taiyang　101
　　　1)Course of the Meridian　101
　　　2)Course of the Collaterals　102
　　　3)Divergent Meridian　102
　　　4)Muscle Region　102
　　　5)Cutaneous Region　102
　　　6)Acupoints　102
　2. Symptoms and Signs of the Bladder Meridian of Foot Taiyang　103
　　　1)Symptoms and Signs of the Disorders of the Meridian　103
　　　2)Symptoms and Signs of the Disorders of the Collaterals　105
　　　3)Symptoms and signs of the Disorders of the Muscle Region　105

Chapter Seven　Acupoints of the Du Meridian and Ren Meridian 106
　I. **Acupoints of the Du Meridian**　106
　　DU 1 Changqiang(长强)(Long Strength)　106
　　DU 2 Yaoshu(腰俞)(Lumbar Shu)　108
　　DU 3 Yaoyangguan(腰阳关)(Lumbar Yang Pass)　109
　　DU 4 Mingmen(命门)(Life Gate)　110
　　DU 5 Xuanshu(悬枢)(Hanging Pivot)　111
　　DU 6 Jizhong(脊中)(Middle of Spine)　111
　　DU 7 Zhongshu(中枢)(Middle Pivot)　112
　　DU 8 Jinsuo(筋缩)(Muscle Spasm)　112

DU 9 Zhiyang(至阳)(Reaching Yang)　113
DU 10 Lingtai(灵台)(Spirit Platform)　114
DU 11 Shendao(神道)(Spirit Path)　115
DU 12 Shenzhu(身柱)(Body Pillar)　116
DU 13 Taodao(陶道)(Kiln Path)　117
DU 14 Dazhui(大椎)(Big Vertebra)　118
DU 15 Yamen(哑门)(Dumb Gate)　119
DU 16 Fengfu(风府)(Wind Mansion)　120
DU 17 Naohu(脑户)(Brain Door)　121
DU 18 Qiangjian(强间)(Rigid Fissure)　122
DU 19 Houding(后顶)(Posterior Vertex)　123
DU 20 Baihui(百会)(Hundred Convergences)　123
DU 21 Qianding(前顶)(Antevo-Vertex)　125
DU 22 Xinhui(囟会)(Fodtanel Convergences)　126
DU 23 Shangxing(上星)(Upper Star)　126
DU 24 Shenting(神庭)(Spirit Courtyard)　127
DU 25 Suliao(素髎)(White Crevice)　128
DU 26 Shuigou(水沟)(Ditch)　129
DU 27 Duiduan(兑端)(Upperlip Projection)　130
DU 28 Yinjiao(龈交)(Gum Meeting)　131

II. Acupoints of the Ren Meridian　136

RN 1 Huiyin(会阴)(Converging Yin)　136
RN 2 Qugu(曲骨)(Crooked Bone)　137
RN 3 Zhongji(中极)(Middle Extremity)　138
RN 4 Guanyuan(关元)(Life Pivot)　139
RN 5 Shimen(石门)(Stone Gate)　141
RN 6 Qihai(气海)(Qi Sea)　142
RN 7 Yinjiao(阴交)(Yin Meeting)　143
RN 8 Shenque(神阙)(Spirit Palace)　144
RN 9 Shuifen(水分)(Water Divisions)　145
RN 10 Xiawan(下脘)(Lower Part of Stomach)　146
RN 11 Jianli(建里)(Building Li)　146
RN 12 Zhongwan(中脘)(Middle Part of Stomach)　147
RN 13 Shangwan(上脘)(Upper Part of Stomach)　149
RN 14 Juque(巨阙)(Great palace)　150
RN 15 Jiuwei(鸠尾)(Dove Tail)　151
RN 16 Zhongting(中庭)(Middle Courtyard)　152
RN 17 Danzhong(膻中)(Middle of Chest)　153
RN 18 Yutang(玉堂)(Jade Hall)　154
RN 19 Zigong(紫宫)(Purple Palace)　154
RN 20 Huagai(华盖)(Organ's Conopy)　155
RN 21 Xuanji(璇玑)(Rotating Jade)　156
RN 22 Tiantu(天突)(Heaven Projection)　156

RN 23 Lianquan(廉泉)(Corner Fountain) 157
RN 24 Chengjiang(承浆)(Saliva Receiver) 159

Chapter Eight   Acupoints of Three Yin Meridians of Hand   164

Ⅲ. Acupoints of the Lung Meridian of Hand Taiyin 164

LU 1 Zhongfu(中府)(Central Mansion) 164
LU 2 Yunmen(云门)(Cloud Gate) 165
LU 3 Tianfu(天府)(Heaven Mansion) 166
LU 4 Xiabai(侠白)(White Insertion) 167
LU 5 Chize(尺泽)(Foot Marsh) 167
LU 6 Kongzui(孔最)(Convergence Hole) 169
LU 7 Lieque(列缺)(Branching Cleft) 170
LU 8 Jingqu(经渠)(Passing Ditch) 171
LU 9 Taiyuan(太渊)(Supreme Abyss) 172
LU 10 Yuji(鱼际)(Fish Border) 174
LU 11 Shaoshang(少商)(Lesser Shang) 175

Ⅳ. Acupoints of the Pericardium Meridian of Hand Jueyin 178

PC 1 Tianchi(天池)(Heaven Pool) 178
PC 2 Tianquan(天泉)(Heaven Fountain) 179
PC 3 Quze(曲泽)(Marshon Bend) 179
PC 4 Ximen(郄门)(Cleft Gate) 180
PC 5 Jianshi(间使)(Intermediary) 181
PC 6 Neiguan(内关)(Inner Conjunction) 183
PC 7 Daling(大陵)(Big Hill) 184
PC 8 Laogong(劳宫)(Labour Palace) 186
PC 9 Zhongchong(中冲)(Centre Rush) 187

Ⅴ. Acupoints of the Heart Meridian of Hand Shaoyin 190

HT 1 Jiquan(极泉)(Extreme Fountain) 190
HT 2 Qingling(青灵)(Green Spirit) 191
HT 3 Shaohai(少海)(Shaoyin Sea) 191
HT 4 Lingdao(灵道)(Spirit Path) 193
HT 5 Tongli(通里)(Inner Communication) 193
HT 6 Yinxi(阴郄)(Yin Cleft) 194
HT 7 Shenmen(神门)(Spirit Gate) 195
HT 8 Shaofu(少府)(Shaoyin Mansion) 197
HT 9 Shaochong(少冲)(Shaoyin Rush) 197

Chapter Nine   Acupoints of Three Yang Meridians of Hand   200

Ⅵ. Acupoints of the Large Intestine Meridian of Hand Yangming 200

LI 1 Shangyang(商阳)(Shangyang) 200
LI 2 Erjian(二间)(Second Interval) 201
LI 3 Sanjian(三间)(Third Interval) 202

LI 4 Hegu(合谷)(Enclosed Valley)　203
LI 5 Yangxi(阳溪)(Yang Stream)　205
LI 6 Pianli(偏历)(Lateral Passage)　206
LI 7 Wenliu(温溜)(Warm-Remaining)　207
LI 8 Xialian(下廉)(Lower Side)　207
LI 9 Shanglian(上廉)(Upper Side)　208
LI 10 Shousanli(手三里)(Hand Three Li)　209
LI 11 Quchi(曲池)(Pool on Bend)　210
LI 12 Zhouliao(肘髎)(Elbow Crevice)　211
LI 13 Shouwuli(手五里)(Hand Five Li)　212
LI 14 Binao(臂臑)(Median Side of Upper Arm)　213
LI 15 Jianyu(肩髃)(Shoulder Corner)　214
LI 16 Jugu(巨骨)(Great Bone)　215
LI 17 Tianding(天鼎)(Heaven Vessel)　216
LI 18 Futu(扶突)(Hyoid Border)　216
LI 19 Kouheliao(口禾髎)(Spike Crevice of Mouth)　217
LI 20 Yingxiang(迎香)(Welcome Fragrance)218

VII. Acupoints of the Sanjiao Meridian of Hand Shaoyang　222

SJ 1 Guanchong(关冲)(Pass Rush)　222
SJ 2 Yemen(液门)(Fluid Gate)　223
SJ 3 Zhongzhu(中渚)(Middle Islet)　224
SJ 4 Yangchi(阳池)(Yang Pool)　225
SJ 5 Waiguan(外关)(Outer Conjunction)　226
SJ 6 Zhigou(支沟)(Branching Ditch)　227
SJ 7 Huizong(会宗)(Converging Meridians)　228
SJ 8 Sanyangluo(三阳络)(Three Yang Collaterals)　229
SJ 9 Sidu(四渎)(Four Canals)　229
SJ 10 Tianjing(天井)(Heaven Well)　230
SJ 11 Qinglengyuan(清冷渊)(Pure Cold Abyss)　231
SJ 12 Xiaoluo(消泺)(Thawing River-bed)　231
SJ 13 Naohui(臑会)(Nao Convergence)　232
SJ 14 Jianliao(肩髎)(Shoulder Crevice)　233
SJ 15 Tianliao(天髎)(Heaven Crevice)　233
SJ 16 Tianyou(天牖)(Heaven Window)　234
SJ 17 Yifeng(翳风)(Wind Screen)　235
SJ 18 Chimai(瘈脉)(Convulsion Collateral)　236
SJ 19 Luxi(颅息)(Skull Signal)　236
SJ 20 Jiaosun(角孙)(Auditory Angle)　237
SJ 21 Ermen(耳门)(Ear Gate)　238
SJ 22 Erheliao(耳和髎)(Ear Harmony Crevice)　238
SJ 23 Sizhukong(丝竹空)(Musical Instrument Hole)239

VIII. Acupoints of the Small Intestine Meridian of Hand Taiyang　243

SI 1 Shaoze(少泽)(Lesser Marsh)　243

SI 2 Qiangu(前谷)(Front Valley) 244
SI 3 Houxi(后溪)(Back Stream) 245
SI 4 Wangu(腕骨)(Wrist Bone) 246
SI 5 Yanggu(阳谷)(Yang Valley) 247
SI 6 Yanglao(养老)(Aging Nourishment) 248
SI 7 Zhizheng(支正)(Branch from Small Intestine Meridian) 249
SI 8 Xiaohai(小海)(Small Intestine Sea) 250
SI 9 Jianzhen(肩贞)(Upright Shoulder) 251
SI 10 Naoshu(臑俞)(Nao Shu) 252
SI 11 Tianzong(天宗)(Heaven Attribution) 252
SI 12 Bingfeng(秉风)(Watching Wind) 253
SI 13 Quyuan(曲垣)(Bend Wall) 253
SI 14 Jianwaishu(肩外俞)(Outer Shoulder Shu) 254
SI 15 Jianzhongshu(肩中俞)(Intro-Shoulder Shu) 254
SI 16 Tianchuang(天窗)(Heaven Window) 255
SI 17 Tianrong(天容)(Heaven Appearance) 256
SI 18 Quanliao(颧髎)(Zygoma Crevice) 257
SI 19 Tinggong(听宫)(Listening Palace) 258

Chapter Ten Acupoints of Three Yin Meridians of Foot 262

Ⅸ. Acupoints of the Spleen Meridian of Foot Taiyin 262

SP 1 Yinbai(隐白)(Hidden White) 262
SP 2 Dadu(大都)(Big Capital) 263
SP 3 Taibai(太白)(Supreme Whiteness) 264
SP 4 Gongsun(公孙)(Grandfather Grandson) 265
Sp 5 Shangqiu(商丘)(Shang Mound) 266
SP 6 Sanyinjiao(三阴交)(Three Yin Meeting) 267
SP 7 Lougu(漏谷)(Leaky Valley) 269
SP 8 Diji(地机)(Earth Pivot) 270
SP 9 Yinlingquan(阴陵泉)(Yin Hill Fountain) 271
SP 10 Xuehai(血海)(Blood Sea) 272
SP 11 Jimen(箕门)(Squatting Gate) 273
SP 12 Chongmen(冲门)(Rushing Gate) 274
SP 13 Fushe(府舍)(Mansion Room) 275
SP 14 Fujie(腹结)(Abdominal Convergence) 276
SP 15 Daheng(大横)(Big Cross) 276
SP 16 Fuai(腹哀)(Abdomen Sob) 277
SP 17 Shidou(食窦)(Feed Point) 277
SP 18 Tianxi(天溪)(Heaven Stream) 278
SP 19 Xiongxiang(胸乡)(Chest Village) 279
SP 20 Zhourong(周荣)(Encircling Nourishment) 279
SP 21 Dabao(大包)(General Control) 280

Ⅹ. Acupoints of the Liver Meridian of Foot Jueyin 284

LR 1 Dadun(大敦)(Big Thick)　284
LR 2 Xingjian(行间)(Inter Column)　285
LR 3 Taichong(太冲)(Supreme Rush)　286
LR 4 Zhongfeng(中封)(Middle Seal)　288
LR 5 Ligou(蠡沟)Gourd Ditch　289
LR 6 Zhongdu(中都)(Middle Capital)　289
LR 7 Xiguan(膝关)(Knee Pass)　289
LR 8 Ququan(曲泉)(Spring on Bend)　290
LR 9 Yinbao(阴包)(Yin Wrappage)　292
LR 10 Zuwuli(足五里)(Foot Five Li)　292
LR 11 Yinlian(阴廉)(Yin Side)　293
LR 12 Jimai(急脉)(Acute Pulse)　293
LR 13 Zhangmen(章门)(Chapter Gate)　294
LR 14 Qimen(期门)(Cyclic Gate)295

XI. Acupoints of the Kidney Meridian of Foot Shaoyin　300

KI 1 Yongquan(涌泉)(Bubbling Fountain)　300
KI 2 Rangu(然谷)(Blazing Valley)　301
KI 3 Taixi(太溪)(Supreme Stream)　303
KI 4 Dazhong(大钟)(Big Bell)　304
KI 5 Shuiquan(水泉)(Water Fountain)　305
KI 6 Zhaohai(照海)(Shining Sea)　306
KI 7 Fuliu(复溜)(Returning Carrent)　307
KI 8 Jiaoxin(交信)(Meeting Spleen Meridian)　308
KI 9 Zhubin(筑宾)(Guest Building)　309
KI 10 Yingu(阴谷)(Yin Valley)　310
KI 11 Henggu(横骨)(Transverse Bone)　311
KI 12 Dahe(大赫)(Big Glory)　312
KI 13 Qixue(气穴)(Qi Point)　313
KI 14 Siman(四满)(Quadruple Fullness)　313
KI 15 Zhongzhu(中注)(Centre Injection)　314
KI 16 Huangshu(肓俞)(Vitals Shu　315
KI 17 Shangqu(商曲)(Shang Crook)　315
KI 18 Shiguan(石关)(Stone Pass)　316
KI 19 Yindu(阴都)(Yin Capital)　317
KI 20 Futonggu(腹通谷)(Passing Valley)　317
KI 21 Youmen(幽门)(Hades Gate)　318
KI 22 Bulang(步廊)(Walking Corridor)　319
KI 23 Shenfeng(神封)(Spirit Seal)　320
KI 24 Lingxu(灵墟)(Spirit Burial-ground)　320
KI 25 Shencang(神藏)(Spirit Storage)　321
KI 26 Yuzhong(彧中)(In Literature)　321
KI 27 Shufu 俞府(Shu Mansion)　322

Chapter Eleven   Acupoints of Three Yang Meridians of Foot   327
XII. Acupoints of the Stomach Meridian of Foot Yangming   327

- ST 1 Chengqi(承泣)(Tear Receiver)   327
- ST 2 Sibai(四白)(Four Whites)   328
- ST 3 Juliao(巨髎)(Great Crevice)   329
- ST 4 Dicang(地仓)(Earth Granary)   329
- ST 5 Daying(大迎)(Big Welcome)   330
- ST 6 Jiache(颊车)(Mandible Angle Chariot)   331
- ST 7 Xiaguan(下关)(Lower Pass)   332
- ST 8 Touwei(头维)(Head Corner)   333
- ST 9 Renying(人迎)(Man's Welcome)   333
- ST 10 Shuitu(水突)(Water Projection)   335
- ST 11 Qishe(气舍)(Qi Room)   335
- ST 12 Quepen(缺盆)(Broken Basin)   336
- ST 13 Qihu(气户)(Qi Door)   337
- ST 14 Kufang(库房)(Store House)   337
- ST 15 Wuyi(屋翳)(Chamber Root)   338
- ST 16 Yingchuang(膺窗)(Chest Window)   339
- ST 17 Ruzhong(乳中)(Middle of Nipple)   339
- ST 18 Rugen(乳根)(Breast Root)   340
- ST 19 Burong(不容)(No Admittance)   341
- ST 20 Chengman(承满)(Fullness Receive)   342
- ST 21 Liangmen(梁门)(Beam Gate)   342
- ST 22 Guanmen(关门)(Pivotal Gate)   343
- ST 23 Taiyi(太乙)(Supreme Yi)   344
- ST 24 Huaroumen(滑肉门)(Slippery Flesh Gate)   344
- ST 25 Tianshu(天枢)(Heaven Pivot)   345
- ST 26 Wailing(外陵)(Outer Hill)   346
- ST 27 Daju(大巨)(Big Greatness)   347
- ST 28 Shuidao(水道)(Water Path)   347
- ST 29 Guilai(归来)(Return)   348
- ST 30 Qichong(气冲)(Qi Rush)   349
- ST 31 Biguan(髀关)(Femoral Pass)   350
- ST 32 Futu(伏兔)(Prostrate Rabbit)   350
- ST 33 Yinshi(阴市)(Yin Market)   351
- ST 34 Liangqiu(梁丘)(Beam Mound)   352
- ST 35 Dubi(犊鼻)(Calf Nose)   352
- ST 36 Zusanli(足三里)(Foot Three Li)   353
- ST 37 Shangjuxu(上巨虚)(Upper Great Void)   356
- ST 38 Tiaokou(条口)(Narrow Openning)   357
- ST 39 Xiajuxu(下巨虚)(Lower Great Void)   358
- ST 40 Fenglong(丰隆)(Abundant Bulge)   359
- ST 41 Jiexi(解溪)(Dispersing Stream)   360

ST 42 Chongyang（冲阳）(Rushing Yang)　361
ST 43 Xiangu（陷谷）(Sinking Valley)　362
ST 44 Neiting（内庭）(Inner Court-Yard)　363
ST 45 Lidui（厉兑）(Sick Mouth)　364

XIII. **Acupoints of the Gallbladder Meridian of Foot Shaoyang**　371

GB 1　Tongziliao（瞳子髎）(Pupil Crevice)　371
GB 2　Tinghui（听会）(Listening Convergence)　372
GB 3　Shangguan（上关）(Upper Pass)　372
GB 4　Hanyan（颔厌）(Jaw Detested)　373
GB 5　Xuanlu（悬颅）(Hanging Skull)　374
GB 6　Xuanli（悬厘）(Deviation From Hanging Skull)　374
GB 7　Qubin（曲鬓）(Twist Temple)　375
GB 8　Shuaigu（率谷）(Leading Valley)　375
GB 9　Tianchong（天冲）(Heaven Rush)　376
GB 10　Fubai（浮白）(Floating White)　377
GB 11　Touqiaoyin（头窍阴）(Head Orifice Yin)　377
GB 12　Wangu（完骨）(Whole bone)　378
GB 13　Benshen（本神）(Spirit Source)　379
GB 14　Yangbai（阳白）(Yang White)　380
GB 15　Toulinqi（头临泣）(Head Falling Tears)　380
GB 16　Muchuang（目窗）(Eye Window)　381
GB 17　Zhengying（正营）(Top Convergence)　382
GB 18　Chengling（承灵）(Spirit Receiver)　382
GB 19　Naokong（脑空）(Brain Hollow)　383
GB 20　Fengchi（风池）(Wind Pool)　383
GB 21　Jianjing（肩井）(Shoulder Well)　385
GB 22　Yuanye（渊腋）(Armpit Abyss)　386
GB 23　Zhejin（辄筋）(Flank Muscle)　387
GB 24　Riyue（日月）(Sun and Moon)　387
GB 25　Jingmen（京门）(Capital Gate)　388
GB 26　Daimai（带脉）(Belt Meridian)　390
GB 27　Wushu（五枢）(Five Pivots)　391
GB 28　Weidao（维道）(Binding Path)　392
GB 29　Juliao（居髎）(Reside Crevice)　392
GB 30　Huantiao（环跳）(Jumping Circle)　393
GB 31　Fengshi（风市）(Wind Market)　394
GB 32　Zhongdu（中渎）(Middle Canal)　395
GB 33　Xiyangguan（膝阳关）(Knee Yang Pass)　396
GB 34　Yanglingquan（阳陵泉）(Yang Hill Fountain)　397
GB 35　Yangjiao（阳交）(Yang Crossing)　398
GB 36　Waiqiu（外丘）(Outer Mound)　399
GB 37　Guangming（光明）(Brightness)　399
GB 38　Yangfu（阳辅）(Yang Aid)　400

GB 39 Xuanzhong（悬钟）(Hanging Bell)　401
GB 40 Qiuxu（丘墟）(Big Mound)　402
GB 41 Zulinqi（足临泣）(Foot Falling Tears)　403
GB 42 Diwuhui（地五会）(Five Convergences)　404
GB 43 Xiaxi（侠溪）(Stream Insertion)　405
GB 44 Zuqiaoyin（足窍阴）(Foot Orifice Yin)　406

XIV. Acupoints of the Bladder Meridian of Foot Taiyang　414

BL 1 Jingming（睛明）(Eye Brightness)　414
BL 2 Cuanzhu（攒竹）(Gathering Eyebrows)　415
BL 3 Meichong（眉冲）(Eyebrow Rush)　416
BL 4 Qucha (Quchai)（曲差）(Crooked Branch)　417
BL 5 Wuchu（五处）(Five Stops)　417
BL 6 Chengguang（承光）(Receiving Light)　418
BL 7 Tongtian（通天）(Reaching Heaven)　418
BL 8 Luoque（络却）(Return Collateral)　419
BL 9 Yuzhen（玉枕）(Jade Occiput)　420
BL 10 Tianzhu（天柱）(Celestial Pillar)　420
BL 11 Dazhu（大杼）(Great Axle)　422
BL 12 Fengmen（风门）(Windy Gate)　423
BL 13 Feishu（肺俞）(Lung Shu)　424
BL 14 Jueyinshu（厥阴俞）(Jueyin Shu)　425
BL 15 Xinshu（心俞）(Heart Shu)　426
BL 16 Dushu（督俞）(Du Shu)　427
BL 17 Geshu（膈俞）(Diaphragm Shu)　428
BL 18 Ganshu（肝俞）(Liver Shu)　429
BL 19 Danshu（胆俞）(Gallbladder Shu)　431
BL 20 Pishu（脾俞）(Spleen Shu)　432
BL 21 Weishu（胃俞）(Stomach Shu)　433
BL 22 Sanjiaoshu（三焦俞）(Triple Warmer Shu)　434
BL 23 Shenshu（肾俞）(Kidney Shu)　435
BL 24 Qihaishu（气海俞）(Energy Sea Shu)　436
BL 25 Dachangshu（大肠俞）(Large Intestine Shu)　437
BL 26 Guanyuanshu（关元俞）(Guan Yuan Shu)　438
BL 27 Xiaochangshu（小肠俞）(Small Intestine Shu)　439
BL 28 Pangguangshu（膀胱俞）(Bladder Shu)　439
BL 29 Zhonglushu（中膂俞）(Intro-back Muscle Shu)　440
BL 30 Baihuanshu（白环俞）(White Ring Shu)　441
BL 31 Shangliao（上髎）(Upper Crevice)　441
BL 32 Ciliao（次髎）(Secondary Crevice)　442
BL 33 Zhongliao（中髎）(Middle Crevice)　443
BL 34 Xialiao（下髎)(Lower Crevice)　444
BL 35 Huiyang（会阳）(Converging Yang)　444
BL 36 Chengfu（承扶）(Supporting by Hand)　445

BL 37 Yinmen （殷门）(Big Red Gate)　445
BL 38 Fuxi （浮郄）(Superficial Crevice)　446
BL 39 Weiyang （委阳）(Popliteal Yang)　446
BL 40 Weizhong （委中）(Popliteal Center)　447
BL 41 Fufen （附分）(Lateral Separation)　448
BL 42 Pohu （魄户）(Soul Shelter)　449
BL 43 Gaohuang （膏肓）(Vital Organs)　450
BL 44 Shentang （神堂）(Spiritual House)　451
BL 45 Yixi （譩譆）(Yi Xi)　452
BL 46 Geguan （膈关）(Diaphragm Pass)　452
BL 47 Hunmen （魂门）(Soul Gate)　453
BL 48 Yanggang （阳纲）(Yang Principles)　453
BL 49 Yishe （意舍）(Thought Refuge)　454
BL 50 Weicang （胃仓）(Stomach Granary)　454
BL 51 Huangmen （肓门）(Huang Gate)　455
BL 52 Zhishi （志室）(Will Cabinet)　456
BL 53 Baohuang （胞肓）(Bladder Vitals)　456
BL 54 Zhibian （秩边）(Lowermost in Order)　457
BL 55 Heyang （合阳）(Combining Yang)　458
BL 56 Chengjin （承筋）(Supporting Tenden)　459
BL 57 Chengshan （承山）(Supporting Hill)　459
BL 58 Feiyang （飞扬）(Flying up)　461
BL 59 Fuyang （跗阳）(Yang of Foot Dorsum)　461
BL 60 Kunlun （昆仑）(Big and High)　462
BL 61 Pucan （仆参）(Worship on Bended Kness)　463
BL 62 Shenmai （申脉）(Stretching Channel)　464
BL 63 Jinmen （金门）(Golden Gate)　465
BL 64 Jinggu （京骨）(Jing Bone)　466
BL 65 Shugu （束骨）(Shu Bone)　467
BL 66 Zutonggu （足通谷）(Passing Valley)　467
BL 67 Zhiyin （至阴）(Reaching Yin)　468

Chapter Twelve　Extraordinary Points　480

I. Points of Head and Neck，EX-HN　480

EX-HN 1 Sishencong （四神聪）(Wisdom Spirit)　480
EX-HN 2 Dangyang （当阳）(Just above Yangbai)　481
EX-HN 3 Yintang （印堂）(Front Hall)　481
EX-HN 4 Yuyao （鱼腰）(Fish Lumbar)　482
EX-HN 5 Taiyang （太阳）(Large Yang)　482
EX-HN 6 Erjian （耳尖）(Ear Tip)　483
EX-HN 7 Qiuhou （球后）(Behind Eyeball)　483
EX-HN 8 Shangyingxian （上迎香）(Upper Yingxiang)　484
EX-HN 9 Neiyingxiang （内迎香）(Inner Yingxiang)　484

EX-HN 10 Juquan（聚泉）(Convergence Spring)　484
EX-HN 11 Haiquan（海泉）(Sea Spring)　485
EX-HN 12 Jinjin（金津）(Gold Fluid)　485
EX-HN 13 Yuye（玉液）(Jade Fluid)　486
EX-HN 14 Yiming（翳明）(Brightness Screen)　486
EX-HN 15 Jingbailao（颈百劳）(Neck Labours)　487

Ⅱ. Points of Chest and Abdomen，EX-CA　487

EX-CA 1 Zigong（子宫）(Uterus)　487

Ⅲ. Points of Back，EX-B　488

EX-B 1 Dingchuan（定喘）(Relief Asthma)　488
EX-B 2 Jiaji（夹脊）(Side of Spine)　488
EX-B 3 Weiwanxiashu（胃脘下俞）(Below Stomach)　489
EX-B 4 Pigen（痞根）(Mass Root)　490
EX-B 5 Xiajishu（下极俞）(Lower Extremity)　490
EX-B 6 Yaoyi（腰宜）(Lumbar Benefit)　491
EX-B 7 Yaoyan（腰眼）(Lumbar Eyes)　491
EX-B 8 Shiqizhui（十七椎）(Seventeenth Vetebrea)　491
EX-B 9 Yaoqi（腰奇）(Lumbar Marvel)　492

Ⅳ. Points of Upper Extremities，EX-UE　492

EX-UE 1 Zhoujian（肘尖）(Elbow Tip)　492
EX-UE 2 Erbai（二白）(Two White)　493
EX-UE 3 Zhongquan（中泉）(Middle Spring)　493
EX-UE 4 Zhongkui（中魁）(Middle Chief)　494
EX-UE 5 Dagukong（大骨空）(Large Bone Hole)　494
EX-UE 6 Xiaogukong（小骨空）(Small Bone Hole)　495
EX-UE 7 Yaotongdian（腰痛点）(Lumbago Point)　495
EX-UE 8 Wailaogong（外劳宫）(Outer Laogong)　496
EX-UE 9 Baxie（八邪）(Eight Evils)　496
EX-UE 10 Sifeng（四缝）(Four Seams)　497
EX-UE 11 Shixuan（十宣）(Ten Drains)　497

Ⅴ. Points of Lower Extremities，EX－LE　498

EX-LE 1 Kuangu（髋骨）(Hip Bone)　498
EX-LE 2 Heding（鹤顶）(Crane Crown)　498
EX-LE 3 Baichongwo（百虫窝）(Worm Nest)　499
EX-LE 4 Neixiyan（内膝眼）(Inner Knee Eyes)　499
EX-LE 5 Xiyan（膝眼）(Knee Eyes)　499
EX-LE 6 Dannang（胆囊）(Gallbladder)　500
EX-LE 7 Lanwei（阑尾）(Appendix)　501
EX-LE 8 Neihuaijian（内踝尖）(Inner Ankle Tip)　501
EX-LE 9 Waihuaijian（外踝尖）(Outer Ankle Tip)　501
EX-LE 10 Bafeng（八风）(Eight Winds)　502
EX-LE 11 Duyin（独阴）(Extremity Yin)　502
EX-LE 12 Qiduan（气端）(Qi Termination)　502

Chapter One

General Introduction to the System of Meridians, Collaterals and Acupoints

  Meridians and collaterals are pathways in which the qi and blood of the human body circulates. They pertain to the Zangfu organs interiorly and extend over the body exteriorly, forming a network and linking tissues and organs into an organic whole. Acupoints are the specific sites through which the meridian qi is accumulated and transported crossing skin, tendons, muscles and joints. Acupoints connect the Zangfu organs interiorly through the routes of the meridians and collaterals, while the meridians and collaterals manifest through their acupoints on the body surface. The acupoints receive needle stimulation and transmit it to the interior of the human body. It is said that the meridians and collaterals are lines while acupoints are points. Acupoints are mostly distributed over the pathway of certain meridians, and in areas where the meridians and collaterals are connected. The meridians, collaterals and acupoints together constitute one system, which is generally called "the meridian-collateral system".

  The theory of the meridian points is of great significance in guiding physiological research, pathological inquiry, disease diagnosis, prognostic analysis and the determination of a treatment principle. It particularly plays an important role in differential diagnosis in fields of acupuncture and moxibustion.

  The meridian theories in T.C.M have substantial contents, such as the concepts of the meridians and collaterals, the actions of the meridians and collaterals, clinical application of meridians and collaterals, the formation of the meridian and collateral system as well as muscle regions, divergent meridians, Biao-Ben and Gen-Jie. These contents are explained in detail in *Fundamentals of Acupuncture & Moxibustion*. The contents concerning Specific Acupoints and Combining Points Method are discussed in *Clinical Acupuncture & Moxibustion*. This book focuses more on meridians, collaterals and acupoints, especially those which have a close relation with the selection of treatment based on differential diagnosis.

Ⅰ. Discovery and Development of the Meridians, Collaterals and Acupoints

The meridians, collaterals and acupoints were discovered one after the other in the past after long periods of medical practice.

It is generally thought that acupoints were discovered before the meridian and collateral system. The meridian and collateral system were discovered in relation to acupoints. Discovery of acupoints underwent different processes such as smaller to larger number and from without having a location and name to having a location and name. In the beginning very few of the basic acupoints were first discovered, however, gradually more and more acupoints were added after predecessors realized the connection between the meridians and collaterals. The acupoints recorded in *Internal Classic* should be considered as basic points, which had a great influence on the formation of the meridians and collaterals.

During the New Stone Age, Bian stones were used as special tools to prick bleeding and to cut running sores (called Bianshi, 砭石). The ancestors used such methods as heat, massage, tapping the body surface, or burning a certain part of the body surface to heal pain. As time passed, individuals learned that certain parts of the human body have the function of curing some diseases. That was the beginning of the discovery of acupoints.

In the Warring States period, the people took the painful part of the body as an acupoint. They believed that acupoints were located at painful parts in the body. At that time, the location and names of acupoints were neither unified nor systematized, it was only called "puncture moxibustion point". After prolonged clinical practice, predecessors realized that the acupoints could treat not only the local disease, but also diseases on the distal parts of the body. That is "treating the major disease", which is mentioned in *Plain Questions · Syncope*.

It has been found in existing medical documents that the meridian theory had been systematized two thousands years before. Acupoints were discovered in many ways. However, it is unlikely they were discovered without the application of acupuncture and moxibustion treatment and the spread of acupuncture knowledge. For example, at that time when acupuncture was applied, needling sensation usually transmitted to distal portions of the body along certain routes. Several acupoints, which had similiar indications, were usually arranged in a line regularly. They were inducted and classified by ancient medical experts according to their functions. These acupoints gradually formed the connecting lines of the meridians and collaterals. According to the analysis of ancient documents, the formation of the early theories of meridians and collaterals were closely related to the four extremities. The eleven meridians on the arms and feet, recorded in the silk books found in the Mawang Tomb, the understanding of the muscle regions, the five Shu points and the Biao-Ben, Gen-Jie, discussed in *Internal Classic* can all prove this viewpoint.

With the development of the ancient medical theories, the relation between meridians and collaterals in the body, the natural environment, Yin and Yang, the Five Elements and the functions of Zangfu organs were all established. These concepts were finally organized into a theoretical system, and thereby establishing a relationship betweeen the Zangfu organs and the meridians and collaterals. These concepts occurred at the same time that acupoints were being organized.

In the book *Internal Classic*, the locations, names and meridians to which the acupoints belonged and the indications were all expounded, thereby laying a foundation for the formation and development of the theory of meridian and acupoints.

Acupoints are also called "Joints" (Jie, 节), "Convergence" (Hui, 会), "Qi Holes" (Qixue, 气穴), "Qi House" (Qifu, 气府), Cracks of bones (Gukong, 骨空) etc, in *Internal Classic*. They were named "Kong Points" (Kongxue, 孔穴) in *A-B Classic of Acupuncture and Moxibustion*. They were named "Point Path" (Xuedao, 穴道) or "point" (Xuewei, 穴位) in the Song Dynasty.

In each chapter of *Internal Classic*, about 160 acupoints are recorded. In the Jin Dynasty, the book *A-B Classic of Acupuncture and Moxibustion* gave a complete record on the locations and indications of acupoints. The total number of acupoints were 349. In the Qing Dynasty, the book *Acupuncture and Moxibustion Meeting the Source* recorded 361 acupoints located on the 14 meridians, which are still applied today. (See Tab. 1-1).

Table 1-1 Typical Medical Books of Past Dynasties and Total Number of Acupoints Recorded

Years (the Christian Era)	Authors	Books	Number of Acupoints		
			One-side Points	Two-side Points	Total
475-221 B.C (the Warring States)		Internal Classic	about 25	about 135	about 160
Wei 256-260 (Three Kingdom) 682 (Tang)	Huang Pumi Sun Simiao	A-B Classic of Acupuncture and Moxibustion A Supplement to Thousand Golden Prescriptions	49	300	349
1026 (Song) 1341 (Yuan)	Wang Weiyi Hua Boren	Bronze Figure of Acupuncture and Moxibustion Exposition of the Fourteen Meridians	51	303	354
1601 (Ming)	Yang Jizhou	Great Compendium of Acupuncture and Moxibustion	51	308	359
1817 (Qing)	Li Xuechuan	Acupuncture and Moxibustion Meeting the Source	52	309	361

(1) Two points were added in *Illustrated Manual of Points for Acupuncture and Moxibustion on a Bronze Statue with Acupoints* and *An Elaboration of the Fourteen Meridians*: Lingtai (DU 10) and Yaoyangguan (DU 3). They were both from *Plain Questions*, which is annotated by Wang Bing. Three bilateral points were added: Gaohuangshu (BL 43) and Jueyinshu (BL 14) were from *Thousand Golden Prescriptions*, Qingling (HT 2) was from *Imperial Benevolent Prescriptions*.

(2) Five bilateral points were added in *Great Compendium of Acupuncture and Moxibustion*: Meichong (BL 3) was from *Classic of Sphygmology*, Dushu (BL 16), Qihaishu (BL 24) and Guanyuanshu (BL 26) were from *Imperial Benevolent Prescriptions*, and Fengshi (BL 13) from *A Handbook of Prescriptions for Emergencies*.

(3) One unilateral point and one bilateral point were added in *Acupuncture and Moxibustion Meeting the Source*. The unilateral point was Zhongshu (DU 7) and the bilateral point Jimai (LR 12), both of them were from *Plain Questions* annotated by Wang Bing.

Internal Classic gave a concrete introduction to the meridians and collaterals, including chapters of "Meridians", "Divergent Meridians", "Muscle Region" and "Pulse Diagnosis" in *Miraculous Pivot* and chapters of "Discussion on Cleft of Bones (骨空论)", "Discussion on Meridians and Collaterals (经络论)" and "Discussion on Cutaneous Regions (皮部论)" in *Plain Questions* are all major medical documents, which laid the foundation for the theory of meridians and collaterals. Later *Classic of Medical Problems* made an elucidation on the eight Extra-meridians. Other explanations in the following ages were all concluded in *Internal Classic* and *Classic of Medical Problems*.

II. Classification and Nomenclature of the System of Meridians, Collaterals and Acupoints

The system of meridians and collaterals is composed of meridian and collateral branches of the large channel which includes the twelve regular meridians and eight extra meridians. In addition, there are twelve divergent meridians, twelve muscle regions and twelve cutaneous regions, which are attached to the twelve regular meridians. Included in the collateral branches of the large channel are the 15 major collaterals, superficial collaterals and minute collaterals, etc. These have already been explained in *Fundamentals of Acupuncture & Moxibustion*.

The system of meridians and collaterals is primarily named after Yin Yang. Three yins and three yangs are derived from original one Yin and one Yang, bearing corresponding relationship between each other.

$$\text{Yin} \begin{bmatrix} \text{Taiyin} \longrightarrow \text{Yangming} \\ \text{Shaoyin} \longrightarrow \text{Taiyang} \\ \text{Jueyin} \longrightarrow \text{Shaoyang} \end{bmatrix} \text{Yang}$$

The three Yin and the three Yang are used to name the meridians, divergent meridians, collateral branches of the large channel and the muscle regions. The three Yin and the three Yang in combination with feet and hands constitute the 12 meridians. The meridians distributed on the medial aspect of the upper extremities are the three Yin meridians of hand, while those distributed on the lateral aspect of the upper extremities are the three Yang meridians of the hand. Those travelling along the medial aspect of the lower extremities are the three Yin meridians of foot, while those travelling along the lateral aspect of the lower extremities are the three Yang meridians of foot.

The eight extra meridians are named in accordance with their functions. For instance, the nomenclature of the Du and Ren meridians is explained as follows. Du means "Governing". Running along the midline of the back, the Du meridians governs all the Yang meridians. Ren means "Fostering" and "Responsibility". Going along the midline of the abdomen, the Ren meridian is responsible for pregnancy and the fetus.

Acupoints are classified into three categories: 1. acupoints of the fourteen meridians. 2. extraordinary acupoints 3. Ashi points.

(1) Acupoints of the fourteen meridians. They refer to the major acupoints distributed across the body, including the acupoints on the twelve regular meridians, Ren and Du Meridians, totalling 670 acupoints, among which, the acupoints on the twelve regular meridians are

distributed symmetrically in pairs on the left and right sides of the body. (309 points on the left side and 309 points on the right, for a total of 618). The acupoints of Du and Ren Meridians are single ones, aligned on the posterior and anterior midlines respectively, (for a total of 52 points).

Among the acupoints of the fourteen Meridians, some acupoints are named Back-Shu points, Front-Mu points, Five-Shu points, Yuan-(Source) points, Luo-(Connecting) points, Xi-(Cleft) points, Lower He-(Sea) points, Crossing points, Eight Confluent points and Eight Influential points. These names are classified according to the functions of the acupoints, which have already been explained in *Clinical Acupuncture & Moxibustion*.

(2) Extraordinary acupoints. They refer to the acupoints which have specific names and definite locations, but are not attributed to the system of the fourteen Meridians. They are also named "extra points" in short. These extra points have a special therapeutic effect on certain diseases. For example, Taiyang (EX-HN 5) is used to treat headache, Yaotongdian (EX-UE 7) is used to treat lumbago, etc. Extra points have a close relationship with the system of meridians and collaterals. Some extra points are located along the route of the meridians. For example, Yintang (EX-HN 3) is located on the Du Meridian. Zhoujian (EX-UE 1) is located on the Sanjiao Meridian of Hand Shaoyang.

(3) Ashi points. They are also named "tender points", "reflect points", or "unfixed points". They have neither specific names nor definite locations, but they are considered as acupoints based on the tender or other reflecting points. Ashi points are mostly located near the pathological changes of the body, or located in the distal part of the pathological changes of the body. Their numbers can never be determined.

Nomenclature of Acupoints

Acupoints were given their names by ancient people on the basis of the locations and functions of acupoints in combination with many kinds of objects in the natural world and medical theories. Classification of the names of acupoints is listed as follows:

a. Points named according to anatomical terms: Wangu (SI 4), Wangu (GB 12) Xinshu (BL 15), Pishu (BL 20).

b. Names bearing analogy to astronomical and meteorological phenomena: Riyue (GB 24), Taiyi (ST 23), Shangxing (DU 23), Taibai (SP 3).

c. Names bearing analogy to mountains and valleys: Chengshan (BL 57), Hegu (LI 4), Chize (LU 5), Xiaohai (SI 8).

d. Names bearing analogy to architectural structure: Neiguan (PC 6), Tianchuang (SI 16), Zigong (RN 19), Neiting (ST 44)

e. Names bearing analogy to animals or plants: Yuji (LU 10), Futu (ST 32), Cuanzhu (BL 2).

f. Names bearing analogy to utensils: Duzhu (BL 11), Quepen (ST 12) Tianding (LI 17), Xuanzhong (GB 39).

g. Points named according to their physiological functions: Guanyuan (RN 4), Zhishi (BL 52), Qihai (RN 6), Xuehai (SP 10).

h. Points named according to their therapeutic properties: Yingxiang (LI 20), Guilai (ST 29), Guangming (GB 37), Shuifen (RN 9).

The explanation on how a certain acupoint is named will be described in each of the following chapters.

III. Locations of the Meridians, Collaterals and Acupoints

1. Locations of the Meridians and Collaterals

The system of meridians and collaterals includes the twelve regular meridians, eight extra meridians, fifteen collaterals, twelve divergent meridians, twelve muscle regions, twelve cutaneous regions and uncountable minute collaterals. (*Fundamentals of Acupuncture & Moxibustion* for more details).

Each of the twelve regular meridians has its own circulating route. Moreover, there is a close relationship between each other. The twelve regular meridians are the core of the whole system of meridians and collaterals. The eight extra meridians also have their own circulating route, and in particular the functions of the Ren and Du Meridians are quite important. Therefore, these two meridians and the twelve regular meridians are usually called the fourteen meridians.

The distributions of the collaterals, the major collaterals, divergent meridians, muscle regions and cutaneous regions are all based on meridians. Locations of meridians and collaterals are outlined by the meridian theory, and the fourteen meridians in particular. Distribution of acupoints are located on the circulating route of the fourteen meridians.

Meridians circulate generally interiorly and exteriorly across the body. Since there aren't any acupoints on the interior route of the body, There exists no influence on acupoint selection. Locations of meridians and collaterals discussed here are primarily those concerning the exterior route of the body on the fourteen meridians. The acupuncture and moxibustion therapeutists should have good knowledge of this. Locations of meridians and collaterals will be discussed as follows according to the body parts.

1) Distribution on the Head

a. Anterior Part of the Head: The meridians circulating along the anterior part of the head are the Du Meridian, Foot Taiyang, Foot Shaoyang and Foot Yangming. First locate Shenting (DU 24) of the Du Meridian (Location: 0.5 cun directly above the midpoint of the anterior hairline). Next locate Touwei (ST 8) of Foot Yangming (0.5 cun within the anterior hairline at the corner of the forehead). Then divide the line connecting Touwei and Shenting into 3 equal parts (1.5 cun for each), the point on the medial 1/3 is Qucha (BL 4), which is on the route of Foot Taiyang, while the point on the lateral 1/3 is Benshen (GB 13), which is on the second route of Foot Shaoyang circulating along the anterior part of the head. Finally locate Toulinqi (GB 15) at the midpoint of the line connecting Qucha and Benshen, which is on the first route of Foot Shaoyang circulating along the anterior part of the head.

b. The Vertex: The meridians circulating along the vertex are the Du Meridian, Foot Taiyang, Foot Shaoyang and Hand Shaoyang. First locate the Du Meridian, which is on the midline of the vertex. Next locate Jiaosun (SJ 20) (Directly above the ear apex, in the depression of the hairline). Then divide the line connecting the Du Meridian and Hand Shaoyang into 4 equal parts (1.5 cun for each). The point on the medial 1/4 is the circulating route of Foot Taiyang, that of lateral 1/4 is the second circulating route of Foot Shaoyang and that running between them is the first circulating route of Foot Shaoyang.

c. Posterior part of the Head: Those travelling along the posterior part of the head are the Du Meridian, Foot Taiyang, Foot Shaoyang and Hand Shaoyang. First locate the Du Meridian, which is on the midline of the posterior part of the head. Next locate Yifeng (SJ 17) of Hand Shaoyang (In the depression of the midpoint of the line connecting the Mandible and mastoid process). Then divide the line connecting the Du Meridian and Yifeng point into 4 equal parts (1.5 cun for each). The point on the medial 1/4 is the circulating route of Foot Taiyang, that of lateral 1/4 is the second circulating route of the Foot Shaoyang, the line between the Du Meridian and Yifeng point is the first circulating route of Foot Shaoyang.

The middle line of the vertex is the circulating route of the Du Meridian. Draw a line connecting the three points of Foot Taiyang Meridian, along the circulating route of Foot Taiyang Meridian, travelling along the vertex. Draw a line connecting Benshen, the Du Meridian and the two points on the lateral 1/4 of Hand Shaoyang to make an arcline, along the second circulating route of Foot Shaoyang travelling along the vertex. Draw a line connecting the three points (Toulinqi and the line between the Du Meridian and the second circulating route of Hand Shaoyang) along the first circulating route of Foot Shaoyang travelling along the vertex.

2) Distribution in the neck

The meridians circulating along the neck are the Ren Meridian, Foot Yangming, Hand Taiyang, Foot Shaoyang, Foot Taiyang and the Du Meridian. First locate the Ren Meridian along the midline of the anterior neck. Taking the midline as a reference, locate Renying (ST 9), which is 1.5 cun lateral, level with the tip of Adam's apple (just on the course of the common carotid artery), this is the circulating line of Foot Yangmimg. Locate Futu (LI 18), which is 3.0 cun lateral to the midline, level with the tip of Adam's apple (between the sternal head and clavicular head of m. sternocleidomastoideus). This is the circulating route of Hand Yangming. Locate Tianchuang (SI 16), which is 1.0 cun lateral to Futu (in the posterior border of m. sternocleidomastoideus). This is the circulating route of Hand Taiyang. Next, locate the Du Meridian, which is on the midline of the vertex. Locate Tianzhu (BL 10), which is 1.3 cun lateral to Yamen (DU 15), it is the circulating route of Foot Taiyang (on the lateral aspect of m. trapezius). Locate Fengchi (GB 20), which is on the same level with Fengfu (DU 16), between m. trapezius and m. sternocleidomastoideus, this is the circulating route of Foot Shaoyang. Locate Tianyou (SJ 16), which is between Tianzhu (BL 10) and Tianrong (SI 17), (Tianrong is located posterior to the angle of mandible), this is the circulating route of Hand Shaoyang.

3) Distribution on the back and at the lumbar region

The meridians circulating along the lumbar and back regions are the Du Meridian and the first and the second circulating routes of Foot Taiyang. First locate the Du Meridian, which is located along the midline of the lumbar and back regions. Next locate the second circulating route of Foot Taiyang in straight sitting position along the medial border of the scapula (3 cun lateral from the middle line). Then locate the first circulating route of Foot Taiyang between the Du Meridian and the second circulating route of Foot Taiyang (1.5 cun lateral to the middle line.)

4) Distribution in the Thoracic and Abdominal Regions

a. The Thoracic Region: The meridians travelling along the chest region are the Ren Meridian, Foot Shaoyang, Foot Yangming, Hand Taiyin, Foot Taiyin, Foot Jueyin, Foot

Shaoyang and Hand Jueyin. First locate the Ren Meridian (located on the midline of the sternum). Next locate Yunmen (LU 2) (located in the depression below the acromial extremity of the clavicle) of Hand Taiyin. Foot Taiyin is the downward extending line of Hand Taiyin. Then divide the line connecting the Ren Meridian and Hand Taiyang into 3 equal parts (2 cun for each). The line (the midline of the breast) on the lateral 1/3 is the circulating route of Foot Yangming, while that of medial 1/3 is the circulating route of Foot Shaoyin. Between Ruzhong (ST 17) (located in the center of the nipple of Foot Yangming) and Tianxi (SP 18) (2 cun lateral superior to Ruzhong of Foot Taiyin), the Hand Jueyin is located. Directly below Ruzhong, between the two intercostal spaces, Qimen (LR 14) is located. 1.5 cun below Qimen (LR 14), Riyue (GB 24) is located.

b. The Abdominal Region: The meridians travelling along the abdominal region are the Ren Meridian, Foot Shaoyin, Foot Yangming and Foot Taiyang. First locate the Ren Meridian (located on the midline of the abdomen). Next locate Foot Taiyin, which is located 4 cun lateral to the Ren Meridian (lateral border of the rectus abdominal muscle), this is the extension of the midline of the breast. Then locate the circulating route of Foot Yangming (2 cun lateral to the Ren Meridian) between the Ren Meridian and Foot Taiyin. Then divide the line connecting the Ren Meridian and Foot Yangming into 4 equal parts (0.5 cun for each). Locate the circulating route of Foot Shaoyin on the medial 1/4 part.

5) Distribution in the upper limbs

a. Medial aspect of the upper limbs: The meridians running along the medial aspect of the upper limbs are Hand Taiyin, Hand Jueyin and Hand Shaoyin. Distribution on the armpit, elbow, wrist and fingers are listed as follows: (See Tab. 1-2).

Table 1-2 Body Part and Distribution of the Three Yin Meridians of Hand

Body Part / Meridians	Armpit	Elbow	Wrist	Finger
Hand Taiyin	lateral bicipital groove (Tianfu LU 3)	radial side of m. biceps brachii (Chize LU 5)	between long abductor muscle of thumb and lateral side of the tendon of m. flexor carpi ulnaris (Taiyuan LU 9)	medial side of the thumb (Shaoshang LU 11)
Hand Jueyin	between the two heads of m. biceps brachii (Tianquan PC 2)	medial side of m. biceps brachii (Quze PC 3)	between long palmar muscle and medial side of the tendon of m. flexor carpi ulnaris (Daling PC 7)	tip of the middle finger (Zhongchong PC 9)
Hand Shaoyin	medial bicipital border (Jiquan HT 1)	when the elbow is flexed into a right angle, the point is in the medial end of the transverse cubital crease (Shaohai HT 3)	radial side of the tendon of m. flexor carpi ulnaris (Shenmen HT 7)	radial side of the little finger (Shaochong HT 9)

Tianfu (LU 3), Chize (LU 5), Taiyuan (LU 9) and Shaoshang (LU 11) are joined by a line along the circulating route of Hand Taiyin travelling along the upper limbs. Tianquan (PC 2), Quzen (PC 3), Daling (PC 7) and Zhongchong (PC 9) are joined by a line along the circulating route of Hand Jueyin travelling along the upper limbs. Jiquan (HT 1), Shaohai (HT 3), Shenmen (HT 7) and Shaochong (HT 9) are joined by a line along the circulating route of Hand Shaoyin travelling along the upper limbs.

b. Lateral aspect of the upper limbs: The meridians circulating on the lateral side of the upper limbs are Hand Yangming, Hand Shaoyang and Hand Taiyang. Anatomical characteristics of their distribution on finger, wrist, elbow and shoulder are listed as follows: (See Tab. 1-3).

Table 1-3 Body Part and Distribution of the Three Yang Meridians of Hand

Body Part / Meridians	Finger	Wrist	Elbow	Shoulder
Hand Yangming	index finger (Shangyang LI 1)	between the tendons of the m. extensor pollicis longus and brevis (Yangxi LI 5)	lateral side of the brachioradial muscle (Quchi LI 11)	in the centre of deltoid muscle, when the arm is in full abduction, the point is in the depression (Jianyu LI 15)
Hand Shaoyang	ring finger (Guanchong SJ 1)	lateral side of the tendon of the m. extensor digitorum communis (Yangchi SJ 4)	directly above its tip in the depression superior to the olecranon (Tianjing SJ 10)	between Hand Yangming and Hand Taiyang (Jianliao SJ 14)
Hand Taiyang	little finger (Shaoze SI 1)	between the styloid process of the ulna and the triquetral bone (Yanggu SI 5)	between the medial condyle of humerus and the olecranon (Xiaohai SI 8)	lateral border of the suprascepular fossa (Naoshu SI 10)

Shangyang (LI 1), Yangxi (LI 5), Quchi (LI 11) and Jianyu (LI 15) are joined by a line along the circulating route of Hand Shaoyang travelling along the upper limbs. Shaoze (SI 1), Yanggu (SI 5), Xiaohai (SI 8) and Naoshu (SI 10) are joined by a line along the circulating route of Hand Taiyang travelling along the upper limbs.

6) Distribution in the lower limbs

a. Lateral, anterior and posterior aspects of the lower limbs: The meridian circulating along the lateral aspect of the lower limbs is Foot Shaoyang, along the anterior aspect is Foot Yangming and along the posterior aspect is Foot Taiyang. Anatomical characteristics of their distribution on the thigh, knee, ankle and toe are listed as follows: (See Tab. 1-4).

Biguan (ST 31), Dubi (ST 35), Jiexi (ST 41) are joined by a line along the circulating route of Foot Yangming travelling along the lower limbs. Huantiao (GB 30), Yanglingquan (GB 34), Qiuxu (GB 40) and Zuqiaoyin (GB 44) are joined by a line along the circulating route of Foot Shaoyang travelling along the lower limbs. Chengfu (BL 36), Weizhong (BL 40), Kunlun (BL 60) and Zhiyin (BL 67) are joined by a line along the circulating route of Foot Taiyang travelling along the lower limbs.

Table 1-4 Body Part and Distribution of the Three Yang Meridians of Foot

Body Part / Meridians	Thigh	Knee	Ankle	Toe
Foot Yangming	between sartorius muscle and tensor muscle of fascia lata (Biguan ST 31)	when the knee is flexed, the point is at the lower border of the patella (Dubi ST 35)	between the tendons of m. extensor digitorum longus and hallucis longus (Jiexi ST 41)	the second toe (Lidui ST 45)
Foot Shaoyang	between the great trochanter and the hiatus of the sacrum (Huantiao GB 30)	anterior and inferior to the head of the fibula (Yanglingquan GB 34)	in the depression anterior and inferior to the external malleolus (Qiuxu GB 40)	the fourth toe (Zuqiaoyin GB 44)
Foot Taiyang	inferior border of the greatest gluteal muscle, between the biceps muscle of thigh and semitendinous muscle (Chengfu BL 36)	midpoint of the transverse crease of the popliteal fossa (Weizhong BL 40)	between the external malleolus and the tendo calcaneus (Kunlun BL60)	the fifth toe (Zhiyin BL67)

Table 1-5 Body Part and Distribution of the Three Yin Meridians of Foot

Body Part / Meridians	Toe	Ankle	Knee	Thigh
Foot Taiyin	medial side of the first toe (Yinbai SP 1)	in the depression distal and inferior to the medial malleolus (Shangqiu SP 5)	on the lower border of the medial condyle of the tibia, in the depression on the medial border of the tibia (Yinlingquan SP 9)	3.5 cun lateral to Qugu (RN 2) (Chongmen SP 12)
Foot Jueyin	lateral side of the first toe (Dadun LR 1)	1 cun anterior to the medial malleolus, medial side of the tendon of m. tibialis anterior (Zhongfeng LR 4)	the medial end of the transverse popliteal crease, side of the tibia (Ququan LR 8)	2 cun below Qichong (ST 30), on the lateral side of femoral artery (Yinlian LR 11)
Foot Shaoyin	on the side, approximately at the junction of the anterior one third and posterior two thirds of the sole (Yongquan KI 1)	between the medial malleolus and tendo calcaneus (Taixi KI 3)	medial side of the popliteal fossa, between the tendons of m. semitendinosus and semimembranosus (Yingu KI 10)	between the tip of the coccyx and the anus (Changqiang DU 1)

b. Medial aspect of the lower limbs: The meridians circulating along the medial aspect of the lower limbs are Foot Taiyin, Foot Jueyin and Foot Shaoyin. Anatomical charateristics of their distribution on the toes, knees and thigh are listed as follows: (See Tab 1-5).

Yinbai (SP 1), Shangqiu (SP 5), Yinlingquan (SP 9) and Chongmen (SP 12) are joined by a line, which is the circulating route of Foot Taiyin travelling along the lower limbs. Dadun (LR 1), Zhongfeng (LR 4), Ququan (LR 8) and Yinlian (LR 11) are joined by a line, which is the circulating route of Foot Jueyin travelling along the lower limbs. But Foot Jueyin runs across an area 8 cun directly above the medial malleolus, where it runs across and behind Foot Taiyin. Yongquan (KI 1), Taixi (KI 3), Yingu (KI 10) and Changqiang (DU 1) are joined by a line, which is the circulating route of Foot Shaoyin.

2. Methods of Locating Acupoints

At the present time, methods which are commonly used in clinics are anatomical landmarks, proportional measurement and finger measurement. These three methods are usually used in combination, i.e. using the anatomical landmarks as the first step, we then divide the body respectively into fixed numbers of equal units, and then use finger measurements to determine the location of acupoints.

1) Anatomical Landmarks

This refers to the locating acupoints based on various anatomical landmarks on the body surface. Those landmarks fall into two categories: fixed landmarks and moving landmarks.

Fixed landmarks include prominence and depression of the bones, the five sense organs, hair, nails (toes), nipple and umbilicus, etc. Examples are Yanglingquan (GB 34) on the anterior and inferior area of the fibula, Binao (LI 14) on the tip of deltoid muscle, Cuanzhu (BL 2) on the medial extremity of the eyebrow, Yintang (EX-HN 3) between the two eyebrows, and Danzhong (RN 17), midway between the two nipples, etc.

Moving landmarks refer to gaps, depressions, creases and tips that will appear only when joins, muscle, tendons and skin of the body move. For instance, when the mouth is slightly open, a depression appears between the tragus and posterior to the condyloid process of the mandible, where Tinggong (SI 19) can be located, and when the elbow is flexed, Quchi (LI 11) can be located in the depression at the lateral end of the transverse cubital crease.

Important to note is that the explanation of body parts and their positions in TCM is not entirely the same as that in modern medicine. For example:

"medial aspect of the upper limbs" ——the palmar side of the upper limbs, that is the area where the three Yin meridians of foot distribute.

"lateral side of the upper limbs" ——the back of hand, that is the area where the three Yang meridians of hand distribute.

"anterior aspect of the upper limbs" ——the lateral aspect of thumb of the upper limbs is considered as "the anterior"

"posterior aspect of the upper limbs" ——the fifth finger aspect of the upper limbs is considered as the "the posterior"

"medial aspect of the lower limbs" ——the front middle line of the lower limbs is the area where the three Yin meridians of foot distributed

"lateral aspect and posterior aspect of the lower limbs" refer respectively to the back middle line and the posterior area of the lower limbs, where the three Yang meridians of foot distribute.

"dorso-ventral boundary of the hand (or foot)" ——border line between the palm and back of hand or that between the sole and back of foot.

"basic joints of extremities" —— referring to the eminence of the metacarpophalangeal and metatarsophalangeal joints (including the coverings of joint capsule). "Basic joints of anterior extremities" and "basic joints of posterior extremities" should be distinguished (distal end is known as "anterior", while the neighbouring area as "posterior").

The front and back middle lines running along the head, face and body trunk are respectively the areas where the Ren Meridian and Du Meridian distribute, they also serve as proof for distinguishing the three Yin meridians and the three Yang meridians, which distribute on the two sides of the Ren and Du meridians.

Major anatomical landmarks of the body are listed as follows:

Head

    a. midpoint of front hairline (midpoint of anterior border of hair)
    b. midpoint of posterior hairline (midpoint of posterior border of hair)
    c. frontal angle (angle of hair) (corner of forehead of front hairline)
    d. Wangu (the mastoid process of temporal bone)

Face

    a. glabellum (Yintang EX-HN1) midway between two eyebrows
    b. pupil (centre of the pupil) or centre of eye (midpoint of the line connecting inner canthus and outer canthus)

Neck and Neck Region

    a. Adam's apple (prominence of the larynx)
    b. the spinous process of the seventh cervical vertebra.

Thoracic Region

    a. superior fossa of sternum (depression of superior area of sternum notch)
    b. midpoint of the sternocostal (connecting part of sternal body and xiphoid process)
    c. nipple (the center of nipple)

Abdominal Region

    a. umbilicus (Shenque RN 8) (the centre of the umbilicus)
    b. superior border of pubic symphysis (the crossing point between superior border of pubic symphysis and the front midline)
    c. anterior superior iliac spine (prominence of superior area of anterior iliac crest)

Lateral Abdominal and Lateral Thoracic Regions

    a. tip of axillary fossa (the highest point of the centre of axillary fossa)
    b. the eleventh intercostal end (the free end of the eleventh rib)

Back, Lumbar and Sacral Regions

    a. the spinous process of the seventh cervical vertebra
    b. the spinous process of the 12th thoracic vertebra, the spinous process of the 1st—5th

lumbar vertebra, median sacral crest, coccyx
   c. bottom point of spine of scapula (the lateral point of the spinal column, medial lateral border of the scapula)
   d. acromial angle (connecting area between the lateral border of acromion and medial border of the scapula)
   e. posterior superior iliac spine (prominence of superior area of the iliac spine)

Upper Limbs

   a. anterior stripe of axillary (the anterior extremity of plica of axillary fossa)
   b. stripe of posterior axillary (the posterior extremity of plica of axillary fossa)
   c. transverse crease of the elbow
   d. tip of the elbow (olecranon of the ulna)
   e. transverse creases of the dorsal part of the wrist and palm.

Lower Limbs

   a. uppermost part of the lateral aspect of the thigh (the greater trochanter of the femur)
   b. medial condyle of femur
   c. medial malleolus of tibia
   d. gluteal fold of the transverse crease (the moving part of buttock and thigh)
   e. Dubi (ST 35) (Waixiyan) (centre of the lateral depression of the patellar ligament)
   f. transverse popliteal crease (transverse crease of the popliteal fossa)
   g. tip of medial malleolus (bony prominence on top of the medial malleolus)
   h. tip of external malleolus (bony prominence on the lateral malleolus)

2) Proportional Measurement

Proportional measurement means the width or length of various portions of the human body. They are divided respectively into definite numbers of equal units as the standards for the proportional measurement. This is based on proportional measurement provided in *Miraculous Pivot* and associated with the equal division measurement created by the past scholars (divide the part between two bone joints into several equal parts, 1 cun for each, 10 equal parts is 1 cun). (See Fig. 1-1 and Tab. 1-6 for details)

3) Finger Measurement

The length and width of the patient's finger are taken as a standard for point selection. (See Fig. 1-2)

(1) Middle Finger Measurement
When the patient's middle finger is flexed, the distance between the two medial ends of the crease of the interphalangeal joints is taken as one cun. (See Fig. 1-2)

(2) Thumb Measurement
The width of the four fingers (index, middle, ring and little) close together at the level of the dorsal skin crease of the proximal interphalangeal joint of the middle figer is taken as three cun. (See Fig. 1-2)

Methods of locating points are based on standard measurements. An acupuncturist should first of all have a clear idea of these measurements and the patient's body build, and then

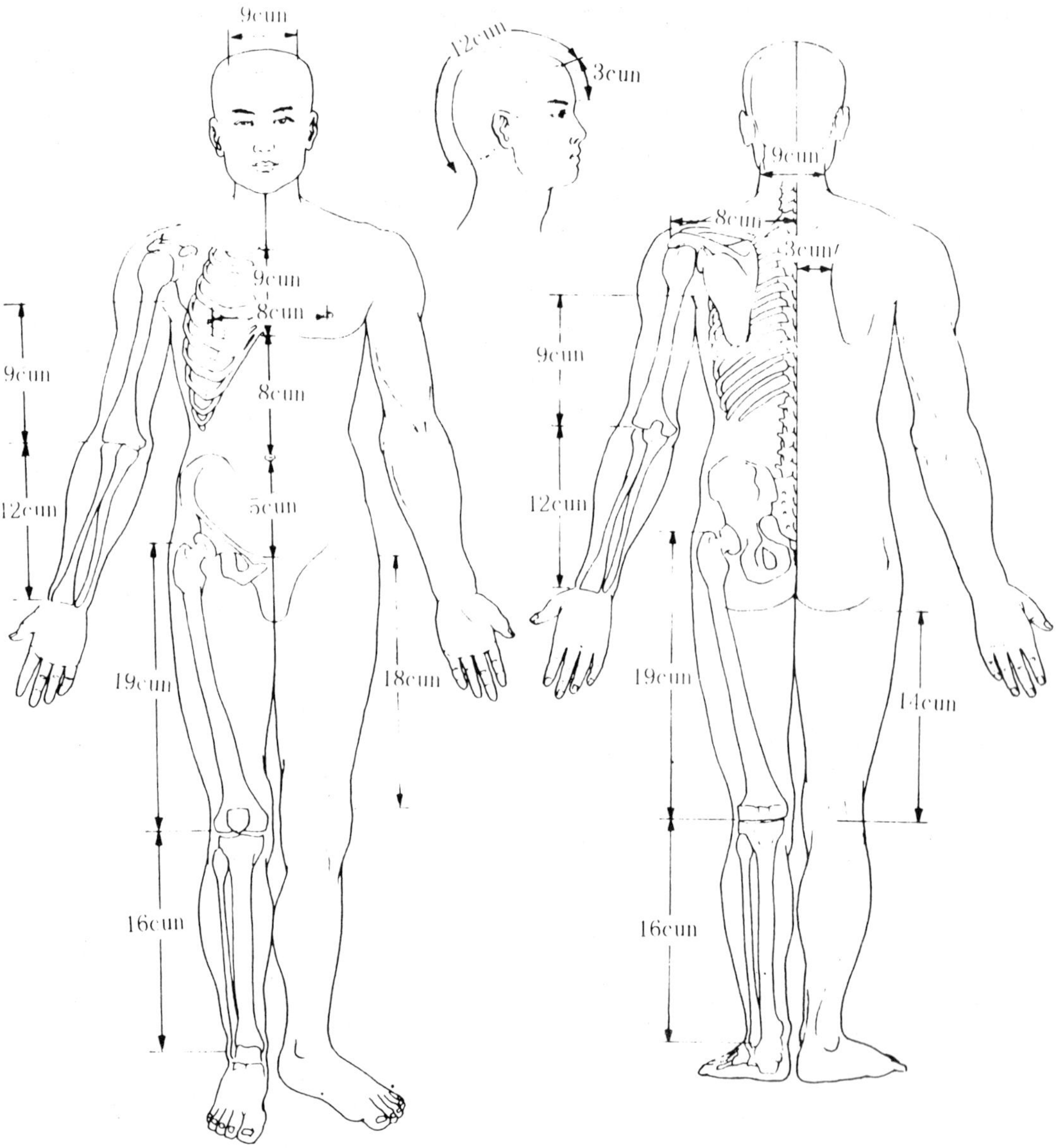

Fig. 1-1 Standards for Proportional Measurement

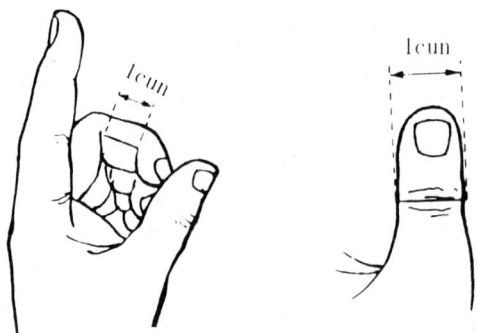

Fig. 1-2 Finger Measurement

General Introduction to the System of Meridians, Collaterals and Acupoints

Table 1-6 Standards for Proportional Measurement

Body part	Distance	Proportional Measurement	Method	Explanation
Head and Face	midway of the anterior hairline → midway of the posterior hairline	12 cun	longitudinal measurement	used to determine the longitudinal distance of acupoints and the head
	glabellum (Yintang) → midway of the anterior hairline	3 cun		used to determine the longitudinal distance of acupoints located on the anterior or posterior hairline and the head
	spinous process of the seventh cervical vertebra → midway of the posterior hairline	3 cun		
	between the two eyebrows (Yintang) → spinous process of the seventh certical vertebra	18 cun		
	anterior hairline between the two corners of the forehead (Touwei ST 8)	9 cun	transverse measurement	used to determine the transverse distance of the acupoint on the anterior part of the head
	between the depressions posterior and inferior to the mastoid processes	9 cun		used to determine the transverse distance of the acupoints on the posterior part of the head
Chest Abdomen and Hypochondrium	superior fossa of the sternum (Tiantu RN 22) → midpoint of the sternocostal angle (歧骨)	9 cun	longitudinal measurement	used to determine the longitudinal distance of the acupoints on the chest
	midpoint of the sternocostal angle (歧骨) → the centre of the umbilicus	8 cun		used to determine the longitudinal distance of the acupoints on the upper abdomen
	centre of the umbilicus → superior border of the symphysis of the pubis (Qugu RN 2)	5 cun		used to determine the longitudinal distance of the acupoints on the lower abdomen
	between the two nipples	8 cun	transverse measurement	used to determine the transverse distance of the acupoints on the chest and abdomen
	tip of the axillary fossa → free end of the eleventh rib (Zhangmen LR 13)	12 cun	longitudinal measurement	used to determine the longitudinal distance of the acupoints on the hypochondriac region
Back	medial border of the scapula → posterior midline	3 cun	transverse measurement	used to determine the transverse distance of the acupoints on the back and waist
	border of the acromion → posterior midline	8 cun		used to determine the transverse distance of the acupoints on the shoulder and back
Upper Extremities	anterior axillary fold, posterior stripe → transverse crease of the elbow, tip of the elbow	9 cun	longitudinal measurement	used to determine the longitudinal distance of the acupoints on the arms
	transverse crease of the elbow → transverse crease of the wrist	12 cun		used to determine the longitudinal distance of the acupoints on the anterior aspect of the arms

Lower Extremities	superior border of the symphysis pubis → superior border of medial epicondyle of femur	18 cun	longitudinal measurement	used to determine the longitudinal distance of the acupoints of the three Yin meridians of the foot travelling along the medial side of the lower limbs
	inferior border of medial condyle of tibia → the tip of medial malleolus	13 cun		
	great trochanter of the femur → transverse crease	19 cun		used to determine the longitudinal distance of the acupoints of the three Yang meridians of the foot travelling along the lateral posterior aspect of the lower limbs (gluteous → popliteal transverse crease)
	Transverse crease → tip of the external malleolus			

use some simple moving landmarks on the patient for locating acupoints.

These moving landmarks refer to those which can be used to locate some points in clinic by certain specific movements or posture of the patient. For example, when the patient is standing erect with the hands close to the sides, Fengshi (GB 31) can be located where the tip of the middle finger touches. When the index fingers and thumbs of both hands are crossed with the index fingers of one hand placed on the styloid process of the radius of the other, Lieque (LU 7) can be located under the tip of the index finger. When the patient is standing erect with the elbow flexed, Zhangmen (LR 13) can be located below the free end of the eleventh rib where the tip of the elbow touches. Other example arc Xuehai (SP 10), Liangqiu (ST 34), Yanglao (SI 6), Zhiyang (DU 9), Hegu (LI 4), Tianzong (SI 11) and Baihui (DU 20). These points can also be located easily in clinic by way of some simple moving landmarks on the patient. The related discussion in other chapters can be referred to.

IV. The Therapeutic Properties of the Meridians, Collaterals and Acupoints

1. The Therapeutic Properties of the Meridians and Collaterals

Therapeutic function of the meridians and collaterals can be determined by transporting qi and blood, reflecting signs and symptoms and transmitting needling sensation of the meridians and collaterals.

The network of the meridians and collaterals are closely connected with the tissues and organs of the body. This includes the twelve regular meridians and their branches which run longitudinally and transversely, interiorly and superficially over the body, connecting with the Zangfu organs internally, and with the joints, limbs and other superficial tissues of the body externally. The eight extra meridians connect the twelve regular meridians to strengthen the association of Yin and yang, qi and blood. The muscle regions and the cutaneous regions connect with the limbs, muscles and the skin, thus all the Zangfu organs and tissues of the human body connect and form a network of an organic whole.

Under normal conditions, the system of the meridians and collaterals functions to transport qi and blood and nourish Yin and Yang, so that coordination and a relative equilibrium of normal life activities are maintained. In clinical treatment, differentiation, point selection along the meridians and reinforcing and reducing needling methods are all worked out on the basis of the theories of the meridians and collaterals. It is pointed out in *Miraculous Pivot* that: With the twelve meridians, human beings are born and diseases occur. By the same twelve meridians, diseases are caused and cured.

It is said in *Miraculous Pivot* that the condition of the meridians and collaterals can determine the life and death of human beings. They are able to treat many diseases by regulating deficiency and excess of the body. The meridians and collaterals must be in a state of free circulation. The above classical expositions show that the meridians and collaterals play an important role in treatment selection based on diagnosis. Since the meridians and collaterals have their own circulating areas to which Zangfu organs belong, qi and blood of the meridians and collaterals originate from those of Zangfu organs. With the aid of the transmitting function of the meridians and collaterals, the system of the meridians and collaterals can not only reflect the signs and symptoms of the Zangfu organs, but also dredge the meridian qi and regulate the function of qi and blood and Zangfu organs of the human body by way of stimulating the meridians and collaterals, thereby achieving a curative effect. Early in the age of *Internal Classic*, predecessors gave a systematic exposition of the signs and symptoms reflected on the twelve regular meridians, the eight extra meridians, collaterals, branch of the large channel, muscle regions and their indications.

The signs and symptoms reflected on the meridians and collaterals can be divided according to the area of disease into: the local area, one meridian, several meridians or the general body. They can also be divided into related areas where the meridians and collaterals run through and related organs where the meridians and collaterals belong.

The properties of the signs and symptoms reflected on the meridians and collaterals are classified into different types: deficiency, excess, cold and heat.

Generally speaking, when qi and blood of the meridians and collaterals are blocked, pain and swelling will occur on the related parts of the body. If stagnation of qi and blood transmits into heat, redness swelling, feverish sensation and pain of the skin will appear.

These are all considered as excess and heat syndromes of the meridians and collaterals. If qi and blood are insufficient in transportation, then numbness, muscular atrophy, hypofunction and local coldness may occur on the areas where pathological changes take place. These signs and symptoms are thought to be deficiency and cold syndromes of the meridians and collaterals. The general condition of cold, heat, deficiency and excess of the Zangfu organs can also be reflected on the body surface through the meridians and collaterals. We will give more details in the following chapters.

The meridians and collaterals have a function of regulating deficiency and excess based on regulating Yin and yang, and transporting qi and blood under normal conditions. When acupuncture and moxibustion therapy are applied, stimulation of the acupoint is transmitted to the relevant Zangfu organs. Needling stimulation can reduce the excess, reinforce the insufficiency and regulate Yin and yang.

In general, the therapeutic properties of the meridians and collaterals are determined by the internal related Zangfu organs and their pertaining meridians, as what is said in *Miraculous Pivot* "the areas of acupoints where the meridian pass through can be used to treat a specific diseases". Therefore, it is quite important in clinic to gain a thorough understanding from a different angle of the meridians and collaterals connecting with Zangfu organs of the body and distribution of Zangfu organs and the meridians and collaterals. In addition, they are also considered as the basis of point selection along the meridians. Distribution of the meridians and collaterals on the Zangfu organs and parts of the body surface are given as follows:

Lung

Meridians:
Hand Taiyin pertains to the lung. Hand Yangming connects with the lung. Hand Shaoyin ascends to the lung. Foot Shaoying enters into the lung and Foot Jueyin runs upward to the lung.

Divergent Meridians: Hand Taiyin runs through the lung, its pertaining organ. Hand Yangming pertains to the lung.

Large Intestine

Meridian: Hand Yangming pertains to the large intestine. Hand Taiyin connects downward with the large intestine.

Divergent Meridians: Hand Yangming runs downward to the large intestine. Hand Taiyin runs downward to connect with the large intestine.

Collateral: Divergent Meridian of Foot Taiyin enters and connects with the intestine and stomach.

Stomach

Meridians: Foot Yangming pertains to the stomach. Foot Taiyin connects with the lung. Hand Taiyang reaches the stomach. Foot Jueyin passes through the diaphragm and branches out in the costal and hypochondriac region. Hand Taiyin, winding back, goes along the upper orifice of the stomach.

Divergent Meridian: Foot Yangming pertains to the stomach

Collateral: Divergent Meridian of Foot Taiyin enters and connects with the intestine and stomach.

Spleen

Meridians: Foot Taiyin pertains to the spleen. Foot Yangming connects with the spleen.
Divergent Meridian: Foot Yangming enters the stomach and connects with the spleen.

Heart

Meridian: Hand Shaoyin originates from the heart. Emerging, it spreads over the heart system.

Divergent Meridians: Hand Taiyang connects with the heart. Hand Shaoyin emerged from the lung and connects with the heart. Foot Taiyin enters into the heart. Foot Taiyang spreads over in the heart. Foot Shaoyang passes through the heart. Foot Yangming runs upwards to connect with the heart. Hand Taiyang enters the armpit, turning downward to connect with the heart. Hand Shaoyin pertains to the heart.

Collateral: Divergent Meridians of Hand Shaoyin enters the heart.

Small Intestine

Meridians: Hand Taiyang pertains to the intestine. Hand Shaoyin connects with the small intestine.

Divergent Meridian: Hand Taiyang enters the small intestine.

Collateral: Divergent Meridian of Hand Taiyin connects with the intestine and stomach.

Bladder

Meridians: Foot Taiyang pertains to the bladder. Foot Shaoyang connects with the bladder.

Divergent Meridian: Foot Taiyang pertains to the bladder.

Kidney

Meridians: Foot Shaoyin pertains to the kindey. Foot Taiyang connects with the kidney. Du Meridian, running along the spinal column, pertains to the kidney and connects with the kidney.

Divergent Meridians: Foot Taiyang connects with the kidney. Foot Shaoyin, running upward, reaches the kidney.

Pericardium

Meridian: Hand Jueyin pertains to the pericardium. Hand Shaoyang connects with the pericardium.

Collateral: Divergent Meridian of Foot Shaoyin ascends to the pericardium. Divergent Meridian of Hand Jueyin enters the pericardium.

Sanjiao

Meridian: Hand Shaoyang pertains to Sanjiao. Hand Jueyin connects with Sanjiao. Hand Taiyin originates from the Middle Jiao.

Divergent Meridian: Foot Shaoyang runs downward to meet Sanjiao Meridian. Hand Shaoyang passes through Sanjiao.

Gallbladder

Meridian: Foot Shaoyang pertains to the gallbladder. Foot Jueyin connects with the gallbladder.

Divergent Meridian: Foot Shaoyang pertains to the gallbladder.

Liver

Meridian: Foot Jueyin pertains to the liver. Foot Shaoyang connects with the liver. Foot Shaoyin passes through the liver and diaphragm.

Divergent Meridian: Foot Shaoyang passes through the diaphragm to connect with the liver.

Diaphragm

Meridian: Hand Taiyang, Hand Shaoyang, Hand Yangming, Hand Jueyin and Hand Shaoyin descend through the diaphragm.

Divergent Meridian: Hand Taiyin, Foot Taiyin and Foot Jueyin ascend through the diaphragm. Foot Shaoyin passes through the liver and diaphragm. Foot Yangming descend through the diaphragm. Foot Shaoyang passes through the diaphragm.

Muscle Regions: Muscle region of Hand Taiyin disperses over the diaphragm and converges again at the lower rib. Muscle region of Hand Shaoyin descends across the thoracic diaphragm to connect with the umbilicus. Muscle region of the palm knots with the diaphragm.

Chest

Meridian: Foot Shaoyang runs downward to the chest. Foot Shaoyin joins the heart and runs into the chest to link with the Pericardium Meridian. Hand Jueyin originates from the chest. Chong Meridian disperses over the chest. Yinqiao Meridian goes upward along the chest.

Divergent Meridians: Hand Jueyin enters into the chest. Foot Shaoyang runs along the chest. Hand Shaoyang disperses in the chest.

Muscle Regions: Muscle region of Foot Taiyin disperses through the chest. Muscle region of Hand Taiyin emerges at Quepen (ST 12) and knots below in the chest. Muscle region of Hand Shaoyin knots in the chest. Muscle region of Hand Jueyin enters the chest below the axilla and spreads over the chest.

Collateral: Hand Shaoyang runs into the chest. The major collateral of the spleen spreads through the chest and hypochondriac region.

Quepen (ST 12)

Meridian: Foot Yangming, Foot Shaoyang and Hand Taiyang enter into Quepen. Hand Yangming and Hand Shaoyang run into and out of Quepen. Yinqiao Meridian enters into Quepen.

Divergent Meridians: Hand Taiyin superiorly runs out of Quepen. Hand Shaoyang enters into Quepen.

Muscle regions: Muscle region of Foot Taiyang superiorly runs out of Quepen. Muscle region of Foot Yangming disperses upward on the abdomen and knots at Quepen.

Breast

Meridian: Foot Yangming runs downward and passes through the nipple. (Breast pertains to Foot Yangming, while nipple pertains to Foot Jueyin).

Divergent Meridian: Hand Yangming starts from the hand and runs upwards to the neck and descends along the breast region.

Muscle regions: Muscle region of Foot Shaoyang connects at the breast region. Muscle region of Hand Shaoyin crosses the Muscle Region of Hand Taiyin in the breast region.

Spine

Meridian: Du Meridian and Foot Shaoyin run through the spinal column. Foot Taiyang runs along both sides of the spinal column.

Muscle Regions: Muscle region of Foot Yangming ascends along the ribs to connect with the spine. An internal branch of the Muscle region of Foot Taiyin adheres to the spine. Muscle region of Foot Shaoyin proceeds upwards along the side of the spine to the nape. Muscle region of Hand Yangming moves around the scapula and attaches to the spine.

Collateral: Divergent Meridian of the Du Meridian runs upward along both sides of the spine to the nape.

Waist

Meridian: Foot Taiyang and Du Meridian run both downwards and upwards to the waist. Dai Meridian runs transversely around the waist like a belt.

Divergent Meridian: Foot Shaoyin passes through the fourteenth cervical vertebra, connecting with the kidney and crossing the Dai Meridian.

Collateral: Divergent Meridian of Foot Shaoyin runs upward along the lumbar and spinal regions.

Abdomen

Meridian: Foot Taiyang runs upward into the abdomen. Foot Yangming descends along the lateral side of the lower abdomen. Foot Shaoyin enters the abdomen. Ren Meridian ascends along the interior of the abdomen. Chong Meridian, starting from the inside of the lower abdomen runs upward. Foot Jueyin goes up to the lower abdomen. Du Meridian arises from the lower abdomen and descends to the pubis.

Divergent Meridian: Foot Yangming enters the abdomen.

Muscle regions: Muscle region of Foot Yangming distributes upward from the abdomen. Muscle region of Foot Taiyin extends to the abdomen and knots with the umbilicus.

Collateral: Divergent Meridian of the Ren Meridian disperses in the abdomen.

Axilla

Meridian: The straight portion of Foot Shaoyang runs downward and passes in front of the axilla. Hand Taiyin comes out transversely from the axilla. Hand Jueyin ascends to the axilla.

Divergent Meridian: Hand Taiyang enters the axilla and crosses the heart. Hand Jueyin derives from the Pericardium Meridian at a point 3 cun below the axilla. Hand Shaoyin, deriving from Heart Meridian in the axillary fossa, connects with the heart. Hand Taiyang, deriving from the small intestine Meridian at the shoulder joint, enters the axilla.

Muscle regions: A branch of muscle region of Foot Taiyang enters the chest below the axilla. The straight branch of muscle region of Foot Shaoyang ascends across the ribs, dispersing around the anterior to the axilla and connecting first at the breast region. Muscle region of Hand Taiyang runs upward along the arm and knots below the axilla. Muscle region of Hand Taiyin enters the chest below the axilla. Muscle region of Hand Jueyin knots below the axilla. Muscle region of Hand Shaoyin runs upwards and enters the chest below the axilla.

Collateral: The Major Collateral of the Spleen begins from Dabao (SP 21), and emerges at 3 cun below the axilla.

Hypochondrium

Meridian: Foot Shaoyang runs inside the hypochondriac region. Foot Jueyin branches out in the costal and hypochondriac region. Hand Jueyin runs inside the chest and ascends to the axilla.

Divergent Meridian: Foot Shaoyang runs inside the hypochondriac region.

Muscle regions: Muscle region of Foot Yangming goes up along the hypochondrium. A branch of Muscle region of Hand Taiyang extends over the hypochondrium. Muscle region of Foot Shaoyang runs through the intercostal space.

Collateral: The Major Collateral of the Spleen spreads through the chest and hypochondriac region.

Rib

Muscle region of Foot Taiyang knots at the ribs.

Buttock

Meridian: Foot Taiyang runs through the gluteal region. Du Meridian arises posteriorly from the lower abdomen and emerges from the perineum.

Muscle region: Muscle region of Foot Taiyang runs upward and knots at the buttock.

Coccyx (Sacrum)

Meridian: Du Meridian is the Meridian through which Foot Taiyang passes.

Divergent Meridian: Foot Taiyang proceeds to a point 5 cun below the sacrum.

Muscle region: A branch of the muscle region of Foot Shaoyang runs posteriorly and knots with the sacrum.

Collateral: A branch of Foot Taiyang enters the anus.

Suprapubic Margin (Pubic Hair Region)

Meridian: Foot Jueyin enters into the pubic hair region. Foot Shaoyang runs superficially along the margin of the pubic hair. The Ren Meridian travels anteriorly to the pubic triangle.

Divergent Meridian: Foot Shaoyang passes through the pubic triangle.

External Genitals

Meridian: Foot Jueyin runs around the external genitals. Yinqiao Meridian runs upward to the external genitals. Ren Meridian starts from the inside of the lower abdomen, below Zhongji (RN 3).

Muscle Regions: Muscle regions of Foot Yangming and Muscle region of Foot Taiyin join with the external genitals. Muscle regions of Foot Shaoyin and Foot Jueyin ascend along the medial aspect of the thigh to knot at the genital region.

Collateral: Divergent Meridian of Foot Jueyin runs upward to the pubic region and knots at the penis.

Vertex

Meridian: Foot Taiyang runs across the vertex at the forehead. Foot Tueyin meets Du Meridian at the vertex. Du Meridian runs up through the vertex and forehead.

Divergent Meridian: Divergent Meridian of Hand Shaoyang derives from the Sanjiao Meridian at the vertex.

Muscle region: Muscle region of Foot Shaoyang proceeds up to the vertex to join its bilateral counterpart.

Forehead Angle

Meridian: Foot Yangming runs up along the hairline to the forehead. Foot Taiyang runs upward to the forehead. Foot Jueyin runs upward and emerges from the forehead. Du Meridian, Yangwei and Yangqiao Meridians all go through the forehead. Foot Shaoyang originates from the outer canthus and ascends to the corner of the forehead.

Muscle Regions: Muscle region of Foot Shaoyang runs upward behind the ear to the forehead angle. Muscle region of Hand Shaoyang runs upward to the outer canthus, then crosses the temple and connects at the corner of the forehead. Muscle region of Hand Taiyang ascends around the teeth and in front of the ear, connecting with the outer canthus and knots at the angle of the forehead. Muscle region of Hand Yangming runs up to the forehead angle and then crosses over the head.

Brain

Meridian: The straight portion of Foot Taiyang enters and communicates with the brain from the vertex. The Du Meridian enters the brain. Foot Yangming runs through the eye system and reaches the brain.

Head and Face

Meridian: The Ren Meridian runs upward directly to the face. All of the Yang Meridians meet at the head and face.
Divergent Meridians: Divergent Meridian of Foot Shaoyang disperses in the face. Divergent Meridian of Hand Shaoyin runs upward across the throat and emerges on the face.
Muscle Regions: Muscle regions of the Three Yang Meridians of Hand and Foot gather at the head and face.

Eyes

Meridian: All meridians connect with the eyes. Ren Meridian enters the eyes. Du Meridian pertains to the eyes. Yinqiao Meridian meets Yangqiao Meridian at the inner canthus. Foot Taiyang starts from the inner canthus. Foot Shaoyang starts from the outer canthus, while Hand Shaoyang reaches the outer canthus. Hand Taiyang reaches the outer canthus, and its branch reaches the inner canthus. Hand Shaoyin pertains to the eye system. Foot Jueyin connects with the eye system.
Divergent Meridians: Divergent Meridian of Foot Yangming connects with the eye. Divergent Meridian of Hand Shaoyin joins the Small Intestine Meridian at the inner canthus. Divergent Meridian of Foot Shaoyang runs upward to connect with the eye system.
Muscle Regions: A branch of muscle region of Foot Taiyang spreads around the margin of the upper eyelid. Muscle region of Foot Yangming superiorly joins with Foot Taiyang to form a muscular net around the eye, and joins with Foot Yangming to be the margin of the lower eyelid. A branch of muscle region of Foot Shaoyang knots at the outer canthus.

Nose

Meridian: A branch of Hand Yangming runs upward and passes through the cheek to both sides of the nose. Foot Yangming starts from the lateral side of ala nasi, turning downward along the lateral side of nose. A branch of Hand Taiyang reaches the lateral side of the nose.
Muscle Regions: Muscle region of Foot Yangming runs upward to the neck and mouth, meeting at the side of the nose and knotting below the nose. Muscle region of Foot Taiyang knots at the nose.

Ears

Meridian: A branch of Foot Taiyang runs downward from the vertex, running to the upper angle of the ear. Foot Yangming, winding along the angle of the mandible, ascends in front of the ear. The retroauricular branch of Foot Shaoyang arises from the retroauricular region and enters the ear. It then comes out and passes the preauricular region. The branch of Hand Taiyang enters the ear. The auricular branch of Hand Shaoyang arises from the retroauricular region and enters the ear. Then it emerges in front of the ear, crosses the previous branch at the cheek and reaches the outer canthus.

Divergent Meridian: Divergent Meridian of Hand Jueyin ascends across the throat and emerges behind the ear.

Muscle Regions: A branch of muscle region of Foot Shaoyang emerges in front of the muscle region of Foot Taiyang where it continues upward behind the ear. A subbranch of the Muscle Region of Foot Yangming separates at the jaw and knots in front of the ear. The Muscle Region of Hand Taiyang knots behind the ear, a branch seperates behind the auricle and enters the ear, the other straight branch emerges below the ear.

Collateral: Divergent Meridian of Hand Yangming enters the ear and joins with the assembled meridian.

Mouth

Meridian: Hand Yangming runs upward to the cheek and curves around the upper lip and crosses the opposite meridian at the philtrum. Foot Yangming emerges and curves around the lips.

Divergent Meridian: Divergent Meridian of Foot Yangming ascends through the heart and alongside the esophagus to reach the mouth.

Muscle Region: Muscle Region of Foot Yangming extends to the neck and mouth.

Lip

Meridian: Foot Yangming curves around the lips. Foot Jueyin curves around the inner surface of the lips. Chong and Ren Meridians ascend to the face and curve around the lips.

Tongue

Meridian: Foot Taiyin reaches the root of the tongue and spreads over its lower surface. Foot Shaoyin runs up and along the throat and terminates at the root of the tongue.

Divergent Meridian: Foot Shaoyin runs further to the root of the tongue. Divergent Meridian of Foot Taiyin converges with Foot Yangming and runs upward to the throat, and finally enters the tongue.

Collateral: Divergent Meridian of Hand Shaoyin runs upward across the throat and emerges on the face.

Muscle Regions: A branch of muscle region of Hand Shaoyang saperates at the angle of the mandible and connects with the root of the tongue. Muscle region of Foot Taiyang knots at the root of the tongue.

Teeth

Meridian: Hand Yangming enters the gums of the lower teeth. Foot Yangming enters the gums of the upper teeth.

Divergent Meridian: Divergent Meridian of Hand Yangming runs upward from the shoulder along the throat.

Occipital Bone

Meridian: Foot Taiyang and Du Meridian pass through the occipital bone.

Muscle Regions: A straight portion of muscle region of Foot Taiyang knots with the occipital bone.

Mastoid Process

Meridian: Hand and Foot ShaoYang Meridians pass through Wangu.

Divergent Meridian: Hand Jueyin meets Foot Shaoyang below the mastoid process.

Muscle Regions: Muscle region of Hand Taiyang knots at the mastoid process and a branch of muscle region of Foot Taiyang knots at the mastoid process behind the ear.

Zygomatic Bone

Meridian: Hand Taiyang runs obliquely upward and downward round the zygomatic bone.

Muscle Regions: A straight portion of the muscle region of Foot Taiyang knots below the zygomatic bone. Muscle region of Foot Yangming joins with the zygomatic bone. A straight portion of muscle region of Hand Yangming knots at the zygomatic bone. Muscle region of Foot Shaoyang knots at the zygomatic bone. The Yangqiao Meridian enters the zygomatic bone.

Infraorrbital Margin

Meridian: A branch of Hand Taiyang runs up to it. A branch of Hand Shaoyang reaches it. A branch of Foot Shaoyang reaches below it.

Divergent Meridian: Foot Yangming ascends to the bridge of the nose.

Cheek

Meridian: Hand Yangming runs upward to the neck and passes through the cheek. Hand Taiyang runs to the neck and further to the cheek. A branch of Hand Shaoyang turns downward to the cheek, and crosses the cheek to the outer canthus. Foot Shaoyang passes through Jiache (ST 6). A branch of Foot Jueyin runs downward into the cheek. Foot Yangming runs along the angle of the mandible (Jiache ST 6).

Muscle Regions: A branch of muscle region of Hand Shaoyang saperates at the angle of the mandible. Muscle region of Hand Yangming runs up to the neck, where a branch seperates at the jaw and knots in front of the ear.

Collateral branch of the large channel: the Divergent Meridian runs upward from the shoulder along the throat.

Lower Cheek

Meridian: The Ren and Du Meridian run upward to the lower cheek. Foot Yangming runs around the lower cheek.

Divergent Meridian: A branch of Foot Shaoyang emerges from the lower cheek and goes to the chin.

Chin

Meridian: The Ren Meridian passes through the chin.

Divergent Meridian: A branch of Foot Shaoyang meets Hand Shaoyang in the infraorbital region.

Muscle Regions: A branch of muscle region of Foot Shaoyang descends from the temple across the cheek and then knots beside the bridge of the nose. Muscle region of Hand Taiyang knots beneath the mandible. Muscle region of Hand Shaoyang runs upward and saperates at the angle of the mandible. Muscle region of Hand Yangming runs up from the left cheek and down to the right mandible.

Face

Meridian: Du Meridian winds down from the vertex along the forehead to the bridge of the nose.

Muscle region: Muscle region of Foot Taiyang spreads around the eye and knots beneath the nose on the side.

Throat

Meridian: Ren, Chong and Yinqiao Meridians all pass through the throat. Foot Yangming runs along the throat. Hand Taiyang ascends to the neck, and then to the cheek. Foot Shaoyin runs along the throat. A branch of Hand Shaoyin runs alongside the esophagus to connect with the "eye system". Foot Jueyin ascends along the posterior aspect of the throat to the nasophargynx. The Du Meridian enters the throat.

Divergent Meridians: Foot Shaoyang runs upward to cross the heart and esophagus. Foot Yangming runs alongside the esophagus to reach the mouth. Foot Taiyin runs upward and knots at the throat. Hand Shaoyin runs upward through the throat. Hand Jueyin ascends across the throat. Hand Yangming runs upward from the shoulder along the throat. Hand Taiyin ascends across the throat.

Collateral: Divergent Meridian of Foot Yangming runs downward to connect with the heart.

Nasopharynx

Meridian: Foot Jueyin ascends along the posterior aspect of the throat to the nasopharynx, where the Chong Meridian emerges.

Neck

Meridian: Foot Taiyang descends along the nape of the neck. Foot Shaoyang runs along the side of the neck. Hand Shaoyang ascends to the nape of the neck. Hand Taiyang ascends along the side of the neck.

Hand Yangming ascends upward to the neck. The Du Meridian, Yangqiao and Yangwei Meridians all pass through the anterior and posterior portions of the neck.

Divergent Meridian: Foot Taiyang emerges and bifurcates, descending to the nape of the neck. Foot Shaoyin emerges at the nape to join Foot Taiyang.

Collateral: Divergent Meridian of the Collaterals runs upward to the nape of the neck. Divergent Meridian of Foot Yangming runs upward to connect with the vertex.

Shoulder

Meridian: Foot Shaoyang runs along the neck to the shoulder. Hand Taiyang circles round the scapular region and meets Dazhui (DU 14) on the superior aspect of the shoulder. Hand Yangming ascends to the highest point of the shoulder. Hand Shaoyang passes through the olecranon to the lateral aspect of the upper arm and shoulder region. The Yangqiao and Yangwei Meridians pass through the shoulder region. Foot Taiyang runs straight downward along the medial border of the scapula.

Divergent Meridian: Hand Yangming ascends along the lateral anterior aspect of the upper arm to the highest point of the shoulder (Jianyu LI 15).

Collateral: Divergent Meridian of Hand Taiyang connects with Jianyu (LI 15). Divergent Meridian of Hand Yangming separates at the top of the shoulder. Divergent Meridian of Du Meridian runs along the left and right scapulas.

The course of the Meridians and collaterals of the four limbs are not concluded here. See related chapters for details.

The Connection between the Meridians and collaterals and Zangfu organs and body parts is summarized as follows:

Lung Meridian of Hand Taiyin

Meridian: Middle Jiao, diaphragm, stomach, lung, the large intestine, lung system, Quepen (ST 12), chest, axilla, medial aspect of the thumb of the upper limbs, tip of the thumb, Yuji (LU 10) index.

Divergent Meridians: lung, large intestine, throat, Quepen (ST 12).

Collateral: center of the palm, Yuji (LU 10).

Muscle Regions: Cardia anterior of Jianyu (LI 15), inner chest, Yuji (LU 10), hypochondriac region.

Large Intestine Meridian of Hand Yangming

Meridian: lung, diaphragm, the large intestine, lower teeth, mouth, nose, index, lateral aspect of the thumb, anterior shoulder, Quepen (ST 12), anterior aspect of the neck, cheek, spine.

Divergent Meridians: large intestine, lung, throat, breast, chest, the spine, Jianyu (LI 15), Quepen (ST 12).

Collateral: ear, teeth, Jianyu (LI 15), cheek.

Muscle Regions: around the scapula, running alongside the spine, zygomatic region, connecting with the head, Jianyu (LI 15), cheek, mandible, wrist.

Stomach Meridian of Foot Yangming

Meridian: the upper teeth, stomach, spleen, throat, mouth, lips, nose, breast, face, cheek, anterior portion of the ear, forehead, neck, Quepen (ST 12), chest, abdomen, Qichong (ST 30), lateral border of the anterior surface of the lower limbs, the second toe, middle toe, big toe, and diaphragm.

Divergent Meridians: Stomach, spleen, heart, mouth, pharygnx, eyes, thighs.

Collateral: throat, head and nape of the neck.

Muscle Regions: external genitals, nose, mouth, hypochondriac region, spine, zygomatic region, margin of the lower eyelid, thigh, upper abdomen, Quepen (ST 12), cheek.

Spleen Meridian of Foot Taiyin

Meridian: Spleen, stomach, pharynx, root of the tongue, centre of the heart, big toe, medial border of the anterior surface of the lower limbs, chest, hypochondrium, abdomen, diaphragm.

Divergent Meridians: stomach, spleen, heart, pharynx, centre of the tongue.

Collateral: intestine, stomach.

Muscle Regions: external genitals, umbilicus, hypochondrium, inner chest, spine, thigh, inner abdomen.

Heart Meridian of Hand Shaoyin

Meridian: heart, the small intestine, pharynx, eye, lung, diaphragm, medial side of the little finger, inner palm, and the little finger.

Divergent Meridian: heart, throat, inner canthus, face.

Collateral: heart, root of the tongue, eyes.

Muscle Regions: breasts, cardia, umbilicus, centre of the chest.

Small Intestine Meridian of Hand Taiyang

Meridian: heart, small intestine, pharynx, stomach, ear, inner canthus, outer canthus, nose, little finger, lateral side of the little finger, scapula, Quepen (ST 12), lateral aspect of the neck, face and cheek, anterior portion of the ear, zygomatic region and diaphragm. Divergent Meridians: heart, small intestine and axilla.

Collateral: Jianyu (LI 15).

Muscle Regions: ear, axilla, posterior axilla, Wangu (GB 12), mandible, neck, scapula, outer canthus.

Bladder Meridian of Foot Taiyang

Meridian: the brain, kidney, bladder, inner canthus, forehead, vertex, angle of the ear, nape of the neck, scapula, beside the spine, waist, buttock, thigh, lateral aspect of the posterior side of the lower limbs, the fifth toe.

Divergent Meridians: anus, bladder, kidney, heart.

Muscle Regions: root of the tongue, nose, knee, ankle, occipital bone, face, margin of the upper eyelid, zygomatic region, Jianyu (LI 15), posterior side of the axilla, Quepen (ST 12), Wangu (GB 12), buttock, nape of the neck and spine.

Kidney Meridian of Foot Shaoyin

Meridian: Spine, kidney, bladder, liver, diaphragm, centre of the chest, lung, throat, root of the tongue, heart, the fifth toe, through the heart, inferior and posterior to the medial malleolus, posterior border of the medial aspect of the lower limbs.

Divergent Meridians: kidney, root of the tongue, second lumbar vertebra, Dai Meridian, nape of the neck.

Collateral: pericardium, lumbar spine.

Muscle Regions: external genitals, heels, spine, alongside the spine, occipital bone.

Pericardium Meridian of Hand Jueyin

Meridian: pericardium collateral, Sanjiao, chest and diaphragm, hypochondrium, below the axilla, midline of the medial aspect of the upper limbs, centre of the palm, the middle finger and ring finger.

Divergent Meridians: Sanjiao, throat, posterior of the ear, centre of the chest, Wangu (GB 12).

Collateral: pericardium, heart system.

Sanjiao Meridian of Hand Shaoyang

Meridian: pericardium, Sanjiao, inner ear, outer canthus, the ring finger, the upper line of the lateral aspect of the upper limbs, shoulder, Quepen (ST 12), diaphragm, Danzhong (RN 17), nape of the neck, anterior and posterior portion of the ear, head, cheek.

Divergent Meridians: Sanjiao, vertex, centre of the chest, Quepen (ST 12).

Muscle Regions: root of the tongue, teeth, outer canthus, posterior portion of the ear, neck, mandible, cheek, wisdom teeth.

Gallbladder Meridian of Foot Shaoyang

Meridian: liver, gallbladder, inner ear, outer canthus, angle of the forehead, head, nape of the neck, anterior and posterior portion of the ear, shoulder, Quepen (ST 12), diaphragm, Jiache (ST 6), neck, axilla, chest, hypochondrium, abdomen, Qichong (ST 30), thigh, the midline of the lateral aspect of the lower limbs, fourth toe and the big toe.

Divergent Meridians: gallbladder, liver, heart, pharynx, eyes, hypochondriac region, inner chest, lower cheek, mandible, face, outer canthus.

Muscle Regions: breast, angle of the forehead, vertex, zygomatic region, outer canthus, thigh, hypochondriac region, Quepen (ST 12), mandible, axilla.

Liver Meridian of Foot Jueyin

Meridian: stomach, liver, gallbladder, throat, eyes, diaphragm, lung, external genitalia, big toe, midline of the medial aspect of the lower limbs, upper and lower abdomen, abdomen, hypochondrium, rib, forehead, vertex, cheek, inside lips.

Divergent Meridians: gallbladder, liver, heart, pharynx, eyes, inner chest, mandible, face.

Collateral: testis, external genitalia.

Muscle Regions: external genitalia.

Ren Meridian

Abdomen, throat, lower cheek, face, eyes, uterus, spine, lips, mouth.

Du Meridian

The lower abdomen, external genitalia, spine, kidney, umbilicus, heart, throat, lower cheek lips, eyes, the brain.

Chong Meridian

Five Zang and six fu organs, Qijie, kidney, dorsum, centre of the chest, thumb.

Dai Meridian

Kidney, the fourteenth vertebra, hypochondriac region.

Yinqiao Meridian

Inner chest, Quepen (ST 12), inner canthus.

Yangqiao Meridian

Eyes, nape of the neck, the brain, outer canthus.

Yinwei Meridian

Lower abdomen, hypochondrium, chest, diaphragm, pharynx.

Yangwei Meridian

Lower abdomen, hypochondrium, posterior portion of the ear, forehead, ear.

2. The Therapeutic Properties of Acupoints

"Passages of the Meridians and collaterals are amenable to treatment."

The therapeutic properties of acupoints are generalized on the basis of the theories of the meridians and collaterals. It can be known from 3 aspects:

1) The Local and Adjacent Therapeutic Properties of Acupoints

All the acupoints (including the acupoints of the fourteen Meridians, extraordinary points and Ashi points) share a common feature in terms of their therapeutic properties. Namely, all the points can be applied to treat disorders of these areas and of nearby organs. For example, Tinggong (SI 19), Tinghui (GB 2), Ermen (SJ 21) and Yifeng (SJ 17) located on the auricular area are used to treat ear disorders. Jingming (BL 1), Sibai (ST 2), Tongziliao (GB 1) and Cuanzhu (BL 2) located around the optic area are used for eye disorders, etc.

2) The Remote Therapeutic Properties of Acupoints

Among the acupoints of the fourteen meridians, those located on the limbs (especially below the elbow and knee joints) are effective not only for local disorders but also for disorders of more remote Zangfu organs and tissues along the course of their pertaining meridians. Some even have systemic therapeutic properties. For example, Hegu (LI 4) is used for disorders not only on the hands and arms, but also on the head, face and five sense organs, as well as exogenous diseases such as fever and coma.

3) The Special Therapeutic Properties of Acupoints

It has been proven in clinical practice that puncturing specific points can have a homeostatic effect on functional conditions in the body. For instance, puncturing Tianshu (ST 25) can relieve both diarrhea and constipation, and puncturing Neiguan (PC 6) can correct both tachycardia and bradycardia. In addition to the general therapeutic properties of acupoints, clinical attention should also be paid to the special therapeutic properties of some acupoints. Examples are Dazhui (DU 14), which is effective for reducing fever, and Zhiyin (BL 67), which is mainly applied to malposition of a fetus.

The therapeutic properties of acupoints are primarily determined by the transverse and longitudinal locations of acupoints on the body surface. The course of the Meridians is taken as the longitudinal location of most acupoints, while the level position with the human body is taken as transverse locations. No matter what location it is, longitudinal or transverse, neighbouring acupoints will have similar therapeutic properties. For example, Zusanli (ST 36), Shangjuxu (ST 37) and Xiajuxu (ST 39) pertain to the Stomach Meridian and they are longitudinal neighbours used for abdominal disorders. Shenque (RN 8), Tianshu (ST 25) and Daheng (SP 15) do not pertain to the same meridian but they are neighbouring transversely used for disorders of intestine and abdomen. The therapeutic properties of acupoints can be understood according to the meridians and body parts of acupoints.

Indications of Acupoints with Relation to Meridians

The acupoints of the fourteen meridians are used not only for the disorders of the individual meridian, but also for the disorders of two meridians in common. Regarding the indications of acupoints with relation to meridians not only have their special features, but also have their general characteristics. Indications of acupoints with relation to meridians are listed as follows: (See Tab. 1-7 to 1-11)

Table 1-7 Indications of Acupoints of the Three Yin Meridians of Hand

Name of the Meridian	Indications of Individual Meridian	Indications of Two Meridians in Common	Indications of Three Meridians in Common
The Lung Meridian of Hand Taiyin	Disorders of the lung and throat		Disorders of the chest
The Pericardium Meridian of Hand Jueyin	Disorders of the heart and stomach	Mental illness	
The Heart Meridian of Hand Shaoyin	Disorders of the heart		

Table 1-8 Indications of Acupoints of the Three Yang Meridians of Hand

Name of the Meridians	Indications of Individual Meridian	Indications of Two Meridians in Common	Indications of Three Meridians in Common
The Large Intestine Meridian of Hand Yangming	Disorders of the forehead, face, nose, mouth and teeth		Disorders of the eye, throat and febrile diseases
The Sanjiao Meridian of Hand Shaoyang	Disorders of the temporal and hypochondriac region	Disorders of the ear	
The Small Intestine Meridian of Hand Taiyang	Disorders of the occipital region and scapular region and mental illness		

Table 1-9 Indications of Acupoints of the Three Yang Meridians of Foot

Name of the Meridians	Indications of Individual Meridian	Indications of Two Meridians in Common	Indications of Three Meridians in Common
The Stomach Meridian of Foot Yangming	Disorders of the forehead, teeth, mouth, throat, stomach and intestine		Mental illness, febrile diseases
The Gallbladder Meridian of Foot Shaoyang	Disorders of the ear, temporal and hypochondriac regions	Disorders of the eyes	
The Bladder Meridian of Foot Taiyang	Disorders of the neck, dorsolumbar region and Zangfu organs.		

Table 1-10 Indications of Acupoints of the Three Yin Meridians of Foot

Name of the Meridians	Indications of Individual Meridian	Indications of Three Meridians in Common
The Spleen Meridian of Foot Taiyin	Disorders of the spleen and stomach	Disorders of the external genitalia and gynaecological diseases
The Liver Meridian of Foot Jueyin	Disorders of the liver	
The Kidney Meridian of Foot Shaoyin	Disorders of the kidney, lung and throat	

Table 1-11 Indications of Acupoints of Ren and Du Meridians

Name of the Meridians	Indications of Individual Meridian	Indications of Two Meridians in Common
Ren Meridian	Prolapse of Yang, collapse, bearing strengthening function	Mental illness, disorders of Zangfu organs and gynecological disorders
Du Meridian	Apoplexy, coma, febrile diseases, disorders of the head and face	

Indications of Acupoints on the Head, Face and Trunk with Relation to Their Locations

Acupoints of the fourteen Meridians located on the head, face and trunk have their own therapeutic properties. For example, most points on the head, face and neck are used for local disorders, and very few acupoints are used for general disorders or disorders on the four limbs. Acupoints on the chest and abdomen are mostly used for disorders of Zangfu organs and acute diseases. Most acupoints on the back and around the lumbar region are used for local disorders, disorders of Zangfu organs and chronic diseases. In addition, few points are used for disorders on the lower limbs. Acupoints on the lower abdomen are used for general disorders in addition to the disorders of Zangfu organs. Those above the elbows and knees are mainly used for local disorders, while those below the elbows to the wrist and knees to ankles are used for disorders of Zangfu organs in addition to local disorders. In addition to local disorders, the points below the wrists and ankles can be used for disorders of the head, face and five sense organs as well as general disorders including fever and mental disorders. Indications of acupoints on the head, face and trunk with relation to their locations are concluded as follows: (See Tab. 1-12 to 1-21, See Fig. 1-3 to 1-10)

Table 1-12　Indications of Acupoints on the Head, Face and Neck

Locations of Acupoints	Indications
Forehead, temporal region	Disorders of the eyes and nose
Occipital region	Mental illness, local diseases
Vertex	Mental illness, hoarseness, disorders of the throat, eyes and vertex
Optic region	Disorders of the eyes
Nasal region	Disorders of the nose
Neck	Disorders of the tongue, throat, esophagus and neck, hoarseness and asthma

Table 1-13　Indications of Acupoints on the Chest, Abdomen and Hypochondriac Region

Locations of Acupoints	Indications
Chest, upper dorsal region	Disorders of the chest, lung and heart
Abdominal region	Disorders of the liver, gallbladder, spleen and stomach
Lower abdominal region	Disorders of menstruation, leukorrhea, genital organs, kidney, bladder and intestine

Table 1-14　Indications of Acupoints on the Shoulder, Dorsal and Lumbar Region

Locations of Acupoints	Indications
Scapular region	Local disorders, pain of the vertex
Dorsal region	Disorders of the lung and heart
Lumbar region	Disorders of the liver, gallbladder, spleen and stomach
Lumbosacral region	Disorders of the kidney, bladder, intestine, anus, menstruation and leukorrhea

Table 1-15　Indications of Acupoints on the Hypochondriac and Lateroabdominal Region

Locations of Acupoints	Indications
Hypochondriac region	Disorders of the liver and gallbladder and local disorders
Lateroabdominal region	Disorders of the spleen and stomach, menstruation and leukorrhea diseases

Table 1-16　Indications of Acupoints on the Medial Aspect of the Upper Limbs

Locations of Acupoints	Indications
Medial aspect of the upper arms	Disorders of medial aspect of the shoulders and arms
Medial aspect of the anterior part of the arm	Disorders of the chest, lung, heart, throat and stomach, mental illness
Medial aspect of the palm and fingers	Mental illness, febrile diseases, coma and emergency treatment

Table 1-17 Indications of Acupoints on the Lateral Aspect of the Upper Limbs

Locations of Acupoints	Indications
Lateral aspect of the upper arms Lateral aspect of the anterior part of the arm Lateral aspect of the palm and fingers	Disorders of lateral aspect of the shoulders, arms and elbows Disorders of the head, eyes, nose, mouth, teeth, throat, hypochondrium and scapular area, mental illness and febrile diseases Disorders of the throat, febrile diseases and emergency treatment

Table 1-18 Indications of Acupoints on the Posterior Aspect of the Lower Limbs

Locations of Acupoints	Indications
Posterior aspect of the thigh Posterior aspect of the leg Posterior aspect of the heel, lateral aspect of foot	Disorders of buttock and femoral region Disorders of back, lumbar region and anus Disorders of the head, neck, back, lumbar region, eyes, mental illness and febrile diseases

Table 1-19 Indications of Acupoints on the Anterior Aspect of the Lower Limbs

Locations of Acupoints	Indications
Anterior aspect of the thigh Anterior aspect of the leg Anterior aspect of foot	Disorders of the legs and knees Disorders of the stomach and intestine Disorders of the forehead, teeth, throat, gastrointestinal tract, mental illness and febrile diseases

Table 1-20 Indications of Acupoints on the Medial Aspect of the Lower Limbs

Locations of Acupoints	Indications
Medial aspect of the thigh	Disorders of menstruation, urinary bladder and anterior genitalia, leukorrhea.
Medial aspect of the leg	Disorders of menstruation, spleen and stomach, anterior genitalia and urinary bladder and leukorrhea.
Medial aspect of the foot	Disorders of menstruation, the spleen and stomach, the liver, anterior genitalia, the kidney, the lung and throat and leukorrhea.

Table 1-21 Indications of Acupoints on the Lateral Aspect of the Lower Limbs

Locations of Acupoints	Indications
Lateral aspect of the thigh Lateral aspect of the leg Lateral aspect of the foot	Disorders of lumbosacral region, of knees and femur joints. Disorders of the neck, eyes, hypochondriac and temporal regions Disorders of temporal and hypochondriac regions, eyes and ears and febrile diseases.

General Introduction to the System of Meridians, Collaterals and Acupoints

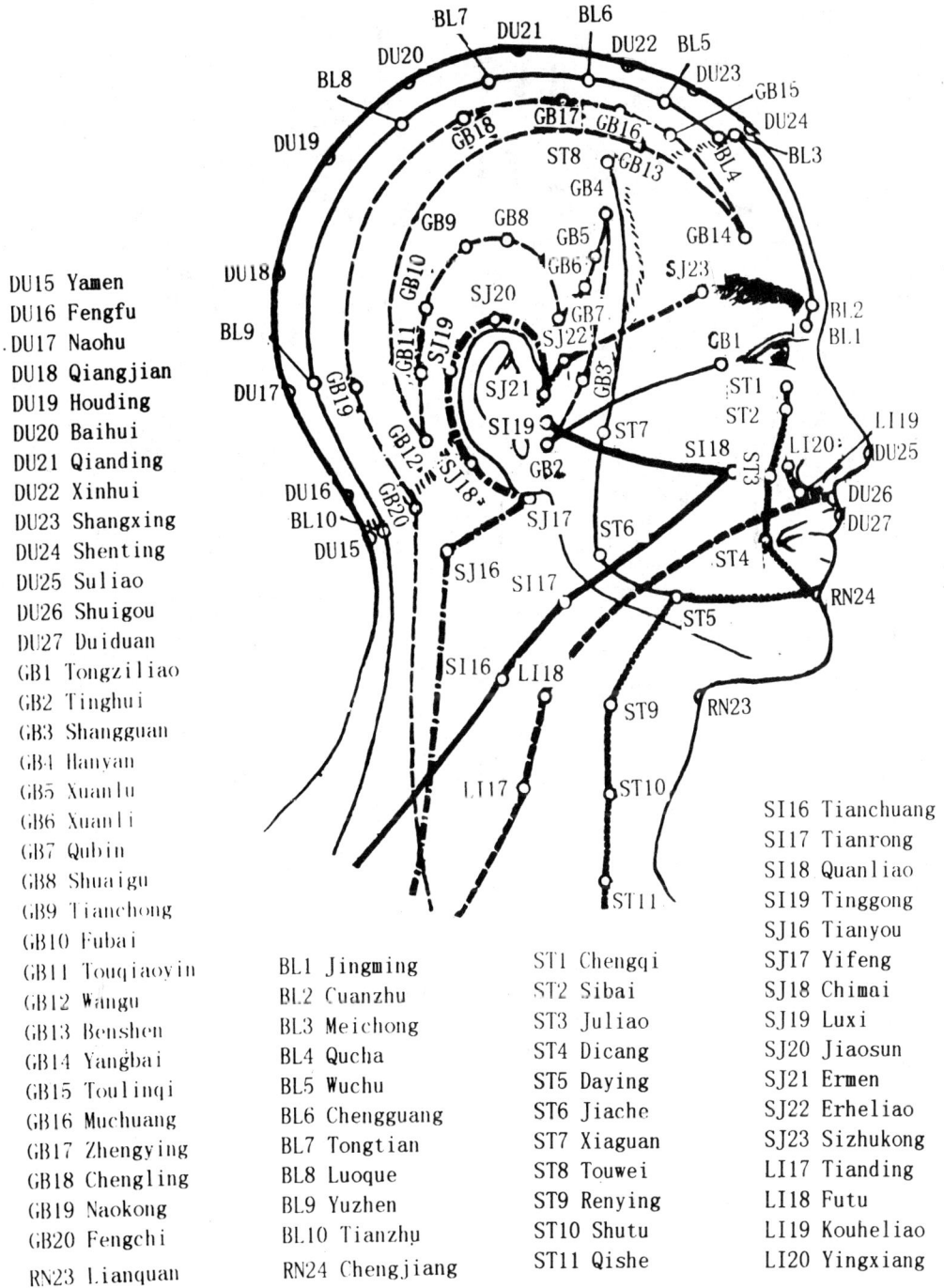

DU15 Yamen
DU16 Fengfu
DU17 Naohu
DU18 Qiangjian
DU19 Houding
DU20 Baihui
DU21 Qianding
DU22 Xinhui
DU23 Shangxing
DU24 Shenting
DU25 Suliao
DU26 Shuigou
DU27 Duiduan
GB1 Tongziliao
GB2 Tinghui
GB3 Shangguan
GB4 Hanyan
GB5 Xuanlu
GB6 Xuanli
GB7 Qubin
GB8 Shuaigu
GB9 Tianchong
GB10 Fubai
GB11 Touqiaoyin
GB12 Wangu
GB13 Benshen
GB14 Yangbai
GB15 Toulinqi
GB16 Muchuang
GB17 Zhengying
GB18 Chengling
GB19 Naokong
GB20 Fengchi
RN23 Lianquan

BL1 Jingming
BL2 Cuanzhu
BL3 Meichong
BL4 Qucha
BL5 Wuchu
BL6 Chengguang
BL7 Tongtian
BL8 Luoque
BL9 Yuzhen
BL10 Tianzhu
RN24 Chengjiang

ST1 Chengqi
ST2 Sibai
ST3 Juliao
ST4 Dicang
ST5 Daying
ST6 Jiache
ST7 Xiaguan
ST8 Touwei
ST9 Renying
ST10 Shutu
ST11 Qishe

SI16 Tianchuang
SI17 Tianrong
SI18 Quanliao
SI19 Tinggong
SJ16 Tianyou
SJ17 Yifeng
SJ18 Chimai
SJ19 Luxi
SJ20 Jiaosun
SJ21 Ermen
SJ22 Erheliao
SJ23 Sizhukong
LI17 Tianding
LI18 Futu
LI19 Kouheliao
LI20 Yingxiang

Fig. 1-3　Acupoints on the Head, Face and Neck

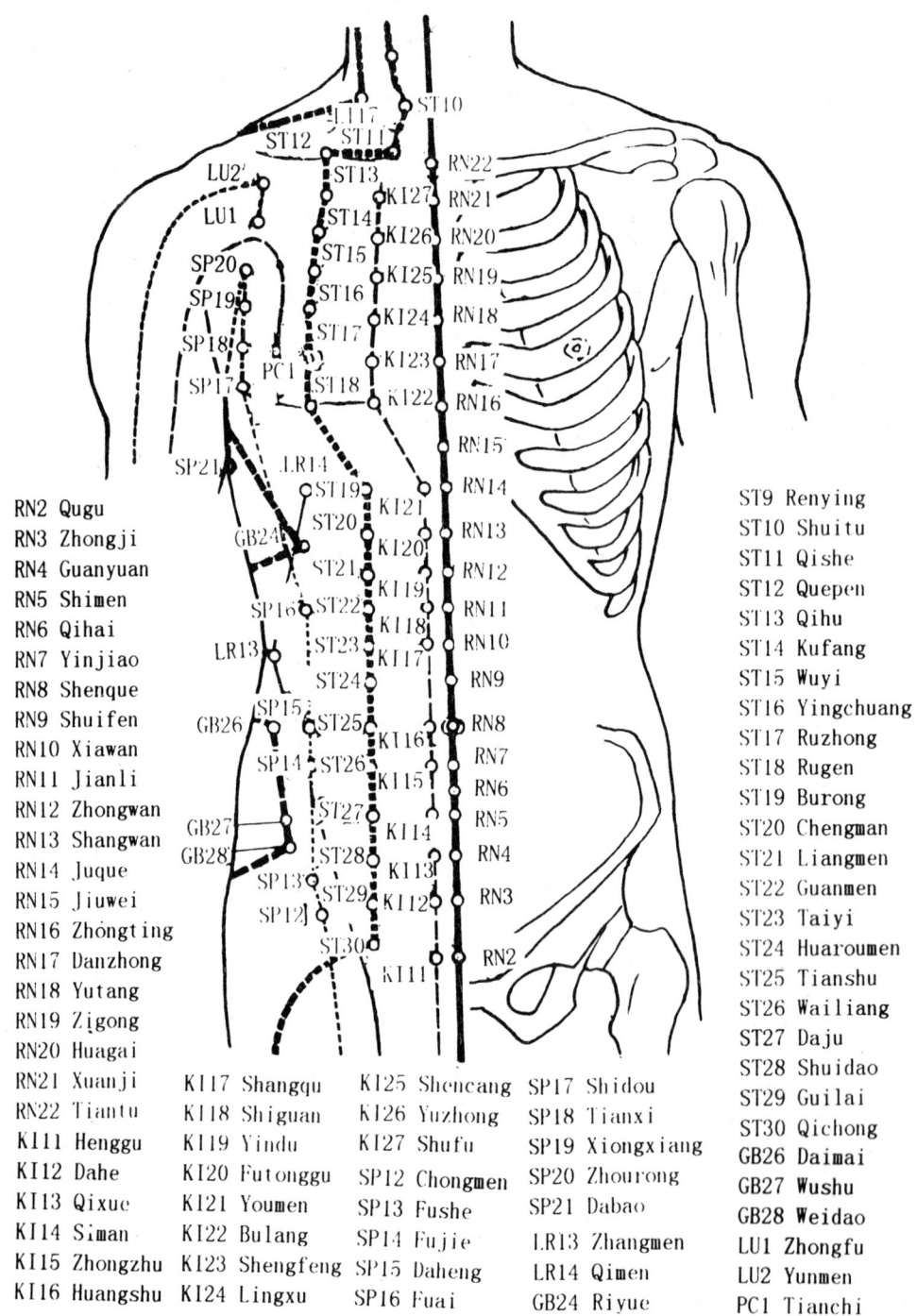

Fig. 1-4 **Acupoints at the Chest and Abdomen**

General Introduction to the System of Meridians, Collaterals and Acupoints 37

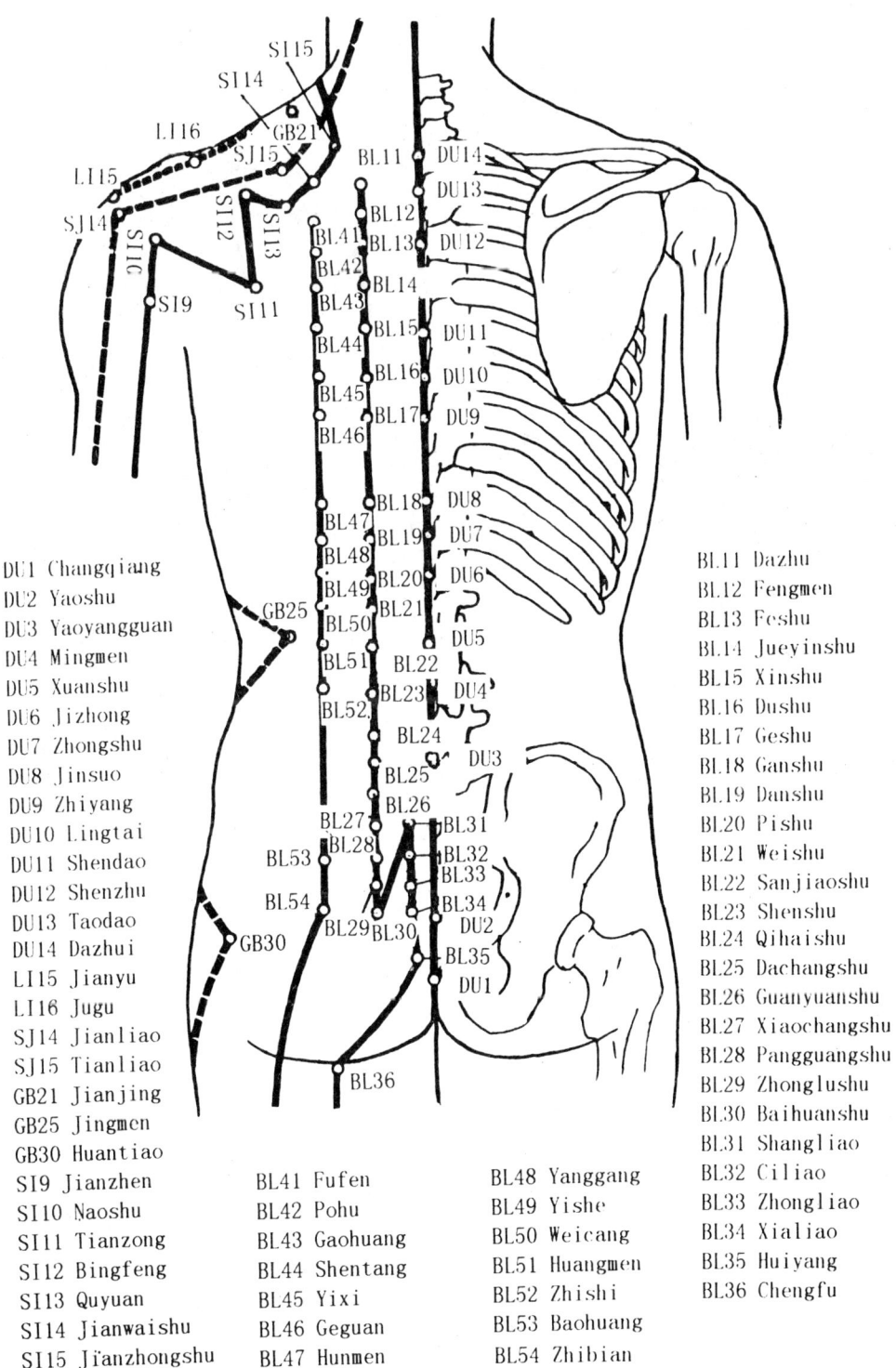

Fig. 1-5 **Acupoints on the Back and at the Lumbar Region**

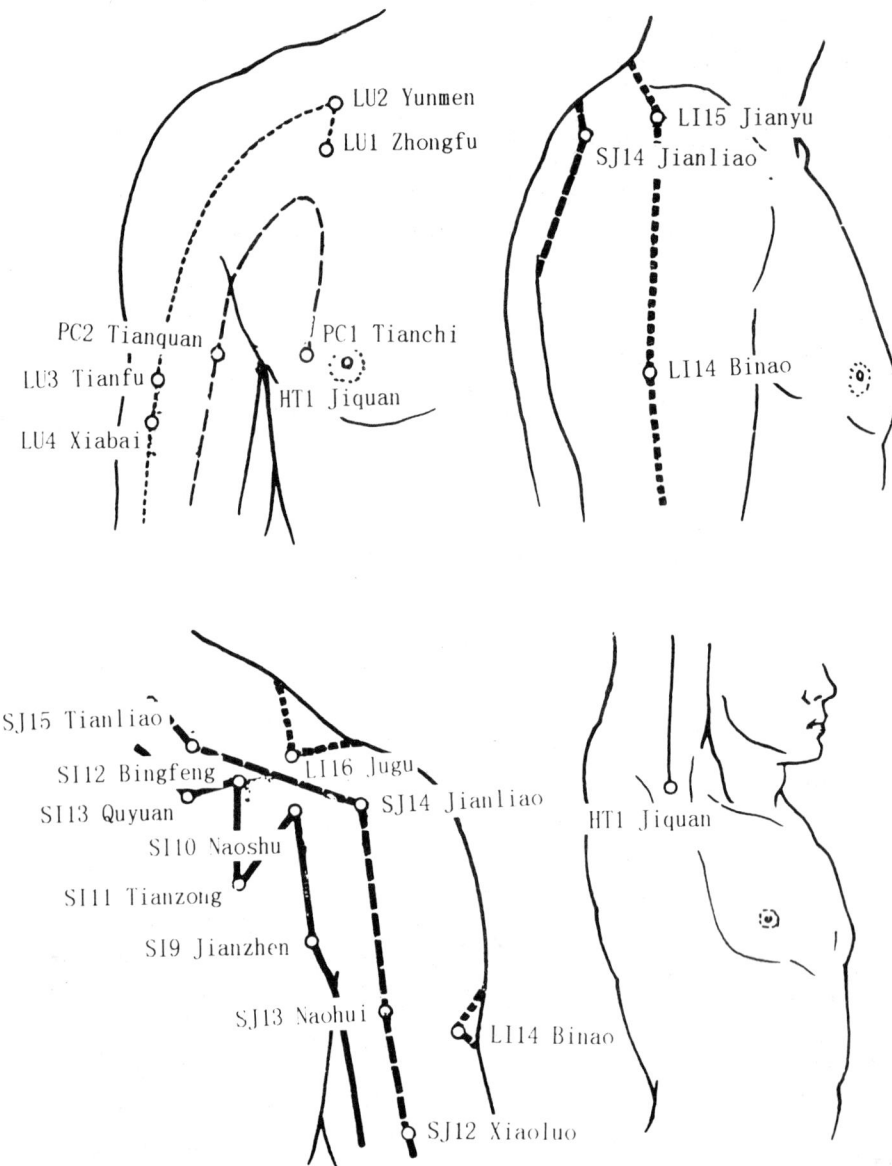

Fig. 1-6 Acupoints at the Shoulder Region

General Introduction to the System of Meridians, Collaterals and Acupoints

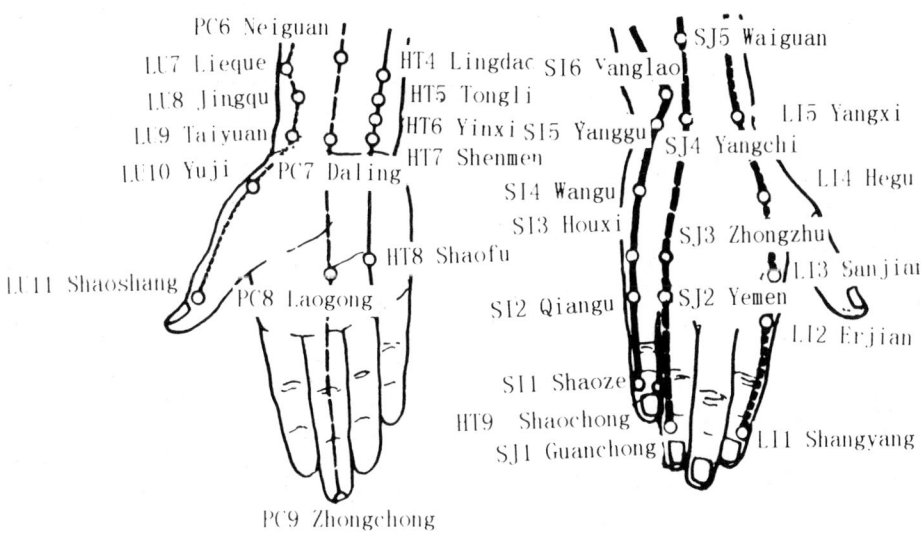

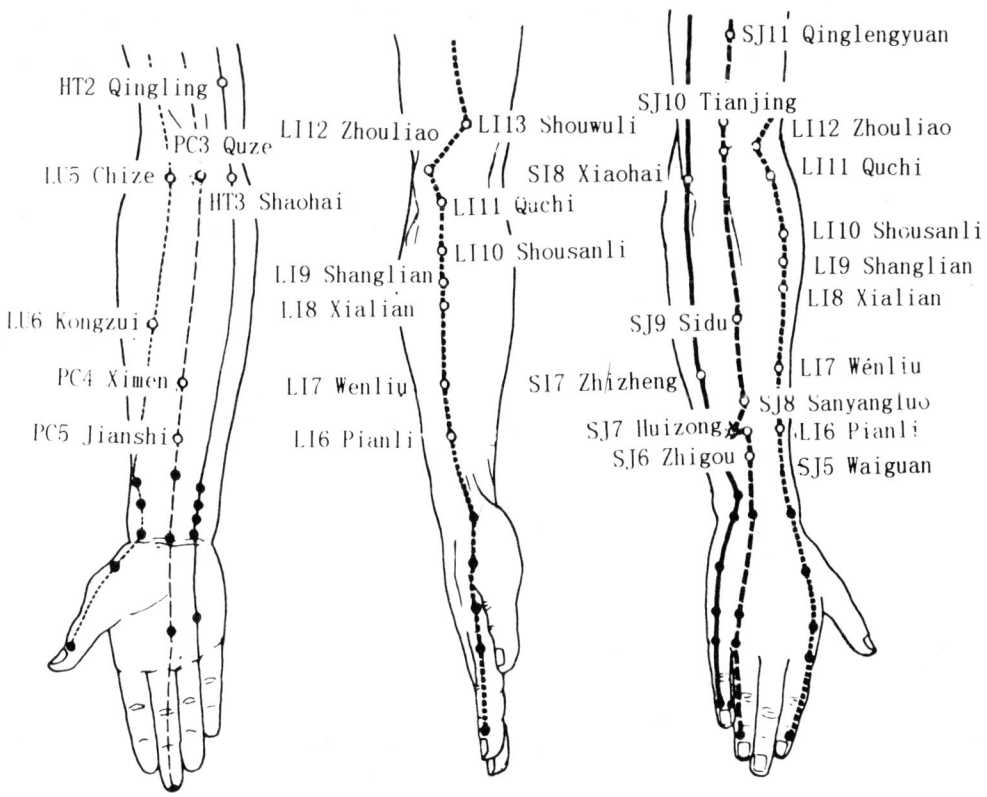

Fig. 1-7 Acupoints in the Upper Limbs

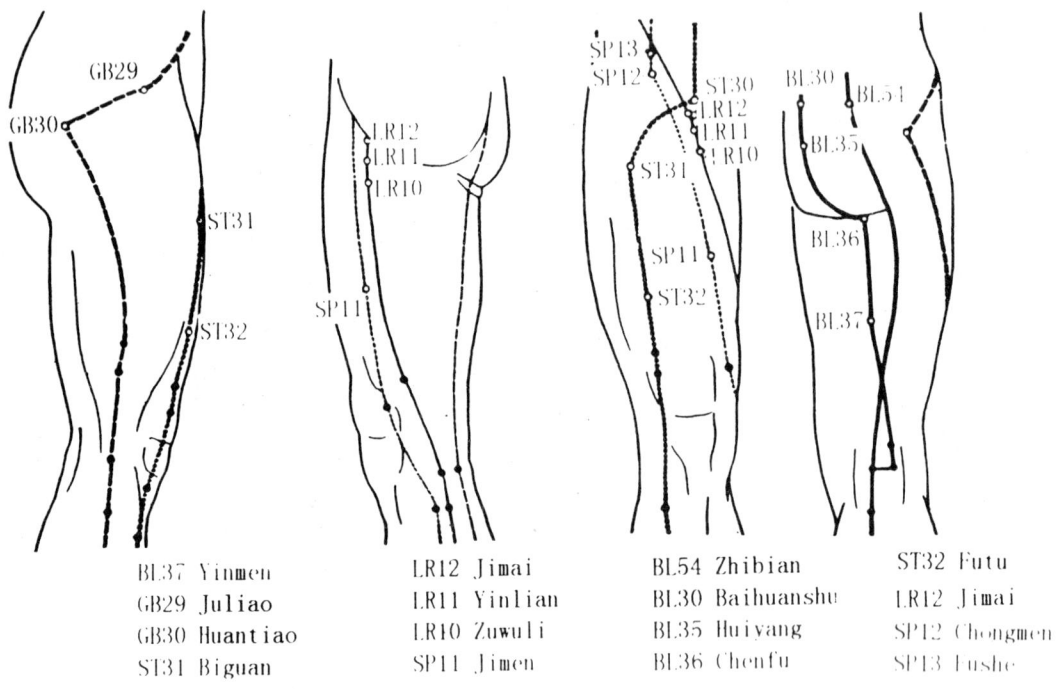

Fig. 1-8 Acupoints on the Hip and Thigh

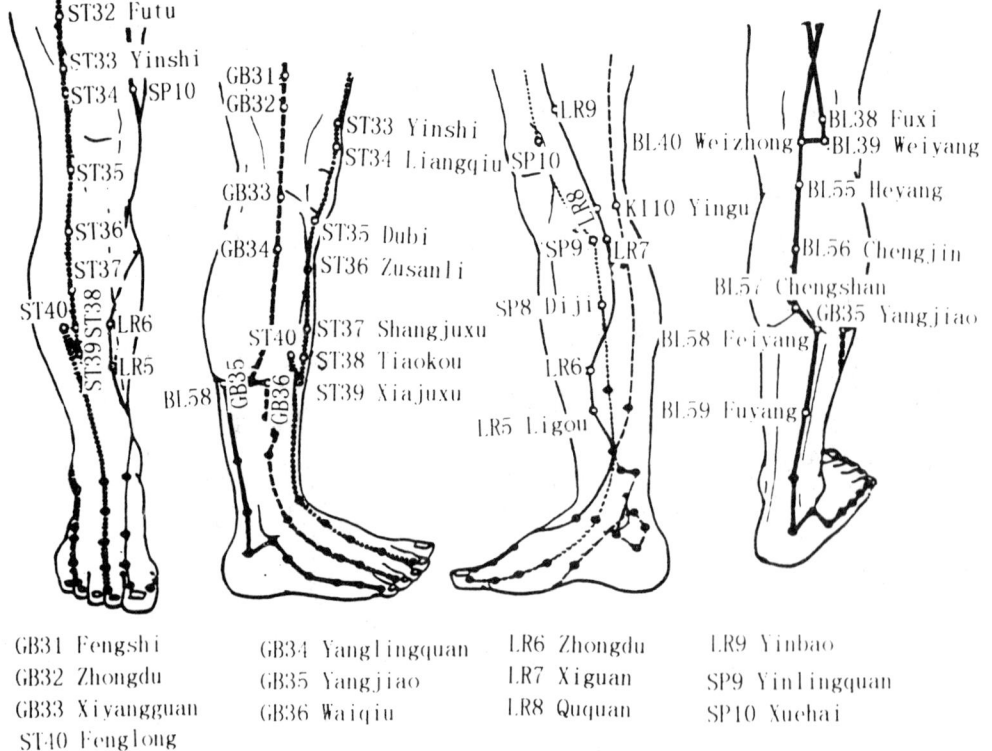

Fig. 1-9 Acupoints in the Leg

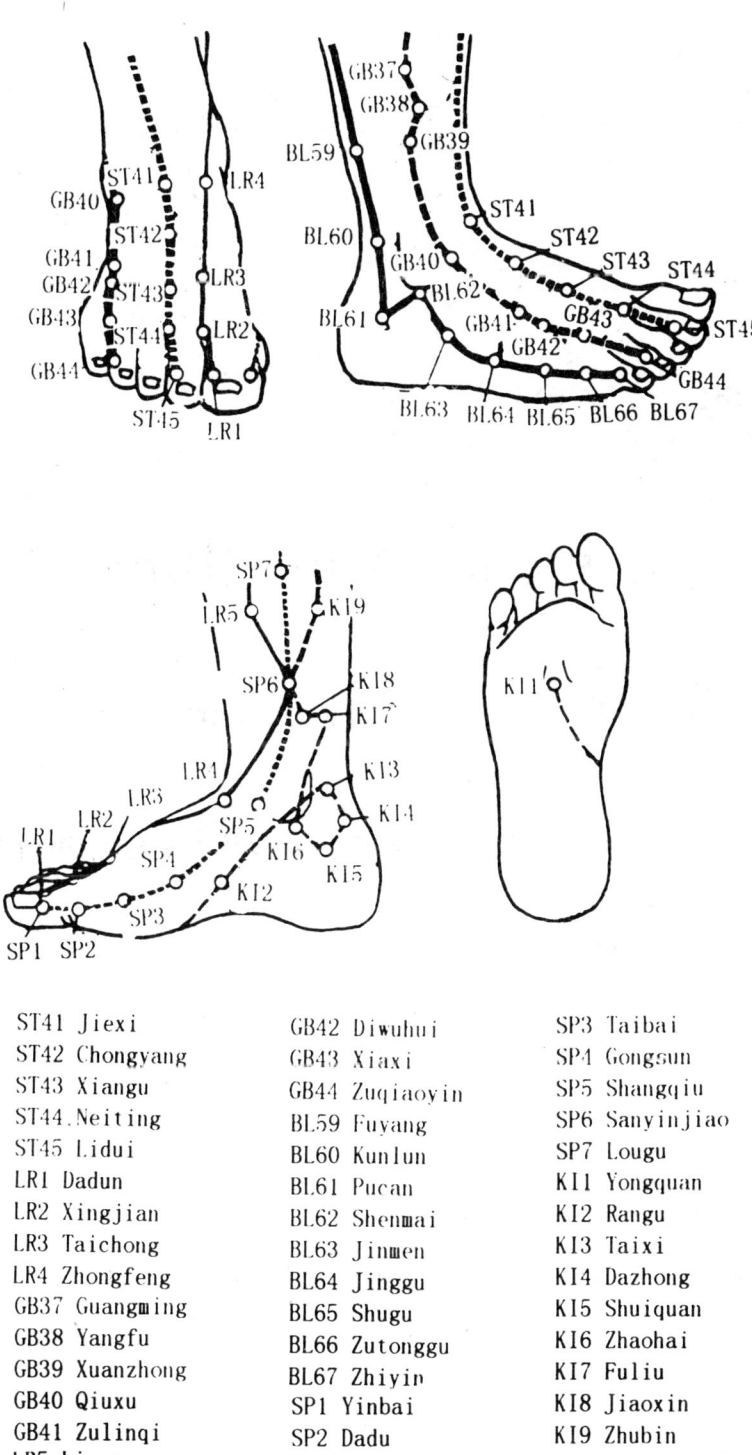

ST41 Jiexi	GB42 Diwuhui	SP3 Taibai
ST42 Chongyang	GB43 Xiaxi	SP4 Gongsun
ST43 Xiangu	GB44 Zuqiaoyin	SP5 Shangqiu
ST44 Neiting	BL59 Fuyang	SP6 Sanyinjiao
ST45 Lidui	BL60 Kunlun	SP7 Lougu
LR1 Dadun	BL61 Pucan	KI1 Yongquan
LR2 Xingjian	BL62 Shenmai	KI2 Rangu
LR3 Taichong	BL63 Jinmen	KI3 Taixi
LR4 Zhongfeng	BL64 Jinggu	KI4 Dazhong
GB37 Guangming	BL65 Shugu	KI5 Shuiquan
GB38 Yangfu	BL66 Zutonggu	KI6 Zhaohai
GB39 Xuanzhong	BL67 Zhiyin	KI7 Fuliu
GB40 Qiuxu	SP1 Yinbai	KI8 Jiaoxin
GB41 Zulinqi	SP2 Dadu	KI9 Zhubin
LR5 Ligou		

Fig. 1-10 **Acupoints on the Heel**

Chapter Two

The Eight Extra Meridians

I. System of the Du Meridian

1. Distribution of the Du Meridian and Its Collaterals

1) Course of the Du Meridian

The Du Meridian originates from the lower abdomen and emerges at the perineum. Ascending, it runs along the interior of the spinal column to Fengfu (DU 16) located at the nape of the neck, and then enters the brain. It further ascends along the midline of the head to the vertex and begins its descent along the forehead, nose, and upper lip, terminating at the frenulum of the upper lip. (See Fig. 2-1).

2) Course of the Large Collaterals

"The collateral of the Du Meridian arises from Changqiang (DU 1) in the perineum, runs upward along both sides of the spine to the nape and spreads over the top of the head. At the scapular region, it connects with Foot Taiyang and pierces through the spine." (*Miraculous Pivot*)

3) The Acupoints

There are 28 points in the Du Meridian. The first point is Changqiang (DU 1) and the last point is Yinjiao (DU 28).
Crossing points: Huiyin (RN 1), Fengmen (BL 12). (See Fig. 2-1).

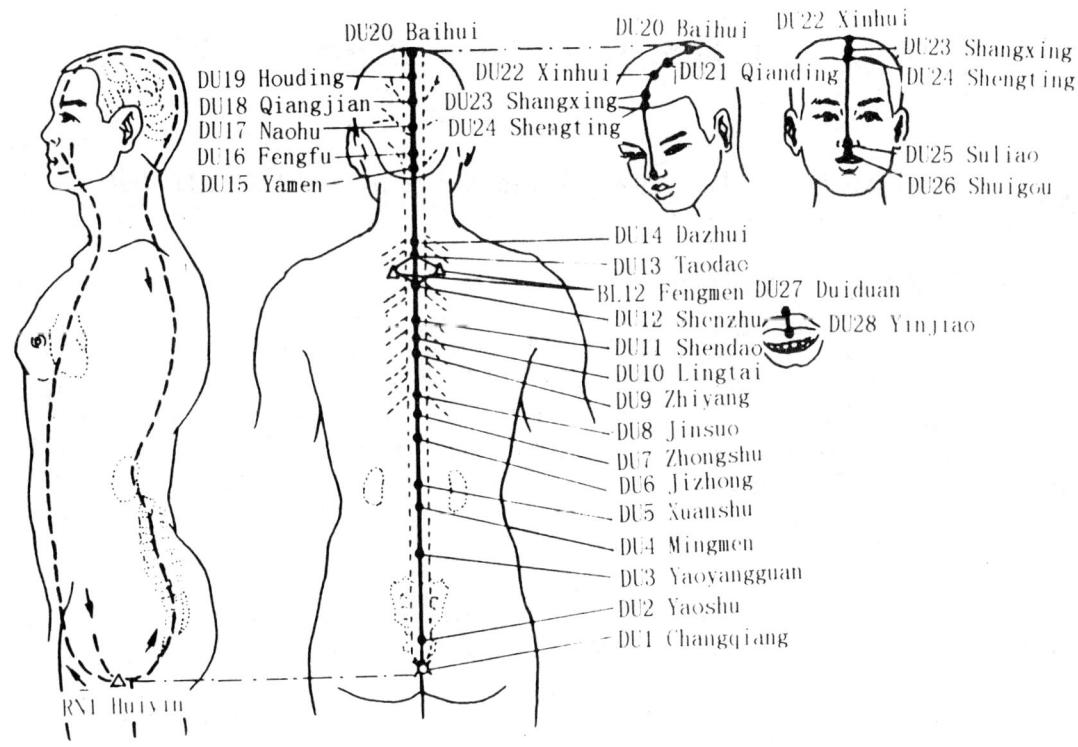

Fig. 2-1 the Du Meridian

2. Symptoms and Signs of Disorders of the Du Meridian and Its Large Collaterals

1) Symptoms and Signs of the Disorders of the Du Meridian

"Disorders of the Du Meridian start from the lower abdomen and go up to the heart. There may appear difficulty in urination and defecation, sterility in women, dysuria, hemorrhoids and enursis and a dry sensation in the pharynx." (*Plain Questions*)

"Diseases of the Du Meridian may cause opisthotonos." (*Plain Questions*)

"The collateral of the Du Meridian arises from Changqiang (DU 1). Excess of the Du Meridian may lead to stiffness of the back, while deficiency may cause heaviness of the head." (*Miraculous Pivot*)

"Wind pathogen may run upward along Fengfu (DU 16) and cause headache due to pathogenic wind, manifested as mental illness, convulsions and dizziness." (*Plain Questions*)

"If the Du Meridian has a disorder, there may appear stiffness of the spine, which may bring about convulsion." (*Classic of Medical Problems*)

2) Symptoms and Signs of the Disorders of the Large Collaterals

"Excess syndromes cause stiffness of the spine, while deficiency syndromes lead to heaviness of the head." (*Miraculous Pivot*)

II. System of the Ren Meridian

1. Distribution of the Ren Meridian and Its Collaterals

1) Course of the Ren Meridian

The Ren Meridian originates in the lower abdomen and emerges from the perineum. It ascends anteriorly along the pubic region, runs along the interior of the abdomen and passes through Guanyuan (RN 4) and other points of the Ren Meridian along the front midline to the throat. Crossing the mandibular region, it curves around the lips and travels through the cheek to the infraobital region. (*Plain Questions*) (See Fig. 2-2).

2) Course of the Collaterals

It starts from Jiuwei (RN 15) (located 7 cun above the umbilicus) and then runs downward and spreads over the abdomen. (See Fig. 2-2).

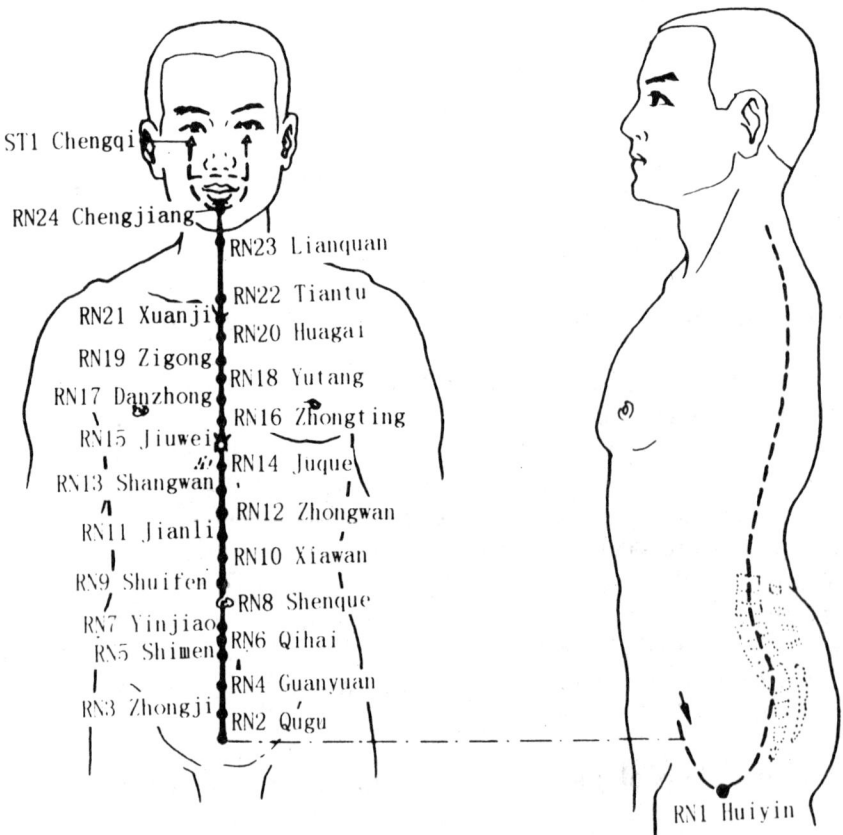

Fig. 2-2 The Ren Meridian

2. Symptoms and Signs of the Disorders of the Ren Meridian and its Collaterals

1) Symptoms and Signs of the Disorders of the Ren Meridian

"Diseases of the Ren Meridian manifest as seven kinds of hernia in men and leukorrhea and abdominal masses in women." (*Plain Questions*)

"Diseases of the Ren Meridian manifest as internal obstruction, which refers to the seven kinds of hernia in men and abdominal masses in women." (*Classic of Medical Problems*)

2) Symptoms and Signs of the Disorders of the Collaterals

"Excess syndromes may cause abdominal pain, while deficiency syndromes may cause itch." (*Miraculous Pivot*)

Appendix 1. The Chong Meridian

1. Course of the Chong Meridian

The Chong Meridian originates in the lower abdomen and emerges at the perineum. Ascending, it runs along the interior of the spinal column. Its superficial branch passes through the region of Qichong (ST 30) and communicates with the Kidney Meridian of Foot Shaoyin. Running along both sides of the abdomen, it ascends to the throat and curves around the lips. (See Fig. 2-3).

There are no acupoints along the course of the Chong Meridian.

Crossing points: Huiyin (RN 1), Qichong (ST 30), Youmen (KI 21), Yindu (KI 19), Shiguan (KI 18), Shangqu (KI 17), Huangshu (KI 16), Zhongzhu (KI 15), Siman (KI 14), Qixue (KI 13), Dahe (KI 12), Henggu (KI 11). (See Fig. 2-3).

2. Symptoms and Signs of the Disorders of the Chong Meridian

"Diseases of the Chong Meridian may cause adverse flow of qi and abdominal pain" (*Plain Questions*)

"Diseases of the Chong Meridian may cause reversed flow of qi and abdominal pain." (*Classic of Medical Problems*)

Appendix 2. The Dai Meridian

1. Course of the Dai Meridian

The Dai Meridian originates below the hypochondrium at the level of the second lumbar vertebra. It then turns obliquely downward through Daimai (GB 26), Wushu (GB 27) and Weidao (GB 28). It encircles the body at the waist, resembling a belt or girdle. (See Fig. 2-4).

There are no acupoints along the course of the Dai Meridian.

Crossing point: Daimai (GB 26), Wushu (GB 27), Weidao (GB 28). (See Fig. 2-4).

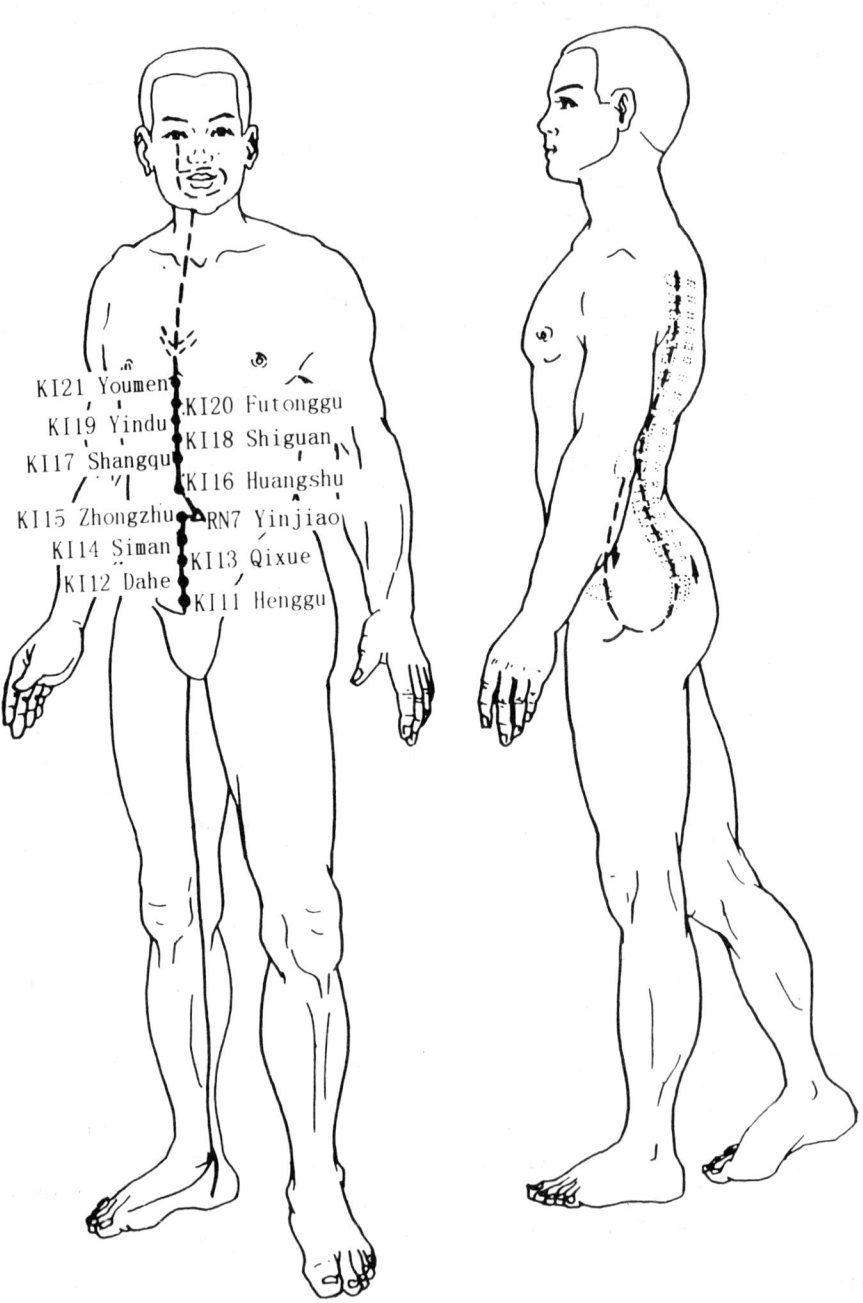

Fig. 2-3 The Chong Meridian

2. Symptoms and Signs of the Disorders of the Dai Meridian

"Deficiency of Yangming may lead to weakness of the tendons. Disorders of the Dai Meridian cause flaccidity of the lower limbs." (*Plain Questions*)

"Diseases of the Dai Meridian manifest as fullness of the abdomen, weakness and softness of the waist as if sitting in water." (*Classic of Medical Problems*)

Appendix 3. The Yangqiao Meridian

1. Course of the Yangqiao Meridian

The Yangqiao Meridian originates at the lateral side of the heel (Shenmai, BL 62). Running upward behind the lateral malleolus and along the posterior border of the fibula, the meridian passes the lateral side of the thigh and the posterior side of the hypochondrium to the posterior axilla fold. It then winds over to the shoulder and traverses the neck to pass by the side of the mouth on its way to the inner canthus. At the inner canthus, it joins the Yinqiao Meridian and the Bladder Meridian of Foot Taiyang. Running with the Bladder Meridian, it continues upwards to the forehead and onto the hair, where it winds behind the ear. It meets the Gallbladder Meridian of Foot Shaoyang at the nape of the neck (Fengchi, GB 20). (See Fig. 2-5).

There are no acupoint along the course of the Yangqiao Meridian.

Crossing points: Shenmai (BL 62), Pucan (BL 61), Fuyang (BL 59), Juliao (BL 29), Naoshu (SI 10), Jugu (LI 16), Jianyu (LI 15), Dicang (ST 4), Juliao (ST 3), Chengqi (ST 1), Jingming (BL 1), Fengchi (GB 20). (See Fig. 2-5).

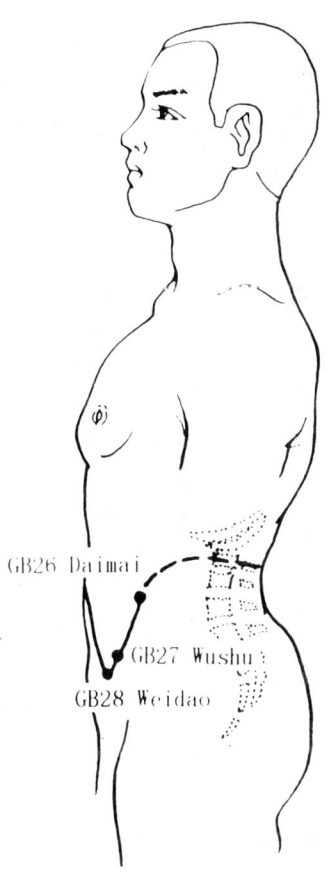

Fig. 2-4 The Dai Meridian

2. Symptoms and Signs of the Disorders of the Yangqiao Meridian

"Over abandance of Yang qi causes wide opened eyes." (*Miraculous Pivot*)

"If pathogenic factors attack the Yangqiao Meridian, there may appear pain in the eyes around the inner canthus." (*Plain Questions*)

"Diseases of the Yangqiao Meridian may cause weakness and softness of the medial aspect of the leg and spasm of the lateral aspect." (*Classic of Medical Problems*)

Appendix 4. The Yinqiao Meridian

1. Course of the Yinqiao Meridian

The Yinqiao Meridian originates from the posterior aspect of the navicular bone below the medial malleolus. It runs upwards posterior to the naviculus (Zhaohai, KI 6), then runs upwards posterior to the medial malleolus along the medial aspect of the lower limbs, it reaches the external genitalia. It then extends upward along the abdomen and chest to the supraclavicu-

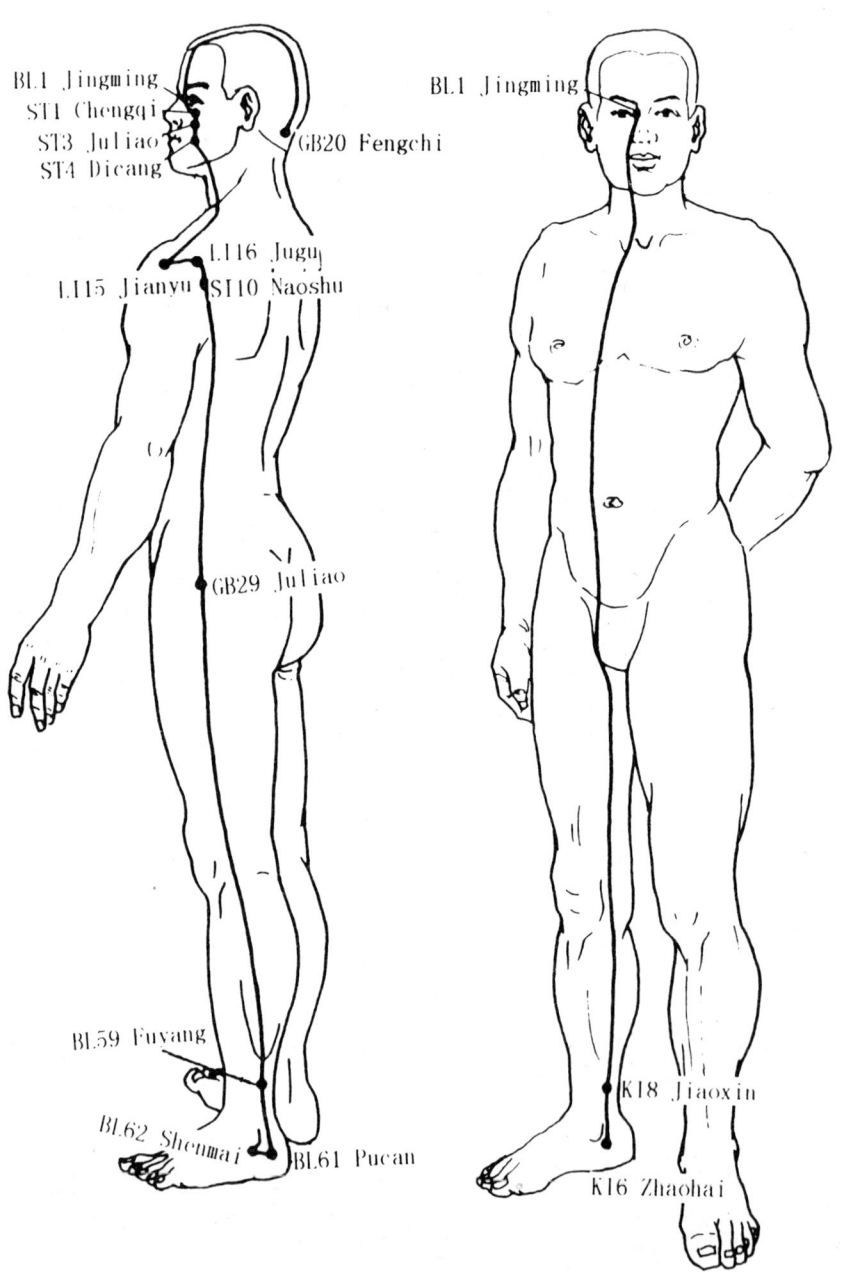

Fig. 2-5 The Yangqiao Meridian **Fig. 2-6 The Yinqiao Meridian**

lar fossa and continues its ascent lateral to the thyroid cartilage in front of Renying (ST 9) and along the zygomatic process. Reaching the inner canthus, it connects with the Bladder Meridian of Foot Taiyang and the Yangqiao Meridian. (See Fig. 2-6).

There are no acupoints along the course of the Yinqiao Meridian.

Crossing points: Zhaohai (KI 6), Jiaoxin (KI 8), Jingming (BL 1). (See Fig. 2-6).

2. Symptoms and Signs of the Disorders of the Yinqiao Meridian

"Over abandance of Yin qi causes closure of the eyes, which refers to drowsiness." (*Miraculous Pivot*)

"Diseases of the Yinqiao Meridian may cause weakness and softness of the lateral aspect of the leg and spasm of the medial aspect." (*Classic of Medical Problems*)

Appendix 5. The Yangwei Meridian

1. Course of the Yangwei Meridian

The Yangwei Meridian originates from the lateral aspect of the heel and passes through the external malleolus. It continues to ascend along the course of the Gallbladder Meridian to the hip region. The meridian continues upwards along the posterior aspect of the axilla to the shoulder and the forehead. Turning toward the back of the neck, it communicates with the Du Meridian. (See Fig. 2-7).

There are no acupoints along the course of Yangwei Meridian.

Crossing point: Jinmen (BL 63), Yangjiao (GB 35), Naoshu (SI 10), Tianliao (SJ 15), Jianjing (GB 21), Benshen (GB 13), Yangbai (GB 14), Toulinqi (GB 15), Muchuang (GB 16), Zhengying (GB 17), Chengling (GB 18), Naokong (GB 19), Fengchi (GB 20), Riyue (GB 24), Fengfu (DU 16), Yamen (DU 15).

2. Symptoms and Signs of the Disorders of the Yangwei Meridian

"Diseases of the Yangwei Meridian may cause coldness and heat simultaneously." (*Classic of Medical Problems*)

"Disorders of the Yangwei Meridian may bring about lumbar pain accompanied by sudden swelling of the painful point." (*Plain Questions*)

Appendix 6. The Yinwei Meridian

1. Course of the Yinwei Meridian

The Yinwei Meridian originates from the medial aspect of the leg, where the three meridians of the foot meet. Running upward along the medial aspect of the thigh, it reaches the abdomen to communicate with the Spleen Meridian of Foot Taiyin. When the meridian passes through the thoracic region, it connects with the Liver Meridian of Foot Jueyin. Ascending further to the throat, it communicates with the Ren Meridian at the neck. (See Fig. 2-8).

There are no acupoints along the course of the Yinwei Meridian.

Crossing point: Zhubin (KI 9), Chongmen (SP 12), Fushe (SP 13), Daheng (SP 15), Fuai (SP 16), Qimen (LR 14), Tiantu (RN 22), Lianquan (RN 23).

2. Symptoms and Signs of the Disorders of the Yinwei Meridian

"Diseases of the Yinwei Meridian may cause cardial pain." (*Classic of Medical Problems*)

"The Yangwei Meridian binds together with yang, while the Yinwei Meridian binds together with yin. If Yin and Yang fail in their maintenance (defence), there may appear mental depression and general weakness." (*Classic of Medical Problems*)

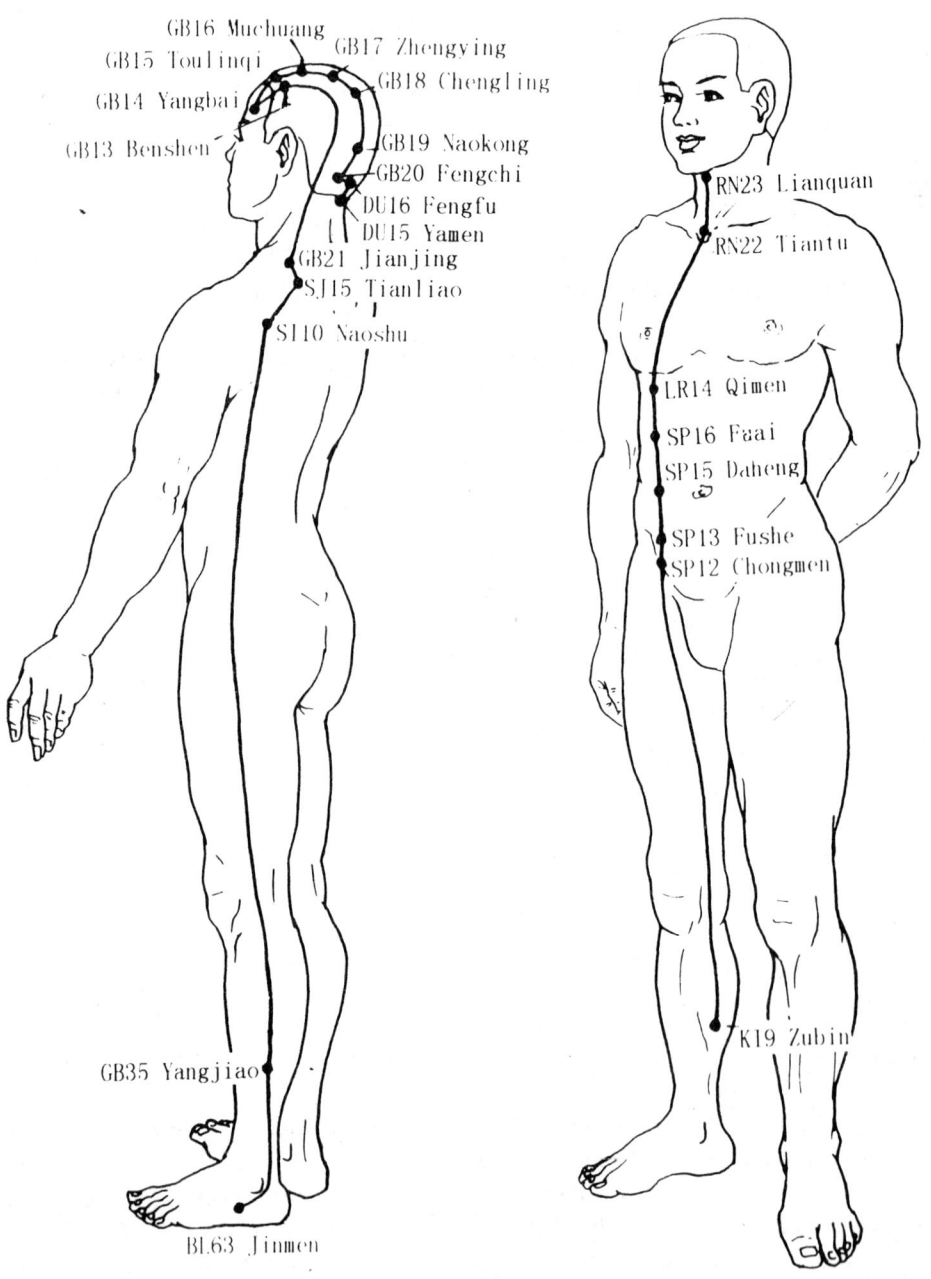

Fig. 2-7 **The Yangwei Meridian**   Fig. 2-8 **The Yinwei Meridian**

Chapter Three

The Three Yin Meridians of Hand

III. System of the Lung Meridian of Hand Taiyin

1. Distribution of the Lung Meridian of Hand Taiyin

1) Course of the Meridian

The Lung Meridian of Hand Taiyin originates from the Middle Jiao and descends to connect with the large intestine. Winding back on itself, it travels along the upper orifice of the stomach, crosses the diaphragm and enters the lung, its pertaining organ. Emerging transversely from the lung system (the portion of the lung communicating with the throat), the meridian descends along the medial aspect of the upper arm in front of the Heart and Pericardium Meridians. Reaching the cubital fossa, it continues downward along the anterior border, in the medial aspect of the forearm to the Cun Kou (寸口), the radial artery at the wrist, where the pulse is palpated. Passing the thenar eminence, the meridian travels along the radial border and terminates at the radial side of the tip of the thumb.

A branch proximal to the wrist splits from the acupoint Lieque (LU 7) and travels directly to the radial side of the tip of the index finger, where it links with the Large Intestine Meridian of Hand Yangming. (*Miraculous Pivot*) (See Fig. 3-1).

2) Course of the Collaterals

It arises from Lieque (LU 7), 1.5 cun above the transverse crease of the wrist. It runs further to the palm and spreads through Yuji (LU 10) and travels to the Large Intestine Meridian of Hand Yangming. (*Miraculous Pivot*)

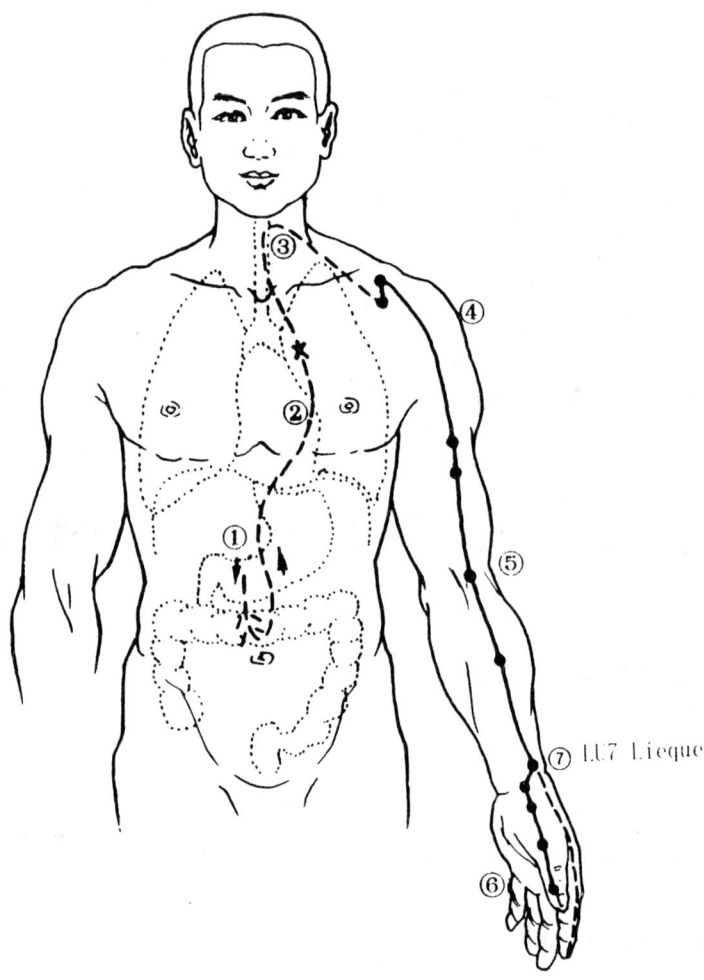

Fig. 3-1 The Lung Meridian of Hand Taiyin

3) Divergent Meridian

The Divergent Meridian of Hand Taiyin derives from the lung meridian at the axilla. It runs anterior to the Pericardium Meridian of Hand Jueyin into the chest, and there it connects with the lung and then disperses in the large intestine. A branch extends upward from the lung and emerges at Quepen (ST 12) (superior border of clavicle). It ascends across the throat and converges with the Large Intestine Meridian of Hand Yangming. (*Miraculous Pivot*) (See Fig. 3-2).

4) Muscle Region

It arises from the tip of the thumb and knots at the lower thenar eminence. Proceeding up laterally to the pulse and along the forearm, it knots at the elbow, then ascends along the medial aspect of the arm and enters the chest below the axilla. Emerging from Quepen (ST 12), it knots

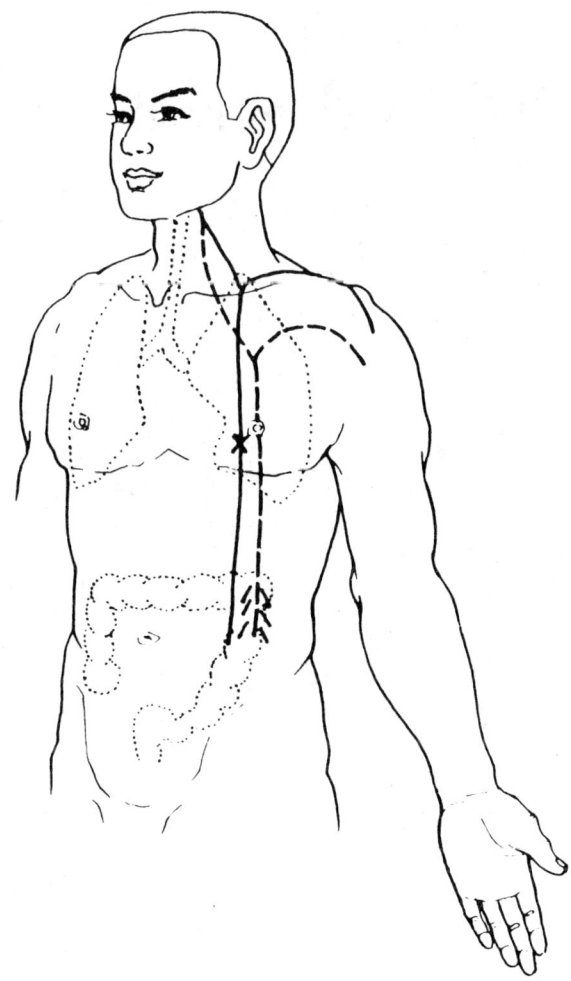

Fig. 3-2 Divergent Meridians of the Lung Meridian of Hand Taiyin and the Large Intestine Meridian of Hand Yangming

anteriorly at Jianyu (LI 15). Above, it knots with the clavicle, and below, it knots in the chest, dispersing over the diaphragm and converging again at the lowest rib. (*Miraculous Pivot*) (See Fig. 3-3).

5) Cutaneous Region

The Cutaneous Region of the Lung Meridian of Hand Taiyin, similar to the course of the meridian and collateral of the Lung Meridian, is predominantly distributed at the radial aspect of the upper limbs and the palmar radial aspect of the thumb and index finger. (See Fig. 3-4).

6) Acupoints

There are 11 points in the Lung Meridian, starting from Zhongfu (LU 1) and ending at Shaoshang (LU 11).

Crossing point: None.

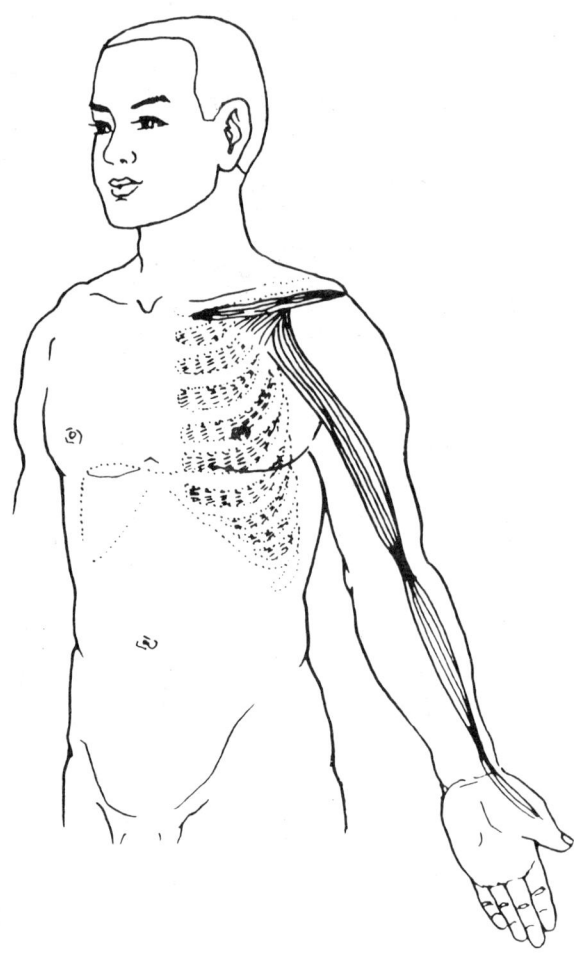

Fig. 3-3 Muscle Region of the Lung Meridian of Hand Taiyin

2. Symptoms and Signs of the Disorders of the Lung Meridian of Hand Taiyin

1) Symptoms and Signs of the Disorders of the Meridian

"If the meridian (qi) has pathological change, there may appear fullness of the lung, leading to cough. Pain of supraclavicular fossa causes difficult movement of the arm, which is due to adverse flow of qi in the arm. The Lung Meridian of Hand Taiyin is mainly used to treat diseases such as cough, adverse flow of qi, asthma, thirst, restlessness, fullness of the chest, cold sensation of the forearm and feverish sensation in the palm. Over abundance of qi may cause pain of the shoulder and back, apoplexy due to attack of the wind cold during sweating, and frequent urination with small amount of urine. Qi deficiency causes pain and cold sensation of the shoulder and back, shortness of breath and difficulty in breath and change of the urine colour." (*Miraculous Pivot*)

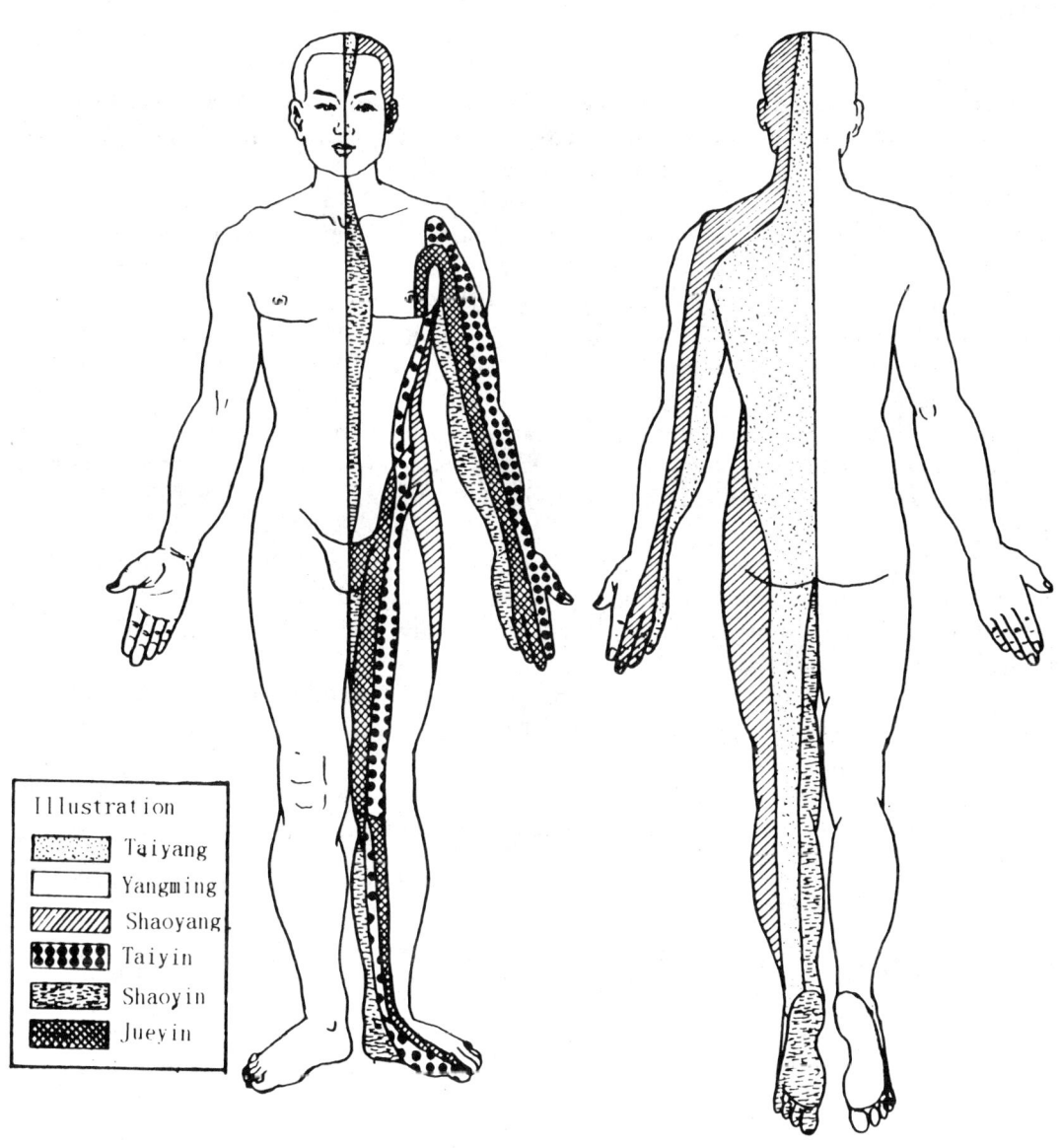

Fig. 3-4 Cutaneous Regions of Six Meridians

2) Symptoms and Signs of the Disorders of the Collaterals

"Excess of the collateral may lead to feverish sensation around the styloid process of the radius of the palm. Deficiency may cause frequent yawning, enuresis and frequent urination." (*Miraculous Pivot*)

3) Symptoms and Signs of the Disorders of the Muscle Region

"Diseases of the Muscle Region may cause muscular spasm and pain, and masses in the lung in severe cases. Hypochondriac pain may cause hemoptysis." (*Miraculous Pivot*)

> **Appendix** Medical Documents

Fullness due to lung deficiency may manifest as asthma and cough. (*Miraculou Pivot*).

Deficiency of lung qi may lead to stuffy nose and insufficient qi. Excess of lung qi may cause asthma, thirst, fullness of the chest and sluggishness. (*Miraculous Pivot*)

Excess of the lung may cause distension of the lung, cold sensation of the Middle Jiao and indigestion; while deficiency of the lung may cause hot sensation in the Middle Jiao, insufficiency of qi and change of urine color. (*Miraculous Pivot*)

If pathogenic factors attack the lung, it may cause pain of the skin, simultaneous cold and hot, adverse flow of qi, asthma, sweating and severe cough. (*Miraculous Pivot*)

Adverse flow of lung qi of Hand Taiyin is due to deficiency. There may be coughing which is usually accompanied by foaming in the mouth. (*Miraculous Pivot*)

Lung heat may gradually lead to syncope, there may be aversion to wind and cold, yellowish tongue and general fever of the body. Heat causes cough and asthma, wandering pain in the chest and back, difficulty breathing freely, severe headache and sweating with chills. (*Miraculous Pivot*)

Lung wind may cause excessive sweating and aversion to wind, pale complexion, intermittent cough, short breath, which may become worse at night. (*Miraculous Pivot*).

Pulmonary symptoms manifest as cough, dyspnea with wheezing and hemoptysis in severe cases. (*Plain Questions*)

Diseases of the lung may cause asthma, cough, adverse flow of qi, pain in the shoulder and back and sweating. Deficiency of the lung may lead to insufficient qi and restlessness, deafness and dry throat. (*Plain Questions*)

Yin fights interiorly and Yang disturbs exteriorly. Uncontrollable sweating may stimulate pathogenic factors to cause steaming in the lung and dyspnea with wheezing to occur. (*Plain Questions*)

IV. System of the Pericardium Meridian of Hand Jueyin

1. Distribution of the Pericardium Meridian of Hand Jueyin

1) Course of the Meridian

The Pericardium Meridian of Hand-Jueyin originates from the chest and joins with the pericardium, its pertaining organ. It then descends across the diaphragm and enters the abdomen, where it successively connects with the Upper, Middle and Lower Jiao.

A branch arises in the chest, it runs inside the chest to emerge superficially in the costal region at a point 3 cun below the anterior axillary fold. From this point, it ascends to the axilla. Following the medial aspect of the upper arm, it runs downward between the paths of the Lung and Heart Meridians to the cubital fossa. Continuing downward, it descends to the forearm between the tendons of the muscle palmaris longus and muscle flexor carpi radialis and enters the palm. From the palm, it passes along the third finger to its tip.

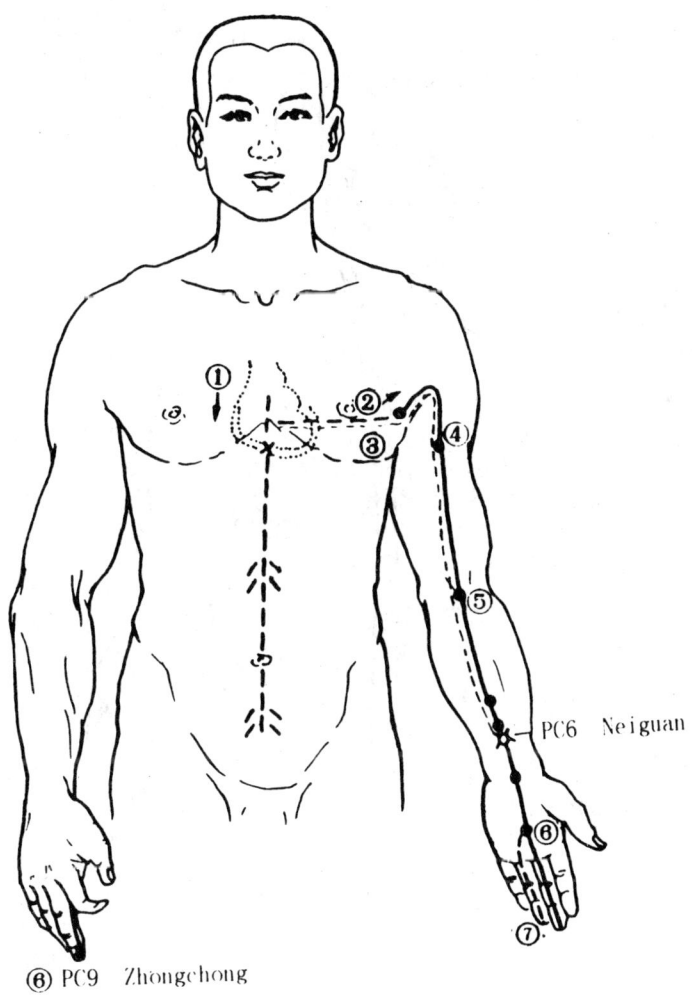

Fig. 3-5 The Pericardium Meridian of Hand Jueyin

Another branch separates in the palm (Laogong, PC 8) and proceeds along the fourth finger to its tip to link with the Sanjiao Meridian of Hand Shaoyang. (*Miraculous Pivot*) (See Fig. 3-5).

2) Course of the Collaterals

"It starts from Neiguan (PC 6). Two cun above the wrist, it disperses between the two tendons (radial flexor muscle of wrist and long palmar muscle) and runs up along the Pericardium Meridian to the pericardium and finally connects with the heart." (*Miraculous Pivot*)

3) Divergent Meridian

After deriving from the Pericardium Meridian at a point 3 cun below the axilla, it enters the

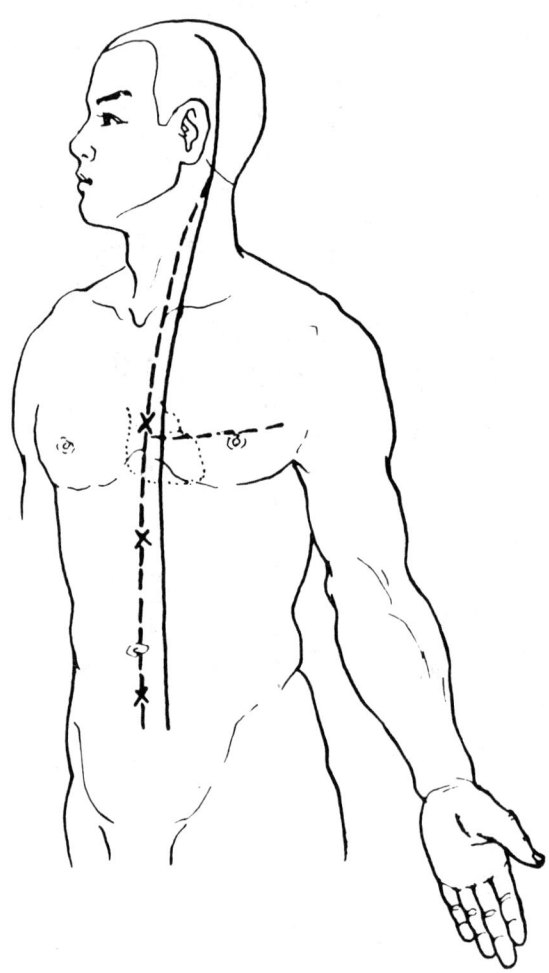

Fig. 3-6 Divergent Meridians of the Pericardium Meridian of Hand Jueyin and the Sanjiao Meridians of Hand Shaoyang

chest and communicates with the Sanjiao. A branch ascends across the throat and emerges behind the ear and then converges with the Sanjiao Meridian of Hand Shaoyang (at the mastoid process), which is called "the fifth convergence". (*Miraculous Pivot*) (See Fig. 3-6).

4) Muscle Region

It arises from the palmar aspect of the middle finger and follows the Muscle Region of Hand Taiyin upward. It first knots at the medial aspect of the elbow, and later below the axilla. Then it descends, dispersing at the front and back of the ribs. A branch enters the chest below the axilla and spreads over the chest, knotting in the thoracic diaphragm. (*Miraculous Pivot*) (See Fig. 3-7).

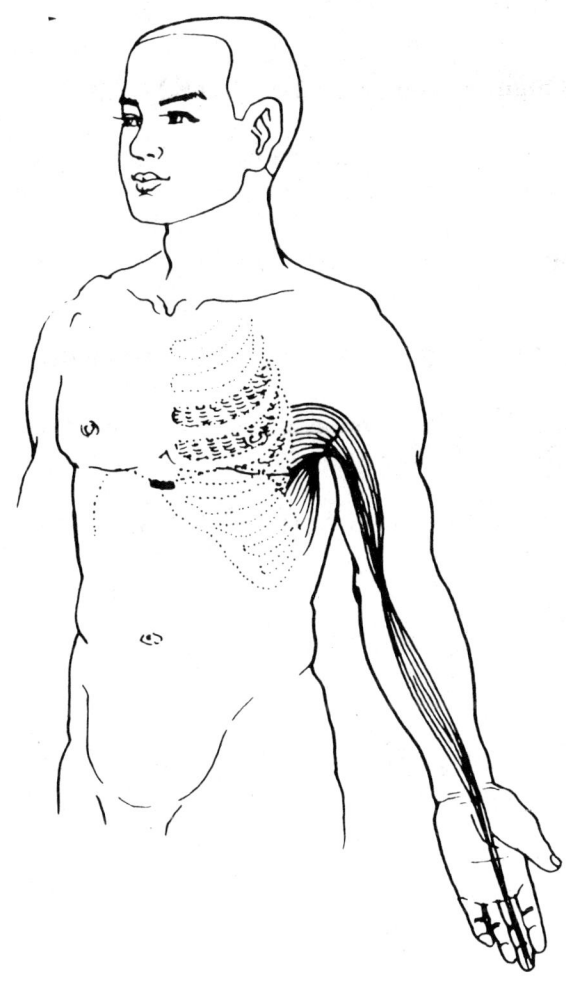

Fig. 3-7 Muscle Region of the Pericardium Meridian of Hand Jueyin

5) Cutaneous Region

The Cutaneous Region of the Pericardium Meridian of Hand Jueyin, similar to the course of the meridian and collateral, is predominantly distributed at the palmer side of the ring finger, centre of the palm, middle part of the medial side of the upper limbs, below the axilla and the lateral chest, etc. (See Fig. 3-4).

6) Acupoints

There are 9 points in the Pericardium Meridian, starting from Tianchi (PC 1) and ending at Zhongchong (PC 9).

Crossing point: None.

2. Symptoms and Signs of the Disorders of the Pericardium Meridian of Hand-Jueyin

1) Symptoms and Signs of the Disorders of the Meridian

If the meridian (qi) has pathological change, there may appear feverish sensation in the palm, spasm of the arm and elbow and swelling of the axilla. In severe cases, there may appear fullness sensation in the hypochondriac region, palpitation, flushed face, icteric sclera and easily laughing. The Pericardium Meridian is mainly used to treat irritability, cardiac pain and feverish sensation in the palm. (*Miraculous Pivot*)

2) Symptoms and Signs of the Disorders of the Collaterals

"Excess syndrome of the heart system may cause cardiac pain; while deficiency may bring about irritability." (*Miraculous Pivot*)

3) Symptoms and Signs of the Disorders of the Muscle Region

Diseases of the Muscle Region may cause muscular spasm, chest pain and obstruction in the lung. (*Miraculous Pivot*)

Appendix Medical Documents

Pathogenic factors attacking the heart actually means that pathogenic factors attack the pericardium of the heart, because the heart is dominated by the pericardium. (*Miraculous Pivot*)

Deficiency of heart qi causes grief, while excess of heart qi causes overjoy. (*Miraculous Pivot*)

Disturbance of the Pericardium Meridian may cause cardiac pain, which may affect the throat. If this symptom is accompanied by fever, it may be difficult to cure and finally leads to death. (*Miraculous Pivot*)

V. System of the Heart Meridian of Hand Shaoyin

1. Distribution of the Heart Meridian of Hand Shaoyin

1) Course of the Meridian

The Heart Meridian of Hand Shaoyin originates in the heart, its pertaining organ, then emerges and spreads over the "heart system" (i.e. the tissues and blood vessels surrounding the heart and connecting with the other internal organs). Traveling downward, it crosses the diaphragm and connects with the small intestine, its related Fu organ.

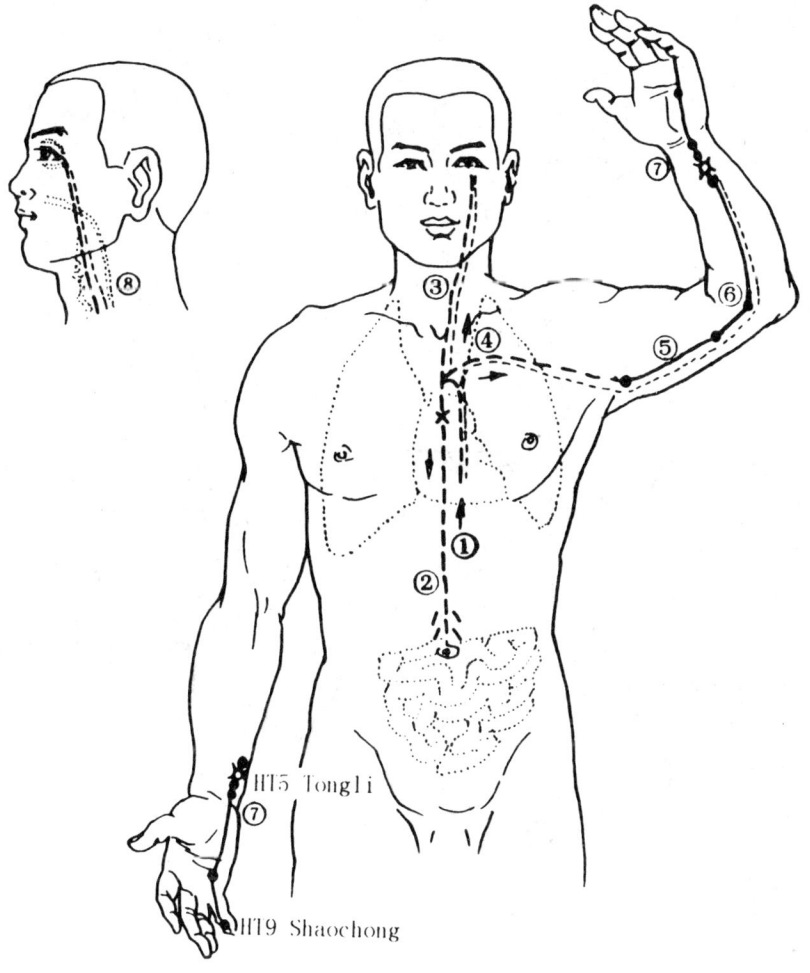

Fig. 3-8 The Heart Meridian of Hand Shaoyin

A branch of the main meridian separates from the "heart system" and ascends alongside the esophagus to the face where it joins the "eye system" (i.e. the tissues connecting the eyes with the brain).

The straight portion of the meridian from the "heart system" travels upward to the lung. It then turns downward and emerges from the axilla. From the axilla, it travels along the posterior border of the medial aspect of the upper arm behind the lung and pericardium meridian, descending to the cubital fossa. It continues to descend along the posterior border of the medial aspect of the forearm to the pisiform region, proximal to the palm and enters it. Then it follows the medial aspect of the fifth finger to its tip and links with the Small Intestine Meridian of Hand Taiyang. (*Miraculous Pivot*) (See Fig. 3-8).

2) Course of the Collaterals

It starts from Tongli (HT 5). About one and a half cun above the wrist, it runs upward along the meridian and enters the heart, it then runs to the root of the tongue and connects with

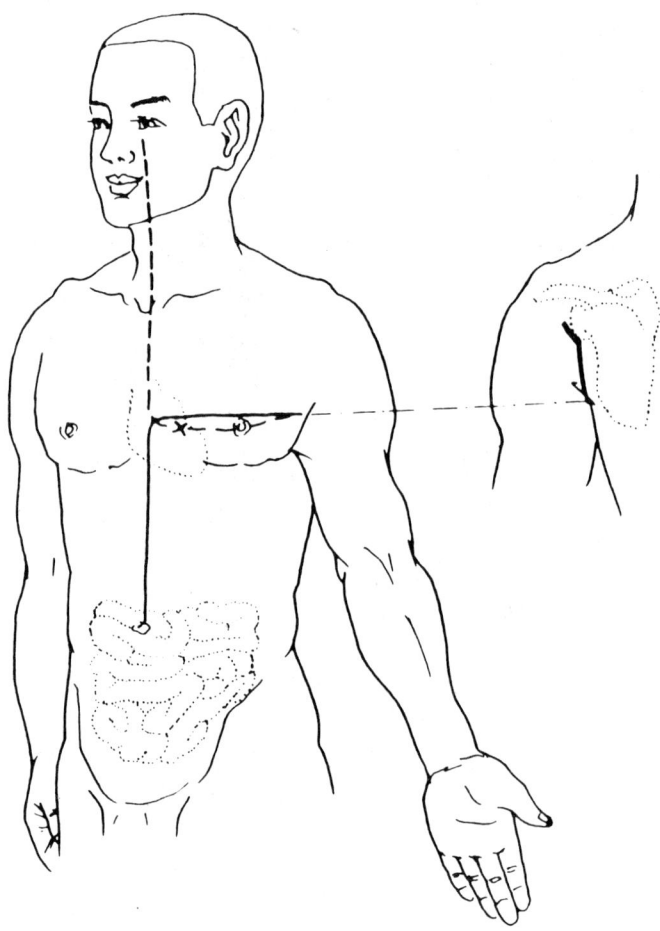

Fig. 3-9 Divergent Meridian of the Heart Meridian of Hand Shaoyin

the eye. One cun above the transverse crease of the wrist, it connects with the Small Intestine Meridian of Hand Taiyang. (*Miraculous Pivot*)

3) Divergent Meridian

After deriving from the Heart Meridian in the axillary fossa (biceps muscle of arm and brachial triceps muscle), it enters the chest and connects with the heart. Then it runs upward across the throat and emerges on the face joining the Small Intestine Meridian at the inner canthus, which is called the fourth convergence. (*Miraculous Pivot*) (See Fig. 3-9).

4) Muscle Region

It begins from the medial side of the small finger, knots first at the pisiform bone of the hand, and then at the medial aspect of the elbow. Continuing upward and entering the chest below

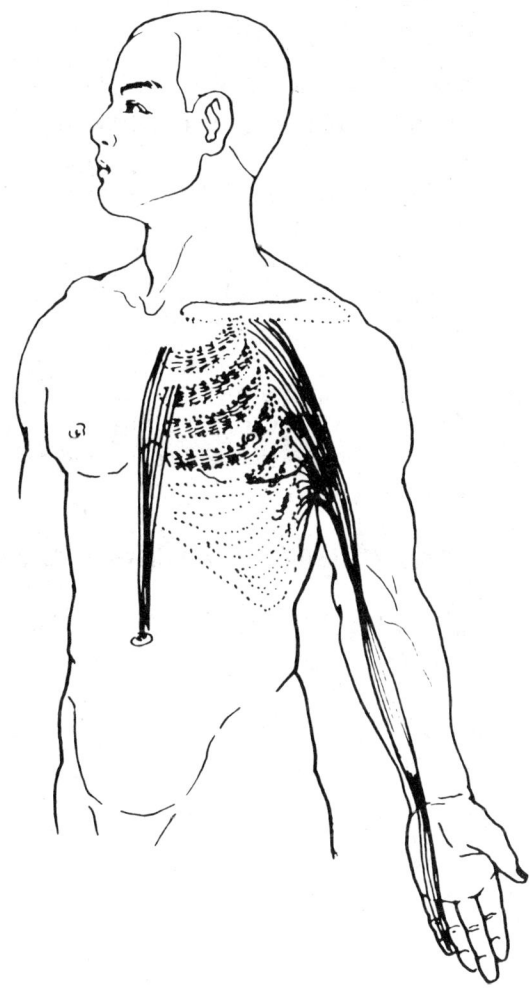

Fig. 3-10   Muscle Region of the Heart Meridian of Hand Shaoyin

the axilla, it crosses the Muscle Region of Hand Taiyin in the breast region and knots in the chest. Then it descends, crossing the diaphragm to connect with the umbilicus. (*Miraculous Pivot*) (See Fig. 3-10).

5) Cutaneous Region

Cutaneous Region of the Heart Meridian of Hand Shaoyin, on the basis of the passing course of the meridian and collateral of the Heart Meridian, is predominantly distributed at the palmar and radial side of the small finger, palm and the ulna side of the medial aspect of the upper limbs. (See Fig. 3-4).

6) Acupoints

There are 9 points in the Heart Meridian, starting from Jiquan (HT 1) and ending at

Shaochong (HT 9).

2. Symptoms and Signs of the Disorders of the Heart Meridian of Hand Shaoyin

1) Symptoms and Signs of the Disorders of the Meridian

If meridian (qi) has pathological changes, there may appear dry sensation in the pharynx, cardiac pain, thirst and desire to drink. These are thought to be diseases due to adverse flow of qi in the arm. The Heart Meridian is mainly used to treat icteric scleras, hypochondriac pain, pain in the posterior border of the elbow, cold limbs and feverish sensation in the palm. (*Miraculous Pivot*)

2) Symptoms and Signs of the Disorders of the Collaterals

"Excess syndrome may cause discomfort of the diaphragm, deficiency syndrome may cause inability to speak." (*Miraculous Pivot*)

3) Symptoms and Signs of the Disorders of the Muscle Region

"Diseases of the muscle region can cause contracture in the chest and hardness in the epigastrium. Diseases in the passing course of the muscle Region can cause spasm and pain of the tendons." (*Miraculous Pivot*)

Appendix Medial Documents

Heart disorders may cause irritability, short breath and inability to sleep soundly. (*Miraculous Pivot*)

Pathogenic factors in the heart may lead to cardiac pain, susceptibility to sorrow and occasional fainting due to vertigo. (*Miraculous Pivot*)

Heart diseases may cause pain in the chest, sensation of fullness or pain in the hypochondriac region, pain in the shoulder, back scapular region and the medial side of the arm. Deficient syndrome may be manifested as fullness in the chest and abdomen, pain in the hypochondrium radiating to the waist. (*Plain Questions*)

Heart disorders may develop cough which leads to cardiac pain, the sensation of obstruction and inflammation in the throat, swelling of the pharynx and sore throat in severe cases. (*Plain Questions*)

Disturbances of the Heart Meridian cause cardiac pain referring to the throat with fever. (*Plain Questions*)

Heart heat may cause sudden cardiac pain, irritability, frequent vomitting, headache and flushed face without sweat. (*Plain Questions*).

Chapter Four

The Three Yang Meridians of Hand

VI. System of the Large Intestine Meridian of Hand Yangming

1. Distribution of the Large Intestine Meridian of Hand Yangming

1) Course of the Meridian

The Large Intestine Meridian of Hand Yangming originates at the radial side of the tip of the index finger and proceeds upward between the first and second metacarpal bones of the hand. It then runs up to the depression between the tendons of the muscle extensor pollicis longus and brevis at the wrist and continues along the lateral anterior aspect of the forearm to the lateral side of the elbow. From the elbow, it ascends along the lateral anterior aspect of the upper arm to the shoulder joint, traveling along the anterior aspect of the lateral border of the acromion and ascending to the 7th cervical vertebrae (Dazhui, DU 14, at the confluence of the three Yang meridians of hand and foot). The meridian then descends to the supraclavicular fossa to connect with the lung. It then passes through the diaphragm and enters the large intestine, its pertaining organ.

A branch separates from the main meridian at the supraclavicular fossa and ascends through the neck, crossing the cheek and entering the lower gum. From the gum, it curves around the upper lip and intersects the same branch from the opposite side of the body at the philtrum. The branch finally terminates at the side of the ala nasi, where the meridian links with the Stomach Meridian of Foot Yangming. (See Fig. 4-1).

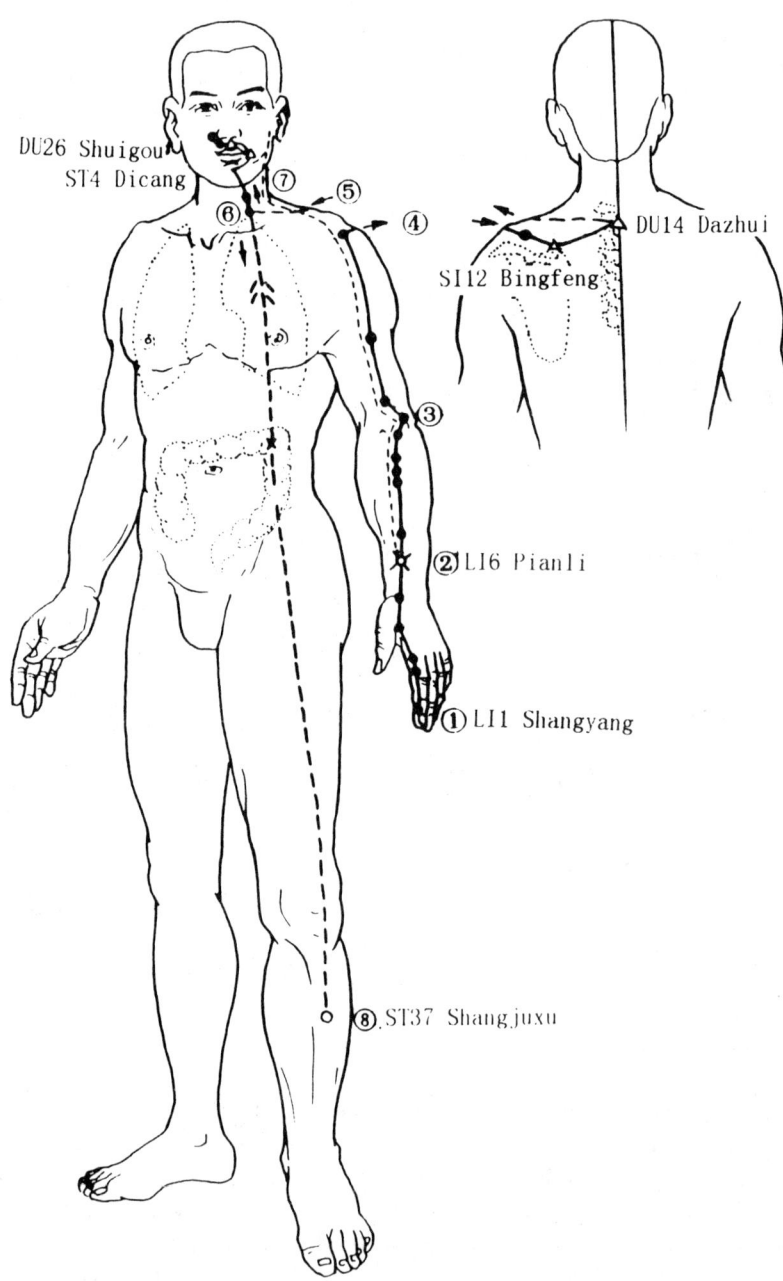

Fig. 4-1 The Large Intestine Meridian of Hand Yangming

2) Course of the Collaterals

It starts from Pianli (LI 6) three cun above the wrist and joins the Lung Meridian of Hand Taiyin. Another branch runs along the arm to Jianyu (LI 15), crosses the jaw and extends to the teeth. The third branch derives at the jaw and enters the ear to join the assembled meridian (the meeting place of Hand Taiyin, Hand Shaoyang, Foot Shaoyang and Foot Yangming). (*Miraculous Pivot*)

3) Divergent Meridian

"After deriving from the Large Intestine Meridian on the head, divergent meridian continues upward to connect with the large intestine, pertaining organ of the lung. Another branch runs upwards from the shoulder along the throat and emerges at the supraclavicular fossa, there it joins the Large Intestine Meridian." (*Miraculous Pivot*) (See Fig. 3-2).

4) Muscle Region

It starts from the extremity of the finger and knots at the dorsum of the wrist. Then it goes upwards along the forearm, and knots at the lateral side of the elbow. Continuing up the arm, it

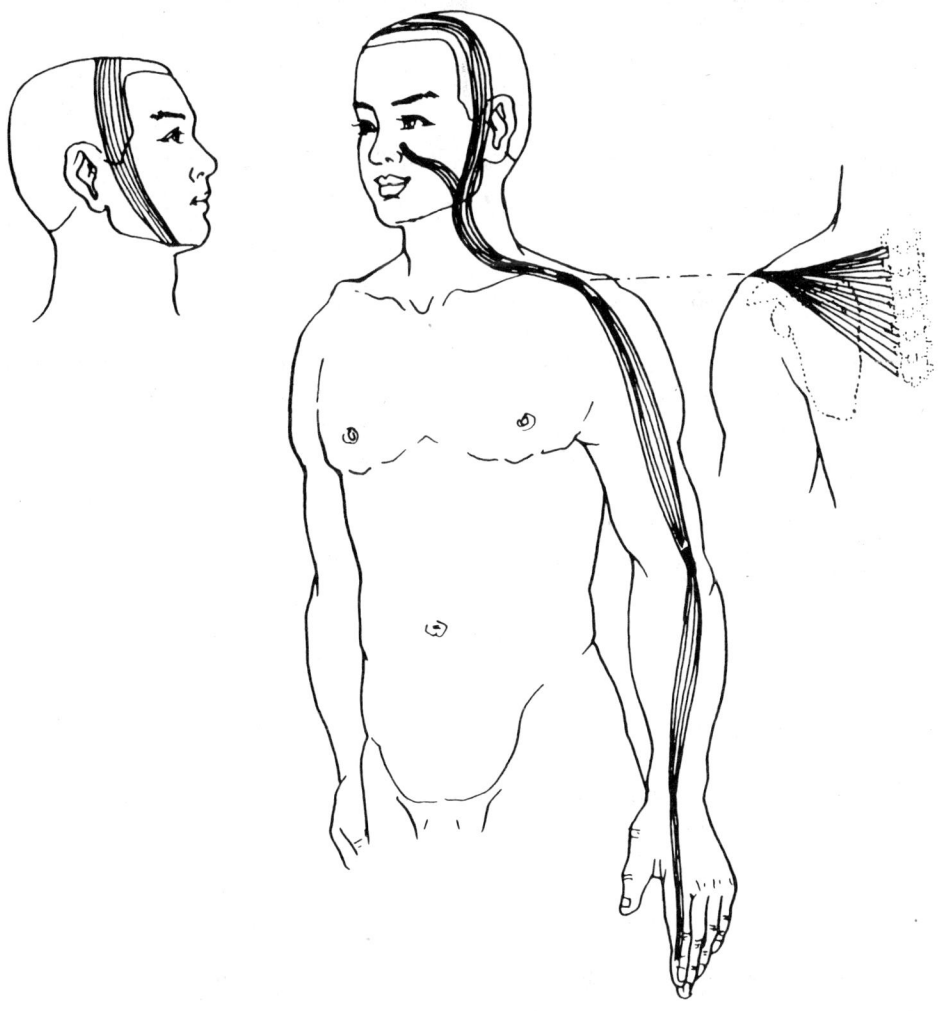

Fig. 4-2 Muscle Region of the Large Intestine Meridian of Hand Yangming

knots at Jianyu (LI 15). A branch moves around the scapula and attaches to the spine. The straight branch continues from Jianyu (LI 15) to the neck, where a branch separates and knots at the side of the nose. The straight branch continues upwards and emerges in front of Muscle Meridian of Hand Taiyang. Then it crosses over the head, connecting at the mandible on the opposite side of the face. (*Miraculous Pivot*) (See Fig. 4-2).

5) Cutaneous Region

The Cutaneous Region of the Large Intestine Meridian of Hand Yangming, according to the passing course of the meridian and collateral, is predominantly distributed at the radial side of the lateral aspect of the upper limbs, dorsum of the thumb and index finger, inferior border of the shoulder and lateral aspect of the neck, face, nasolabial groove and the side of the nose. (See Fig. 3-4).

6) Acupoints

There are 20 acupoints in the Large Intestine Meridian and it starts from Shangyang (LI 1) and ends at Yingxiang (LI 20).

Crossing Points: Bingfeng (SI 12), Dazhui (DU 14), Dicang (ST 4), Shuigou (DU 26), Jiaosun (SJ 20), Chengjiang (RN 24).

2. Symptoms and Signs of the Disorders of the Large Intestine Meridian of Hand Yangming

1) Symptoms and Signs of the Disorders of the Meridian

If pathological changes occur in the meridian, there may be toothache and swelling of the neck. If there is disturbance in the transportation of body fluid, there may appear icteric scleras, dry mouth, running nose, epistaxis, allergic rhinitis, inflammation of the throat, shoulder pain, limited movement of the index finger. Excessive meridian qi may cause fever and swelling. Deficiency may lead to rigor. (*Miraculous Pivot*)

2) Symptoms and Signs of the Disorders of the Collaterals

"Excess syndromes may cause toothache and deafness, while deficiency syndromes may lead to rigor and obstruction of the diaphragm." (*Miraculous Pivot*)

3) Symptoms and Signs of the Disorders of the Muscle Region

"Disorders of the muscle region may cause general pain, spasm, limited movement of the shoulder and neck with inability to turn left and right." (*Miraculous Pivot*)

Appendix Medical Documents

Intermittent pain is due to dysfunction of qi. Borborygmus is caused by the attack of wind cold in the intestine and stomach. (*Miraculous Pivot*)

Borborygmus is due to adversed qi in the chest. Inability to stand due to dyspnea results from pathogenic factors in the large intestine. (*Miraculous Pivot*)

Heat in the large intestine may cause yellow mucous stool while pathogenic cold may lead to borborygmus and diarrhea. (*Miraculous Pivot*)

Febrile disease may cause heaviness of the body and heat in the large intestine. (*Miraculous Pivot*)

Distention of the large intestine may cause borborygmus and abdominal pain. If the large intestine is attacked by the cold in winter, there may appear diarrhea with undigested food. (*Miraculous Pivot*)

If there are disorders in the large intestine, there may appear borborygmus and abdominal pain. If the large intestine is attacked by cold in winter, it may cause diarrhea, pain around umbilicus and inability to stand. (*Miraculous Pivot*)

Dysfunction of Hand Yangming and Hand Shaoyang Meridians may cause inflammation of the throat, swelling of the pharynx and spasm. (*Plain Questions*)

If pathogenic factors attack the collateral of Hand Yangming, there may appear a sensation of fullness in the chest, shortness of breath with wheezing and heat in the chest. (*Plain Questions*)

If pathogenic factors attack the collateral of Hand Yangming, there may appear deafness. (*Plain Questions*)

Ⅶ. System of the Sanjiao Meridian of Hand Shaoyang

1. Distribution of the Sanjiao Meridian of Hand Shaoyang

1) Course of the Meridian

The Sanjiao Meridian of Hand Shaoyang originates from the fourth fingertip, ascends between the fourth and fifth metacarpal bones at the dorsum of the wrist, traverses the forearm between the ulna and the radius, and continues upward across the olecranon and the lateral aspect of the upper arm to the shoulder region. It then intersects and passes posteriorly to the Gallbladder Meridian of Foot Shaoyang, winding toward the supraclavicular fossa. The meridian then spreads in the chest to connect with the pericardium. It then descends through the diaphragm to the abdomen linking successively with the Upper, Middle and Lower Jiao, its pertaining organ.

A branch separates in the chest and ascends to emerge superficially from the supraclavicular fossa. It then runs upward to the neck along the posterior border of the ear to the corner of the forehead. From the forehead, it turns downward to the cheek and terminates in the infraorbital region.

An auricular branch arises from the retroauricular region and enters the ear. It then emerges anteriorly to the ear, crossing the previous branch at the cheek and reaching the outer canthus to link with the Gallbladder Meridian of Foot Shaoyang. (See Fig. 4-3).

2) Course of the Collaterals

"It arises from Waiguan (SI 5), two cun above the dorsum of the wrist. It travels up the posterior aspect of the arm and over the shoulder and disperses in the chest, converging with the Pericardium Meridian." (*Miraculous Pivot*)

3) Divergent Meridian

"After deriving from Sanjiao Meridian at the vertex, divergent meridian of Sanjiao Meridian descends into the supraclavicular fossa, crossing the Upper Jiao, Middle Jiao and Lower Jiao, and finally disperses in the chest." (*Miraculous Pivot*) (See Fig. 3-6).

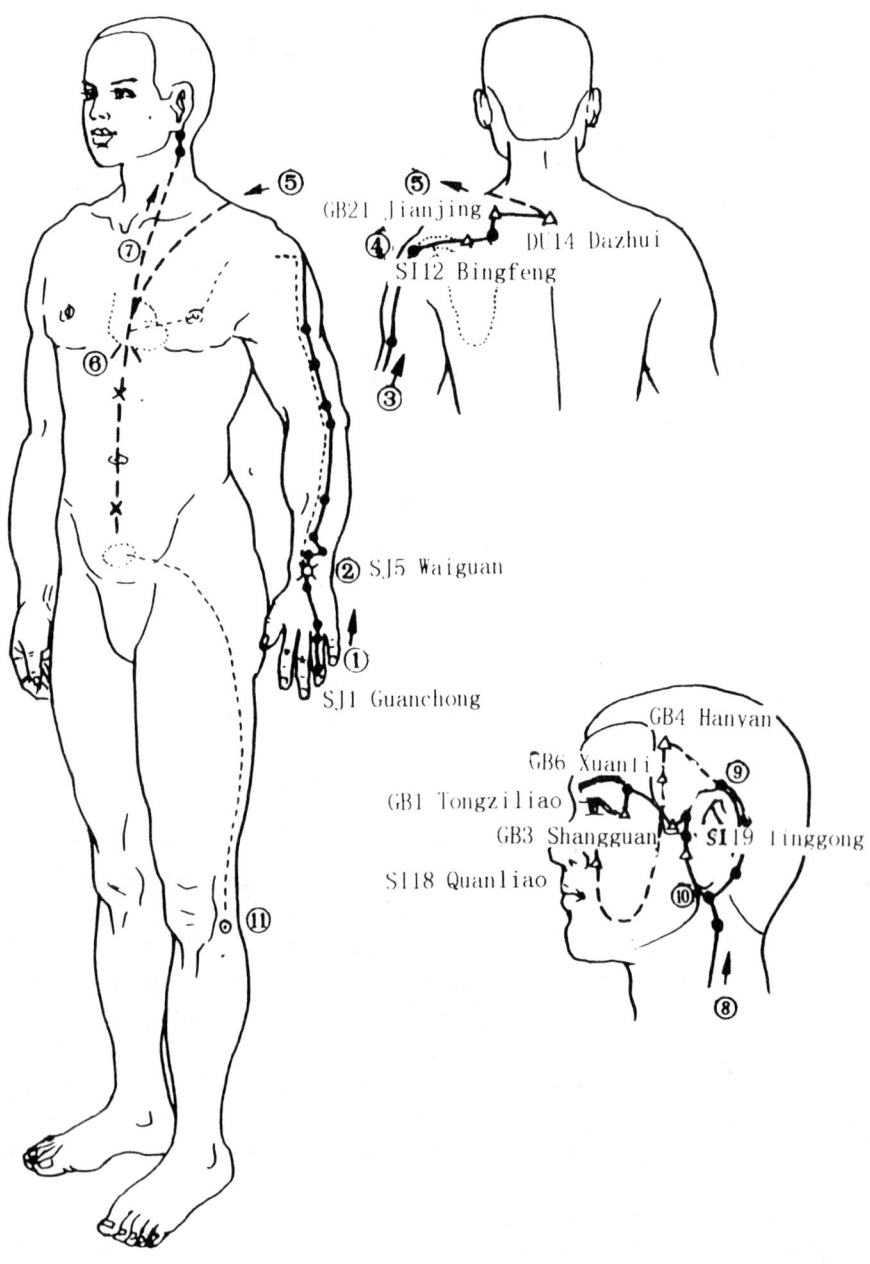

Fig. 4-3 **The Sanjiao Meridian of Hand Shaoyang**

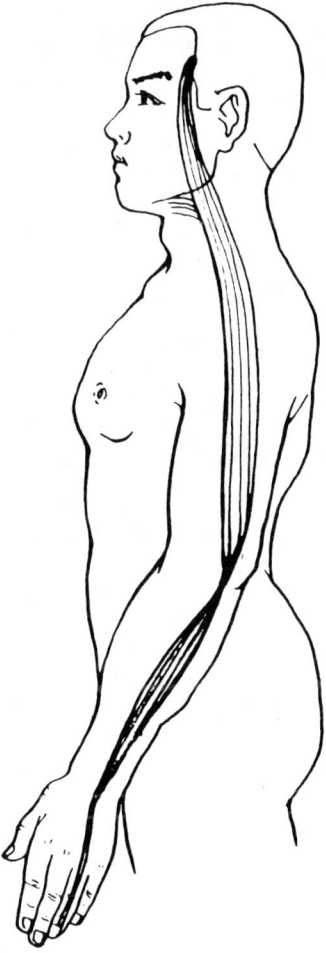

Fig. 4-4 Muscle Region of Sanjiao Meridian of Hand Shaoyang

4) Muscle Region

"It begins from the tip of the ring finger and knots at the dorsum of the wrist. Then it travels up along the forearm and knots at the olecranon of the elbow. Proceeding upwards along the lateral aspect of the upper arm, it crosses the shoulder and the neck, converging with the Muscle Region of Hand Taiyin. A branch splits out the angle of the mandible and connects with the root of the tongue. Another branch proceeds upward in front of the ear to the outer canthus, then crosses the temple and connects at the corner of the forehead." (*Miraculous Pivot*) (See Fig. 4-4).

5) Cutaneous Region

The Cutaneous Region of Sanjiao Meridian of Hand Shaoyang, according to the passing course of the meridian and collateral, is predominantly distributed at the dorsum of the ring and middle fingers, dorsal side of the upper limbs, superior border of the scapula, posterior border of the lateral neck, posterior side and front part of the ear. (See Fig. 3-4).

6) Acupoints

There are 23 acupoints in Sanjiao Meridian, starting at Guanchong (SJ 1) and ending at Sizhukong (SJ 23).

Crossing Points: Bingfeng (SI 12), Zhongwan (RN 12), Jianjing (GB 21), Hanyan (GB 4), Xuanli (GB 6), Quanliao (SI 18), Shangguan (GB 3), Tinggong (SI 19), Tongziliao (GB 1).

2. Symptoms and Signs of Sanjiao Meridian of Hand Shaoyang

1) Symptoms and Signs of the Disorders of the Meridian

"If there are pathogenic changes in the meridian, there may appear deafness, progressive hypoacusia, swelling of pharynx, inflammation of the throat. Disorders of function of qi may cause sweating, pain of the outer canthus, swelling of the cheek, pain in the posterior of the ear, shoulder, upper arm, elbow and the lateral side of the arm, limited movement of the ring finger." (*Miraculous Pivot*)

2) Symptoms and Signs of the Disorders of the Collaterals

"Excess syndromes may cause hypermyotonia while deficiency may cause hypomyotonia." (*Miraculous Pivot*)

3) Symptoms and Signs of the Disorders of the Muscle Region

"Disorders of the muscle region may cause spasm and curled up tongue." (*Miraculous Pivot*)

Appendix Medical Documents

Disorders of Sanjiao Meridian may cause fullness sensation of abdominal qi, masses in the abdomen, difficult urination, retention of urine and distention of the urinary bladder. (*Miraculous Pivot*)

Distention of Sanjiao may lead to overflowing of qi under the skin, which can be felt quite soft and weak. (*Miraculous Pivot*)

Sanjiao Meridian runs downward to connect with the bladder at the lower jiao. Sanjiao excess may cause anuria, and its deficiency may lead to enuresis. (*Miraculous Pivot*)

Dysfunction of Hand Yangming and Hand Shaoyang Meridians may cause inflammation of the throat, swelling of the pharynx and spasm. (*Plain Questions*)

If pathogenic factors attack the collateral of Hand Shaoyang, there may appear inflammation of the throat, curled-up tongue, dry mouth, irritability, pain in the lateral aspect of the arm with inability to reach the head. (*Plain Questions*)

VIII. System of the Small Intestine Meridian of Hand Taiyang

1. Distribution of the Small Intestine Meridian of Hand Taiyang

1) Course of the Meridian

The Small Intestine Meridian of Hand Taiyang originates at the ulna side of the fifth finger and ascends along the ulna side of the tip of the hand to the wrist, emerging at the styloid process of the ulna. From the styloid process, it travels directly upward along the posterior aspect of the forearm, passing between the olecranon of the ulna and the medial epicondyle of the humerus. It then proceeds along the posterior border of the lateral aspect of the upper arm to the shoulder. Then, turning downward to the supraclavicular fossa, it connects with the heart. From the heart, it descends alongside the esophagus, passing through the diaphragm, transversing the stomach and finally entering the small intestine, its pertaining organ.

A branch of the meridian travels upward from the supraclavicular fossa and crosses the neck and cheek to the outer canthus of the eye. It then enters the ear.

Another branch separates from the first branch at the cheek, ascending to the infraorbital region of the eye and traveling to the lateral aspect of the nose. It then reaches the inner canthus to link with the Bladder Meridian of Foot Taiyang. (See Fig. 4-5).

2) Course of the Collaterals

"It originates from Zhizheng (SI 7) (*Plain Questions*), five cun above the wrist and connects with the Heart Meridian. Another branch runs upward, crosses the elbow and connects with Jianyu (LI 15)." (*Miraculous Pivot*)

3) Divergent Meridian

"After deriving from the Small Intestine Meridian at the shoulder joint, it enters the axilla, crosses the heart and runs downwards to the abdomen to link up with the Small Intestine Meridian." (*Miraculous Pivot*) (See Fig. 3-9).

4) Muscle Region

It starts from the tip of the small finger, knots at the dorsum of the wrist, and proceeds up along the forearm to knot at the medial condyle of the humerus in the elbow. Then it continues up along the arm and knots below the axilla. A branch runs behind the axilla, curves around the scapula and emerges in front of the Foot Taiyang Meridian on the neck, knotting behind the ear. Another branch separates behind the auricle, descends across the face and knots beneath the mandible, then continues upwards to link the outer canthus. (*Miraculous Pivot*) (See Fig. 4-6).

5) Cutaneous Region

The Cutaneous Region of the Small Intestine Meridian of Hand Taiyang, according to the passing course of the meridian and collateral, is mainly distributed on the lateral and dorsal sides of the small finger, dorsum, posterior aspect of the lateral side of the upper limbs, posterior

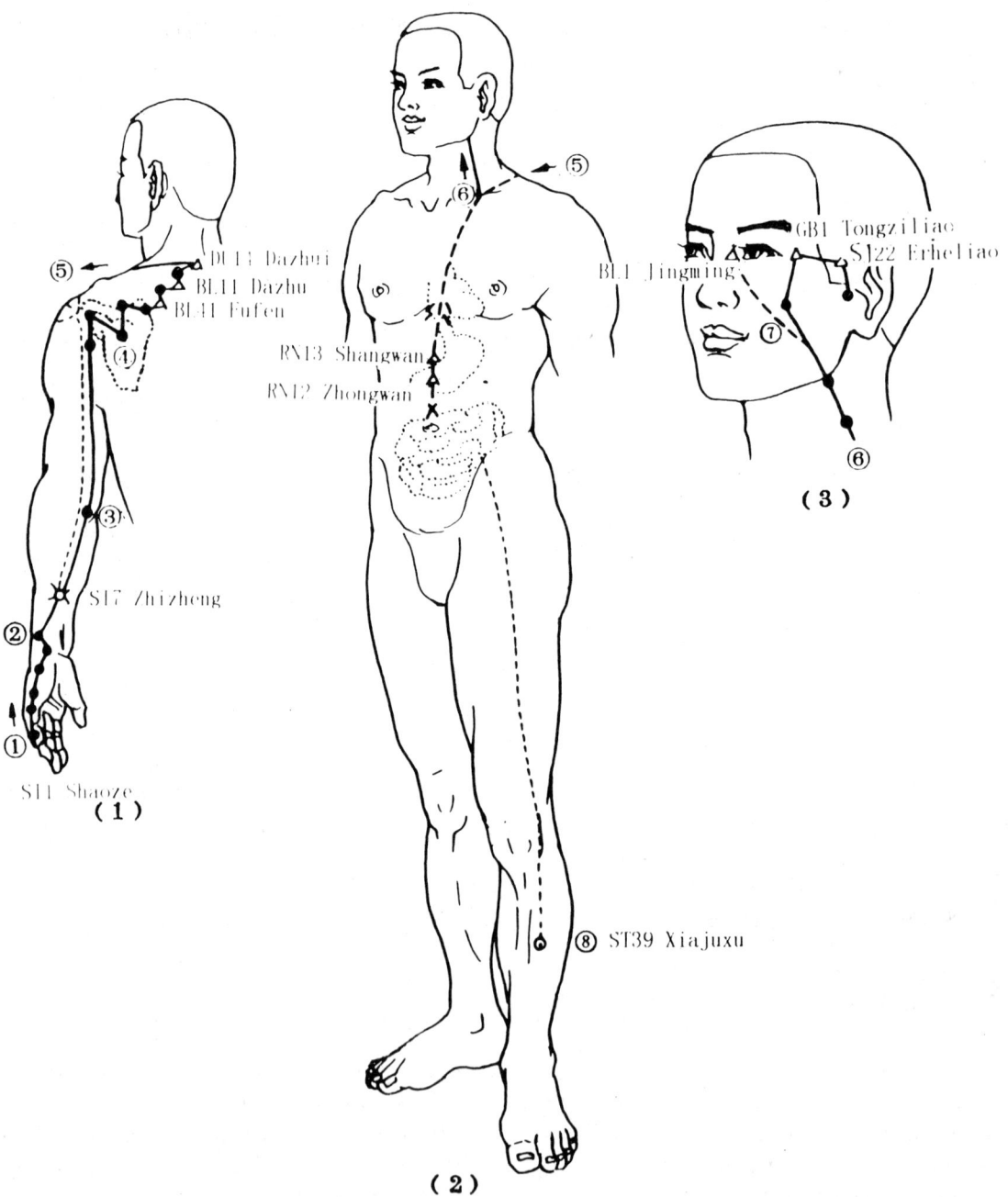

Fig. 4-5 The Small Intestine Meridian of Hand Taiyang

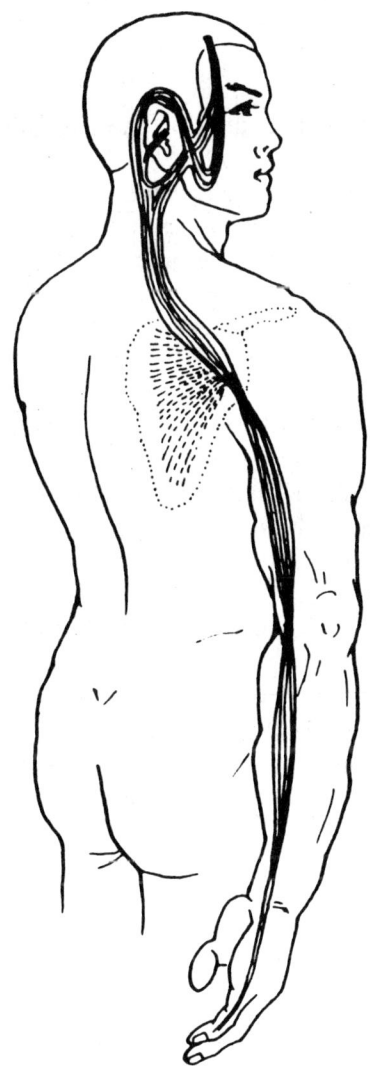

Fig. 4-6 Muscle Region of the Small Intestine of Hand Taiyang

border of the scapula and lateral aspect of the neck, cheek and mandible and in front of the ear. (See Fig. 3-4).

6) Acupoints

There are 19 acupoints in the Small Intestine Meridian. And it starts from Shaoze (SI 1) and ends at Tinggong (SI 19).

Crossing points: Duzhu (BL 11), Shangwan (RN 13), Zhongwan (RN 12), Tongziliao (GB 1), Heliao (SJ 22), Jingming (BL 1).

2. Symptoms and Signs of the Small Intestine Meridian of Hand Taiyang

1) Symptoms and Signs of the Disorders of the Meridian

If pathogenic changes occur in the meridian, there may appear pain in the pharynx, swelling of the lower chin with inability to turn around, shoulder pain which is felt as if having a traction, pain of the upper arm felt as if being broken. The Small Intestine Meridian is mainly used to treat the disturbances in transporting body fluid, such as deafness, icteric sclera, swelling of the cheek, pain in the lower chin and the neck, pain in posterior aspect of the shoulder, elbow and arm. (*Miraculous Pivot*)

2) Symptoms and Signs of the Disorders of the Collaterals

"Excess syndromes of the collateral may lead to relaxed joints and inability of the elbow to move. Deficiency syndromes may produce verruca, which looks like crusted scabies between fingers." (*Miraculous Pivot*)

3) Symptoms and Signs of the Disorders of the Muscle Region

Disorders of the muscle region may cause pain in the posterior aspect of the elbow, pain of the small finger radiating to the axilla along the arm, pain in the posterior border of the axilla which curves around the scapula and goes to the neck, as a result, there is ringing and pain in the ear which radiate to the lower chin, inability to see until the eyes are closed for a period of time. Contraction of the neck muscle may lead to swelling of the neck and scrofula. (*Miraculous Pivot*)

Appendix Medical Documents

Disorders of the small intestine may cause pain in the lower abdomen, dragging pain of the waist referring to the testes. Then the patients usually have desire to defecate. There may appear heat in the anterior part of the ear, pathogenic cold and heat in the shoulder, heat sensation between the ring finger and small finger and also deeper pulse will appear. (*Miraculous Pivot*)

If distention of the small intestine occurs, there may appear lower abdominal distension, which brings about pain in the waist. (*Miraculous Pivot*)

Dysfunction of Hand Taiyang Meridian may lead to deafness, watery eyes, inability of the nape to turn around and inability of the waist to lie flat. (*Plain Questions*)

Function of the large intestine and small intestine is excretion. (*Plain Questions*)

If pathogenic heat of the bladder is transmitted to the small intestine, there may appear difficult urination and if this pathogenic heat invades upwards, there may appear erosion of the oral mucosa. (*Plain Questions*)

If pathogenic cold attacks the small intestine, there may be diarrhea and abdominal pain. If pathogenic heat attacks the small intestine, there may appear pain in the small intestine, fever, extreme thirst, mass in the abdomen and abdominal pain, which leads to anuria. (*Plain Questions*)

Chapter Five

The Three Yin Meridians of Foot

IX. System of the Spleen Meridian of Foot Taiyin

1. Distribution of the Spleen Meridian of Foot Taiyin

1) Course of the Meridian

The Spleen Meridian of Foot Taiyin originates from the tip of the first toe. From the first toe, it follows the border between the dark and light skin of the medial aspect of the foot and ascends up the leg in front of the medial malleolus. It then travels along the posterior side of the tibia, crosses and runs anterior to the Liver Meridian of Foot Jueyin. Passing through the anterior medial aspect of the knee and thigh, it enters the abdomen. It then connects with the spleen, its pertaining organ, and the stomach. It continues ascending across the diaphragm and alongside the esophagus. When it reaches the root of the tongue, it spreads over its lower surface.

A branch separates from the main meridian in the stomach region and ascends through the diaphragm, flowing into the heart to link with the Heart Meridian of Hand Shaoyin. (See Fig. 5-1).

2) Course of the Collaterals

"It branches out at Gongsun (*Plain Questions*), one cun posterior to the base of the first metatarsal bone, and then joins the Stomach Meridian. A branch runs upwards to the abdomen and connects with the stomach and intestine". (*Miraculous Pivot*)

"The Major Collaterals of the Spleen begins from Dabao (SP 21), emerges at three cun below Yuanye (GB 22) through the chest and hypochondriac region." (*Miraculous Pivot*)

3) Divergent Meridian

"After deriving from the Spleen Meridian on the thigh, it converges with the Divergent Meridian of the Stomach Meridian of Foot Yangming, runs upwards to the throat and finally

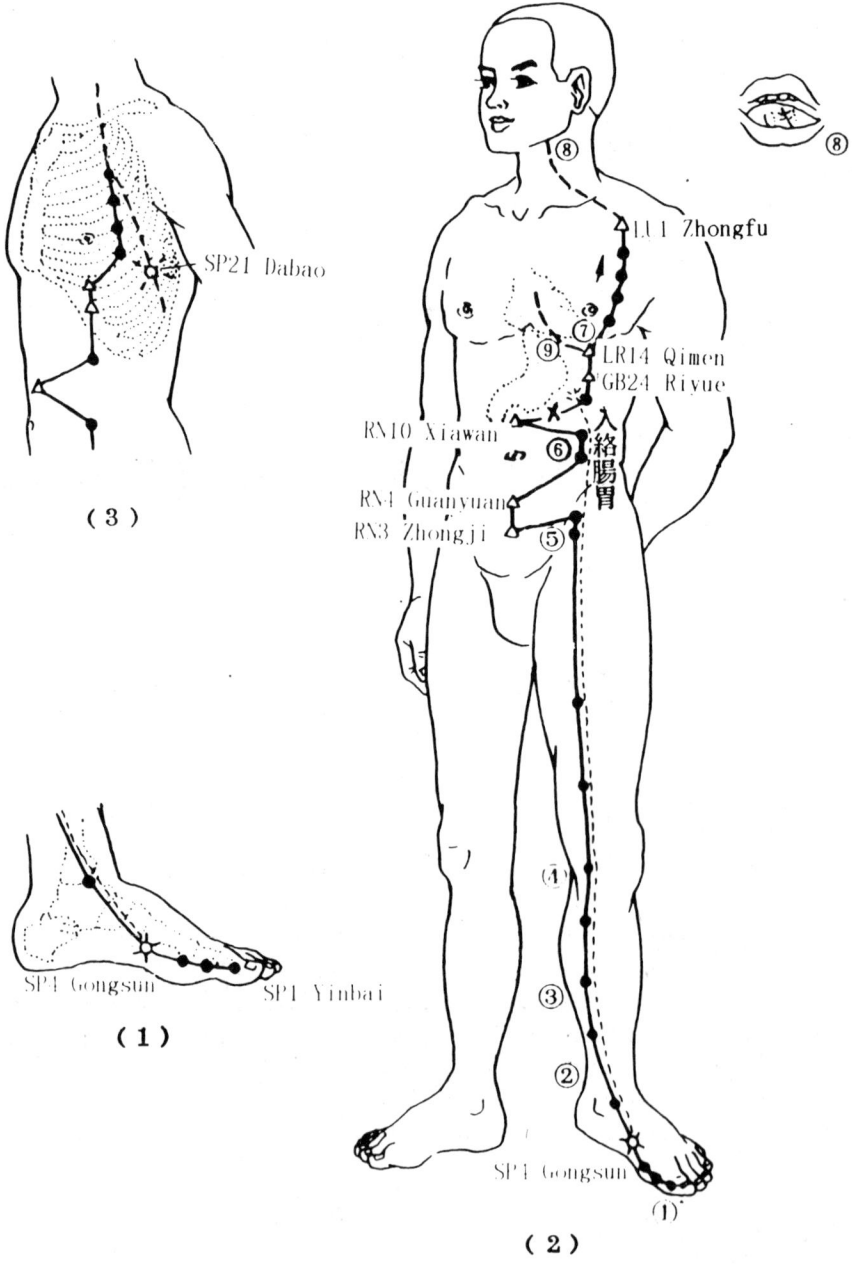

Fig. 5-1 The Spleen Meridian of Foot Taiyin

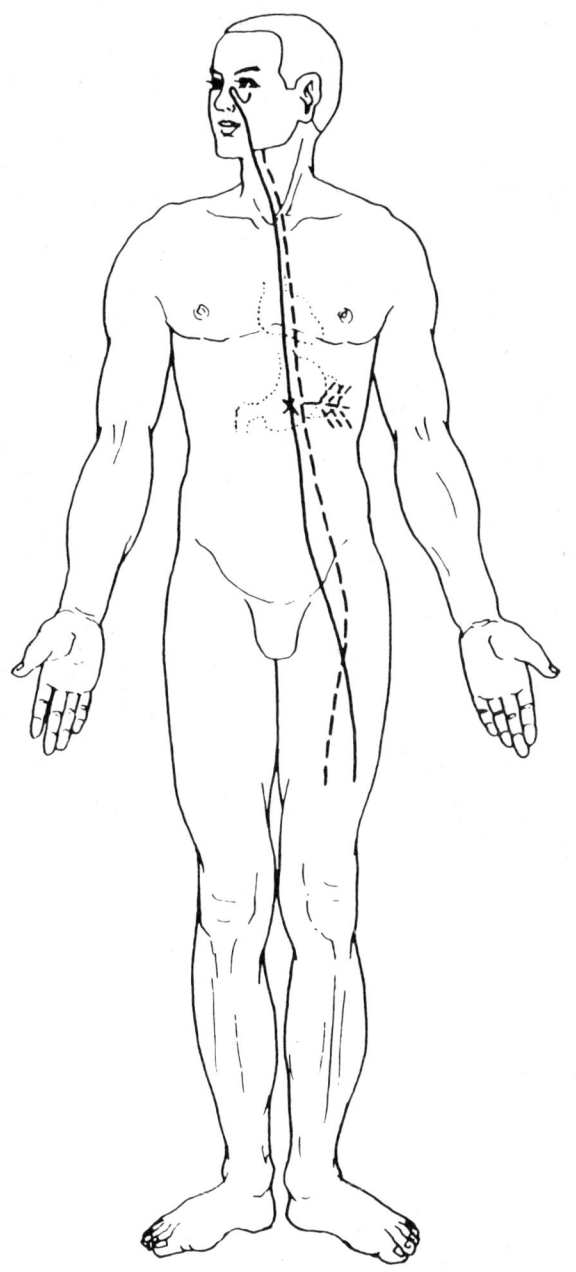

Fig. 5-2 Divergent Meridians of the Stomach Meridian of Foot Yangming and the Spleen Meridian of Foot Taiyin

enters the tongue." (*Miraculous Pivot*) (See Fig. 5-2).

4) Muscle Region

"It starts from the medial side of the big toe and knots at the internal malleolus. Continuing upwards and knotting at the medial side of the knee, a branch travels through the medial aspect of the thigh and knots at the lip. Then it joins with the external genitalia and extends to the abdomen, knotting with the umbilicus. From there, it enters the abdominal cavity, knots with the ribs and disperses through the chest. An internal branch adheres to the spine." (*Miraculous Pivot*) (See Fig. 5-3).

5) Cutaneous Region

The Cutaneous Region of the Spleen Meridian of Foot Taiyin, according to the passing course

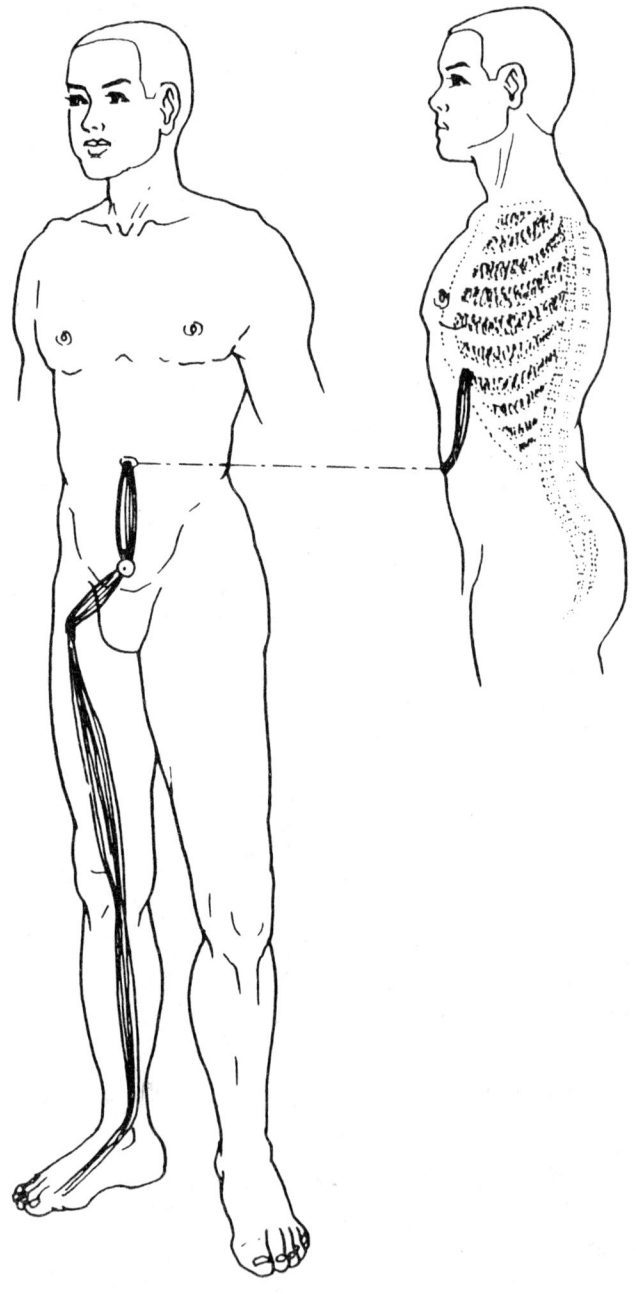

Fig. 5-3 Muscle Region of the Spleen Meridian of Foot Taiyin

of the meridian and collateral, is mainly distributed at the medial side of the big toe, anterior aspect of the internal malleolus, the centre and anterior side of the medial aspect of the leg, the medial side of the thigh, the lateral side of the straight muscle of the abdomen and the lateral chest. (See Fig. 3-4).

6) Acupoints

There are 21 acupoints in the Spleen Meridian and it starts from Yinbai (SP 1) and ends at Dabao (SP 21).

Crossing points: Zhongji (RN 3), Guanyuan (RN 4), Xiawan (RN 10), Riyue (GB 24), Qimen (LR 14), Zhongfu (LU 1).

2. Symptoms and Signs of the Disorders of the Spleen Meridian of Foot Taiyin

1) Symptoms and Signs of the Disorders of the Meridian

"If pathogenic factors attack the meridian, there may appear stiffness of the tongue root, vomiting when taking food, epigastric pain, abdominal distention, frequent eructation and heaviness of the body. Then abdominal distention may get better after free circulation of qi. The Spleen Meridian is mainly used to treat such disorders as pain of the tongue root, inability of the body to move, anorexia, irritability, acute pain below the heart, loose stool, dysentery, water blockage, jaundice, inability to lie flat, difficulty in standing, swelling of the medial side of the hip and knee, muscular spasm and limited movement of the big toe." (*Miraculous Pivot*)

2) Symptoms and Signs of the Disorders of the Collaterals

"Disorders of the collateral may cause an adverse flow of qi resulting in acute vomiting and diarrhea. Excess syndromes lead to sharp pain in the abdomen, deficiency may cause distended abdomen like a drum." (*Miraculous Pivot*)

"If the Large Collateral of the Spleen is excessive, there may appear general pain of the body, and dysfunction of all the joints." (*Miraculous Pivot*)

3) Symptoms and Signs of the Disorders of the Muscle Region

"Disorders of the muscle region may cause pain of the first toe referring to the medial malleolus due to spasm, pain of the knee and the medial side of the thigh, spasmodic pain around external genitalia, which brings about pain in the umbilicus, hypochondriac pain leading to pain in the chest." (*Miraculous Pivot*)

Appendix Medical Documents

Spleen deficiency causes limited movement of the four limbs, discomfort of the internal organs. Spleen excess causes abdominal distention and difficult urination. (*Miraculous Pivot*)

Chronic infantile convulsion due to dysfunction of the spleen may result in excessive sweat, aversion to wind, general fatigue of the body, laziness of the four limbs, yellow tongue with thin coating and anorexia. (*Plain Questions*)

Dysfunction of the Foot Taiyin Meridian causes acute contraction of the limbs and cardiac pain referring to the abdomen. (*Plain Questions*)

Disorders of the spleen may cause heaviness sensation of the body, insatiable hunger, muscular atrophy, inability of the lower limbs to flex and extend with pain while walking. Spleen deficiency causes abdominal distention, borborygmus and diarrhea with undigested food. (*Plain Questions*)

Disorders of the Foot Taiyin Meridian may lead to mental depression, eructation, sweating due to cold and heat and frequent vomiting. Patients may feel better after vomiting. Select the acupoint of the Foot Taiyin Meridian to give treatment. (*Plain Questions*)

Dysfunction of the Foot Taiyin Meridian causes fullness sensation and distention of the abdomen, anorexia, vomiting immediately after meals and inability to fall asleep. (*Plain Questions*)

Spleen distension causes frequent retching, restlessness of the four limbs, heaviness of the body with inability to dress oneself and insomnia. (*Miraculous Pivot*)

If pathogenic factors attack the collateral of the Foot Taiyin Meridian, there may appear lumbago referring to the lower abdominal area between the ribs and laterl abdomen, then inability to lie flat appears. (*Plain Questions*)

X. System of the Liver Meridian of Foot Jueyin

1. Distribution of the Liver Meridian of Foot Jueyin

1) Course of the Meridian

The Liver Meridian of the Foot Jueyin originates from the dorsal region of the big toe, continuing upward along the dorsum of the foot to a point 1 cun in front of the medial malleolus. It then ascends to a point 8 cun superior to the medial malleolus, where it intersects and then travels behind the Spleen Meridian of Foot Taiyin. Continuing to ascend posterior to the Spleen Meridian, the meridian reaches the medial side of the knee and thigh. It then enters the pubic region, curving around the external genitalia and ascending to the lower abdomen. Going up and skirting the stomach, it enters the liver, its pertaining organ, and connects with the gallbladder. The meridian then continues its ascending route through the diaphragm branches out to the costal and hypochondriac regions. It continues ascending through the neck, posterior to the pharynx, and enters the nasopharyax to connect with the "eye system". Finally, the meridian runs upward to the forehead and meets the Du Meridian at the vertex. A branch from the "eye system" descends into the cheek and curves around the inner surface of the lips. Another branch separates in the liver, crosses the diaphragm and runs into the lung, where it links with the Lung Meridian of Hand Taiyin. (See Fig. 5-4).

2) Course of the Collaterals

"It starts from Ligou (LR 5), five cun above the internal malleolus and connects with the Gallbladder Meridian. A branch runs up the leg to the genitals and knots at the penis." (*Miraculous Pivot*)

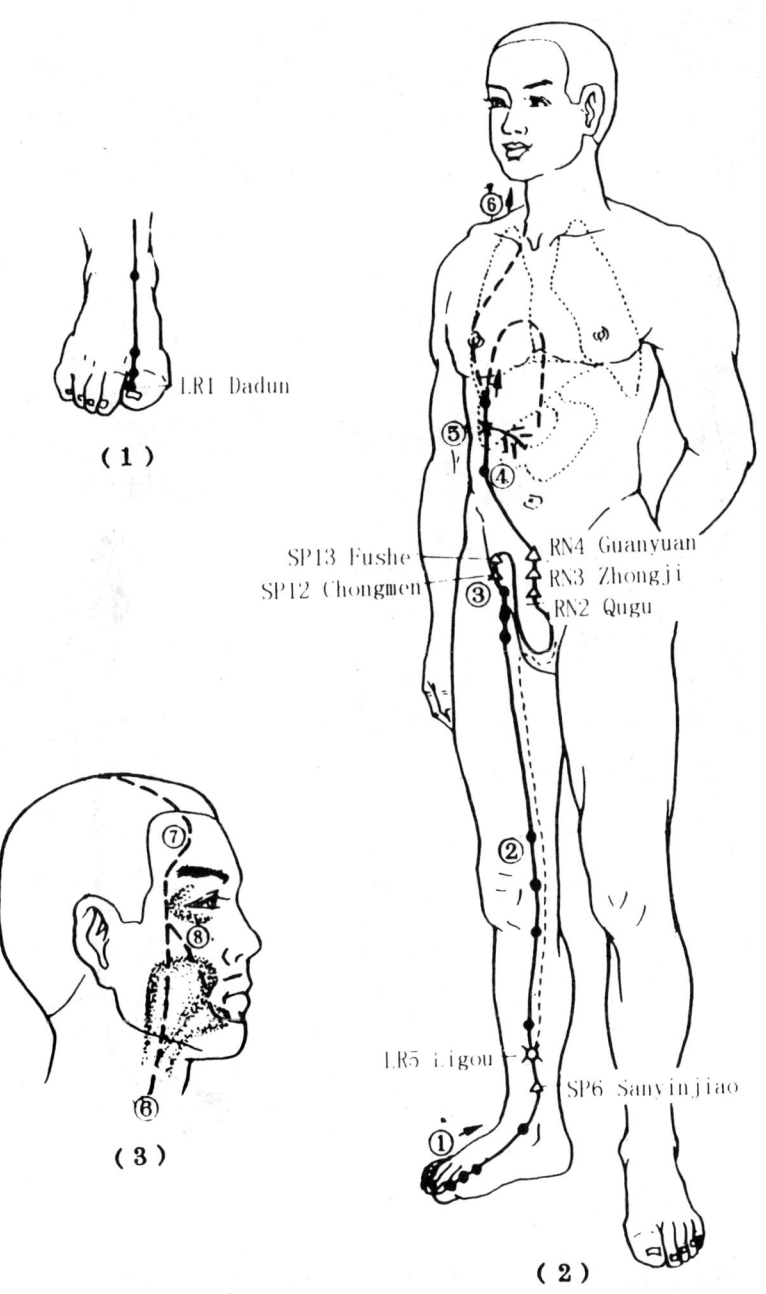

Fig. 5-4 The Liver Meridian of Foot Jueyin

3) Divergent Meridian

"After deriving from the Liver Meridian on the instep, it runs upward to the pubic region and converges with the Gallbladder Meridian of Foot Shaoyang." (*Miraculous Pivot*) (See Fig. 5-5).

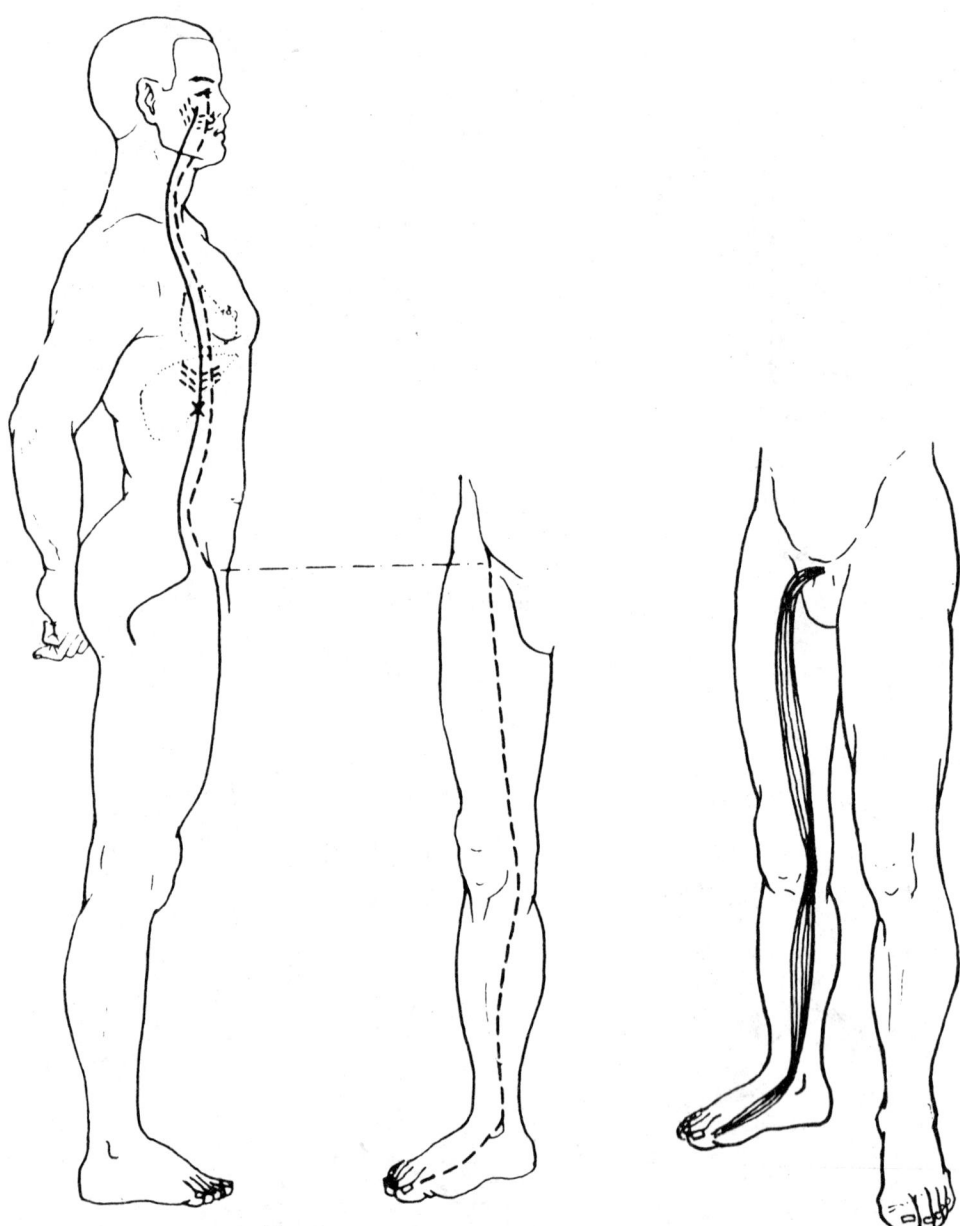

Fig. 5-5 Divergent Meridians of the Gallbladder Meridian of Foot Shaoyang and the Liver Meridian of Foot Jueyin

Fig. 5-6 Muscle Region of the Liver Meridian of Foot Jueyin

4) Muscle Region

"It originates from the dorsum of the big toe and knots at the anterior part of the internal malleolus. Then it runs upward along the medial side of the tibia and knots at the lower, medial aspect of the knee. From there, it runs upward along the medial aspect of the thigh to the genital region, where it converges with other muscle regions." (*Miraculous Pivot*) (See Fig. 5-6).

5) Cutaneous Region

The Cutaneous Region of the Liver Meridian of Foot Jueyin, based on the passing course of the meridian and collateral, is distributed at the dorsum of the big toe, medial aspect of the dorsum of the foot anterior of the medial side of the leg (above eight cun below the internal malleolus), center (above eight cun above the internal malleolus) of the medial side of the tibia, medial aspect of the thigh, inguinal area, chest and hypochondriac region. (See Fig. 3-4).

6) Acupoints

There are 14 acupoints in the Liver Meridian. It starts from Dadun (LR 1) and ends at Qimen (LR 14).

Crossing points: Sanyinjiao (SP 6), Chongmen (SP 12), Qugu (RN 2), Zhongji (RN 3), Guanyuan (RN 4).

2. Symptoms and Signs of the Disorders of the Liver Meridian of Foot Jueyin

1) Symptoms and Signs of the Disorders of the Meridian

"If pathogenic changes occur in the meridian, there may be lumbago with inability to bend forward and backward, pain and swelling of the scrotum, swelling of the lower abdomen in women, dry pharynx and lusterless face. The Liver Meridian is mainly used to treat such disorders as fullness of the chest, vomiting, diarrhea with undigested food, inguinal hernia, enuresis and anuria." (*Miraculous Pivot*)

2) Symptoms and Signs of the Disorders of the Collaterals

"Disorders of the collaterals may be manifested as an adverse flow of qi leading to sudden inguinal hernia. Excess syndrome causes extended length of the scrotum and deficiency syndrome produces sudden and extreme itch." (*Miraculous Pivot*)

3) Symptoms and Signs of the Disorders of the Muscle Region

"Disorders of the Muscle Region may be manifested as pain in the big toe referring to the anterior part of the medial melleolus, pain in the medial aspect of the thigh, pain of the genitalia and hip, spasm and impotence in case of sexual strain, and flaccid constriction of the penis in case of cold injury and continuous erection of penis in case of heat injury." (*Miraculous Pivot*)

Appendix Medical Documents

If liver pulse feels little tense, it indicates "fat qi" (a mass below the left hypochondrium), which is like an overturned cup under the hypochondriac region. Slow pulse suggests susceptibility to vomiting. Slippery pulse may suggest hard and stiff testis. Slight slippery pulse may suggest urinary bleeding. Choppy pulse may appear muscular spasm and muscular Bi syndrome. (*Miraculous Pivot*)

Enlarged liver may compress the stomach and the throat, then there may appear pain in the stomach and hypochondrium. (*Miraculous Pivot*) Distention of the liver causes hypochondriac fullness, which brings about the pain in the lower abdomen. (*Miraculous Pivot*)

If pathogenic factors attack the liver, there may appear pain in the hypochondriac region. Pathogenic cold in the middle Jiao and turbid blood in the internal organs may cause pain of the joints while walking and occasional swelling of the foot. (*Miraculous Pivot*)

Cough due to disorders of the liver may bring about pain in the hypochondriac region, inability of the body to turn side to side in severe cases, and feeling of fullness. (*Plain Questions*)

Disorders of the liver may cause excessive sweating, aversion to wind, susceptibility to sorrow, lusterless face, dry throat, susceptibility to anger and hate towards women at times. (*Plain Questions*)

Pathogenic heat in the liver causes yellowish urine, abdominal pain, drowsiness, fever, convulsion, abdominal fullness and pain, involuntary movement of the limbs, and inability to fall asleep. (*Plain Questions*)

Dysfunction of Foot Jueyin causes swelling and pain in the lower abdomen, abdominal distention, enuresis, drowsiness, flexed knee, constriction and swelling of the scrotum and heat sensation between the legs. (*Plain Questions*)

Dysfunction of Foot Jueyin may lead to hypochondriac pain, vomiting and diarrhea. (*Plain Questions*)

Adverse flow of liver qi causes headache. (*Plain Questions*)

Pathogenic wind causes blurring of vision because of dysfunction of the liver. (*Plain Questions*)

Deficiency syndrome of the liver causes hypochondriac pain involving with the lower abdomen, susceptibility to anger, blurred vision, being unable to hear, and susceptibility to fright like a feeling of being hunted. (*Plain Questions*)

Excess syndrome of Foot Jueyin may lead to ringing in the ears, dizziness and tendency to vomit. (*Plain Questions*)

XI. System of the Kidney Meridian of Foot Shaoyin

1. Distribution of the Kidney Meridian of Foot Shaoyin

1) Course of the Meridian

The Kidney Meridian of Foot Shaoyin originates at the inferior aspect of the fifth toe and runs obliquely towards the sole of the foot. Emerging from the inferior aspect of the navicular tuberosity and behind the medial malleous, it enters the heel. It then proceeds upward along the medial aspect of the leg to the medial side of the lumbar region. It then enters the kidney, its pertaining organ, and connects with the bladder. Returning anteriorly, it ascends along a line 1/2 cun from the anterior midline of the abdomen to the chest. It terminates at Shufu (KI 27) on the lower border of the clavicle. A branch ascends directly from the kidney, crosses the liver and diaphragm and enters the lung. From the lung, it follows the throat to the root of the tongue. Another branch originates in the lung, connects with the heart and disperses in the chest., it links with the Pericardium Meridian of Hand Jueyin. (See Fig. 5-7).

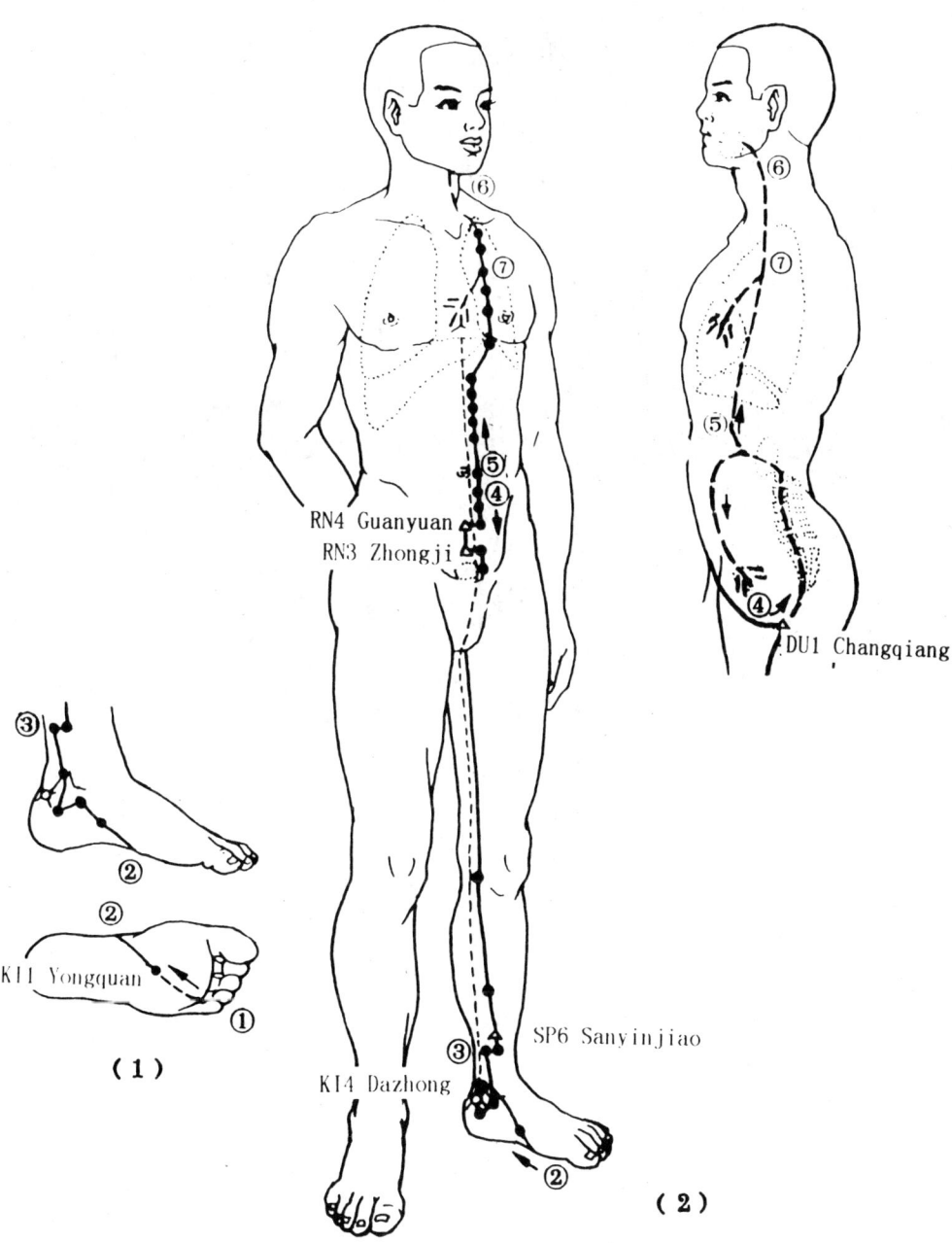

Fig. 5-7 The Kidney Meridian of Foot Shaoyin

2) Course of the Collaterals

"It starts from Dazhong (KI 4), on the posterior aspect of internal malleolus, it crosses the heel and joins the Bladder Meridian. A branch follows the Kidney Meridian upward to a point below the pericardium and then pierces through the lumbar vertebrae." (*Miraculous Pivot*)

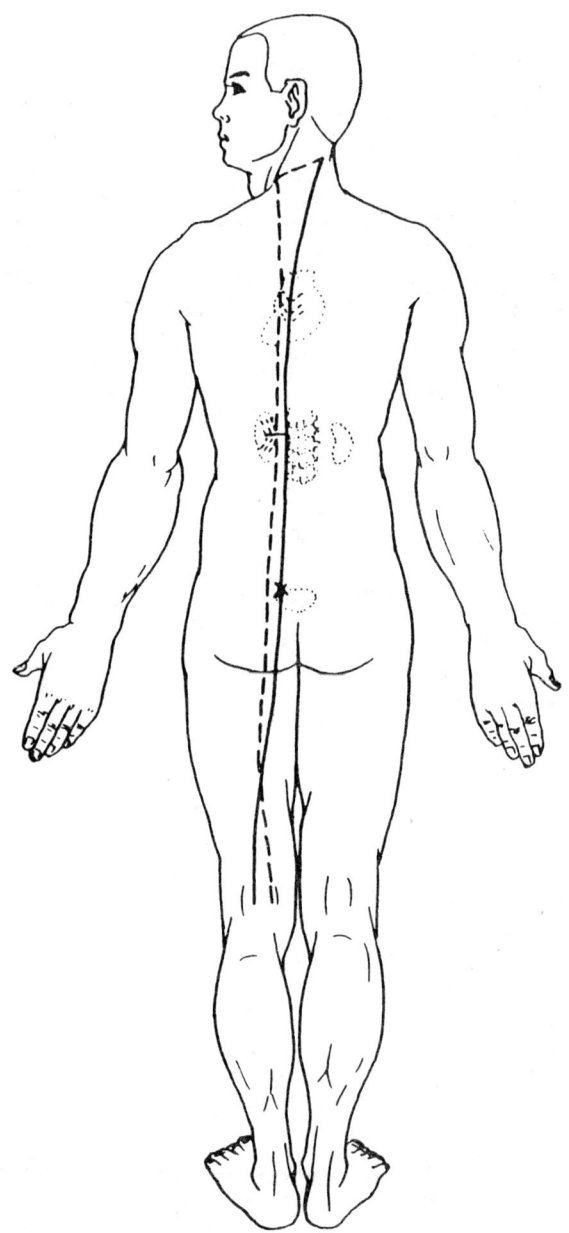

Fig. 5-8 Divergent Meridians of the Bladder Meridian of Foot Taiyang and the Kidney Meridian of Foot Shaoyin

3) Divergent Meridian

"After derived from the Kidney Meridian in the popliteal fossa, it intersects the Divergent Meridian of the Bladder Meridian on the thigh. It then runs upward, connects with the kidney and crosses the Dai Meridian at about the level of the 14th vertebra. The straight branch ascends to the root of the tongue and finally emerges at the nape of the neck to join the Bladder Meridian of Foot Taiyang." (*Miraculous Pivot*) (See Fig. 5-8).

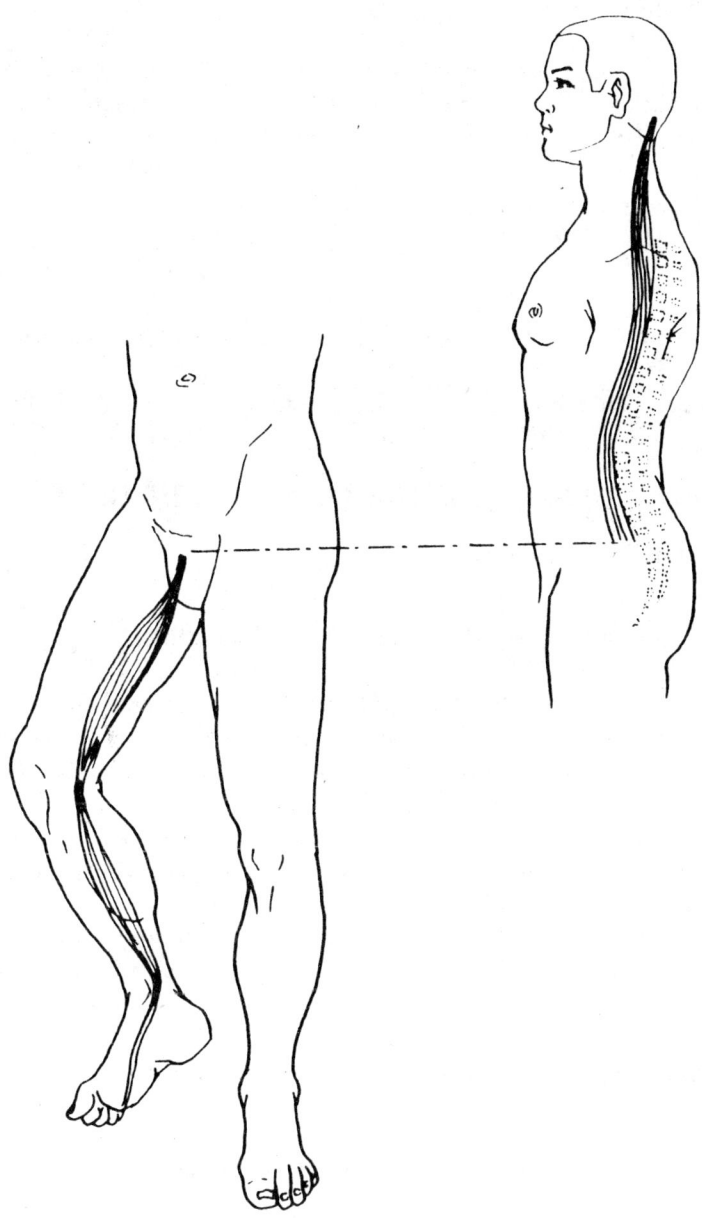

Fig. 5-9 Muscle Region of the Kidney Meridian of Foot Shaoyin

4) Muscle Region

"It starts beneath the small toe. Together with the Muscle Region of Foot Taiyin, it runs obliquely below the internal malleolus and knots at the heel. It converges with the Muscle Region of Foot Taiyang, knots at the lower, medial aspect of the knee, joins with the Muscle Region of Foot Taiyin and ascends along the side of the spine to the nape of the neck and knots with the occipital bone, converging with the Muscle Region of Foot Taiyang." (*Miraculous Pivot*) (See

Fig. 5-9).

5) Cutaneous Region

The Cutaneous Region of the Kidney Meridian of Foot Shaoyin, based on the passing course of the meridian and collateral, is mostly distributed at the sole, tuberosity of the navicular bone and the inferior part of the internal malleolus, leg and the posterior part of the medial aspect of the knee, the genital region, the inferior border of the pubis, and on both sides of the midline of the chest and abdomen. (See Fig. 3-4).

6) Acupoints

There are 27 acupoints in the Kidney Meridian. It starts from Yongquan (KI 1) and ends at Shufu (KI 27).

Crossing points: Sanyinjiao (SP 6), Changqiang (DU 1), Zhongji (RN 3), Guanyuan (RN 4).

2. Symptoms and Signs of the Disorders of the Kidney Meridian of Foot Shaoyin

1) Symptoms and Signs of the Disorders of the Meridian

"If pathogenic changes occur in the meridian, there may appear hunger without desire for food, lusterless complexion, cough with blood, shortness of breath with wheezing, uneasy feeling during sitting, blurring of vision, poor eyesight and severe palpitation with hungry feeling. Deficiency of qi causes a susceptibility to fear and fright with palpitation like a feeling of being hunted, which is caused by dysfunction of the meridian qi between bones. The Kidney Meridian is mainly used to treat such disorders as heat sensation in the mouth, dry tongue, swelling of the throat, adverse flow of qi, dry sensation and pain in the pharynx, irritability, cardiac pain, jaundice, borborygmus, diarrhea, spinal pain and pain in the posterior aspect of the thigh, muscular atrophy, cold limbs, desire for lying down, heat sensation and pain in the sole." (*Miraculous Pivot*)

2) Symptoms and Signs of the Disorders of the Collaterals

"Disorders of the Kidney Meridian cause adverse flow of qi leading to restlessness. Excess syndrome produces anuria or enuresis, deficiency syndrome produces waist pain." (*Miraculous Pivot*)

3) Symptoms and Signs of the Disorders of the Muscle Region

"Disorders of the muscle region may cause spasm of foot. If disorders of the muscle region occur in the foot, there may appear epilepsy and muscular contracture. If it occurs on the muscle region of the back, there may appear inability to bend forward, if it occurs on the muscle region of the abdomen, there may appear inability to bend backward. It is indicated that Yang disorders cause inability of the waist to bend forward, while Yin disorders cause inability of the waist to bend backward." (*Miraculous Pivot*)

Appendix Medical Documents

Distention of the kidney may lead to abdominal fullness referring to the back with pain in the thigh. (*Miraculous Pivot*)

Deficiency of kidney qi causes cold limbs, excess may cause distention and discomfort of the internal organs. (*Miraculous Pivot*) If pathogenic factors attack the kidney, there may appear bone disorders, yin arthralgia, feeling uneasy while pressing, abdominal distention, difficult defecation, pain in the shoulder, back, neck and frequent dizziness. (*Miraculous Pivot*)

Dysfunction of the Foot Shaoyin Meridian causes dry mouth, dark coloured urine, abdominal fullness and cardiac pain. (*Plain Questions*)

Dysfunction of the Foot Shaoyin Meridian may cause deficient fullness sensation, vomiting and watery stools. (*Plain Questions*)

Pathogenic wind in the kidney may cause hyperhidrosis, aversion to wind, edema of the face, spinal pain with inability to stand, darkish complexion, difficult urination and defecation. (*Plain Questions*)

Disorders of the kidney may lead to distended abdomen, swelling of the fibula, asthma, cough, heaviness of the body, night sweating, aversion to wind. (*Plain Questions*)

Cough due to disorders of the kidney may lead to pain in the waist and back which refers to each other, and there may appear expectoration of saliva in severe cases. (*Plain Questions*)

Pathogenic heat in the kidney may lead to waist pain first, then soreness of the waist, bitter taste and thirst, desire for drink, fever sensation all over the body. Severe heat leads to pain and stiffness at the nape of the neck, cold sensation and soreness of the leg, feverish sensation of the sole, no desire to talk, pain at the nape of the neck and irritability. (*Plain Questions*)

If pathogenic factors attack the collateral of the Foot Shaoyin Meridian, there may appear sudden cardiac pain, abdominal distention, fullness sensation in the chest and hypochondriac region. (*Plain Questions*)

If pathogenic factors attack the collateral of the Foot Shaoyin Meridian, there may appear pain in the pharynx, inability to take food, susceptibility to anger and abnormal qi ascending to the diaphragm. (*Plain Questions*)

Chapter Six

The Three Yang Meridians of Foot

XII. System of the Stomach Meridian of Foot Yangming

1. Distribution of the Stomach Meridian of Foot Yangming

1) Course of the Meridian

The Stomach Meridian of Foot Yangming originates from the lateral side of the ala nasi and ascends to the bridge of the nose where it meets the Bladder Meridian of Foot Taiyang. Turning downward along the lateral side of the nose, it enters the upper gum. Reemerging, it curves around the lips and descends to meet the Ren Meridian at the mentolabial groove (Chengjiang, RN 24). It then runs posterolaterally across the lower portion of the cheek at Daying (ST 5). Winding along the angle of the mandible (Jiache, ST 6), it ascends anteriorly to the ear and transverses Shangguan (GB 3). It then follows the anterior hairline and reaches the forehead. A facial branch of the meridian emerges in front of Daying (ST 5) and descends to Renying (ST 9). It then travels along the throat and enters the supraclavicular fossa. Descending, it passes the diaphragm, enters the stomach, its pertaining organ, and connects with the spleen. The straight portion of the meridian arises from the supraclavicular fossa, descends along the mammary line, then passes beside the umbilicus and enters Qichong (ST 30) on the lateral side of the lower abdomen. A branch from the lower orifice of the stomach descends inside the abdomen and joins the previous portion of the meridian at Qichong (ST 30). Running downward, transversing Biguan (ST 31) on the anterior aspect of the thigh and Futu (ST 32) at the femur, it reaches the knee. From there, it proceeds along the lateral side of the tibia, passes through the dorsum of the foot and reaches the lateral side of the tip of the second toe. A tibial branch separates from the main meridian at Zusanli (ST 36), 3 cun below the knee, and enters the lateral side of the third toe. Another branch arises from the dorsum of the foot and terminates at the me-

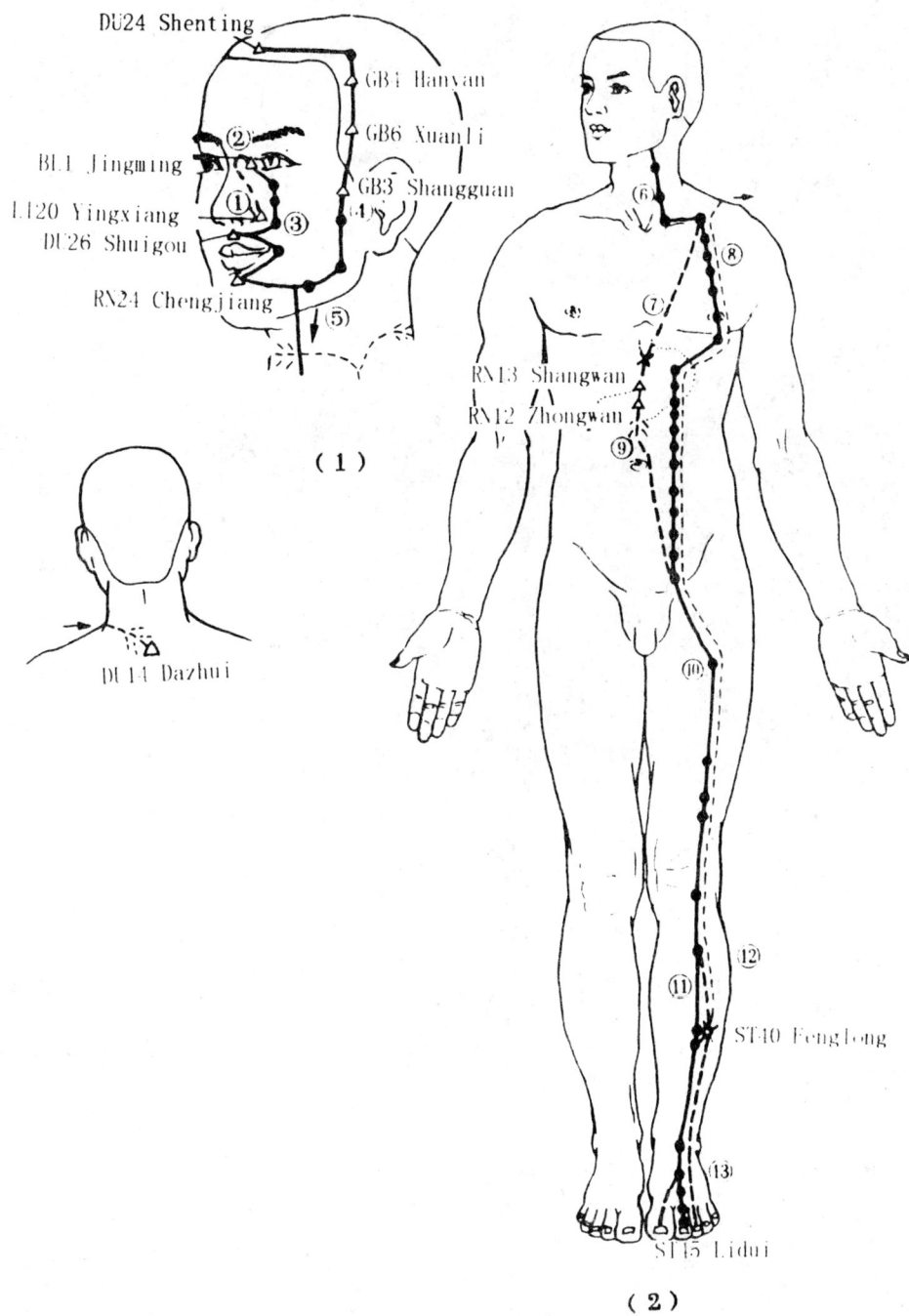

Fig. 6-1 The Stomach Meridian of Foot Yangming

dial side of the tip of the first toe where it links with the Spleen Meridian of Foot Taiyin. (See Fig. 6-1).

2) Course of the Collaterals

"It originates from Fenglong (ST 40), eight cun above the external malleolus and connects

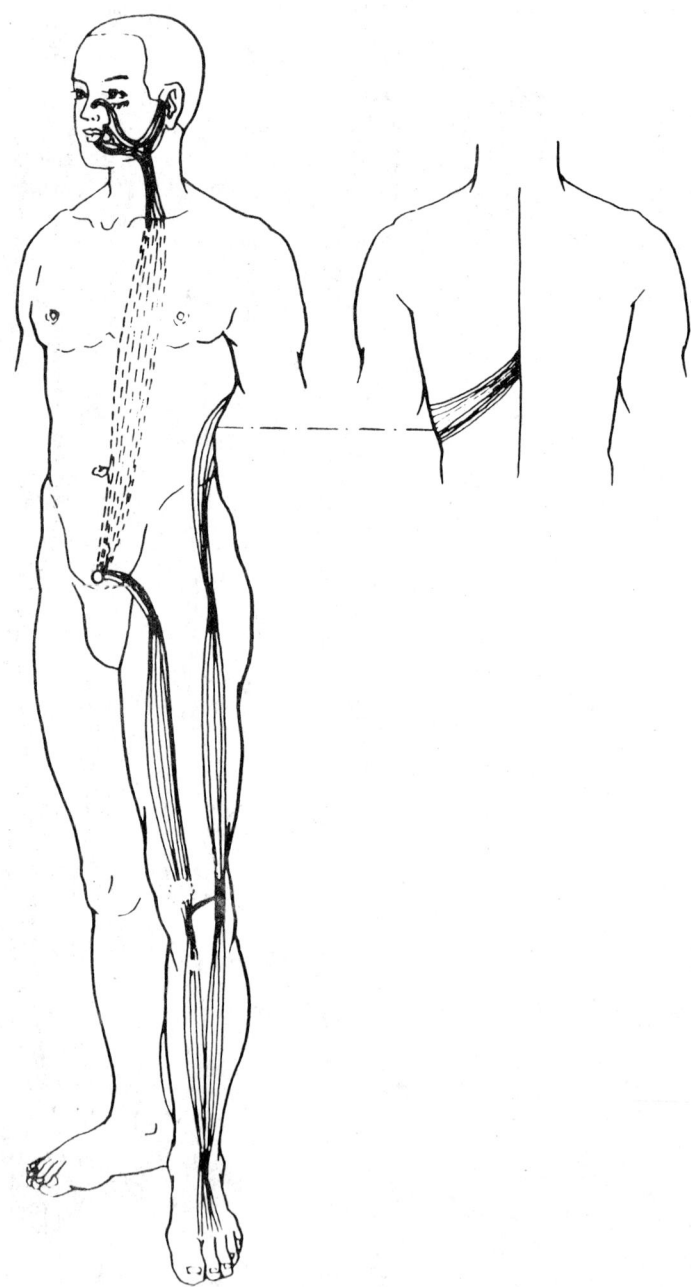

Fig. 6-2 Muscle Region of the Stomach Meridian of Foot Yangming

with the Spleen Meridian. A branch runs along the lateral aspect of the tibia upward to the top of the head, and converges with the other Yang Meridians on the head and neck. From there it runs downward to connect with the throat." (*Miraculous Pivot*)

3) Divergent Meridian of Foot Yangming

"After deriving from the Stomach Meridian on the thigh, it enters the abdomen, connects with the stomach and disperses in the spleen. It then runs upward beside the nose and connects with the eye and finally joins the Stomach Meridian of Foot Yangming. (*Miraculous Pivot*) (See Fig. 5-2).

4) Muscle Region

"It starts from the second, middle and fourth toes, knots at the dorsum of the foot, and ascends obliquely along the lateral aspect of the leg, where it disperses at the tibia and then knots at the lateral aspect of the knee. Ascending directly to knot at the hip joint, it extends to the lower ribs to connect with the spine. The straight branch runs along the tibia and knots at the knee. A branch connects with the fibula, and joins with the Foot Shaoyang Meridian. The straight branch travels upward along Futu (ST 32), knots at the thigh and gathers at the genital region. Dispersing upward on the abdomen and knotting at Quepen (ST 12), it extends to the neck and mouth, meeting at the side of the nose and knotting below the nose. Above, it joins with the Foot-Taiyang Meridian to form a muscular net around the eye. A branch separates at the jaw and knots in front of the ear." (*Miraculous Pivot*) (See Fig. 6-2).

5) Cutaneous Region

The Cutaneous Region of the Stomach Meridian of Foot Yangming, based on the passing course of the meridian and collateral, is mostly distributed at the second and middle toes, at the middle of the dorsum of foot, anterior and lateral side of the tibia, knee and the thigh, straight muscle of abdomen, medial side of the breast and suprascapular fossa, both sides of the throat, mandible, front of the ear, anterior temple, and the area below the eye and beside the nose. (See Fig. 3-4).

6) Acupoints

There are 45 acupoints in the Stomach Meridian. It starts from Chengqi (ST 1) and ends at Lidui (ST 45).
Crossing points: Yingxiang (LI 20), Jingming (BL 1), Shuigou (DU 26), Chengjiang (RN 23), Shangguan (GB 3), Xuanli (GB 6), Hanyan (GB 4), Shenting (DU 24), Dazhui (DU 14), Shangwan (RN 13), Zhongwan (RN 12).

2. Symptoms and Signs of the Disorders of the Stomach Meridian of Foot Yangming

1) Symptoms and Signs of the Disorders of the Meridian

"If pathogenic changes occur in the meridian, there may appear aversion to cold, inability to stretch oneself, frequent yawning, dark complexion, aversion to meeting people and fire, extreme fear while hearing a sound, severe palpitation, self-isolation in a room with closed windows and doors. In severe cases, there may be climbing to a high place, singing or walking away without being dressed. Abdominal distention and intestinal borborygmus are due to adverse flow of qi in the leg and foot. The Stomach Meridian is mainly used to treat disorders related to blood such as mania, malaria, acute febrile disease, hyperhidrosis, allergic rhinitis, deviation of the mouth, ulcer in the mouth and lips, swelling and pain of the knee joints, pain in the breast region, Qijie (the area in the groin where pulsation of the femoral artery can be felt), the thigh, Futu (ST 32) and the dorsum of foot and limited movement of the middle finger. Excessive qi may cause fever in the anterior part of the body. If the stomach function is excessive, there may appear rapid digestion of food, polyorexia and yellowish urine. Deficient qi may cause cold sensation of the body and cold in the stomach which causes fullness feeling of it." (*Miraculous Pivot*)

2) Symptoms and Signs of the Disorders of the Collaterals

"Disorders of the collateral may cause adverse flow of qi leading to inflammation of the throat and sudden loss of voice. Excess syndrome causes madness, deficiency syndrome causes limited movement of foot and muscular atrophy of the shank." (*Miraculous Pivot*)

3) Symptoms and Signs of the Disorders of the Muscle Region

"Disorders of the muscle region may cause spasm of the shank of the middle toe, muscular contracture of the dorsum of foot, spasm at Futu (ST 32), swelling of the anterior part of the thigh, swelling of the testicles, contracture of the abdominal muscle referring to the supraclavicular fossa and cheek, deviation of the mouth. Severe cases may be accompanied with inability to close the eyes. Pathogenic heat causes muscular flaccidity and inability of the eyes to open. If pathogenic cold attacks the muscle on the cheek, there appears muscular contracture leading to inability of the mouth to close. If pathogenic heat attacks the muscle on the cheek, there may appear muscular atonia." (*Miraculous Pivot*)

Appendix Medical Documents

Stomach absorbs qi and body fluid turns it to red color fluid, that is called blood. (*Miraculous Pivot*)

If pathogenic factors attack the spleen and stomach, there may appear muscular disorder and pain. Excessive Yang qi with insufficient Yin qi causes heat in the stomach, there may appear susceptibility to hunger; Excessive Yin qi with insufficient Yang qi causes cold in the stomach, there may appear borborygmus and abdominal pain. If Yin and Yang are both excessive, it means pathogenic cold and heat coexist in the stomach. (*Miraculous Pivot*)

Stomach disorders may appear abdominal distention, epigastric pain, obstruction of the ribs, diaphgram and pharynx, inability to eat and drink. (*Miraculous Pivot*)

Borborygmus is due to wind cold in the intestine and stomach. (*Miraculous Pivot*)

Dysfunction of Foot Yangming Meridian may lead to madness, abdominal distention, inability to fall asleep, flushed face, visual hallucination and incoherent speech. (*Plain Questions*)

Dysfunction of Foot Yangming Meridian causes aversion to cold and shivering, and then a feeling like cold water being sprinkled over the body. Then the body turns to heat, which may be eliminated by sweating. In this cases, the patient feels happy while being in the sun and warm qi. (*Plain Questions*)

The Stomach Meridian of Foot Yangming dominates the muscle, it runs along the nose to connect with the eyes. Disorders of Foot Yangming Meridian may cause fever, pain in the eyes, dry nose and inability to lie flat. (*Plain Questions*)

Discomfort in the stomach causes an inability to fall asleep. (*Plain Questions*)

Dysfunction of the stomach causes dyspnea with cough, fever, susceptibility to fear, epistaxis and hematemesis. (*Plain Questions*)

If pathogenic factors attack the collateral of Foot Yangming, there may appear allergic rhinitis and cold sensation of the upper teeth. (*Plain Questions*)

XIII. System of the Gallbladder Meridian of Foot Shaoyang

1. Distribution of the Gallbladder Meridian of Foot Shaoyang

1) Course of the Meridian

The Gallbladder Meridian of Foot Shaoyang originates at the outer canthus, ascends to the corner of the forehead and curves downward behind the ear. It then proceeds along the side of the neck in front of the Sanjiao Meridian of Hand Shaoyang to the shoulder. Turning back, it transverses and passes behind the Sanjiao Meridian and descends to the supraclavicular fossa. One branch of the main meridian emerges behind the auricle and enters the ear. Coming out from the anterior part of the ear, it travels to the posterior aspect of the outer canthus. Another branch separates at the outer canthus and proceeds downward to Daying (ST 5). It meets the Sanjiao Meridian and continues to the infraorbital region. Passing through Jiache (ST 6), it then descends to the neck and enters the supraclavicular fossa where it meets the main meridian. It further descends into the chest, crosses the diaphragm and connects with the liver before entering the gallbladder, its pertaining organ. Continuing along the inside of the ribs, it emerges in the inguinal region at the lower abdomen, winds around the genitals and emerges again in the hip region. The straight portion of the meridian runs downwards from the supraclavicular fossa to the axilla and the lateral aspect of the chest. Crossing the hypochondriac region, it meets the previous branch at the hip region. Then it descends along the lateral aspect of the thigh and knee and passes along the anterior aspect of the fibula to its lower end. From the end of the fibula, it crosses in front of the lateral malleolus and transverses the dorsum of foot, terminating at the lateral side of the tip of the fourth toe. Finally, a branch separates on the dorsum of the foot at Zulinqi (GB 41) and runs between the first and second metatarsal bones to the distal portion of the first toe. It then crosses under the toenail and turns back to the proximal portion of the toenail to link with the Liver Meridian of Foot Jueyin. (See Fig. 6-3).

2) Course of the Collaterals

"It starts from Guangming (GB 37), five cun above the external malleolus, and joins the Liver Meridian. It then runs downward and disperses over the dorsum of the foot." (*Miraculous Pivot*)

3) Divergent Meridian

"After deriving from the Gallbladder on the thigh, it crosses over the hip joint and enters the lower abdomen in the pelvic region and converges with the Divergent Meridian of the Liver Meridian. Then, it crosses between the lower ribs, connects with the gallbladder and spreads

98   Acupoints & Meridians

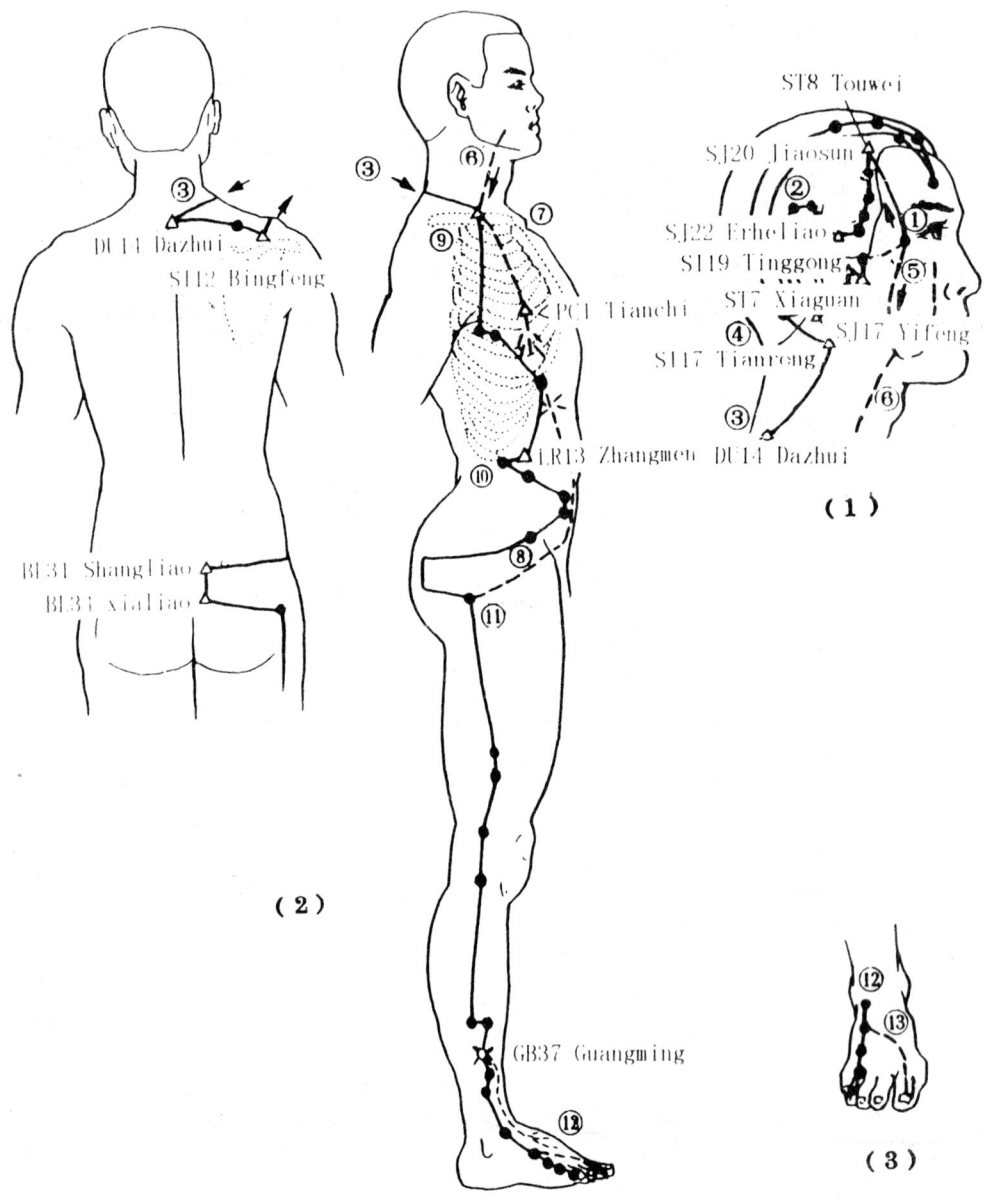

Fig. 6-3 The Gallbladder Meridian of Foot Shaoyang

through the liver. Proceeding upward, it crosses the heart and esophagus and disperses in the face. It then connects with the eyes and the Gallbladder Meridian at the outer canthus." (*Miraculous Pivot*) (See Fig. 5-5).

4) Muscle Region

"It originates from the fourth toe and knots at the external malleolus. Then it ascends along the lateral side of the tibia where it knots at the knee. A branch begins at the upper part of the fibula and continues upward along the thigh. One of its branches runs anteriorly and knots with the sacrum. The straight branch ascends across the ribs and disperses around and anterior to the axilla, connecting first at the breast region and then knotting at Quepen (ST 12). Another branch extends from the axilla upward across the clavicle, emerging in front of Muscle Region of the Foot Taiyang Meridian where it continues upward behind the ear to the temple. Then, it runs up to the vertex. A branch descends from the temple across the cheek and then knots besides the bridge of the nose. A subbranch knots at the outer canthus." (*Miraculous Pivot*) (See Fig. 6-4).

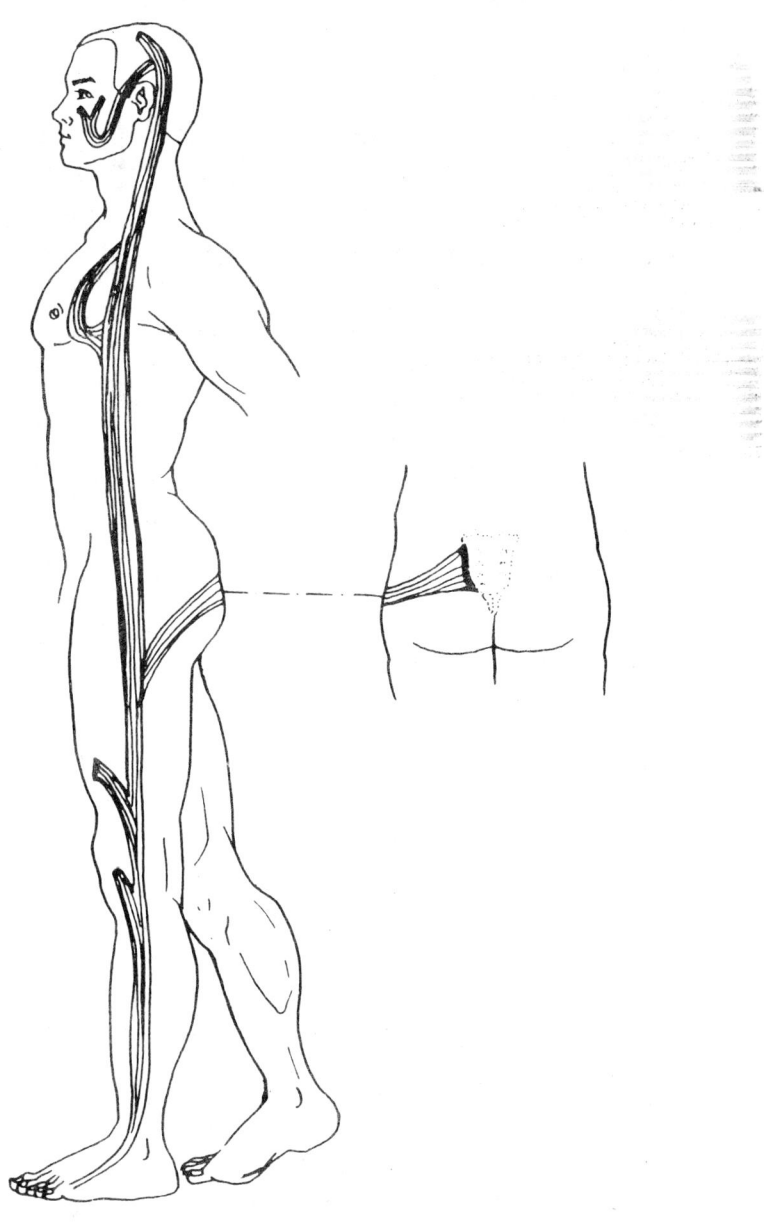

Fig. 6-4 Muscle Region of the Gallbladder Meridian of Foot Shaoyang

5) Cutaneous Region

The Cutaneous Region of the Gallbladder Meridian of Foot Shaoyang, based on the passing course of the meridian and collateral, is mostly distributed at the dorsal side of the fourth toe, the lateral side of the dorsum of foot, anterior of the external malleolus, center of the lateral side of the lower limbs, hip joint, hypochondriac region, anterior part of the axilla, lateral part of the neck and temple region. (See Fig. 3-4).

6) Acupoints

There are 44 acupoints in the Gallbladder Meridian. It starts from Tongziliao (GB 1) and ends at Zuqiaoyin (GB 44).

Crossing points: Touwei (ST 8), Erheliao (SJ 22), Jiaosun (SJ 20), Dazhui (DU 14), Bingfeng (SI 12), Yifeng (SJ 17), Tinggong (SI 19), Xiaguan (ST 7), Tianchi (PC 1), Zhangmen (LR 13), Shangliao (BL 31), Zhongliao (BL 33), Xialiao (BL 34).

2. Symptoms and Signs of the Disorders of the Gallbladder Meridian of Foot-Shaoyang

1) Symptoms and Signs of the Disorders of the Meridian

"If pathogenic change occurs in the meridian, there may appear bitter taste in the mouth, frequent sighing, epigastric and hypochondriac pain, slightly dusty face, emaciation, and heat sensation of foot. These symptoms are caused by dysfunction of Foot Shaoyang. Kidney dominates bone. The Kidney Meridian is mainly used to treat such disorders as headache, mandibular pain, pain of the outer canthus, swelling and pain in supraclavicular fossa, swelling of the axilla, scrofula, sweating, malaria, pain in the chest and hypochondriac region, joint pain of the ribs, the thigh, lateral side of the knee and the legs, Juegu (GB 39) and the part anterior to the external malleolus including limited movement of the fourth toe." (*Miraculous Pivot*)

2) Symptoms and Signs of the Disorders of the Collaterals

"Excess syndrome causes syncope, deficiency syndrome causes muscular flaccidity with difficulty walking and difficult rising up after sitting." (*Miraculous Pivot*)

3) Symptoms and Signs of the Disorders of the Muscle Region

"Disorders of the Muscle Region may cause spasm referring to the lateral side of the knee, inability of the knee to flex and extend, muscular contractions of the popliteal muscles referring to the front of the thigh, the hip and the back. There may also appear pain in the hypochondriac region referring to supraclavicular fossa, muscular contractures of the spinal column from the left to the right, inability of the right eye to open. The muscle of the left side runs alongside with Qiao Meridian. The left connecting with the right, thus the injury of the muscle of the left cause limited movement of the right foot. This is called crossing of the muscle region." (*Miraculous Pivot*)

> **Appendix** Medical Documents

Diseases of the gallbladder may cause frequent sighing, bitter taste, vomiting of bilious fluid, severe palpitation, fright with palpitation like a feeling of being hunted, discomfort in the pharynx and frequent sleepiness. Give moxibustion to the end of the Foot Shaoyang in case of depression of the meridian. Select Yanglingquan (GB 34) in case of cold and heat. (*Miraculous Pivot*)

Dysfunction of Shaoyang may cause deafness, abnormal pulse, inability of the eye system. (*Miraculous Pivot*)

Distention of the gallbladder may cause pain and distention below the hypochondriac region, bitter taste, and frequent sighing. (*Miraculous Pivot*)

Foot Shaoyang Meridian dominates the gallbladder, ⋯ pain in the chest and hypochondriac region brings about deafness. (*Plain Questions*)

Dysfunction of Foot Shaoyang meridian may cause sudden deafness, swelling and a sensation of heat in the cheek, hypochondriac pain, inability to walk. (*Plain Questions*)

Dysfunction of Foot Shaoyang meridian causes limited movement of the joints, inability of the waist to move, inability to turn the neck and periappendicular abscess. (*Plain Questions*)

Diseases of Foot Shaoyang make patients feel irritable and discomfortable. There may appear slight cold and slight heat, aversion to meeting people, severe palpitation on seeing people and excessive sweating. Apply acupuncture to Foot Shaoyang meridian. (*Plain Questions*)

Vertigo with a swaying sensation and blurred vision, eyes closed and deafness are due to upper deficiency and lower excess of Foot Shaoyang. (*Plain Questions*)

If pathogenic factors attack the collateral, there may appear hypochondriac pain, inability to breathe smoothly, cough and sweating. (*Plain Questions*)

If pathogenic factors attack the collateral, there may appear pain in the collaterals and inability to raise up the thigh. (*Plain Questions*)

XIV. System of the Bladder Meridian of Foot Taiyang

1. Distribution of the Bladder Meridian of Foot Taiyang

1) Course of the Meridian

The Bladder Meridian of Foot Taiyang originates at the inner canthus of the eye and ascends across the forehead, joining the Du Meridian at the vertex. A branch originates from the vertex, running to the temple region above the ear. A straight portion of the meridian enters and communicates with the brain from the vertex. It then emerges and bifurcates to descend along the posterior aspect of the neck. Travelling downward alongside the medial aspect of the scapula region and parallel to the vertebral muscles to communicate with the kidney, and finally joins the bladder, its pertaining organ. A branch of the lumbar region descends through the gluteal region and terminates in the popliteal fossa. Another branch separates from the main meridian at the posterior aspect of the neck and descends straight downward along the medial side of the scapula, parallel to the spine, to the gluteal region. It then crosses the gluteal region and descends along the lateral posterior aspect of the thigh to join the other branch of the meridian at the popliteal fossa. Continuing downward through the gastrocnemius muscle, the meridian emerges behind the external malleolus, following the fifth metatarsal bone, crossing its tuberosity to the lateral side of the tip of the fifth toe. At the tip of the fifth toe, it links with the Kidney Meridian of Foot Shaoyin. (See Fig. 6-5).

2) Course of the Collaterals

"It arises from Feiyang (BL 58), seven cun above the external malleolus, it connects with the Foot Shaoyin Meridian. (*Miraculous Pivot*)

3) Divergent Meridian

"After deriving from the Bladder Meridian in the popliteal fossa, it proceeds to a point five cun below the sacrum. Winding around to the anal region, it connects with the bladder and disperses in the kidneys. Then it follows the spine and disperses in the cardiac region and then emerges at the neck and converges with Foot Taiyang." (*Miraculous Pivot*) (See Fig. 5-8).

4) Muscle Region

"It starts from the little toe, running upward to knot at the external malleolus and then obliquely at the knee. A lower branch travels along the lateral aspect of foot to knot at the heel, further ascending to knot at the popliteal fossa. Another branch starts at the convergence of the medial and lateral heads of the gastrocnemius muscle and ascends to knot at the medial side of the popliteal fossa. These two branches join in the gluteal region and then ascend along the side of the spine to the nape, where a branch enters the root of the tongue. The straight branch above the neck knots with the occipital bone and crosses over the top of the head to knot at the bridge of the nose. A branch spreads around the eye and knots at the side below the nose. Another branch extends from the lateral side of the posterior axillary fold to knot with Jianyu (LI 15). Another branch enters the chest below the axilla, emerges from the supraclavicular fossa and transverses the face to knot beside of the nose. Another branch emerges from Quepen (ST 12), running upward obliquely, and emerges from the side below the nose." (*Miraculous Pivot*) (See Fig. 6-6).

5) Cutaneous Region

The Cutaneous Region of the Bladder Meridian of Foot Taiyang, based on the passing course of the meridian and collateral, is mostly distributed at the dorsum of the little toe, the lateral aspect of the dorsum of the foot, inferior border of the external malleolus, the posterior side of the heel and leg, thigh, hip, waist and back and both sides of the middle line of the occipital region, crossing the head and running to the inner canthus. (See Fig. 3-4).

6) Acupoints

There are 67 acupoints in the Gallbladder Meridian. It starts from Jingming (BL 1) and ends at Zhiyin (BL 67).

Crossing points: Shenting (DU 23), Toulinqi (GB 15), Baihui (DU 20), Qubin (GB 7), Shuaigu (GB 8), Tianchong (GB 9), Fubai (GB 10), Touqiaoyin (GB 11), Wangu (GB 12), Naohu (DU 17), Fengfu (DU 16), Dazhui (DU 14), Taodao (DU 13), Huantiao (GB 30).

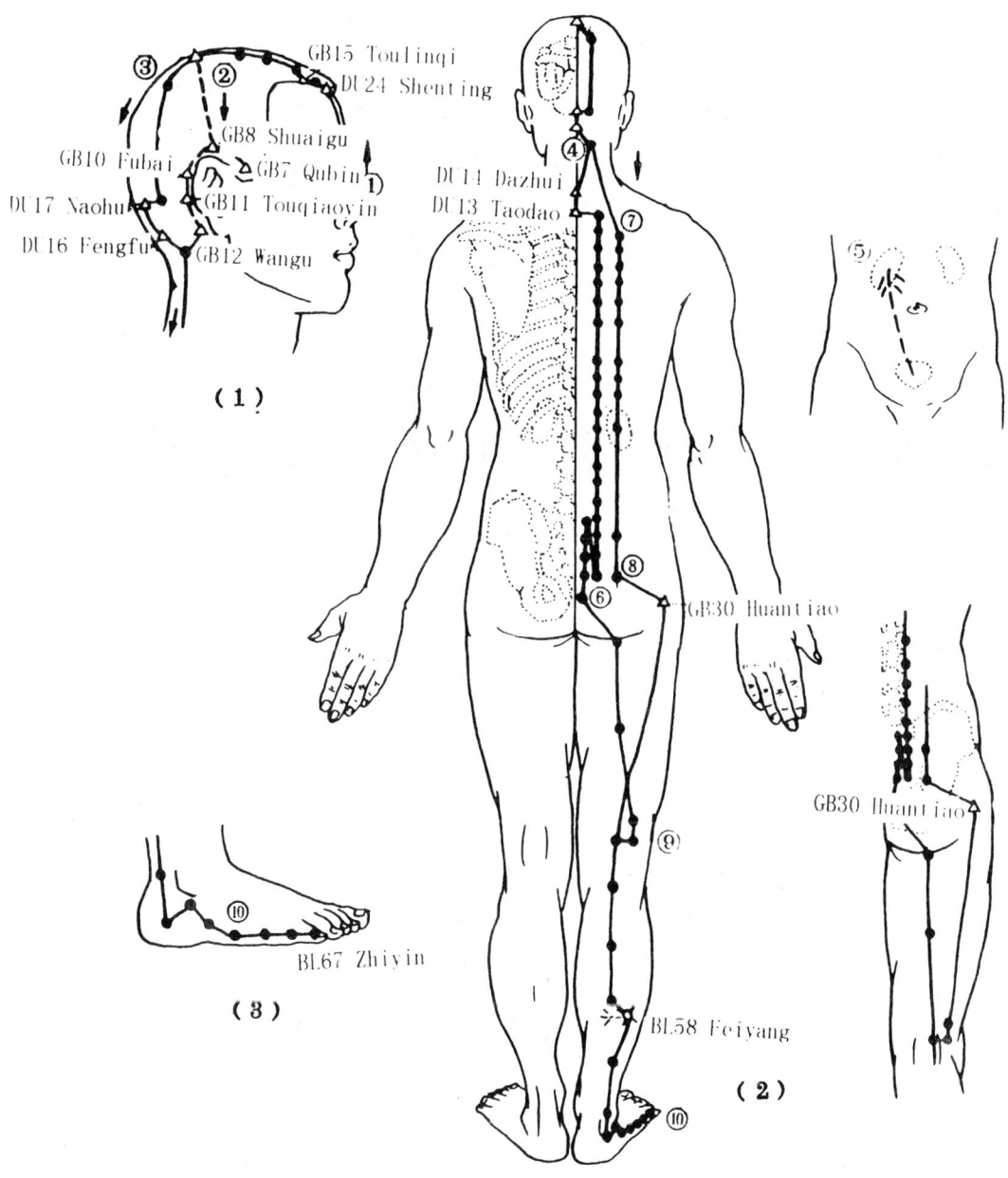

Fig. 6-5 The Bladder Meridian of Foot Taiyang

2. Symptoms and Signs of the Bladder Meridian of Foot Taiyang

1) Symptoms and Signs of the Disorders of the Meridian

"If pathogenic changes occur in the meridian, there may appear headache, severe distending

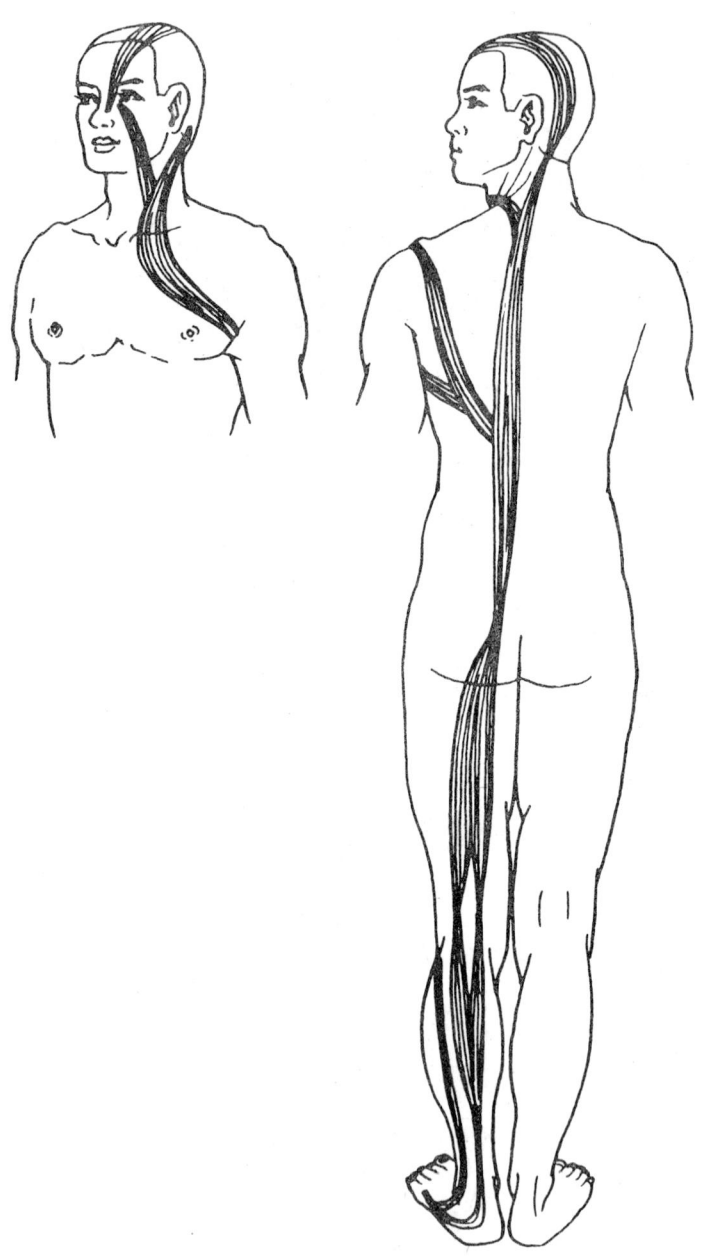

Fig. 6-6 Muscle Region of the Bladder Meridian of Foot Taiyang

pain of the eyes as if the eyeballs were squeezed out, severe lumbago as if the lumbar vertebrae were broken off, inability of the thigh to flex, inflexible knee as if there were a knot in the popliteal fossa, severe distending pain of the calf as if the calf were broken. These symptoms are considered due to cold limbs caused by upward adverse flow of qi from the Foot Taiyin Meridian. The Bladder Meridian is mainly used to treat diseases caused by muscular disorders, hemorroids, malaria, mental illness, fontanel and occipital pain, icteric sclera, lacrimation, allergic rhinitis, pain of the back, waist, hip, popliteal fossa, calf and foot and limited movement of the little toe." (*Miraculous Pivot*)

2) Symptoms and Signs of the Disorders of the Collaterals

"Excess syndrome may cause nasal obstruction, headache and backache, deficiency syndrome may cause running nose and epistaxis." (*Miraculous Pivot*)

3) Symptoms and Signs of the Disorders of the Muscle Region

"Disorders of the Muscle Region manifest as swelling and pain of the little toe, muscular spasm in popliteal fossa, opisthotonos, contraction of the neck muscles, inability to raise the arm, spasm and pain in the supraclavicular fossa and inability to turn the neck." (*Miraculous Pivot*)

Appendix Medical Documents

Disorders of the bladder may cause slight distention and pain of the lower abdomen, eagerness to pass water when the bladder is being pressed. There may be heat sensation on the shoulder and lateral aspect of the little toe, tibia and ankle. (*Miraculous Pivot*)

If the Bladder Meridian of Foot Taiyang is exhausted, there may appear fixed eyes upwards, opisthotonos and spasm. (*Miraculous Pivot*)

On the first day when the Foot Taiyang diseases occur, there appears pain of the vertex and stiffness along the spinal column. (*Plain Questions*)

Disturbance of Foot Taiyang causes heaviness of the head, inability to walk, vertigo and syncope. (*Plain Questions*)

Malaria of the Foot Taiyang type manifestes as swelling and lumbago, heaviness of the head, pathogenic cold which first occurs on the back, then turns to fever or high fever. The heat may be relieved while sweating. This disease is difficult to cure. (*Plain Questions*)

Obstruction of the bladder causes retention of urine, uncontrollable urine and enuresis. (*Plain Questions*)

Disturbance of the Foot Taiyang Meridian causes chills and fever. (*Plain Questions*)

Adverse flow of qi of Foot Taiyang Meridian causes syncope, hematemesis and epistaxis. (*Plain Questions*)

If pathogenic factors attack the collateral of Foot Taiyang, there may appear headache, pain in the neck and shoulder. (*Plain Questions*)

If pathogenic factors attack the collateral of Foot Taiyang Meridian, there may appear muscular contracture of the back referring to the hypochondrium. (*Plain Questions*)

Chapter Seven

Acupoints of the Du Meridian and Ren Meridian

Ⅰ. Acupoints of the Du Meridian

DU 1 Changqiang (长强)
(Long Strength)

【Source】 *Miraculous Pivot*
【Name Explanation】 The collateral of the Du Meridian courses from both sides of the spine and flows up to the top of the head. Its distribution is very long (长, Chang) and its function very strong (强, Qiang).
【Classification】 1. The Crossing Point of the Shaoyin Meridian. (*A-B Classic of Acupuncture and Moxibustion*). 2. The Luo-(Connecting) point of the Du Meridian. (*Miraculous Pivot*).
【Location】 0.5 cun below the tip of the coccyx, at the midpoint between the tip of the coccyx and the anus. (See Fig. 7-1)
【Localization】 In a kneeling position or in the prone position, the point can be located on the midpoint of the line connecting the tip of the coccyx and the anus.
【Indications】
　　1) Digestive Diseases: Diarrhea, dysentery, constipation, hematemesis.
　　2) Urinary Diseases: Dysuria, stranguria, discharge and pruritus in the external vaginal area.
　　3) Reproductive Diseases: Nocturnal emission, impotence, pruritus and inflammation.
　　4) Mental Diseases: Mania, epilepsy, convulsion, clonic convulsion, opisthotonos.
　　5) Other Diseases: Pain in the lower back and spine, hernia, hemorrhoid, prolapse of the rectum.

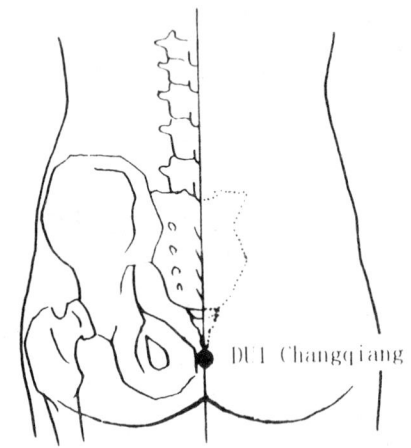

Fig. 7-1 Insertion of Needle of Changqiang Point

[Mechanism of Action]
The anus is the lower orifice of the digestive system. It is reported that the acupoint is the main point for diarrhea and dysentery. Needling Changqiang (DU 1) can effectively treat constipation and prolapse of the rectum caused by chronic diarrhea and dysentery.

The Du Meridian governs the Yang-energy of whole the body. The mental diseases listed above are caused by the over-hyperactivity of Yang, thus, Changqiang (DU 1) is the main point for mania and epilepsy, etc.

Changqiang (DU 1) is the crossing point of Foot Shaoyin and Foot Taiyang meridians. The kidney governs the water metabolism, and the urinary bladder is in charge of the water circulation. Therefore, the point is commonly used to treat the diseases of the urogenital system.

[Method] Puncture obliquely 0.8-1.2 cun along the anterior aspect of the coccyx. Use caution as perpendicular puncturing can easily injure the rectum. Apply 3-7 moxa cones. (See Fig. 7-2)

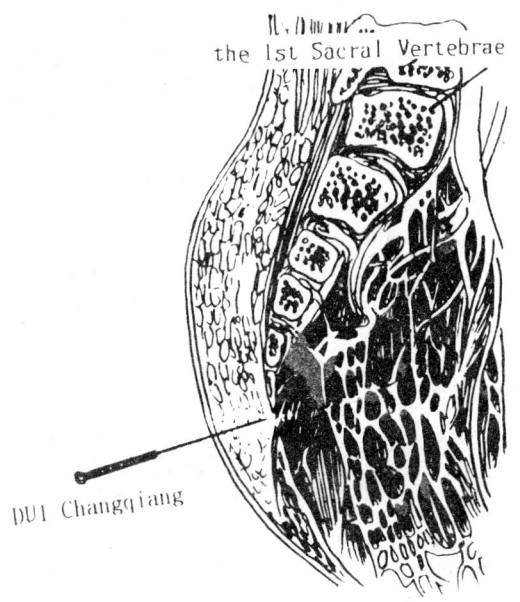

Fig. 7-2
Insertion of Needle of Changqiang Point

[Acupoint Prescriptions]
1) Constipation: Changqiang (DU 1), Xiaochangshu (BL 27). (*Thousand Golden Prescriptions*).
2) Epilepsy in children induced by fright: Changqiang (DU 1), Shenzhu (DU 12). (*Experience on Acupuncture and Moxibustion Therapy*).
3) Dysentery with red or white discharge: Changqiang (DU 1), Mingmen (DU 4). (*Treatise on Miraculous Moxibustion*).
4) Prolapse of the rectum: Changqiang (DU 1), Chengshan (BL 57), Huanmen (EX). (*Abstract of Clinical Experience on Acupuncture and Moxibustion*)
5) Enuresis in children: Changqiang (DU 1), Sanyinjiao (SP 6). (*ibid*)
6) Hernia: Changqiang (DU 1), Dadun (LR 1). (*Secret Songs of Chang Sangjun*).
7) Hemorrhoids: Changqiang (DU 1), Chengshan (BL 57). (*Songs of Jade Dragon*).
8) Fresh blood in stool: Changqiang (DU 1), Chengshan (BL 57). (*Songs of Hundreds of Symptoms*).
9) Constipation caused by pathogenic heat or qi-stagnation: Changqiang (DU 1), Dadun (LR 1), Yanglingquan (GB 34). (*Songs on Point Selection of Miscellaneous Diseases*).

[Regional Anatomy] Skin-subcutaneous tissue-anococcygeal ligament. In the superficial layer, there are the posterior branches of the coccygeal nerve. In the deep layer, there are the anal nerve of the pudendal nerve and the anal artery and vein of the internal pudendal artery and vein.

[Remark] Puncturing Changqiang (DU 1) and Huiyin (RN 1) can effectively treat constipation caused by latent bifid spine.

DU 2　Yaoshu（腰俞）
（Lumbar Shu）

【Source】 *Plain Question*

【Name Explanation】 *Plain Question*: "The orifice at the sacrum... is the acupoint Yaoshu (DU 2)." Here, the sacrum means the sacral region and the orifice refers to the hiatus. All points are called "Shu", so it is known as Yaoshu.

【Location】 On the sacrum, along the posterior midline, in the hiatus of the sacrum. (See Fig. 7-3)

【Localization】 In the prone or lateral recumbent position, first locate the sacral horn obove the coccyx, then locate the point at the posterior midline which parallels the two sacral horns.

【Indications】

   1) Digestive Diseases: Diarrhea, Constipation, bloody stool, etc.

   2) Urinary Diseases: Dysuria, stranguria, reddish urine, enuresis.

   3) Reproductive Diseases: Irregular menstruation, leukorrhagia, nocturnal emission.

   4) Mental Disease: Epilepsy.

   5) Other Diseases: Malaria, fever without sweating, hemorrhoid and prolapse of the rectum, stiffness and pain in the lower back and spine, motor impairment and muscular atrophy or numbness in the lower limbs.

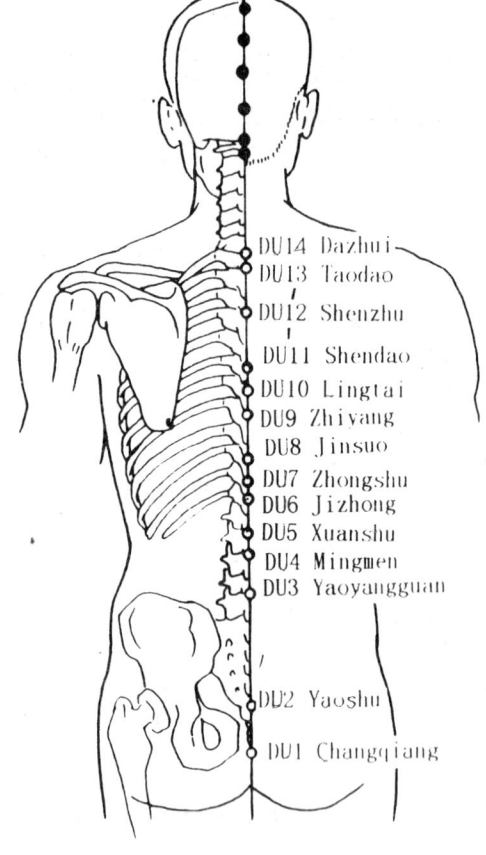

Fig. 7-3

【Mechanism of Action】

The Du Meridian governs the Yang-energy of the whole body and its points can be used to treat spinal diseases.

Yaoshu (DU 2) is near the lower end of the digestive tract and belongs to the Du meridian which is a main Yang meridian. Therefore, the point can be used to treat digestive system disorders by its near-treating function that regulates Yang energy.

Anterior to Yaoshu (DU 2) are the reproductive and urogential systems. According to the law that a point may always be used to treat the diseases along the passing course of its meridian, needling the point can regulate the functions and treat the diseases of these two systems.

【Method】 Puncture obliquely upwards 0.5-1.0 cun. Apply 3-7 moxa cones.

【Acupoint Prescriptions】

   1) Pain in the lumbosacral region: Yaoshu (DU 2), Changqiang (DU 1), Pangguangshu (BL 28), Qichong (ST 30), Shangliao (BL 31), Xialiao (BL 34) and Juliao (GB 29). (*Thousand Golden Prescriptions*).

   2) Malaria (Pyrexial malaria, malaria due to phlegm): Yaoshu (DU 2), Zhongwan (RN 12). (*Experience on Acupuncture and Moxibustion Therapy*).

3) Motor impairment and muscular atrophy in the lower limbs: Yaoshu (DU 2), Fengfu (DU 16). (*ibid*)

4) Prostatitis: Yaoshu (DU 2), Zhongji (RN 3), Baihui (DU 20), Dahe (KI 12), Sanyinjiao (SP 6). Needle these points with mild stimulation and apply moxibustion after needling, one time each day. (*Science of Acupuncture and Moxibustion*).

【Regional Anatomy】 Skin-subcutaneous tissue-dorsal sacrococcgyeal ligament-sacral canal. In the superficial layer, there are the posterior branches of the 5th sacral nerve. In the deep layer, there is the coccygeal plexus.

DU 3   Yaoyangguan (腰阳关)
(Lumbar Yang Pass)

【Source】 *Plain Question*

【Name Explanation】 The acupoint is located at the waist and connects internally the Dantian (elixir field) where the kidney Yin and kidney Yang converge. The acupoint belongs to the Du Meridian which is the sea of Yang meridians and in charge of the Yang energy of the whole body, therefore, it is called as Yaoyangguan.

【Location】 In the lumbar area, on the posterior midline, below the spinous process of the 4th lumbar vertebra, and level with the crista iliaca. (See Fig. 7-3)

【Localization】 In the prone or lateral recumbent position, the point can be located along the posterior midline, in the depression below the spinous process of the 4th lumbar vertebra, level with the crista iliaca.

【Indications】

1) Digestive Diseases: Bloody stool, dysentery, fullness sensation in the lower abdomen, vomiting, etc.

2) Reproductive Diseases: Irregular menstruation, leukorrhea with reddish discharge, nocturnal emission, impotence, dysuria, etc.

3) Other Diseases: Tetanus, hernia, scrofula, pain in the lumbar and sacral region, motor impairment and muscular atrophy in the lower limbs, pain in knee with motor impairment.

【Mechanism of Action】 The acupoint is located at the lower lumbar area with the digestive and reproductive system in its anterior field. According to the law that a point may always be used to treat diseases on the passing course of its meridian, Yaoyangguan (DU 3) can be used to treat the diseases of the above two systems. Intestinal diseases are the main indications. The indications of lumbar and sacral pain, and motor impairment and muscular atrophy of lower extremities are based on the local-treating function of acupoints.

【Method】 Puncture perpendicularly 0.5-1.0 cun. Apply 3-7 moxa cones.

【Acupoint Prescription】 Cystoparalysis (retention of urine, enuresis): Yaoyangguan (DU 3), Ciliao (BL 32), Zhongliao (BL 33), Guanyuan (RN 4), Zhongji (RN 3), Qugu (RN 2). (*Chinese Acupuncture and Moxibustion*).

【Regional Anatomy】 Skin-subcutaneous tissue-supraspinal ligament-interspinal ligament-interarcuate ligament. In the superficial layer, there are the medial branches of the posterior branches of the 4th lumbar nerve and the accompanying artery and vein. In the deep layer, there are the external (posterior) vertebral venous plexus between the adjacent spinous processes, the branches of the posterior branches of the 4th lumbar artery and vein.

DU 4 Mingmen (命门)
(Life Gate)

【Source】 *A-B Classic of Acupuncture and Moxibustion*
【Name Explanation】 Kidney qi is the basic source for the whole body. The point is located between the kidneys and is an important life gate.
【Location】 On the lumbar area, along the posterior midline, in the depression below the spinous process of the 2nd lumbar vertebra. (See Fig. 7-3)
【Localization】 In the lateral recumbent or sitting position, in the depression between the spinous process of the 2nd and 3rd lumbar vertebra, it is located just below the spinous process, level with the umbilicus.
【Indications】
   1) Digestive Diseases: Diarrhea, hematochezia, etc.
   2) Reproductive Diseases: Impotence, nocturnal emission, premature ejaculation, leukorrhagia, dysmenorrhea, habitual abortion.
   3) Urogenital Diseases: Enuresis, frequent urination, dysuria.
   4) Mental Diseases: Epilepsy, infantile convulsion, fear due to fright, etc.
   5) Deficiency Syndromes: Insomnia, dizziness, tinnitus, consumption of the heart, the liver, the lung, the spleen and the kidney, seven kinds of impairment (七伤, Qi Shang), cold extremities, chills, etc.
   6) Other Diseases: Fever without sweating, high fever, malaria, headache, hernia, edema, prolapse of rectum, hemorrhoid, etc.
【Mechanism of Action】
   The kidney stores the kidney Yin and the kidney Yang and has the property of water and fire. The point is located between the kidneys and belongs to the Du meridian, which is a Yang meridian. Therefore, the point is interrelated with the life gate fire and is important for reinforcing the life gate fire, i. e. the kidney Yang. The point is used especially for the diseases in the urogenital and digestive systems which result from Yang deficiency. The diseases or syndromes caused by Yang deficiency such as cold extremities, aversion to cold, five kinds of consumption, seven kinds of impairment, insomnia, dizziness and tinnitus, are usually treated by puncturing of Mingmen (DU 4).
   Acupoints have a dual-regulation function, so, Mingmen (DU 4) can also be used to treat some syndromes caused by excessive heat such as fever without sweating, high fever, malaria, etc, except for those caused by Yang deficiency.
【Method】 Puncture perpendicularly 0.5-1.0 cun. Moxibustion is applicable.
【Acupoint Prescriptions】
   1) Excessive fullness without sweating: Mingmen (DU 4), Pangguangshu (BL 28), Shangwan (RN 13), Quchai (BL 4), Shangxing (DU 23), Taodao (DU 13), Tianzhu (BL 10), Shangliao (BL 31), Xuanli (GB 6) and Fengchi (GB 20). (*Experience on Acupuncture and Moxibustion Therapy*).
   2) Impotence: Apply moxibustion to Mingmen (DU 4), Shenshu (BL 23), Qihai (RN 6), Rangu (KI 2). (*Illustrated Supplementary to the Classified Canon*).
   3) Thrombotic phlebitis: Mingmen (DU 4), Yangguan (DU 3), Dachangshu (BL 25), Ciliao (BL 32), Yinlian (LR 11), Ququan (LR 8), Futu (ST 32), Xuehai (SP 10), puncture with mild stimulation. (*New Science of Acupuncture and Moxibustion*)
   4) Enuresis: Mingmen (DU 4), Changqiang (DU 1), Sanyinjiao (SP 6), puncture with thumb-tack needle for subcutaneous embedding. (*Abstract of Clinical Experience on*

Acupuncture and Moxibustion)

5) Frequent stools in old men: Mingmen (DU 4) Shenshu (BL 23). (*Songs of Jade Dragon*)

6) Lumbar pain and frequent urination: Mingmen (DU 4), Shenshu (BL 23). (*Songs of Shengyu*)

【Regional Anatomy】 The layer structures of the needle insertion are the same as those in Yaoyangguan (DU 3). In the superficial layer, there are the medial branches of the posterior branches of the 2nd lumbar nerve and the accompanying artery and vein. In the deep layer, there are the external (posterior) vertebral venous plexus between the adjacent spinous process, the branches of the posterior branches of the 2nd lumbar nerve and the branches or tributaries of the dorsal branches of the 2nd lumbar artery and vein.

DU 5   Xuanshu (悬枢)
(Hanging Pivot)

【Source】 *A-B Classic of Acupuncture and Moxibustion*
【Name Explanation】 Xuan (悬), suspended; Shu (枢), pivot. The point is on the lower back, when in supine position, the local region is suspended as a pivot for lumbar movement.
【Location】 On the lumbar area, along the posterior midline, in the depression below the spinous process of the 1st lumbar vertebrae. (See Fig. 7-3)
【Localization】 In prone or a sitting position, the point can be located in the depression between the spinous processes of the 1st and 2nd lumbar vertebra.
【Indications】
  1) Digestive Diseases: Abdominal distention, abdominal pain, indigestion, diarrhea, etc.
  2) Other Diseases: Stiffness, pain and motor impairment in the waist and spine, dysentery and prolapse of the rectum, etc.
【Mechanism of Action】 All points have the function of treating the diseases of their local and nearby region. Under this point are the stomach and intestines, so, Xuanshu (DU 5) is a common point for gastric diseases.
【Method】 Puncture obliquely 0.5-1.0 cun. Moxibustion is applicable.
【Regional Anatomy】 Skin-subcutaneous tissue-supraspinal ligament-interspinal ligament. In the superficial layer, there are the medial branches of the posterior branches of the 1st lumbar nerve and the accompanying artery and vein. In the deep layer, there are the external (posterior) vertebral venous plexus between the adjacent spinous processes, the branches of the posterior branches of the 1st lumbar nerve and the branches or tributaries of the dorsal branches of the 1st lumbar artery and vein.

DU 6   Jizhong (脊中)
(Middle of Spine)

【Source】 *Plain Questions*
【Name Explanation】 Ji (脊), spine; Zhong (中), middle. The spine consists of 21 vertebra. The point is below the 11th vertebra at exactly the middle of the spinal cord.
【Location】 On the back along the posterior midline, in the depression below the spinous process of the 11th thoracic vertebra. (See Fig. 7-3)
【Localization】 In prone or erect sitting position, the point can be located in the depression be-

tween the spinous processes of the 11th and 12th thoracic vertebra.
【Indications】
　　1) Digestive Diseases: Gastric pain, abdominal fullness sensation, diarrhea, dysentery, hematochezia, indigestion in children, poor appetite, jaundice, vomiting, hematermesis, nausea.
　　2) Other diseaese: Hemorrhoid, prolapse of rectum.
【Mechanism of Action】 Refer to Xuanshu (DU 5).
【Method】 Puncture obliquely 0.5-1.0 cun. Moxibustion is applicable.
【Acupoint Prescription】
　　Epilepsy caused by pathological wind: Jizhong (DU 6). Yongquan (KI 1). (*Experience on Acupuncture and Moxibustion Therapy*).
【Regional Anatomy】 Skin-subcutaneous tissue-supraspinal ligament-interspinal ligament. In the superficial layer, there are the medial cutaneous branches of the posterior branches of the 11th thoracic nerve and the accompanying artery and vein. In the deep layer, there are the external (posterior) vertebral venous plexus between the adjacent spinous processes, the branches of the posterior branches of the 11th thoracic nerve and the branches or tributaries of the dorsal branches of the 11th posterior intercostal artery and vein.

DU 7　Zhongshu (中枢)
(Middle Pivot)

【Source】 *Plain Question*
【Name Explanation】 Zhong (中), middle; Shu (枢), pivot. The point is below the 10th vertebra and acts like a pivot in the middle of the spine.
【Location】 On the back, on the posterior midline, in the depression below the spinous process of the 10th thoracic vertebra. (See Fig. 7-3)
【Localization】 In an erect sitting or prone position, the point can be located in the depression between the spinous processes of the 10th and 11th thoracic vertebra.
【Indications】
　　1) Digestive Diseases: Gastric pain, abdominal fullness sensation, vomiting, poor appetite, jaundice, etc.
　　2) Other Diseases: Aversion to cold and fever, hypopsia, stiffness and pain in the lower back and spine with motor impairment.
【Mechanism of Action】 Refer to Xuanshu (DU 5).
【Method】 Puncture obliquely 0.5-1.0 cun. Moxibustion is applicable.
【Regional Anatomy】 The layer structures of the needle insertion are the same as those in Jizhong (DU 6). In the superficial layer, there are the medial cutaneous branches of the posterior branches of the 10th thoracic nerve and the accompanying artery and vein. In the deep layer, there are the external (posterior) vertebral venous plexus between the adjacent spinous processes, the branches of the posterior branches of the 10th thoracic nerve and the branches or tributaries of the dorsal branches of the 10th posterior intercostal artery and vein.

DU 8　Jinsuo (筋缩)
(Muscle Spasm)

【Source】 *A-B Classic of Acupuncture and Moxibustion*

[Name Explanation] Jin (筋), muscle and tendon; Suo (缩), contracture. On either side of this point is Ganshu (BL 18), and the liver governs the muscles and tendons. This point is useful in treating muscle contracture of all types.
[Location] On the back along the posterior midline, in the depression below the spinous process of the 9th thoracic vertebra. (See Fig. 7-3)
[Localization] In an erect sitting or the prone position, the point can be located in the depression between the spinous processes of the 9th and 10th thoracic vertebra.
[Indications]
   1) Digestive Diseases: Gastric pain, vomiting and jaundice.
   2) Mental Diseases: Manic-depressive psychosis, infantile epilepsy, convulsion, superduction, hysteria, etc.
   3) Other Diseases: Motor impairment, stiffness and pain in the lower back and spine.
[Mechanism of Action] The liver is below this point, with Ganshu (BL 18) on either side of it. So, it is mainly used to treat liver diseases. The liver is in charge of anger, tendons and qi-circulation, and its disorders usually manifest as mental diseases or syndromes. Jinsuo (DU 8) is internally close to the stomach. Therefore, the point is useful in treating gastric diseases.
[Method] Puncture obliquely 0.5-1.0 cun. Moxibustion is applicable.
[Acupoint Prescription]
   Epilepsy and depressive psychosis: Jinsuo (DU 8), Qugu (RN 2), Yingu (KI 10), and Xingjian (LR 2). (*Experience on Acupuncture and Moxibustion Therapy*).
[Regional Anatomy] The layer structures of the needle insertion are the same as those in Jizhong (DU 6). In the superficial layer, there are the medial cutaneous branches of the posterior branches of the 9th thoracic nerve and the accompanying artery and vein. In the deep layer, there are the external (posterior) vertebral venous plexus between the adjacent spinous processes, the branches of the posterior branches of the 9th thoracic nerve and the branches or tributaries of the dorsal branches of the 9th posterior intercostal artery and vein.
[Remark] Puncturing Jinsuo (DU 8) can regulate the activities of the stomach and relieve pathological changes. There is a report in which an x-ray showed a stomach which had a shrimp shape with the greater curvature up and the lesser curvature down. After Jinsuo (DU 8) and Zusanli (ST 36) are punctured, the needling-sensation reaches the stomach region which may cause the stomach to spasm and contract. The x-ray examination indicated that the greater curvature had gone down and the lesser curvature had gone up, and the symptoms had disappeared within 20 minutes.

DU 9   Zhiyang (至阳)
(Reaching Yang)

[Source] *A-B Classic of Acupuncture and Moxibustion*
[Name Explanation] Zhi (至), reaching; Yang (阳), Yang of Yin-Yang. The point is level with the diaphragm. The qi of this meridian passes here and ascends, i.e. it reaches "Yang within Yin above the diaphragm from "Yin within Yang" below the diaphragm.
[Location] On back, along the posterior midline, in the depression below the spinous process of the 7th thoracic vertebra. (See Fig. 7-3)
[Localization] In prone position or lying in the prostrate position, the point can be located at the crossing point of the line connecting the posterior midline with the inferior angle of the scapula between the spinous processes of the 7th and 8th thoracic vertebra.
[Indications]
   1) Respiratory Diseases: Cough, asthma, distension and fullness in the chest and

hypochondrium, etc.

   2) Digestive Diseases: Gastric pain, abdominal distension, borborygmus, and jaundice, etc.

   3) Other Diseases: Fever, stiffness and pain in the back and spine, soreness in the leg, general asthenis, shortness of breath with disinclination to talk, etc.

【Mechanism of Action】 Below the point and above the chest cavity, are the lung in the chest and the stomach in the abdomen. The lung is in charge of breath, and the spleen has the function to transport and transform nutrients and nourish the limbs. According to the local-treatment and regional-treatment functions of acupoints, Zhiyang (DU 9) is a commonly used point for treating diseases of the digestive and respiratory systems. General deficiency and shortness of breath result from dysfunction of the spleen and stomach.

【Method】 Puncture obliquely upward 0.5-1.0 cun. Moxibustion is applicable.

【Acupoint Prescriptions】

   1) Acute infectious hepatitis (syndrome with more heat and less wetness): Zhiyang (DU 9), Yongquan (KI 1). Puncture with reducing method by inserting and withdrawing the needles with different speeds, retain the needles for 15 minutes. (*Abstract of Clinical Experience on Acupuncture and Moxibustion*).

   2) Chronic hepatitis: Zhiyang (DU 9), Zusanli (ST 36). Acupoint injection: Injecting 200-400 mg of IMP-Na in average into the two points, every other day, five weeks constituting one course, then another course may be continued after one injection is suspended. (*ibid*).

【Regional Anatomy】 The layer structures of the needle insertion are the same as those in Jizhong (DU 6). In the superficial layer, there are the medial cutaneous branches of the posterior branches of the 7th thoracic nerve and the accompanying artery and vein. In the deep layer, there are the external (posterior) vertebral venous plexus between the adjacent spinous processes, the branches of the posterior branches of the 7th thoracic nerve and the branches or tributaries of the dorsal branches of the 7th posterior intercostal artery and vein.

【Remark】 Puncturing Zhiyang (DU 9) and Shendao (DU 11) can reduce the peristalsis of the esophagus and improve the development of the mucosal folds.

DU 10   Lingtai (灵台)
(Spirit Plaform)

【Source】 *Plain Question . Treatise on Acupoints*

【Name Explanation】 Ling (灵), the heart spirit; Tai (台), platform. The point is below Shendao (DU 11) and Xinshu (BL 15) and is therefore likened to a platform for the heart spirit.

【Location】 On the back, along the posterior midline, in the depression below the spinous process of the 6th thoracic vertebra. (See Fig. 7-3)

【Localization】 In prone or erect sitting position, locate the point in the depression between the spinous processes of the 6th and 7th thoracic vertebra.

【Indications】

   1) Respiratory Diseases: Cough, asthma, insomnia and restlessness, stiff neck, etc.

   2) Digestive Diseases: Gastric pain, biliary ascariasis, etc.

   3) Other Diseases: Febrile disease with chills and fever, malaria, furuncle, boils.

【Mechanism of Action】 The heart corresponds to "fire" in the Five Elements and is in charge of the blood vessels. "Pruritus and pain of ulcers are cardiac in origin". The excessive heart fire can cause furuncles and boils. Due to the position at the point it is commonly used for treating furuncles and boils, and also can be used to treat respiratory diseases as its location is close to the

lungs.
【Method】 Puncture obliquely 0.5-1.0 cun. Moxibustion is applicable.
【Regional Anatomy】 The layer structures of the needle insertion are the same as those in Jizhong (DU 6). In the superficial layer, there are the medial cutaneous branches of the posterior branches of the 6th thoracic nerve and the accompanying artery and vein. In the deep layer, there are the external (posterior) vertebral venous plexus between the adjacent spinous processes, the branches of the posterior branches of the 6th thoracic nerve and the branches or tributaries of the dorsal branches of the 6th posterior intercostal artery and vein.

DU 11 Shendao (神道)
(Spirit Path)

【Source】 *A-B Classic of Acupuncture and Moxibustion*
【Name Explanation】 Shen (神), the heart mind; Dao (道), pathway. The heart houses the mind and the point is lateral to Xinshu, like a pathway of the mind.
【Location】 On the back, along the posterior midline, in the depression below the spinous process of the 5th thoracic vertebra. (See Fig. 7-3)
【Localization】 In prone or an erect sitting position. The point is located in the depression between the spinous process between the 5th and 6th thoracic vertebra.
【Indications】
  1) Respiratory Diseases: Cough, asthma, cold and fever, headache, etc.
  2) Cardiac Diseases: Cardiac pain, palpitation, etc.
  3) Mental Diseases: Apoplexy, epilepsy, spasm, insomnia, poor memory, hysteria.
【Mechanism of Action】
  The heart governs blood vessels, blood circulation and the mind. If there is heart disorders, cardiovascular and nervous diseases may result.
  The lungs are lateral at both sides of the point, hence, it is a commonly used point for treating respiratory diseases.
【Method】 Puncture obliquely 0.5-1.0 cun. Moxibustion is applicable.
【Acupoint Prescriptions】
  1) Acute stiffness in the back and spine: Shendao (DU 11), Jizhong (DU 6), Yaoshu (DU 2), Changqiang (DU 1), Dazhu (BL 11), Geguan (BL 46), Shuifen (RN 9), Pishu (BL 20), Xiaochangshu (BL 27) and Pangguangshu (BL 28). (*Thousand Golden Prescriptions*)
  2) Poor memory: Shendao (DU 11), Youmen (KI 21), Lieque (LU 7), Gaohuangshu (BL 43). (*Experience on Acupuncture and Moxibustion Therepy*).
  3) Aversion to cold and fever: Shendao (DU 11), Shaohai (HT 3). (*ibid*)
  4) Epilepsy caused by wind: Shendao (DU 11), Xinshu (BL 15). (*Songs of Hundreds of Symptoms*).
【Regional Anatomy】 The layer structures of the needle insertion are the same as those in Jizhong (DU 6). In the superficial layer, there are the medial cutaneous branches of the posterior branches of the 5th thoracic nerve and the accompanying artery and vein. In the deep layer, there are the external (posterior) vertebral venous plexus between the adjacent spinous processes, the branches of the posterior branches of the 5th thoracic nerve and the branches or tributaries of the dorsal branches of the 5th posterior intercostal artery and vein.
【Remark】 Puncturing Shendao (DU 11), Mingmen (DU 4), Zhibian (BL 54) and Baihui (DU 20), etc. can have a positive effect in treating dysuria caused by latent bifid spine. In addition, puncturing Shendao (DU 11) can reduce the movements of the esophagus.

Du 12　Shenzhu (身柱)
(Body Pillar)

[Source] A-B Classic of Acupuncture and Moxibustion

[Name Explanation] Shen (身), body; Zhu (柱), pillar. The point is below the 3rd thoracic vertebra and connects upwards with the head and neck, then downwards with the back and the lumbar vertebra, like a pillar of the body.

[Location] On the back along the posterior midline, in the depression below the spinous process of the 3rd thoracic vertebra. (See Fig. 7-3)

[Localization] Sit with the back bending over a desk or in the prone position, the point is located in the depression below the spinous process of the 3rd thoracic vertebra i.e. the intersection between the posterior midline and the line joining both the highest point of the scapulae. (Spine of scapulae.)

[Indications]

　　1) Respiratory Diseases: Cough with dyspnea, irritable feverish sensation in chest.

　　2) Mental Diseases: Fainting due to emotional upset, manic-depressive psychosis, epilepsy, clonic convulsion, aphasia from apoplexy.

　　3) Other Diseases: Stiffness and pain along the spinal column which causes forced sitting position, furuncle and lumbodorsal cellulitis, fever with headache.

[Mechanism of Action] This point can be used for clearing heat, removing toxic material and relieving spasm. It is a commonly used point to treat the diseases mentioned above.

[Method] Puncture obliquely 0.5-0.8 cun. Moxibustion is applicable.

[Acupoint Prescriptions]

　　1) Anemia: Shenzhu (DU 12), Geshu (BL 17), Weishu (BL 21), Mingmen (DU 4), Zhongfu (LU 1), Guanyuan (RN 4), Zusanli (ST 36), Neiting (ST 44), Fenglong (ST 40), Zhongwan (RN 12), Fengchi (GB 20). (*New Science of Acupuncture and Moxibustion*)

　　2) Manic depression: Shenzhu (DU 12), Benshen (GB 13). (*Songs of Hundreds of Symptoms*).

[Regional Anatomy] The layer structures of the needle insertion are the same as those in Jizhong (DU 6). In the superficial layer, there are the medial cutaneous branches of the posterior branches of the 3rd thoracic nerve and the accompanying artery and vein. In the deep layer, there are the external (posterior) vertebral venous plexus between the adjacent spinous process, the branches of the posterior branches of the 3rd thoracic nerve and the branches or tributaries of the dorsal branches of the 3rd posterior intercostal artery and vein.

[Remark] We used an electroencephalogram (EEG) to observe the effect of acupuncture. It was found that applying moxibustion to Baihui (DU 20) and Shenzhu (DU 12) for 24 seconds enhanced the α-wave and showed an increase in amplitude. A constant longer period showed the late stage of attention process slower. In the comparative group (moxibustion to Hegu (LI 4)), the α-wave showed no obvious improvement.

DU 13 Taodao (陶道)
(Kiln Path)

【Source】 *A-B Classic of Acupuncture and Moxibustion*
【Name Explanation】 Tao (陶), moulding; Dao (道), pathway. Qi of Zangfu organs is gathered at the Governor Vessel and ascends along this way.
【Classification】 The Crossing Point of the Du Meridian and the Foot Taiyang Meridian
【Location】 On the back and along the posterior midline, in the depression below the spinous process of the 1st thoracic vertebra. (See Fig. 7-3)
【Localization】 Sit with the back bending over a desk or in the prone position, first locate Dazhui (Du 14), then move downwards to find one spinous process, the point is located at the depression below this spinous process.
【Indications】
　　1) Respiratory Diseases: Stiffness and pain of the head and neck, fever, aversion to cold without sweating, dyspnea, malaria.
　　2) Mental Diseases: Manic-depressive psychosis, epilepsy, convulsion, opisthotonos.
　　3) Other Diseases: Night sweat due to hectic fever, chest pain, soreness along the spinal column, inability to raise arm due to pain in shoulder joint, urticaria.
【Mechanism of Action】 This is the crossing point of the Du Meridian and Bladder Meridian. Clinical experiments demonstrated that this point is similar to Dazhui (DU 14) in clearing heat, removing toxic material, centilating the lung and inducing diaphoresis. Thus, it is a commonly used point to treat diseases of the respiratory system and various febrile diseases. Also, it is often used to treat backache, the inability to raise arm due to pain in the shoulder joint, and stiffness and pain of the head and neck. This is one of the points on the Du Meridian used to treat manic-depressive psychosis, epilepsy, spasm and opisthotonos.
【Method】 Puncture obliquely 0.5-1.0 cun. Moxibustion is applicable.
【Acupoint Prescriptions】
　　1) Aversion to cold with a feeling of cold sprinking over the body: Taodao (DU 13), Shentang (BL 44), Fengchi (GB 20). (*Experience on Acupuncture and Moxibustion Therapy*)
　　2) Five kinds of strain and seven kinds of impairment due to consumptive diseases: Important points for moxibustion: Taodao (DU 13) 14 moxa cones, Shenzhu (DU 12) 14 moxa cones, Feishu (BL 13) on both sides 49-100 moxa cones and Gaohuang (BL 43) on both sides 21-49 moxa cones. (*Generation of Universe*)
【Regional Anatomy】 The layer structures of the needle insertion are the same as those in Jizhong (DU 6). In the superficial layer, there are the medial cutaneous branches of the posterior branches of the 1st thoracic nerve and the accompanying artery and vein. In the deep layer, there are the external (posterior) vertebral venous plexus between the adjacent spinous process, the branches of the posterior branches of the 1st thoracic nerve and the branches or tributaries of the dorsal branches of the 1st posterior intercostal artery and vein.
【Remark】 Puncturing Taodao (DU 13) can increase acidocytes. It's reported that in 133 cases of tertian ague with all treatment using Dazhui (DU 14), Jianshi (PC 5), Taodao (DU 13) and Houxi (SI 3) as main points, 99 cases were cured, 12 showed same positive results, 111 cases in total (curative rate of 83.5%), 22 cases showed no effect (16.5%). Note: the following tests were done before and again after the acupuncture treatment: RHA intraccitamepis test, serum immunolobulin test, lymphocytes and T-lymphocyte subpopulation test. The results indicated acupuncture can regulate the immunologic function of the human body.

DU 14　Dazhui（大椎）
（Big Vertebra）

【Source】 *Plain Question*

【Name Explanation】 Da（大）, large; Zhui（椎）, vertebra. The point is below the prominence of the 7th cervical vertebra, which is the largest of the vertebra.

【Classification】 Crossing Point of the Three Yang Meridians of Hand, the Three Yang Meridians of Foot and the Du Meridian.

【Location】 On the posterior midline, in the depression below the 7th cervical vertebra. (See Fig. 7-3)

【Localization】 Sit with the back bent over a desk or in the prone position. The point is located below the 7th cervical vertebra the highest projection on the neck which allows the neck to flex and extend, approximately at the same level with the shoulders.

【Indications】

1) Respiratory Diseases: Cough and dyspnea.

2) Deficiency syndromes: Consumptive diseases due to five kinds of strain, weakness and fatigue due to seven kinds of impairment, spontaneous sweating, night sweats.

3) Mental Diseases: Infantile convulsion, opisthotonos, manic-depressive psychosis, epilepsy.

4) Other Diseases: Pain in the shoulder, back and waist, stiffness of spinal column, urticaria, measles, malaria, sunstroke, cholera, rubella, jaundice, fever, aversion to wind and cold, headache, stiffness of nape.

【Mechanism of Action】 This is the crossing point of all the Yang meridians, thus, it is the point of pure-yang which dominates the exterior and is a commonly used point to relieve exterior syndromes and reduce fever. It can also deal with such exterior illnesses as spontaneous sweating and urticaria. The famous ancient physician Zhang Jingyue said that the person who needs tonifying yin must gain Yin from Yang, therefore, night sweating, hectic fever and other Yin deficiency symptoms can be treated with this point. According to the acupuncture principle that where the meridians pass, diseases found in the area can be treated. This point can be used to treat pain in the shoulder, back and waist.

【Method】 Puncture slightly obliquely upwards 0.5-1.0 cun. (See Fig. 7-4). Hegu needling can be used, bleeding puncture can be used for high fever.

【Acupoint Prescriptions】

1) Stiffness and pain of the neck, dizziness, epigastric fullness and obstruction sensation: Dazhui (DU 14), Feishu (BL 13), Ganshu (BL 18). (*Treatise on Exogenous Febrile Diseases*)

2) Fever due to exogenous febrile diseases: Dazhui (DU 14), Hegu (LI 4), Zhongchong (PC 9). (*A Complete Work on Acupuncture and Moxibustion by Yang Jingzhai*)

3) Hernia: Dazhui (DU 14), Changqiang (DU 1). (*Songs of Original Tai Yi*)

4) Malaria due to spleen cold: Dazhui (DU 14), Jianshi (PC 5), Rugen (ST 18). (*Great Compendium of Acupuncture and Moxibustion*)

【Regional Anatomy】 Musccle: fascial lumbodorsalis supraspinal and interspinal ligaments. Blood vessels: the branch of the transverse cervical artery, the interior ramus of the eighth cervical nerve and the medial branch of the posterior ramus of the thoracic nerve.

DU 15 Yamen (哑门)
(Dumb Gate)

【Source】 *Plain Question*
【Name Explanation】 Ya (哑), mutism; Men (门), door. This point may either cause or treat mutism, so it is likened to a two-way door to mutism.
【Classification】 The Crossing Point of the Du and Yangwei Meridians
【Location】 On the nape, 0.5 cun directly superior to the midpoint of the posterior hairline, below the 1st cervical vertebra.
【Localization】 Sitting with the head slightly forwards (See Fig. 7-5), locate the point at 0.5 cun superior to the hairline on the posterior median line.
【Indications】

1) Dieases of Head and Sense Organs: Headache, heaviness of the head, stiffness of nape, flaccid tongue with aphasia, hoarseness, low voice speaking.

2) Mental Diseases: Back rigidity, apoplexy, syncope, manic-depressive psychosis, epilepsy, hysteria, clonic convulsion.

3) Other Diseases: Epistaxis, vomiting.

【Mechanism of Action】 Since this point enters the root of the tongue, it is also named Shegen, which means this point is closely related with the tongue. In clinic, the symptoms of flaccid tongue with aphasia, hoarseness, sublingual swelling are all treated with this point. It is also the crossing point of both the Yangwei meridian which dominates the yang of the whole body, and Du meridian which connects upwards with the brain. Thus, it has the actions of opening orifice and regulating the meridians and is often used to treat diseases of the nervous system.
【Method】 Puncture perpendicularly or obliquely downwards 0.5-1 cun. Avoid strong stimulation. (See Fig. 7-4)

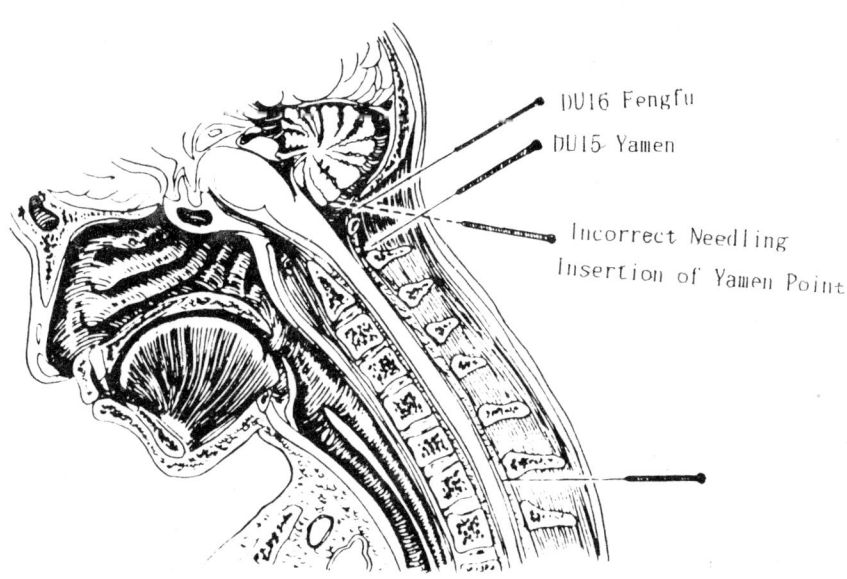

Fig. 7-4

【Acupoint Prescriptions】
1) Heaviness of the head: Yamen (DU 15), Tongtian (BL 7), Fuyang (BL 59). (*Experience on Acupuncture and Moxibustion Therapy*)
2) Opisthotonos: Yanmen (DU 15), Fengfu (DU 16). (*Greet Compendium of Acupuncture and Moxibustion*)
3) Clonic convulsion: Yamen (DU 15), Yanggu (SI 5), Wangu (SI 4), Daimai (GB 26), Laogong (PC 8). (*ibid*)
4) Epilepsy: main points are Yamen (DU 15), Houxi (SI 3); supplementary points are Fengchi (GB 20), Yaoqi (EX 20), Renzhong (DU 26), Neiguan (PC 6). (*Abstract of Clinical Experience on Acupuncture and Moxibustion*)

【Regional Anatomy】 Skin - subcutaneous tissue - between left and right trapezius muscle - nuchal ligament (between left and right splenius muscles of head - between left and right semispinal muscles of head). Inthe superficial layer, there are the 3rd occipital nerve and the subcutaneous vein. In the deep layer, there are the branches of the posterior branches of the 2nd and 3rd cervical nerves, the external (posterior) vertebral venous plexus and branches or tributaries of the occipital artery and vein.

【Remark】 Puncturing Yamen (DU 15) and Huagai (RN 20) can increase the total number of WBC and neutrophils and decrease acidocytes. It is reported that needling Yamen (DU 15) may decrease lymphocytes in all cases with the results being relative to the patients' body condition. It is also reported that puncturing Yamen (DU 15) and Huagai (RN 20) can improve the medullary hematopoiesis function.

DU 16　Fengfu（风府）
(Wind Mansion)

【Source】 *Miraculous Pivot and Plain Question*
【Name Explanation】 Feng (风), pathogenic wind; Fu (府), place. This is a point for eliminating pathogenic wind.
【Classification】 The Crossing Point of the Du and Yangwei Meridians
【Location】 On the nape, 1 cun directly above the midpoint of the posterior hairline, directly below the external occipital protuberance, in the depression between the trapezius muscle of both sides. (See Fig. 7-5)
【Localization】 Sitting with head slightly forwards, locate the point at 1 cun superior to the hairline on the posterior midline, in the depression directly inferior to the external occipital protuberance.
【Indications】
1) Diseases of Head and Sense Organs: Headache, verti-

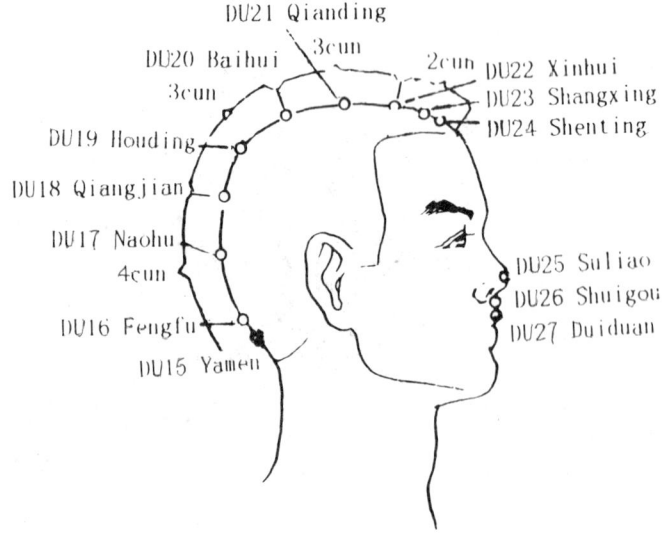

Fig. 7-5

go, stuffy nose, epistaxis, sore throat, stiffness of nape.

2) Mental Diseases: Manic-depressive psychosis, epilepsy, hysteria, apoplexy, flaccid tongue with aphasia, dysphoria, palpitation due to sorrow and fright.

3) Other Diseases: Flaccidity of lower limbs, numbness of the feet, jaundice, common cold, fever.

[Mechanism of Action] The point lies in the place where pathogenic wind easily attacks and where wind is dispelled. As a pathogenic factor, wind may assume various deteriorated cases and all the diseases above are related with wind. Thus, this point is one of the main points used to treat the diseases mentioned above. This point belongs to the Du Meridian and is the crossing point of Foot Taiyang and Yangwei Meridians, which determines its actions in expelling wind and evil from the exterior.

[Method] Puncture perpendicularly or obliquely downwards 0.5-1 cun. Direct moxibustion is prohibited. (See Fig. 7-4)

[Acupoint Prescriptions]

1) Epilepsy due to accumulation of wind phlegm in the thorax: Moxibustion to Fengfu (DU 16), Shuigou (DU 26), Chengjiang (RN 24). (*Thousand Golden Prescriptions*)

2) Mania: Fengfu (DU 16), Kunlun (BL 60), Shugu (BL 65). (*ibid*)

3) Sore throat: Fengfu (DU 16), Tianchuang (SI 16), Laogong (PC 8). (*ibid*)

4) Dysphonia and aphasia: Fengfu (DU 16), Chengjiang (RN 24). (*Experience on Acupuncture and Moxibustion*)

5) Involuntary walking due to mania: Fengfu (DU 16), Yanggu (SI 5). (*Great Compendium of Acupuncture and Moxibustion*)

6) Epistaxis: Fengfu (DU 16), Erjian (LI 2), Yingxiang (LI 20). (*ibid*)

[Regional Anatomy] Skin – subcutaneous tissue – between left and right tendons of trapezius muscles – nuchal ligament (between left and right semispinal muscles of head) – between left and right larger and lesser posterior straight muscles of head. In the superficial layer, there are the branches of the greater occipital nerve and the 3rd occipital nerve and the branches or tributaries of the occipital artery and vein. In the deep layer, there are the branches of the suboccipital nerve.

[Remark] Experiments showed using Fengfu (DU 16) for regulating gastric secretion allows the higher gastric acid and pepsase to descend and the lower to ascend. In pituitary hyertension, Fengfu (DU 16) has the effect of lowering blood pressure.

DU 17　Naohu (脑户)
(Brain Door)

[Source] *A-B Classic of Acupuncture and Moxibustion*

[Name Explanation] Nao (脑), brain; Hu (户), door. The Governer Vessel runs upwards along the spine and enters the brain. The point is like a door on the occipital region for the qi of meridian to the brain.

[Classification] The Crossing Point of the Du and Foot Taiyang Meridians

[Location] On the head, 2.5 cun above the midpoint of the posterior hairline, 1.5 cun above Fengfu (DU 16), at the depression in the upper border of the external occipital protuberance. (See Fig. 7-5)

[Localization] Sitting or in the prone position, locate the point at the depression in the upper margin of the external occipital protuberance on the posterior midline.

[Indications]

1) Diseases of Head and Sense Organs: Heaviness in the head, dizziness, headache,

flushed face, icteric sclera, opthalmalgia which causes inability to see something at a distance, pain and edema of the face, stiffness of nape, bleeding in the root of tongue.

    2) Mental Diseases: Manic-depressive psychosis, epilepsy, clonic convulsion, aphasia, apoplexy.

    3) Other Diseases: Goiter, jaundice.

[Mechanism of Action] The point has the functions of refreshing the head and opening orifice. Since Du Meridian is connected with the brain, it is one of the common points used to treat the diseases of the face and head and mental diseases.

[Method] Puncture horizontally 0.5-0.8 cun. Direct moxibustion is prohibited.

[Acupoint Prescriptions]

    1) Goiter: Naohu (DU 17), Tongtian (BL 7), Xiaoluo (SJ 12), Tiantu (RN 22). (*Thousand Golden Prescriptions*)

    2) Pain and heaviness in the head: Naohu (DU 17), Tongtian (BL 7), Naokong (GB 19). (*Experience on Acupuncture and Moxibustion Therapy*)

    3) Icteric sclera: Naohu (DU 17), Danshu (BL 19), Yishe (BL 49), Yanggang (BL 48). (*ibid*)

[Regional Anatomy] Skin – subcutaneous tissue – between occipital belly of left and right occipitofrontal muscles – subaponeurotic loose tissue. There are the branches of the greater occipital nerve and the branches or tributaries of the occipital artery and vein in this area.

[Remark] Needling Naohu (DU 17) for pituitary hypertention can lower blood pressure, decrease the total number of WBC, neutraphils and acidocytes. It is also reported that puncturing this point can increase lymphocytes in 80% of the cases.

DU 18   Qiangjian (强间)
(Rigid Fissure)

[Source] *A-B Classic of Acupuncture and Moxibustion*

[Name Explanation] Qiang (强), stiffness; Jian (间), middle. The point is between the perietal and occipital bones and indicated by a stiff neck and headache.

[Location] On the head, 4 cun above the midpoint of the posterior hairline, 1.5 cun above Naohu (DU 17). (See Fig. 7-5)

[Localization] Sitting or in the prone position, locate the point at 1.5 cun directly superior to the depression in the upper margin of the external occipital protuberance on the posterior midline.

[Indications]

    1) Diseases of Head and Sense Organs: Headache, dizziness, stiffness and pain of the neck with the inability to turn the head.

    2) Mental Diseases: Manic-depressive psychosis, epilepsy, clonic convulsion.

    3) Other Diseases: Vomiting, restlessness.

[Mechanism of Action] This point is used to refresh the head and tranquilize the mind. It is commonly used for mental diseases, vertigo and vomiting.

[Method] Puncture horizontally 0.5-0.8 cun. Moxibustion is applicable.

[Acupoint Prescription] Headache: Qiangjian (DU 18), Fenglong (ST 40). (*Songs of Hundreds of Symptoms*)

[Regional Anatomy] Skin – subcutaneous tissue – epicranial aponeurosis – subaponeurotic loose tissue. There are the great occipital nerve and the anastomotic network of the left and right occipital arteries and veins in this area.

DU 19 Houding (后顶)
(Posterior Vertex)

【Source】 *A-B Classic of Acupuncture and Moxibustion*
【Name Explanation】 Hou (后), posterior; Ding (顶), vertex. The point is posterior to the vertex.
【Location】 On the head, 5.5 cun directly above the midpoint of the posterior hairline, 3 cun above Naohu (DU 17). (See Fig. 7-5)
【Localization】 Sitting wtch the back bent over a desk, locate the point at 0.5 cun posterior to the midpoint of the line joining anterior and posterior hairline on the posterior midline.
【Indications】
   1) Diseases of Head and Sense Organs: Vertical pain, migraine, vertigo, blurred vision, stiffness and pain of the neck.
   2) Mental Diseases: Manic-depressive psychosis, restlessness, insomnia, clonic convulsion.
   3) Other Diseases: Epidemic febrile diseases due to exopathogen.
【Mechanism of Action】 Most of the points in Du Meridian have the function of treating mental diseases.
   The point is located in the head. Where the point lies, the diseases there are treated.
【Method】 Puncture horizontally 0.5-0.8 cun. Moxibustion is applicable.
【Acupoint Prescriptions】
   1) Dizziness due to wind pathogen: Houding (DU 19), Yuzhen (BL 9), Hanyan (GB 5). (*Experience on Acupuncture and Moxibustion Therapy*)
   2) Neck pain, aversion to cold: Houding (DU 19), Waiqiu (GB 36). (*ibid*)
   3) Occipital neuralgia: Houding (DU 19), Qubin (GB 7), Naokong (GB 19), Tongtian (BL 7), Tianzhu (BL 10), Fengchi (GB 20), Baihui (DU 20), Wangu (GB 12), Qimai (SJ 18), Tianyou (SJ 16), Qiaoyin (GB 44), Quyuan (SI 13), Dazhu (BL 11), Shousanli (LI 10). (*New Science of Acupuncture and Moxibustion*)
【Regional Anatomy】 Skin − subcutaneous tissue − epicranial aponeurosis − subaponeurotic loose tissue. There are the great occipital nerve and the anastomotic network of the occipital arteries and veins with the superficial temporal arteries and veins in this area.

DU 20 Baihui (百会)
(Hundred Convergences)

【Source】 *A-B Classic of Acupuncture and Moxibustion*
【Name Explanation】 Bai (百), hundred; Hui (会), meeting. The point is at the vertex and is a meeting place of the Three Yang Meridians of foot, the Liver Meridian and the Governer Vessel.
【Classification】 Crossing Point of the Du Meridian and Bladder Meridian of Foot Taiyang
【Location】 On the head, 5 cun directly above the midpoint of the anterior hairline, at the midpoint of the line connecting the apexes of both ears. (See Fig. 7-5)
【Localization】 Sitting, locate the point at 1 cun anterior to the midpoint of the line joining anterior and posterior hair line.
   The point is located at the intersection between the midline of the head and the line joining

both apex auriculae.

[Indications]

1) Diseases of Head and Sense Organs: Headache, dizziness, tinnitus, deafness, obstruction of external acoustic meatus, dizziness due to wind pathogen, heaviness in the head, blurred vision, conjunctival congestion, nasal obstruction.

2) Digestive Diseases: Epistaxis, poor appetite with a flat feeling in the mouth, prolapse of anus, protracted diarrhea and dysentery, gastroptosis.

3) Urogenital Diseases: Nephroptosis, enuresis, prolapse of uterus and impotence.

4) Mental Diseases: Palpitation, amnesia, syncope, shock, aphasia due to apoplexy, lockjaw, hemiplegia, epilepsy, hysteria, clonic convulsion.

5) Other Diseases: Hypertension.

[Mechanism of Action] This point lies in the uppermost part of the body where Yang qi converges. Puncturing this point is to regulate Yang qi, thus, various cases of prolapse of visceral organs can be treated. The symptoms of protracted diarrhea and dysentery, enuresis, impotence, coma, corpse-like syncope are all correlated with the failure of Yang qi in ascending to the brain, and needling this point can make Yang qi go upwards, prolapse of organs astringe, consciousness be restored and resuscitation be induced, thus, it is always the first point to be selected in the treatment.

As it is the crossing point of the three Yang meridians of both hand and foot, also the meridians of the Hand jueyin and Foot jueyin, which have a wide connection with the five sense organs of the face and head. This point is mostly used for diseases of the ears, eyes and nose.

Modern clinical practice demonstrated that for cardiovascular diseases of hypertension and apoplexy, puncturing this point may regulate the overabundance of Yang qi, lower the blood pressure and improve cerebral blood flow. For the patients suffering from shock, needling the point may raise their blood pressure.

[Method] Puncture horizontally 0.5-0.8 cun. Moxibustion is applicable.

[Acupoint Prescriptions]

1) Beriberi: Baihui (DU 20), Fengfu (DU 16), Shu and Mu points of the five-zang and six-fu organs. (*Experience on Acupuncture and Moxibustion Therapy*)

2) Wind syndrome of the head: Baihui (DU 20), Naokong (GB 19), Tianzhu (BL 10). (*ibid*)

3) Red jaundice: Baihui (DU 20), Quchi (LI 11), Hegu (LI 4), Sanli (ST 36), Weizhong (BL 40). (*Great Compendium of Acupuncture and Moxibustion*)

4) Prolapse of anus: Baihui (DU 20), Changqiang (DU 1) (moxibustion with seven cones), Qizhong (RN 8). (*ibid*)

5) Wandering erysipelas: Baihui (DU 20), Weizhong (BL 40). (*ibid*)

6) Prolapse of anus in children: Baihui (DU 20), Changqiang (DU 1), Dachangshu (BL 25). (*ibid*)

7) Red spot all over the body: Baihui (DU 20), Quchi (LI 11), Sanli (ST 36), Weizhong (BL 40). (*ibid*)

8) Malaria: Baihui (DU 20), Jingqu (LU 8), Qiangu (SI 8). (*A Miraculous Classic*)

9) Coma: Baihui (DU 20), Shuigou (DU 26), Shixuan (EX-UE 11), Zusanli (ST 36), After insertion, the needles are manipulated every 3-5 minutes; if no obvious effect is observed, Neiguan (PC 6) and Yongquan (KI 1) are added. (*Science of Acupuncture and Moxibustion*)

10) Attack of hysteria: Baihui (DU 20), penetrating Neiguan (PC 6) through Waiguan (SJ 5). (*ibid*)

11) Impotence: Baihui (DU 20), Geshu (BL 17), Shenshu (BL 23), Mingmen (DU 4), Yaoyangguan (DU 3), Guanyuan (RN 4), Zhongji (RN 3) (moxibustion with moxa cones every day). (*Chinese Acupuncture and Moxibustion*)

12) Prolapse of anus: Baihui (DU 20), Zusanli (ST 36), Changqiang (DU 1), Chengshan (BL 57). (*Abstract of Clinical Experience on Acupuncture and Moxibustion*)

13) Prolapse of anus in children: First Baihui (DU 20), then Jiuwei (RN 15), (moxibustion with moxa cones). (*Songs of Xihong*)

14) Acute laryngeal infection: Baihui (DU 20), Taichong (LR 3), Zhaohai (KI 6), Yinjiao (RN 7). (*ibid*)

【Regional Anatomy】Skin — subcutaneous tissue — subaponeurotic loose tissue. There are branches of the greater occipital and frontal nerves, and the anastomotic network of the left and right superficial temporal arteries and veins with the left and right occipital arteries and veins in this area.

【Remark】Puncturing Baihui (DU 20) can make the electroencephalogram (EEG) of most patients with grand mal epilepsy become normal. A normal man's myoelectric can rise ($P<0.05$) from 15-35 minutes after acupuncture. Using electroacupuncture to treat patients with cerebral embolism can also raise the myoelectric amplitude. The effect will usually be seen five minutes after Baihui is punctured.

Needling Baihui (DU 20) has a fixed effect on asphyxia neonatorum, and is curative with electropuncture.

Moxibustion to Baihui (DU 20) can correct the position of fetus.

DU 21　Qianding (前顶)
(Anteviov-Vertex)

【Source】*A-B Classic of Acupuncture and Moxibustion*

【Name Explanation】Qian (前), front; Ding (顶), vertex. The point is in front of the vertex.

【Location】On the head 3.5 cun directly above the midpoint of the anterior hairline and 1.5 cun anterior to Baihui (DU 20). (See Fig. 7-5)

【Localization】Sitting or sitting with head at rest, locate the point 0.5 cun posterior to anterior one-fourth of the line joining anterior and posterior hairline.

【Indications】

1) Diseases of Head and Sense Organs: Vertigo, stuffy nose with clear discharge, rhinorrhea with turbid discharge, epistaxis, conjunctival congestion, blurred vision, flushed and swollen face.

2) Mental Diseases: Manic-depressive psychosis, clonic convulsion, chronic and acute convulsion in children, apoplexy.

3) Other Diseases: Hypertension, edema.

【Mechanism of Action】The point has the functions of refreshing the head and tranquilizing the mind. It is mainly used to treat diseases of the nose and eyes and can get a dramatic effect. Compared with Baihui (DU 20), it is not usually used to treat ear diseases.

It is the common characteristic of Du Meridian that this point can cure mental diseases, for its meridian is connected with the brain and totally dominates all Yang meridians.

【Method】Puncture horizontally 0.5-0.8 cun. Moxibustion is applicable.

【Acupoint Prescriptions】

1) Migraine due to pathogenic wind: Qianding (DU 21), Houding (DU 19), Hanyan (GB 4). (*Thousand Golden Prescriptions*)

2) Wind-syndrome of the head, vertigo: Qianding (DU 21), Wuchu (BL 5). (*Experience on Acupuncture and Moxibustion Therapy*)

3) Acute infantile convulsion: Administering moxibustion to Qianding (DU 21) only with

3 cones. If no obvious effect is observed, continuing moxibustion to both of the supercilinary areas and Renzhong (DU 26) point below the nose. The moxa cones should be wheat grain-sized. (*The Peaceful Holy Benevolent Prescriptions*)

4) Conjunctival congestion: Puncturing Qianding (DU 21) and Baihui (DU 20) with three-edged needles. (*Confucian's Duties to Their Parents*)

【Regional Anatomy】 Skin – subcutaneous tissue – epicranial aponeurosis – subaponeurotic loose tissue. There are frontal nerve, the anastomotic network of the left and right superficial temporal arteries and veins with the left and right frontal arteries and veins in this area.

DU 22　Xinhui（囟会）
（Fodtanel Convergences）

【Source】 *Miraculous Pivot*
【Name Explanation】 Xin (囟), fontanel; Hui (会), closing. The point is located at the major gate.
【Location】 On the head, 2 cun directly above the midpoint of the anterior hairline and 3 cun anterior to Baihui (DU 20). (See Fig. 7-5)
【Localization】 Sitting or sitting with head at rest, locate the point at one sixth of the line joining anterior and posterior hairline. Or locate the point at 1 cun posterior to Shangxing (DU 23).
【Indications】
1) Diseases of Head and Sense Organs: Headache, vertigo, flushed and swollen face, rhinorrhea with turbid discharge, epistaxis, nasal polyp, carbuncle of nose, cold sensation pain in the head, itch of the scalp with much scurf.
2) Mental Diseases: Epilepsy, infantile convulsion, apoplexy, insomnia, lethargy.
3) Other Diseases: Hypertension.
【Mechanism of Action】 See Baihui (DU 20).
【Method】 Puncture horizontally 0.5-0.8 cun, Moxibustion is applicable.
【Acupoint Prescriptions】
1) Lethargy: Xinhui (DU 22), Baihui (DU 20). (*Experience on Acupuncture and Moxibustion Therapy*)
2) Infantile convulsion: Xinhui (DU 22), Qianding (DU 21), Benshen (GB 23), Tianzhu (BL 10). (*ibid*)
3) Wind-syndrome of the head: Xinhui (DU 22), Baihui (DU 20), Qianding (DU 21). (*ibid*)
4) Apoplexy: Xinhui (DU 22), Baihui (DU 20). (*Songs of Jade Dragon*)

【Regional Anatomy】 Skin – subcutaneous tissue – epicranial aponeurosis – subaponeurotic loose tissue.

There are frontal nerve and the anastomotic network of the left and right superficial temporal arteries and veins with the left and right frontal arteries and veins in this area.

DU 23　Shangxing（上星）
（Upper Star）

【Source】 *A-B Classic of Acupuncture and Moxibustion*
【Name Explanation】 Shang (上), upper; Xing (星), star. The head is considered as heaven. The point is on the head like a star in the sky.

【Location】 On the head, 1 cun directly above the midpoint of the anterior hairline. (See Fig. 7-5)

【Localization】 Sitting or sitting with head at rest, locate the point 1 cun directly superior to the anterior hairline.

【Indications】

1) Diseases of Head and Sense Organs: Headache, vertigo, edema of face, conjunctival congestion, lacrimation induced by wind, inability of eyes to see something at a distances, epistaxis, rhinorrhea with turbid discharge, nasal polyp, anosmia, carbuncle of nose.

2) Mental Diseases: Manic-depressive psychosis, epilepsy, infantile convulsion, apoplexy.

3) Other Diseases: Malaria, febrile diseases, anhidrosis, vomiting.

【Mechanism of Action】 See Baihui (DU 20). At present, this point is mainly used to treat nasal and febrile diseases.

【Method】 Puncture horizontally 0.5-0.8 cun or apply bleeding puncture. Moxibustion is applicable.

【Acupoint Prescriptions】

1) Flushed and swollen face: Shangxing (DU 23), Xinhui (DU 22), Qianding (DU 21), Naohu (DU 17), Fengchi (GB 20). (*Thousand Golden Prescriptions*)

2) Rednees, pain and itch of inner canthus: Shangxing (DU 23), Ganshu (BL 18). (*Experience on Acupuncture and Moxibustion Therapy*)

3) Stuffy nose, anosmia: Shangxing (DU 23), Baihui (DU 20), Xinhui (DU 22), Chengguang (BL 6). (*ibid*)

4) Wind-syndrome of head, edema of the face: Shangxing (DU 23), Tianyou (SJ 16). (*ibid*)

5) Malarial Diseases: Shangxing (DU 23), Qiuxu (GB 40), Xiangu (ST 43). (*Great Compendium of Acupuncture and Moxibustion*)

6) Epistaxis: Shangxing (DU 23), (moxibustion with 14 cones), Juegu (GB 39), Xinhui (DU 22). (*ibid*)

7) Serious cases of sinusitis with purulent discharge: Shangxing (DU 23), Qucha (BL 4), Hegu (LI 4). (*ibid*)

8) Five types of epilepsy: Shangxing (DU 23), Jiuwei (RN 15), Yongquan (KI 1), Xinshu (BL 15), Baihui (DU 20). (*ibid*)

9) Pulmonary tuberculosis (headache and dizziness): Main points: Shangxing (DU 23), Touwei (ST 8), moxibustion to Baihui (DU 20), Taiyang (EX-HN 1), Tianzhu (BL 10). Hegu (LI 4) and Lieque (LU 7) can be added if needed. (*Abstract of Clinical Experience on Acupuncture and Moxibustion*)

10) Wind syndrome of head: Shangxing (DU 23), Shenting (DU 24). (*Songs of Jade Dragon*)

11) Epistaxis: Shangxing (DU 23), Heliao (LI 19). (*Songs on Point Selection of Miscellaneous Diseases*)

【Regional Anatomy】 Skin - subcutaneous tissue - epicranial aponeurosis - subaponeurotic loose tissue. There are branches of the frontal nerve and the branches or tributaries of the frontal artery and vein in this area.

DU 24　Shenting (神庭)
(Spirit Courtyard)

【Source】 *A-B Classic of Acupuncture and Moxibustion*

【Name Explanation】 Shen (神), mind; Ting (庭), vestibule. "The brain is the mansion of the primordial mind." Shen here means brain. The point is on the forehead, like a vestibule of the brain.

[Classification] Crossing Point of the Du, Foot Taiyang and Foot Yangming Meridians

[Location] On the head, 0.5 cun directly above the midpoint of the anterior hairline. (See Fig. 7-5)

[Localization] Sitting with head at rest, locate the point at 0.5 cun directly superior to the anterior hairline.

If the patient's hairline is unclear, first locate Baihui (DU 20), this point is located at 4.5 cun anterior to Baihui (DU 20).

[Indications]

1) Diseases of Head and Sense Organs: Headache, vertigo, conjunctival congestion, nebula, night blindness, rhinorrhea with turbid discharge, running nose, stuffy nose, epistaxis.

2) Mental Diseases: Manic-depressive psychosis, epilepsy, apoplexy, infantile convulsion, opisthotonos, neurogenic vomiting.

3) Other Diseases: Wagging tongue, dyspnea with thirst, dysphoria and fullness sensation.

[Mechanism of Action] See Baihui (DU 20).

[Method] Puncture horizontally 0.5-0.8 cun, or apply bleeding puncture. Moxibustion is applicable.

[Acupoint Prescriptions]

1) Malaria: Shenting (DU 24), Baihui (DU 20). (*A-B Classic of Acupuncture and Moxibustion*)

2) Nasal diseases (epistaxis, watery nasal discharge): Shenting (DU 24), Cuanzhu (BL 2), Yingxiang (LI 20), Hegu (LI 4), Zhiyin (BL 67), Tonggu (BL 66). (*Thousand Golden Prescriptions*)

3) Wind type epilepsy with fixation of the eyes: Shenting (DU 24), Sizhukong (SJ 23). (*Experience on Acupuncture and Moxibustion Therapy*)

4) Vertigo due to pathogenic wind: Shenting (DU 24), Shangxing (DU 23), Xinhui (DU 22). (*ibid*)

5) Wind type epilepsy: Shenting (DU 24), Baihui (DU 20), Qianding (DU 21), Yongquan (KI 1), Sizhukong (SJ 23), Shenque (RN 8) (moxibustion with one cone), Jiuwei (RN 15) (moxibustion with three cones). (*Great Compendium of Acupuncture and Moxibustion*)

[Regional Anatomy] Skin - subcutaneous tissue - between frontal belly of left and right occipitofrontal muscles - subaponeurotic loose tissue. There are the supratrochlear nerve from the frontal nerve and the branches or tributaries of the frontal artery and vein in this area.

DU 25 Suliao (素髎)
(White Crevice)

[Source] *A-B Classic of Acupuncture and Moxibustion*

[Name Explanation] Su (素), nasal cartilage; Liao (髎), foramen. The point is in a foramen at the lower end of the nasal cartilage.

[Location] On the face, at the centre of the nose apex. (See Fig. 7-5)

[Localization] Sitting with head at rest or in the supine position, the point is located at the apex of nose.

[Indications]

1) Diseases of Head and Sense Organs: Stuffy nose, epistaxis, running nose, rhinorrhea

with turbid discharge, nasal polyp, carbuncle of the nose, rosacea, stye, epidemic hemorrhagic conjunctivitis.

2) Digestive Diseases: Cholera, vomiting.

3) Mental Diseases: Convulsion, coma, shock, infantile convulsion, clonic convulsion, asphyxia neonatorum dysphoria, irritability.

【Mechanism of Action】 The point is used to treat nasal diseases and its machanism are based on the acupuncture principle that where the point locates, where the indications are.

In the light of modern clinical research, this point has the functions of elevating the blood pressure and regulating respiratory failure, so it is effective for treating shock and asphyxia neonatorum.

The point has the functions of inducing resuscitation, relieving convulsion and calming the mind. For instance, for the cases of convulsion coma, infantile convulsion, clonic convulsion, though the blood pressure of the patient is not low, this point still has a good therapeutic effect, which shows that this point has double regulating functions.

【Method】 Puncture obliquely upwards 0.3-0.5 cun, or apply bleeding puncture.

【Acupoint Prescription】

Shock: Main points: Suliao (DU 25), Neiguan (PC 6); Supplementary points: Shaochong (HT 9), Shaoze (SI 1), Zhongchong (PC 9), Huizong (SJ 7), Renying (ST 9), Shuigou (DU 26), Yongquan (KI 1), Zhongdu (SJ 3). Manipulation: Inserting the needle, stimulating the point moderately and strongly, retaining the needle and constantly or intermittently twisting the needle until the blood pressure is stable. (*Abstract of Clinical Experience on Acupuncture and Moxibustion*)

【Regional Anatomy】 Skin – subcutaneous tissue – septal cartilage of nose and lateral nasal cartilage. There are the lateral nasal branches of the anterior echmoidal nerve and dorsal nasal branches of the facial artery and vein in this area.

【Remark】 Needling Suliao (DU 25) has fixed curative effect for asphyxia neonatorum. Electropuncturing Suliao (DU 25) can treat respiratory failure, improve respiratory frequency and rhythm and treat various other kinds of abnormal respiration. It is reported the positive rate of respiratory changes caused by puncturing Suliao (DU 25) was 92%, there was no change in the group which did not receive needling in this point.

DU 26　Shuigou (水沟)
(Ditch)

【Source】 *A-B Classic of Acupuncture and Moxibustion*

【Name Explanation】 Shui (水), water; Gou (沟), groove. The point is in the philtrum which looks like a water groove.

【Classification】 Crossing Point of the Du Meridian, the Large Intestine Meridian of Hand Yangming and the Stomach Meridian of Foot Yangming

【Location】 On the face, at the junction of the upper one-third and middle one-third of the philtrum. (See Fig. 7-5)

【Localization】 Sitting with head at rest or in the supine position, locate the point at the intersection between superior one-third and median one-third on the philtrum.

【Indications】

1) Diseases of Head and Sense Organs: Facial paralysis, toothache, stuffy nose, epistaxis, edema on face due to wind, locked jaw.

2) Mental Diseases: Coma, syncope, manic-depressive psychosis, epilepsy, acute and chronic convulsion, sunstroke, opisthotonos, hysteria.

3) Other Diseases: Jaundice, diabetes, pestilence, stuffness and pain of the spinal column, lumbago due to sudden sprain and contusion, stiff neck.

【Mechanism of Action】 The point has the functions of restoring consciousness, inducing resuscitation, raising Yang qi, activating the flow of qi, relaxing the muscles and spine. It is one of the commonly used points to increase energy.

The point lies between the mouth and nose and its Du Meridian connects with the brain at the cortex, so it dominates inducing resuscitation and restoring consciousness.

The Du Meridian is the sea of Yang meridians and controls all the Yang of the body. Thus, it recuperate depleted Yang and rescues the patient from collapse by elevating Yang and promoting the circulation of qi.

In circulation of qi, the Du Meridian is linked with the nearby meridian of Foot Taiyang and the meridian of Hand Taiyang. This point is the crossing point of Hand Yangming and Foot Yangming mericlians, thus, it can be used to treat deviation of the mouth, toothache, stiff neck and sudden sprain of the waist.

【Method】 Puncture obliquely upwards 0.3-0.5 cun, or press the point with a finger nail. Moxibustion is applicable.

【Acupoint Prescriptions】
1) Epileptic Diseases: Shuigou (DU 26), Yinjiao (DU 28). (*A-B Classic of Acupuncture and Moxibustion*)
2) Running nose, anosmia: Shuigou (DU 26), Tianyou (SJ 16). (*Thousand Golden Prescriptions*)
3) Stiffness and pain of spinal column: Shuigou (DU 26), Weizhong (BL 40). (*Songs of Jade Dragon*)
4) Apoplexy, unconsciousness: Shuigou (DU 26), Zhongchong (PC 9). (*Great Compendium of Acupuncture and Moxibustion*)
5) Edema of the face: Shuigou (DU 26), Qianding (DU 21). (*Songs of Hundreds of Symptoms*)
6) Flaccidity with bent body: Shuigou(DU 26), Quchi(LI 11). (*Songs of Jade Dragon*)

【Regional Anatomy】 Skin – subcutaneous tissue – orbicular muscle of mouth. There are the branches of the infraobital nerve and the superior labial artery and vein in this area.

【Remark】 Animal experimentation have shown that puncturing Shuigou (DU 26) can temporarily improve respiration, and that respiration can usually be recovered during the respiratory stopping-stage in the animals. The results of the experiments which hemorrhagic shock was treated with acupuncture indicated there is a longer descending process of blood pressure in the needling Shuigou (DU 26) group. Getting shock stage needed longer time and more blood loss. It is reported that needling Shuigou (DU 26) cau also raise the blood pressure of animal with normal blood pressure. Therefore, repeatedly stimulating Shuigou (DU 26) can immediately cure coma, because not only its pralsor effect can improve cerebral blood flow, but also its afferent impulses can strengthen the brain activity by the ascending activiating system of the brain stem reticular structure.

DU 27　Duiduan（兑端）
（Upperlip Projection）

【Source】 *A-B Classic of Acupuncture and Moxibustion*
【Name Explanation】 Dui (兑), mouth; Duan (端), tip. The point is at the upper lip.
【Location】 On the face, on the labial tubercle of the upper lip, on the vermilion border between the philtrum and upper lip. (See Fig. 7-5)

【Localization】 Sitting with head at rest or in the supine position, the point is located at the intersection between the lower extremity of the philtrum and upper lip.

【Indications】

1) Diseases of Head and Sense Organs: Thirst, lip tremor, aphthae and halitisis, toothache, gingivitis, locked jaw, nebula, stuffy nose, epistaxis, extreme thirst, dry tongue.

2) Digestive Diseases: Jaundice, yellow urine.

3) Mental Diseases: Coma, syncope, manic-depressive psychosis, hysteria.

4) Other Diseases: Coccyalgia (pain in the end of coccyx).

【Mechanism of Action】 Based on the local and adjacent curative effect of this point, diseases of the mouth, teeth, and nose are treated. The treatment of pain at the end of coccyx is based on the corresponding action of this point. This is because the digestive system and Duiduan (DU 27) and the end of coccyalgia respectively lie beside the mouth and anus.

【Method】 Puncture obliquely 0.2-0.3 cun. Moxibustion is prohibited.

【Acupoint Prescriptions】

1) Epilepsy: Duiduan (DU 27), Yinjiao (DU 28), Chengjiang (RN 24), Daying (ST 5), Sizhukong (SJ 23), Xinhui (DU 22), Tianzhu (BL 10), Shangqiu (SP 5). (*Thousand Golden Prescriptions*)

2) Toothache and gingivitis: Duiduan (DU 27), Muchuang (GB 16), Zhengying (GB 17), Ermen (SJ 21). (*ibid*)

3) Epileptic diseases with salivation: Duiduan (DU 27), Benshen (GB 13). (*Experiences on Acupuncture and Moxibustion Therapy*)

4) Superior dental caries: Duiduan (DU 27), Ermen (SJ 21). (*ibid*)

5) Stranguria with deep-coloured urine: Duiduan (DU 27), Xiaohai (SI 8). (*Songs of Hundreds of Symptoms*)

【Regional Anatomy】 Same as Shuigou (DU 26).

DU 28　Yinjiao (龈交)
(Gum Meeting)

【Source】 *Plain Question*

【Name Explanation】 Yin(龈), gum; Jiao(交), meet. The point is on the incisive suture of the upper gum where Governor Vessel and Conception Vessel meet.

【Classification】 Crossing Point of the Du and Ren Meridians

【Location】 Inside of the upper lip, at the junction of the labial frenum and upper gum. (See Fig. 7-6)

【Localization】 Sitting with head at rest, pick up the upper lip, locate the point where the superior frenulum meets the gums.

【Indications】

1) Diseases of Head and Sense Organs: Gingivitis, deviation of the mouth, lockjaw, halitosis, gingival bleeding, sinusitis, flushed face, swollen cheek, sore and tinea on face, sore on both cheeks.

2) Mental Disease: Manic-depressive psychosis.

3) Other Disease: Stiff nape.

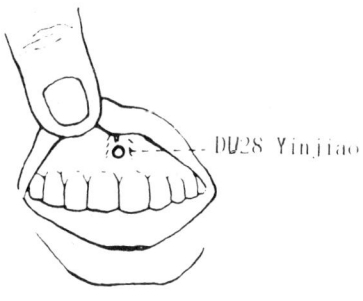

Fig. 7-6

【Mechanism of Action】 As this point lies in the place where Du and Ren Meridrans converge, it may dominates the mental diseases. This point lies right in the center of the face, thus, it treats diseases of the face and head, which is based on the adjacent therapeutic effect of the point. (*Thousand Golden Prescriptions*)

[Method] Puncture obliquely 0.2-0.3 cun. Moxibustion is prohibited.

[Acupoint Prescriptions]

1) Lockjaw: Yinjiao (DU 28), Shangguan (GB 3), Daying (ST 5), Yifeng (SJ 7).

2) Stiffness of the nape with inability to turn the head: Yinjiao (DU 28), Fengfu (DU 16). (*Experience on Acupuncture and Moxibustion*)

3) Halitosis: Yinjiao (DU 28), Chengjiang (RN 24). (*Great Compendium of Acupuncture and Moxibustion*)

[Regional Anatomy] Transitional border of superior labial frenulum and upper gum — between deep surface of orbicular muscle of mouth and aveolar arch of maxillary bone. There are the superior labial branches of the maxillary nerve, the infraorbital plexus formed by the branches of the infraobital and facial nerves, and the superior labial artery and vein in this area.

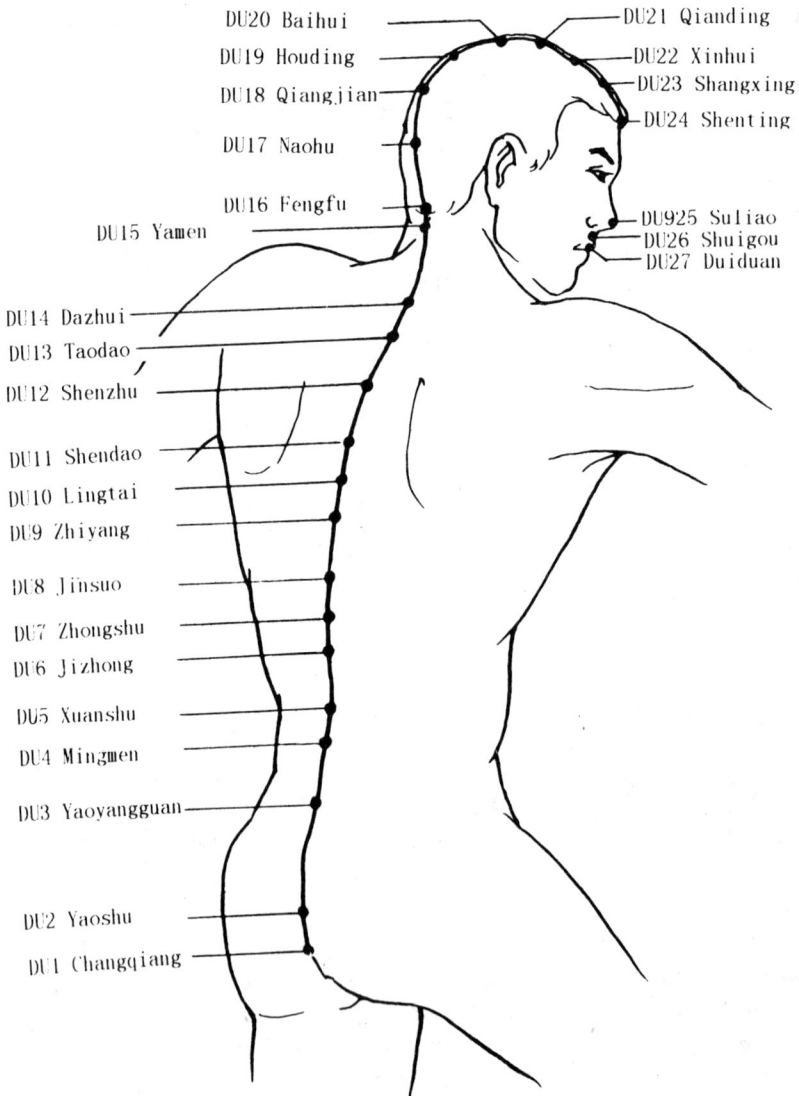

Fig. 7-7 **Acupoints of the Du Meridian**

Table 7-1 Indications and Actions of Acupoints of the Du Meridian

Name of the points	Specific points	Common indications	Specific indications and functions
DU 1 Changqiang (长强)	Crossing point, Luo-(Connecting) point	Mental diseases: manic depression and epilepsy	Dreding the Ren and Du meridians, regulating the intestines. Hemorrhoids, prolapse of anus, bloody stool, manic-depression and epilepsy, dysuria and stranguria, damp and itching genitals, lumbosacral pain
DU 2 Yaoshu (腰俞)		Gynecological and external genital diseases: irregular menstruation, seminal emission, leukorrhea, impotence	Irregular menstruation, stiffness and pain along the spinal column, flaccidity of the lower limbs
DU 3 Yaoyangguan (腰阳关)			Reinforcing the kidney and strengthening the lower back, clearing away cold and damp pathogens. Irregular menstruation, seminal emission, impotence, lumbosacral pain, painful knees with inability to flex, leukorrhea, tetanus
DU 4 Mingmen (命门)		Intestinal diseases: diarrhea, constipation, hemorrhoids	Tonifying vital qi and reinforcing the kidney, controlling emission and strengthening yang. Impotence, seminal emission, premature ejaculation, leukorrhea, sterility, stiffness and pain along the spinal column, weakness and coldness of the waist, enuresis
DU 5 Xuanshu (悬枢)		Mental diseases: manic-depression, Gastrointestinal diseases: abdominal pain, fullness sensation in the abdomen, diarrhea, prolapse of anus	Warming and recuperating the spleen and kidney. Abdominal distension and pain, indigestion of food, diarrhea, prolapse of anus, stiffness and pain along the spinal column
DU 6 Jizhong (脊中)			Invigorating the spleen and eliminating dampness, reinforcing the kidney and strengthening the spine. Diarrhea, jaundice, infantile malnutrition, epilepsy, prolapse of anus, stiffness and pain along the spine
DU 7 Zhongshu (中枢)			Invigorating the spleen and eliminating dampness. Stomachache, fullness of the abdomen, anorexia, vomiting, jaundice, hypopsia
DU 8 Jinsuo (筋缩)			Relieving convulsions and stopping wind pathogens, invigorating the spleen and regulating the middle Jiao. Depressive diseases, infantile convulsion, spasm, stiffness and pain of the spine and back, stomachache, tetanus
DU 9 Zhiyang (至阳)		The same as below.	Relieving the chest and regulating the circulation of qi, clearing heat and eliminating dampness. Jaundice, cough, asthma, distending pain in the chest and hypochondrium, stiffness of the spine, back pain, soreness of the shank, heaviness and pain of the four limbs
DU 10 Lingtai (灵台)			Dispersing lung qi to relieve cough, clearing away heat and toxins. Cough, inability to sleep soundly due to dyspnea, pain in the chest and back, furuncles and sores

Name of the points	Specific points	Common indications	Specific indications and functions
DU 11 Shendao (神道)		Mental disease: manic-depressive psychosis Disease of the heart and lung: cough, asthma, palpitation, febrile diseases	Nourishing the heart and tranquilizing the mind, clearing heat and dredging the collaterals. Cardiac pain, palpitations, forgetfulness, insomnia, cough, neurosis, fever, headache
DU 12 Shenzhu (身柱)			Dispersing lung qi to relieve cough, tranquilizing the mind. Cough, dyspnea, epilepsy, infantile convulsion, tetanus, neurosis, stiffness and pain along the spinal column
DU 13 Taodao (陶道)	Crossing point		Relieving the exterior, clearing heat, tranquilizing the mind. Headache, febrile diseases, malaria, fever and aversion to cold, hectic fever, night sweat, urticaria
DU 14 Dazhui (大椎)			Relieving the exterior, clearing heat, activating yang, dispersing lung qi, relieving convulsion and strengthening the brain. Headache, stiff neck, febrile diseases, cough with dyspnea, hectic fever, night sweats, epilepsy, urticaria, hysteria, cerebral palsy
DU 15 Yamen (哑门)	Crossing point	Mental diseases: manic-depression, and epilepsy Diseases of the vertex: headache, stiffness of the neck	Dredging the orifice, clearing the mind. Sudden loss of voice, stiff tongue with inability to speak, deafness and muteness, epilepsy, hysteria, stiffness and pain in the head and nape
DU 16 Fengfu (风府)			Expelling wind-evils, clearing heat in the heart to open the orifices. Vertigo, swelling and pain of the throat, nasal obstruction, epistaxis, deafness and muteness, apoplexy, hemiplegia, flaccid tongue, manic-depression
DU 17 Naohu (脑户)		Mental diseases: manic-depression and epilepsy Diseases of the head, face and sense organs: headache, dizziness, blurred vision, rhinorrhea with turbid discharge	Dispelling wind and clearing heat, opening the orifices to relieve convulsion. Pain in the back of head, dizziness, loss of voice, stiffness of the neck, blurring of vision, red, swollen and painful eyes, icteric sclera, epilepsy
DU 18 Qiangjian (强间)			Tranquilizing the mind by calming the heart, expelling wind and dredging the collaterals. Blurred vision, irritability, insomnia, stiffness and pain of the neck and occiput
DU 19 Houding (后顶)			Vertex pain, vertigo, manic-depression and epilepsy
DU 20 Baihui (百会)	Crossing point		Lowering hyperactive liver to relieve the wind syndrome, ascending Yang and invigorating qi, restoring consciousness and calming the mind, clearing heat and opening the orifices. Diarrhea, apoplexy, aphasia, prolapse of anus, prolapse of the uterus, insomnia, coma, neurosis, shock, trismus
DU 21 Qianding (前顶)			Lowering hyperactive liver and subsiding Yang. Headache, vertigo, epilepsy, rhinorrhea with turbid discharge

Acupoints of the Du Meridian and Ren Meridian

Name of the points	Specific points	Common indications	Specific indications and functions
DU 22 Xinhui (囟会)		The same as above.	Headache, vertigo, epilepsy, rhinorrhea with turbid discharge
DU 23 Shangxing (上星)			Removing heat from the liver to improve eyesight, dredging the nasal passage. Pain of the forehead, painful eyes, lacrimation, nasal obstruction, bleeding from nose, rhinorrhea with turbid discharge, febrile diseases, infantile convulsion
DU 24 Shenting (神庭)	Crossing point		Removing heat from the liver to improve eyesight, relieving wind syndrome to stop convulsions, dredging the orifices to calm the mind. Red, swollen and painful eyes, nightblindness, nebula, rhinorrhea, epistaxis, opisthotonus, mania, headache
DU 25 Suliao (素髎)		Mental diseases: convulsions, coma, manic-depression and epilepsy. Diseases of nose, mouth and tooth: Deviation of the eyes and mouth, swelling and pain of the gums, rhinorrhea with turbid discharge	Dispersing heat and opening the orifices, recuperating depleted yang and rescueing the patient from collapse. Nasal obstruction, nasal polyps, rhinorrhea, acne rosacea, convulsions, coma, asphyxia in newborns
DU 26 Shuigou (水沟)			Reducing heat to open the orifices, stopping pain and calming the mind, recuperating depleted yang and rescueing the patient from collapse. Syncope, coma, manic-depression, eclampsia, gravidarum, asphyxia, trismus, apoplexy, cholera, heatstroke, uterine bleeding, lumbar sprain
DU 27 Duiduan (兑端)			Clearing away stomache heat, arresting convulsion and stopping pain. Aphtha, foul breath, swelling and pain of gums, toothache, diabetes, stiffness and pain along the spinal column
DU 28 Yinjiao (龈交)			Clearing heat to improve eyesight, dredging the nasal passages. Swelling and pain of gums, rhinorrhea, acne rosacea, nasal obstruction, watery eyes, redness and itching pain of the eye, nebula, irritability, cardiac pain, stiffness of the neck

II. Acupoints of the Ren Meridian

RN 1 Huiyin (会阴)
(Converging Yin)

【Source】 *A-B Classic of Acupuncture and Moxibustion*
【Name Explanation】 Hui (会), crossing; Yin (阴), genitalia. The point is located in the space between the genitalia and the anus, called Huiyin.
【Classification】 The Crossing Point of the Ren, Du and Chong Meridians
【Location】 On the perineum, at the midpoint between the posterior border of the scrotum and the anus in males, and between the posterior commissure of the large labia and anus in females. (See Fig. 7-8)

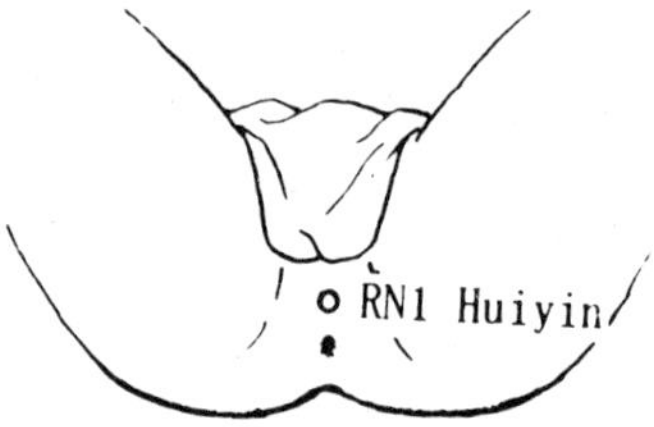

Fig. 7-8

【Localization】 The point is located between the anus and the root of the scrotum in males, midpoint of the line joining the anus and the posterior symphysis of the greater lips of the pudendum in females.
【Indications】
    1) Urinary Diseases: Difficult urination, enuresis.
    2) Reproductive Diseases: Vulvar pain, pruritus vulva, vulvar eczema, uterus prolapse, nocturnal emission, irregular menstruation.
    3) Mental Diseases: Coma, manic-depressive psychosis, epilepsy.
    4) Other Diseases: Asphyxia due to drowning, neonatal asphyxia, hernia, hemorrhoid, prolapse of rectum.
【Mechanism of Action】 As this point is located between the vulvar and rectum, it can be used in fameles to treat various kinds of diseases in the genital and anus regions. Ren, Du and Chong Meridians pass through this point, and are called the three branches off the same origin. The Du Meridian dominates yang all over the body and goes up to the brain. The Chong Meridian is the sea of blood, and therefore it can also be used to treat mental diseases and gynecopathy.
【Method】 Puncture perpendicularly 0.5-1 cun. Be cautious to apply in pregnant women. Moxibustion is applicable.
【Acupoint Prescription】 Accident coma: Moxibustion to Huiyin (RN 1) and Sanyinjiao (SP 6). (*Experience on Acupuncture and Moxibustion Therapy*)
【Regional Anatomy】 Skin - subcutaneous - central tendon of perineum.
    There are the branches of the pudendal nerve and the branches or tributaries of the pudendal artery and vein.

RN 2 Qugu (曲骨)
(Crooked Bone)

【Source】 *A-B Classic of Acupuncture and Moxibustion*
【Name Explanation】 Qu (曲), crooked; Gu (骨), bone. Qugu refers to the pubic bone, and the point is at the superior margin of the pubic symphysis.
【Classification】 The Crossing Point of the Ren Meridian and the Liver Meridian of Foot Jueyin
【Location】 On the lower abdomen in the anterior midline, 5 cun below the center of the umbilicus, directly above the superior border of the pubic symphysis. (See Fig. 7-9)
【Localization】 Supine position, the point can be located at the midpoint of the upper margin of the pubic bone on the linea alba.
【Indications】
　1) Urinary Diseases: Lower abdominal distention, dribbling of urine, retention of urine, enuresis.
　2) Reproductive Diseases: Nocturnal emission, impotence, irregular menstruation, leukorrhagia with reddish discharge, sterility.
　3) Mental Disease: Depressive disorder.
　4) Other Diseases: Vulvar eczema, hernia, lower abdominal pain, edema, cramp in cholera morbus.
【Mechanism of Action】 This point belongs to the Ren Meridian, and can be used to treat man's hernia and woman's morbid leukorrhagia and abdominal mass. It is located below the lower abdomen, just between the reproductive system and the bladder. Therefore, it is the most commonly used point to treat both reproductive and urinary diseases.

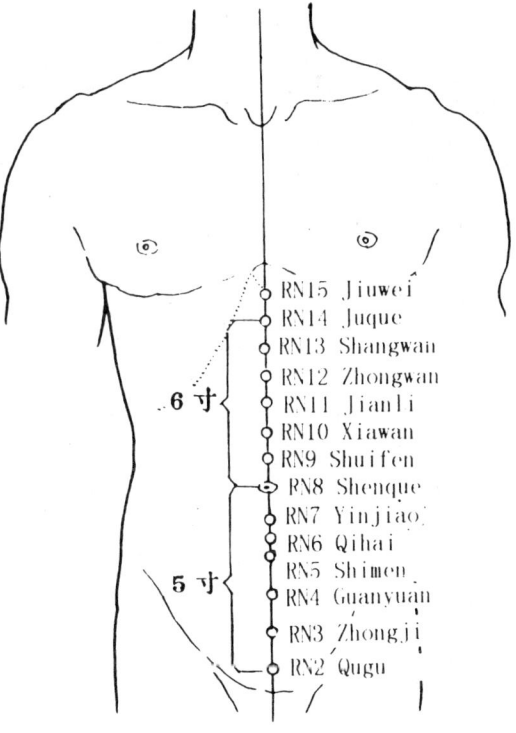

Fig. 7-9

【Method】 Puncture perpendicularly 1-1.5 cun, be cautious to apply in pregnant women. Moxibustion is applicable.
【Acupoint Prescriptions】
　1) Nocturnal emission: main points Qugu (RN 2), Sanyinjiao (SP 6) and Qihai (RN 6). Supplementary acupoints: Guanyuan (RN 4) and Shenshu (BL 23) with calmative method. (*Abstract of Clinical Experience on Acupuncture and Moxibustion*)
　2) Enuresis: Qugu (RN 2), Zhongji (RN 3), Sanyinjiao (SP 6), Baihui (DU 20) and Yintang (EX-HN3). (*ibid*)
　3) Prolapse of uterus: Qugu (RN 2), Henggu (KI 11) (both sides) and Qichong (ST 30). (*ibid*)
　4) Ejaculatory dysfunction: Qugu (RN 2), Yinlian (LR 11), Dadun (LR 1). (*Selection of Treatise of 30 Years*)
【Regional Anatomy】 Skin - subcutaneous tissue - linea alba - transverse fascia - extraperitoneal

fat tissue - parietal peritoneum. In the superficial layer, there are the anterior cutaneous branches of the iliohypogastric nerve and the tributaries of the superficial epigastricvein. In the deep layer, there are the branches of the iliohypogastric nerve.

【Remark】 It has dual-direction regulating effect on urinary tension. Punctruing this point can make the flaccid bladder contract and the tensive bladder relax. The effect depends on the needling manipulation, twisting the needle can make the bladder contract and the internal pressure rise, while stop twisting the needle can produce relaxation of the bladder and its internal pressure will decrease.

RN 3 Zhongji (中极)
(Middle Extremity)

【Source】 *Plain Questions*
【Name Explanation】 Zhong (中), center; Ji (极), exactly. The point is exactly "at the center" of the body.
【Classification】 Front-Mu Point of the urinary bladder, Crossing Point of the Ren Meridian and the three Yin Meridians of Foot
【Location】 On the lower abdomen and the anterior midline, 4 cun below the center of the umbilicus. (See Fig. 7-9)
【Localization】 Supine position, locate the point at the intersection between inferior one-fifth and superior four-fifths on the line joining the umbilicus and midpoint of the upper margin of the pubic bone.
【Indications】
　　1) Urinary Diseases: Dysuria, frequent micturition, urgency of urination, urodynia, enuresis.
　　2) Reproductive Diseases: Nocturnal emission, impotence, sterility, premature ejaculation, irregular menstruation, dysmenorrhea, uterine bleeding, prolapse of uterus, postpartum persistent lochia, retention of placenta, infertility.
　　3) Mental Disease: Corpse-like syncope.
　　4) Other Diseases: Hernia, abdominal mass, sensation of gas rushing.
【Mechanism of Action】 This point is the Front-Mu point of the bladder, belonging to the Ren Meridian. It is used to treat male hernia and female morbid leukorrhagia and abdominal masses. Therefore, it is the main point to treat the diseases of the urogenital system.
【Method】 Puncture perpendicularly 1-1.5 cun, be cautious to apply in pregnant women. Moxibustion is applicable.
【Acupoint Prescriptions】
　　1) Corps-like syncope: Zhongji (RN 3), Pucan (BL 61). (*A-B Classic of Acupuncture and Moxibustion*)
　　2) Pruritus vulvae: Zhongji (RN 3), Zhaohai (KI 6), Yaokaojiao (EX), Ququan (LR 8). (*Experience on Acupuncture and Moxibustion Therapy*)
　　3) Retention of placeta: Zhongji (RN 3), Jianjing (GB 21). (*Great Compendium of Acupuncture and Moxibustion*)
　　4) Penis pain of deficiency type: Zhongji (RN 3), Taixi (KI 3), Fuliu (KI 7), Sanyinjiao (SP 6). (*ibid*)
　　5) Irregular menstruation: Zhongji (RN 3), Shenshu (BL 23), Qihai (RN 6) and Sanyinjiao (SP 6). (*ibid*)
　　6) Uterine bleeding: Zhongji (RN 3), Zigong (EX-16). (*ibid*)
　　7) Postpartum persistent lochia: Zhongji (RN 3), Sanyinjiao (SP 6), Guanyuan (RN

4), Yingu (KI 10), Zhigou (SJ 6), Zusanli (ST 36), Fengfu (DU 16), Shenshu (BL 23), Yangguan (DU 3). (*New Science of Acupuncture and Moxibustion*)

〖Regional Anatomy〗 Skin – subcutaneous tissue – line alba – transverse fascia – extraperitoneal fat tissue – parietal peritoneum. In the superficial layer, there are the anterior cutaneous branches of the iliohypogastric nerve and the branches and tributaries of the superficial epigastric artery and vein. In the deep layer, there are the branches of the iliohypogastric nerve.

〖Remark〗 Puncturing this point has a regulating effect in patients with nervous system diseases complicated by bladder functional disorders. Puncturing Zhongji (RN 3) and Qugu (RN 2) with reducing method can decrease the tension of tensive bladder and strengthen that of a flaccid bladder. The most effective points for bladder function were found to be: Pangguangshu (BL 28), Ciliao (BL 32), Ququan (LR 8), Zhongji (RN 3) and Guanyuan (RN 4) (ordered according to the level of contracture). The following points were selected to do comparative treatment: (1) Pangguangshu (BL 28), Zhongji (RN 3) and Ciliao (BL 32); (2) Sanyinjiao (SP 6), Yinlingquan (SP 9) and Yingu (KI 10). The result showed that these points decreased the residual urine in patients with paraparesis.

RN 4 Guanyuan (关元)
(Life Pivot)

〖Source〗 *Miraculous Pivot and Plain Questions*

〖Name Explanation〗 Guan (关), storage; Yuan (元), primordial qi. This point is a storage place for the primordial qi of the body.

〖Classification〗 Front-Mu Point of the Small Intestine, one of the important points for tonification

〖Location〗 The lower abdomen on the anterior midline, 3 cun below the center of the umbilicus. (See Fig. 7-9)

〖Localization〗 Supine position, locate the point at the intersection between the inferior two-fifths and superior three-fifths of the line joining the umbilicus and the midpoint of the upper margin of the pubic bone.

〖Indications〗

1) Respiratory Diseases: Cough, asthma, hemoptoic cough, lack of strength in speaking, tuberculosis of the lung.

2) Digestive Diseases: Cholera morbus, vomiting, diarrhea, abdominal pain, dysentery, bloody stools, chronic diarrhea and dysentery, jaundice, thirsty.

3) Urinary Diseases: Frequent micturition, retention of urine, hematuria, dribbling of urine, enuresis.

4) Reproductive Diseases: Nocturnal emission, impotence, premature ejaculation, gonorrhea, irregular menstruation, amenorrhea, uterine bleeding, leukorrhagia with reddish discharge, prolapse of uterus, itch of vulvae, postpartum persistent lochia, retention of placenta.

5) Mental Diseases: Prostration syndrome due to apoplexy, or summer heat, syncope, insomnia, dreaminess, poor memory.

6) Other Diseases: Consumptive disease, weakness and thin, lassitude in the waist and legs, palpitation and shortness of breath, apoplexy, lumbodorsal cellulitis, any type of furuncles.

〖Mechanism of Action〗 Being closely related to Yuan qi, this is one of the most important acupoints used to irrigate Yuan qi. Yuan qi is the basis of the vital activities of the body. Deficient Yuan qi may result in many diseases, such as, frequent micturition, enuresis in the urinary system, and nocturnal emission, impotence, premature ejaculation, irregular menstruaction and leukorrhagia with reddish discharge in the reproductive system. It is easy for Yuan qi to be injured as a result of cholera morbus causing vomiting and acute diarrhea. In order to recuperate depleted yang and rescue the patient from collapse, moxibustion to Guanyuan (RN 4) is applied. TCM considers that inspiration occurs through the lung, and improvement of inspiration is due to the kidney function, If the kidney fails to nourish lung qi, it may result in a lung Yin defiency. If the collaterals of the lung are damaged by deficient heat, this will lead to hemoptysis.

Deficiency of the kidney with dysfunction to support the heart can cause palpitation, shortness of breath and deteroration of the memory.

Lassitude in the limbs and exhaustion are both caused by Yuan qi deficiency. All these symptoms resulting from Yuan qi deficiency can be treated by applying Guanyuan (RN 4) as the main point, when there is prostration caused by apoplexy or summer heat, Guanyuan (RN 4) must be applied immediately with moxa to recuperate depleted Yang and rescue the patient from collapse.

[Method] Puncture perpendicularly 0.5-1 cun. Be cautious to apply in pregnant women. Moxibustion is applicable.

[Acupoint Prescriptions]

1) Retention of urine due to dysfunction of qi, dark urine: Guanyuan (RN 4), Yinlingquan (SP 9). (*A-B Classic of Acupuncture and Moxibustion*)

2) Stranguria caused by the passage of urinary stones: Moxibustion to Guanyuan (RN 4) with 30 moxa cones, then to Qimen (LR 14) 30 moxa cones. (*Thousand Golden Prescriptions*)

3) Feeling of gas ascending: Guanyuan (RN 4), Zhongji (RN 3), Yinjiao (RN 7), Shimen (RN 6), Siman (KI 14), Qimen (LR 14). (*Experience on Acupuncture and Moxibustion Therapy*)

4) Taiyin Syndrome of exogenous febrile disease: Guanyuan (RN 4), Mingmen (DU 4). (*Comprehension of Bianque's Medicine*)

5) Incontinence of stools: Guanyuan (RN 4), Dachangshu (BL 25). (*Great Compendium of Acupuncture and Moxibustion*)

6) Chronic bacterial dysentery: Guanyuan (RN 4), Qihai (RN 6), Shenshu (BL 23), Pishu (BL 20), Dachangshu (BL 25), Sanyinjiao (SP 6), Zusanli (ST 36). Apply moxibustion to 2-3 points mentioned above for 15 minutes every day. (*Science of Acupuncture and Moxibustion*)

7) Impotence: Guanyuan (RN 4), Sanyinjiao (SP 6), Shenshu (BL 23), Zusanli (ST 36). Apply acupuncture once every other day. Needle-embedding therapy can be applied to Sanyinjiao (SP 6) for 4-6 hours. (*ibid*)

8) Enuresis: Guanyuan (RN 4), Sanyinjiao (SP 6). (*Experience on Acupuncture and Moxibustion Therapy*)

9) Steriliey of Males: Guanyuan (RN 4), Diji (SP 8), Zusanli (ST 36), Sanyinjiao (SP 6), Rangu (KI 2). (*ibid*)

[Regional Anatomy] Skin – subcutaneous tissue – linea alba – transversefascia – extraperitoneal fat tissue – parietal peritoneum. In the superficial layer, there are the anterior cutaneous branches of the anterior branch of the 12th thoracic nerve and the branch tributaries of the superficial epigastric artery and vein. In the deep layer, there are the branches of the anterior branch of the 12th thoracic nerve.

[Remark] This point can be used to regulate the bladder tension, effectively treat enuresis and improve the function of the hypophysial-gonadel aris system. It is reported that puncturing such points as Zhongji (RN 3), Guanyuan (RN 4), Dahe (KI 12) and so on, can make the level of plasma luteotropic and follicule-stimulating hormone (FSH) change and improve ovulation. The point can also be used to treat azoospermatism with a certain effect.

RN 5 Shimen (石门)
(Stone Gate)

【Source】 A-B Classic of Acupuncture and Moxibustion
【Name Explanation】 Shi (石), stone; Men (门), door. Stone here means "hard", the point is used for treating lumps in the lower abdomen.
【Classification】 Front-Mu Point of Sanjiao
【Location】 The lower abdomen on the anterior midline, 2 cun below the center of the umbilicus. (See Fig. 7-9)
【Localization】 Supine position, locate the point at the intersection between superior two-fifths and inferior three-fifths of the line joining the umbilicus and the midpoint of the upper margin of the pubic bone.
【Indications】

1) Digestive Diseases: Abdominal distention, diarrhea, dysentery, constipation, indigestion, vomiting.

2) Urinary Diseases: Dribbling of urine, frequent micturition, urgency of urination, urodynia, hematuria, enuresis, retention of urine.

3) Reproductive Diseases: Nocturnal emission, impotence, premature ejaculation, sterility, irregular menstruation, amenorrhea, leukorrhagia with reddish discharge, metrorrhagia and metrostaxis, postpartum persistent lochia, retention of placenta.

4) Other Diseases: feeling of gas ascending, hernia, retraction of the penis.

【Mechanism of Action】 Dantian, another name of Shimen (RN 5), Qihai (RN 6) and Guanyuan (RN 4), are where Yuan qi is nourished, invigorated and regulated. Therefore, it plays an important role in the restoration of Yuan qi and also in the treatment of the diseases caused by the deficiency of Yuan qi in the reproductive, urinary and digestive systems.

Shimen (RN 5) is located in the lower abdomen, below which is the reproductive system, the bladder and the small intestine. In accordance with the principles on the local function of the acupoints, all the diseases of Zangfu organs in the area, both deficient and excess syndrome can be treated by using this acupoint.

【Method】 Puncture perpendicularly 1-2 cun. Contraindicated to apply in pregnant women. Moxibustion is applicable.
【Acupoint Prescriptions】

1) Lower abdominal pain radiating to the external genitalia: Shimen (RN 5), Shangqiu (SP 5). (*Thousand Golden Prescriptions*)

2) Contraction and pain in the lower abdomen: Shimen (RN 5), Shuifen (RN 9). (*Experience on Acupuncture and Moxibustion Therapy*)

3) Artificial abortion: Shimen (RN 5), Sanyinjiao (SP 6). (*Great Compendium of Acupuncture and Moxibustion*)

【Regional Anatomy】 Skin - subcutaneous tissue - linea alba - transverse fascia - extraperitoneal fat tissue - parietal peritoneum. In the superficial layer, there are the anterior cutaneous branches of the anterior branches of the 11th thoracic nerve and the tributaries of the superficial epigastric vein. In the deep layer, there are the branches of the anterior branches of the 11th thoracic nerve.

RN 6 Qihai (气海)
(Qi Sea)

【Source】 Mai Jing. Also named "Boyang" in Miraculous Pivot

【Name Explanation】 Qi (气), primary qi; Hai (海), sea. The point, found below the navel, is the sea of the primary qi of the whole body.

【Location】 On the lower abdomen and the anterior midline, 1.5 cun below the center of the umbilicus. (See Fig. 7-9)

【Localization】 Supine position, first locate Guanyuan (RN 4), the point is located at the midpoint between the umbilicus and Guanyuan (RN 4).

【Indications】

1) Respiratory Diseases: Cough, asthma, shortness of breath

2) Digestive Diseases: Pain and distention of the stomach, hiccup, vomiting, indigestion, constipation, dysentery, acute vomiting and diarrhea

3) Reproductive Diseases: Nocturnal emission, impotence, premature ejaculation, sterility, irregular menstruation, dysmenorrhea, amenorrhea, metrorrhagia and metrostaxis, leukorrhea with reddish discharge, prolapse of uterus, postpartum persistent lochia, retention of placenta.

4) Mental Diseases: Collapse syndrome of apoplexy, or summer heat, acute infantile omphalitis.

5) Other Diseases: Hernia, pain of the waist, pain around umbilicus, cold limbs, shortness of breath due to qi deficiency of five Zang organs, asthma, emaciation, acratia, infantile metopism.

【Mechanism of Action】 Since such acupoints as Qihai (RN 6), Guanyuan (RN 4) and Shimen (RN 5) perform an important function in tonifying Yuan qi, they can be used to treat collapse syndrome of Yuan qi deficiency.

Compared with Guanyuan (RN 4) and Shimen (RN 5), this acupoint can also be used to promote the circulation of qi, as well as to tonify Yuan qi.

【Method】 Puncture perpendicularly 1-2 cun. Moxibustion is applicable.

【Acupoint Prescriptions】

1) Slow Chi pulse, cold retention in the lower Jiao: Qihai (RN 6), Guanyuan (RN 4). (Classic of the Pulse)

2) Uterine bleeding: Qihai (RN 6), Shimen (RN 5). (ibid)

3) Abdominal mass: Qihai (RN 6), Tianshu (ST 25) (Moxibustion with one hundred moxa-cones). (Experience on Acupuncture and Moxibustion Therapy)

4) Collapse syndrome of Yuan qi: Moxibustion to Qihai (RN 6), Guanyuan (RN 4), Shimen (RN 5) (300 moxa-cones for each point). (Comprehension of Bianque's Experience)

5) Irregular menstruation: Qihai (RN 6), Zhongji (RN 3), Daimai (GB 26) (one moxa-cone), Shenshu (BL 23), Sanyinjiao (SP 6). (ibid)

6) Leukorrhagia with reddish discharge: Qihai (RN 6), Zhongji (RN 3), Baihuanshu (BL 30), Shenshu (BL 23). (Great Compendium of Acupuncture and Moxibustion)

7) Enuresis: Qihai (RN 6), Guanyuan (RN 4), Yinlingquan (SP 9), Dadun (LR 1), Xingjian (LR 2). (Illustrated Supplementary to the Classified Canon)

8) Acute bacterial dysentery: Qihai (RN 6), Tianshu (ST 25), Shangjuxu (ST 37). (Selection of Treatise of 30 Years)

9) Deficiency syndrome: Qihai (RN 6), Guanyuan (RN 4). (Songs on Guiding for Acupuncture)

10) Five stranguria: Qihai (RN 6), Zusanli (ST 36). (*Songs of Xihong*)
11) Five stranguria: Qihai (RN 6), Xuehai (SP 10). (*Songs of Lingguang*)

[Regional Anatomy] Skin – subcutaneous tissue – linea alba – transverse fascia – extraperitoneal fat tissue – parietal peritoneum. In the superficial layer, there are the anterior cutaneous branches of the anterior branch of the 11th thoracic nerve and the periumbilical venousnetwork. In the deep layer, there are the branches of the anterior branch of the 11th thoracic nerve.

[Remark] Qihai (RN 6) can be used to strengthen the immunity.

Puncturing the point can relieve the following symptoms and quicken recovery: acute or chronic gastroentertis, bacterial dysentery, diarrhea and constipation. It indicates Qihai (RN6) and has a good regulatory effect. It's also reported that puncturing Qihai (RN 6) and Tianshu (ST 25) in patients with acute bacterial dysentery can cause all the immunoglobulins (IgG, IgA, IgM) rose in different extents. This increase degree was very obvious within three days of the acupuncture treatment.

Puncturing Qihai (RN 6) perpendicularly in patients with hephritis can improve the urinary function of the kidney, increase renalsulfonphthalein excretion, decrease urinary protein and lower blood pressure, the effect may generally last for 2-3 hours and in some cases for several days. It is also reported that ginger-separated moxibustion to Qihai (RN 6) is effective to treat azoospermia.

RN 7 Yinjiao (阴交)
(Yin Meeting)

[Source] *A-B Classic of Acupuncture and Moxibustion*

[Name Explanation] Yin (阴), yin of Yin-Yang; Jiao (交), crossing. This point is the crossing point of the Renmai (Conception Vessel), the Chongmai (Throughfare Vessel) and the Kidney Meridian.

[Classification] The Crossing Point of the Ren and Chong Meridians

[Location] The lower abdomen on the anterior midline, 1 cun below the center of the umbilicus. (See Fig. 7-9)

[Localization] Supine position, locate the point at the midpoint on the line joining the umbilicus and Shimen (RN 5), or locate the point at the intersection of the superior one-fifths and inferior four-fifths distance between the umbilicus and the midpoint of the upper margin of the pubic bone.

[Indications]
1) Digestive Diseases: Diarrhea, borborygmus, abdominal distention, chronic diarrhea and dysentery.
2) Urinary Diseases: Retention of urine, abdominal fullness, edema.
3) Reproductive Diseases: Irregular menstruation, leukorrhagia with reddish discharge, postpartum persistent lochia, retention of placenta
4) Other Diseases: Hernia, lumbago.

[Mechanism of Action] Deep under the area of this point are the starting part of the mesentery of small intestine, greater omentum and inferior vena cavam, and the uterus and bladder are also here. This point is commonly used to treat intestinal diseases, post partum persistent lochia and retention of placenta according to the local function of the points.

Corresponding to the front and back of the forth and fifth lumber vertebrae, this acupoint can be used to treat pain of the waist and sacrum according to the corresponding function of the points.

[Method] Puncture perpendicularly 1-2 cun. Moxibustion is applicable.

【Acupoint Prescriptions】

1) Epilepsy due to fright: Yinjiao (RN 7), Qihai (RN 6), Daju (ST 27). (*Thousand Golden Prescriptions*)
2) Retention of urine (pain and rigidity in lower abdomen radiating to the external genital organs): Yinjiao (RN 7), Shimen (RN 5), Weiyang (BL 39). (*ibid*)
3) Metrorrhagia and metrostaxis: Yinjiao (RN 7), Shimen (RN 5). (*Experience on Acupuncture and Moxibustion Therapy*)
4) Vertigo due to blood deficiency: Yinjiao (RN 7), Sanyinjiao (SP 6), Yangchi (SJ 4). (*Secret Secret on Acupuncture and Moxibustion*)
5) Sterility: Yinjiao (RN 7), Shiguan (KI 18). (*Songs of Hundreds of Symptoms*)
6) Fullness of the chest and diaphragm: Yinjiao (RN 7), Chengshan (BL 57). (*Secret Songs of Chang Sangjun*)

【Regional Anatomy】 Skin — subcutaneous tissue — linea alba--transverse fascia — extraperitoneal fat tissue — parietal peritoneum. In the superficial layer, there are the anterior cutaneous branches of the anterior branch of the 11th thoracic nerve and the periumbilical venous network. In the deep layer, there are the branches of the anterior branch of the 11th thoracic nerve.

RN 8 Shenque (神阙)
(Spirit Palace)

【Source】 *Illustrated Manual of Points for Acupuncture and Moxibustion on a Bronze Status with Acupoints*

【Name Explanation】 Shen (神), spirit; Que (阙), palace gate. The point is at the center of the navel which is an important passage for the circulation of the fetal qi and blood, like a palace gate of the qi of spirit.

【Location】 The middle abdomen at the center of the umbilicus. (See Fig. 7-9)

【Localization】 Supine position, locate the point at the center of the umbilicus.

【Indications】

1) Digestive Diseases: Diarrhea, dysentery, constipation, cholera morbus difficult stools.
2) Urinary Diseases: Enuresis, retention of urine, edema, stranguria.
3) Reproductive Diseases: Irregular menstruation, metrorrhagia and metrostaxisuterine, , sterility.
4) Mental Diseases: Collapse syndrome of apoplexy, collapse syndrome of summer heat, syncope, loss of consciousness, opisthotonos, exhaustion syndrome.
5) Other Diseases: Cold in the lower extremities, tidal fever and night sweating, anaphylaxis, allergic urticaria, allergic bronchial asthma, allergic enterities etc., hernia, pain around umbilicus, general acratia.

【Mechanism of Action】 Sun Si-miao said that the name of every acupoint has its deep significance. "Shenque" refers to the entrance where Shen and qi pass through and the place where the fetus is nourished to grow. Thus this acupoint has such physiological characteristics as the source from which life comes, the position where vessels converge and the place where primary qi is linked with. As a result, it can be used to treat the diseases caused by digestive and mental diseases, specifically in the deficient syndromes and exhaustion syndrome. It has been clinically proven that this point is the most efficient point to treat tidal fever and night sweating due to yin deficiency, anaphylaxis and any type of allergic reactions.

【Method】 Needling is prohibited. Moxibustion is applicable.

【Acupoint Prescriptions】

1) Abdominal distention like a drum: Shenque (RN 8), Gongsun (SP 4). (*Experience*

on Acupuncture and Moxibustion Therapy)

2) Borborygmus and diarrhea: Shenque (RN 8), Shuifen (RN 9), Sanyinjiao (SP 6). (Great Compendium of Acupuncture and Moxibustion)

3) Five types of stranguries: Salt moxibustion to Shenque (RN 7) with 7 cones, moxibustion to Sanyinjiao (SP 6) (A Collection of Gems in Acupuncture and Moxibustion)

【Regional Anatomy】 Skin – connective tissue – parietal peritoneum. In the superficial layer, there are the anterior cutaneous branches of the anterior branch of the 10th thoracic nerve and the periumbilical venous network on the abdomen wall. In the deep layer, there are the branches of the anterior branch of the 10th thoracic nerve.

RN 9 Shuifen (水分)
(Water Divisions)

【Source】 A-B Classic of Acupuncture and Moxibustion
【Name Explanation】 Shui (水), water and food; Fen (分), separation. The point is 1 cun above the navel and corresponds internally to the small intestine, where water and food are separated into turbid and clear.
【Location】 On the upper abdomen and the anterior midline, 1 cun above the center of the umbilicus. (See Fig. 7-9)
【Localization】 Supine position, locate the point at the intersection of inferior one-eighth and superior seven-eighths distance between the seventh costosternal juncture and the umbilicus.
【Indications】
1) Digestive Diseases: Pain around umbilicus, borborygmus, diarrhea, regurgitation, anorexia, prolapse of the rectum, difficult defecation.
2) Urinary Diseases: Edema, retention of urine.
3) Other Diseases: Hernia, stiffiness and pain along the spinal column.
【Mechanism of Action】 The small intestine serves to digest and absorb nutrients. As this point is located below the small intestine, it can be applied to treat borborygmus, diarrhea, regurgitation and edema.
【Method】 Puncture perpendicularly 1-2 cun. Moxibustion is applicable.
【Acupoint Prescriptions】
1) Numbness and pain in abdomen: Shuifen (RN 9), Shimen (RN 5). (Thousand Golden Prescriptions)
2) Regurgitation and vomiting: Shuifen (RN 9), Qihai (RN 6). (Experience on Acupuncture and Moxibustion Therapy)
3) Pain around abdomen: Shuifen (RN 9), Shenque (RN 8), Qihai (RN 6). (Great Compendium of Acupuncture and Moxibustion)
4) Exanthema and filthy diseases: Shuifen (RN 9), Bailao (EX), Daling (PC 7), Weizhong (BL 40). (ibid)
5) Ascites: Shuifen (RN 9), Tianshu (ST 25), Sanyinjiao (SP 6), Diji (SP 8), Zusanli (ST 36). (New Acupuncture and Moxibustion)
6) Edema of abdomen: Shuifen (RN 9), Jianli (RN 11). (Secret Songs of Chang Sangjun)
7) Edema: Shuifen (RN 9), Fuliu (KI 7). (Songs of Point Selection on Miscellaneous Diseases)
8) Edema: Shuifen (RN 9), Qihai (RN 6). (Songs of Xihong)
【Regional Anatomy】 Skin – subcutaneous tissue – linea alba – transverse fascia – extraperitoneal fat tissue – parietal peritoneum. In the superficial layer, there are the anterior cutaneous branch-

es of the anterior branch of the 9th thoracic nerve and the superficial epigastric vein. In the deep layer, there are the branches of the anterior branch of the 9th thoracic nerve.

RN 10 Xiawan (下脘)
(Lower Part of Stomach)

【Source】 *Miraculous Pivot*

【Name Explanation】 Xia (下), inferior; Wan (脘), stomach. The point is at the inferior position of the stomach.

【Classification】 Crossing Point of the Ren Meridian and the Spleen Meridian of Foot Taiyin

【Location】 The upper abdomen on the anterior midline, 2 cun above the center of the umbilicus. (See Fig. 7-9)

【Localization】 Supine position, locate the point at the intersection of inferior one-fourth and superior three-fourths distance between the seventh costosternal juncture and umbilicus, or locate the point 1 cun directly above Shuifen (RN 9).

【Indications】
　1) Digestive Diseases: Stomachache, abdominal distention and pain, vomiting, hiccups, indigestion, borborygmus, diarrhea.
　2) Urinary Disease: Dark urine

【Mechanism of Action】 The transverse colon, the stomach and the pancreas are below this acupoint. According to the local function of acupoints, it can be used to treat gastroenteric diseases.

【Method】 Puncture perpendicularly 1-2 cun. Moxibustion is applicable.

【Acupoint Prescriptions】
　1) Emaciation: Xiawan (RN 10), Weishu (BL 21), Pishu (BL 20), Xialian (LI 8). (*Experience on Acupuncture and Moxibustion Therapy*)
　2) Regurgitation (of food from stomach): Xiawan (RN 10), Zusanli (ST 36). (*ibid*)
　3) Dysentery and tenesmus: Moxibustion to Xiawan (RN 10), Tianshu (ST 25), Zhaohai (KI 6). (*Classic on Miraculous Moxibustion*)
　4) Borborygmus: Xiawan (RN 10), Xiangu (ST 43). (*Songs of Hundreds of Symptoms*)
　5) Acute Bacterial Dysentery: Xiawan (RN 10), Tianshu (ST 25), Qihai (RN 6), Guanyuan (RN 4), Zusanli (ST 36). (*Abstract of Clinical Experience on Acupuncture and Moxibustion*)

【Regional Anatomy】 Skin — subcutaneous tissue — linea alba — transverse fascia — extraperitoneal fat tissue — parietal peritoneum. In the superficial layer, there are the anterior cutaneous branches of the anterior branch of the 9th thoracic nerve and the superficial epigastric vein. In the deep layer, there are the branches of the anterior branch of the 9th thoracic nerve.

【Remark】 For intestinal dysfunction, puncturing Xiawan (RN 10) can make it normal. Puncturing the point can make gastroduodenal ulcers and gastric juice secretion mantain high secreting state, but the gastric total acidity and free acidity tend to be normal. There are experiments indicating that puncturing Xiawan (RN 10) could improve the immunity.

RN 11 Jianli (建里)
(Building Li)

【Source】 *A-B Classic of Acupuncture and Moxibustion*

【Name Explanation】 Jian (建), establishing; Li (里), interior. This point located in the epigastric region, aids in establishing the qi of the Middle Jiao.
【Location】 The upper abdomen on the anterior midline, 3 cun above the center of the umbilicus. (See Fig. 7-10)
【Localization】 Supine position, locate the point at the intersection of the inferior three-eighths and superior five-eighths distance between the seventh costosternal juncture and the umbilicus, or locate the point 1 cun directly superior to Xiawan (RN 10).
【Indications】
　　1) Digestive Diseases: Stomachache, abdominal distention, vomiting, anorexia, borborygmus, cholera morbus.
　　2) Other Diseases: Cardiac pain, fullness of chest with difficulty breathing, edema.
【Mechanism of Action】 Below this acupoint is the stomach, the liver and the pancreas. Therefore, it is used to treat diseases of the upper abdomen.
【Method】 Puncture perpendicularly 1-2 cun. Moxibustion is applicable.
【Acupoint Prescription】 Oppressed feeling in the chest with difficult breath: Jianli (RN 11), Neiguan (PC 6). (*Songs of Hundreds of Symptoms*)
【Regional Anatomy】 Skin – subcutaneous tissue – linea alba – transversefascia – extraperitoneal fat tissue – parietal peritoneum. In the superficial layer, there are the anterior cutaneous branches of the anterior branch of the 8th thoracic nerve and the superficial epigastric vein. In the deep layer, there are the branches of the anterior branch of the 8th thoracic nerve.

RN 12 Zhongwan (中脘) (Middle Part of Stomach)

【Source】 *The Classic of Sphygmology*
【Name Explanation】 Zhong (中), middle; Wan (脘), stomach. The point is at the middle of the stomach.
【Classification】 Front-Mu Point of the stomach. Influential Point of the fu organs, the crossing point of Hand Taiyang, Hand Shaoyang and Foot Yangming meridians
【Location】 The upper abdomen on the anterior midline, 4 cun above the center of the umbilicus. (See Fig. 7-9)
【Localization】 Supine position, locate the point at the midpoint between the seventh costosternal juncture and umbilicus.
【Indications】
　　1) Respiratory Diseases: Asthma, profuse phlegm, consumptive diseases, hematemesis.
　　2) Digestive Diseases: Gastric pain, abdominal distention, vomiting, hiccup, nausea,, acid-regurgitation, anorexia, indigestion, infantile malnutrition, abdominal pain, borborygmus, diarrhea, cholera morbus, bloody stools, constipation, edema, jaundice.
　　3) Cardiovascular Diseases: Palpitation, cardiac pain.
　　4) Gynecopathies: Hysteroptosis, pernicious vomiting.
　　5) Mental Diseases: Insomnia, hysteria, manic-depressive disorder, epilepsy, apoplexy, syncope, acute or chornic infantile convulsion, postpartum syncope due to excess of bleeding.
　　6) Other Diseases: Urticaria, dark yellow complexion, lassitude, syncope due to summer heat, fever, dark urine, burnt and foul smell in the nose.
【Mechanism of Action】 This acupoint is the Front-Mu point if the stomach and is effective to treat diseases of the spleen and stomach. It can also be used to treat not only diseases of the stomach such as stomachache, vomiting, indigestion, diarrhea, etc, but also many other diseases due to hypofunction of the stomach and spleen. The spleen and stomach correspond to earth ac-

cording to the theory of the Five Elements. If the spleen and the stomach fail to perform their function normally, and earth (the spleen) fails to generate metal (the lung), diseases of the lung such as asthma, excessive phlegm, consumption and hematemesis will appear.

Palpitation, insomnia, hysteria, manic-depressive disorder and epilepsy are caused by the insufficient growth and development of the spleen and stomach, lack of nourishment of the heart, or excessive salivation due to malfunction of the spleen. The retention of dampness in the middle Jiao is manifested as urticaria and jaudice. The ascending heat from the stomach leads to the burnt and foul smell in the nose.

To generate a permanent cure for diseases caused by the pathological changes of the stomach caused by itself or resulting from the failure of the spleen and the stomach, this point is the best choice.

[Method] Puncture perpendicularly 1-2 cun. Moxibustion is applicable.

[Acupoint Prescriptions]

1) Jaundice: Zhongwan (RN 12), Daling (PC 7), Laogong (PC 8), Zusanli (ST 36), Rangu (KI 2), Taixi (KI 3). (*A Supplement to Thousand Golden Prescriptions*)

2) Regurgitation: If there is not effect after taking medicine, apply moxibustion immediately to Zhongwan (RN 12) and Zusanli (ST 36) (7 or 9 moxa-cones for every point). (*Prescriptions for Saving Life*)

3) Long-lasting dysentery: Moxibustion to Zhongwan (RN 12), Pishu (BL 20), Tianshu (ST 25), Sanjiaoshu (BL 22), Dachangshu (BL 25), Zusanli (ST 36), Sanyinjiao (SP 6). (*Classic on Miraculous Moxibustion*)

4) Gastritis, peptic ulcer: Zhongwan (RN 12), Jianli (RN 11) or with Zhangmen (LR 13), Tianshu (ST 25); add Neiguan (PC 6) in case of vomiting. (*Science of Acupuncture and Moxibustion*)

5) Acute or chronic gastritis: Zhongwan (RN 12), Jianli (RN 11), Zusanli (ST 36) (both sides for the three points); add right Liangmen (ST 21) in case of abdominal pain in right side; add left Liangmen (ST 21) in case of abdominal pain in left side; add Ashi points in case of pain in the shoulder and back. (*Abstract of Clinical Experience on Acupuncture and Moxibustion*)

6) Phlegm syndrome: Zhongwan (RN 12), Zusanli (ST 36). (*Songs of Aucpuncture Techniques*)

7) Vomiting: Zhongwan (RN 12), Qihai (RN 6), Danzhong (RN 17). (*ibid*)

8) Cholera morbus: Zhongwan (RN 12), Zusanli (ST 36). (*Songs of Point Selection on Miscellaneous Diseases*)

9) Fullness of abdomen: Zhongwan (RN 12), Qihai (RN 6), Danzhong (RN 17). (*ibid*)

10) Abdominal tenderness: Zhongwan (RN 12), Xiawan (RN 10). (*Songs of Lingguang*)

[Regional Anatomy] Skin – subcutaneous tissue – linea alba – transverse fascia – extraperitoneal fat tissue – parietal peritoneum. In the superficial layer, there are the anterior cutaneous branches of the anterior branch of the 9th thoracic nerve and the superficial epigastric vein. In the deep layer, there are the branches of the anterior branch of the 9th thoracic nerve.

[Remark] The regulating effect of the point over the gastrointestinal function is related to the different original functional conditions and the needling manipulations, i. e. it could strengthen gastrointestinal peristalsis if they are originally flaccid or in moderate peristalsis states, but it has no obvious influence in normal peristalsis conditions. Weak stimulation could improve gastric peristalsis, while the strong needling acts with inhibitory effect. Puncturing the point could improve gastric acid secretion, increase pulmanary rest ventilation volume, oxygen consumption and maximum ventilation volume.

The point also has a regulating effect on bladder tension, the tension will weaken if the bladder is originally tense, and it will strengthen if the bladder is orginally relaxed.

The point could also impact blood, and increase both WBC and neutrophils. It's also effective in leukopenia caused by hypersplenism.

RN 13 Shangwan （上脘）
(Upper Part of Stomach)

【Source】 *Miraculous Pivot*
【Name Explanation】 Shang （上）, superior; Wan （脘）, stomach. The point is at the upper portion of the stomach.
【Classification】 Crossing Point of the Ren Meridian, Foot Yangming and Hand Taiyang Meridians
【Location】 The upper abdomen on the anterior midline, 5 cun above the center of the umbilicus. (See Fig. 7-9)
【Localization】 Supine position, locate the point at the intersection of the superior three-eighths and inferior five-eighths distance between the seventh costosternal juncture and the umbilicus, or locate the point 1 cun directly above Zhongwan (RN 12).
【Indications】
    1) Respiratory Diseases: Cough, asthma, profuse phlegm, hemoptysis
    2) Digestive Diseases: Gastric pain, abdominal distention and pain, borborygmus, diarrhea, cholera morbus, vomiting, hiccup, anorexia, hyperemesis, jaundice.
    3) Cardiovascular Dsieases: Angenia pectoris, restlessness palpitation.
    4) Mental Diseases: Manic-depressive psychosis, epilepsy, dizziness and blurred vision.
    5) Other Disease: Fever with anhidrosis.
【Mechanism of Action】 See Zhongwan (RN 12).
【Method】 Puncture perpendicularly 1-1.5 cun. Moxibustion is applicable.
【Acupoint Prescriptions】
    1) Full pulse in Cun position, full sensation in the chest and hypochondrium: Shangwan (RN 13), Qimen (LR 14), Zhangmen (LR 13). (*Classic of Pulse*)
    2) Hematemesis: Shangwan (RN 13), Burong (SI 19), Daling (PC 7). (*Thousand Golden Prescriptions*)
    3) Indigestion due to coldness in the middle Jiao and overeating: Shangwan (RN 13), Zhongwan (RN 12). (*Experience on Acupuncture and Moxibustion Therapy*)
    4) Severe pain of the chest without vomiting or diarrhea: Shangwan (RN 13), Zhongwan (RN 12), Xiawan (RN 10), Pishu (BL 20), Sanyinjiao (SP 6). (*ibid*)
    5) Nine kinds of heart pain: Shangwan (RN 13), Zhongwan (RN 12). (*Songs of Jade Dragon*)
    6) Depressive Disorder: Shangwan (RN 13), Shenmen (HT 7). (*Songs of Hundreds of Symptoms*)
【Regional Anatomy】 Skin - subcutaneous tissue - linea alba - transverse fascia - extraperitoneal fat tissue - parietal peritoneum. In the superficial layer, there are the anterior cutaneous branches of the anterior branch of the 7th thoracic nerve and the superficial epigastric vein. In the deep layer, there are the branches of the anterior branch of the 7th thoracic nerve.
【Remark】 Puncturing Shangwan (RN 13) has a certain therapeutic effect on gastroduodenal ulcer, it can alleviate symptoms, promote the healing of ulcer and influence the gastric acid secrection.

RN 14 Juque (巨阙)
(Great Palace)

【Source】 *Classic of the Pulse*
【Name Explanation】 Ju (巨), great; Que (阙), palace gate. This is a Front-(Mu) Point of the heart, like a door for the qi of the heart.
【Classification】 Front-Mu point of the heart
【Location】 On the upper abdomen and the anterior midline, 6 cun above the center of the umbilicus. (See Fig. 7-9)
【Localization】 Supine position, locate the point at the intersection of superior one-fourth and inferior three-fourths distance between the seventh costosternal juncture and the umbilicus, or locate the point at the midpoint of Zhongwan (RN 12) and the seventh costosternal juncture.
【Indications】
 1) Respiratory Diseases: Fullness of the chest, shortness of breath, cough, asthma, hemoptysis.
 2) Digestive Diseases: Stomachache, upper abdominal distention, cholera morbus, vomiting, dysphagia, acid swallow, diarrhea, dysentery, pain of the chest due to ascariasis, jaundice.
 3) Cardiovascular Diseases: Oppressed feeling in the chest, pain of the chest, restlessness, palpitation.
 4) Mental Diseases: Palpitation, corpse-like syncope, manic-depressive psychosis, epilepsy, poor memory, insomnia.
 5) Other Diseases: Beriberi, hernia.
【Mechanism of Action】 This acupoint is one of the twelve Front-(Mu) Points. This is related to the heart. The heart controls mental activities and blood circulation. Therefore it can be used to treat angiocardiopathy and mental diseases.
 Located above the stomach and liver, the acupoint is usually used to treat digestive diseases. Various kinds of diseases of the respiratory system due to the failure of earth (spleen) to generate metal (Lung) or adverse rising of the stomach qi can be treated with this acupoint.
【Method】 Puncture obliquely downwards 0.5-1 cun. Moxibustion is applicable.
【Acupoint Prescriptions】
 1) Cholera morbus: Juque (RN 14), Guanchong (SJ 1), Zhigou (SJ 6), Gongsun (SP 4), Jiexi (ST 41). (*A-B Classic of Acupuncture and Moxibustion*)
 2) Rapid Guan pulse, heat in the stomach: Juque (RN 14), Shangwan (RN 13). (*Classic of the Pulse*)
 3) Shortness of breath: Juque (RN 14), Jiexi (ST 41), Rangu (KI 2), Chize (LU 5). (*Experience on Acupuncture and Moxibustion Therapy*)
 4) Heavy oppressive feeling in the chest: Juque (RN 14), Hegu (LI 4) (tonifying method), Sanyinjiao (SP 6) (reducing method). (*Great Compendium of Acupuncture and Moxibustion*)
 5) Rheumatic cardiac disease: Juque (RN 14), Jianshi (PC 5), Yanglingquan (GB 34). (*Abstract of Clinical Experience on Acupuncture and Moxibustion*)
【Regional Anatomy】 Skin - subcutaneous tissue - linea alba - transverse fascia - extraperitoneal fat tissue - parietal peritoneum. In the superficial layer, there are the anterior cutaneous branches of the anterior branch of the 7th thoracic nerve and the superficial epigastric vein. In the deep layer, there are the branches of the anterior branch of the 7th thoracic nerve.
【Remark】 Puncturing Juque (RN14) has obvious effect on gastroptosia. The point should be

punctured with a long needle 7 cun in length from Juque (RN 14) to the left Huangshu (KI 16), after the needle is inserted in the point, lift the needle handle to a 45° angle with the skin, and slowly ascend the needle. The first time for 10 minutes, and then for 3-5 minutes every time, once every two days, and 10 times as a treatment course.

RN 15 Jiuwei (鸠尾)
(Dove Tail)

[Source] *Miraculous Pivot and Plain Questions*
[Name Explanation] Jiu (鸠), turtledove; Wei (尾), tail. The point is below the xiphoid process of the sternum, which resembles a turtledove's tail.
[Classification] Luo-(Connecting)Point of the Ren Meridian
[Location] The upper abdomen on the anterior midline, 1 cun below the xiphosternal synchondrosis. (See Fig. 7-9, 7-10)

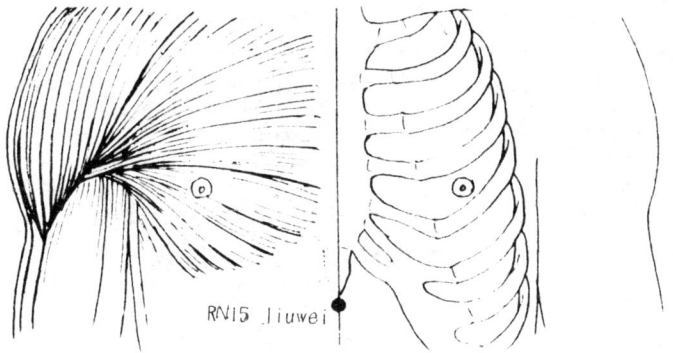

Fig. 7-10

[Localization] Supine position, locate the point at the intersection of the superior one-eighth and inferior seven-eighths distance between the seventh costosternal juncture and umbilicus, or locate the point 1 cun directly above Juque (RN 14).
[Indications]
  1) Diseases of the Head and Sense Organs: Migraine, sore throat.
  2) Cardiovascular Diseases: Cardiac pain, palpitation, restlessness, oppressive feeling in the chest, pain of the chest, shortness of breath, listlessness.
  3) Digestive Diseases: Vomiting, hiccups, regurgitation (of food from stomach) pain of the stomach, abdominal distention.
  4) Mental Diseases: Maniac-depressive disorder, epilepsy, hysteria.
  5) Other Diseases: Prolapse of rectum, sexual excess, exhaustion of spirit, sunken fontanel in infant.
[Mechanism of Action] Juque (RN 14) and Jiuwei (RN 15) are proved acupoints for treating epilepsy, which is related to phlegm. To treat epilepsy, phlegm must be eliminated first. The function of Jiuwei (RN 15) is to regulate the stomach and spleen and to clear away pathogenic phlegm.
  This point is the Yuan-(Source) point. It is believed in traditional Chinese medicine that excessive sexual activity impairs the essence of people. This point can be used to treat many

symptoms, such as exhaustion of spirit, shortness of breath, listlessness due to excessive sexual activity.
【Method】 Puncture obliquely downwards 0.5 cun.
【Acupoint Prescriptions】
　　1) Infantile epilepsy: Moxibustion to Jiuwei (RN 15). (*Peaceful Holy Benevolent Prescriptions*)
　　2) Shortness of breath in youth due to excessive sexual activity: Moxibustion to Jiuwei (RN 15) (with 50 moxa-cones, Shenque (RN 8) with salt 27 moxa-cones). (*Experience on Acupuncture and Moxibustion Therapy*)
　　3) Cold in the heart: Jiuwei (RN 15), Shaochong (HT 9), Shangqiu (SP 5). (*ibid*)
　　4) Epilepsy due to food: Jiuwei (RN 15), Zhongwan (RN 12), Shaoshang (LU 11). (*Great Compendium of Acupuncture and Moxibustion*)
　　5) Epilepsy: Jiuwei (RN 15), Zhongwan (RN 12), Jianyu (LI 15). (*ibid*)
　　6) Five kinds of epilepsy: Jiuwei (RN 15), Yongquan (KI 1). (*Songs of Xihong*)
【Regional Anatomy】 Skin – subcutaneous tissue – linea alba – transverse fascia – extraperitoneal fat tissue – parietal peritoneum. In the superficial layer, there are the anterior cutaneous branches of the anterior branch of the 7th thoracic nerve. In the deep layer, there are the branches of the anterior branch of the 7th thoracic nerve.
【Remark】 The point has regulating effects over the gastrointestinal function. For example, acupuncture and moxibustion to Zusanli (ST 36) and Jiuwei (RN 15) can treat acute gastroenteritis with a curative effect and also can regulate blood pressure. It is especially suitable for terciary hypertension.

RN 16 Zhongting (中庭)
(Middle Courtyard)

【Source】 *A-B Classic of Acupuncture and Moxibustion*
【Name Explanation】 Zhong (中), middle; Ting (庭), courtyard. The point is below the heart, as if in the courtyard in front of the palace.
【Location】 The chest and on the anterior midline, level with the 5th intercostal space, on the xiphosternal synchondrosis. (See Fig. 7-11)
【Localization】 Supine position, locate the point at the junction of the sternal body and xiphoid on the anterior midline.
【Indications】
　　1) Digestive Diseases: Abdominal distention, dysphagia, vomiting anorexia, vomiting of milk.
　　2) Cardiovascular Diseases: Cardiac pain, palpitation, oppressed feeling in the chest, pain of chest.
　　3) Other Diseases: Globous hysteria, pain in the pharynx.

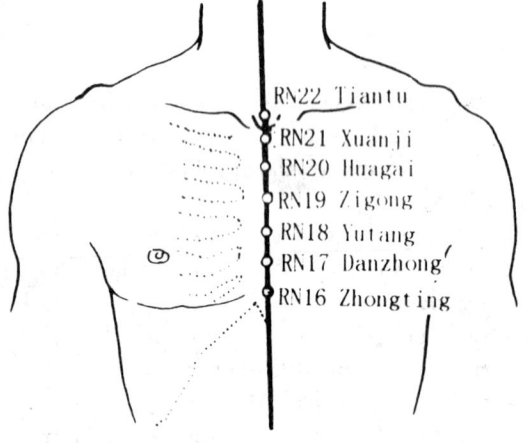

Fig. 7-11

【Mechanism of Action】 This point is located near the heart, and can be used to treat diseases of cardiovascular system.

In accordance with the clinical experience obtained from both the ancient and the present time, this is the most effective point to regulate the stomach and lower rising adverse rising of stomach qi and is very effective for vomiting and infantile vomiting of milk.
【Method】 Puncture subcutaneously 0.3-0.5 cun. Moxibustion is applicable.
【Acupoint Prescriptions】
　　1) Vomiting: Moxibustion to Zhongting (RN 16). (*The Peaceful Holy Benevolent Prescriptions*)
　　2) Vomiting: Zhongting (RN 16), Shufu (KI 27), Yishe (BL 49). (*Experience on Acupuncture and Moxibustion Therapy*)
【Regional Anatomy】 Skin - subcutaneous tissue - radiate sternocostal ligament and costoxiphoid ligament - xiphosternal synchondrosis. There are the anterior cutaneous branches of the 6th intercostal nerve and the perforating branches of the internal thoracic artery and vein in this area.

RN 17 Danzhong (膻中)
(Middle of Chest)

【Source】 *Miraculous Pivot*
【Name Explanation】 Dan (膻), exposure; Zhong (中), middle. The point is located at the exposed middle part of the chest, called shanzhong in ancient times.
【Classification】 Front-Mu Point of the pericardium. Influential Point of qi
【Location】 The chest on the anterior midline, level with the 4th intercostal space, at the midpoint of the line connecting both nipples. (See Fig. 7-11)
【Localization】 Supine position, locate the point at the intersection between the mid-sternal line and the line joining both nipples for males. Locate the point at the intersection between the mid-sternal line and the line which has the same level with the fourth intercostal space for females.
【Indications】
　　1) Repiratory Diseases: Cough, asthma, shortness of breath.
　　2) Digestive Diseases: Dysphagia, abdominal distention, vomiting with saliva and spittle.
　　3) Cardiovascular Diseases: Obstruction of qi in the chest, pain in the chest, cardiac pain, palpitation, irritability.
　　4) Other Diseases: Postpartum lactation, goiter, cramp in cholera morbus. corpse-like syncope.
【Mechanism of Action】 This point is the influential point of qi. Because the lungs control qi and respiration, it is a commonly used point to treat diseases of the respiratory system. Lactation is related to various internal organs. Main function of these points is regulating qi, so it is an important point for improving insufficient lactation.
　　Puncturing this point can also treat diseases of the digestive system such as goiter, syncope, cramp in cholera morbus. It is an effective way of regulating qi.
　　This point is Front-Mu point of the pericardium. The pericardium can promote the functions of the heart. It is usually used to treat diseases of the cardiovascular system.
【Method】 Puncture subcutaneously 0.3-0.5 cun. Moxibustion is applicable.
【Acupoint Prescriptions】
　　1) Shortness of breath: Danzhong (RN 17), Huagai (RN 20). (*Thousand Golden Prescriptions*)
　　2) Pain of the heart and chest: Danzhong (RN 17), Tianjing (SJ 10). (*Experience on Acupuncture and Moxibustion Therapy*)
　　3) Retention of body fluid and pain in the chest: Danzhong (RN 17), Juque (RN 14). (*Songs of Hundreds of Symptoms*)

【Regional Anatomy】 Skin – subcutaneous tissue – sternal body. There are the anterior cutaneous branches of the 4th intercostal nerve and the perforating branches of the internal thoracic artery and vein in this area.

【Remark】 Puncturing Danzhong (RN 17), Tiantu (RN 22) and Hegu (LI 4) can widen the esophageal internal diameter of patients of esophageal cancer, strengthen its peristalsis to alleviate dysphagia, but needling Zusanli (ST 36), Xinshu (BL 15) and Geshu (BL 17) had no above obvious effect. Taking ECG of patients as a pattern, it's found that the effect caused by needling Danzhong (RN 17), Jiuwei (RN 15), Jianjing (GB 21), Shendao (DU 11) and Renying (ST 9) was better than that caused by needling Shousanli (LI 10) and Zhongwan (RN 12).

Puncturing Danzhong (RN 17) piercing to Jiuwei (RN 15), Neiguan (PC 6), Zusanli (ST 36) and Sanyinjiao (SP 6) on patients of cardiac diseases impacts the inflowing time, amplitude, resistance and intensity under encephalogram.

RN 18 Yutang (玉堂)
(Jade Hall)

【Source】 *Classic of Medical Problems*
【Name Explanation】 Yu (玉), jade; Tang (堂), palace. The point is located at the site of the heart, and since jade is valuable, it is considered a jade palace.
【Location】 On the chest and on the anterior midline, level with the 3rd intercostal space. (See Fig. 7-11)
【Localization】 Supine or sitting position, locate the point on the mid-sternal line which has the same level with the third intercostal space.
【Indications】
　　1) Respiratory Diseases: Pain in the chest, cough, asthma, inflammation of the throat, swelling of the pharynx.
　　2) Digestive Disease: Vomiting.
　　3) Other Disease: Swelling and pain in the breasts.
【Mechanism of Action】 This point is located on the front of the chest, between the lungs and close to the breasts. According to the local function of acupoints, it can be used to treat disorders in these areas.
【Method】 Puncture subcutaneously 0.3-0.5 cun. Moxibustion is applicable.
【Regional Anatomy】 Skin – subcutaneous tissue – sternal body. There are the anterior cutaneous branches of the 3rd intercostal nerve and the perforating branches of the internal thoracic artery and vein in this area.

RN 19 Zigong (紫宫)
(Purple Palace)

【Source】 *A-B Classic of Acupuncture and Moxibustion*
【Name Explanation】 Zi (紫), purple; Gong (宫), palace. Zigong is the name of a star and refers to the Emperor's residence. The point corresponds to the heart which is the organ of the monarch, and is therefore called Zigong.
【Location】 On the chest and on the anterior midline, level with the 2nd intercostal space. (See Fig. 7-11)
【Localization】 Supine or sitting position, locate point on the mid-sternal line which is level with

the second intercostal space.

【Indications】
1) Respiratory Diseases: Pain in the chest, cough, asthma, sore throat and dysphagia.
2) Digestive Diseases: Vomiting, indigestion.
3) Other Disease: Pain in the breasts.

【Mechanism of Action】 This point is located between the lungs, where the esophagus is and near the breast. According to its local indications, it can be applied to treat the diseases in that area.

【Method】 Puncture subcutaneously 0.3-0.5 cun. Moxibustion is applicable.

【Acupoint Prescriptions】
1) Cough with upward qi and irritability: Zigong (RN 19), Yutang (RN 18), Taixi (KI 3). (*Thousand Golden Prescriptions*)
2) Indigestion: Zigong (RN 19), Zhongting (RN 16), Danshu (BL 19). (*Experience on Acupuncture and Moxibustion Therapy*)
3) Distention and fullness feeling in the chest and hypochondrium: Zigong (RN 19), Zhongting (RN 16), Yongquan (KI 1). (*ibid*)

【Regional Anatomy】 Skin – subcutaneous tissue – origin of greater pectoral muscle – sternal body. There are the anterior cutaneous branches of the 2nd intercostal nerve and the perforating branches of the internal thoracic artery and vein in this area.

RN 20 Huagai (华盖)
(Organ's Conopy)

【Source】 *A-B Classic of Acupuncture and Moxibustion*

【Name Explanation】 Hua (华), magnificent; Gai (盖), umbrella. Huagai refers to the Emperor's umbrella. The location of the point corresponds to the lung, which is above the heart and like an umbrella over it.

【Location】 On the chest and on the anterior midline, level with the 1st intercostal space. (See Fig. 7-11)

【Localization】 Supine or sitting position, locate the point on the mid-sternal line which is level with the first intercostal space.

【Indications】
1) Respiratory Diseases: Cough, asthma, hematemesis, pain in the chest, sore throat and dysphagia.
2) Digestive Diseases: Vomiting, dysphagia.

【Mechanism of Action】 This point is located between the lungs, where the esophagus lies. According to its local indications, it can be used to treat the diseases in that area.

【Method】 Puncture subcutaneously 0.3-0.5 cun. Moxibustion is applicable.

【Regional Anatomy】 Skin – subcutaneous tissue – origin of greater pectoral muscle – area between manubrium of sternum and sternal body (sternal angle). There are the anterior cutaneous branches of the 1st intercostal nerve and the perforating branches of the internal thoracic artery and vein in this area.

【Remark】 For patients of hypertension caused by hyperthyreosis, puncturing Huagai (RN 20) has the effect of descending blood pressure.

Moreover, needling the point could increase the total number of WBC, neutrophils and acidocytes. Puncturing Huagai (RN 20) and Yamen (DU 15) can improve the hematopoietic function of bone marrow.

RN 21 Xuanji (璇玑)
(Rotating Jade)

【Source】 A-B *Classic of Acupuncture and Moxibustion*
【Name Explanation】 Xuan (璇), rotation; Ji (玑), axis. Xuanji is the name of the 2nd and 3rd stars of the big Dipper, opposite the Zigong star. This point is also opposite the Zigong point and therefore named Xuanji.
【Location】 On the chest and on the anterior midline, 1 cun below Tiantu(RN 22). (See Fig. 7-11)
【Localization】 Supine or sitting position with head at rest, locate the point between the 1st sternocostal joints on the mid-sternal line.
【Indications】
　　1) Respiratory Diseases: Cough, asthma, pain in the chest, throat redness, swelling, and pain on swallowing, wheezing sounds in the throat of infants.
　　2) Digestive Disease: Dyspepsia.
【Mechanism of Action】 This acupoint is located between the lungs. According to the principle of the local indications of acupoints, it was frequently used to treat dyspepsia in ancient China and is still being used to date.
【Method】 Puncture subcutaneously 0.3-0.5 cun. Moxibustion is applicable.
【Acupoint Prescriptions】
　　1) Redness, swelling and pain on swallowing: Xuanji (RN 21), Jiuwei (RN 15). (*Thousand Golden prescriptions*)
　　2) Asthma: Apply moxibustion to Xuanji (RN 21), Qihai (RN 6), Qimen (LR 14), Zhiyang (DU 19). (*Complete Works of Jingyue*)
　　3) Asthma: Apply moxibustion to Xuanji (RN 21), Danzhong (RN 17), Jianjing (GB 21), Taiyuan (LU 9), Jianzhongshu (SI 14) and Zusanli (ST 36). (*Illustrated Supplementary to the Classified Canon*)
　　4) Magersucht: Xuanji (RN 21), Qihai (RN 6). (*Songs of Jade Dragon*)
　　5) Dyspepsia: Xuanji (RN 21), Zusanli (ST 36). (*Secret Songs of Chang Sangjun*)
【Regional Anatomy】 Skin - subcutaneous tissue - origin of greater pectoral muscle - manubrium of sternum. There is the medial supraclavicular nerve and the perforating branches of the internal thoracic artery and vein in this area.

RN 22 Tiantu (天突)
(Heaven Projection)

【Source】 *Miraculous Pivot and Plain Questions*
【Name Explanation】 Tian (天), heaven; Tu (突), chimney. The location of the point corresponds to the upper end of the trachea, like the chimney for the qi of the lung.
【Location】 On the neck and on the anterior midline, at the center of the suprasternal fossa. (See Fig. 7-11)
【Localization】 Sitting with head at rest, the point is located 1 cun superior to Xuanji (RN 21), in the center of the suprasternal fossa.
【Indications】
　　1) Respiratory Diseases: Cough, asthma, sensation of gas ascending in the chest, cough

with pus and blood, pulmonary abscess, swelling and pain of throat on swallowing, sudden hoarseness of voice.

    2) Digestive Diseases: Dysphagia, vomiting.

    3) Cardiovascular Disease: Cardiac pain.

    4) Other Diseases: Subglossal spasm, goiter, globus hystericus, swelling of nape and pain of shoulders.

【Mechanism of Action】 This acupoint is anterior to the trachea and can be used to treat globus hyteria and goiter. According to the law of the local indications of acupoints, it is one of the main points used to treat diseases of respiration.

【Acupoint Prescriptions】

    1) Cough, sensation of masses of gas ascending and sudden asthma: Tiantu (RN 22), Huagai (RN 20). (*Thousand Golden Prescriptions*)

    2) Asthma: Apply moxibustion to Tiantu (RN 22) with 50 moxa-cones, Zhongwan (RN 12) with 50 moxa-cones for severe cases (*Comprehension of Bianque's Medicine*)

    3) Cough: Tiantu (RN 22), Shufu (KI 27), Huagai (RN 20), Rugen (ST 18), Fengmen (BL 20), Feishu (BL 13), Shenzhu (DU 12), Zhiyang (DU 9), Lieque (LU 7). (*Illustrated Supplementary to the Classified Canon*)

    4) Spasm of diaphragm: main point: Tiantu (RN 22), supplementary points: Neiguan (PC 6), Zhongwan (RN 12). Needling Tiantu with strong stimulation. If without good curative effect, add Neiguan (PC 6) and Zhongwan (RN 12). (*Science of Acupuncture and Moxibustion*)

    5) Hyperthyroidism: Tiantu (RN 22), Quchi (LI 11), Yanglingquan (GB 34), Zhongfeng (LR 4), Qishe (ST 11). (*Abstract of Clinical Experience on Acupuncture and Moxibustion*)

    6) Endemic goiter: Tiantu (RN 22), Tianzhu (BL 10), Hegu (LI 4), Yifeng (SJ 17). (*ibid*)

    7) Infantile croup syndrome: Tiantu (RN 22), Jinsuo (DU 8). (*Songs of Shengyu*)

    8) Asthma and cough: Tiantu (RN 22), Danzhong (RN 17). (*Songs of Jade Dragon*)

【Regional Anatomy】 Skin − subutaneous tissue − the two sternalheads of sternocleidomastoid muscle − superior side of suprasternal notch − bilateral sternothyroid muscle − anterior space of trachea. In the superficial layer, there is the medial supraclavicular nerve, the platysma and the jugular arch of veins in the subcutaneous tissue. In the deep layer, there are important structure, including the orachiocephalic trunk, the left common carotid artery, the aortic arch and the brachiocephalic.

【Remark】 Electropuncturing Tiantu (RN 22) could curatively treat respiratory failure, and is especially suitable for peripheral respiratory failure. It has a positive effect on hyperthyroidism by shrinking the enlarged thyroid, which alleviates symptoms and decreases the basic metabolism. When treating endemic goiter, the curative rate can reach 86.9%, with the urinary iodine output being greatly lowered, the ability of the thyroid to absorb and utilize iodine were improved. Puncturing the point can regulate the bronchial smooth muscles, treating bronchial asthma effectively. Observed under X-ray, puncturing Tiantu (RN 22) and Danzhong (RN 17) could strengthen normal person's esophageal peristalsis, and widen its internal diameter. Some effects have been observed in the upper and lower sections of the esaphaous in esophageal cancer patients.

RN 23 Lianquan (廉泉)
(Corner Fountain)

【Source】 *Miraculous Pivot and Plain Questions*

【Name Explanation】 Lian (廉), clear; Quan (泉), spring. In ancient times the two blood vessels below the tongue were called Lianquan. The point is at the superior margin of the laeyngeal prominence, close to the Lianquan vessels.

【Classification】 The crossing point of the Ren Meridian and Yinwei Meridian

【Location】 On the neck and on the anterior midline, above the laryngeal protuberance, in the depression above the upper border of the hyoid bone. (See Fig. 7-12)

【Localization】 Sitting with head at rest, locate the point at the superior border of the Adam's apple, between the lower margin of hyoid body and superior thyroid notch.

【Indications】

1) Diseases of the Head and Sense Organs: Subglossal swelling and pain, spasmodic pain at the root of the tongue, protrusion of the tongue, stiff tongue, dry tongue and mouth, sore tongue, sudden loss of voice, redness, inflammation of the throat, difficulty in swallowing.

2) Digestive Diseases: Dyspepsia, diabetes.

3) Mental Diseases: Apoplexy aphasia, infantile convulsion, manic-depressive psychosis, epilepsy.

【Mechanism of Action】 This acupoint is located at the root of the tongue. According to the principle of the local indication of acupoints, it can be used to treat diseases of the tongue and the throat.

【Method】 Puncture perpendicularly 0.5-0.8 cun, the needle can not be retained. (See Fig. 7-13)

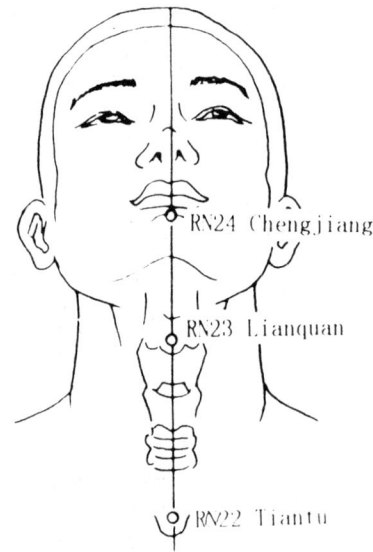
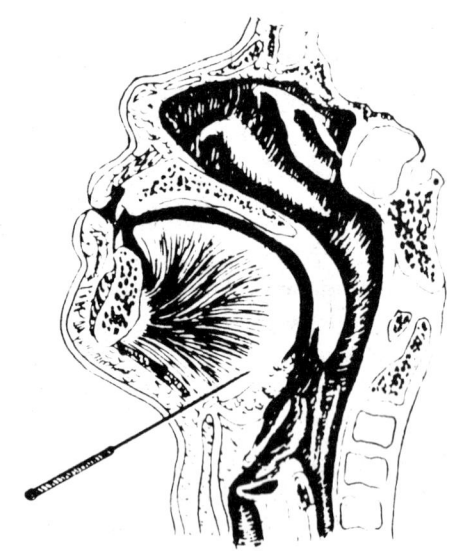

Fig. 7-12   Fig. 7-13 Insertion of Needle of Lianquan Point

【Acupoint Prescriptions】

1) Loss of voice due to subglossal swelling and protrusion of the tongue with salivation: Lianquan (RN 23), Rangu (KI 2), Yingu (KI 10). (*Thousand Golden Prescriptions*)

2) Pain in the chest: Lianquan (RN 23), Zhongfu (LU 1). (*Experience on Acupuncture and Moxibustion Therapy*)

3) Loss of the voice due to swelling of the tongue: Lianquan (RN 23), Jinjin (EX-HN 12), Yuye (EX-HN 13). (*Great Compendium of Acupuncture and Moxibustion*)

4) Hyperthyroidism: Lianquan (RN 3), Hegu (LI 4), Zusanli (ST 36), Sanyinjiao (SP 6), Tianchuang (SI 16), Naohu (DU 17). (*Abstract of Clinical Experience on Acupuncture and Moxibustion*)

5) Subglossal swelling and pain: Lianquan (RN 23), Zhongchong (PC 9). (*Songs of Hundreds of Symptoms*)

【Regional Anatomy】 Skin – subcutaneous tissue – orbicular muscle of mouth – depressor muscle of lower lip – mental muscle. In the superficial layer, there are the cervical branches of the facial nerve and the branches of the superior branch of the transverse nerve of the neck. In the deep layer, there are the branches or tributaries of the lingual artery and vein and the branches of the hypoglossal and mylohyoid nerves.

【Remark】 Puncturing Lianquan (RN 23) has a good regulating effect on the thyroid function. For patients of hyperthyroidism, needling this point can narrow the enlarged thyroid, eliminate symptoms and obviously lower the basic metabolism.

RN 24 Chengjiang (承浆)
(Saliva Receiver)

【Source】 *A-B Classic of Acupuncture and Moxibustion*
【Name Explanation】 Cheng (承), receiving; Jiang (浆), fluid. The point is in the depression at the midpoint of the chin, where excessive saliva is received.
【Classification】 Crossing Point of the Ren Meridian and the Stomach Meridian of Foot Yangming
【Location】 On the face, in the depression at the midpoint of the mentolabial sulcus. (See Fig. 7-12)
【Localization】 Sitting with head at rest, the point is located in the depression in the center of the mentolabial sulcus.
【Indications】
　　1) Diseases of the Head and Sense Organs: Deviation of the mouth and eye, spasm of lips, swelling of the face, toothache, gingival bleeding, gingivitis, salivation, sore tongue.
　　2) Digestive Diseases: Diabetes, thirst.
　　3) Urinary Diseases: Enuresis, infantile enuresis.
　　4) Mental Disease: Epilepsy, infantile convulsion.
　　5) Other Disease: Hemiplegia.
【Mechanism of Action】
　　1) The acupoint is located beneath the lips, connecting the large intestine meridian of Hand-Yangming with the stomach meridian of Foot Yangming. The meridians of both Hand Yangming and Foot Yangming circulate through the upper and lower teeth and their divergent meridians reach the face, so it can be one of the main points used to treat diseases of the head, face and five sense organs.
　　2) The Ren Meridian controls Yin and the Du Meridian controls Yang all over the body. This point is a crossing point of the two meridians which creates a balance between Yin and Yang. For the treatment of epilepsy, hemiplagia and infantile convulsion due to the failure in the balance between Yin and Yang, this point can be selected as one of the main acupoints.
　　3) According to the principle that where the meridian passes, where the indications are, most of the acupoints have characteristics of distant function. The lower part of the Ren meridian locates the bladder, this point can be used to treat enursis and infantile enuresis.
【Method】 Puncture obliquely upwards 0.3-0.5 cun. Moxibustion is applicable.
【Acupoint Prescriptions】
　　1) Gingival bleeding: Chengjiang (RN 24), Weizhong (BL 40). (*A-B Classic of Acupuncture and Moxibustion*)
　　2) Acute infantile omphalitis: Moxibustion to Chengjiang (RN 24) and Jiache (ST 6). (*the Peaceful Holy Benevolent Prescriptions*)
　　3) Enuresis: Chengjiang (RN 24), Yinlingquan (SP 9), Weizhong (BL 40), Taichong (LR 3), Pangguangshu (BL 28), Dadun (LR 1). (*Great Compendium of Acupuncture and*

Moxibustion)

4) Tongue and teeth disorders: Moxibustion to Chengjiang (RN 24) and Laogong (PC 8). (*ibid*)

5) Diabetes: Moxibustion to Chengjiang (RN 24), Taixi (KI 3), Zhizheng (SI 7), Yangchi (SJ 4), Zhaohai (KI 6), Shenshu (BL 23), Xiaochangshu (BL 27) and tip of small fingers. (*Classic on Miraculous Moxibustion*)

【Regional Anatomy】 Skin - subutaneous tissue - orbicular muscle of mouth - depressor muscle of lower lip - mental muscle. There is the mental nerve of the inferior alveolar nerve and the mental artery and vein in this area.

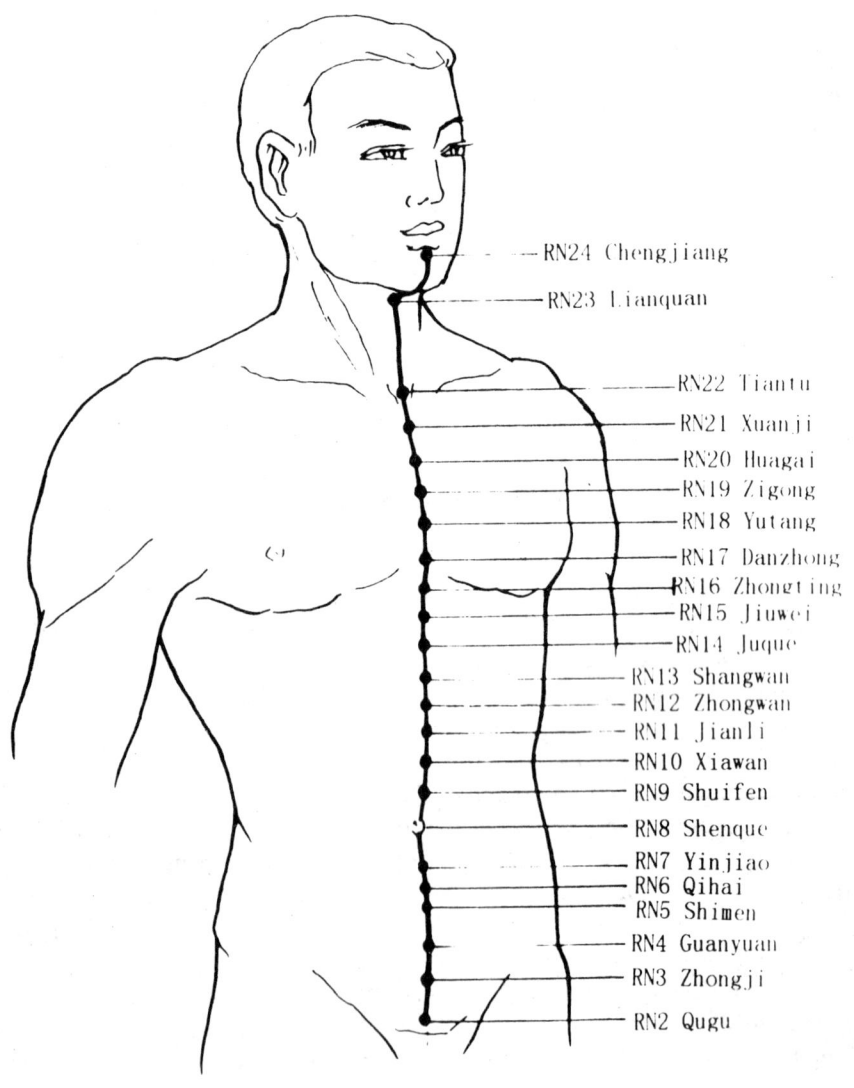

Fig. 7-14 **Acupocnts of the Ren Meridian**

Table 7-2
Indications and Actions of Acupoints of the Ren Meridian

Name of the points	Specific points	Common indications	Specific indications and functions
RN 1 Huiyin (会阴)	Crossing point	Gynecological, external genital and intestinal diseases: dysuria, edema, enuresis, irregular menstruation, seminal emission, leukorrea, amenorrhea, menorrhagia and metrostaxis, impotence, abdominal pain, diarrhea	Regulating menstruation and reinforcing the kidney, clearing away damp-heat. Sweat and itching of vulvae, pain over the perineum, vulvitis, prolapse of uterus, itching of anus, dysuria, coma
RN 2 Qugu (曲骨)	Corssing point		Invigorating vital qi and reinforcing the kidney, regulating menstruation and arresting leukorrhea, clearing away damp-heat. Distension and pain in the lower abdomen, dribbling urination, red and whitish vaginal discharge, wetness and itching of the scrotum, constriction of penis, emission, impotence
RN 3 Zhongji (中极)	Front-Mu point of the urinary bladder, Crossing point		Reinforcing the kidney to invigorate vital qi, clearing away damp-heat. Enuresis, dysuria, frequent urine, dribbling urination, emission, impotence, prolapse of the uterus, lochiorrhea, retention of placenta
RN 4 Guanyuan (关元)	Front-Mu point of the small intestine, Crossing point		Strengthening the kidney and reinforcing the vital qi, regulating the Chong and Ren Meridians, regulating qi and removing cold pathogen. Comsumptive disease, prolapse of the uterus, sterility, lochiorrhea, diabetes, cold sensation and pain in the lower abdomen, dysmenorrhea It is also a point for health care.
RN 5 Shimen (石门)	Front-Mu point of Sanjiao		Warming the kidney and replenishing the essence, regulating menses and arresting leukorrhea. Abdominal pain, edema, diarrhea, amenorrhea, retraction of penis, hernia, enuresis
RN 6 Qihai (气海)			Replenishing the kidney and controlling the essence, ascending yang and reinforcing qi, regulating the Chong and Ren Meridians. Consumptive disease, emaciation, sluggishness, prolapse of uterus, hypertension, insomnia, abdominal pain after childbirth, retention of placenta It is also a point for health care.
RN 7 Yinjiao (阴交)	Crossing point		Warming the kidney to benefit essence, regulating the Chong and Ren Meridians. Abdominal pain, edema, irregular menstruation, sweat and itching of the vulvae, prolapse of uterus, leukorrhea
RN 8 Shenque (神阙)		The same as below.	Warming yang to control essence, invigorating the spleen and stomach. Apoplexy, extreme cold of the four limbs, coma, edema, tympanites, dysuria, in continence, sterility, abdominal pain, diarrhea

Name of the points	Specific points	Common indications	Specific indications and functions
RN 9 Shuifen (水分)		Grastrointestinal diseases: stomachache, abdominal pain, abdominal distension, vomiting, diarrhea Mental diseases: manic-depressive psychosis and epilepsy	Invigorating the spleen and resolving dampness, removing edema. Dysuria, edema, diarrhea, stomach distension due to deficiency, anorexia, vomiting, distending pain of the stomach, borborygmus
RN 10 Xiawan (下脘)	Crossing point		Regulating the intestine and stomach, removing food retention. Vomiting, indigestion of food, abdominal mass, pain and distention
RN 11 Jianli (建里)			Invigorating the spleen and regulating the stomach, resolving dampness and easing the middle-Jiao. Gastric distention and pain, loss of appetite, vomiting, oppressive sensation in the chest, edema
RN 12 Zhongwan (中脘)	Front-Mu point of the stomach, Influential point of the fu-organs Crossing, point		Regulating the middle-Jiao, resolving dampness and food retention. Hiccups, acid regurgitation, deficiency of the spleen and stomach, jaundice, infantile malnutrition, chronic infantile convulsion due to dysfunction of the spleen, tympanites, flaccidity syndrome, hypertension, insomnia
RN 13 Shangwan (上脘)	Crossing point		Regulating the spleen and stomach, resolving sputum, promoting circulation of qi, calming the mind. Vomiting, anorexia, hiccups, undigested food, palpitation, epilepsy, jaundice, morning sickness
RN 14 Juque (巨阙)	Front-Mu point of the heart		Regulating the middle-Jiao to send down the adverse flow of qi, easing the chest to resolve phlegm. Chest pain, palpitation, vomiting, acid regurgitation, hiccups, regurgitation, manic-depression and epilepsy
RN 15 Jiuwei (鸠尾)	The Luo-(Connecting) point	Diseases of the chest, heart and lung: chest pain, cough, asthma	Chest pain, abdominal distention, manic-depression and epilepsy
RN 16 Zhongting (中庭)			Easing the chest and regulating qi, descending adverse flow of qi and regulating the middle-Jiao. Distension and fullness sensation in the chest and hypochondrium, hiccups, vomiting, regurgitation, globus hystericus, infantile vomiting of milk
RN 17 Danzhong (膻中)	Front-Mu point of the pericardium Influential point of qi		Regulating qi to descend adverse flow of qi, easing the chest to benefit the diaphragm, promoting lactation. Vomiting, hiccups, shortness of breath, cardiac pain, palpitation, lack of lactation, pulmonary abscess, cough and dyspnea
RN 18 Yutang (玉堂)			Arresting cough and resolving phlegm. Cough, asthma, chest pain, vomiting, phlegm due to cold-pathogen

Name of the points	Specific points	Common indications	Specific indications and functions
RN 19 Zigong (紫宫)		The same as above.	Clearing heat-pathogens in the lung and benifiting the phraynx. Cough, asthma, chest pain, inflammation of the throat
RN 20 Huagai (华盖)			Easing the chest and regulating qi, benefiting the pharynx. Chest pain, cough, asthma, inflammation of the throat, swelling of the throat
RN 21 Xuanji (璇玑)			Cough, asthma, chest pain, swelling and pain of the throat
RN 22 Tiantu (天突)	Crossing point	Diseases of the tongue and phraynx: Sudden loss of voice, swelling and pain of the throat, difficulty in swallowing, ulceration on the oral mucosa and the tongue	Easing the chest and regulating qi, resolving phlegm to benefit the phraynx. Cough, asthma, pulmonary abscess, chest pain, swelling and pain of the throat, sudden loss of voice, goiter, globus hystericus, hiccups, vomiting
RN 23 Lianquan (廉泉)	Crossing point		Clearing heat and resolving phlegm, inducing resuscitationt to benefit the tongue and throat. Sublingual swelling and pain, flaccid tongue with salivation, stiff tongue with inability to speak, sudden loss of voice, difficulty in swallowing, asthma, deafness and muteness
RN 24 Chengjiang (承浆)	Crossing point	Diseases of the mouth and tooth	Expelling wind and dredging collaterals, tranquillizing the mind and arresting pain. Deviation of the mouth, swelling of the face, swelling and pain of the gums, salivation, hemiplegia, ulcer in the mouth, trismus, epilepsy, diabetes, thirst with desire for drink

Chapter Eight

Acupoints of Three Yin Meridians of Hand

Ⅲ. Acupoints of the Lung Meridian of Hand Taiyin

LU 1　Zhongfu (中府)
(Central Mansion)

【**Source**】 *Plain Questions*
【**Name Explanation**】 Zhong (中), middle; Fu (府), place. Zhong refers to the middle Jiao. The Lung Meridian starts from the middle Jiao. The point is located where the qi of Spleen and Stomach in the middle Jiao gathers into the Lung Meridian.
【**Classification**】 It is the Front-Mu Point of the Lung and the Crossing Points of the Lung Meridian of Hand-Taiyin and the Spleen Meridian of Foot Taiyin.
【**Location**】 In the superior lateral part of the anterior thoracic wall, 1 cun below Yunmen (LU 2), on the level with the 1st intercostal space, 6 cun lateral to the anterior midline. (See Fig. 8-1)
【**Localization**】
　　1) Sit with the arms akimbo, first locate Yunmen (LU 2) which is located in the depression inferior to the lateral segment of clavicle (i.e: acromial extremity of the clavicle), the point is located 1 cun directly inferior to Yunmen (LU 2), at the same level with the first intercostal space.

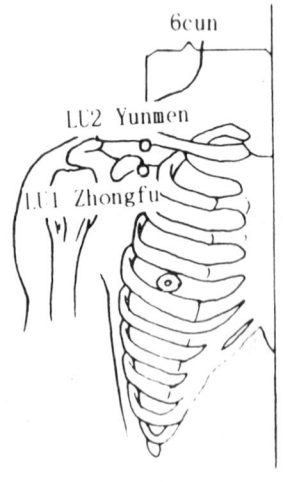

Fig. 8-1

2) Supine position, the point is located on a straight line, 2 cun lateral to the nipple (male), in the first intercostal space.

【Indications】

1) Diseases of Head and Sense Organs: Nasal obstruction, rhinorrhea, sinusitis, hyposmia, sore throat.

2) Respiratory Diseases: Cough, asthma, shortness of breath, feeling of fullness and pain in the chest, hemoptysis.

3) Digestive Diseases: Vomiting, anorexia, abdominal distension, edema of the four limbs.

4) Other Diseases: Shoulder pain, goiter, abdominal pain referring to the lumbar area.

【Mechanism of Action】

1) It is the Front-Mu point of the lung, and a commonly used point for treating lung diseases. The application of cupping to Zhongfu (LU 1) point is effective for bronchitis and pneumonia.

2) The Lung Meridian of Hand Taiyin begins in the epigastric region, so it can also be used for stomachache due to exogenous pathogen.

【Method】 Puncture perpendicularly 0.3-0.5 cun. Moxibustion is applicable.

【Acupoint Prescriptions】

1) Edema: Zhongfu (LU 1), Jianshi (PC 5), Hegu (LI 4). (*Thousand Golden Prescriptions*)

2) Sore throat: Zhongfu (LU 1), Yangjiao (GB 35). (*ibid*)

3) Dyspnea: Zhongfu (LU 1), Pohu (BL 42). (*Experience on Acupunture and Moxibustion Therapy*)

4) Dysphagia: Zhongfu (LU 1), Yishe (BL 49). (*Songs of Hundreds of Symptoms*)

【Regional Anatomy】 Skin-subcutaneous tissue-greater pectoral muscle-smaller pectoral muscle-axillary cavity. In the superficial layer, there are the intermediate supraclavicular nerve, the lateral cutaneous branches of the first intercostal nerve and the cephalic vein and so on. In the deep layer, there are the thoracolacromial artery and vein, the medial and lateral pectoral nerves.

【Remark】 By isotopic intravascular injection, it was found that puncturing Zhongfu (LU 1) increased hepatic blood flow. Needling Zhongfu (LU 1) had a good effect on bronchial asthma. Experprmental research has shown that puncturing Zhongfu (LU 1) can relax smooth bronchial muscles and increase pulmonary ventilation to alleviate asthma.

LU 2　Yunmen (云门)
(Cloud Gate)

【Source】 *Plain Questions*

【Name Explanation】 Yun (云), cloud; Men (门), door. Yun refers to the qi of Lung. The point is on the upper part of the chest, serving as a door for the qi of Lung.

【Location】 In the superior lateral portion of the anterior thoracic wall, superior to the coracoid process of the scapula, in the depression of the infraclavicular fossa, 6 cun lateral to the anterior midline. (See Fig. 8-1)

【Localization】 Sit with the arms akimbo, locate the point in the middle of the triangular depression inferior to the lateral segment of the clavicle.

【Indications】

1) Diseases along the Course of the Meridian: Shoulder pain, frozen shoulder, pain in the supraclavicular fossa, hypochondriac pain referring to the back, coldness of extremities.

2) Respiratory Diseases: Cough, asthma, pain and fullness in the chest, oppression and heat sensation in the chest.

3) Other Diseases: Heat sensation in the extremities caused by cold, sudden pain in cardiac region and abdomen, irregular pulse, goiter.

【Mechanism of Action】 Yunmen (LU 2) has an action of promoting lung qi and clearing heat from the four limbs. It is used for shoulder pain, frozen shoulder, pain in the supraclavicular fossa, heat sensation in the extremities due to cold, etc. Coldness of the four limbs due to obstruction of lung qi and deeper pathogenic heat and cold limbs can be treated by needling Yunmen (LU 2).

【Method】 Puncture perpendicularly 0.3-0.5 cun. Moxibustion is applicable.

【Acupoint Prescription】

1) Heat in the four limbs: Yunmen (LU 2), Jianyu (LI 15), Weizhong (BL 40), Yaoshu (DU 2) (*Plain Questions*).

2) Asthma: Yunmen (LU 2), Renying (ST 9), Shencang (KI 25), (*Experience on Acupunture and Moxibustion Therapy*).

3) Shortness of breath: Yunmen (LU 2), Fengmen (BL 12), Zhongfu (LU 1), Juque (RN 14), Qimen (LR 14). (*ibid*)

4) Shoulder pain, frozen shoulder: Yunmen (LU 2), Bingfeng (SI 12). (*ibid*)

【Regional Anatomy】 Skin-subcutaneous tissue-deltoid muscle-clavipectoral fascia-coracoclavicular ligament. In the superficial layer, there are the cephalic vein and the intermediate supraclavicular nerve. In the deep layer, there are the branches of the thoracoacromial artery and vein and the branches of the medial and lateral pectoral nerves.

LU 3 Tianfu (天府)
(Heaven Mansion)

【Source】 *Miraculous Pivot*

【Name Explanation】 Tian (天), heaven; Fu (府), place. Tian refers to the upper. The point is on the upper arm, where there is a confluence of the Lung qi.

【Location】 On the medial side of the upper arm, on the radial border of the biceps brachii muscle, 3 cun below the anterior end of the axillary fold. (See Fig. 8-2)

【Localization】

1) Sitting posture, raise the arm forward, bow the head, the point is located where the apex of the nose touches the internal side of the upper arm.

2) Sitting posture, bend the elbow slightly, the point is located in the lateral side of biceps brachii muscle 6 cun superior to the cubital crease.

【Indications】

1) Diseases along the Course of the Meridian: Pain and numbness of shoulder and arm.

2) Disease of Head and Sense Organs: Epistaxis, vertigo.

3) Respiratory Diseases: Asthma, cough.

4) Mental Diseases: Trance, amnesia, grief.

5) Other Diseases: General edema, heaviness sensation of the body, lethargy.

【Mechanism of Action】 It is one of the points of the lung meridi-

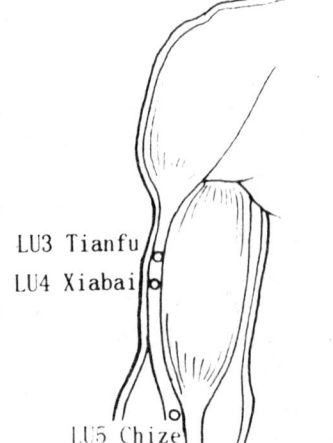

Fig. 8-2

an and is used to promote lung qi and tranquilize the mind, which can be achieved by promoting the circulation of lung qi.
【Method】 Puncture perpendicularly 0.5-0.8 cun. Moxibustion is applicable
【Acupoint Prescriptions】
　　1) Goiter: Tianfu (LU 3), Naohui (SJ 13), Qishe (ST 11) (*Thousands Golden Prescriptions*).
　　2) Wind syndrome: Tianfu (LU 3), Quchi (LI 11), Lieque (LU 7), Baihui (DU 20). (*ibid*)
　　3) Epistaxis: Tianfu (LU 3), Hegu (LI 4) (*Songs of Hundreds of Symptoms*).
【Regional Anatomy】 Skin-subcutaneous tissue-biceps brachii muscle. In the superficial layer, there are the muscular branches of the brachial artery and vein and the branches of the musculocutaneous nerve.

LU 4　Xiabai（侠白）
(White Insertion)

【Source】 *A-B Classic of Acupuncture and Moxibustion*
【Name Explanation】 Xia (侠), to press from both sides; Bai (白), white. White color pertains to the Lung. With both arms hanging freely, this point is precisely on both sides of the Lung.
【Location】 On the medial side of the upper arm, on the radial border of the biceps brachii muscle, 3 cun below the anterior end of the axillary fold, or 5 cun above the transverse cubital crease. (See Fig. 8-2)
【Localization】 Sitting posture, the point is located 5 cun superior to the cubital crease, the lateral side of the tendon of the biceps brachii muscle.
【Classification】 The Divergent Meridian of the Lung Meridian of Hand Taiyin is derived here.
【Indications】
　　1) Diseases along the Course of the Meridian: Pain in the medial aspect of the upper arm and shoulder, tinea versicolor.
　　2) Respiratory Diseases: Cough, asthma, shortness of breath.
　　3) Digestive Diseases: Stomachache, nausea.
【Mechanism of Action】 The lung is in charge of the skin, so Xiabai (LU 4) is used for treating tinea versicolor. See Tianfu (LU 3) for more details.
【Method】 Puncture perpendicularly 0.5-0.8 cun. Moxibustion is applicable.
【Acupoint Prescription】
　　Brachial plexus neuralgia: Xiabai (LU 4), Ximen (PC 4), Jianshi (PC 5), Daling (PC 7), Neiguan (PC 6), Tianquan (PC 2), (*New Acupuncture and Moxibustion*).
【Regional Anatomy】 Skin-subcutaneous tissue-brachial muscle. In the superficial layer, there is the cephalic vein and the lateral cutaneous nerve of the arm. In the deep layer, there are the muscular branches of the brachial artery and vein and the branches of the musculocutaneous nerve.

LU 5　Chize（尺泽）
(Foot Marsh)

【Source】 *Miraculous Pivot*

【Name Explanation】 Chi (尺), ruler or ulnar; Ze (泽), marsh. Chi refers to the ulnar aspect (from the wrist to the elbow). The point is in the depression of the ulnar aspect of the cubital fossa. The qi of the meridian is infused here, like water flowing into a marsh.

【Classification】 One of the Five Shu points and He-(Sea) point of the Lung Meridian of Hand Taiyin, pertaining to water in the Five Elements.

【Location】 In cubital crease, in the depression on the radial side of the tendon of the biceps brachii muscle. (See Fig. 8-2)

【Localization】 Bend the elbow slightly with palm facing upward, the point is located on the cubital crease, on the radial border of the tendon of biceps brachii.

【Indications】
1) Diseases along the Course of the Meridian: Spasmodic pain of the elbow and arm, pain in the medial aspect of the shoulder, sudden swelling of the four limbs, inability to extend the arm, paralysis of upper arms.

2) Diseases of Head and Five Sense Organs: Pain and swelling of the throat, aphasia.

3) Respiratory Diseases: Cough, asthma, hemoptysis, afternoon fever, feeling of fullness in the chest and hypochondrium.

4) Digestive Diseases: Acute vomiting and diarrhea, dryness of the tongue, spitting blood.

5) Urinary Diseases: Enuresis, incontinence of urine, amenorrhea, hernia, abdominal masses.

6) Mental Diseases: Sadness, acute and chronic infantile convulsions, epilepsy.

7) Other Diseases: General pain, stiffness and pain of the back and lumbar region, swelling and pain of the knee, mastitis, erysipelas, fever.

【Mechanism of Action】
1) It is an important point for regulating lung qi, and is effective for lung diseases. It is used for fever, infantile convulsions, spasm, erysipelas and sore throat due to stagnation of lung-heat.

2) The lung dominates emotional activity, deficiency of lung qi may cause sadness.

3) The lung starts from the Middle-Jiao, so many points of the lung meridian are used to treat disorders of the spleen and stomach. Applying blood-letting method to this point is effective for acute vomiting and diarrhea.

4) The lung helps maintain normal water metabolism. Obstruction of lung qi may affect the function of dredging water passages of the lung, leading to enuresis and incontinence of urine. Promoting the dispersing and descending function of the lung is essential in treating urinary system diseases.

5) Elbows correspond to the knees, thus, Chize (LU 5) can be used for cases of swelling and pain of the knees. According to the pathogenesis, lung-heat is one of the causes of crane-knees arthritis. This point has the function of nourishing lung yin to clear away lung heat.

【Method】 Puncture perpendicularly 0.3-0.5 cun, or prick the point to cause bleeding. Moxibustion is applicable.

【Acupoint Prescriptions】
1) Epilepsy: Chize (LU 5), Rangu (KI 2). (*Thousand Golden Prescriptions*)

2) Chronic convulsions: Apply moxibustion to Chize (LU 5) point. (*The Peaceful Holy Benevolent Prescriptions*)

3) Irritability: Chize (LU 5), Shaoze (SI 1). (*Experience on Acupuncture and Moxibustion Therapy*)

4) Turbid spitting: Chize (LU 5), Jianshi (PC 5), Lieque (LU 7), Shaoshang (LU 11). (*Great Compendium of Acupuncture and Moxibustion*)

5) Adverse flow of lung qi: Chize (LU 5), Shangqiu (SP 5), Taibai (SP 3), Sanyinjiao (SP 6). (*ibid*)

6) Wind-numbness: Chize (LU 5), Yangfu (GB 38). (*ibid*)

7) Motor impairment of lumbar and hypochondriac region: Chize (LU 5), Weizhong (BL 40), Renzhong (DU 26). (*ibid*)

【Regional Anatomy】 Skin-subcutaneous tissue-brachioradial muscle-radial nerve-biceps brachii muscle. In the superficial layer, there is the cephalic vein and the lateral cutaneous nerve of the forearm. In the deep layer, there is the radial nerve, the anterior branches of the radial collateral artery and vein and the radial recurrent artery and vein.

【Remark】 Clinical observations have proved that puncturing Chize (LU 5) has the function of decreasing blood pressure and treating hypertension with curative effect. It has been found in experimental observations that needling this point has a function of regulating colic peristalsis and strengthening the peristalsis of the rectum and lower sigmoidcolon of descending colon which have a little or no movement.

LU 6   Kongzui (孔最)
(Convergence Hole)

【Source】 *A-B Classic of Acupuncture and Moxibustion*
【Name Explanation】 Kong (孔), hole; Zui (最), the most. This point is located deeply.
【Classification】 It is the Xi-(Cleft) point of the Lung Meridan of Hand Taiyin.
【Location】 On the radial side of the palmar surface of the forearm, on the line connecting Chize (LU 5) and Taiyuan (LU 9), 7 cun above the transverse crease of the wrist. (See Fig. 8-3)
【Localization】 Stretch the arm straight with the palm facing upwards, the point is located 1 cun superior to the middle point between Chize (LU 5) and Taiyuan (LU 9), in the medial border of the radius.

【Indications】
1) Diseases along the Course of the Meridian: Shoulder pain, pain of the elbow and arm, hemiplegia.
2) Disorders of Head and Sense Organs: Pain and swelling of the throat, aphasia.
3) Respiratory Diseases: Hemoptysis, cough, asthma, febrile diseases without sweating.
4) Other diseases: Hemorrhoids.

【Mechanism of Action】 Kongzui (LU 6) is the Xi-(cleft) point of the Lung Meridian of Hand-Taiyin. The Xi-(cleft) points of the Yin meridians are effective in hemorrhagic syndromes. Puncturing Kongzui (LU 6) is good for treating hemoptysis due to bronchiectasis. Lung and Large Intestine Meridians are exteriorly-interiorly related, so Kongzui is used to treat hemorrhoids.

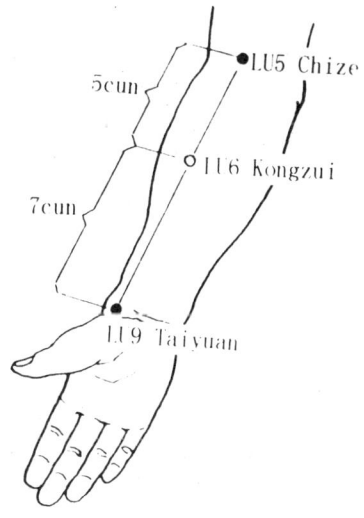

Fig. 8-3

【Method】 Puncture perpendicularly 0.5-1 cun. Moxibustion is applicable.
【Acupoint Prescriptions】
1) Cough: Kongzui (LU 6), Tianquan (PC 2), Taixi (KI 3), Xingjian (LI 2), Shufu (KI 27), Shenfeng (KI 23), Fujie (SP 14), Shaoshang (LU 11) Fubai (GB 13), (*Experience on Acupuncture and Moxibustion Therapy*).
2) Aphasia: Kongzui (LU 6), Yamen (DU 15). (*ibid*)
3) Acute hemoptysis: Give strong stimulation on Kongzui (LU 6), Chize (LU 5), Neiguan (PC 6), and retain the needles for 15 minutes. (*Abstract of Clinical Experience on*

Acupuncture and Moxibustion).

【Regional Anatomy】 Skin-subcutaneous tissue-brachioradial muscle-radial flexor muscle of the wrist-between superficial flexor muscle of the fingers and round pronator muscle-long flexor muscle of the thumb. In the superficial layer, there is the cephalic vein and the branches of the lateral cutaneous nerve of the forearm. In the deep layer, there is the radial artery and vein and the superficial branches of the radial nerve.

LU 7 Lieque (列缺)
(Branching Cleft)

【Source】 *Miraculous Pivot*

【Name Explanation】 Lie (列), arrangement; Que (缺), depression. Lightning and rifts in the clouds were called Lieque in ancient times. The Meridian of Hand Taiyin diverges from this point to the Meridian of Hand Yangming. The point is in the depression superior to the styloid process of the radius.

【Classification】 Luo-(Connecting) point of the Lung Meridian of Hand Taiyin and one of the Eight Confluent Points, communicating with the Ren Meridian.

【Location】 On the radial side of the forearm, proximal to the styloid process of the radius, 1.5 cun above the crease of the wrist, between the brachioradial muscle and the tendon of the long abductor muscle of the thumb. (See Fig. 8-4)

【Localization】

1) Cross the index fingers and thumbs of both hands, and place the index finger of one hand on the styloid process of the radius of the other, the point is located where the tip of the index finger rests.

2) Make a fist holding the thumb upwards, first locate Yangxi (LI 5) which is located in the depression between the two tendons, anatomical snuffbox above styloid process of the radius, Lieque (LU 7) is 1.5 cun superior to Yangxi (LI 5).

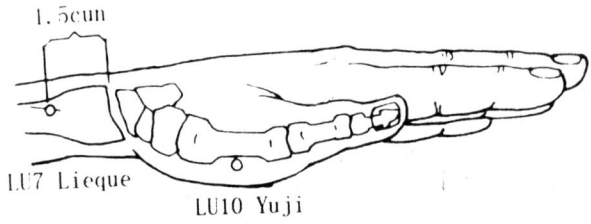

Fig. 8-4

【Indications】

1) Diseases along the Course of the Meridian: Pain of the arm and shoulder, numbness of fingers, hemiparalysis.

2) Disorders of Head and Sense Organs: Headache, migraine, deviation of the eye and mouth, facial spasm, facial paralysis, trigeminal neuralgia, sore throat, toothache.

3) Respiratory Diseases: Cough, asthma, common cold, fever and chills.

4) Digestive Diseases: Abdominal pain, diarrhea, dysentery, hemoptysis, dysphagia.

5) Cardiovascular Diseases: Cardiac pain, chest pain, hypertension.

6) Urinary Diseases: Hematuria, penile pain, hotness of urine, difficulty and pain in micturition, dysuria, stranguria.

7) Genital Diseases: Nocturnal emission, retention of dead fetus.

8) Other Diseases: Malaria, rubella, lumbago, sudden swelling of the four limbs, mastitis.

【Mechanism of Action】

1) The lung is in charge of qi. This point has the function of activating lung qi, thus it can

be used to treat sore throat and respiratory diseases.

2) The Lung Meridian starts from the epigastric region (the Middle-Jiao), and can treat abdominal pain, diarrhea, dysentery and hemoptysis. The lung has the function of promoting water metabolism. The disorders of the urinary system can be treated by activating lung qi. The heart controls the blood circulation. Both the lung and heart are in the thoracic cavity, and can affect each other. This point can be used to treat cardiac pain and hypertension by activating lung qi and smoothing the chest qi.

3) Lieque (LU 7) communicates with the Ren Meridian which dominates pregnancy, and can be used to treat sterility.

4) The Lung Meridian has no distribution on the head, but its divergent meridian does. On the other hand, Lieque is the Luo-(connecting) point of the Lung Meridian. It connects with the Large Intestine Meridian, and crosses at Dazhui (DU 14) with all the Yang meridians through the Large Intestine Meridian. It is an effective point to treat the disorders of the head and sense organs. It is mentioned in Song of the Four Key Points that: "select Lieque (LU 7) for the diseases of head and sense organs."

5) The lung dominates the skin and hair, and can be used to treat rubella and lumbago by expelling the wind evils through the body surface.

【Method】 Puncture obliquely 0.5-0.8 cun. Moxibustion is applicable.

【Acupoint Prescriptions】
1) Infantile convulsion: Lieque (LU 7), Pianli (LI 6). (*A-B Classic of Acupuncture and Moxibustion*).
2) Malaria: Lieque (LU 7), Houxi (SI 3), Shaoze (SI 1), qiangu (SI 2). (*Thousand Golden Prescriptions*).
3) Penile pain: Lieque (LU 7), Yinlingquan (SP 9), Shaofu (HT 8). (*Experience on Acupuncture and Moxibustion Therapy*)
4) Pulmonary tuberculosis with hemoptysis: Lieque (LU 7), Taiyuan (LU 9), Chize (LU 5), Zusanli (ST 36). (*Science of Acupuncture and Moxibustion*).

【Regional Anatomy】 Skin-subcutaneous tissue-long abductor muscle of the thumb-tendon of brachioradial muscle-quadrate pronator muscle. In the superficial layer, there is the cephalic vein, the lateral cutaneous nerve of the forearm and the superficial branches of the radial nerve. In the deep layer, there are the branches of the radial artery and vein.

【Remark】 Puncturing Lieque (LU 7) can increase pulmonary ventilation, relieve the resistance of respiratory tracts, eliminate spasms of the bronchial smooth muscles, and alleviate asthma.

By clinical observations and experimental studies, researchers have found that puncturing Lieque (LU 7) in combination with Shenshu (BL 23) or Zhaohai (KI 3) can improve renal function (increase phenol sulfonph thalein excretion rate), decrease urinary protein, and decrease blood pressure. The effect can last for 2-3 hours, and after another puncture, the effect can be even better. There are also experiments which show that puncturing Lieque (LU 7) can cause bladder contraction to increase urinary output.

Puncturing Lieque (LU 7) can regulate vasomotor function. Through vascular capacity tracing method, researchers have found that needling Lieque (LU 7) can bring about the change of capacity of the blood vessels vascular contraction.

LU 8 Jingqu (经渠)
(Passing Ditch)

【Source】 *Miraculous Pivot*
【Name Explanation】 Jing(经), passage; Qu(渠), ditch. A ditch where the meridian passes.

[Classification] One of the Five Shu Points and the Jing-(River) Point of the Lung Meridian of Hand Taiyin, pertaining to metal in the Five Elements.

[Location] On the radial side of the palmar surface of the forearm, 1 cun above the crease of the wrist, in the depression between the styloid process of the radius and the radial artery. (See Fig. 8-5)

[Localization] Extend the hand laterally with the palms facing upward. The point is located 1 cun superior to the transverse crease of the wrist, located where the radial artery beats in the middle pulse position.

[Indications]

1) Diseases along the Course of the Meridian: Pain in the medial aspect of the shoulder, forearm and wrist, neuralgia and paralysis of radial nerve.

2) Diseases of Head and Sense Organs: Sore throat.

3) Respiratory Diseases: Cough, asthma, fullness and pain in the chest.

4) Digestive Diseases: Epigastric pain, vomiting.

5) Other Diseases: Malaria, phrenospasm, esophagospasm.

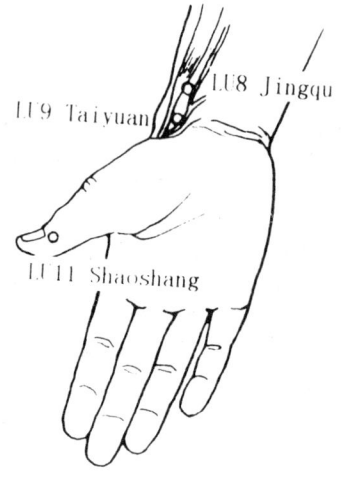

Fig. 8-5

[Mechanism of Action] See Lieque (LU 7).

[Method] Puncture perpendicularly or obliquely 0.3-0.5 cun. Avoid puncturing the radial artery. Moxibustion is contraindicated.

[Acupoint Prescription]

1) Cough and asthma: Jingqu (LU 8), Tianfu (LU 3), (*A-B Classic of Acupuncture and Moxibustion*).

2) Back pain: Jingqu (LU 8), Qiuxu (GB 40), Yuji (LU 10), Kunlun (BL 60), Jinggu (BL 64), (*Great Compendium of Acupuncture and Moxibustion*).

[Regional Anatomy] Skin-subcutaneous tissue-ulnar border of the tendon of brachioradial muscle-quadrate pronator muscle. In the superficial layer, there is the lateral cutaneous nerve of the forearm and the superficial branches of the radial nerve. In the deep layer, there are the radial artery and vein.

LU 9 Taiyuan (太渊)
(Supreme Abyss)

[Source] *Miraculous Pivot*

[Name Explanation] Tai (太), great; Yuan (渊), deep pool. Tai means abundance. The qi of the meridian in this point is abundant.

[Classification]

1) One of the Five Shu Points and the Shu-(Stream) Point of the Lung Meridian of Hand Taiyin, pertaining to earth in the Five Elements.

2) Yuan-(Source) Point of the Lung Meridian.

3) One of the Eight Influential Points, the Influential Point of the pulse and vessels.

[Location] At the radial end of the crease of the wrist, where the pulse of the radial artery is palpable. (See Fig. 8-5)

[Localization] Palm facing upwards. The point is located at the transverse crease of the wrist in the place where we can feel the pulse.

【Indications】
1) Diseases along the Course of the Meridian: Pain in arm and elbow, hemiparalysis, injury of wrist and soft tissue.
2) Disorders of Head and Sense Organs: Cataract, dryness of the throat, inflammation of the throat.
3) Respiratory Diseases: Cough, asthma, hemoptysis, pain in the chest and back.
4) Cardiovascular diseases: Cardiac pain, pulseless disease.
5) Digestive system diseases: distention in the abdomen, belching vomiting with bleeding.
6) Other Diseases: Amenorrhea, dysmenorrhea, deafness and mutism, intercostal neuralgia.

【Mechanism of Action】
1) The Lung Meridian of Hand Taiyin is externally and internally related with the Large Intestine Meridian of Hand Yangming, communicating with the Ren Meridian. The points of the Large Intestine Meridian are commonly used to treat diseases of the head and sense organs. According to the therapeutic property that the Five-Shu points connect with the meridian, this point is commonly used to treat disorders of head and sense organs.
2) It is the influential point of the vessels and pulse. The heart controls blood circulation, so the point is used for pulseless disease and cardiac pain.
3) The muscle region of Hand Taiyin "runs downwards to knot in the chest and arrives at the hypochondriac region", and is used for intercostal neuralgia.

【Method】 Puncture perpendicularly 0.2-0.3 cun. Moxibustion is applicable

【Acupoint Prescriptions】
1) Restlessness: Taiyuan (LU 9), Feishu (BL 13), Shangguan (GB 3), Tiaokou (ST 38), Yinbai (SP 1). (*Experience on Acupuncture and Moxibustion Therapy*)
2) Belching: Taiyuan (LU 9), Yangxi (LI 5), Xialian (LI 8), Kunlun (BL 60), (*Great Compendium of Acupuncture and Moxibustion*)
3) Syncope due to cold: Taiyuan (LU 9), Yemen (SJ 3). (*ibid*)
4) Cough due to wind phlegm: Taiyuan (LU 9), Lieque (LU 9). (*Songs of Jade Dragon*)

【Regional Anatomy】 Skin-subcutaneous tissue-between the tendons of the radial flexor muscle of wrist and long abductor muscle of the thumb. In the superficial layer, there is the lateral cutaneous nerve of the forearm, the superficial branches of the radial nerve and the superficial palmar branches of the radial artery. In the deep layer, there is the radial artery and vein.

【Remark】 Taiyuan (LU 9) is one of the Eight Influential Points. Puncturing Taiyuan (LU 9) has a great effect on diseases caused by abnormal blood circulation and hemorrhage. According to clinical observations, needling Taiyuan (LU 9) can treat hemoptysis and cerebral hemorrhage. Taiyuan (LU 9) has an obvious effect of regulating blood pressure and clinical observations have proven that needling it can decrease tertiary hypertension. Taiyuan (LU 9) is also the Shu-(Stream) point Yuan-(Source) of the Lung Meridian. It has an obvious action of regulating lung function. Researchers used flowing rate recorder and steaming air flow to test Taiyuan (LU 9) and Feishu (BL 13) seperately. The results of the resistance before and after the experiment indicated that the increase of airway resistance decreased in both the breathing-in and breathing-out stage, and resistance decreased more obviously in the breathing-out stage. This proves that needling this point can improve pulmonary ventilation to strengthen respiratory function.

LU 10　Yuji (鱼际)
(Fish Border)

[Source] *Miraculous Pivot*

[Name Explanation] Yu (鱼), fish; Ji (际), border. The muscle flexor pollicis in the palm is prominent like a fish, the point is located just at its border. Yuji is used as an anatomical landmark at present.

[Classification] One of the Five Shu Points and the Ying-(Spring) Point of the Lung Meridian of Hand Taiyin pertaining to fire in the Five Elements.

[Location] In the depression proximal to the 1st metacarpophalangeal joint, on the radial side of the midpoint of the 1st metacarpal bone, and at the junction of the red and white skin. (See Fig. 8-4)

[Localization] Make a fist slightly with palm facing upwards and joint of the wrist bending downwards, the point is located between the white and red skin in the middle of the first metacarpal bone.

[Indications]

　　1) Diseases along the Course of the Meridian: Shoulder pain, spasmodic pain of the elbow, numbness of the fingers.

　　2) Disorders of Head and Sense Organs: Headache, dry throat, sore throat, aphasia.

　　3) Digestive Diseases: abdominal pain, vomiting.

　　4) Respiratory Diseases: Cough, asthma, hemoptysis, pain in chest and back, common cold, fever.

　　5) Mental Disorders: Susceptibility to sorrow and fright, mental confusion..

　　6) Other Diseases: Mastitis, arrhythmia.

[Mechanism of Action] The point is located on the hand. According to therapeutic properties, points on the hand are good at treating the diseases on head and face. It can also be used to clear away lung heat. Clinically, it can be used to treat cases of cough, asthma, fever and sore throat due to excess syndrome.

[Method] Puncture perpendicularly 0.2-0.3 cun. Moxibustion is applicable.

[Acupoint Prescriptions]

　　1) Hemoptysis: Reduce Yuji (LU 10), reinforce Chize (LU 5). (*A-B Classic of Acupuncture and Moxibustion*)

　　2) Cardiac pain: Yuji (LU 10), Taiyuan (LU 9). (*ibid*)

　　3) Cough: Yuji (LU 10), Lieque (LU 7), Shaoze (SI 1), Quepen (ST 12). (*Experience on Acupuncture and Moxibustion Therapy*)

　　4) Headache: Yuji (LU 10), Yemen (SJ 2), Zhongzhu (SJ 3), Tongli (HT 5). (*ibid*)

[Remark] Radio-immune analysis shows that puncturing Yuji (LU 10) has the effect of relieving asthma. It is found that asthmatic attack is related with the decline of cyclic adenosine monaphosphate (CAMP) in the plasma and lung tissue. Puncturing Yuji (LU 10) for two weeks can increase plasmsa levels of CAMP, and the ratio of CAMP and cyclic guanosine monophosphate (CGMP). At the same time, clinical symptoms such as asthmatic wheezing are eliminated and the maximum ventilation volume increased. Puncturing the point can also improve pulmonary function to calm abnormal breathing. Needling Ximen (PC 4), Yuji (LU 10), and Taixi (KI 3) can improve the pendular movement of the mediastinum due to thoracatomy. This effect is more advantageous than that of the old method in which the peripheral nerve at the pulmonary hilum has to be blocked.

LU 11　Shaoshang（少商）
（Lesser Shang）

【Source】 *Miraculous Pivot*
【Name Explanation】 Shao（少）, immaturity; Shang（商）, one of the Five Sounds, pertaining to metal. Shao means minority. The Lung pertains to metal in the Five Elements and to shang sound in the Five Sounds. This is the last point of the Lung Meridian where qi becomes less.
【Classification】 One of the Five Shu Points and the Jing-(Well) point of the Lung Meridian of Hand Taiyin, pertaining to wood in the Five Elements.
【Location】 On the radial side of the distal segment of the thumb, 0.1 cun posterior to the corner of the fingernail. (See Fig. 8-5)
【Localization】 Make a fist slightly with the palm facing upwards and thumb pointing upwards. The point can be located in the intersection of the lines between the radial border of thumb nail and the basal part.
【Indications】
　　1) Diseases along the Course of the Meridian: Numbness and spasmodic pain of the fingers.
　　2) Disorders of Head and Sense Organs: Sore throat, epistaxis, mumps, toothache, tinnitus.
　　3) Respiratory Diseases: Cough, asthma.
　　4) Mental Disorders: Coma, loss of consciousness, trismus epilepsy, mania, infantile convulsion.
　　5) Other Diseases: Heatstroke, febrile diseases, apoplexy.
【Mechanism of Action】
　　1) Blood-letting method can be applied to smooth the circulation of blood and qi for finger numbness caused by stasis of blood and can also be used for coma and apoplexy to induce resuscitation. For the cases of sunstroke and infantile convulsion, blood-letting method is the main method to clear away heat.
　　2) This point is one of the 13 ghost points, (From the ancient to the present, it is one of the important points which have the effects of inducing resuscitation and tranquilizing the mind).
【Method】 Puncture perpendicularly 0.1 cun, or prick the point to cause bleeding. Moxibustion is applicable.
【Acupoint Prescription】
　　1) Vomiting: Shaoshang (LU 11), Laogong (PC 8). (*Great Compendium of Acupuncture and Moxibustion*)
　　2) Wheezing sound in the throat: Shaoshang (LU 11), Tiantu (RN 22), apply moxibustion with three moxa cones. (*ibid*)
　　3) Tonsillitis: Shaoshang (LU 11), Jinjin (EX-HN 12), Yuye (EX-HN 13). (*ibid*)
　　4) Hysteria: Apply moxibustion to Shaoshang (LU 11) and Xinshu (BL 15). Puncture Shenmen (HT 7), Yongquan (KI 1), Zhongwan (RN 12). (*New Acupuncture and Moxibustion*)
【Regional Anatomy】 Skin-subcutaneous tissue-root of the nail
　　There are the dorsal digital branches of the proper palmar digital nerve of the median nerve, the arteriovenous network formed by the principal arteries and veins of the thumb and the 1st dorsal metacarpal arteries and veins in this area. (See Fig 8-6 and Table 8-1)

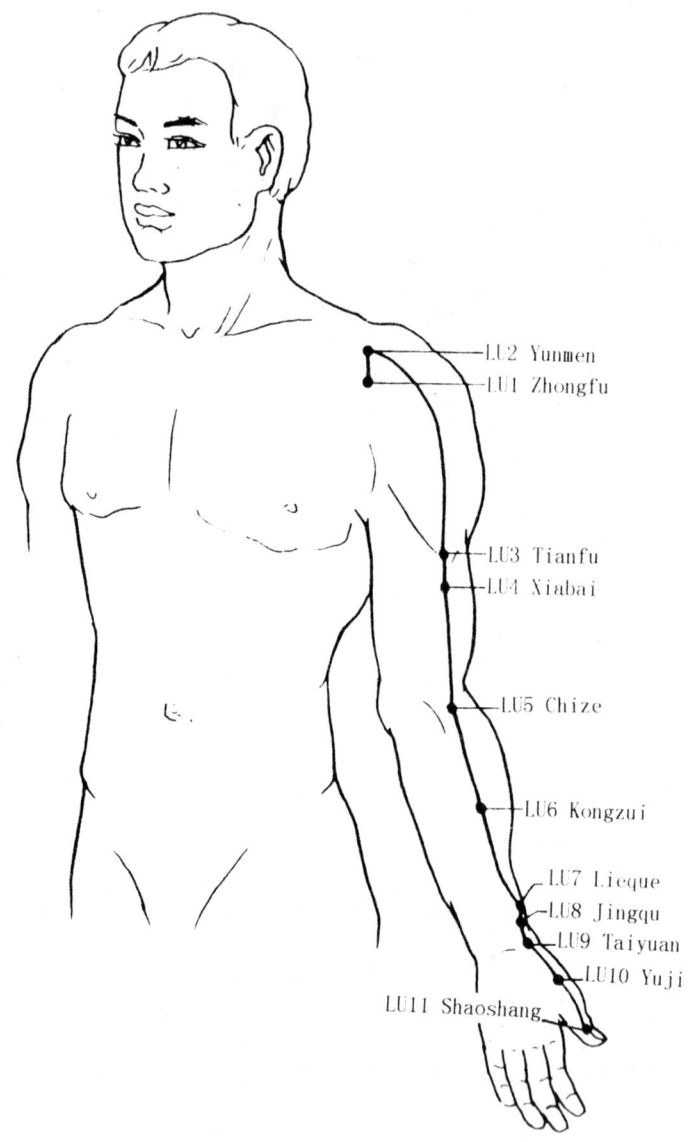

Fig. 8-6 Acupoints of the Lung Meridian of Hand Taiyin

Table 8-1 Indications and Actions of Acupoints of the Lung Meridian of Hand Taiyin

Name of the points	Specific points	Common indications	Specific indications and functions
LU 1 Zhongfu (中府)	Front-Mu point Crossing point	Diseases of the chest and lung: cough, asthma, chest pain	Easing the chest and regulating qi, reduces heat and disperses lung-qi. Cough, asthma, distention of the chest, vomiting, hiccups, vomiting of turbid fluid, shoulder and back pain, bronchitis, pneumonia
LU 2 Yunmen (云门)			Easing the chest and regulating qi, reducing heat and dispersing lung-qi. Inability to lie down due to cough and dyspnea, fullness sensation and heat-pain in the chest, shoulder and back pain

Acupoints of Three Yin Meridians of Hand

Name of the points	Specific points	Common indications	Specific indications and functions
LU 3 Tianfu (天府)		Diseases of the throat, chest and lung: cough, hemoptysis, dyspnea, chest pain, swelling and pain of the throat	Dyspnea, epistaxis, pain in the upper arm
LU 4 Xiabai (侠白)			Regulating lung qi and promoting qi and blood circulation. Cough, dyspnea, nausea, restlessness and fullness, pain in the upper arm
LU 5 Chize (尺泽)	He-(Sea) point		Reducing heat and regulating lung qi, dredging meridians and collaterals, descending the adverse flow of qi and promoting diuresis. Hectic fever, irritability, infantile convulsion, acrotism (no pulse), acute vomiting and diarrhea, spasmatic pain of the elbow and arm
LU 6 Kongzui (孔最)	Xi-(Cleft) point		Reducing heat, regulating lung qi, stopping bleeding. Febrile diseases without sweating, hemoptysis, loss of voice, headache, spasmatic pain of the elbow and arm, hemorrhoids
LU 7 Lieque (列缺)	Luo-(Connecting) point One of the eight confluent points		Dispersing lung qi by expelling wind, benefiting pharynx and diaphragm, regulating the Ren Meridian. Stiffness and pain of the head and neck, migraine, deviation of the mouth and eyes, hiccups, edema, consumptive disease, acrotism, swelling pain, and weakness of the wrist
LU 8 Jingqu (经渠)	Jing-(River) point		Cough, dyspnea, pain in chest and back, febrile diseases without sweating, feverish sensation in the centre of palm, pain and weakness of the wrist
LU 9 Taiyuan (太渊)	Shu-(Stream) point Yuan-(Source) point Influential point of the vessels and pulse		Expelling wind to stop cough, regulating lung qi and resolving phlegm, dredging the collaterals. Acrotism, cough and dyspnea due to deficiency of lung qi, restlessness, cardiac pain, palpitation, feverish sensation in the centre of palm, hiccups, abdominal pain, amenorrhea
LU 10 Yuji (鱼际)	Ying-(Spring) point		Headache, swelling and pain of the throat, dryness in the phraynx, loss of voice, mastitis
LU 11 Shaoshang (少商)	Jing-(Well) point		Clearing heat from the lung and relieving sore throat, reviving the unconsciousness. Fever, headache, swelling and pain of the throat, apoplexy and coma, manic-depression, heatstroke, infantile convulsion, spasm and pain of the fingers

IV. Acupoints of the Pericardium Meridian of Hand Jueyin

PC 1 Tianchi (天池)
(Heaven Pool)

【Source】 *Miraculous Pivot*

【Name Explanation】 Tian (天), heaven; Chi (池), pool. The point is lateral to the breast and the milk secreted from the breast is as if from a heavenly pool.

【Classification】 It is one of the Crossing Points, and the crossing place of Hand Jueyin and Foot Shaoyang meridians.

【Location】 On the chest, in the 4th intercostal space, 1 cun lateral to the nipple and 5 cun lateral to the anterior midline. (See Fig. 8-7)

【Localization】 Supine position, the point is located in the intercostal space of the 4th rib, 1 cun lateral to the nipple.

【Indications】

1) Cardiovascular Diseases: Cardiac pain, oppression and pain of the chest, fullness in the chest.

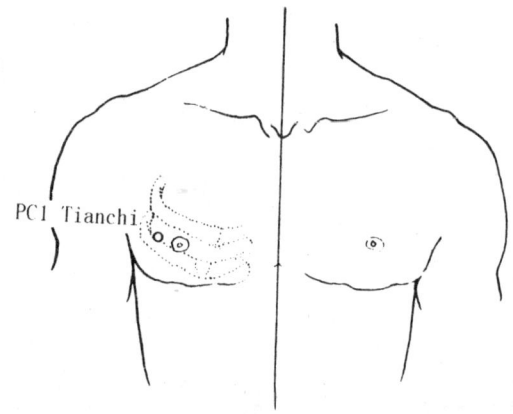

Fig. 8-7

2) Respiratory and Diaphragm Diseases: Cough, asthma, excessive phlegm, wheezing sound in the throat.

3) Other Diseases: Scrofula in the axilla, mastitis, pain in the chest and hypochondrium, anhidrosis, malaria.

【Mechanism of Action】 The point is located beside the breast, corresponding to the heart and lung in the chest. According to the rule that where the acupoint locates where the indications are. This point is used for treating diseases of the heart, lung and breast.

【Method】 Puncture obliquely 0.3-0.5 cun, deeper puncturing is contraindicated. Moxibustion is applicable.

【Regional Anatomy】 Skin-subcutaneous tissue-greater pectoral muscle-smaller pectoral muscle. In the superficial layer, there are the lateral cutaneous branches of the 4th intercostal nerve and the tributaries of the thoraco epigastric vein. In women, there are also glandular tissues in the subcutaneous layer. In the deeper layer, there are the medial and later pectoral nerves and the branches or tributaries of the lateral thoracic artery and vein.

PC 2 Tianquan (天泉)
(Heaven Fountain)

【Source】 *A-B Classic of Acupuncture and Moxibustion*
【Name Explanation】 Tian (天), heaven; Quan (泉), spring. The qi of meridian originating from Tianchi (PC 1) flows downward as spring water from heaven.
【Location】 On the medial side of the arm, 2 cun below the anterior end of the axillary fold, between the long and short heads of the biceps muscle of the arm. (See Fig. 8-8)
【Localization】 Extend the arm with palm facing upwards. Connect the line between the superior extremity of the anterior axillary fold and Quze (PC 3) which is located on the cubital cross striation. This point is located 7 cun superior to the cubital cross striation on the line.
【Indications】
   1) Diseases along the Course of the Meridian: Pain in the chest and medial aspect of the upper limbs.
   2) Cardiovascular Diseases: Cardiac pain, palpitation, fullness in the chest and hypochondrium.
   3) Respiratory Diseases: Cough, pain in the chest.
   4) Other Diseases: Hicups, failure of the lower limbs to walk, blurring of vision.
【Mechanism of Action】 The Pericardium Meridian of Hand Jueyin "originates from the chest, emerges and pertains to the pericardium and connects with San jiao". The lungs are located in

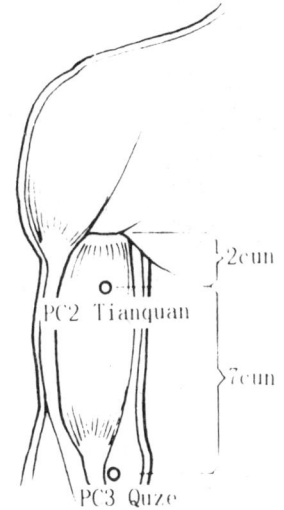

Fig. 8-8

the upper Jiao, so this point is used to treat the diseases of the heart and lung. The Foot and Hand Jueyin Meridians are connected with each other. The liver determines the condition of the tendons. The point can be used to treat failure of the lower limbs to walk.
【Method】 Puncture perpendicularly 0.5-1 cun. Moxibustion is applicable.
【Regional Anatomy】 Skin-subcutaneous tissue-brachial biceps muscle-brachial muscle-tendon of coracobrachial and vein. In the superificial layer, there are the branches of the medial brachial cutaneous nerve. In the deep layer, there are the musculocutaneous nerve and the muscular branches of the brachial artery and vein.

PC 3 Quze (曲泽)
(Marshon Bend)

【Source】 *Miraculous Pivot*
【Name Explanation】 Qu (曲), curve; Ze (泽), marsh. The qi of the meridian infuses into the shallow depression of the elbow like water flowing into a marsh.
【Classification】 He-(Sea) Point of the Pericardium Meridian of Hand Jueyin, pertaining to wa-

ter in the Five Elements.

【Location】 At the midpoint of the cubital crease, on the ulnar side of the tendon of the biceps muscle of the arm. (See Fig. 8-8)

【Localization】 Bend the elbow slightly with palm facing upwards. The point is located in the ulnar side of the tendon of brachial biceps on the cubital cross striation.

【Indications】

1) Diseases along the Course of the Meridian: Pain in the arm and elbow, tremor in the upper limbs.

2) Cardiovascular Diseases: Cardiac pain, palpitation.

3) Digestive Diseases: Stomachache, vomiting, hematemesis, cholera, diarrhea.

4) Respiratory Diseases: Cough.

5) Other Diseases: Heatstroke, febrile diseases, dry mouth, adverseness of qi.

【Mechanism of Action】

The Pericardium Meridian "connects with the three Jiao. Using bleeding method on this point can clear away heat. It is an effective point for treating cholera, heatstroke and vomiting. See Tianquan(PC 2), Jianshi(PC 5), Neiguan(PC 6) for more details.

【Method】 Puncture perpendicularly 1-1.5 cun, or prick the vein to cause bleeding. Moxibustion is applicable.

【Acupoint Prescriptions】

1) Palpitation: Quze (PC 3), Daling (PC 7) "which is used to treat timidness due to palpitation. (*Thousand Golden Prescriptions*)

2) Dryness of the mouth: Quze (PC 3), Zhangmen (LI 13). (*ibid*)

3) Hematemesis: Quze (PC 3), Shenmen (HT 7), Yuji (LU 10). (*Great Compendium of Acupuncture and Moxibustion*)

4) Pain in the chest and cardiac region: Quze (PC 3), Neiguan (PC 6), Daling (PC 7). (*ibid*)

【Regional Anatomy】 Skin-subcutaneous tissue-medial nerve-brachial muscle. In the superficial layer, there are the medial vein of the elbow and the medial cutaneous nerve of the forearm. In the deep layer, there is the brachial artery and veins, the arteriovenous network formed by the palmar branches of the ulnar recurrent artery and vein with the anterior branches of the inferior ulnar collateral artery and vein, and the trunk of the median nerve.

PC 4　Ximen (郄门)
(Cleft Gate)

【Source】 *A-B Classic of Acupuncture and Moxibustion*

【Name Explanation】 Xi (郄), cleft; Men (门), door. This is a Xi-(Cleft) point of the Pericardium Meridian, also a door where the qi of this meridian enters and exits.

【Classification】 Xi-(Cleft) Point of the Pericardium Meridian of Hand Jueyin.

【Location】 On the palmar side of forearm and on the line connecting Quze (PC 3) and Daling (PC 7), 5 cun above the crease of the wrist. (See Fig. 8-9)

【Localization】 Extend the arm with palm facing upwards. The point is located in 5 cun directly superior to Daling (PC 7) which is located in the middle of the transverse crease of the wrist, between the tendon of palmaris longus and the radial side of the carpal flexor tendon.

【Indications】

1) Diseases along the Course of the Meridian: Hemiplegia, pain and numbness of arm and shoulder.

2) Cardiovascular Diseases: Cardiac pain, palpitation, irritablility, chest pain.

3) Digestive Diseases: Hematemesis.
4) Respiratory Diseases: Hemoptysis.
5) Mental Disorders: Epilepsy, timidness, hysteria.
6) Other Diseases: Uterine bleeding, furuncle, mastitis.

【Mechanism of Action】
1) The Cleft-point is good for treating bleeding syndromes, such as hematemesis, hemoptysis, epistaxis, uterine bleeding, etc.
2) The pericardium is the peripheral tissue of the heart. It performs the function of the heart and is always attacked instead of the heart. Because the Pericardium Meridian connects with the heart, the point can be used to treat heart diseases, such as cardiac pain, palpitation, irritability, etc. It is reported that its effect on treating atrial fibrillation is obvious. The heart dominates mental activities, so it is a commonly used point for mental diseases.
3) The meridian and the muscle region of Hand-Jueyin distribute in the chest. So most of the points of the Pericardium Meridian are used to treat mastitis.
4) This point has the action of clearing away heat and toxic materials. So it can be used to treat furuncles.

【Method】 Puncture perpendicularly 0.5-1 cun. Moxibustion is applicable.

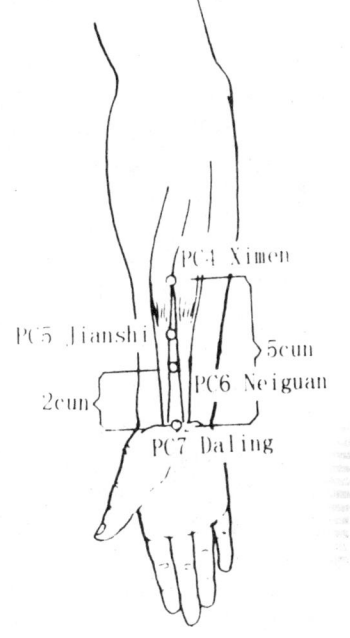

Fig. 8-9

【Acupoint Prescription】
Hemoptysis caused by pulmonary tuberculosis: Ximen (PC 4), Chize (LU 5) and Feishu (BL 13) are used as main points. Bailao (EX-HN 15), Zhongfu (LU 1) and Zhongwan (RN 12) are used as supplementary points. (*Abstract of Clinical Experience on Accupuncture and Moxibustion*.)

【Regional Anatomy】 Skin-subcutaneous tissue-between tendons of radial flexor muscle of wrist and long palmar muscle-superficial flexor muscle of fingers-deep flexor muscle of fingers-interosseous membrane of forearm. In the superficial layer, there are the branches of the lateral and medial cutaneous nerves of the forearm and the median vein of the forearm. In the deep layer, there are the median nerve and the accompanying artery and vein and the anterior interosseous artery and nerve.

【Remark】 Needling Ximen (PC 4) has a regulating effect on pulmonary function, it can also relieve the pendular movement of the mediastinum caused by thoracotomy. During thoracotomy, the open pneumothorax and pulmonary collapse can be found at the operative side, but the partial pressure of oxygen in aterial blood may rise so as to avoid hypoxi, only carbon dioxide may rise in different degrees. Puncturing Ximen (PC 4) also has a regulating effect on cardiac function. Puncturing Ximen (PC 4) may slow the cardiac rate and strengthen the myocardial contraction power for the patients having coronary heart disease and angina pectoris.

PC 5   Jianshi（间使）
（Intermediary）

【Source】 *Miraculous Pivot*
【Name Explanation】 Jian (间), space; Shi (使), minister of a monarch. The point pertains to the pericardium Meridian and is in the space between the two tendons. It is so named because

the pericardium is the minister of the heart.

【Classification】 Jing-(River) Point of the Pericardium Meridian of Hand Jueyin, pertaining to metal in the Five Elements.

【Location】 On the palmar side of forearm and on the line connecting Quze (PC 3) and Daling (PC 7), 3 cun above the crease of the wrist, between the tendons of the long palmar muscle and radial flexor muscle of the wrist. (See Fig. 8-9)

【Localization】 Extend the arm with palm facing upwards. The point is located 3 cun directly superior to Daling (PC 7) which is located in the middle of the transverse crease of the wrist, between the tendon palmaris longus and the radial side of carpal flexor tendon.

【Indications】

1) Diseases along the Course of the Meridian: Swelling of axilla, pain of the arm, spasm of the elbow, feverish sensation in the palm.

2) Diseases of Head and Sense Organs: Sore throat.

3) Cardiovascular Diseases: Cardiac pain, palpitation and palpitation with hungry feeling, slow and irregular pulse.

4) Digestive Diseases: Stomachache, vomiting, cholera, diarrhea.

5) Mental Disorders: Epilepsy, mania, depression, apoplexy, infantile convulsion, aphasia, hysteria.

6) Other Diseases: Menorrhagia, metrorrhagia urticaria, scabies, malaria.

【Mechanism of Action】 It's effective for scabies and urticaria by clearing away heat and cooling blood. See Neiguan (PC 6) and Ximen (PC 4) for other details.

【Method】 Puncture perpendicularly 0.5-1 cun. Moxibustion is applicable.

【Acupoint Prescriptions】

1) Frequent vomiting: Apply moxibustion to Jianshi (PC 5), or Chize (LU 5). (*A Handbook of Prescriptions for Emergency*)

2) Infantile convulsive seizure due to fright: Apply moxibustion to Jianshi (PC 5) with 7 cones, Jianjing (GB 21) 100 cones, the tip of the fingers 3 cones. (*A Supplement to Thousand Golden Prescriptions*)

3) Nausea: Applying moxibustion to Jianshi (PC 5) with 30 cones, Danshu (BL 19), Tonggu (BL 66), Yinbai (SP 1) and the spot 1.5 cun below the nipple. (*Great Compendium of Acupuncture and Moxibustion*).

4) Sudden attack of mania: Jianshi (PC 5), Houxi (SI 3), Hegu (LI 4). (*ibid*)

5) Five types of malaria: Jianshi (PC 5), Dazhu (BL 11). (*Songs of Shengyu*)

6) Ravings and night sweating: Fengfu (DU 16), Jianshi (PC 5). (*Songs For Easy Acupoint Selection*)

【Regional Anatomy】 Skin-subcutaneous tissue-between tendons of radial flexor muscle of the wrist and long palmar muscle-superficial flexor muscle of the fingers-deep flexor muscle of the fingers-quadrate pronator, muscle-interosseous membrane of forearm. In the superficial layer, there are the branches of the lateral and medial cutaneous nerves and the median vein of the forearm. In the deep layer, there are the median nerve and the accompanying artery and vein and the anterior interosseous artery and nerve.

【Remark】 Puncturing Jianshi (PC 5) has an obvious effect on cardiac function. In the treatment of coronary heart disease, it can strengthen myocardial contraction power, slow cardiac rate, improve electrocardio-gram and decrease the left ventricular and diastolic pressure. An experiment proved that electropuncturing Neiguan (PC 6) and Jianshi (PC 5) could increase coronary blood flow and myocardial blood oxygen supply, descend coronary resistance and myocardial oxygen consumption rate, decrease the maximum difference of blood oxygen content in coronary arteria, and lower myocardial oxygen balance between supply and demand, help reduce the myocardial damage degree in ischemia area, and decrease the necrotic area.

PC 6　Neiguan (内关)
(Inner Conjunction)

〖Source〗 *Miraculous Pivot*
〖Name Explanation〗 Nei (内), medial; Guan (关), pass. The point is at an important site at the medial aspect of the forearm, like a pass.
〖Classification〗
　　3) Luo-(Connecting) Point of the Pericardium Meridian of Hand Jueyin and one of the Eight Confluent Points joining the Yinwei Meridian.
〖Location〗 On the palmar side of the forearm and on the line connecting Quze (PC 3) and Daling (PC 7), 2 cun above the crease of the wrist, between the tendons of the long palmar muscle and radial flexor muscle of the wrist. (See Fig. 8-9)
〖Localization〗 Extend the arm with palm facing upwards. The point is located 2 cun directly superior to Daling (PC 7) which is located in the middle of the transverse crease of the wrist, between the tendon palmaris longus and the radial side of carpal flexor tendon.
〖Indications〗
　　1) Diseases along the Course of the Meridian: Spasmodic pain of arm, elbow and wrist, hemiplegia.
　　2) Diseases of Head and Sense Organs: Migraine, vertigo.
　　3) Cardiovascular Diseases: Cardiac pain, palpitation, pain in the chest and hypochondrium.
　　4) Digestive Diseases: Stomachache with distention, vomiting, hiccups, gastric and abdominal distention, diarrhea.
　　5) Respiratory Diseases: Cough, asthma, fullness in the chest, short breath.
　　6) Genital Diseases: Irregular menstruation, vomiting due to pregnancy, postpartum vertigo, nocturnal emission.
　　7) Mental and general diseases: Insomnia, amnesia, depression, mania, epilepsy, melanchholia apoplexy.
　　8) Other Diseases: Heatstroke, malaria, anhidrosis.
〖Mechanism of Action〗
　　1) The meridian connects with the Sanjiao, and the collateral connects with the heart. The heart and lung are in the upper Jiao, the spleen and stomach in the middle Jiao, the liver and the kidney are in the lower Jiao. So the point can be used to treat diseases of the heart and lung in the upper Jiao, such as cardiac pain, palpitation, fullnessin the chest, shortness of breath, etc. The therapeutic effect is obvious. It is also the main point for treating stomachache, epigastric distention and vomiting due to disorders of the spleen and stomach in the middle Jiao. It's also used for irregular menstruation, postpartum vertigo and nocturnal emission due to disorders in the lower Jiao.
　　2) Heatstroke, febrile diseases and malaria belong to febrile diseases. The heart controls the blood circulation. Puncturing this point to cause bleeding can clear away the heat evil.
　　3) Puncturing this point to treat apoplexy is not only for activiting heart qi and inducing resusitation, but also for smoothing the meridians and collaterals.
〖Method〗 Puncture perpendicularly 0.5-1 cun. Moxibustion is applicable.
〖Acupoint Prescriptions〗
　　1) Anorexia: Neiguan (PC 6), Yuji (LU 10), Zusanli (ST 36). (*Great Compendium of Acupuncture and Moxibustion*).
　　2) Abdominal pain: Neiguan (PC 6), Zusanli (ST 36), Zhongwan (RN 12). (*ibid*)

3) Arrhythmia: Neiguan (PC 6), Shenmen (HT 2). (*Abstract of Clinical Experience on Acupuncture and Moxibustion*)

4) Leptospirosis: Neiguan (PC 6), Zusanli (ST 36), by injecting 10% quantity of penicillin for intramuscular injection into the point. (*Selection of Treatise of 30 Years*).

5) Pulselessness: Neiguan (PC 6), Taiyuan (LU 9). (*ibid*)

[Regional Anatomy] Skin-subcutaneous tissue-between tendons of radial flexor muscle of the wrist and long palmar muscle-superficial flexor muscle of fingers-deep flexor muscle of fingers-quadrate pronator muscle. In the superficial layer, there are the branches of the medial and lateral cutaneous nerves and the median vein of the forearm. In the deeper layer, there are the median nerve and accompanying artery and vein, the superficial flexor muscle of the fingers, the long flexor muscle of the thumb and the deep flexor muscle of the fingers. There are the anterior interosseous artery, vein and nerve on the anterior side of the interosseous membrane of the forearm.

[Remark] Observation on the pulse recovery of pulseless patient by way of acupuncture indicated that puncturing Neiguan (PC 6), Jianshi (PC 5) and Quze (PC 3) could obviously make pulses reappear 15 times in 19 experiments; Needling Liequ (LU 7), Taiyuan (LU 9) and Chize (LU 5) could make pulses reappear only 12 times in 19 experiments; Puncturing Shaohai (HT 3), Tongli (HT 5) and Qingling (HT 2) could make pulses recover only 5 times in 12 experiments. It's thought that the points of Hand-Jueyin meridian are the first choice to treat pulseless disease. The second are those of the Lung Meridian, and then those of the Heart Meridian.

179 cases with hypertension treated with acupuncture were divided into the following five groups: ① Neiguan (PC 6) in combination with Sanyinjiao (SP 6), Hegu (LI 4) and Taichong (LR 3); ② Neiguan (PC 6) with Sanyinjiao (SP 6); ③ Fengchi (GB 20) with Jianjing (GB 21) and Ganshu (BL 18); ④ Hegu (LI 4) with Zusanli (ST 36); ⑤ Quchi (LI 11) with Chize (LU 5), Ququan (LR 8) and Yanglingquan (GB 34). The curative rate of the first group was the highest, reach 88.2%, those of other groups were lower in turn.

Puncturing Neiguan (PC 6) in patients with coronary heart disease for two minutes, the preceding ejection period (PEP) and isovolumetric contraction time (ICT) are obviously shortened; the ejection time (ET) evidently lengthened, the ratio of ET/ICT obviously increased. The changes still have statistic significance after 15 minutes when the needle is withdrawn. But when Waiguan (SJ 5) and Sanyinjiao (SP 6) are punctured, the effect on the above five items doesn't show up until 15 minutes later.

Puncturing Neiguan (PC 6) has no obvious effect on the stroke output of the patients with coronry heart diseases, but can slow the heart rate, therefore, both the output per minute and the cardiac index are decreased. So, needling the point is effective in relieving the clinical symptoms of coronary heart diseases and improving electrocardiogram, it's probably because cardiac rate decreases and coronary blood flow increases, but it is not closely related to cardiac output.

Puncturing Neiguan (PC 6) of the 31 cases of coronary heart diseases patients whose electrocardio-gram's S-T segment showed ischemic descent for 0.05mv, their LVET prolonged, the PEP shortened and the ratio of PEP/LVET descended. But needling Waiguan (SJ 5), the three targets had no change.

PC 7　Daling（大陵）
（Big Hill）

[Source] *Miraculous Pivot*

[Name Explanation] Da (大), large; Ling (陵), mound. The protrusion of the palmar root is large, like a mound. The point is in the depression of the wrist proximal to it.

【Classification】
Shu-(Stream) and Yuan-(Source) Point of the Pericardium Meridian of Hand Jueyin pertaining to earth in the Five Elements.

【Location】 At the midpoint of the crease of the wrist, between the tendons of the long palmar muscle and radial flexor muscle of the wrist. (See Fig. 8-9)

【Localization】 Extend the arm with palm facing upwards. The point is located in the middle of the transverse crease of the wrist, between the tendon of the palmar is longus muscle and the radial side of the carpal flexor tendon.

【Indications】
1) Diseases along the Course of the Meridian: Spasmodic pain of the arm and elbow, pain of the wrist, feverish sensation in the palm.

2) Diseases of Head and Sense Organs: Headache, sore throat, pain, swelling and redness of the eyes, stiffness of the tongue.

3) Cardiovascular Diseases: Cardiac pain, palpitation, fullness sensation in the chest, short breath, pain in the chest and hypochondrium.

4) Digestive Diseases: Stomachache, vomiting, appendicitis, cholera, heamatemesis, foul breath.

5) Mental Diseases: Timidness, depression, mania, epilepsy, caprice, susceptibility to fright and anger.

6) Other Diseases: Eczema, urticaria, scabies, sore, anhidrosis, heatstroke.

【Mechanism of Action】 The application of this point is similar to that of Neiguan (PC 6) and with which it is often used, so is Jianshi (PC 5). Choosing two or more points bearing the similar function on the same meridian can enchance the curative effect.

【Method】 Puncture perpendicularly 0.5-0.8 cun. Moxibustion is applicable.

【Acupoint Prescriptions】
1) Scabies: Daling (PC 7), Zhigou (SJ 6), Yanggu (SI 5), Houxi (ST 3). (*Thousand Golden Prescriptions*)

2) Sore throat and dryness of the mouth: Daling (PC 7), Pianli (LI 6). (*ibid*)

3) Short breath: Daling (PC 7), Chize (LU 5). (*Great Compendium of Acupuncture and Moxibustion*)

4) Red urine: Daling (PC 7), Guanyuan (RN 4). (*ibid*)

5) Pain in the chest and cardiac region: Daling (PC 7), Neiguan (PC 6), Quze (PC 3). (*ibid*)

6) Salivation: Daling (PC 7), Danzhong (RN 17), Zhongwan (RN 12), Laogong (PC 8). (*ibid*)

7) Paroxysmal tachycadia: Daling (PC 7), Shenmen (HT 7), Danzhong (RN 17). (*Abstract of Clinical Experience on Acupuncture and Moxibustion*)

8) Abdominal pain: Daling (PC 7), Waiguan (SJ 5), Zhigou (SJ 6). (*Songs of Jade Dragon*)

9) Constipation: Daling (PC 7), Waiguan (SJ 5), Zhigou (SJ 6). (*ibid*)

10) Foul breath: Daling (PC 7), Renzhong (DU 26). (*ibid*)

【Regional Anatomy】 Skin-subcutaneous tissue-between the tendons of the palmar is longus muscle and the radial flexor muscle of the wrist-between the tendons of the common flexor muscle of the fingers-distal side of radiocarpal joint. In the superficial layer, there are the medial and lateral cutaneous nerves of the forearm, the palmar branches of the median nerve and the palmar venous network of the wrist. In the deep layer, the median nerve may be injured if the needle is inserted between and beyond the long palmar muscle and the radial flexor muscle of the wrist.

【Remark】 Puncturing this point has a clear effect on the cardiac function with ballistocardiogram, cardiovectography and X-ray scopeophotography, some researchers found that puncturing Neiguan (PC 6) and Daling (PC 7) can improve the contracting waves of ballistocardiogram of patients with heart diseases. Observation from the X-ray scopeophotography before acupuncture presented that the left ventriculus cordis and aortic peak descended being out of shape, the contractive winding became tilted, and the diastolic hump weakened. After puncturing, the left ventricular peak enlarged, the contractive slope descended, and the diastolic hump also enlarged. This indicates that cardiac contraction is strengthened and cardiac function improved after acupuncture.

Needling Daling (PC 7) could make the electroencephalogragm of some patients with grand mal epilepsy become regular.

PC 8   Laogong（劳宫）
（Labour Palace）

【Source】 *Miraculous Pivot*
【Name Explanation】 Lao（劳）, labor; Gong（宫）, center. The hand is for labor, and Lao refers to the hand. The point is in the center of the palm.
【Classification】 Ying-(Spring) Point of the Pericardium Meridian of Hand Jueyin, pertaing to fire in the Five Elements.
【Location】 At the center of the palm, between the 2nd and 3rd metacarpal bones, the point is located where the tip of the middle finger touches when a fist is made. (See Fig. 8-10)
【Localization】 Make a fist with fingers flexed. Pressing the palm cross striation with the tips of the middle and the ring fingers. The point can be located between the second and the third metacarpal bones close to the radial side of the third metacarpal bone.
【Indications】

1) Diseases along the Course of the Meridian: Anhidrosis in the palm, numbness of the fingers, tineu manuum, feverish sensation in the palm.

2) Diseases of Head and Sense Organs: Headache, trigeminal neuralgia, aphtha, foul breath, epistaxis, swelling of the throat, aphagia.

3) Cardiovascular Diseases: Pain in the chest and hypochondrium, cardiac pain.

4) Digestive Diseases: Epigastric pain, vomiting, anorexia, bleeding stool.

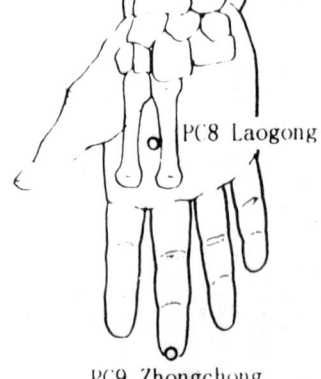

Fig. 8-10

5) Mental Diseases: Coma, infantile epilepsy, hysteria.

6) Other Diseases: Lower abdominal mass, bleeding urine, fever, windstroke, heatstroke.

【Mechanism of Action】 This point has the action of clearing away heat to induce resuscitation, tranquilizing the mind and relieving pain. It can be used to treat headache, trigeminal neuralgia, windstroke, fever, foul breath, aphtha and mental disorders.
【Method】 Puncture perpendicularly 0.3-0.5 cun. Moxibustion is applicable.
【Acupoint Prescriptions】

1) Excessive fetal movement, fullness sensation in the abdomen, dysuria, excess of heart qi: Laogong(PC 8), Guanyuan(RN 4).(*Synopsis of Prescriptions of the Golden Champer*)

2) Heat and dry sensation in the mouth, aphthosis: Laogong (PC 8), Shaoze (SI 1), Sanjian (LI 3), Taichong (LR 3). (*Thousand Golden Prescriptions*)

3) Oppressive sensation in the chest, sore: Laogong (PC 8), Daling (PC 7). (*Songs of*

Jade Dargon)

4) Five kinds of carbuncle: Laogong (PC 8), Yongquan (KI 1). (*Songs on Point Selection of Miscellaneous Diseases*)

【Regional Anatomy】 Skin-subcutaneous tissue-palmar aponeurosis-between tendons of superficial and deep flexor muscle of fingers on radial side second lumbrical muscle-first palmar interosseous muscle and second dorsal interosseous muscle. In the superficial layer, there are the palmar branches of the median nerve and the venous network of the palmar side. In the deep layer, there are the common palmar digital artery and the preper palmar digital nerve of the median nerve.

PC 9　Zhongchong（中冲）
（Centre Rush）

【Source】 *Miraculous Pivot*
【Name Explanation】 Zhong（中）, middle; Chong（冲）, gushing. The point is at the tip of the middle finger and is the Jing-well point of the pericardium Meridian, where the qi of the meridian originates and gushes upward along the meridian.
【Classification】 Jing-(Well) Point of the Pericardium Meridian of Hand Jueyin, pertaining to wood in the Five Elements.
【Location】 At the center of the tip of the middle finger. (See Fig. 8-10)
【Localization】 Palm facing upwards, the point is located in the middle of the tip of middle finger, 0.1 cun inferior to the nail, or at the intersection of the lines between the radial border of the middle finger nail and basal part.
【Indications】

1) Diseases along the Course of the Meridian: Numbness of the fingers.
2) Diseases of Head and Sense Organs: Tinnitus, pain and swelling, stiffness of the tongue, headache.
3) Cardiovascular Diseases: Cardiac pain, palpitation.
4) Digestive Diseases: Epigastric pain, cholera, vomiting, diarrhea.
5) Mental Diseases: Coma, infantile convulsion.
6) Other Diseases: High fever, heatstroke, windstroke.

【Mechanism of Action】 See Shaoshang (LU 11).
【Method】 Puncture obliquely 0.1 cun, or prick to cause bleeding. Moxibustion is applicable.
【Acupoint Prescriptions】

1) Sudden attack of cardiac pain: Apply moxibustion to the tip of the middle finger with 3 cones. (*A Handbook of Prescriptions for Emergencies*)
2) Hand disorders: Zhongchong (PC 9), Laogong (PC 8), Shaochong (HT 9), Taiyuan (LU 9), Jingqu (LU 8), Liequ (LU 7). (*Thousand Golden Prescriptions*)
3) Convulsion: Apply moxibustion, to Zhongchong (PC 9), Yintang (EX-HN3) several tens of cones. (*Great Compendium of Acupuncture and Moxibustion*)

【Regional Anatomy】 Skin-subcutaneous tissue.

There are the terminal branches of the proper palmar digital nerve of the median nerve, and the arteriovenous network of the proper palmar digital arteries and veins in this area. Inside the subcutaneous tissue are the fiber bundles between the skin and the periosteum of the distal phalanx.

【Remark】 Needling Zhongchong (PC 9) has a clear effect on the visual field, and the effect is related to meridian transmission. For example, after puncturing Zhongchong (PC 9), the Jing-(Well) point of the Pericardium Meridian-Zhongchong (PC 9), both the red and green peripheral visual fields were normal before meridion transmission, but they became narrow after meridian transmission.

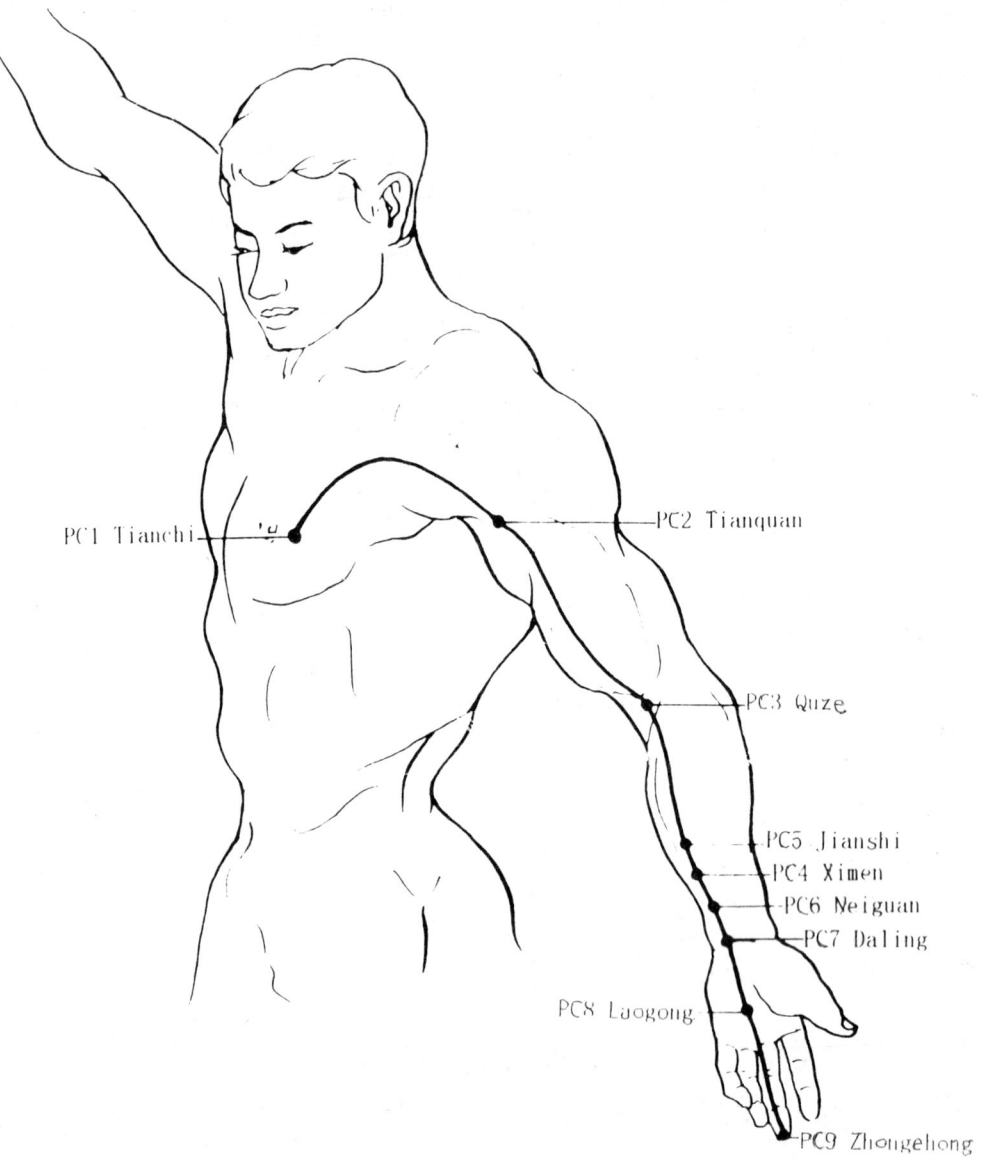

Fig. 8-11　Acupoints of the Pericardium Meridian of Hand Jueyin

Acupoints of Three Yin Meridians of Hand

Table 8-2

Indications and Actions of Acupoints of the Pericardium meridian of Hand Jueyin

Name of the points	Specific points	Common indications	Specific indications and actions
PC 1 Tianchi (天池)	Crossing point	Diseases of the heart and chest: Cardiac pain, fullness sensation in the chest, distending pain in the chest and hypochondrium	Easing the chest and regulating qi, clearing heat from the lung to stop cough. Fullness sensation in the chest, scrofula, cough, asthma
PC 2 Tianquan (天泉)			Easing the chest and regulating qi, dredging the meridians and collaterals. Cardiac pain, distending pain in the chest and hypochondrium, arm pain
PC 3 Quze (曲泽)	He-(Sea) point	Diseases of the heart, chest and stomach: palpitation, cardiac pain, fullness sensation in the chest, vomiting, epigastric pain. Mental diseases: manic-depression, coma, febrile diseases	Regulating heart qi, reducing damp-heat, regulating the intestines. Fever, restlessness and thirst, dry mouth, hiccups, epigastric pain, spasmatic pain of the elbow and arm, acute enterogastritis
PC 4 Ximen (郄门)	Xi-(Cleft) point		Calming the heart and tranquilizing the mind, easing the chest, regulating qi, dredging the collaterals to stop bleeding. Palpitation, hematemesis, hemoptysis, epistaxis, dysphoria with feverish sensation in the chest, palms and soles
PC 5 Jianshi (间使)	Jing-(River) point		Clearing away heat to calm the heart, regulating the stomach to resolve phlegm. Sudden heart attack, severe palpitation with hungry feeling, febrile diseases, manic-depression, epilepsy, vomiting, malaria, urticaria, mental diseases
PC 6 Neiguan (内关)	Luo-(Connecting) point Influential point		Calming the heart and tranquilizing the mind, regulating the stomach to normalize qi, stopping pain. Angina pectoris, gastrospasm, severe palpitation, shortness of breath, hiccups, dizziness, migraine, spasm and pain of the elbow and arm, numbness in the hands
PC 7 Daling (大陵)	Shu-(Stream) point, Yuan-(Source) point		Clearing heat from the heart and tranquilizing the mind, regulating the stomach and easing the chest. Chest and hypochondriac pain, shortness of breath, irritability, neurosis, acute appendicitis, inflammation of the throat, sores, heel pain, spasm and pain of the wrist
PC 8 Laogong (劳宫)	Ying-(Spring) Point		Reviving the patient from unconsciousness by clearing heat, tranquilizing and calming the mind. Hysteria, apoplectic coma, sunstroke, irritability due to febrile diseases, foul breath, goose-skin palms, hysteria
PC 9 Zhongchong (中冲)	Jing-(Well) point		Reviving the patient from unconsciousness, clearing heat to reduce fever. Apoplectic coma, sunstroke, syncope, febrile diseases, acute infantile convulsions, syndromes similar to wind disease, stiff tongue, night crying, feverish sensation in the palm

V. Acupoints of the Heart Meridian of Hand Shaoyin

HT 1 Jiquan (极泉)
(Extreme Fountain)

【Source】 *A-B Classic of Acupuncture and Moxibustion*
【Name Explanation】 Ji (极), summit; Quan (泉), spring. The point is in the center of the armpit; the local depression is like a spring.
【Location】 At the apex of the axillary fossa, where the pulsation of the axillary artery is palpable. (See Fig. 8-12)
【Localization】 Elbow bent press the occiput with the palm, select the point in the middle of the axillary fossa.
【Indications】
　1) Diseases of the Limbs along the Course of the Meridian: Hemiplegia, cold-pain of the elbow, inability to raise the limbs, pain and distention of fingers.
　2) Cardiovascular Diseases: Oppressive feeling in the chest, shortness of breath, palpitation, cardiac pain
　3) Other Diseases: Insufficient lactation, intercostal neuralgia, foul smell in armpits.
【Mechanism of Action】 It's a commonly used point for treating paralysis of the upper limb, which has the action of smoothing meridians and collaterals.
【Method】 Puncture perpendicularly 0.5-1 cun. Moxibustion is applicable.
【Acupoint Prescriptions】
　1) Dryness of the throat: Jiquan (HT 1), Taiyuan (LU 9), Pianli (LI 6), Taichong (LR 3), Tiantu (RN 22). (*Experience on Acupuncture and Moxibustion Therapy*)
　2) Cardiac pain: Jiquan (HT 1), Xiabai (LU 4). (*ibid*)
【Regional Anatomy】 Skin-subcutaneous tissue-brachial plexus and axillary artery and vein-tendon of latissimus muscle of the back-teres major muscle. In the superficial layer, there is the intercostobrachial nerve. In the deep layer, there is the radial nerve, the ulnar nerve, the median nerve, the medial cutaneous nerve of the forearm, the medial cutaneous nerve of the arm and the axillary artery and vein.

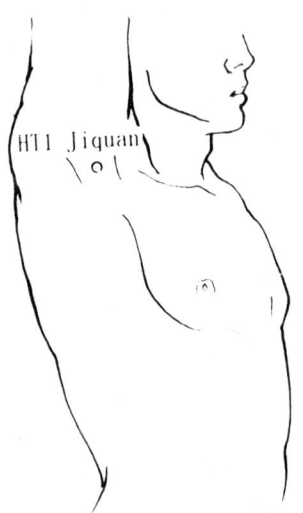

Fig. 8-12

HT 2 Qingling (青灵)
(Green Spirit)

【Source】 *The Peaceful Holy Benevolent Prescriptions*

【Name Explanation】 Qing (青), origin; Ling (灵), mind. The heart is the officer of the monarch with the function of resuscitating and housing the mind. It is the source of the qi of meridian.

【Location】 On the medial side of the arm and on the line connecting Jiquan (HT 1) and Shaohai (HT 3), 3 cun above the cubital crease, in the groove medial to the biceps muscle of the arm. (See Fig. 8-13)

【Localization】 Elbow bent, first select Shaohai (HT 3) which is located in the ulnar side of the cubital cross striation. Qingliing (HT 2) is located 3 cun directly superior to Shaohai (HT 3), on the same straight line with Jiquan (HT 1).

【Indications】

1) Diseases along the Course of the Meridian: Pain and difficult movement of the shoulder and upper limbs, swelling of the axilla.

2) Diseases of Hand and Sense Organs: Headache, icteric sclera.

【Mechanism of Action】 The point has the function of smoothing the meridians and collaterals. It is a commonly used point for headache, pain and difficult movement of the shoulder and upper limb, pain and swelling of the axilla.

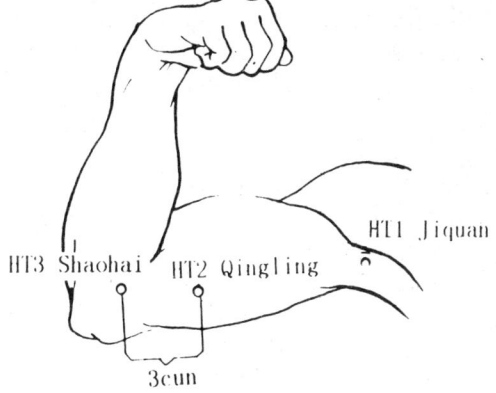

Fig. 8-13

【Method】 Puncture perpendicularly 0.3-0.5 cun. Moxibustion is applicable.

【Regional Anatomy】 Skin-subcutaneous tissue-medial intermuscular septum of the arm and brachial muscle. In the superficial layer, there is the medial cutaneous nerve of the arm, the medial cutaneous nerve of the forearm and the basilic vein. In the deep layer, there are the brachial artery and vein, the medial nerve, the superior ulnar collateral artery and vein and the brachial triceps muscle.

HT 3 Shaohai (少海)
(Shaoyin Sea)

【Source】 *Miraculous Pivot*

【Name Explanation】 Shao (少), young; Hai (海), sea. Shao refers to Hand-Shaoyin Meridian. This is the He-(Sea) Point of the Heart Meridian. The qi of the meridian circulates to this point, like water flowing into the sea.

【Classification】 He-(Sea) Point of the Heart Meridian of Hand Shaoyin, pertaining to water in the Five Elements.

【Location】 With the elbow flexed, at the midpoint of the line connecting the medial end of the cubital crease and the medial epicondyle of the humerus. (See Fig. 8-13)

【Localization】 Elbow bent, raise the arm, hold the head with hands, the point is located in the end of ulnar side of the cubital cross striation.

【Indications】

1) Diseases along the Course of the Meridian: Pain and stiffness of the neck, numbness and spasm of the arm and hand, inability to raise the limbs, hypochondriac pain, neck sprain.

2) Diseases of Hand and Sense Organs: Headache, toothache, trigeminal neuralgia, vertigo.

3) Cardiovascular Diseases: Cardiac pain, palpitation.

4) Mental Diseases: Depression, mania, epilepsy, amnesia, sudden loss of voice.

5) Other Diseases: Furuncle, scrofula, vomiting.

【Mechanism of Action】 The heart is a monarch organ, controlling blood circulation, taking charge of the mind, corresponding to fire in the five elements, opening to the tongue. Deficiency of the heart qi and stagnation of the collateral can cause cardiac pain and palpitation. Deficiency of the heart qi and disturbance of the mind can cause depression, mania, epilepsy, amnesia. The tongue is the organ of the voice. The divergent meridian of Hand Shaoyin "connects with the root of the tongue" and if the heart qi is deficient, sudden loss of the voice may appear. Headaches and toothaches can be caused by the rising of heart fire. Furuncle results from stagnation of heat and toxins. The point has the functions of tranquilizing the mind, smoothing the meridian, clearing away the heat. It is an important point for the disorders mentioned above.

【Method】 Puncture perpendicularly 0.3-0.5 cun. Moxibustion is applicable.

【Acupoint Prescription】

1) Salivation: Shaohai (HT 3), Duiduan (DU 27), Benshen (GB 13). (*Experience on Acupuncture and Moxibustion Therapy.*)

2) Toothache and dental caries: Shaohai (HT 3), Xiaohai (SI 8), Yanggu (SI 5), Yemen (SJ 2), Erjian (LI 2), Neiting (ST 44), Lidui (ST 45). (*Great Compendium of Acupuncture and Moxibustion.*)

3) Plexus brachialis neuralgia: Shaohai (HT 3), Shenmen (HT 9), Yinxi (HT 8), Tongli (HT 7), Qingling (HT 2). (*New Acupuncture and Moxibustion.*)

4) Intractable numbness of the arms: Shaohai (HT 3), Shousanli (LI 10). (*Songs of Hundreds of Symptoms.*)

5) Scrofula: Shaohai (HT 3), Tianjing (SJ 10). (*Songs of Shengyu.*)

6) Cardiac pain and tremor of the hand: Shaohai (HT 3), Yinshi (ST). (*Xi Hong's Songs.*)

【Regional Anatomy】 Skin-subcutaneous tissue-round pronator muscle-brachial muscle. In the superficial layer, there are the medial cutaneous nerve of the forearm and the basilic vein. In the deep layer, there is the medial nerve, the anastomotic branches of the ulnar recurrent artery and vein and the inferior ulnar collateral artery and vein.

【Remark】 The point has a regulating effect on hurmone. Taking the urine 17-hydroxycorticosterone and urine 17-ketosteraid and leukocyte as targets, some researchers punctured Zusanli (ST 36), Hegu (LI 4) and Shaohai (HT 3) to observe the change in adrenocortical function. The results indicated that acupuncture could make an originally lower content ascend and an originally higher content descend.

HT 4 Lingdao (灵道)
(Spirit Path)

【Source】 *A-B Classic of Acupuncture and Moxibustion*
【Name Explanation】 Ling (灵), mind; Dao (道), pathway. The heart dominates the mind. The point is in the depression on the radial side of the tendon of the m. flexor carpi ulnaris; it is like a pathway leading toward the mind.
【Classification】 Jing-(River) Point of the Heart Meridian of Hand Shaoyin, pertaining to metal in the Five Elements.
【Location】 On the palmar side of the forearm and on the radial side of the tendon of the ulnar flexor muscle of the wrist, 1.5 cun proximal to the crease of the wrist. (See Fig. 8-14)
【Localization】 Palm facing upwards, the point is located on the radial side of the ulnar carpal flexor tendon, 1.5 cun superior to the transverse crease of the wrist.
【Indications】
    1) Diseases along the Course of the Meridian: Pain and numbness of the elbw and arm.
    2) Diseases of Hand and Sense Organs: Dizziness, vertigo, redness, swelling and pain of the eyes, stiffness of the tongue, aphasia, sudden loss of voice.
    3) Cardiovascular Diseases: Cardiac pain, palpitation.
    4) Digestive Diseases: Stomachache, nausea.
    5) Mental Diseases: Hysteria, clonic convulsion, schizophrenia.
【Mechanism of Action】 See Shaohai (HT 3) and Shenmen (HT 7).
【Method】 Puncture perpendicularly 0.3 cun. Moxibustion is applicable.
【Acupoint Prescription】 Sudden loss of voice, trismus: Lingdao (HT 4), Tiantu (RN 22), Tianchuang (SI 16). (*Experience on Acupuncture and Moxibustion Therapy*)
【Regional Anatomy】 Skin-subcutaneous tissue-between ulnar flexor muscle of the wrist and superficial flexor muscle of fingers-deep flexor muscle of fingers-quadrate pronator muscle. In the superficial layer, there is the medial cutaneous nerve and the tributaries of the basilic vein. In the deep layer, there is the ulnar artery and vein and the ulnar nerve.

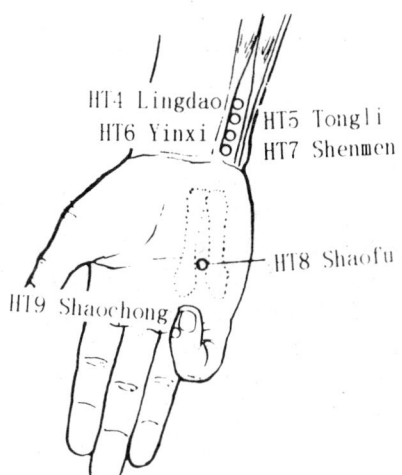

Fig. 8-14

HT 5 Tongli (通里)
(Inner Communication)

【Source】 *Miraculous Pivot*
【Name Explanation】 Tong (通), leading to; Li (里), interior. From this point the collateral of the meridian diverges and relates to the Small Intestine Meridian.
【Classification】
    Luo-(Connecting) Point of the Heart Meridian of Hand Shaoyin.
【Location】On the palmar side of the forearm and in the radial side of the tendon of the ulnar flex-

or muscle of the wrist, 1 cun proximal to the transverse crease of the wrist. (See Fig. 8-14)
【Localization】 Palm facing upwards, the point is located in the radial side of the ulnar carpal flexor tendon, 1 cun superior to the carpal cross striation.
【Indication】
　1) Diseases along the Course of the Meridian: Pain of the posterior aspect of the shoulder, upper arms and elbow, wrist pain, spasm of the fingers.
　2) Diseases of Hand and Sense Organs: Headache, vertigo, pain and redness of the eyes, sore throat, flushing of the face, tonsillitis, stiffness of the tongue, sublingual swelling, sore tongue.
　3) Respiratory Diseases: Cough, asthma.
　4) Cardiovascular Diseases: Cardiac pain, palpitation, short breath, irritability.
　5) Urinary Diseases: Incontinence of urine, hematuria.
　6) Gynecologic Diseases: Irregular menstruation, dysmenorrhea, menorrhagia.
　7) Mental Diseases: Mania, depression, epilepsy, hysteria, sudden loss of voice, amnesia, insomnia.
【Mechanism of Action】 It's the Luo-(Connecting) point of the Heart Meridian. The collateral links with the root of the tongue. The tongue is the sprout of the heart and the organ of the linguistic function. So it is used to treat sudden loss of voice, stiffness, swelling and soreness of the tongue. See Shaohai (HT 3) and Shenmen (HT 7) for more details.
【Method】 Puncture perpendicularly 0.2-0.5 cun. Moxibustion is applicable.
【Acupoint Prescriptions】
　1) Menorrhagia: Tongli (HT 5), Xingjian (LR 2), Sanyinjiao (SP 6). (*Great Compendium of Acupuncture and Moxibustion*.)
　2) Arrhythmia: Tongli (HT 5), Xinshu (BL 15). (*Abstract of Clinical Experience on Acupuncture and Moxibustion*.)
　3) Somnolence with no desire to speak: Tongli (HT 5), Dazhong (KI 4). (*Songs of Hundreds of Symptoms*.)
【Regional Anatomy】 Skin-subcutaneous tissue-between ulnar flexor muscle of the wrist and superficial flexor muscle of fingers-deep flexor muscle of fingers-quadrate pronator muscle. In the superficial layer, there is the medial cutaneous nerve of the forearm and the tributaries of the basilic vein. In the deep layer, there is the ulnar artery and vein and the ulnar nerve.

HT 6　Yinxi (阴郄)
(Yin Cleft)

【Source】 *A-B Classic of Acupuncture and Moxibustion*
【Name Explanation】 Yin (阴), Yin of Yin-Yang; Xi (郄), cleft. This is the short form of Xi-(Cleft) point of the Hand Shaoyin Meridian.
【Classification】 Xi-(Cleft) Point of the Heart Meridian of Hand Shaoyin.
【Location】 On the palmar side of the forearm and in the radial side of the tendon of the ulnar flexor muscle of the wrist, 0.5 cun proximal to the crease of the wrist. (See Fig. 8-14)
【Localization】 Palm facing upwards, the point is located in the radial side of the ulnar carpal flexor tendon, 0.5 cun above the transverse crease of the wrist.
【Indications】
　1) Diseases along the Course of the Meridian: Pain and numbness of the posterior-medial aspect of the shoulder, arm and elbow, spasmodic pain of the little finger.
　2) Diseases of Hand and Sense Organs: Headache, vertigo, tonsillitis, hemorrhage, acute glossolysis, sudden loss of voice.

3) Cardiovascular Diseases: Palpitation, cardiac pain, shortness of breath, feverish sensation in the chest.

4) Digestive Diseases: Epigastric pain, cholera, vomiting, diarrhea, heamatemesis.

5) Gynecologic Diseases: Irregular menstruation, dysmenorrhea, metrorrhagia.

6) Urinary Diseases: Incontinence of urine, hematuria.

7) Mental Diseases: Irritability, timidness, tremor, depression, epilepsy.

8) Other Diseases: Hectic fever due to Yin deficiency, night sweating, chilliness.

【Mechanism of Action】 In comparison with other points of the Heart Meridian, Yinxi (HT 6) is more effective on treating hectic fever due to Yin deficiency and night sweating. It has the functions of nourishing the heart Yin to clear away heat of deficient type. See Shenmen (HT 7) and Shaohai (HT 3) for more details.

【Method】 Puncture perpendicularly 0.3-0.5 cun. Moxibustion is applicable.

【Acupoint Prescriptions】

1) Irritability, stiffness of the tongue: Yinxi (HT6), Zhongchong (PC 9). (*Experience on Acupuncture and Moxibustion Therapy*)

2) Timidness: Yinxi (HT 6), Jianshi (PC 5), Erjian (LI 2), Lidui (ST 44). (*ibid*)

3) Hemorrhage: Yinxi (HT 6), Yingxiang (LI 20). (*ibid*)

【Regional Anatomy】 Skin-subcutaneous tissue-radial border of the tendon of the ulnar flexor muscle of the wrist-ulnar nerve. In the superficial layer, there is the medial cutaneous nerve of the forearm and the tributaries of the basilic vein. In the deep layer, there is the ulnar artery and vein.

【Remark】 Needling Yinxi (HT 6) can decrease the frequeouy of grand mal epilepsy attack, and make the electroencephalogram of those patients become regular. It's reported that puncturing Yinxi (HT 6) can regulate the tension of the bladder by lowering a tension of a tensive bladder and raising the tension of a flaccid bladder.

HT 7   Shenmen (神门)
(Spirit Gate)

【Source】 *A-B Classic of Acupuncture and Moxibustion*

【Name Explanation】 Shen (神), mind; Men (门), door. The heart houses the mind. This point is a door for the mind.

【Classification】

1) Shu-(Stream)Point and Yuan-(Source) Point of the Heart Meridian of Hand Shaoyin, pertaining to earth in the Five Elements.

【Location】 On the wrist, at the ulnar end of the crease of the wrist, in the depression in the radial side of the tendon of the ulnar flexor muscle of the wrist. (See Fig. 8-14)

【Localization】 Palm facing upwards, the point is located in the radial side of the posterior border of the pisiform bone, on the transverse crease of the wrist.

【Indications】

1) Diseases along the Course of the Meridian: Paralysis, spasm and numbness of the chest, elbow, arm, wrist and fingers.

2) Diseases of Hand and Sense Organs: Headache, vertigo, icteric sclera, flushed face, sore tongue, swelling of the tongue.

3) Cardiovascular Diseases: Cardiac pain, palpitation, timidness.

4) Digestive Diseases: Stomachache, dry mouth, anorexia, hematemesis, passing stools with blood and pus, jaundice.

5) Urinary Diseases: Enuresis, hematuria, pain in the vagina.

6) Gynecologic Diseases: Puerperal loss of blood, irregular menstruation, metrorrhagia.

7) Respiratory Diseases: Asthma, cough, hemoptysis.

8) Mental Disorders: Dementia, crying due to sadness and mania with laughter, depression, epilepsy, sudden loss of voice, insomnia, amnesia, hysteria.

9) Other Diseases: Malaria, consumptive disease, fever and aversion to cold.

[Mechanism of Action] It is the Yuan-(Source) point and the most commonly used point of the Heart Meridian of Hand Shaoyin in the clinic.

1) The heart controls blood circulation. There are many causes of heart diseases such as cardiac pain, palpitation, irritability, trance, etc, but deficiency of the heart qi is the major pathogenesis. Shenmen (HT 7) is considered as the first choice in the treatment.

2) The heart dominates the mind. Besides the treatment according to the cause of the disease, activating the heart qi to regulate mental activities is necessary to treat the mental disorders.

3) The Heart Meridian "goes up the esophagus," "links with the ocular connectors," "ascends to the lung", "connects with the small intestine"; The collateral links with the root of the tongue and the musculature connects with the chest, goes up the arm and down the umbilicus. So the point can be used to treat disorders of the head, eyes, tongue, throat, lung and stomach.

4) The heart controls blood circulation. All the hemorrhagic disorders results from the dysfunction of the heart. For this reason, Shenmen (HT 7) is the first choice in treating gynecopathy, hematuria, hematemesis.

[Method] Puncture perpendicularly 0.3-0.5 cun. Moxibustion is applicable.

[Acupoint Prescriptions]

1) Mania: Shenmen (HT7), Yanggu (SI 4). (*Thousand Golden Prescriptions*)

2) Tonsillitis: Shenmen (HT 7), Hegu (LI 4), Fengchi (GB 20). (*ibid*)

3) Palpitation: Shenmen (HT 7), Ligou (LR 5), Juque (RN 14). (*Experience on Acupuncture and Moxibustion Therapy*)

4) Asthma: Shenmen (HT 7), Yinlingquan (SP 9), Kunlun (BL 60), Zulinqi (GB 44). (*Great Compendium of Acupuncture and Moxibustion*)

5) Dementia: Shenmen (HT 7), Shaoshang (LU 11), Yongquan (KI 1), Xinshu (BL 15). (*ibid*)

6) Enurisis: Shenmen (HT 7), Yuji (LU 10), Taichong (LR 3), Dadun (LR 1), Guanyuan (RN 4). (*ibid*)

7) Pulmonary tuberculosis (Insomnia): Shenmen (HT 7), Zusanli (ST 36), Xingjian (LR 2), Baihui (DU 20) (Moxibustion), and Sanyinjiao (SP 6) are used as main points, Zhaohai (KI 6) and Yintang (EX-HN 3) are used as supplementary points. (*Abstract of Clinical Experience on Acupuncture and Moxibustion.*)

[Regional Anatomy] Skin-subcutaneous tissue-radial border of the tendon of the ulnar flexor muscle of the wrist. In the superficial layer, there is the medial cutaneous nerve of the forearm, the tributaries of the basilic vein and the palmar branches of the ulnar nerve. In the deep layer, there is the ulnar artery and vein and the ulnar nerve.

[Remark] Puncturing Shenmen (HT 7) can treat coronary heart diseases and stenocardia. Observations from electrocardio-grams showed it could lengthen the continual time of P-waves, R-waves, P-R period and Q-T period. It was found in experiment that puncturing Shenmen (HT 7) could increase the compound wave amplitude of the ballistocardiogram of the patients with coronary ischemia. It was reported that needling Neiguan (PC 6) and Shenmen (HT 7) could correct arrhythmia, specially suitable to treat those disorders due to emotional excitement. Needling Shenmen (HT 7) has an impact on the cerebral cortex function. Heavy stimulation generally causes depressant processness in the motor area of cerebrum, but does not cause an obvious change in healthy people. Light stimulation may give rise to pallial depressant processes.

By observation from EEG, puncturing the point has a regulating effect and can strengthen the weak 2-waves and its amplitude. On the other hand, it can weaken the strong 2-waves and for some epilepsy patients, needling the point can make the EEG regular. Needling the point for a week can improve pulmonary function and increase pulmonary ventilation volum. For cardiac dyspnea, puncturing Shenmen (HT 7) may make the meridian transmission reach the chest, and can instantly descend the breathing frequency with curative effect.

HT 8　Shaofu (少府)
(Shaoyin Mansion)

【Source】 A-B Classic of Acupuncture and Moxibustion
【Name Explanation】 Shao (少), young; Fu (府), place. The point pertains to the Hand-Shaoyin Meridian, where the Qi of meridian is infused.
【Classification】 Ying-(Spring) Point of the Heart Meridian of Hand Shaoyin, pertaining to fire in the Five Elements.
【Location】 In the palm, between the 4th and 5th metacarpal bones, in the part the palm touches the tip of the little finger when a fist is made. (See Fig. 8-14)
【Localization】 Palm facing upwards, fingers bent to the cross striation of the palm, the point is located in the depression between the little finger tip and the ring finger tip.
【Indications】
　　1) Diseases along the Course of the Meridian: Spasmodic pain of the elbow and the arm, feverish sensation in the palm, spasm of the little finger.
　　2) Diseases of Hand and Sense Organs: Pain, dryness of the throat, globus hystericus, epistaxis, dryness of the nose.
　　3) Cardiovascular Diseases: Palpitation, pain and stuffiness in the chest, short breath.
　　4) Reproductive Diseases: Pruritus vulvae, prolapse of uterus, menorrhagia, enurisis, dysuria.
　　5) Mental Diseases: Susceptibility to laugh and fear, hysteria.
　　6) Other Diseases: Acute appendicitis, malaria.
【Mechanism of Action】 The point is good for clearing away fire from the heart. In clinic, pain and dryness of the throat, epistaxis, dryness of the nose, pruritus vulvea, irregular menstrution, etc, are related to excess fire of the heart. For them, Shaofu (HT 8) is the first consideration to be used.
【Method】 Puncture perpendicularly 0.3-0.5 cun. Moxibustion is applicable.
【Regional Anatomy】 Skin-subcutaneous tissue-palmar aponeurosis-between the tendons of superficial and deep flexor muscle of the 4th and 5th fingers-4th lumbrical muscle-4th dorsal interosseous muscle. In the superficial layer, there are the palmar branches of the ulnar nerve. In the deep layer, there are the common palmar digital artery and vein and the proper palmar digital nerve from the ulnar nerve.

HT 9　Shaochong (少冲)
(Shaoyin Rush)

【Source】 A-B Classic of Acupuncture and Moxibustion
【Name Explanation】 Shao (少), young; Chong (冲), rushing. The point is on the small finger of Hand-Shaoyin Meridian, where the Qi of meridian originates and rushes upwards along

the meridian.

[Classification] Jing-(Well) Point of the Heart Meridian of Hand Shaoyin, pertaining to wood in the Five Elements.

[Location] On the radial side of the distal segment of the little finger, 0.1 cun from the corner of the nail. (See Fig. 8-14)

[Localization] Make a fist slightly, palm facing downwards and the little finger sticking up. The point is located in the intersection lines between the radial border of the little finger nail and the basal part.

[Indications]

    1) Diseases along the Course of the Meridian: Pain in the posterior border of the medial aspect of the arm, feverish sensation in the palm, spasm and numbness of the hand and finger.

    2) Diseases of Hand and Sense Organs: Icteric sclera, stiffness of the tongue, tonsillitis.

    3) Cardiovascular Diseases: Cardiac pain, palpitation, pain in the hypochondrium.

    4) Digestive Diseases: Hematemesis, passing stool with blood and pus, jaundice.

    5) Mental Diseases: Coma, infantile convulsion.

    6) Other Diseases: High fever, apoplexy, sunstroke, shock.

[Mechanism of Action] All the Jing-(Well)points have the functions of clearing away heat, tranquilizing the mind and inducing resuscitation. Shaochong(HT 9) is effective for mental disorders and diseases of sense organs. It can be used single handed alternately or in combination.

[Method] Puncture obliquely 0.1 cun, or prick to cause bleeding. Moxibustion is applicable.

[Acupoint Prescription] Fever: Shaochong (HT 9), Quchi (LI 11). (*Songs of Hundreds of Symptoms.*)

[Regional Anatomy] Skin-subcutaneous tissue-root of nail. There are the dorsal digital branches of the proper palmar digital nerve of the ulnar nerve and the anterior venous network formed by the dorsal digital branches of the proper palmar digital arteries and veins in this area.

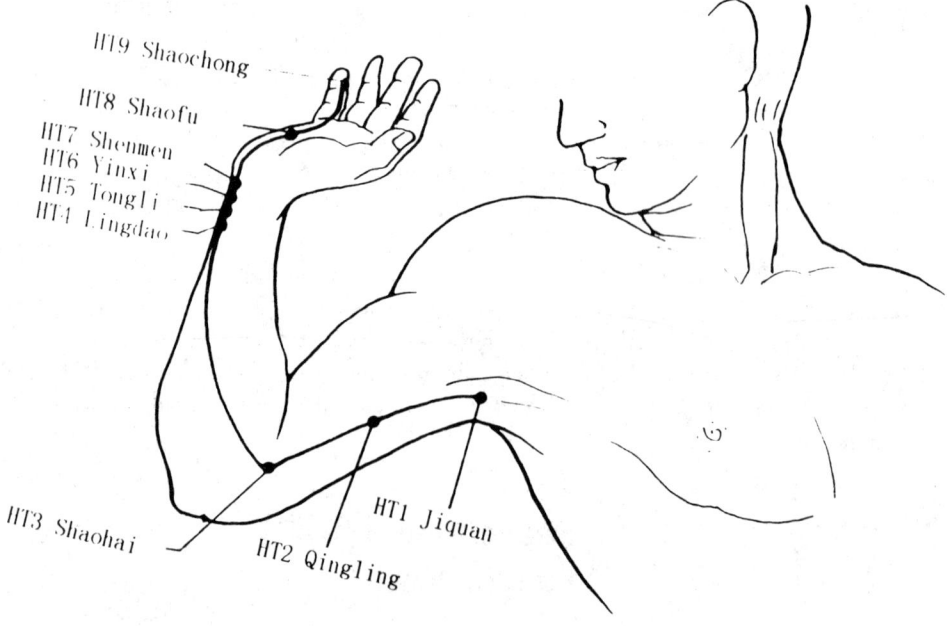

Fig. 8-15 Acupoints of the Heart Meridian of Hand Shaoyin

Table 8-3
Indications and Actions of Acupoints of the Heart Meridian of Hand Shaoyin

Name of the points	Specific points	Common indications	Specific indications and actions
HT 1 Jiquan (极泉)		Diseases of the upper limbs, heart and chest; pain in the shoulder and arm, chest and hypochondriac pain, cardiac pain, palpitations	Dredging the meridians to promote blood circulation. Cardiac pain, dry throat and thirst, hypochondriac and rib pain, scrofula, shoulder and arm pain, insufficient lactation
HT 2 Qingling (青灵)			Headache, chills, icteric sclera, hypochondriac pain, shoulder and arm pain
HT 3 Shaohai (少海)	He-(Sea) point		Clearing heat from the heart and tranquilizing the mind, dredging the meridians and collaterals, promoting qi and blood circulation. Severe palpitation with hungry feeling, blurred vision, amnesia, mania, epilepsy, pain in the head and neck, axilla and hypochondriac pain, spasmatic pain of the elbow and arm, scrofula
HT 4 Lingdao (灵道)	Jing-(River) point		Clearing heat and tranquilizing the mind. Cardiac pain, susceptibility to sorrow and fear, sudden loss of voice, convulsions, hysteria, nausea, spasmatic pain of the elbow and arm
HT 5 Tongli (通里)	Luo-(Connecting) point		Regulating heart-qi and tranquilizing the mind. Palpitation, sudden loss of voice, stiff tongue with inability to speak, excessive menses, mania, insomnia, pain of the wrist and arm
HT 6 Yinxi (阴郄)	Xi-(Cleft) point		Clearing heat from the heart and tranquilizing the mind, benefiting yin to control superficial syndrome. Cardiac pain, palpitations, blurred vision, flushed face, hectic fever and night sweating, hemoptysis, epistaxis, sudden loss of voice
HT 7 Shenmen (神门)	Shu-(Stream) point Yuan-(Source) point		Clearing heat from the heart, tranquilizing the mind and dredging the collaterals. Cardiac pain, irritability, palpitation due to alarm, severe palpitation, amnesia, insomnia, manic-depression, epilepsy, chest and hypochondriac pain, acrotism
HT 8 Shaofu (少府)	Ying-(Spring) point		Palpitation, chest pain, restlessness and fullness, pruritus vulvae, dysuria, urinary bleeding, feverish sensation in the palm, spasmatic pain of the small fingers
HT 9 Shaochong (少冲)	Jing-(Well) point		Clearing heat, Reviving the patient from unconsciousness, restoring consciousness, manic-depression, heat in the palms, heat in the mouth, chest pain

Chapter Nine

Acupoints of Three Yang Meridians of Hand

VI. Acupoints of the Large Intestine Meridian of Hand Yangming

LI 1　Shangyang（商阳）
（Shangyang）

【Source】 *Miraculous Pivot*
【Name Explanation】Shang（商）, one of the Five Sounds, pertaining to metal; Yang（阳）, Yang of Yin-Yang. The large intestine pertains to metal and is ascribed to shang sound. Yang implies the Yang meridian.
【Classification】Jing-(Well)Point of the Large Intestine Meridian of Hand Yangming, pertaining to metal in the Five Elements.
【Location】 On the radial side of the distal segment of the index finger, 0.1 cun from the corner of the nail. (See Fig. 9-1)
【Localization】 Make a fist slightly with the index finger extending forwards, the point is located at the intersection of the lines drawn from the radial side of the index finger nail and its basal part.
【Indications】
　　1) Diseases along the Course of the Meridian: Shoulder and supraclavicular pain, numbness of the fingers.
　　2) Diseases of the Head and Sense Organs: Sore throat, swelling of the submandibular region, toothache, tinnitus, deafness and glaucoma.
　　3) Respiratory Diseases: Cough, asthma, fullness feeling in the chest.
　　4) Digestive Diseases: Acute diarrhea.

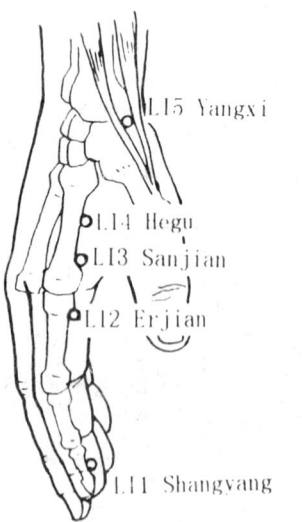

Fig. 9-1

5) Mental Diseases: Loss of consciousness, infantile convulsion.
6) Other Diseases: High fever, windstroke, sunstroke.

【Mechanism of Action】See Shaoshang (LU 11).

【Method】Puncture perpendicularly 0.1 cun, or prick the point to cause bleeding. Moxibustion is applicable.

【Acupoint Prescriptions】
1) Glaucoma: Shangyang (LI 1), Juliao (SJ 14), Shangguan (GB 3), Chengguang (BL 6), Lieque (LU 7), Tongziliao (GB 1). (*Thousand Golden Prescriptions*)
2) Tinnitus, deafness: Shangyang (LI 1), Yangqu (SI 5), Baihui (DU 20), (*Experience on Acupuncture and Moxibustion Therapy*)
3) Typhoid: Shangyang (LI 1), Gegu (LI 4), Zusanli (ST 36). (*Abstract of Clinical Experience on Acupuncture and Moxibustion*)
4) Malaria: Shangyang (LI 1), Taixi (KI 3), (*Songs of Hundreds of Symptoms*)

【Regional Anatomy】Skin-subcutaneous tissue-the root of the nail.

There are the dorsal digital branches of the proper palmar digital nerve of the median nerve, the arteriovenous network formed by the arteries and veins in the radial side of the index finger and the branches of the first dorsal metacarpal artery and vein in this area.

【Remark】It is found under the observation by X-ray that needling Shangyang (LI 1) can strengthen gastric peristalsis.

LI 2   Erjian (二间)
(Second Interval)

【Source】*Miraculous Pivot*

【Name Explanation】Er (二), two, second; Jian (间), clearance. Jian indicates the point. This is the second point of the Large Intestine Meridian.

【Classification】Ying-(Spring)Point of the Large Intestine Meridian of Hand Yangming, pertaining to water in the Five Elements.

【Location】In the depression of the radial side, distal to the 2nd metacarpophalangeal joint when a loose fist is made. (See Fig 9-1)

【Localization】Make a fist slightly with palm facing upwards. The point is located on the radial side anterior to the metacarpophalangeal articulation of the index finger, i. e. at the junction of the red and white skin anterior to the first phalanx of the index finger.

【Indications】
1) Diseases along the Course of the Meridian: Pain of arm and shoulder, numbness and pain of the fingers
2) Diseases of the Head and Sense Organs: Headache, sore throat, swelling of the submandibular region, epistaxis, icteric sclera, vertigo, toothache, facial paralysis.
3) Digestive Diseases: Disease of the intestine, stool with blood and pus.
4) Mental Disorders: Timidness.
5) Other Diseases: Lumbar pain, somnolence, fever, dry mouth.

【Mechanism of Action】The point is mainly used to treat somnolence and icteric sclera due to excessive heat or damp heat of the spleen and stomach. Its action is similar to Hegu (LI 4). Refer to Hegu (LI 4) for more details.

【Method】Puncture perpendicularly 0.3 cun. Moxibustion is applicable.

【Acupoint Prescriptions】
1) Chills and aversion to cold: Erjian (LI 2), Yinxi (HT 6) (*Songs of Hundreds of Symptoms*)

2) Toothache, headache accompanied by sore throat: Erjian (LI 2), Sanli (LI 10). (*Changsang's Secret Songs*)

3) Somnolence: Erjian (LI 2), Sanjian (LI 3) (*Experience on Acupuncture and Moxibustion Therapy*)

4) Pain of the shoulder involving the back: Erjian (LI 2), Shangyang (LI 1), Weizhong (BL 40), Kunlun (BL 60). (*Great Compendium of Acupuncture and Moxibustion*)

【Regional Anatomy】 Skin-subcutaneous tissue-the 1st lumbrical muscle tendon-the base of the proximal phalanx of the index finger. In the superficial layer, there is the dorsal digital nerve of the radial nerve, the proper palmar digital nerve of the median nreve, the branches of the 1st dorsal metacarpal artery and vein and the branches of the radial artery and vein of the index finger. In the deep layer, there are the muscular branches of the median nerve.

LI 3   Sanjian (三间)
(Third Interval)

【Source】 *Miraculous Pivot*

【Name Explanation】 San (三), three, third; Jian (间), clearance. Jian indicates the point. This is the third point of the Large Intestine Meridian.

【Classification】 Shu-(Stream) Point of the Large Intestine Meridian of Hand Yangming, pertaining to wood in the Five Elements..

【Location】 Proximal to the 2nd metacarpophalangeal joint, in the depression of the radial side when a loose fist is made. (See Fig 9-1)

【Localization】 Make a loose fist, the point is located in the metacarpophalangeal articulation of the index finger, i. e: at the junction of the red and white skin posterior to the second metacarpal capitulum of the index finger

【Indications】

1) Diseases along the Course of the Meridian: Pain of the arm and shoulder, redness and swelling of fingers.

2) Diseases of Head and Sense Organs: Pain in the eyes, toothache, sore throat, running nose and epistaxis, dry mouth.

3) Respiratory Diseases: Cough, asthma, fullness of the chest.

4) Digestive Diseases: Fullness of the abdomen, borborygmus, diarrhea, dysentery, constipation.

5) Other Diseases: Fever, somnolence.

【Mechanism of Action】 See Erjian (LI 1) and Hegu (LI 4).

【Method】 Puncture perpendicularly 0.3-0.5 cun, or puncture obliquely toward Hegu (LI 4). Moxibustion is applicable.

【Acupoint Prescriptions】

1) Sore throat: Sanjian (LI 3), Yangxi (LI 5). (*Thousand Colden Prescriptions*).

2) Pain in the eyes: Sanjian (LI 3), Qiangu (SI 2). (*ibid*)

3) Timidness: Sanjian (LI 3), Hegu (LI 4). (*A Supplement to Thousand Golden Prescriptions*)

4) Asthma: Sanjian (LI 3), Shangyang (LI 1). (*Great Compendium of Acupuncture and Moxibustion*)

【Regional Anatomy】 Skin-subcutaneous tissue-the 1st dorsal interosseous muscle-between the 1st lumbrical muscle and 2nd metacarpal bone-between the tendons of the superficial and deep flexor muscles of the index finger and the 1st palmar interoseus muscle. In the superficial layer, there is the dorsal digital nerve of the radial nerve and the proper palmar digital nerve of the median nerve, the dorsal venous network of the hand, the branches of the 1st dorsal metacarpal artery and vein and the branches of the radial artery and vein of the index finger. In the deep layer, there are the deep branches of the ulnar nerve and the muscular branches of the median nerve.

LI 4 Hegu (合谷)
(Enclosed Valley)

【Source】 *Miraculous Pivot*

【Name Explanation】 He (合), junction; Gu (谷), valley. This point is between the 1st and the 2nd metacarpal bones. Location of the point is depressed like a valley.

【Classification】 Yuan-(Source) Point of the Large Intestine Meridian of Hand Yangming.

【Location】 On the dorsum of the hand, between the 1st and the 2nd metacarpal bones, and on the radial side of the midpoint of the 2nd metacarpal bone. (See Fig 9-1)

【Localization】

1) Open the thumb and the index finger. Put the cross striation of the distal interphalangeal joint of one hand pressing on the part between thumb and index finger of the other hand. The point is where the tip of the thumb reaches.

2) Adduct the thumb and the index finger together, the point is located in the top of the muscle on the dorsum of the hand.

3) Open the thumb and the index finger, the point is located between the thumb and the index finger in the middle part between the 1st and 2nd metacarpal bones.

【Indications】

1) Diseases along the Course of the Meridian: Pain of the shoulder, arm, elbow and the wrist, numbness of the fingers, hemiplegia, arthralgia syndrome, flaccidity syndrome, frozen shoulder.

2) Diseases of the Head and Sense Organs: Headache, dizziness, redness, swelling and pain of the eye, night blindness, epistaxis, sinusitis, toothache, trismus, mumps, swelling of the face, furuncles in the face, deviated eye and mouth, deafness, tinnitus, sore throat, loss of voice.

3) Digestive Diseases: Stomachache, vomiting, diarrhea, dysentery, constipation.

4) Respiratory Diseases: Common cold.

5) Gynecopathy: Amenorrhea, dysmenorrhea, delayed labour, retention of placenta, lochiostasis, insufficient lactation, mastitis.

6) Cardiovascular Diseases: Cardiac pain, acrotism.

7) Mental Diseases: Apoplexy, infantile convulsion, tetanus, coma, depression, mania, epilepsy, spasm, opisthotonos.

8) Other Diseases: Malaria, edema, diabetes, retention of urine, urticaria, scabies, erysipelas.

【Mechanism of Action】

1) Where the meridian passes, where the indications are. It is an effective point used for smoothing the meridians and collaterals, so it can be used to treat flaccidity syndrome, arthralgia syndrome, paralysis and pain of the upper limbs.

2) The meridians of Foot and Hand Yangming link each other at Yingxiang (LI 20). The meridians and muscular regions of Yangming distribute on almost all of the face. It's effective for the disorders of the head, face and sense organs.

3) The meridian of the lung and large intestine are interiorly-exteriorly related, so this

is an important point for treating diseases of the respiratory system.

4) The point can be used for eliminating obstruction, clearing away heat, relieving convulsion and stopping pain. So it's effective for retention of urine, constipation, insufficient lactation, amenorrhea, delayed labour, anhidrosis due to stagnation of qi. For mental disorders, such as wind stroke, infantile convulsion and opisthotonos, it has the action of tranquilizing the mind and relieving convulsion. For headache, stomachache, dysmenorrhea, cardiac pain, it can be used to stop the pain.

It should be pointed out that Hegu (LI 4) can be used not only for reducing the excessive syndrome, but also recuperating depleted Yang, rescuing the patient from collapse, inducing resusitation when reinforcing method is used. For treating collapse-syndrome caused by windstroke, sunstroke, cholera, loss blood, spontaneous perspiration due to yang deficiency, coldness of four extremities, it can be used as the main point.

【Method】Puncture perpendicularly 0.5-1 cun. Moxibustion is applicable. Acupuncture and moxibustion are contraindicated in pregnant women.

【Acupoint Prescriptions】

1) Aphonia: Hegu (LI 4), Yongquan (KI 1), Yangjiao (GB 35). (*A-B Classic of Acupuncture and Moxibustion*)

2) Trismus: Hegu (LI 4), lieque (LU 7). (*Experience on Acupuncture and Moxibustion Therapy*)

3) Scabies: Hegu (LI 4), Quchi (LI 11). (*ibid*)

4) Epistaxis: Hegu (LI 4), Shangxing (DU 23), Fengfu (DU 16). (*Great Compendium of Acupuncture and Moxibustion.*)

5) Sunstroke: Hegu (LI 4), Taichong (LR 3), Dazhui (DU 14), Fengchi (GB 20), Zusanli (ST 36). (*Science of Acupuncture and Moxibustion.*)

【Regional Anatomy】Skin-subcutaneous tissue-the 1st dorsal interosseous muscle-the abductor muscle of the thumb. In the superficial layer, there are the superficial branches of the radial nerve, the radial part of the dorsal venous network of the hand and the branches or tributaries of the 1st dorsal metacarpal artery and vein. In the deep layer, there are the deep branches of the ulnar nerve.

【Remark】Of 17 cases of toothache who were treated by puncturing Hegu (LI 4) on both sides, 15 cases proved effective for relieving pain while the needle is retained.

Of 507 cases of acute tonsillitis who were treated by needling Hegu (LI 4) in combination with Shaoshang (LU 11) and Jiache (ST 6), 486 cases were cured, 15 cases were effective and 6 cases without effect. Among 23 cases of acute laryng-oparyngitis who were treated by puncturing Hegu (LI 4) in combination with Tianrong (SI 17) and Lianquan (RN 23), 17 cases were cured, 5 cases were effective, 1 case was obviously relieved. Selecting Hegu (LI 4) on the diseased side and Tianjing (SJ 10) on the healthy side, 130 cases of stye were treated, of whom, 110 cases were cured, 15 cases were relieved and 5 cases without effect.

Puncturing Hegu (LI 4) can relieve dysphagia caused by esophageal cancer, the effective rate was 82.9%. It was found under the observation of the flucroscopy and photograph with barium after acupuncture, the esophagus became wide, its povistalsis strengthened, The passing speed of the barium through the tumorous stricture quickened. Puncturing of Hegu (LI 4), Tangzhong (RN 17), Tiantu (RN 22) and Juque (RN 14) presented better effect comared with the 20 points which were tested.

LI 5　Yangxi（阳溪）
（Yang Stream）

【Source】*Miraculous Pivot*

【Name Explanation】Yang（阳）, Yang of Yin-Yang; Xi（溪）, brook. Yang refers to the Yang meridian. The local depression is like a brook in the mountains.

【Classification】Jing-(River) Point of the Large Intestine Meridian of Hand Yangming, pertaining to fire in the Five Elements.

【Location】At the radial end of the crease of the wrist, in the depression between the tendons of the short extensor and long extensor muscles of the thumb when the thumb is tilted upward. (See Fig. 9-1)

【Localization】When the thumb is tilted upward, the point is located in the radial side of the wrist joint, between the tendons of the long extensor muscle of the thumb and short extensor muscle of the thumb.

【Indications】

　　1) Diseases along the Course of the Meridian: Pain of the shoulder and arm, hemiplegia, pain and weakness of the wrist and the elbow, stiffness of the fingers.

　　2) Diseases of Head and Sense Organs: Headache, tinnitus, deafness, stiffness of the tongue, frequent protrusion of the tongue, sore throat, toothache, redness and pain of eyes, cataract.

　　3) Digestive Diseases: Diarrhea, indigestion.

　　4) Mental Diseases: Epilepsy, convulsion, ravings, susceptibility to laughter.

　　5) Other Diseases: Fever, malaria.

【Mechanism of Action】

　　The action of this point is similar to that of Hegu(LI 4). But it's mainly used for treating wrist diseases. That is because where the acupoints locate, where the indications are.

【Method】Puncture perpendicularly 0.3-0.5 cun. Moxibustion is applicable.

【Acupoint Prescriptions】

　　1) Mania: Yangxi (LI 5) and points of Hand and Foot Yangming Meridians and Foot Taiyin Meridian. (*A-B Classic of Acupuncture and Moxibustion*)

　　2) Mental Diseases: Yangxi (LI 5), Yanggu (SI 5) for frequent protrusion of the tongue, ravings. (*Thousand Golden Prescriptions*)

　　3) Redness and pain of the eye: Yangxi (LI 5), Yanggu (SI 5). (*ibid*)

　　4) Pain of eye: Yangxi (LI 5), Erjian (LI 2), Daling (PC 7), Sanjian (LI 3), Qiangu (SI 2), Shangxing (DU 23). (*Great Compendium of Acupuncture and Moxibustion.*)

【Regional Anatomy】Skin-subcutaneous tissue-between the short extensor muscle tendon of the thumb and the long extensor muscle tendon of the thumb-the front part of the long radial extensor muscle of the wrist. In the superficial layer, there are the branches of the cephalic vein and the superficial branches of the radial nerve. In the deep layer, there are the branches or tributaries of the radial artery and vein.

【Remark】It is found under the observation by a barium swallow and X-ray, puncturing Yangxi (LI 5) can weaken gastric peristulsis.

LI 6 Pianli (偏历)
(Lateral Passage)

【Source】*Miraculous Pivot*
【Name Explanation】Pian(偏), divergence; Li(历), passway. The large Intestine Meridian separates a collateral from here and diverges to the Lung Meridian.
【Classification】Luo-(Connecting) Point of the Large Intestine Meridian of Hand Yangming.
【Location】With the elbow slightly flexed, on the radial side of the dorsal surface of the forearm and on the line connecting Yangxi (LI 5) and Quchi (LI 11), 3 cun above the crease of the wrist. (See Fig. 9-2)
【Localization】Lateral posture of the wrist with the elbow flexed, the point can be located at the junction of inferior one-fourths and superior three-fourths of the distance between Yangxi (LI 5) and Quchi (LI 11).
【Indications】
  1) Diseases along the Course of the Meridian: Pain of the shoulder, arm, elbow and the wrist.
  2) Disorders of the Head and Sense Organs: Headache, epistaxis, redness of the eyes, blurring of vision, deafness, tinnitus, deviation of mouth and eyes, toothache, sore throat, dry throat, cheek swelling..
  3) Urogenital Diseases: Dysuria, edema.
  4) Other Diseases: Malaria.

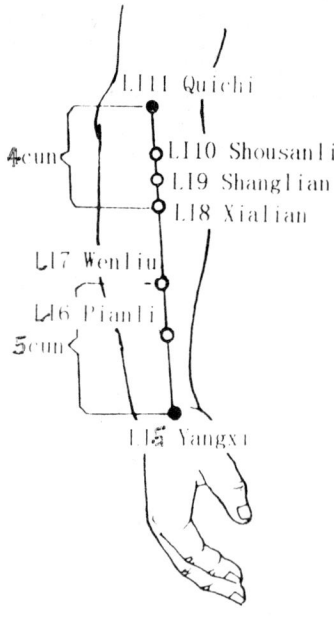

Fig. 9-2

【Mechanism of Action】It's the Luo-(Connecting) point which connects with the Lung Meridian. The lung helps maintain normal water metabolism and the lung has the function of dredging water passages. The point can be used to regulate the lung qi through the Luo-(Connecting) point, so it is used to treat dysuria and edema. See Hegu (LI 4) for more details.
【Method】Puncture perpendicularly 0.3 cun or obliquely 0.3-0.5 cun. Moxibustion is applicable.
【Acupoint Prescriptions】
  1) Soreness and heaviness of the arm and elbow: Pianli (LI 6), Sanli (Li 10). (*Experience on Acupuncture and Moxibustion Therapy*)
  2) Tinnitus: Pianli (LI 6), Yangxi (LI 5), Shangyang (LI 1), Luoque (BL 8), Wangu (SI 4), Qiangu (SI 2). (*ibid*)
  3) Epistaxis: Pianli (Li 6), Hegu (LI 4), Sanli (LI 3), Kunlun (BL 60), Tonggu (KI 20). (*ibid*)
【Regional Anatomy】Skin-subcutaneous tissue-the short extensor muscle of the thumb-the long radial extensor muscle tendon of the wrist-the long abductor muscle tendon of the thumb. In the superficial layer, there are the tributaries of the cephalic vein, the lateral cutaneous nerve of the forearm and the superficial branches of the radial nerve. In the deep layer, there are the branches of the posterior interosseous nerve of the radial nerve.

LI 7　Wenliu（温溜）
（Warm-Remaining）

【Source】 *A-B Classic of Acupuncture and Moxibustion*
【Name Explanation】Wen（温）, to warm; Liu（溜）, circulation. This point is able to warm the meridian and promote its circulation, and is good for treating cold pain of the elbow and arm.
【Classification】Xi-(Cleft) Point of the Large Intestine Meridian of Hand Yangming.
【Location】With the elbow flexed, on the radial side of the dorsal surface of the forearm and on the line connecting Yangxi (LI 5) and Quchi (LI 11), 5 cun above the crease of the wrist. (See Fig. 9-2)
【Localization】Lateral posture of the wrist with elbow flexed. The point can be located at 1 cun anterior to the middle of the junction of Yangxi (LI 5) and Pianli (LI 6).
【Indications】
　　1) Diseases along the Course of the Meridian: Pain and motor impairment of the shoulder and arm, stiffness and pain of the neck.
　　2) Diseases of the Head and Sense Organs: Headache caused by wind, headache, dizziness, pain of the eye, dry lips, salivation, toothache, redness, pain and swelling of the eyes.
　　3) Respiratory Diseases: Tuberculosis, asthma.
　　4) Digestive Diseases: Abdominal pain, abdominal distension, borborygmus.
　　5) Mental Diseases: Ravings, mania, epilepsy.
　　6) Other Diseases: Mastitis, furuncles.
【Mechanism of Action】It is the Xi-(Cleft) point of the Large Intestine Meridian of Hand-Yangming. The Xi-(Cleft) point of Yang Meridians are used to treat acute pain syndrome.
【Method】Puncture perpendicularly 0.5-0.8 cun. Moxibustion is applicable.
【Acupoint Prescriptions】
　　1) Inability to speak due to inflammation of the throat: Wenliu (LI 7), Quchi (LI 11). (*A-B Classic of Acupuncture and Moxibustion.*)
　　2) Mania: Wenliu (LI 7), Yemen (SJ 2), Jingmen (BL 63). (*Thousand Golden Prescriptions*).
　　3) Stiffness of the neck due to cold: Wenliu (LI 7), Qimen (LR 13). (*Songs of Hundreds of Symptoms*)
【Regional Anatomy】Skin-subcutaneous tissue-the long radial extensor muscle tendon of the the wrist-the short radial extensor muscle of the wrist. In the superficial layer, there are the cephalic vein, the lateral cutaneous nerve of the forearm and the posterior cutaneous nerve of the forearm. In the deep layer, there are the superficial branches of the radial nerve before the tendons of the long and short radial extensor muscle of the wrist.

LI 8　Xialian（下廉）
（Lower Side）

【Source】 *A-B Classic of Acupuncture and Moxibustion*
【Name Explanation】Xia（下）, inferior; Lian（廉）, edge. The point is inferior to Shanglian at the dorsal side of the forearm, close to the radial aspect.
【Location】On the radial side of the dorsal surface of the forearm and on the line connecting

Yangxi (LI 5) and Quchi (LI 11), 4 cun below the cubital crease. (See Fig. 9-2)
【Localization】 Lateral posture of the wrist with the elbow flexed. The point can be located at the junction of superior one third and inferior two-thirds of the distance between Jianyu (LI 5) and Quchi (LI 11).
【Indications】
  1) Diseases along the Course of the Meridian: Pain of the arm and elbow, hemiplegia.
  2) Diseases of the Head and Sense Organs: Headache cause by wind, headache, dizziness, pain of the eyes, dry lips, salivation.
  3) Digestive Diseases: Abdominal pain, abdominal distension, masses due to disorders of qi, unbearable pain of the abdomen, distending pain in the abdomen and hypochondrium, pain around umbilicus, indigestion, diarrhea, lung diseases.
  4) Mental Disorders: Ravings, mania.
  5) Other Diseases: Mastitis.
【Mechanism of Action】 See Shousanli (LI 10), Wenliu (LI 7), Quchi (LI 11).
【Method】 Puncture perpendicularly 0.5-0.8 cun. Moxibustion is applicable.
【Acupoint Prescriptions】
  1) Diarrhea with blood: Xialian (LI 8), Youmen (KI 2), Taibai (SP 3). (*Experience on Acupuncture and Moxibustion Therapy*)
  2) Loss of appetite due to heat in the stomach: Xialian (LI8), Xuanzhong (GB 39). (*ibid*)
  3) Ravings: Xialian (LI 8), Qiuxu (GB 40). (*ibid*)
  4) Headache cause by wind: Xialian (LI 8), Wuchu (GB 5), Shenting (DU 24), (*ibid*).
【Regional Anatomy】 Skin-subcutaneous tissue-brachioradial muscle-the short radial extensor muscle of the wrist-supinator muscle. In the superficial layer, there are the lateral and posterior cutaneous nerves of the forearm. In the deep layer, there are the deep branches of the radial nerve.
【Remark】 By the barium swallow and X-ray examination, it was found that needling Xialian (LI 8) could strengthen gastric peristalsis.

LI 9   Shanglian (上廉)
(Upper Side)

【Source】 *A-B Classic of Acupuncture and Moxibustion*
【Name Explanation】 Shang (上), superior; Lian (廉), edge. The point is superior to Xialian (LI 8) at the dorsal side of the forearm, close to the radial aspect.
【Location】 On the radial side of the dorsal surface of the forearm and on the line connecting Yangxi (LI 5) and Quchi (LI 11), 3 cun below the cubital crease. (See Fig. 9-2)
【Localization】 Lateral posture of the wrist with the elbow flexed. The point is located in the junction of superior one fourth and inferior three fourths of the distance between Jianyu (LI 5) and Quchi (LI 11).
【Indications】
  1) Diseases along the Course of the Meridian: Hemiplegia, numbness of the hand and foot, soreness and pain of the arm, hand and shoulder.
  2) Diseases of the Head and Sense Organs: Headache.
  3) Digestive Diseases: Abdominal pain, borborygmus, diarrhea, pain around umbilicus.
  4) Respiratory Diseases: Lung diseases, chest pain, asthma.

5) Urinary Diseases: Dysuria, deep-coloured urine.

【Mechanism of Action】See Shousanli (LI 10) and Quchi (LI 11).

【Method】Puncture perpendicularly 0.5-0.8 cun. Moxibustion is applicable.

【Acupoint Prescriptions】

1) Dysuria: Shanglian (LI 9), Xialian (LI 8). (*Experience on Acupuncture-Moxibustion Therapy.*)

2) Diarrhea: Shanglian (LI 9), Xialian (LI 8). (*Great Compendium of Acupuncture and Moxibustion.*)

【Remark】Barium swallow and X-ray examination showed that puncturing Shanglian (LI 9) can strengthen gastric peristalsis.

LI 10   Shousanli (手三里)
(Hand Three Li)

【Source】*A-B Classic of Acupuncture and Moxibustion*

【Name Explanation】Shou (手), arm; San (三), three; Li (里), taken as cun in ancient times. The point is on the forearm. With the arm outstretched, the point is 3 cun below Quchi.

【Location】On the radial side of the dorsal surface of the forearm and on the line connecting Yangxi (LI 5) and Quchi (LI 11), 2 cun below the cubital transverse crease. (See Fig. 9-2)

【Localization】Lateral posture of the wrist with the elbow flexed. The point can be located at the junction of suprior one sixth and inferior five sixths of the distance between Jianyu (LI 5) and Quchi (LI 11).

【Indications】

1) Diseases along the Course of the Meridian: Pain of the arm and shoulder, numbness of the arm, hemiplegia.

2) Diseases of the Head and Sense Organs: Toothache, loss of voice, swelling of the cheek, eye diseases, pain of the tongue, facial paralysis.

3) Digestive Diseases: Abdominal distension, vomiting, diarrhea, stomach pain, distention of the stomach.

4) Other Diseases: Scrofula, discomfort of the arm due to improper needling, common cold, lower back pain.

【Mechanism of Action】

1) The points located between the elbow and wrist are mainly used to treat disorders of the corresponding zangfu organs. This point belongs to the Large Intestine Meridian, so it's good for treating intestinal disorders, especially for abdominal distention, vomiting and diarrhea.

2) According to the rule that where the meridian passes, where the indications are, this point can be used for treating diseases of the head and sense organs, pain of the shoulder and arm, hemiplegia.

3) Improper acupuncture treatment can cause pain and heaviness sensation of the upper limbs. Flicking at this point with the finger can relieve the uneasiness in the local area. It can also be used to treat lumbar and back pain because its Muscle Region passes beside the spinal column.

【Method】Puncture perpendicularly 0.5-0.8 cun. Moxibustion is applicable.

【Acupoint Prescriptions】

1) Tonsillitis: Sanli (LI 10), Wenliu (LI 7), Quchi (LI 11), Zhongzhu (SJ 3), Fenglong

(ST 40). (*Thousand Golden Prescriptions.*)

2) Edema due to pregnancy: Shousanli (LI 10), Zusanli (ST 36), Pishu (BL 20), Weishu (BL 21), Xuanzhong (GB 39). Applying moxibustion to Qihai (RN 6), Jiaoxi (KI 8), Sanyinjiao (SP 6), Yinlingquan (SP 9), Guanyuan (RN 4). (*New Acupuncture and Moxibustion.*)

【Regional Anatomy】Skin-subcutaneous tissue-the long radial extensor muscle of the wrist-the short radial extensor muscle of the wrist-the front part of the extensor muscle of the fingers-the supinator muscle. In the superficial layer, there are the lateral and posterior cutaneous nerves of the forearm. In the deep layer, there are branches tributaries of the radial recurrent artery and vein and at the deep branches of the radial nerve.

【Remark】It is found under the observation of a barium swallow and X-ray that needling Shousanli (LI 10) can strengthen gastric peristalsis. With the method of obstructing blood flow, puncturing the point can strengthen rectal peristalsis. It's also reported that needling Shousanli (LI 10) can make the peristalsis of jejunum and ileum instantly changed, the strong becomes weak and the weak becomes strong.

LI 11　Quchi（曲池）
（Pool on Bend）

【Source】*Miraculous Pivot*

【Name Explanation】Qu（曲）, crooked; Chi（池）, pond. When the arm is flexed, a depression at the elbow is like a pool and the point is inside it.

【Classification】He-(Sea) Point of the Large Intestine Meridian of Hand Yangming, pertaining to earth in the Five Elements.

【Location】With the elbow flexed, at the lateral end of the cubital crease, at the midpoint of the line connecting Chize (LI 5) and the external humeral epicondyle. (See Fig. 9-2)

【Localization】

1) When the elbow is flexed at a 90° angle, the point is located at the end of the cubital cross striation. (See Fig. 9-3)

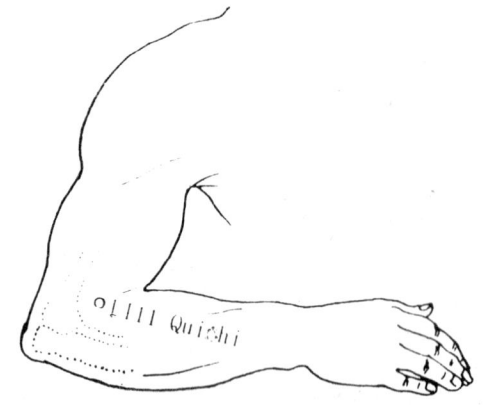

Fig. 9-3　**Location of Quchi Point**

2) When the elbow is flexed, locate the point at the middle junction of Tianyu (LI 5) and external epicondyle of humerus.

【Indications】

1) Diseases along the Course of the Meridian: Hemiplegia, pain around shoulder, thin and weak arm, stiffness or flaccidity of the elbow and arm, pain and limited movement of the elbow, redness and swelling of the arm, back pain, lumbago.

2) Diseases of the Head and Sense Organs: Headache, dizziness, tinnitus, deafness, pain of the anterior side of the ear, redness and pain of the eyes, blurring of vision, toothache, swelling of the neck, sore throat.

3) Respiratory Diseases: Restlessness and fullness in the chest, cough, asthma.

4) Digestive Diseases: Abdominal pain, vomiting, diarrhea, dysentery, constipation, appendicitis.

5) Mental Diseases: Manic depression and insanity, timidness.

6) Other Diseases: Scrofula, goiter, eczema, urticavia, scabies, erysipelas, furuncle,

dry skin, hypertension, febrile diseases, prolonged fever due to cold, malaria, common cold, diabetes, edema.

【Mechanism of Action】

1) It is an effective point for dredging the meridians and collaterals. It can not only be used for treating spasmodic pain in the elbow, but also for swelling and pain of the joints, muscles and skin, flaccidity and arthragia syndrome.

2) The point can be used for expelling wind and regulating Ying-Wei. It is one of the main points for treating fever, common cold, dermatosis and surgical diseases.

3) The point can be used for regulating the function of the intestine. It's one of the main points for treating intestinal diseases. Modern research proved that it is one of the important points for treating dysentery.

This point can be effectively used for regulating Ying-Wei, descending adverse rising of qi and activating the collaterals. It's not only for reducing the excess, but also for improving constitution of the body.

【Method】 Puncture perpendicularly 0.8-1.5 cun. Moxibustion is applicable.

【Acupoint Prescriptions】

1) Pain of the shoulder and back: Quchi (Li 11), Tianliao (SJ 15) (*Thousand Golden Prescriptions*)

2) Manic psychosis: Quchi (LI 11), Hegu (LI 4), Sanli (LI 10), Jugu (GB 39). (*Experience on Acupuncture and Moxibustion Therapy*)

3) High fever: Quchi (LI 11), Sanli (LI 10), Fuliu (LI 7). Edema all over the body: Quchi (LI 11), Hegu (LI 4), Sanli (LI 10), Neiting (ST 44), Xingjian (LR 2), Sanyinjiao (SP 6). Blockage in the body: Quchi(LI 11), Hegu(LI 4). (*Great Compendium of Acupuncture and Moxibustion*)

4) Furuncles all over the body: Quchi (LI 11), Hegu (LI 4), Sanli (LI 10), Xingjian (LR 2). (*ibid*)

5) Hypertension: Quchi(LI 11), Renying (ST 9), Zusanli (ST 36). (*Science of Acupuncture and Moxibustion*)

6) Diseases of the head and sense organs: Quchi (LI 11), Hegu (LI 4). (*Songs on Point Selection of Miscellaneous Diseases*)

【Regional Anatomy】 Skin-subcutaneous tissue-the long radial extensor muscle of the wrist and short radial extensor muscle of the wrist-the brachioradial muscle. In the superficial layer, there are the tributaries of the cephalic vein and the posterior cutaneous nerve of the forearm. In the deep layer, there are the radial nerve and the anastomotic branches of the radial recurrent artery and vein and the radial collateral artery and vein.

【Remark】 It is reported that needling Quchi (LI 11) can make the peristalsis of jejunum and ileum instantly changed, the strong become weak and the weak become strong. Observations under X-ray or in the period of operation indicates that needling Zusanli (ST 36) and Quchi (LI 11) can make the appendix of the patients with appendicitis have the following changes: the peristalsis strengthened, the tension increased, or the arc improved or removed in curly swing way, or the segmental bubble moved quickly to discharge its content. It is also reported that moxibustion to Quchi (LI 11) can weaken gastric peristalsis.

LI 12 Zhouliao （肘髎）
(With the Elbow Crevice)

【Source】 *A-B Classic of Acupuncture and Moxibustion*

【Name Explanation】 Zhou (肘), elbow; Liao (髎), foramen. The point is at the elbow and close to the foramen.

【Location】 With the elbow flexed, at the lateral side of the upper arm, 1 cun above Quchi (LI 11) on the border of the humerus. (See Fig. 9-4)

【Localization】 With the elbow flexed, locate the point 1 cun directly superior to Quchi (LI 11), on the lateral border of tendon of brachial triceps.

【Indications】

Diseases along the Course of the Meridian: Pain and motor impairment of elbow and arm, stiffness, numbness and pain of the elbow, hemiparalysis of the upper extremities, somnolence.

【Mechanism of Action】 Where the meridian passes and the acupoints locate, where the indications are.

【Method】 Puncture perpendicularly 0.5-0.8 cun. Moxibustion is applicable.

【Regional Anatomy】 Skin-subcutaneous tissue-the brachioradial muscle-brachial muscle. In the superficial layer, there is the posterior cutaneous nerve of the forearm. In the deep layer, there are the branches or tributaries of the radial collateral artery and vein.

LI 13 Shouwuli (手五里)
(Hand Five Li)

【Source】 *Miraculous Pivot*.

【Name Explanation】 Shou (手), arm; Wu (五), five; Li (里), taken as cun in ancient times. The point is on the upper arm, 5 cun below Tianfu (LU 3).

【Location】 On the lateral side of the upper arm and on the line connecting Quchi (LI 11) and Jianyu (LI 15), 3 cun above Quchi (LI 11). (See Fig. 9-4)

【Localization】 With the elbow flexed, locate the point at 3 cun directly superior to Quchi (LI 11) on the lateral side of the tendon of the brachial triceps.

【Indications】

1) Diseases along the Course of the Meridian: Stiffness, pain and motor impairment of the elbow and arm, swelling of the arm due to wind and dampness.

2) Respiratory Diseases: Cough, hemoptysis.

3) Digestive Diseases: Distension and pain in the epigastric region, jaundice.

4) Other Diseases: Malaria, scrofula, timidness, somnolence.

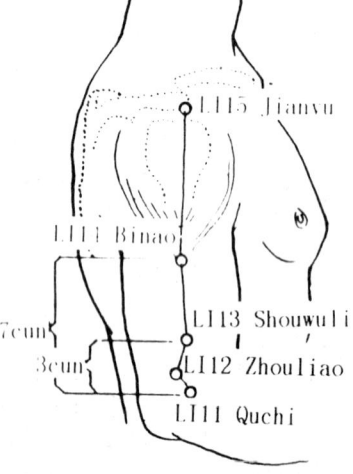

Fig. 9-4

【Mechanism of Action】 This point is mainly used to treat diseases of the shoulder and arm because it has the action of dredging the meridians and activating the collaterals.

【Method】 Puncture perpendicularly 0.3-0.7 cun. Moxibustion is applicable.

【Acupoint Prescriptions】

1) Scrofula: Wuli (LI 13), Binao (LI 14). (*Songs of Hundreds of Symptoms*)

2) Somnolence: Wuli (LI 13), Taixi (KI 3), Dazhong (KI 4), Zhaohai (KI 6), Erjian (LI 2). (*Experience on Acupuncture Moxibustion Therapy*)

3) Pain in the elbow and arm: Wuli (LI 13), Tianjing (SJ 10), Xialian (LI 8). (*ibid*)

4) Redness, swelling and pain of the arm and hand: Wuli (LI 13), Quchi (LI 11), Tongli (HT 5), Zhongzhu (SJ 3). (*Great Compendium of Acupuncture and Moxibustion*)
【Regional Anatomy】 Skin-subcutaneous tissue-brachial muscle. In the superficial layer, there are the lateral inferior cutaneous nerve of the arm and the posterior cutaneous nerve of the forearm. In the deep layer, there are the radial collateral artery and vein and the radial nerve.
【Remark】 It is proved by experiments that electropuncturing Shouwuli (LI 13) and Quchi (LI 11) has an inhibitory effect on the evoked potential in the cerebral cortial somatic area or united area which was caused by stimulating the dental pulp and the greater splanchnic nerve.

LI 14 Binao (臂臑)
(Median Side of Upper Arm)

【Source】 *A-B Classic of Acupuncture and Moxibustion*
【Name Explanation】 Bi (臂), arm; Nao (臑), muscle prominence of the arm. The point is on the muscle prominence of the arm.
【Classification】 Crossing Point of the Collaterals of Hand Yangming.
【Location】On the lateral side of the arm, at the insertion of the deltoid muscle and on the line connecting Quchi (LI 11) and Jianyu (LI 15), 7 cun above Quchi (LI 11). (See Fig. 9-4)
【Localization】 With the elbow flexed, the point is located in the inferior extremity of the deltoid muscle, on the line joining Jianyu (LI 15) and Quchi (LI 11).
【Indications】
   1) Diseases along the Course of the Meridian: Stiffness and pain of the neck, hemiparalysis of the arm.
   2) Diseases of the Head and Sense Organs: Headache, swelling pain and redness of the eyes, lacrimation.
   3) Other Diseases: Chills and fever, scrofula.
【Mechanism of Action】 It can be used for dredging the collaterals and improving acuity of vision, so it's used to treat eye diseases and scrofula.
【Method】Puncture perpendicularly 0.5-0.8 cun or obliquely upwards 1-1.5 cun. Moxibustion is applicable.
【Acupoint Prescriptions】
   1) Motor impairment of shoulder and arm: Binao (LI 14), Naoshu (SI 10). (*A-B Classic of Acupuncture and Moxibustion.*)
   2) Stiffness of the neck: Binao (LI 14), Qiangjian (DU 18). (*Experience on Acupuncture and Moxibustion Therapy*)
   3) Pain of nerves of plexus brachialis (forearm): Binao (LI 14), Shouwuli (LI 13), Shousanli(LI 10), Shanglian(LI 9), Wenliu(LI 7), Hegu(LI 4), Yangxi(LI 5). (*New Acupuncture and Moxibustion*)
【Regional Anatomy】 Skin-subcutaneous tissue-deltoid muscle. In the superficial layer, there are the inferior and superior lateral cutaneous nerves of the arm. In the deep layer, there are muscular branches of the brachial artery.
【Remark】Puncturing Binao(LI 14)may have the action of relieving pain in mastectomy. Some researchers found that needling Binao (LI 14), Neiguan (PC 6) and Hegu (LI 4) has a satisfactory analgesia effect in the modified or enlarged radical operation, or the single removal operation. Based on experimental observations, the analgesic effect may be obtained through the stimulation on the hypothalamic lateral area.

LI 15 Jianyu (肩髃)
(Shoulder Corner)

【Source】 *A-B Classic of Acupuncture and Moxibustion*
【Name Explanation】 Jian (肩), shoulder; Yu (髃), corner. The point is at the corner of the shoulder.
【Classification】 The Crossing Point of Hand Yangming and Yangqiao meridians.
【Location】On the shoulder, superior to the deltoid muscle, in the depression anterior and inferior to the acromion when the arm is abducted or raised at the level of the shoulder. (See Fig. 9-4)
【Localization】
  1) The upper arm fully abducted, the point is located in the anterior depression on the shoulder joint.
  2) Shoulder relaxed, the point is located 2 cun directly inferior to the acromial extremity of clavicle, on the Large Intestine Meridian of Hand-Yangming. (See Fig. 9-5)
【Indications】
  1) Diseases along the Course of the Meridian: Windstroke, hemiplegia, stiffness of the hand and arm, atrophy and weak arm, soreness and pain of tendon and bone, pain and swelling of the arm and shoulder, motor impairment of the arm and the hand.
  2) Other Diseases: Urticaria due to wind-heat, scrofula, goiter. (See Fig 9-5)

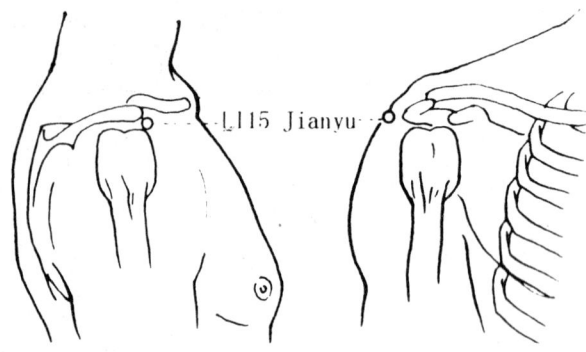

Fig. 9-5

【Mechanism of Action】 It's used to treat diseases of shoulder and upper limbs. It has the action of clearing and activating the meridians and collaterals, regulating the flow of qi to relieve stagnation. So it's usually used to treat Bi syndrome, flaccidity and hemiplegia.
【Method】 Puncture perpendicularly 0.5-1 cun. Moxibustion is applicable.
【Acupoint Prescriptions】
  1) Hemiplegia: Jianyu (LI 15), Quchi (LI 11), Lieque (LU 7). (*A Supplement to the Thousand Golden Prescriptions.*)
  2) Pain in the shoulder and arm: Jianyu (LI 15), Tianjing (SJ 10), Yanggu (SI 5), Guanchong (SJ 1). (*Great Compendium of Acupuncture and Moxibustion.*)
  3) Scrofula: Jianyu (LI 15), Quchi (LI 11), Tianchi (PC 1), Tianjing (SJ 10), Sanjian (LI 3). (*Science of Acupuncture and Moxibustion.*)

4) Rheumatoid arthritis: Jianyu (LI 15), Quchi (LI 11), Bizhong (EX), Hegu (LI 4), Huantiao (GB 30), Zusanli (ST 36). (*ibid*)

5) Arthritis: Jianyu (LI 15) to Jiquan (HT 1). (*Songs of Hundreds of Symptoms.*)

6) Urticaria: Jianyu (LI 15), Yangxi (LI 5). (*Songs of Hundreds of Symptoms*).

【Regional Anatomy】 Skin-subcutaneous tissue-deltoid muscle-subdeltoid bursa-supraspinous muscle tendon. In the superficial layer, there is the lateral supraclavicular nerve and the superior lateral cutaneous nerve of the arm. In the deep layer, there is the posterior humoral circumflex artery and vein and the branches of the axillary nerve.

【Remark】 Clinical observation was made on the impact of myoelectricity on Jianyu (LI 15). It was found that the myoelectric amplitude obviously ascended ($P<0.05$) in five minutes after acupuncture and it may last for 30 minutes. Puncturing Jianyu (LI 15) has an analgesic effect for the operation for esophageal cancer. The following two groups of points were selected to observe the effect of acupuncture anesthesia: ①Jianyu (LI 15), Tianzong (SI 11) and Zusanli (ST 36). ② Xiayifeng (EX), Sanyangluo (SI 8) and some points of the Ren and Du Meridians. The results indicated the effect of the first group was better than that of the second group ($P<0.01$), which proved the points had some specificity in acupuncture anesthesia.

LI 16 Jugu (巨骨)
(Great Bone)

【Source】 *Plain Questions*

【Name Explanation】 Ju (巨), huge; Gu (骨), bone. The clavicle was called Jugu in ancient times. The point is close to the acromial end of the clavicle.

【Classification】 The Crossing Point of Hand Yangming and Yangqiao meridians.

【Location】 On the shoulder, in the depression between the acromial extremity of the clavicle and the scapular spine. (See Fig. 9-6)

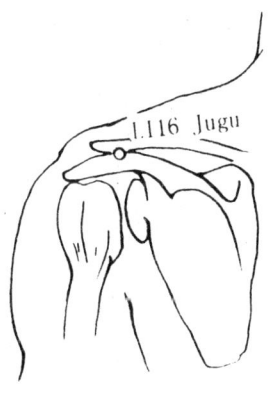

Fig. 9-6

【Localization】 Sit with shoulder relaxed. Locate the point at the posterior border of acromioclavicular joint, the depression between the clavicle and spina scapulae.

【Indications】

1) Diseases along the Course of the Meridian: Pain of the shoulder and back, pain and motor impairment of the upper extremities, hemiparalysis.

2) Mental Disorders: Convulsive disease.

3) Other Diseases: Scrofula, goiter, urticaria, hemoptysis.

【Mechanism of Action】 See Jianyu (LI 15).

【Method】 Puncture perpendicularly 0.4-0.6 cun. Moxibustion is applicable.

【Acupoint Prescriptions】 Motor impairment of the arm: Jugu (LI 16), Qiangu (SI 2). (*Thousand Golden Prescriptions*)

【Regional Anatomy】 Skin-subcutaneous tissue-acromioclavicular ligament-the supraspinous muscle. In the superficial layer, there are the lateral supraclavicular nerve. In the deep layer, there are the branches of the suprascapular nerve and the branches or tributaries of the suprascapular artery and vein.

LI 17 Tianding (天鼎)
(Heaven Vessel)

【Source】*A-B Classic of Acupuncture and Moxibustion*
【Name Explanation】Tian(天), heaven; Ding(鼎), an ancient cooking vessel with two loop handles. Tian implies upper. The head looks like a ding.
【Location】On the lateral side of the neck, at the posterior border of the sternocleidomastoid muscle beside the Adam's apple at the midpoint of the line connecting Futu (LI 18) and Quepen (ST 12). (See Fig. 9-7)
【Localization】Sit with the head flexed slightly lateral and upward, first locate Futu (LI 18) which is located 3 cun lateral to the Adam' apple, between the sternal head of sternocleidomastoid muscle and the clavicular head, and 1 cun directly inferior to Futu (LI 18), the point can be located at the posterior border of sternocleidomastoid muscle.
【Indications】
   1) Diseases of the Head and Sense Organs: Sore throat, sudden loss of voice, wheezing due to retention of phlegm in the throat.
   2) Other Diseases: Scrofula, goiter, throat mass due to disorder of qi.
【Mechanism of Action】Where the acupoint locates, where the indications are. This point can be used to treat diseases around the area of the point.
【Method】Puncture perpendicularly 0.3-0.5 cun. Moxibustion is applicable.
【Acupoint Prescriptions】
   1) Sore throat: Tianding (LI 17), Qishe (ST 11), Geshu (BL 17). (*Thousand Golden Prescriptions.*)
   2) Loss of voice: Tianding (LI 17), Jianshi (PC 5). (*Songs of Hundreds of Symptoms.*)
【Regional Anatomy】Skin-subcutaneous tissue-the posterior border of the sternocleidomastoid muscle-interspace of the scalene muscle. In the superficial layer, there is the transverse nerve of the neck, the external jugular vein and the platysma muscle. In the deep layer, there are the branches or tributaries of the ascending cervical artery and vein and the brachial plexus in the interspace of the scalene muscle.

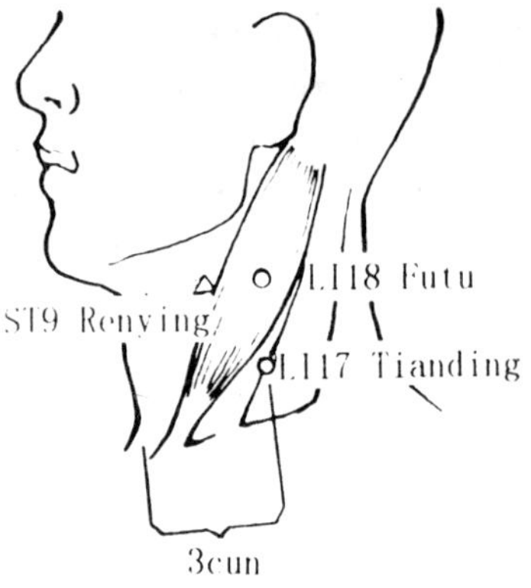

Fig. 9-7

LI 18 Futu (扶突)
(Hyoid Border)

【Source】*Miraculous Pivot and Plain Questions*
【Name Explanation】Fu (扶), side; Tu (突), prominence. Tu refers to prominentia laryngea. The point is beside the Adam's apple.
【Location】On the lateral side of the neck, beside the Adam's apple, between the anterior and posterior borders of the sternocleidomastoid muscle. (See Fig. 9-7)
【Localization】Sit with the head flexed slightly lateral and upwards, first locate Lianquan (RN 23) which is located in the middle of thyroid cartilage and hyoid bone. This point is lo-

cated 3 cun lateral to Lianquan (RN 23), between the sternal head of sternocleidomastoid muscle and the clavicular head.

【Indications】

1) Diseases of Head and Sense Organs: Sore throat, sudden loss of voice, mass in throat due to disorder of qi, bleeding from the root of the tongue.

2) Respiratory Diseases: Asthma, cough, wheezing due to retention of sputum in the throat.

3) Other Diseases: Scrofula, goiter, hiccup.

【Mechanism of Action】 This point is located beside the throat and trachea. It can be used to treat diseases located here, such as scrofula, and goiter. The effect can be obtained by activating the circulation of the local qi and blood, clearing away heat, activating lung qi and dissipating the mass.

【Method】 Puncture perpendicularly 0.5-0.8 cun. Moxibustion is applicable.

【Acupoint Prescriptions】

1) Bleeding from the root of the tongue: Futu (LI 18), Dazhong (KI 4), Qiaoyin (GB 44). (*Thousand Golden Prescriptions*).

2) Throat diseases: Futu (LI 18), Tiantu (RN 22), Tianxi (SP 18). (*ibid*)

【Regional Anatomy】 Skin-subcutaneous tissue-between the sternal head and the clavicular head of the sternocleidomastoid muscle-the posterior border of the carotid sheath. In the superficial layer, there is the transverse nerve of the neck and the platysma muscle. In the deep layer, there is the carotid sheath.

【Remark】 By stimulating the radial nerve with surface electrode to evoke hypothenar activity, the change of myoelectric amplitude when puncturing the patients with cerebral thrombosis in recovery period indicates that needling Futu (LI 18) and Tianzhu (BL 10) can make the mycelectric amplitude ascend ($P<0.05$) from 5 to 45 minutes after needling. Puncturing Futu (LI18) on both sides can inhibit the 2-waves and increase the β-waves of healthy person's electroencephalogram (EEG). It has been proven that acupuncture can strengthen the excitation process of the cerebral cortex.

It is found that needling Futu (LI 18) can make the healthy thyroid absorb more iodine. Puncturing the point has a stable effect on acupuncture anesthesia, which suggests that the point has relative specificity. Puncturing the point has good analgesia effect on internal thoracic operations (Lung esophagus and mediastinum), and has depressive affect on the thoracic sympathetic nerve. The analgesia effect is probably one kind of periodic obstruction.

LI 19 Kouheliao (口禾髎)
(Spike Crevice of Mouth)

【Source】 *A-B Classic of Acupuncture and Moxibustion*

【Name Explanation】 Kou (口), mouth; He (禾), grain; Liao (髎), foramen. The grain enters the stomach through the mouth. The point is in the foramen beside the mouth.

【Location】 On the upper lip, directly below the lateral border of the nostril, at the level of Shuigou (DU 26). (See Fig. 9-8)

【Localization】 Sit with the head flexed upward or in supine position. First locate Shuigou (DU 26) which is located at the junction of superior one third and middle one third on the philtrum. The point is located 0.5 cun lateral to Shuigou (DU 26).

【Indications】

1) Diseases of the Head and Sense Organs: Sore of the nose, nasal polyps, anosmia, nasal obstruction, deviation of the mouth.

2) Mental Disorders: Syncope, trismus.

【Mechanism of Action】It's used to treat diseases of the nose.

【Method】Puncture perpendicularly 2 cun. Moxibustion is not advisable.

【Acupoint Prescription】Epistaxis: Kouheliao (LI 19), Duiduan (DU 27), Laogong (PC 8). (*Experience on Acupuncture and Moxibustion Therapy.*)

【Regional Anatomy】Skin-subcutaneous tissue-the orbicular muscle of the mouth. In the superficial layer, there are the branches of the infraorbital nerve of the maxillary nerves etc. In the deep layer, there are artery and vein of the upper lip and the buccal branches of the facial nerve.

LI 20 Yingxiang (迎香)
(Welcome Fragrance)

【Source】*A-B Classic of Acupuncture and Moxibustion*

【Name Explanation】Ying (迎), to meet; Xiang (香), fragrance. This point is at either side of the nose. It is used to treat disorders of the nose to improve the sense of smell, to enable the nose to "sense fragrance".

【Location】In the nasolabial groove, beside the midpoint of the lateral border of the ala nasi. (See Fig. 9-8)

【Localization】Sit with the head upward. The point is located in the nasolabial groove, the midpoint of the lateral border of wing of nose.

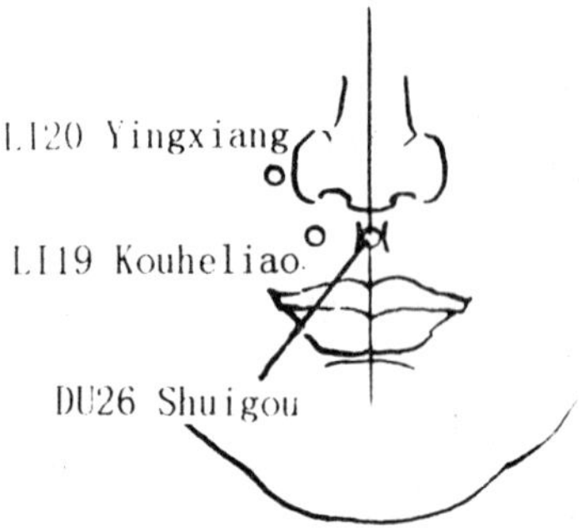

【Indications】

1) Diseases of Head and Sense Organs: Nasal obstruction, epistaxis, rhinitis, deviation of the mouth and eyes, itching and swelling of the face, nasal polyps, headache.

2) Other Diseases: Biliary ascariasis.

【Mechanism of Action】This point is used to treat local diseases.

【Method】Puncture obliquely towards nose 0.3 cun. Moxibustion is contraindicated.

Fig. 9-8

【Acupoint Prescriptions】

1) Itching and swelling of the face: Yingxiang (LI 20), Hegu (LI 4). (*Great Compendium of Acupuncture and Moxibustion.*)

2) Nasal obstruction and anosmia: Yingxiang (LI 20), Shangxing (DU 23), Wuchu (BL 5), Heliao (LI 19). (*Great Compendium of Acupuncture and Moxibustion.*)

3) Redness of the eyes: Yingxiang (LI 20) (blooding-letting), Linqi (GB 41), Taichong (LR 3), Hegu (LI 4). (*Songs of Point Selection on Miscellaneous Diseases.*)

【Regional Anatomy】Skin-subcutaneous tissue-the levator muscle of the upper lip. In the superficial layer, there are the branches of the infraorbital nerve from the maxillary nerve. In the deep layer, there are buccal branches of the facial nerve and the branches or tributaries of the facial artery and vein.

【Remark】The clinical statistics indicated that the effective rate of chronic bronchitis treated by puncturing Yingxiang (LI 20) could reach 70-90%. Compared with the group treated with Chinese drugs, the short-term effect and long-term effect by acupuncture were better than those with Chinese drugs.

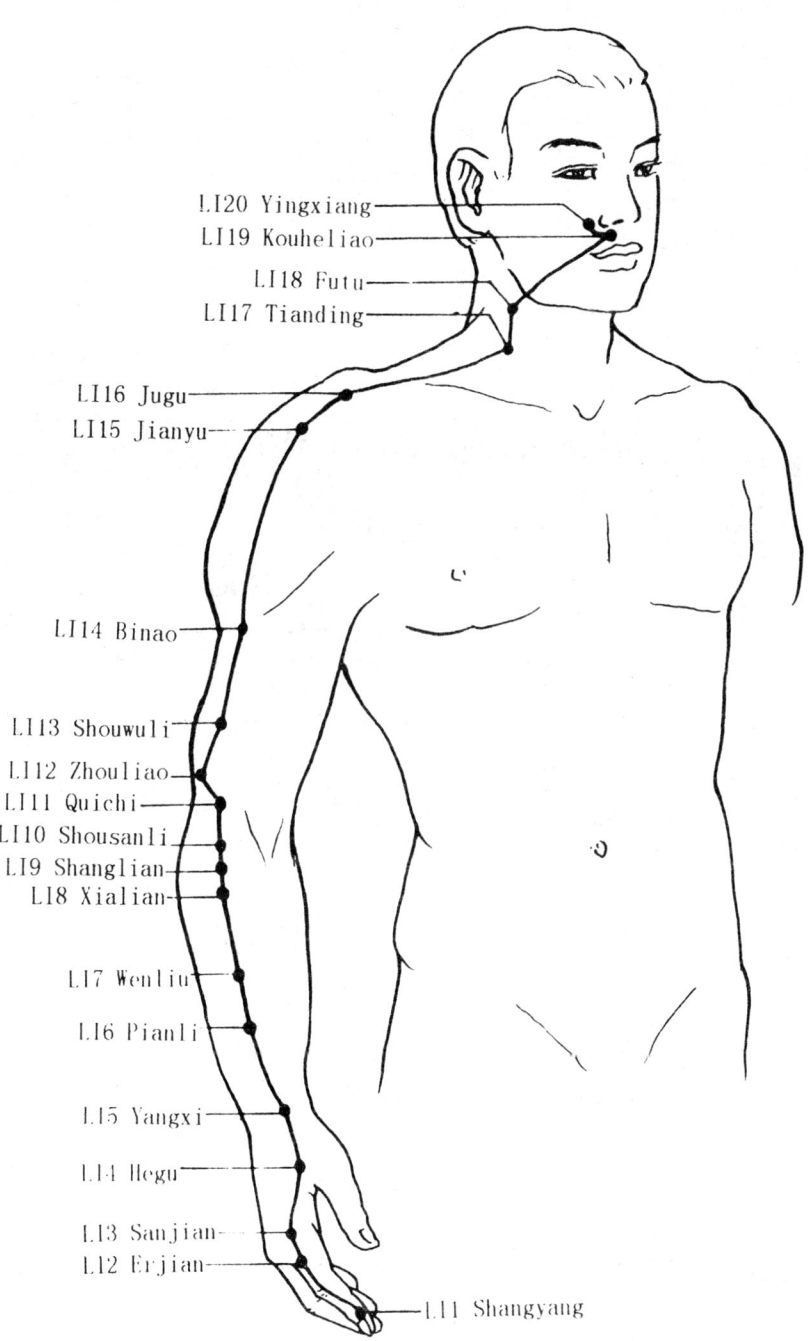

Fig. 9-9 **Acupoints of the Large Intestine Meridian of Hand Yangming**

Table 9-1
Indications and Actions of Acupoints of the Large Intestine Meridian of Hand Yangming

Name of the points	Specific points	Common indications	Specific indications and functions
LI 1 Shangyang (商阳)	Jing-(Well) point	Disorders of the head, face, eyes, ears and teeth: headache, dizziness, redness, swelling and pain of the eye, tinnitus, deafness, toothache, wry mouth with distorted eye, febrile diseases	Reviving the patient from unconsciousness, purging heat. Sore throat, febrile diseases, coma, numbness of fingers
LI 2 Erjian (二间)	Ying-(Spring) point		Eye diseases
LI 3 Sanjian (三间)	Shu-(Stream) point		Clearing heat-evils in yangming, promoting the movement of large intestine. Epistaxis, dry throat, drowsiness, toothache, pain of the shoulder and back, fever, fullness of the abdomen, borborygmus
LI 4 Hegu (合谷)	Yuan-(Source) point		Reviving the patient from unconsciousness, alleviating mental depression, purging heat, relieving convulsion, alleviating pain. Retention of urine, constipation, dysentery, dry mouth, halitosis, coma, headache, pain of the shoulder and arm, febrile disease
LI 5 Yangxi (阳溪)	Jing-(River) point		Expelling wind and purging fire-evil. Redness, swelling and pain of the eye, toothache due to pathogenic wind-fire, sore throat, headache, pain in the wrist
LI 6 Pianli (偏历)	Luo-(Connecting) point		Clearing away lung-heat, removing obstructions in the meridians, regulating water passages. Epistaxis, edema, retention of urine, pain in the wrist and forearm
LI 7 Wenliu (温溜)	Xi-(Cleft) point		Clearing heat-evil, regulating the functions of the stomach and intestines. Puffy face, borborygmus, pain of abdomen, stomatitis, furuncles, aching pain of shoulder and back
LI 8 Xialian (下廉)			Pain of elbow and arm, abdominal pain
LI 9 Shanglian (上廉)			Paralysis of upper extremities, borborygmus, abdominal pain
LI 10 Shousanli (手三里)			Dredging the meridians, regulating the stomach and intestine. Numbness of arm and hand, muscular stiffness of elbow, aphonia, stomachache, abdominal pain, diarrhea

Acupoints of Three Yang Meridians of Hand

Name of the points	Specific points	Common indications	Specific indications and functions
LI 11 Quchi (曲池)	Confluent point	The same as above.	Expelling wind, regulating blood flow, regulating intestine. Febrile disease, urticaria, abdominal pain, vomiting and diarrhea, irregular menstruation, feeling of oppression and fullness in the chest, paralysis of upper extremities
LI 12 Zhouliao (肘髎)		Disorders of the upper-arm and shoulder: aching pain, numbness and motor impairment of the upper extremities	Pain, numbness and muscular stiffness of elbow and arm
LI 13 Shouwuli (手五里)			Dredging the meridians and easing joint movement, regulating the flow of qi and bood. Drowsiness, fullness of upper abdomen, cough, spitting blood
LI 14 Binao (臂臑)			Improving eyesight and stopping pain. Eye disorders
LI 15 Jianyu (肩髃)	Crossing point		Dispersing wind-evil and activating collaterals, regulating qi and blood, easing joint movement. Pain of shoulder and back, omalgia
LI 16 Jugu (巨骨)	Crossing point		Motor impairment of shoulder
LI 17 Tianding (天鼎)		Disorders of pharynx and larynx: sudden onset of aphonia, painful swelling of the throat, goiter	Regulating qi and eliminating phlegm, relieving sore throat. Painful swelling of the throat, hiccup, difficulty in swallowing
LI 18 Futu (扶突)			Regulating qi and eliminating phlegm. Cough, asthma and dyspnea, thyroid enlargement
LI 19 Kouheliao (口禾髎)		Diseases of nose: stuffy nose, epistaxis, rhinorrhea loith tnrhid discharge, wry mouth	Dispersing wind-evil and clearing away heat-evil, relieving stuffy nose. Disorders of the nose, wry mouth, lockjaw, coma
LI 20 Yingxiang (迎香)	Crossing point		Eliminating wind and heat-evils, relieving stuffy nose. Disorders of nose, wry mouth with distorted eye, pruritus of face, formication on the face, pain of face, ascariasis of biliary tract

VII. Acupoints of the Sanjiao Meridian of Hand Shaoyang

SJ 1 Guanchong (关冲)
(Pass Rush)

【Source】 *Miraculous Pivot*

【Name Explanation】Guan (关), same as bend; Chong (冲), gushing. As the ring finger cannot be stretched out along, guan here refers to the ring finger. The point is at the tip of the ring finger and is the Jing-(Well) point of the Sanjiao Meridian, where the Qi of meridian originates and gushes upward along the meridian.

【Classification】 Jing-(Well) Point of the Sanjiao Meridian of Hand Shaoyang, pertaining to metal in the Five Elements.

【Location】 On the ulnar side of the distal segment of the 4th finger, 0.1 cun from the corner of the nail. (See Fig. 9-10)

【Localization】 The palm facing downwards, the point can be located at the intersection between the lines drawn from the ulnar border of the fourth finger and its basal part.

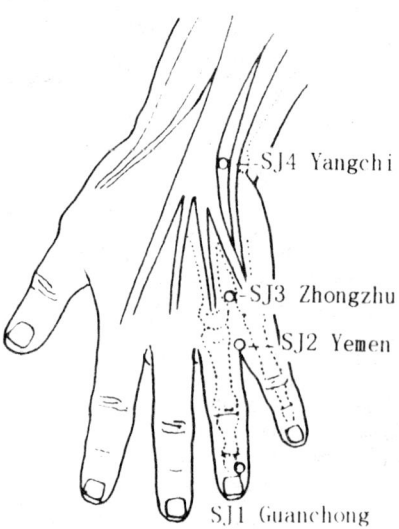

Fig. 9-10

【Indication】
1) Diseases along the Course of the Meridian: Numbness at the tip of the fingers, inability to raise the four limbs.
2) Diseases of the Head and Sense Organs: Headache, dizziness, vertigo, tinnitus, deafness, redness and pain of the eyes, cataract, stiff tongue, curled tongue, fissured tongue, stiffness of the root of the tongue, dry and fissured lips, sore throat, mumps, submandibular swelling.
3) Digestive Diseases: Cholera, vomiting, anorexia, infantile indigestion.
4) Mental Diseases: Windstroke, sunstroke, coma, loss of consciousness.
5) Other Diseases: Febrile diseases, malaria.

【Mechanism of Action】 It is one of the points used for emergency treatment. It can be used to treat such febrile diseases as windstroke, sunstroke, coma, loss of the consciousness by pricking the point to cause bleeding. It is also a commonly used point for treating numbness of the end of the fingers.

Shaoshang (LU 11), Shangyang (LI 1), Zhongchong (PC 9), Guanchong (SJ 1), Shaochong (HT 9), Shaoze (SI 1) on both hands are called the 12 Jing-(Well) points. They can all be used for waking the patient from unconsciousness, smoothing the meridians and collaterals, and clearing away heat evils. They are used to treat coma, loss of consciousness, numbness of the fingertips and febrile diseases. Clinically, each one has its own characteristics.

Shaoshang (LU 11) is used to promote the dispersing function of the lung, relieving sore throat and expelling wind.

Shangyang (LI 1) is used to clear and remove stagnant heat in the Yangming meridians, relieving sore throat and exterior syndromes by clearing away heat.

Zhongchong (PC 9) is used to clear heat in the heart to tranquilize the mind and eliminate stagnant heat in the Pericardium to wake the patient from unconsciousness. Its effect is better than the other ones.

Guanchong (SJ 1) is used to clear heat in the upper Jiao and stagnant heat in the Shaoyang meridian. It's effective at treating diseases of the ears and eyes.

Shaochong (HT 9) is used to clear heat in the heart to tranquilize the mind, remove heart fire, relieve stagnant heat and promote the heart qi.

Shaoze (SI 1) is used to clear heart heat to stop irritability and promoting lactation.

【Method】Puncture subcutaneously 0.1 cun or prick the point to cause bleeding. Moxibustion is applicable.

【Acupoint Prescriptions】

1. Sore throat: Guanchong (SJ 1), Qiaoyin (GB 44), Shaoze (SI 1) (*Thousand Golden Prescriptions*)

2. Cholera, vomiting: Guanchong (SJ 1), Zhigou (SJ 6), Chize (LU 5), Zusanli (ST 36), Taibai (SP 3), Taixi (KI 3), Taichong (LR 3). (*Great Compendium of Acupuncture and Moxibustion*)

【Regional Anatomy】Skin-subcutaneous tissue-the root of the nail. In the superficial layer, there are the branches of the dorsal digital branches of the proper palmar digital nerve from the ulnar nerve, and the arteriovenous network of the dorsal branches of the proper palmar digital arteries and veins.

SJ 2　Yemen（液门）
（Fluid Gate）

【Source】*Miraculous Pivot*

【Name Explanation】Ye（液）, water; Men（门）, door. This is the Ying-(Spring) point of this meridian, pertaining to water. It has the function of regulating water passage like a door.

【Classification】Ying-(Spring) Point of the Sanjiao Meridian of Hand Shaoyang, pertaining to water in the Five Elements.

【Location】On the dorsum of the hand, between the 4th and 5th fingers, at the junction of the red and white skin, proximal to the margin of the web. (See Fig. 9-10)

【Localization】Make a loose fist with palm facing downwards. The point is located in the gap at the level of the junction between the fourth and fifth fingers, at the junction of the red and white skin.

【Indications】

1) Diseases along the Course of the Meridian: Pain in the arms and hands, redness and swelling of the dorsum of the hand, spasm of the fingers.

2) Diseases of the Head and Sense Organs: Headache, dizziness, vertigo, flushed face, lacrimation, redness and swelling of the eye, leukoma, deafness, tinnitus, toothache, pain and swelling of the gum, aphasia, sore throat.

3) Mental Diseases: Timidness, delirium.

4) Other Diseases: Febrile diseases, malaria.

【Mechanism of Action】This point is more effective for the diseases of the head, face and five sense organs, because the meridian is distributed at ears, eyes, throat and the muscle region "enters the root of the tongue". See Waiguan (SJ 5) for other details.

【Method】 Puncture perpendicularly 0.3-0.5 cun. Moxibustion is applicable.

【Acupoint Prescriptions】

1) Diseases of the throat: Yemen (SJ 2) and Sidu (SJ 9) are used for shortness of breath and globus hystericus (*Thousand Goldlen prescriptions*).

2) Febrile diseases: Yemen (SJ 2), Zhongzhu (SJ 3) and Tongli (HT 5) are used for both febrile diseases without headache and feverish sensation of the face without sweat. (*ibid*)

3) Sore throat: Yemen (SJ 2), Yuji (LU 10) (*Songs of Hundreds of Symptoms*)

【Regional Anatomy】 Skin-subcutaneous tissue-between the bases of the 4th and 5th proximal phalangeal bones-the 4th dorsal interosseous muscle and the 4th lumbrical muscle. In the superficial layer, there is the dorsal digital nerve of the ulnar nerve and the dorsal venous network of the hand. In the deep layer, there are the dorsal digital artery and vein.

SJ 3　Zhongzhu（中渚）
（Middle Islet）

【Source】 *Miraculous Pivot*

【Name Explanation】 Zhong（中）, middle; Zhu（渚）, a plot of small land in water. The point is in the middle of the Five-Shu points and the qi of meridian flows like water along the water margin.

【Classification】 Shu-(Stream) Point of the Sanjiao Meridian of Hand Shaoyang, pertaining to wood in the Five Elements.

【Location】 On the dorsum of the hand, proximal to the 4th metacarpophalangeal joint, in the depression between the 4th and 5th metacarpal bones. (See Fig. 9-10)

【Localization】 Palm facing downwards, the point is located 1 cun directly above Yemen (SJ 2), in the depression posterior to the fourth and fifth metacarpal bones.

【Indications】

1) Diseases along the Course of the Meridian: Pain in the shoulder, back, elbow and arm, limited movement of the finger, torticollis.

2) Diseases of the Head and sense Organs: Headache, vertigo, flushed face, redness and pain of the eye, blurring of vision, deafness, tinnitus, sore throat.

3) Other Diseases: Febrile diseases, malaria, furuncle, verruca.

【Mechanism of Action】 It is a commonly used point for treating pain in spine, shoulder and back. It can be used for dredging and activating the meridians and collaterals, expelling wind and relieving pain. The spinal pain refers to the pain in the thoracic vertebra region. Ancient people used to select this point.

According to the rule that where the meridian passes, where the indications are, it is also a commonly used point for treating disorders of the head, face and five sense organs. The headache treated by dealing with the points of the Sanjiao meridian mainly refers to migraine which due to stagnation of the qi, because the Sanjiao meridian distributes on the lateral side of the head and "it is used for the diseases due to the dysfunction of qi".

Flat warts and common warts are termed "Kujinjian" in Chinese. Zhongzhu (SJ 3) treats warts which appear on the face and dorsum of the hand along the course of the meridian. This point and Ashi points can be used in combination. Pricking the root of the wart with three edged needle to cause bleeding proves effective.

【Method】 Puncture perpendicularly 0.3-0.5 cun. Moxibustion is applicable.

【Acupoint Prescriptions】
1) Difficulty in passing stools: Zhongzhu (SJ 3), Taibai (SP 3) (*A-B Classic of Acupuncture and Moxibustion*)
2) Sore throat: Zhongzhu (SJ 3) Zhigou (SI 6), Neiting (ST 44) (*Thousand Golden Prescriptions*)
3) Unconsciousness: Zhongzhu (SJ 3), Sanli (ST 36), Dadun (LR 1). (*Songs of Jade Dragon*)
4) Prolonged malaria: Zhongzhu (SJ 3), Shangyang (LI 1), Qiuxu (GB 40). (*ibid*)
5) Swelling of the throat: Zhongzhu (SJ 3), Taixi (KI 3). (*ibid*)
6) Redness and swelling of the arm, deep-rooted carbuncle: Zhongzhu (SJ 3), Yemen (SJ 2), Quchi (LI 11), Hegu (LI 4)   (*Great Compendium of Acupuncture and Mopxibustion*)
7) Redness and swelling of the arm: Zhongzhu (SJ 3), Yemen (SJ 2). (*ibid*)

【Regional Anatomy】Skin-subcutaneous tissue-the 4th dorsal interosseous muscle. In the superficial layer, there is the dorsal digital nerve of the ulnar nerve and the ulnar part of the dorsal venous network of the hand. In the deep layer, there is the 4th dorsal metacapal artery.

【Remark】Zhongzhu (SJ 3) has a clear analgesic effect in ophthalmic operations under acupuncture anesthesia. It is reported that choosing Zhongzhu (SJ 3) and Lieque (LU 7) as the main points are superior to any other points near the eyes in ophthalonic operations. Puncturing this point may cause excitation of the bowel sounds.

SJ 4 Yangchi (阳池)
(Yang Pool)

【Source】*Miraculous Pivot*
【Name Explanation】Yang (阳), Yang of Yin-Yang; Chi (池), pool. The point is in the depression on the back of the wrist; the qi of meridian flows like water into a pool.
【Classification】Yuan-(Source) Point of the Sanjiao Meridian of Hand Shaoyang.
【Location】At the midpoint of the dorsal crease of the wrist, in the depression on the ulnar side of the tendon of the extensor muscle of the finger. (Fig. 9-10)
【Localization】Palm facing downwards locate the point at the depression in the intersection between the proximal part of the third and fourth metacarpal bones and the carpal cross striation, or locate the point at the ulnacarpal joint, between the tendons of the common extensor muscle of the fingers and the proper extensor muscle of the fifth finger.
【Indications】
1) Diseases along the Course of the Meridian: Pain, weakness, redness and swelling of the wrist, motor injury or failure to flex the wrist, pain in the neck, shoulder, elbow and forearm.
2) Diseases of the Head and Sense Organs: Deafness, redness and swelling of the eye, sore throat.
3) Digestive Diseases: Infantile diarrhea, indigestion, malnutrition, diabetes, dry mouth, constipation.
4) Urinary Diseases: Enuresis.
5) Other Diseases: Febrile diseases, malaria, common cold.

【Mechanism of Action】It is the Yuan-(Source) point of the Sanjiao meridian. The Yuan-(Source) qi passes all over the body through sanjiao. This point has a close relation with the Yuan qi. It is an important point for regulating the Yuan qi, so it can be used to treat dia-

betes, dry mouth, enuresis and pediatric diseases. See Waiguan (SJ 5) for other details.
【Method】 Puncture perpendicularly 0.3-0.5 cun. Moxibustion is applicable.
【Acupoint Prescriptions】 Spasm of the arm and hand: Yangchi (SJ 4), Hegu (LI 4), Chize (LU 5), Quchi (LI 11), Zhongzhu (SJ 3)   (*Great Compendium of Acupuncture and Moxibustion*)
【Regional Anatomy】 Skin-subcutaneous tissue-ligament of dorsum of the wrist-between tendons of extensor muscle of fingers and extensor muscle of the little finger-radiocarpal joint. In the superficial layer, there are the dorsal branches of the ulnar nerve, the dorsal venous network of the wrist and the terminal branches of the posterior cutaneous nerve of the forearm. In the deep layer, there are the branches of the dorsal carpal branch of the ulnar artery.
【Remark】 Puncturing Yangchi (SJ 4) perpendicularly can strengthen the peristalsis of a paralyzed or weak rectum and descending colon.

SJ 5 Waiguan (外关)
(Outer Conjunction)

【Source】 *Miraculous Pivot*
【Name Explanation】 Wai (外), lateral; Guan (关), pass. The point is at the vital site on the lateral side of the humerus.
【Classification】
   1) Luo-(Connecting) Point of the Sanjiao Meridian of Hand-Shaoyang.
   2) One of the Eight Confluent Points, connecting with the Yangwei Meridian.
【Location】 On the dorsal side of the forearm and on the line connecting Yangchi (SJ 4) and the tip of the olecranon, 2 cun proximal to the dorsal crease of the wrist, between the radius and the ulnar. (Fig. 9-11)
【Localization】 Extend the arm with palm facing downwards. The point is located directly 2 cun superior to the middle of carpal dorsal cross striation, between the ulna and radius, opposite to Neiguan (PC 6).
【Indications】
   1) Diseases along the Course of the Meridian: Difficult movement of the elbow and arm, pain in the upper limbs, shaking of the hand, pain in the finger, hemiplegia, hypochondriac pain, torticollis.
   2) Diseases of the Head and Sense Organs: Headache, pain, redness and swelling of the eyes, tinnitus, deafness, epistaxis, toothache.
   3) Digestive Diseases: Abdominal pain, constipation, cholera, appendicitis, anorexia.
   4) Mental Diseases: Acute convulsion, irritability and susceptibility to anger.
   5) Other Diseases: Febrile diseases, common cold, warts.

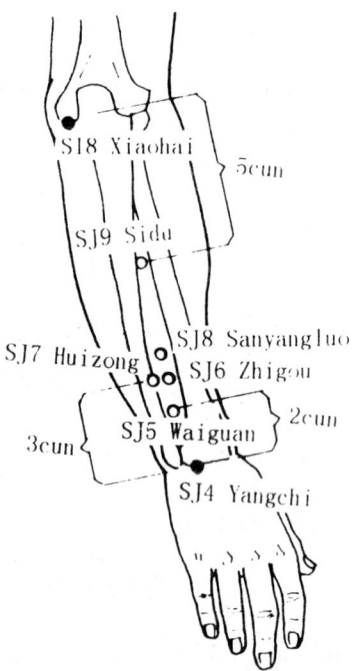

Fig. 9-11

【Mechanism of Action】
   1) It is one of the Eight confluent points and communicates with the Yangwei Meridian. The Yangwei Meridian connects and networks Yang all over the body. It is one of the main points for expelling the external evils and clearing away the heat in treating common cold, febrile diseases and malaria, etc.

2) It is also a commonly used point for treating headache, eye diseases and ear disorders as the Shaoyang Meridian distributes on the lateral side of the hand, eye and ear. That is the reason why where the meridian passes, where the indications are.

3) Puncturing this point has an obvious effect on activating qi to relieve stagnation. It can be used for fullness and pain in the chest and hypochondrium, dysfunction of the gastro-intestinal tract, mental depression, irritability and susceptibility to anger.

【Method】Puncture perpendicularly 0.5-1 cun. Moxibustion is applicable.

【Acupoint Prescriptions】
1) Deafness: Waiguan (SJ 5), Huizong (SJ 7). (*Thousand Golden Prescriptions*)
2) Diseases of the mouth: Waiguan (SJ 5), Neiting (ST 44), Zusanli (ST 36), Shangqiu (SP 5) which is mainly used for lock jaw. (*ibid*)

【Regional Anatomy】Skin-subcutaneous tissue-extensor muscle of the little finger and extensor muscle of the fingers-long extensor muscle of the thumb and extensor muscle of the index finger. In the superficial layer, there is the posterior cutaneous nerve of the forearm and athe tributaries of the cephalic and basilic veins. In the deep layer, there are the posterior interosseous artery and vein and the posterior interosseous nerve.

【Remark】Puncturing Waiguan (SJ 5) and Guangming (GB 37) can effectively treat Juvenile miopia, the rate of needling response to the eye area is 38.2%. Moreover, it can improve the eyesight and lower the diopters. Puncturing Waiguan (SJ 5) also has an analgesic effect.

SJ 6　Zhigou（支沟）
（Branching Ditch）

【Source】*Miraculous Pivot*

【Name Explanation】Zhi（支）, limbs; Gou（沟）, ditch. Zhi here refers to the upper limb. The point is located between the radius and the ulna.

【Classification】Jing-(River) Point of the Sanjiao Meridian of Hand Shaoyang, pertaining to fire in the Five Elements.

【Location】On the dorsal side of the forearm and on the line connecting Yangchi (SJ 4) and the tip of the olecranon, 3 cun proximal to the dorsal crease of the wrist, between the radius and ulnar. (See Fig. 9-11)

【Localization】Extend the arm with palm facing downwards. The point is located 3 cun directly superior to the middle of the transverse dorsal crease of the wrist, between the ulna and radius, opposite to Jianshi (PC 5).

【Indications】
1) Diseases along the Course of the Meridian: Soreness and pain of the shoulder, arm and back, pain in the hypochondriac region, difficult movement of the neck.
2) Diseases of the head and sense organs: Deafness, tinnitus, sudden loss of the voice, pain and redness of the eyes, sore throat.
3) Digestive Diseases: Constipation, vomiting, diarrhea.
4) Gynopathy: Amenorrhea, postpartum, vertigo, dysmenorrhea.
5) Mental Diseases: Irritability and easily angered.
6) Other Diseases: Fullness of the chest and hypochondriac region, febrile diseases.

【Mechanism of Action】
1) It is a major point for activating qi and is a commonly used point for treating hypochondriac distension, irritability, gastro-intestinal diseases and gynecopathy caused by qi stagnation. It is one of the first points chosen for chronic constipation.
2) This point is good at activating qi while Waiguan (SJ 5) is used both for promoting

qi to alleviate depression and for clearing heat. Both of them can be used to treat gastro-intestinal diseases by promoting qi and alleviating depression. Zusanli (ST 36), which belongs to the stomach meridian, can also be used to treat gastro-intestinal diseases but its indications are wider than those of Zhigou (SJ 6).

【Method】 Puncture perpendicularly 0.8-1.2 cun. Moxibustion is applicable.

【Acupoint Prescriptions】
    1) Scrofula: Zhigou (SJ 6), Zhangmen (LR 13). (*Essential Treasured Prescriptions*)
    2) Pain in the shoulder and back: Zhigou (SJ 6) and Guanchong (SJ 1) which are used for soreness and heaviness sensation in the shoulder and arm. (*ibid*)
    3) Heart diseases: Zhigou (SJ 6), Taixi (KI 3), Rangu (KI 2). (*ibid*)
    4) Cholera vomiting and diarrhea: Zhigou (SJ 6), Tianshu (RN 25). (*Experience on Acupuncture and Moxibustion Therapy*)
    5) Postpartum vertigo: Zhigou (SJ 6), Sanli (ST 36), Sanyinjiao (SP 6). (*Great Compendium of Acupuncture and Moxibustion*)
    6) Hypochondriac pain: Zhigou (SJ 6), Zhangmen (LR 13), Waiguan (SJ 5). (*ibid*)
    7) Chronic constipation: Zhigou (SJ 6), Zusanli (ST 36) (*Abstract of Clinical Experience on Acupuncture and Moxibustion*)
    8) Constipation due to deficiency: reinforcing Zhigou (SJ 6), reducing Zusanli. (*Songs on Point Selection of Miscllaneous Diseases*)

【Regional Anatomy】 Skin-subcutaneous tissue-the extensor muscle of the little finger-the long extensor muscle of the thumb-interosseous membrane of the forearm. In the superficial layer, there is the posterior cutaneous nerve of the forearm and the tributaries of the cephalic and basilic veins. In the deep layer, there is the posterior interosseous artery and vein and the posterior interosseous nerve.

【Remark】 Puncturing this point together with Zusanli (ST 36) and Sanyinjiao (SP 6) and retaining the needles for 30 minutes can strengthen uterus contraction in pregnant women, and has an analgesic effect for intrathoracic operations.

SJ 7 Huizong (会宗)
(Converging Meridians)

【Source】 *A-B Classic of Acupuncture and Moxibustion*
【Name Explanation】 Hui (会), meeting; Zong (宗), gathering. This is the Xi-(Cleft) point of this meridian, a place where the qi of the meridian gathers.
【Classification】 Xi-(Cleft) Point of the Sanjiao Meridian of Hand-Shaoyang.
【Location】On the dorsal side of the forearm, 3 cun proximal to the dorsal crease of the wrist, on the ulnar side of Zhigou (SJ 6) and on the radial border of the ulna. (See Fig. 9-11)
【Localization】 Extend the arm with palm facing downwards, locate the point 3 cun above the transverse dorsal crease of the wrist, ulnar side of Zhigou (SJ 6), at the radial side of the ulna.

【Indications】
    1) Diseases along the Course of the Meridian: Pain of the upper limbs, skin and muscles.
    2) Diseases of the Head and Sense Organs: Tinnitus, deafness.
    3) Mental Diseases: Manic and depressive psychosis.

【Mechanism of Action】 See Waiguan (SJ 5) and Zhigou (SJ 6) for other details.
【Method】 Puncture perpendicularly 0.5-1 cun. Moxibustion is applicable.

【Regional Anatomy】Skin-subcutaneous tissue-the ulnar extensor muscle of the wrist-the extensor muscle of the index finger-interosseous membrane of the forearm. In the superficial layer, there is the posterior cutaneous nerve of the forearm and the tributaries of the basilic vein. In the deep layer, there are the branches tributaries of the posterior interosseous artery, vein and nerve of the forearm.

SJ 8 Sanyangluo (三阳络)
(Three Yang Collaterals)

【Source】 *A-B Classic of Acupuncture and Moxibustion*
【Name Explanation】Sanyang (三阳), three Yang meridian of hand; Luo (络), connection. This point connects the three Yang meridian of the hand.
【Location】On the dorsal side of the forearm, 4 cun proximal to the dorsal crease of the wrist, between the radius and ulna. (See Fig. 9-11)
【Localization】Extend the arm with palm facing downwards. Locate the point 4 cun directly above the middle of the transverse dorsal crease of the wrist, between the ulna and the radius.
【Indications】
　1) Diseases along the Course of the Meridian: Lower back pain due to acute lumbar sprain. Pain and inability to raise the arm.
　2) Diseases of the Head and Sense Organs: Sudden loss of voice, deafness, dental carities, eye diseases.
　3) Other Diseases: Aversion to cold, fever without sweating, somnolence.
【Mechanism of Action】See Waiguan (SJ 5) and Zhigou (SJ 6)
【Method】Puncture perpendicularly 0.8-1.2 cun. Moxibustion is applicable.
【Regional Anatomy】Skin-subcutaneous tissue-the extensor muscle of the fingers-the long abductor muscle the thumb-the short extensor muscle of the thumb-interosseous membrane of the forearm.
【Remark】Puncturing Sanyangluo (SJ 8) has a good analgesic effect in thoracic operations. For mitral valvotomy, puncturing Sanyangluo (SJ 8) through Ximen (PC 4) can obtain satisfactory anesthesic effect. This effect is related to the stimulation conducted with acupuncture. The stimulation caused by greater electro-pulses can get better analgesic effect. In pneumonectomy, by puncturing Sanyangluo (SJ 8) through Ximen (PC 4), the acupuncture anesthesic effect of 133 cases were analysed, it was found that the rate of I and II grades was 85.7%. In one of the experiments, 21 healthy subjects were punctured to observe the analgesic effect. The results indicated that twisting the needle at Sanyangluo (SJ 8) has a positive analgesic effect on the thoracic area.
　Puncturing Sanyangluo (SJ 8) can increase endorphins in the blood, and its content has a parallel relation with its analgesic effect.

SJ 9 Sidu (四渎)
(Four Canals)

【Source】 *A-B Classic of Acupuncture and Moxibustion*
【Name Explanation】Si (四), four; Du (渎), river. The Yangtze, the Yellow, the Huaihe and the Jishui Rivers were called Sidu in ancient times. The qi of meridian is able to irrigate

more regions when it reaches this point.
【Location】On the dorsal side of the forearm, the line connecting Yangchi (SJ 4) and the tip of the olecranon, 5 cun distal to the tip of the olecranon, between the radius and ulna. (See Fig. 9-11)
【Localization】Extend the arm with palm facing downwards, locate the point at 7 cun directly above the transverse dorsal crease of the wrist, between the ulna and radius.
【Indications】
    1) Diseases along the Course of the Meridian: Pain of the forearm.
    2) Diseases of the Head and Sense Organs: Sudden loss of voice, sudden onset of deafness, toothache, globus hystericus.
【Mechanism of Action】See Waiguan (SJ 5) and Zhigou (SJ 6) for other details.
【Method】Puncture perpendicularly 1-1. 5 cun. Moxibustion is applicable.
【Regional Anatomy】Skin-subcutaneous tissue-the extensor muscle of the little finger and the ulnar extensor muscle of the wrist-the long abductor and the extensor muscle of the thumb. In the superficial layer, there are the posterior cutaneous nerve of the forearm and the tributaries of the cephalic and basilic veins. In the deep layer, there are the branches of the posterior interosseous nerve of the forearm.

SJ 10　Tianjing（天井）
（Heaven Well）

【Source】*Miraculous Pivot*
【Name Explanation】Tian（天）, heaven; Jing（井）, well. Upper is indicated as heaven. The point is in the depression above the olecranon in the upper limb, which is compared to a well.
【Classification】He-(Sea) Point of the Sanjiao Meridian of Hand Shaoyang, pertaining to earth in the Five Elements.
【Location】On the lateral side of the upper arm, in the depression 1 cun proximal to the tip of the olecranon when the elbow is flexed. (Fig. 9-12)
【Localization】With the arm akimbo, the point is located in the depression 1 cun posterior and superior to the olecranon.

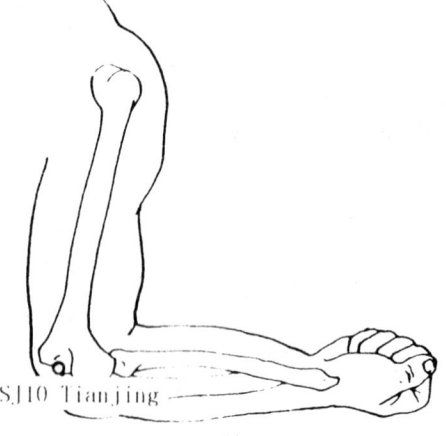

Fig. 9-12

【Indications】
    1) Diseases along the Course of the Meridian: Pain and numbness of the arm and shoulder, elbow pain. pain in the hypochondriac region.
    2) Diseases of the Head and Sense Organs: Migraine, deafness, tinnitus, pain of the eyes, sore throat, swelling of the cheek.
    3) Respiratory Diseases: Cough and spitting bloody pus.
    4) Cardiovascular Diseases: Cardiac pain, chest pain.
    5) Mental Diseases: Epilepsy, palpitation, convulsion, windstroke.
    6) Other Diseases: Scrofula, goiter, warts, sores, urticaria.
【Mechanism of Action】Puncturing this point has an effect of clearing heat, tranquilizing the mind, activating meridians and removing masses. So, it is used to treat cough and spitting bloody pus, sore throat, swelling of the cheek, cardiac pain, and sudden onset of deafness

due to sanjiao fire.

【Method】Puncture perpendicularly 0.5-1 cun. Moxibustion is applicable.

【Acupoint Prescriptions】

1) Arm atrophy: Tianjing (SJ 10), Waiguan (SJ 5), Quchi (LI 11). (*Thousand Golden Prescriptions*)

2) Arthralgia syndrome due to pathogenic wind: Tianjing (SJ 10), Chize (LU 5), Shaohai (HT 3), Weizhong (UB 40), Yangfu (GB 38). (*Great Compendium of Acupuncture and Moxibustion*)

3) Trance: Tianjing (SJ 10), Juque (RN 14), Xinshu (BL 15). (*ibid*)

【Regional Anatomy】Skin-subcutaneous tissue-the brachial triceps muscle. In the superficial layer, there is the posterior brachial cutaneous nerve. In the deep layer, there are the arteriovenous network of the elbow joint and the muscular branches of the radial nerve.

SJ 11 Qinglengyuan (清冷渊)
(Pure Cold Abyss)

【Source】*A-B Classic of Acupuncture and Moxibustion*

【Name Explanation】Qing (清), cool; Leng (冷), cold; Yuan (渊), deep water. The function of this point is to eliminate heat in the Sanjiao as if the patient were in cold deep water.

【Location】With the elbow flexed, on the lateral side of the upper arm, 2 cun above the tip of the olecranon and 1 cun above Tianjing (SJ 10). (Fig. 9-13)

【Localization】With the arm akimbo, the point is located 2 cun posterior and superior to the olecrenon, 1 cun directly above Tianjing (SJ 10).

【Indications】

1) Diseases along the Course of the Meridian: Motor impairment of the shoulder.

2) Diseases of the Head and Sense Organs: eyepain, headache.

3) Other Diseases: Chills, fever.

【Mechanism of Action】Ancient doctors consider it useful to treat headache chills and motor impairment of the shoulder.

【Method】Puncture perpendicularly 0.8-1.2 cun. Moxibustion is applicable.

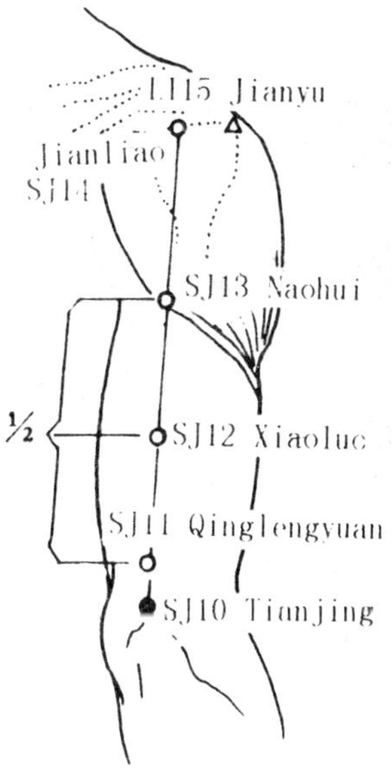

【Regional Anatomy】Skin-subcutaneous tissue-brachial triceps muscle. In the superficial layer, there is the posterior brachial cutaneous nerve. In the deep layer, there are the median collateral artery and vein and the muscular branches of the radial nerve.

Fig. 9-13

SJ 12 Xiaoluo (消泺)
(Thawing River-bed)

【Source】*A-B Classic of Acupuncture and Moxibustion*

【Name Explanation】Xiao (消), to eliminate; Luo (泺), marsh. This point pertains to the

Triple Energizer (Sanjiao) Meridian and functions to regulate water passage.

【Location】 On the lateral side of the upper arm, at the midpoint of the line connecting Qinglengyuan (SJ 11) and Naohui (SJ 13). (See Fig. 9-13)

【Localization】 Sit with the shoulder relaxed, first locate Naohui (SJ 13) which is located at the intersection between the humerus and the poster-inferior border of the deltoid muscle. This point is located at the middle point of the line joining Qinglengyuan (SJ 11) and Naohui (SJ 13).

【Indication】
　　1) Diseases on the Course of the Meridian: Stiffness and pain of the neck and nape, pain of the arm.
　　2) Diseases of the Head and Sense Organs: Headache.

【Mechanism of Action】 This point is mainly used to treat pain. It means where the meridian passes, where the indications are.

【Method】 Puncture perpendicularly 1-1.5 cun. Moxibustion is applicable.

【Regional Anatomy】 Skin-subcutaneous tissue-the long head of brachial triceps muscle-the medial head of the brachial triceps muscle. In the superficial layer, there is the posterior brachial cutaneous nerve. In the deep layer, there is the median collateral artery and vein and the muscualr branches of the radial nerve.

SJ 13　Naohui（臑会）
（Nao Convergence）

【Source】 *A-B Classic of Acupuncture and Moxibustion*

【Name Explanation】 Nao（臑）, muscle prominence of the upper arm; Hui（会）, confluence. The point is at the muscle prominence of the upper arm and is a confluence of this meridian with Yangweimai.

【Classification】 Crossing Point of Hand Yangming and Hand Shaoyang; Crossing Point of Hand Shaoyang and Yangwei meridians.

【Location】 On the lateral side of the upper arm, and on the line connecting the tip of the olecranon and Jianliao (SJ 14), 3 cun below Jianliao (SJ14), and on the posterior inferior border of the deltoid muscle. (See Fig. 9-13)

【Localization】 Sit with the shoulder relaxed. The point is located 3 cun directly inferior to Jianliao (SJ 14) which is located on the posterior side of the shoulder, on the same line with Tianjing (SJ 10).

【Indications】
　　1) Diseases along the Course of the Meridian: Pain in the scapular region, numbness and pain of the arm.
　　2) Diseases of the Head and Sense Organs: Eye disease.
　　3) Other Diseases: Scrofula, goiter.

【Mechanism of Action】 This point is one of commonly used points to treat pain of the arm and scapula. Puncturing this point has an effect of dredging and activating the meridian, and regulating the flow of qi to alleviate pain. See Waiguan (SJ 5) for other details.

【Method】 Puncture perpendicularly 1-1.5 cun. Moxibustion is applicable.

【Regional Anatomy】 Skin-subcutaneous tissue-the long head lateral head of the brachial triceps muscle-radial nerve-the medial head of the brachial triceps muscle. In the superficial layer, there is the posterior brachial cutaneous nerve. In the deep layer, there is the radial nerve and the deep brachial artery and vein.

SJ 14　Jianliao（肩髎）
（Shoulder Crevice）

【Source】 *A-B Classic of Acupuncture and Moxibustion*
【Name Explanation】 Jian（肩）, shoulder; Liao（髎）, foramen. The point is in a foramen on the shoulder.
【Location】On the shoulder, posterior to Jianyu(LI 15), in the depression inferior and posterior to the acromion when the arm is abducted. (See Fig. 9-13)
【Localization】
　　1) When the arm is abducted there appear two depression in the shoulder region. This point is located in the more posterior depression of the shoulder joint.
　　2) The shoulder relaxed, locate the point 2 cun directly below the posterior border of the acrom clavicular joint, between the acromion and the greater tuberosity of the humerus.
【Indications】
　　Diseases along the Course of the Meridian: Pain and heaviness of the arm and inability of the shoulder to raise.
【Mechanism of Action】It is a commonly used point for treating pain and inability to raise the shoulder. It is often used in combination with Jianyu (LI 15) in order to smooth qi and blood circulation around the shoulder. An additional needling between Jianliao (SJ 14) and Jianyu (LI 15) is often added, and all the three points are termed "Jiansanzhen" which can get better effects.
【Method】 Puncture perpendicularly 1-1.5 cun. Moxibustion is applicable.
【Regional Anatomy】 Skin-subcutaneous tissue-the deltoid muscle-the teres minor muscle-the teres major muscle-the tendon of the latissimus muscle of the back. In the superficial layer, there is the lateral supraclavicular nerve. In the deep layer, there is the axillary nerve and the posterior circuflex humeral artery and vein.

SJ 15　Tianliao（天髎）
（Heaven Crevice）

【Source】 *A-B Classic of Acupuncture and Moxibustion*
【Name Explanation】 Tian（天）, heaven; Liao（髎）, foramen. Upper refers to heaven. The point is in a foramen above the shoulder blade.
【Classification】 Crossing Point of Hand Shaoyang and Yangwei meridian and Foot Shaoyang and Yang wei meridian.
【Location】 On the scapula, at the midpoint between Jianjing (GB 21) and Quyuan (SI 13), at the superior angle of the scapula. (See Fig. 9-14)
【Localization】 Sit with the shoulder relaxed. Locate the point at the medial superior angle of the scapula.
【Indications】
　　1) Diseases of the Limbs along the Course of the Meridian: Pain in the arm and shoulder, pain in the

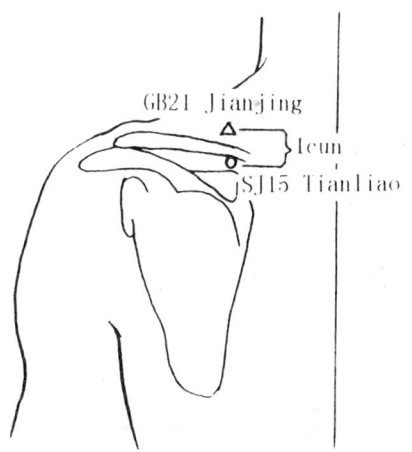

Fig. 9-14

neck.

2) Other Diseases: Irritability and fullness in the chest, febrile diseases without sweat, fever and aversion to cold.

【Mechanism of Action】This point corresponds with the lung in the chest and is located in the shoulder and neck region. Where the acupoint locates, where the indications are.

【Method】 Puncture perpendicularly 0.5-0.8 cun. Moxibustion is applicable.

【Regional Anatomy】 Skin-subcutaneous tissue-trapezius muscle-supraspinous muscle. In the superficial layer, there are the supraclavicular nerve and the lateral cutaneous branches of the posterior branches of the 1st thoracic nerve. In the deep layer, there are the branches tributaries of the dorsal scapular and suprascapular artery and vein, and the suprascapular nerve.

SJ 16   Tianyou (天牖)
(Heaven Window)

【Source】 A-B Classic of Acupuncture and Moxibustion

【Name Explanation】Tian(天), heaven; You(牖), window. Upper refers to heaven. Tianyou means heavenly window. The point is on the upper part of the lateral aspect of the neck and good to "open the upper aperture". It is therefore likened to a heavenly window.

【Location】 On the lateral side of the neck, directly below the posterior border of the mastoid process, level with the angle of the mandible, and on the posterior border of the sternocleidomastoid muscle. (Fig. 9-15)

【Localization】 Sitting position, locate the point at the same level with the angle of mandible on the posterior border of the sternocleidomastoid muscle.

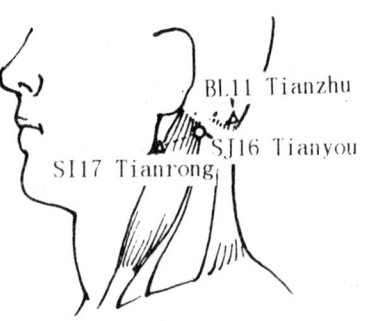

Fig. 9-15

【Indications】

1) Diseases of the Head and Sense Organs: Headache, dizziness, headache due to wind swelling of the face, pain of the eyes, blurry vision, sudden deafness, tinnitus, epistaxis, sore throat.

2) Other Diseases: Difficult movement of the neck due to stiffness.

【Mechanism of Action】 It is a crossing point of the Hand and Foot Shaoyang Meridians with the Yangwei meridian. The Sanjiao meridian of Hand Shaoyang runs along the posterior border of the ear. A branch enters the ear and reaches the outer canthus. Its Muscle Region runs along the root of the tongue. It can be used to treat diseases of the head, face and five sense organs.

For difficult movement of the neck due to stiffness of the nape, different points should be used. This point can be used for cases with obvious tender pain. Ashi points are used for pain caused by other factors.

【Method】 Puncture perpendicularly 0.5-1 cun. Moxibustion is applicable.

【Acupoint Prescriptions】

1) Pain of the shoulder and arm: Tianyou (SJ 16), Quepen (ST 12), Shendao (DU 11), Dazhu (BL 11), Tiantu (RN 22), Shuidao (ST 28), Jugu (LI 16). (*Thousand Golden Prescriptions*)

2) Sudden deafness: Tainyou (SJ 16), Sidu (SI 9). (*ibid*)

3) Headache due to wind: Tianyou (SJ 16), Fengmen (BL 12), Kunlun (BL 60), Guanyuan (RN 4), Guanchong (SJ 1). (*ibid*)

4) Sharp pain and difficult movement in lower back: Tianyou (SJ 16), Fengchi (GB 20), Hegu (LI 4), Kunlun (BL 60). (*Great Compendium of Acupuncture and Moxibustion*)

【Regional Anatomy】 Skin-subcutaneous tissue-between sternocleidomastoid muscle and the trapezius muscle-the splenius muscle of the head and the neck-semispinalis muscles of the head and the neck. In the superficial layer, there are the tributaries of the external jugular vein, the great auricular nerve and the lesser occipital nerve. In the deep layer, there are the branches or tributaries of the occipital artery and vein, and the ascending branches of the deep cervical artery and vein.

SJ 17 Yifeng (翳风)
(Wind Screen)

【Source】 *A-B Classic of Acupuncture and Moxibustion*
【Name Explanation】 Yi (翳), shielding; Feng (风), pathogenic wind. The point is behind the earlobe and is the place for shielding off pathogenic wind.
【Classification】 The Crossing Point of the Hand and Foot Shaoyang Meridians.
【Location】 Posterior to the ear lobe, in the depression between the mastoid process and mandibular angle. (See Fig. 9-16)
【Localization】 Sitting or in lateral recumbant position with the ear lobe slightly bent inward, locate the point anterior to the mastoid process.
【Indications】

1) Diseases of the Head and Sense Organs: Deviation of the eye and mouth, tinnitus, wetness and itch in the ear, blurring of vision, cataract, toothache, sore throat and mumps.

2) Mental Diseases: Convulsion, mania, stuttering.

【Mechanism of Action】

1) It is an important point for treating diseases of the head, face and five sense organs. Puncturing it has an effect of expelling wind, clearing heat, and dredging

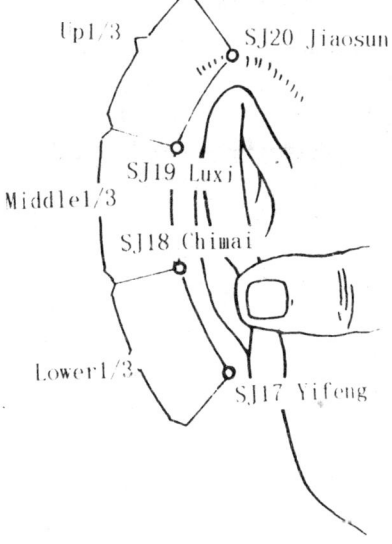

Fig. 9-16

the meridians and collaterals. Different needling direction can be applied to different kinds of diseases. Proper direction can enhance the therapeutic effect. Needling towards Xiaguan (ST 7), the needling response may travel to the ear region and front part of the tongue, and can be used to treat diseases of the ear, tongue and jaw. When it is towards Daying (ST 5), the needling response may reach the lower jiao and lower teeth and can be used to treat diseases in that area. When it is towards the tip of the nose, the needling response may travel to the throat, treating cough due to local itch. It can be used to treat diseases of the throat and cheek region.

2) After withdrawing the needle, if the needling hole is made to give off a little blood, better effect can be gained in treating deafness, tinitus and mumps due to stagnation of heat evil.

【Method】 Puncture perpendicularly 0.8-1.2 cun. Moxibustion is applicable.
【Acupoint Prescriptions】

1) Deafness: Yifeng(SJ 17), Huizong(SJ 7), Xiaguan(ST 7). (*A-B Classic of Acupuncture and Moxibustion*)

2) Sudden loss of voice: Yifeng (SJ 17), Tongli (HT 5). (*ibid*)

3) Allergic toothache: Yifeng (SJ 17), Qubi (GB 7), Touwei (SI 8), Fengchi (GB 20), Taiyang (EX-HN 5). (*New Acupuncture and Moxibustion*)

【Regional Anatomy】Skin-subcutaneous tissue-the parotid gland. In the superficial layer, there is the great aurcular nerve and the tributaries of the external jugular vein. In the deep layer, there is the posterior auricular artery of the external carotid artery and the facial nerve.

SJ 18 Chimai (瘛脉)
(Convulsion Collateral)

【Source】 *A-B Classic of Acupuncture and Moxibustion*

【Name Explanation】 Chi (瘛), convulsion; Mai (脉), collateral. The point is behind the ear where the collaterals are distributed. It is useful therefore in treating convulsion.

【Location】 On the head, at the centre of the mastoid process, at the junction of the middle third and lower third of the line connecting Jiaosun (SJ 20) and Yifeng (SJ 17) along the curve of the ear helix. (See Fig. 9-16)

【Localization】 Sitting or in lateral recumbant position, locate the point at the intersection of the posterior auricular hairline and external auditory canal opening.

【Indications】

1) Diseases of the Head and Sense Organs: Tinnitus, deafness, blurred vision.

2) Digestive Diseases: Vomiting, diarrhea, dysentery.

3) Mental Diseases: Infantile convulsion.

【Mechanism of Action】 It is mainly used to treat ear disorders. For treating infantile convulsion, vomiting, diarrhea and dysentery, bleeding method can be used. That is pricking the point or the small collaterals around the point with a three edged needle to cause bleeding. It can also be used for emergency treatment.

【Method】 Puncture subcutaneously 0.3-0.5 cun or prick the point to cause bleeding. Moxibustion is applicable.

【Acupoint Prescription】 Infantile convulsion: Chimai (SJ 18), Changqiang (DU 1). (*A-B Classic of Acupuncture and Moxibustion*)

【Regional Anatomy】 Skin-subcutaneous tissue-the posterior auricular muscle. There is the great auricular nerve, the posterior auricular branches of the facial nerve and the posterior auricular artery and vein in this area.

【Remark】 In abdominal operations, the simultaneous usage of the points on both the abdomine and head may contribute to the success of acupuncture anesthesia. Adding Jiuwei (RN 15) and right Zhangmen (LR 13), or Weishu (BL 21), right Zhangmen (LR 12) in combination with Chimai (SJ 18), obviously improved analgesic effect of acupuncture anesthesia can be seen in the upper and lower abdominal areas.

SJ 19 Luxi (颅息)
(Skull Signal)

【Source】 *A-B Classic of Acupuncture and Moxibustion*

【Name Explanation】 Lu (颅), skull; Xi (息), tranquility. The point is on the skull and is used to calm the mind.
【Location】 On the head, at the junction of the upper third and middle third of the line connecting Jiaosun (SJ 20) and Yifeng (SJ 17) along the curve of the ear helix. (See Fig. 9-16)
【Localization】 Sitting or in lateral recumbant position, the point is located in the posterior auricular hairline on the midpoint of the line joining Chimai (SJ 18) and Jiaosun (SJ 20) along the helix.
【Indications】
　　1) Diseases of the Head and Sense Organs: Headache, tinnitus, deafness, swelling and pain of the ear, otorrhea.
　　2) Mental Diseases: Infantile convulsion, convulsion.
　　3) Other Diseases: Asthma, pain in the hypochondriac region, vomiting, salivation, febrile diseases.
【Mechanism of Action】 See Chimai (SJ 18).
【Method】 Puncture subcutaneously 0.3-0.5 cun. Moxibustion is applicable.
【Regional Anatomy】 Skin-subcutaneous tissue-the posterior auricular muscle. There is the great auricular nerve, the lesser occipital nerve, the posterior auricular branches of the facial nerve, and the auricular branches of the posterior auricular artery and vein in this area.

SJ 20　Jiaosun（角孙）
(Auditory Angle)

【Source】 *Miraculous Pivot*
【Name Explanation】 Jiao (角), corner; Sun (孙), tertiary collateral. The point is on the temporal region, corresponding to the ear apex, where the reticular meridians are distributed.
【Classification】 The Crossing Point of the Hand and Foot Shaoyang and Hand Yangming Meridians.
【Location】 On the head, above the ear apex within the hairline. (See Fig. 9-16)
【Localization】 Sitting or in lateral recumbant position, bend the ear forward, the point is located at the hairline directly superior to the ear. This area is affected when the mouth is opened or closed.
【Indications】Diseases of the Head: Swelling and pain of the ear, redness and pain of the eyes, blurred vision, toothache, dry lips, aphtha, difficulty in chewing, mumps, stiffness of the neck and headache.
【Mechanism of Action】 The disorders mentioned above are all caused by heat evils in the body. Puncturing this point has the effect of clearing heat, toxic material and expelling wind. Clinically, bleeding method, match moxibustion method and reducing method by filiform needdle are mostly used at this point and they have all proven effective.
【Method】 Puncture subcutaneously 0.3-0.5 cun. Moxibustion is applicable.
【Acupoint Prescription】Pain of the gum: Jiaosun (SJ 20), Xiaohai (SI 8). (*Great Compendium of Acupuncture and Moxibustion*)
【Regional Anatomy】 Skin-subcutaneous tissue-superior auricular muscle-superficial temporal fascia and temporal muscle. There are the the branches of the auriculotemporal nerve and the anterior auricular branches of the superficial temporal artery and vein in this area.

SJ 21 Ermen (耳门)
(Ear Gate)

【Source】 *A-B Classic of Acupuncture and Moxibustion*
【Name Explanation】 Er (耳), ear; Men (门), door. The point is in front of the ear, like a door for the ear.
【Location】 On the face, anterior to the supratragic notch, in the depression behind the posterior border of the condyloid process of the mandible. (See Fig. 9-17)
【Localization】 Sitting or in lateral recumbant position, slightly open the mouth, then locate the point in the depression 0.5 cun directly superior to Luxi (SJ 19).
【Indications】
Diseases of the Head and Sense Organs: Tinnitus, deafness, otorrhea, soreness or pain in the ear, toothache, difficulty in chewing, swelling and pain of the neck and submandibular region, deviation of the mouth and eyes.
【Mechanism of Action】 This point is mostly used to treat ear disorders. That is because where the acupoint is located, where the indications are.

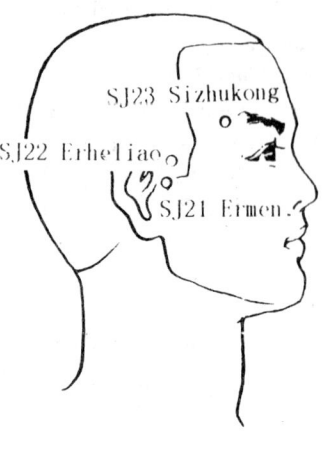

Fig. 9-17

【Method】 Puncture perpendicularly 0.5-1 cun. Moxibustion is applicable.
【Acupoint Prescriptions】
1) Otorrhea and soreness in the ear: Ermen (SJ 21), Yifeng (SJ 17), Hegu (LI 4). (*Great Compendium of Acupuncture and Moxibustion*)
2) Deafness: Ermen (SJ 21), Fengchi (GB 20), Xiaxi (GB 43), Tinggong (SI 19), Tinghui (GB 2). (*ibid*)
【Regional Anatomy】 Skin-subcutaneous tissue-the parotid gland. There is the auriculotemporal nerve, the anterior auricular branches of the superficial temporal artery and vein, and the temporal branches of the facial nerve in this area.

SJ 22 Erheliao (耳和髎)
(Ear Harmony Crevice)

【Source】 *A-B Classic of Acupuncture and Moxibustion*
【Name Explanation】 Er (耳), ear; He (和), harmony; Liao (髎), foremen. The point is in the depression in front of tragicus and is used for improving hearing.
【Location】 On the lateral side of the head, on the posterior margin of the temples, in front of the anterior border of the root of the ear auricle and posterior to the superficial temporal artery. (See Fig. 9-17)
【Localization】 Sitting or in lateral recumbant position, select the point anterior-superior to SJ 21, at the same level with the root of the auricle in the place where the pulsation of the artery can be felt on the posterior border of the hairline of the temple.
【Indications】
1) Diseases of the Head and Sense Organs: Heaviness sensation and pain of the head, lockjaw, swelling of the submandibular region, swelling and pain of the tip of the nose, runny

nose and facial paralysis.

2) Mental Diseases: Convulsions.

【Mechanism of Action】 The point is indicated for excess syndromes because it can clear heat and expel wind.

【Method】 Avoid puncturing the artery. Puncture obliquely or subcutaneously 0.3-0.5 cun. Moxibustion is applicable.

【Regional Anatomy】 Skin-subcutaneous tissue-the anterior auricular muscle-the superficial temporal fascia and the temporal muscle. In the superficial layer, there is the auriculotemporal nerve, the temporal branches of the facial nerve, and the branches or tributaries of the superficial temporal artery and vein. In the deep layer, there are the anterior and posterior deep temporal nerves from the mandibular division of the trigeminal nerve.

SJ 23 Sizhukong (丝竹空) (Musical Instrument Hole)

【Source】 *A-B Classic of Acupuncture and Moxibustion*

【Name Explanation】 Sizhu (丝竹), slender bamboo; Kong (空), space. The point is at the lateral end of the eyebrow, which looks like a slender bamboo. The local region of the point has a shallow depression.

【Location】 On the face, in the depression at the lateral end of the eyebrow. (See Fig. 9-17)

【Localization】 Sitting or in lateral recumbant position, locate the point at the lateral border of the zygomatic process on the frontal bone, in the depression at the lateral end of the eyebrow.

【Indications】

1) Diseases of the Head and Sense Organs: Headache, vertigo, redness and pain of the eye, lacrimation, twitching of the eyelid, toothache.

2) Mental Diseases: Manic depression and insanity.

【Mechanism of Action】 The point is located in the eye region and is mainly used to treat head and eye diseases. Puncturing (SJ 23) Sizhukong through Shuaigu (GB 8) point is used to treat migraines, and puncturing Sizhukong (SJ 23) and Cuanzhu (BL 2) can treat pain of the forehead.

【Method】 Puncture subcutaneously 0.5-1 cun. It is not advisable to apply moxibustion.

【Acupoint Prescriptions】

1) Eye diseases: Sizhukong (SJ 23), Qianding (DU 21).   (*Thousand Golden Prescriptions*)

2) Salivation: Sizhukong (SJ 23), Baihui (Du 20). (*Great Compendium of Acupuncture and Moxibustion*)

3) Redness and pain of the eyes: Sizhukong (SJ 23), Cuanzhu (BL 2). (*ibid*)

【Regional Anatomy】 Skin-subcutaneous tissue-the orbicular muscle of the eye. There is the supraorbital nerve, the zygomaticofacial nerve, the temporal and zygomatic branches of the facial nerve, and the frontal branches of the superficial temporal artery and vein in this area.

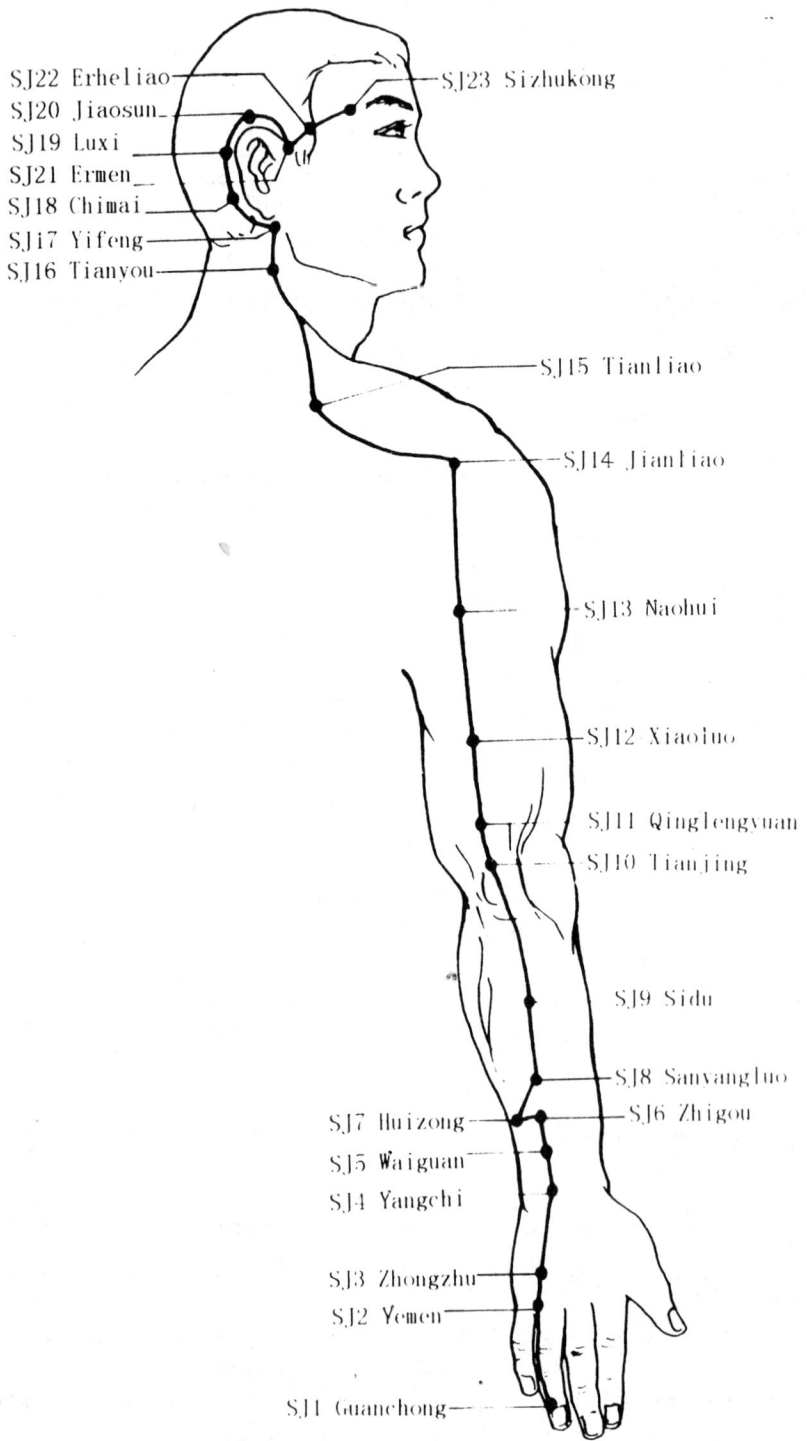

Fig. 9-18 Acupoints of the Sanjiao Meridian of Hand Shaoyang

Table 9-2
Indications and Actions of Acupoints of the Sanjiao Meridian of Hand Shaoyang

Name of the points	Specific points	Common indications	Specific indications and functions
SJ 1 Guanchong (关冲)	Jing-(Well) point	Disorders of the ears, eyes, throat, temporal and hypochondriac regions: headache, tinnitus, redness, swelling and pain of eyes, deafness, sore and swollen throat, hypochondriac pain, febrile disease	Clearing heat and purging fire-evil, restoring consciousness. Syncope, apoplexy, sunstroke, vexation, mumps, stiff tongue, dry mouth, febrile disease
SJ 2 Yemen (液门)	Ying-(Spring) point		Clearing heat and purging fire-evil, dredging the meridian. Redness, swelling and pain of dorsum of hand, stiffness and pain of fingers and arm, dizziness, malaria, mental disease
SJ 3 Zhongzhu (中渚)	Shu-(Stream) point		Regulating the flow of qi, benefiting the function of the ear. Deafness, tinnitus, halo vision, febrile disease, stiff fingers, pain of shoulder, back, elbow and arm
SJ 4 Yangchi (阳池)	Yuan-(Source) point		Relaxing muscles and tendons, activating collaterals, reducing fever. Painful wrist, sprain and contusion of the wrist, diabetes, dry mouth, malaria
SJ 5 Waiguan (外关)	Luo-(connecting) point One of the eight confluence points		Expelling wind-evil from the body surface, dredging the meridian. Common cold, fever, hypertension, hypochondriac pain, pain of upper extremities
SJ 6 Zhigou (支沟)	Jing-(River) point		Promoting the flow of qi, dissipating blood stasis, promoting the movement of intestine. Sudden onset of aphonia, lockjaw, hypochondrial pain, constipation, amenorrhea, angina cordis, pain of shoulder, arm, waist and back
SJ 7 Huizong (会宗)	Xi-(Cleft) point		Clearing away heat from the three jiaos, dredging the Shaoyang Meridian. Deafness, tinnitus, epilepsy, pain of skin and muscle, pain of upper extremities
SJ 8 Sanyangluo (三阳络)			Dredging the collaterals, reviving the patient from unconsciousness, stopping pain. Sudden onset of deafness, sudden onset of aphonia, toothache, pain of waist due to sudden sprain and contusion, pain of upper extremities, drowsiness
SJ 9 Sidu (四渎)			Deafness, toothache, sudden onset of aphonia, pain of upper extremities
SJ 10 Tianjing (天井)	Confluent point		Expelling wind-evil and heat-evil, dredging the collaterals and tranquilizing the mind. Migraine, torticollis
SJ 11 Qinglengyuan (清冷渊)			Pain of upper extremities

Name of the points	Specific points	Common indications	Specific indications and functions
SJ 12 Xiaoluo (消泺)		Disorders of shoulder and arm	Stiffness and pain of neck, toothache, pain of shoulder and arm
SJ 13 Naohui (臑会)			Dissipating masses and eliminating phlegm. Goiter, disorders of the head
SJ 14 Jianliao (肩髎)			Dispelling wind-evil and dampness-evil, dredging the meridian and easing the joint movement, stiffness and pain of the shoulder, apoplexy, scapulohumeral periarthritis
SJ 15 Tianliao (天髎)	Crossing point		Stiffness and pain of neck, shoulder and arm
SJ 16 Tianyou (天牖)		Disorders of ears, eyes and temporal region: headache deafness, tinnitus, puffy cheek, wry mouth with distorted eye, pain of eye	Dispersing wind and bringing down swelling, clearing away heat. Wind-syndrome of head, puffy face, painful eye, sudden loss of hearing, dreaminess, sore throat, stiffness of neck
SJ 17 Yifeng (翳风)	Crossing point		Expelling the wind-evil and dredging the collaterals, improving hearing and sight, stopping pain. Tinnitus, deafness, inner pain of the ear, deafness and muteness, wry mouth with distorted eye, toothache, puffy cheek, mumps, prosopalgia
SJ 18 Chimai (Qimai) (瘛脉)			Calming wind-syndrome, relieving spasm. Migraine, infantile convulsion, clonic convulsion, vomiting, salivation, drooling, diarrhea, deafness, tinnitus
SJ 19 Luxi (颅息)			Clearing heat and calming wind syndrome. Headache, tinnitus, deafness, infantile convulsion, vomiting, salivation, drooling, clonic convulsion, dyspnea
SJ 20 Jiaosun (角孙)	Crossing point		Dispersing wind-evil and clearing heat, clearing heat from the head and improving sight. Cataracts, optic neuritis, retinal hemorrhage, conjunctivitis, toothache, puffy cheek
SJ 21 Ermen (耳门)			Activating the flow of qi, improving the function of the ear, clearing heat. Tinnitus, deafness, toothache, inner pain of the ear, deaf and mute
SJ 22 Erheliao (耳和髎)	Crossing point		Dispersing wind-evil and clearing heat. Headache, tinnitus, lockjaw, wry mouth with distorted eye, clonic convulsion
SJ 23 Sizhukong (丝竹空)			Calming liver-wind, improving sight, stopping pain. Headache, migraine, photophobia, flickering eyelid, optic atrophy

VIII. Acupoints of the Small Intestine Meridian of Hand Taiyang

SI 1   Shaoze (少泽)
(Lesser Marsh)

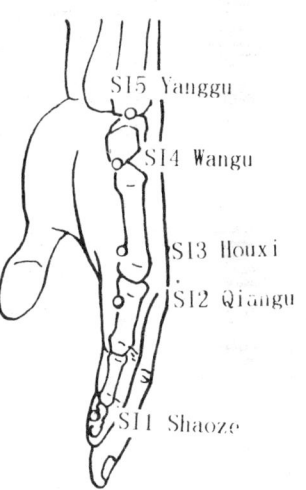

【Source】 *Miraculous Pivot*
【Name Explanation】Shao (少), young of small; Ze (泽), marsh. The point is located on the small finger where the Qi of meridian just originats, like a small marsh.
【Classification】Jing-(Well)Point of the Small Intestine Meridian of Hand Taiyang, pertaining to metal in the Five Elements.
【Location】 On the ulnar side of the distal segment of the little finger, 0.1 cun from the corner of the nail. (See Fig. 9-19)
【Localization】 Make a slight fist with palm facing downwards. The point can be located at the intersection of the lines drawn from the lateral and basal parts of the ulnar side of the little finger nail.
【Indications】
   1) Diseases along the Course of the Meridian: Pain in the posterior aspect of the shoulder and arm, numbness of the small finger.
   2) Diseases of the Head and Sense Organs: Stiffness of the neck, sore throat, cloudiness of the cornea, pterygium, deafness, tinnitus, epistaxis, stiffness of the tongue, aphasia, excessive salivation.

Fig. 9-19

   3) Respiratory Diseases: Cough.
   4) Cardiovascular Diseases: Cardiac pain, shortness of breath, oppressive feeling in the chest and diaphragm.
   5) Mental Diseases: Apoplexy, coma, depression.
   6) Other Diseases: Insufficient lactation, mastitis, jaundice, febrile diseases.
【Mechanism of Action】
   1)The Small Intestine Meridian distributes on the ulnar side of the little finger, posterior aspect of the shoulder and arm, sides of the nose, ear, throat and infraobital region. So Shaoze (SI 1) is a commonly used point to treat the diseases of the limbs, head, face and five sense organs.
   2)Due to its location, the point deals with the functions of the Zangfu organs, particularly the function of separating clarity from turbidity of the small intestine. It has been proven that this point promotes the milk-secretion. It can also be used to treat mastitis due to stagnation of the milk. That is to say it has the function of promoting lactation and resolving masses.
   3) The meridians of the small intestine and the heart are interiorly-exteriorly related and linked each other. So this point can be used to treat cardiac pain by regulating the heart qi

and smoothing blood circulation.

【Method】Puncture obliquely 0.1 cun or prick the point to cause bleeding. Moxibustion is applicable.

【Acupoint Prescriptions】

1) Pain of the inner canthus: puncture Shaoze (SI 1), the Jing- (Well) point of the Hand Taiyang Meridian; Pain of the outer canthus: puncture Guanchong (SJ 1), the Jing- (Well) point of the Hand Shaoyang Meridian. (*Plain Questions*)

2) Pain and stiffness of the neck: Shaoze (SI 1), Qianggu (SI 2), Houxi (SI 3), Yanggu (SI 5), Wangu (SI 4), Kunlun (GB 60), Xiaohai (SI 8), Cuanzhu (BL 2). (*Thousand Golden Prescriptions*)

【Regional Anatomy】Skin-subcutaneous tissue-root of the nail. There are the dorsal digital branches of the proper palmar digital nerve of the ulnar nerve and the arteriovenous network formed by the dorsal digital branches of the ulnar palmar arteries and veins of the little finger in this area.

【Remark】It is reported that puncturing Shaoze (SI 1) and Danzhong (RN 17) can increase the lactation hormone in blood in hypoglalactous women. Electropuncturing Shaoze (SI 1) can increase the serection of alphahypophamine.

SI 2　Qiangu (前谷)
(Front Valley)

【Source】*Miraculous Pivot*

【Name Explanation】Qian (前), front; Gu (谷), valley. The depression in front of the 5th metacarpophalangeal joint is like a valley.

【Classification】Ying-(Spring) Point of the Small Intestine Meridian of Hand Taiyang, pertaining to water in the Five Elements

【Location】At the junction of the red and white skin along the ulnar border of the hand, at the ulnar end of the crease of the 5th metacarpophalangeal joint when a loose fist is made. (See Fig. 9-19)

【Localization】Make a loose fist. The point can be located at the distal part of the 5th metacarpophalangeal joint and the dorso-ventral boundary, on the ulnar end of the metacarpophalangeal transverse crease.

【Indications】

1) Diseases along the Course of the Meridian: Pain of the forearm, spasm of the elbow, numbness, redness, swelling and difficult movement of the fingers, feverish sensation in the palm.

2) Diseases of the Head and Sense Organs: Tinnitus, deafness, pain of the eyes, cloudiness of the cornea, nasal obstruction, epistaxis, sore throat, mumps.

3) Respiratory Diseases: Cough, hemoptysis.

4) Mental Diseases: Depression, mania, epilepsy.

5) Other Diseases: Insufficient lactation, anhidrosis in febrile diseases, malaria.

【Mechanism of Action】See Shaoze (SI 1) and Houxi (SI 3).

【Method】Puncture perpendicularly 0.2-0.3 cun. Moxibustion is applicable.

【Acupoint Prescriptions】

1) Tinnitus: Qiangu (SI 2), Houxi (SI 3), Pianli (LI 6), Daling (PC 7); Cloudness of the cornea: Qiangu (SI 2), Jinggu (BL 64). (*Thousand Golden Prescriptions*)

2) Dysuria and redness of urine: Qiangu (SI 2), Weizhong (BL 40); Nasal obstruction:

Qiangu (SI 2), Yinjiao (Du 22). (*Experience on Acupuncture and Moxibustion Therapy*)

   3) Depression: Qiangu (SI 2), Houxi (SI 3), Shuigou (DU 26), Jiexi (ST 41), Jinmen (BL 63), Shenmai (BL 62). (*Great Compendium of Acupuncture and Moxibustion*)

【Regional Anatomy】Skin-subcutaneous tissue-the base of the proximal phalanx of the little finger. There are the dorsal digital nerve and the proper palmar digital nerve of the ulnar nerve and the palmar artery and the little finger inthis area.

SI 3   Houxi (后溪)
(Back Stream)

【Source】 *Miraculous Pivot*
【Name Explanation】 Hou (后), back; Xi (溪), brook. The depression at the back of the 5th metacarpophalangeal joint is like a brook.
【Classification】
   1) Shu-(Stream) Point of the Small Intestine Meridian of Hand-Taiyang, pertaining to wood in the Five Elements.
   2) One of the Eight Confluent Points, connecting with the Du Meridian.
【Location】 At the junction of the red and white skin along the ulnar border of the hand, at the ulnar end of the distal palmar crease, proximal to the 5th metacarpophalangeal joint when a loose fist is made. (See Fig. 9-19)
【Localization】 Make a loose fist. The point can be located at the posterior border of the 5th metacarpophalangeal joint in the dorso-ventral boundary, on the end of palmar transverse crease.
【Indications】
   1) Diseases along the Course of the Meridian: Stiffness, pain and difficult movement of the neck, pain of the shoulder and arm, hemiplegia, torticollis, lower back pain.
   2) Diseases of the Head and Sense Organs: Headache, deafness, redness of the eye, cloudiness of the cornea, epistaxis.
   3) Urinary Diseases: Dysuria with reddish urine.
   4) Mental Diseases: Depression, mania, epilepsy, insomnia, hysteria.
   5) Other Diseases: night sweating, jaundice, febrile diseases, malaria, scabies, warts.
【Mechanism of Action】
   1) This point opens to the Du Meridian, which dominates the Yang qi and anterior region of the body. It can be used to treat not only excessive heat syndrome, malaria, but also night sweating due to yin defficiency by clearing away the heat.
   2) Puncturing Houxi (SI 2) has an obvious effect on lower back pain. The point opens to the Du meridian. The Hand Taiyang meridian links with the Foot Taiyang meridian. Puncturing Hegu (LI 4) through Houxi (SI 3) is more effective for treating acute lower back pain.
   3) It is an essential point for relieving spasm. It has the function of tranquilizing the mind and stopping spasm resulting from various causes.
   4) By removing damp-heat in the small intestines, this point can treat jaundice, hot urination and scabies.
   5) It is one of the Eight Confluent points, connecting with the Du meridian. Puncturing Houxi (SI 3) in combination with Shenmai (BL 66) is effective for eye pain, stiffness of the neck, torticollis, shoulder and arm pain.
【Method】 Puncture perpendicularly 0.5-0.7 cun. Moxibustion is applicable.
【Acupoint Prescriptions】

1) Malaria: Houxi (SI 3), Hegu (LI 4). (*Great Compendium of Acupuncture and Moxibustion*)

2) Lower back pain: Houxi (SI 3), Huantiao (GB 30); jaundice: Houxi (SI 3), Laogong (PC 8). (*Songs of Hundred Symptoms*)

3) Epilepsy: Houxi (SI 3), Jiuwei (RN 11), Shenmen (HT 7) (*Songs of Shengyu*)

【Regional Anatomy】Skin-subcutaneous tissue-the abductor muscle of the little finger-the short flexor muscle of the little finger. In the superficial layer, there are the dorsal branches of the ulnar nerve, the palmar branches of the ulnar nerve and the subcutaneous superficial vein. In the deep layer, there are the proper ulnar palmar artery and vein and the proper palmar digital nerve of the little finger.

SI 4　Wangu（腕骨）
（Wrist Bone）

【Source】 *Miraculous Pivot*

【Name Explanation】Wan (腕), wrist; Gu (骨), bone. The point is between the bones of the wrist.

【Classification】 Yuan-(Source) Point of the Small Intestine Meridian of Hand-Taiyang.

【Location】 On the ulnar border of the hand, in the depression between the proximal end of the 5th metacarpal bone and the hamate bone, at the junction of the red and white skin. (See Fig. 9-19)

【Localization】 Lateral posture of the hand, palm facing forward, the point is located directly superior to Houxi (SI 3), in the depression between the basis of the fifth metacarpal bone and the hamate bone.

【Indications】

1) Diseases along the Course of the Meridian: Rigidity of the neck, limited movement of elbow and arm, pain of arm and finger, weakness of wrist, hemiplegia, lower back pain.

2) Diseases of the Head and Sense Organs: Lacrimation with cold, cloudiness of the cornea, tinnitus, deafness, nasal obstruction, epistaxis, swelling of the submandibular region.

3) Digestive Diseases: Jaundice, diabetic syndrome, vomiting, aphasia.

4) Mental Diseases: Malaria, infantile convulsion, palpitation, trismus

5) Other Diseases: Febrile diseases with anhidrosis, cholecystitis, pleurisy.

【Mechanism of Action】See Houxi (SI 3) and Shaoze (SI 1)

【Method】 Puncture perpendicularly 0.3-0.5 cun. Moxibustion is applicable.

【Acupoint Prescriptions】

1) Dyspnea due to hypochondriac pain: Wangu (SI 4), Yanggu (SI 5); Tinnitus with inability to hear: Wangu (SI 4), Yanggu (SI 5), Jianzhen (SI 9), Qiaoyin (GB 44), Xiaxi (GB 43). (*Thousand Golden Prescriptions*)

2) Pain of the arm and shoulder: Wangu (SI 4), Tianzong (SI 11); Contracture of fingers: Wangu (SI 4), Zhongzhu (SJ 3). (*Experience on Accupuncture and Moxibustion Therapy*)

3) Yellowish skin due to febrile diseases: Wangu (SI 4), Shenmai (BL 62), Waiguan (SJ 5), Yongquan (KI 1). (*Great Compendium of Acupuncture and Moxibustion*)

4) Jaundice due to deficiency of the spleen: Wangu (SI 4), Zhongwan (RN12). (*Songs of Jade Dragon*)

【Regional Anatomy】Skin-subcutaneous tissue-the abductor muscle of the little finger-pisometacarpal ligament. In the superficial layer, there are the medial cutaneous nerve of the forearm, the palmar branches of the ulnar nerve, the dorsal branches of the ulnar nerve and the superficial vein. In the deep layer, there are the branches or tributaries of the ulnar artery and vein.

【Remark】Perpendicularly needling Wanggu (SI 4) can strengthen the peristalsis of the rectum and the descending colon which may not have peristalsis, and cause a desire to defecate. It is reported that giving slight stimulation at Wangu (SI 4) can cause cortical evoked potential, which is quite different from that caused by needling non-point areas.

SI 5　Yanggu（阳谷）
（Yang Valley）

【Source】*Miraculous Pivot*
【Name Explanation】Yang (阳), Yang of Yin-Yang; Gu (谷), valley. The exterior is Yang. The seam on the exterior aspect of the wrist is like a valley, where the point is located.
【Classification】Jing-(River) Point of the Small Intestine Meridian of Hand Taiyang, pertaining to fire in the Five Elements
【Location】On the ulnar border of the wrist, in the depression between the styloid process of the ulna and the triangular bone. (See Fig. 9-19)
【Localization】Lateral posture of the hand, palm facing forwards, the point can be located directly superior to Wangu (SI 4), the depression of the triangular bone.
【Indications】
　　1) Diseases along the Course of the Meridian: welling of the neck and submandibular area, hypochondriac pain, pain of posterior aspect of the arm and wrist, hemiplegia.
　　2) Diseases of the Head and Sense Organs: Redness, pain and swelling of the eye, vertigo, tinnitus, deafness, toothache, aphtha.
　　3) Mental Diseases: Manic depression and incoherent speech, infantile convulsion, difficulty in sucking due to stiffness of the tongue.
　　4) Other Diseases: Febrile diseases with anhidrosis, hemorrhoid, scabies.
【Mechanism of Action】See Houxi (SI 3) and Shaoze (SI 1).
【Method】Puncture perpendicularly 0.3-0.4 cun. Moxibustion is applicable.
【Acupoint Prescriptions】
　　1) Manic depressive psychosis: Yanggu (SI 5), Zhubin (KI 9), Tonggu (KI 20). (*A-B Classic of Acupuncture and Moxibustion*)
　　2) Acute pain and redness swelling of eyes: Yanggu (SI 5), Taichong (LR 3), Kunlun (BL 60). (*Thousand Golden Prescriptions*)
　　3) Pain of the upper teeth: Yanggu (SI 5), Zhengying (GB 17). (*Experience on Acupuncture and Moxibustion Therapy*)
　　4) Raving: Yanggu (SI 5), Yemen (SJ 2); Hypochondriac pain: Yanggu (SI 5), Wangu (SI 4), Zhigou (SJ 6), Geshu (BL 17), Shenmai (BL 61); Contracture of fingers and infantile convulsion: Yanggu (SI 5), Wangu (SI 4), Kunlun (BL 60). (*Great Compendium of Acupuncture and Moxibustion*)
　　5) Swelling of submandibular area and trismus: Yanggu (SI 5), Xiaxi (Gb 43) (*Songs of Hundreds of Symptoms*)
【Regional Anatomy】Skin-subcutaneous tissue-the anterior border of the tendon of the ulnar extensor muscle of the wrist. In the superficial layer, there are the dorsal branches of the ulnar nerve and the basilec vein. In the deep layer, there are the dorsal branches of the ulnar artery.

SI 6 Yanglao (养老)
(Aging Nourishment)

【Source】 A-B Classic of Acupuncture and Moxibustion
【Name Explanation】 Yang (养), to support; Lao (老), the aged. This point is used to treat geriatric diseases such as blurring of vision, deafness, lumbago, and shoulder pain.
【Classification】 Xi-(Cleft) Point of the Small Intestine Meridian of Hand Taiyang.
【Location】 On the ulnar side of the posterior surface of the forearm, in the depression proximal to and on the radial side of the head of the ulna. (See Fig. 9-20)
【Localization】
　　1) Bend the elbow with the palm facing the chest. The point is located at the radial bor-

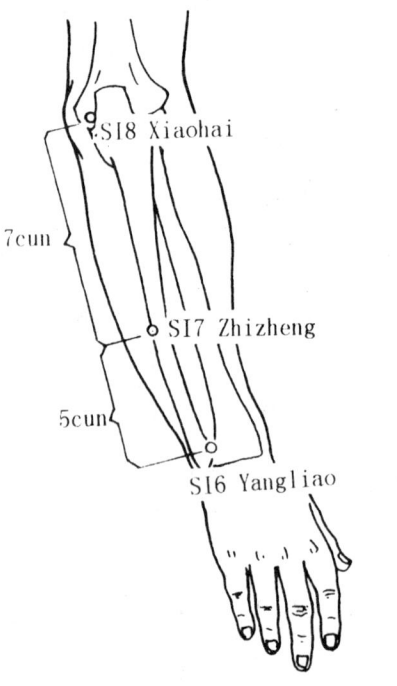
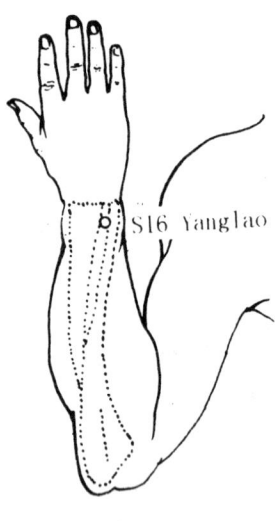

　　Fig. 9-20　　　　　　　　　　　　　　　　　　　　Fig. 9-21

der of the little head of ulna, in the gap formed at the same level with the top of the little head of ulna. (See Fig. 9-21)
　　2) Palm facing downwards, press the top of the little head of ulna with the other hand, and then turn the palm towards the chest, the point is located at the depression in the top of the little head of ulna.
【Indications】
　　1) Diseases along the Course of the Meridian: Torticollis, acute lumbar sprain.
　　2) Diseases of the Head and Sense Organs: Blurring of vision, redness, pain and swelling of eyes.
【Mechanism of Action】 The point is used for clearing away heat from the head, brightening eyes and relaxing both muscles and tendons to promote blood circulation. It is mostly com-

monly used to treat eye diseases, torticollis and lumbar sprain.
【Method】 Puncture perpendicularly 0.3-0.5 cun. Moxibustion is applicable.
【Acupoint Prescriptions】
 1) Pain in the shoulder and back: Yanglao (SI 6), Tianzhu (BL 10). (*Thousand Golden Prescriptions.*)
 2) Blurring of vision: Yanglao (SI 6), Hegu (LI 4), Quchai (BL 4). (*Experience on Acupuncture and Moxibustion Therapy.*)
 3) Blurring vision: Yanglao (SI 6), Tianzhu (BL 10). (*Songs of Hundreds of Symptoms*)

【Regional Anatomy】 Skin-subcutaneous tissue-the tendon of the ulnar extensor muscle of the wrist. In the superficial layer, there are the medial cutaneous nerve of the forearm, the posterior cutaneous nerve of the forearm, the dorsal branches of the ulnar nerve and the tributaries of the basilec vein. In the deep layer, there is the network of the dorsal carpal arteries and veins.
【Remark】 Selecting the local points Yanglao (SI 6) and Waiguan (SJ 5) may obtain a satisfactory result in the treatment of arthralgia syndrome.

SI 7   Zhizheng (支正)
(Branch from Small Intestine Meridian)

【Source】 *Miraculous Pivot*
【Name Explanation】 Zhi (支), divergence; Zheng (正), regular meridian. The collateral of the Small Intestine Meridian diverges from this point to the Heart Meridian.
【Classification】 Luo-(Connecting) Point of the Small Intestine Meridian of Hand-Taiyang.
【Location】 On the ulnar side of the posterior surface of the forearm and on the line connecting Yanggu (SI 5) and Xiaohai (SI 8), 5 cun proximal to the dorsal crease of the wrist. (See Fig. 9-20)
【Localization】 Raise the hand, the point is located at 5 cun superior to Yanggu (SI 5), medial side of the ulna, on the line joining Yanggu (SI 5) and Xiaohai (SI 8).
【Indications】
 1) Diseases along the Course of the Meridian: Neck rigidity, spasmodic pain in the elbow and fingers, numbness of fingers, swelling of the submandibular region.
 2) Diseases of the Head and Sense Organs: Headache, hordeolum.
 3) Mental Diseases: Manic depressive psychosis, timidness, susceptibility to laugh and amnesia.
 4) Other Diseases: Scabies, five kinds of impairment, diabetic syndrome, febrile diseases.
【Mechanism of Action】 It is the Luo-(Connecting) point of the small Intestine Meridian of Hand-Taiyang and opens to the Heart Meridian. So it's used to treat mental diseases. Scabies is caused by damp heat of the small intestine and hordeolum is caused by heat evil in the blood. This point has the function of clearing away heat from the heart and regulating the small intestine. So it can be used to treat hordeolum and scabies.
【Method】 Puncture perpendicularly 0.3-0.5 cun. Moxibustion is applicable.
【Acupoint Prescriptions】
 1) Ravings: Zhizheng (SI 7), Yuji (LU10), Hegu (LI 4), Shaohai (HT 3), Quchi (LI 11), Wangu (SI 4). (*Thousand Golden Prescriptions.*)
 2) Epilepsy induced by terror: Zhizheng (SI 7), Neiguan (PC 6), Yangxi (LI 5). (*Experience on Acupuncture and Moxibustion Therapy.*)

【Regional Anatomy】 Skin-subcutaneous tissue-the ulnar flexor muscle of the wrist-the deep flexor muscle of the fingers- interosseous membrane of the forearm. In the superficial layer there is the medial cutaneous nerve of the forearm and the tributaries of the basilic vein. In the deep layer, there is the ulnar artery and vein and the ulnar nerve.

SI 8 Xiaohai （小海）
（Small Intestine Sea）

【Source】 *Miraculous Pivot*
【Name Explanation】Xiao（小）, small; Hai（海）, sea. Xiao refers to the Small Intestine Meridian, and this is its He-(Sea) point. The arrival of qi and blood at this point is like water flowing into the sea.
【Classification】 He-(Sea) Point of the Small Intestine Meridian of Hand Taiyang, petaining to earth in the Five Elements.
【Location】 On the medial side of the elbow, in the depression between the olecranon of the ulna and the medial epicondyle of the humerus. (See Fig. 9-20)
【Localization】 Bend the elbow slightly. The point is located at the middle of the loecranon at the same level of the transverse crease of the cubital fossa and medial epicondyle of humerus. (Fig. 9-22). This point produces the sensation of an electric shock radiating to the little finger when the area around this point is flicked.
【Indications】
    1) Diseases along the Course of the Meridian: Pain in the shoulder and back, spasmodic pain in the elbow, pain in the lateral-posterior aspect of the arm.
    2) Diseases of the Head and Sense Organs: Headache, dizziness, vertigo, deafness, tinnitus, hordeolum.
    3) Mental Diseases: Manic depressive psychosis, epilepsy.
    4) Other Diseases: Scrofula, ulceration of the skin, lower abdominal pain, irritability.

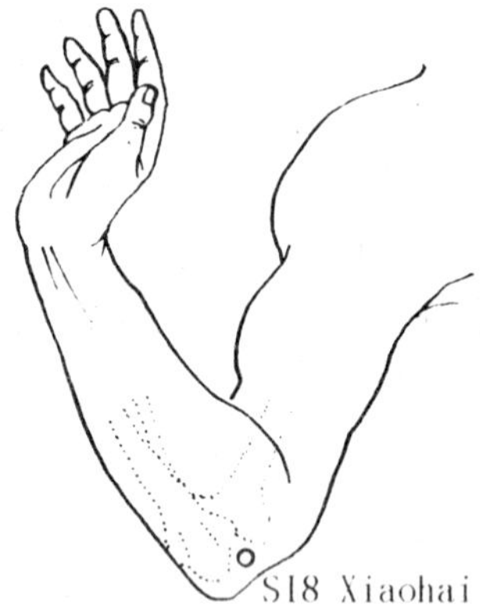

Fig. 9-22

【Mechanism of Action】
    1) The small intestine meridian connects with the heart which is related to fire. The small intestine has the function of seperating the clear from turbidity. Scrofula and ulceration of skin can be caused by phlegmatic dampness in the meridian and collaterals due to the heart fire. It's a commonly used point for treating the diseases mentioned above because it has the function of clearing away the heart fire and phlegmatic dampness.
    2) The heart controls the mind. If the phlegm-fire disturbs the function of the heart or runs up along the course of the meridian, diseases of the head, face and sense organs, and mental disorders may be present. This point can be used for removing dampness and phlegm, and clearing away the heart fire.
【Method】 Puncture perpendicularly 0.3-0.5 cun. Moxibustion is applicable.
【Regional Anatomy】 Skin-subcutaneous tissue-the groove of the ulnar nerve.

In the superficial layer, there are the ulnar branches of the medial cutaneous nerve of the forearm, the medial cutaneous nerve of the arm and the tributaries of the basilic vein. In the deep layer, there are the ulnar nerve, the arteriovenous network formed by the superior ulnar collateral arteries and veins and the posterior branches of the ulnar recurrent artery and vein on the posterior lateral side of the ulnar nerve.

【Remark】Puncturing Xiaohai (SI 8) perpendicularly can improve the obstinate vagotonia of the lower end of the descending colon and irritable colitis.

SI 9   Jianzhen (肩贞)
(Upright Shoulder)

【Source】 *Plain Questions*

【Name Explanation】Jian (肩), shoulder; Zhen (贞), first. This is the first point where the Small Intestine Meridian joins the shoulder.

【Location】Posterior and inferior to the shoulder joint, 1 cun above the posterior end of the axillary fold with the arm abducted. (See Fig. 9-23)

【Localization】Sit with shoulder relaxed and the upper arm abducted, the point is located at 1 cun directly superior to the end of posterioraxillary stripe.

【Indications】

1) Diseases along the Course of the Meridian: Pain, numbness and inability to raise hand and arm, pain in the scapular region.

2) Diseases of the Head and Sense Organs: Tinnitus, deafness, toothache.

3) Other Diseases: Scrofula.

【Mechanism of Actions】It's generally used to treat diseases of the limbs on the course of the meridian and local diseases.

【Method】Puncture perpendicularly 0.5-1 cun. Moxibustion is applicable.

【Acupoint Prescriptions】

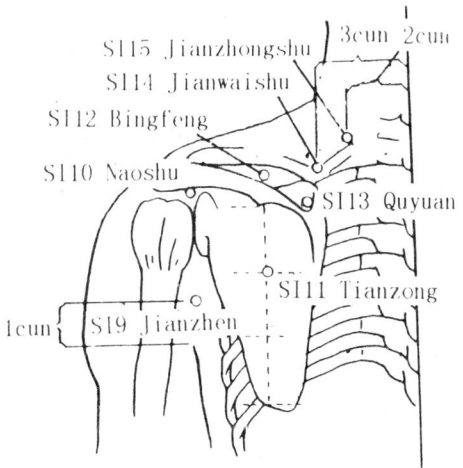

Fig. 9-23

1) Tinnitus and deafness: Jianzhen (SI 9), Wangu (GB 12). (*A-B Classic of Acupuncture and Moxibustion.*)

2) Hot and motor impairment of the shoulder: Jianzhen (SI 9), Guanchong (SJ 1), Jiannao. (*Thousand Golden Prescriptions.*)

3) Pain of the nervous subscapulares: Jianzhen (SI 9), Jianyu (LI 15), Tianzong (SI 11), Jianliao (SJ 10), Quyuan (SI 13). (*New Acupuncture and Moxibustion.*)

【Regional Anatomy】Skin-subcutaneous tissue-the posterior part of the deltoid muscle-the long head of the brachial triceps muscle-teres major muscle-the tendon of the latissims muscle of the back. In the superficial layer, there is the lateral cutaneous branch of the 2nd intercostal nerve and the superior lateral cutaneous nerve of the arm. In the deep layer, there is the radial nerve.

SI 10　Naoshu（臑俞）
(Nao Shu)

【Source】 *A-B Classic of Acupuncture and Moxibustion*
【Name Explanation】Nao（臑）, muscle prominence of the upper arm; Shu（俞）, point. The point is on the upper arm, where the qi of meridian is infused.
【Classification】The Crossing Point of the Hand Taiyang, Yangwei and Yangqiao Meridians.
【Location】 On the shoulder, above the posterior end of the axillary fold, in the depression below the lower border of the scapular spine. (See Fig. 9-23)
【Localization】 Sit with shoulder relaxed and the upper arm abducted. The point is located directly superior to Jianzhen (SI 9) which is located at the end of posterior axillary fold on the inferior border of spire of scapulae.
【Indications】
　　Diseases along the Course of the Meridian: Swelling of the shoulder, pain and weakness of the arm and shoulder, scrofula in the neck.
【Mechanism of Action】 This point can be used to dredge the meridian and collaterals, resolve mass and remove blood stasis.

SI 11　Tianzong（天宗）
(Heaven Attribution)

【Source】 *A-B Classic of Acupuncture and Moxibustion*
【Name Explanation】 Tian（天）, the upper part; Zong（宗）, respect. Tianzong means an important point on the upper part of the body.
【Location】 On the scapula, in the depression of the centre of the subscapularfossa, and on the level of the 4th thoracic vertebra. (See Fig. 9-23)
【Localization】 Sitting or prone position.
　　1) It is at the junction of the superior one third and middle one third of the distance between the inferior border of spina scapulae andinferior angle of scapula.
　　2) The point is located at the line joining the inferior border of spina scapulae with inferior angle of scapula on the same level with the inferior part of the 4th thoracic spinous process. Forming a triangle with Jianzhen (SI 9) and Naoshu (SI 10).
【Indications】
　　1) Diseases along the Course of the Meridian: Pain in the scapular region and inability to raise arms, numbness and soreness of the upper limbs along the course of the meridian.
　　2) Other Diseases: Mastitis.
【Mechanism of Action】
　　1) Where the acupoint locates, where the indications are. This point is mainly used to treat diseases of the scapular region and upper limbs.
　　2) This point can also be used to treat diseases in the opposite region. Tianzong (SI 11) is located in the scapular region opposit to the breast, so it can be used to treat mastitis.
【Method】 Puncture obliquely 0.5-1.5 cun. Moxibustion is applicable.
【Acupoint Prescription】
　　Arm pain: Tianzong (SI 11), Wuli (LI 13). (*Experience on Acupuncture and Moxibustion*

Therapy)

【Regional Anatomy】Skin-subcutaneous tissue- the trapezius muscle-infraspinous muscle. In the superficial layer, there are the cutaneous branches of the posterior branches of the 4th thoracic nerve and the accompanying arteries and veins. In the deep layer, there are the branches of the suprascapular nerve and the branches or tributaries of the circumflex scapular artery and vein.

SI 12　Bingfeng (秉风)
(Watching Wind)

【Source】 *A-B Classic of Acupuncture and Moxibustion*
【Name Explanation】Bing (秉), to receive; Feng (风), pathogenic wind. The point is located at a place where it is easily invaded by pathogenic wind.
【Classification】Crossing point of Hand Yangming, Hand Taiyang, Hand and Foot Shaoyang Meridions.
【Location】On the scapula, at the centre of the suprascapular fossa, directly above Tianzong (SI 11), in the depression when the arm is raised. (See Fig. 9-23)
【Localization】Sitting or prone position. Locate the point 1 cun superior to the middle of the superior border of spina scapulae, i.e: suprascapulae fossa. The point forms a triangle with Naoshu (SI 10) and Tianzong (SI 11).
【Indications】
　　Diseases along the Course of the Meridian: Pain in the scapular region, soreness and numbness of the upper limbs on the course of the meridian, stiffness and motor impairment of the neck.
【Mechanism of Action】Where the point locates, where the indications are. It is generally used for treating diseases in the shoulder and scapular region.
【Method】Puncture perpendicularly 0.5-0.7 cun. Moxibustion is applicable.
【Acupoint Prescription】
　　Pain of the nervous suprascapularis: Bingfeng (SI 12), Jugu (LI 16), Dazhu (BL 11), Jianwaishu (SI 14), Jianzhongshu (SI 15), Quyan (SI 13). (*New Acupuncture and Moxibustion*)
【Regional Anatomy】Skin-subcutaneous tissue-the trapezius muscle-the supraspinous muscle. In the superficial layer, there are the cutaneous branches of the posterior branches of the 2nd thoracic nerve and the accompanying arteries and veins. In the deep layer, there are the branches of the suprascapular nerve and the branches or tributaries of the suprascapular artery and vein.

SI 13　Quyuan (曲垣)
(Bend Wall)

【Source】 *A-B Classic of Acupuncture and Moxibustion*
【Name Explanation】Qu (曲), curved; Yuan (垣), wall. The point is located on the spine of the scapula which is like a curved wall.
【Location】On the scapula, at the medial end of the suprascapular fossa, at the midpoint of the line connecting Naoshu (SI10) and the spinous process of the 2nd thoracic vertebra. (See Fig. 9-23)

【Localization】Sit with the shoulder relaxed. The point is located at the midpoint of the line joining Naoshu (SI 10) and the spinous process of the 2nd thoracic vertebra.
【Indication】
Disease of the Limbs along the Course of the Meridian: Spasmodic pain in the shoulder and scapular region.
【Mechanism of Action】See Bingfeng (SI 12).
【Method】Puncture perpendicularly 0.3-0.5 cun. Moxibustion is applicable.
【Regional Anatomy】Skin-subcutaneous tissue-the trapezius muscle-supraspinous muscle.

In the superficial layer, there are the cutaneous branches of the posterior branches of the 2nd and 3rd thoracic nerves and the accompanying arteries and veins. In the deep layer, there are the muscular branches of the suprascapular nerve, the branches or tributaries of the suprascapular artery and vein and the dorsal scapular artery and vein.

SI 14　Jianwaishu（肩外俞） (Outer Shoulder Shu)

【Source】A-B Classic of Acupuncture and Moxibustion
【Name Explanation】Jian (肩), shoulder; Wai (外), lateral side, Shu (俞), point. The point is on the shoulder, slightly lateral to the vertebral border of the scapula.
【Location】On the back, below the spinous process of the 1st thoracic vertebra, 3 cun lateral to the posterior midline. (See Fig. 9-23)
【Localization】Sitting or prone position, the point is located at the intersection between the vertical line of vertebral margin of scapula and horizontal line of Taodao (DU 13).
【Indications】
Diseases along the Course of the Meridian: Stiffness of the neck, soreness and pain in shoulder and back.
【Mechanism of Action】See Bingfeng (SI 12).
【Method】Puncture perpendicularly 0.3-0.6 cun. Moxibustion is applicable.
【Regional Anatomy】Skin-subcutaneous tissue-the trapezius muscle-the rhomboid muscle. In the superficial layer, there are the cutaneous branches of the posterior branches of the 1st and 2nd thoracic nerves and accompanying arteries and veins. In the deep layer, there are the branches of tributaries of the transverse cervical artery and vein and muscular branches of the dorsal scapular nerve.

SI 15　Jianzhongshu（肩中俞） (Intro-shoulder Shu)

【Source】A-B Classic of Acupuncture and Moxibustion
【Name Explanation】Jian (肩), shoulder; Zhong (中), central; Shu (俞), point. The point is on the shoulder and is central to the vertebral border of the scapula.
【Location】On the back, below the spinous process of the 7th cervical vertebra, 2 cun lateral to the posterior midline. (See Fig. 9-23)
【Localization】Sitting or prone position, first locate Dazhui (DU 14) which is located in the spinous process of the 7th cervical vertebra, locate the point 2 cun lateral to Dazhui (DU 14). The point is located at the transverse process of the 1st thoracic vertebra.
【Indications】

1) Diseases along the Course of the Meridian: Pain in the shoulder and back, torticollis.
2) Diseases of the Head and Sense Organs: Blurring of vision.
3) Respiratory Diseases: Cough, asthma, fever and chills.

【Mechanism of Action】The point corresponds to the lung, therefore, it is effective in the treatment of lung diseases. It's also used for the treatment of local and adjacent diseases.

【Method】Puncture obliquely 0.3-0.6 cun. Moxibustion is applicable.

【Acupoint Prescriptions】

1) Pulmonary tuberculosis: Jianwaishu (SI 14), Jianzhongshu (SI 15), Dazhui (DU 11), Fufen (BL 41), Feishu (BL 13), Jueyinshu (BL 14), Xinshu (BL 15), Geshu (BL 17), Qihu (ST 13), Shufu (KI 27), Kufang (ST 14). (*New Acupuncture and Moxibustion*).

2) Paralysis of the muscle Trapezius: Jianzhongshu (SI 15), Jianwaishu (SI 14), Tianliao (SJ 15), Fufen (BL 41), Pohu (BL 42), Gaohuang (BL 43), Yixi (BL 45), Geguan (BL 46). (*ibid*)

【Regional Anatomy】Skin-subcutaneous tissue-the trapezius muscle-the rhomoboid muscle.

In the superficial layer, there are the posterior branches of the 8th cervical nerve and the cutaneous branches of the posterior branches of the 1st thoracic nerve. In the deep layer, there are the accessory nerve, the branches of the dorsal scapular nerve and the transverse cervical artery and vein.

SI 16 Tianchuang (天窗)
(Heaven Window)

【Source】*Miraculous Pivot and Plain Questios*

【Name Explanation】Tian (天), upper part; Chuang (窗), window. The point is on the neck and is indicated in otological diseases. Its function is to restore hearing loss which is compared to like opening a window.

【Location】On the lateral side of the neck, posterior to the sternocleidomastoid muscle and Futu (LI 18), on the level of the laryngealprotuberance. (See Fig. 9-24)

【Localization】Sitting position, the point is located at the same level with Futu (RN 23), which is located between the thyroid cartilage and hyoid muscle, on the posterior border of sternocleidomastoid muscle.

【Indications】

1) Diseases along the Course of the Meridian: Pain and stiffness of the neck, soreness and numbness of the arm and hand.

2) Diseases of the Head and Sense Organs: Sore throat, deafness, tinnitus, sudden loss of the voice, deviation of the eye and mouth.

【Mechanism of Action】

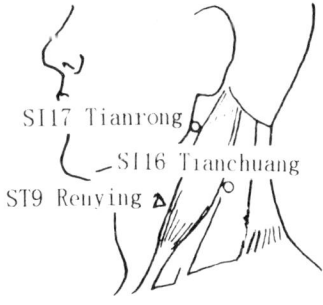

Fig. 9-24

1) The point is located beside the throat, therefore, it can be used for treating pain and swelling in the throat and sudden loss of voice.

2) Deeper puncturing at this point can treat pain and numbness of the arm and hand.

【Method】Puncture perpendicularly 0.5-0.8 cun. Moxibustion is applicable.

【Acupoint Prescriptions】

1) Goiter: Tianchuang (SI 16), Naohui (SJ 13). (*A-B Classic of Acupuncture and Moxi-*

bustion)

   2) Loss of voice: Apply moxibustion 50 cones to Tianchuang (SI 16) first, then 50 cones to Baihui (DU) and 50 cones to Tianchuang (SI 16) again. (*A Supplement to Thousand Golden Prescriptions*)

   3) Trismus: Tianchuang (SI 16), Yifeng (SJ 17). (*Experience on Acupuncture and Moxibustion Therapy*).

【Regional Anatomy】Skin-subcutaneous tissue-the posterior border of the sternocleidomastoid muscle-levator muscle of the scapula- splenius muscle of the neck and the head. In the superficial layer, there are the greater auricular nerve, the lesser occipital nerve and the external jugular vein. In the deep layer, there are the branches or tributaries of the ascending cervical artery and jugular vein.

SI 17   Tianrong (天容)
(Heaven Appearance)

【Source】*Miraculous Pivot*

【Name Explanation】Tian (天), upper part; Rong (容), abundance. The point is on the head, where the qi of the meridian is abundant.

【Location】On the lateral side of the neck, posterior to the angle of mandibular, in the depression on the anterior border of the sternocleidomastoid muscle. (See Fig. 9-24)

【Localization】Sitting or lateral position, the point is located at the same level with the angle of mandible, the anterior margin of the end of sternocleidomastoid muscle, the inferior border of posterior belly of digastric muscles.

【Indications】

   1) Diseases along the Course of the Meridian: Muscle sprain of the neck, furuncle on the neck.

   2) Diseases of the Head and Sense Organs: Tinnitus, deafness, sore throat, globus hystericus.

   3) Respiratory Diseases: Asthma, fever and aversion to cold.

   4) Other Diseases: Scrofula.

【Mechanism of Action】Where the point is located, where the indications are. It is generally used to treat diseases of the throat, ear, and others near the point.

【Method】Puncture perpendicularly 0.5-0.8 cun. Moxibustion is applicable.

【Acupoint Prescriptions】

   1) Cough, asthma, salivation: Tianrong (SI 17), Xingjian (LR 2). (*A-B Classic of Acupuncture and Moxibustion*)

   2) Limited movement due to shoulder pain: Tianrong (SI 17), Bingfeng (SI 12). (*ibid*)

   3) Tinnitus and deafness: Tianrong (SI 17), Tinghui (GB 2), Tinggong (SI 19), Zhongzhu (SJ 3). (*Thousand Golden Prescriptions*)

【Regional Anatomy】Skin-subcutaneous tissue-the posterior border of the facial artery-tendons of the digastric muscle and the stylohyid muscle. In the superficial layer, there are the greater auricular nerve and the external jugular vein. In the deep layer, there are the facial artery and vein, the internal jugular vein, the accessory nerve, the vagus nerve, the hypoglossal nerve and the superior cervical ganglion.

【Remark】Puncturing Tianrong (SI 17) has an antispasmodic action to the oddis' sphincter and can promote the contraction of Common bile duct and secretion of bile. Besides, it also has a satisfactory analgesic effect. Electropuncturing Tianrong (SI 17) has a definite effect on the meningovascular expansion and contraction and its change relates to electropuncture parameters; The weak electric current can cause the small arteries in cerebral pia mater to dilate, and a strong current can cause them to contract.

SI 18　Quanliao（顴髎）
（Zygoma Crevice）

【Source】 *A-B Classic of Acupuncture and Moxibustion*
【Name Explanation】 Quan (顴), zygoma; Liao (髎), foramen. The point is in the seam of the zygomatic bone.
【Classification】 The Crossing Point of Hand Shaoyang and Hand Taiyang Meridians
【Location】 On the face, directly below the outer canthus, in the depression below the zygomatic bone. (See Fig. 9-25)
【Localization】 Sitting with the head erect, the point is located at the intersection between the horizontal line of inferior margin of zygomatic bone and vertical line of the lateral canthus, aproximately at the same level of YingXiang (LI 20).
【Indications】
　　Diseases of the Head and Sense Organs: Deviation of the eye and mouth, twitching of eyelids, flushed face, toothache, swelling of the cheek, trigeminal neuralgia.
【Mechanism of Action】 Where the acupoints locate, where the indications are. For treating trigeminal neuralgia, the tip of the needle should point to the inner canthus of the opposite side and puncture it deeply to get the needling sensation in the upper teeth and lip.

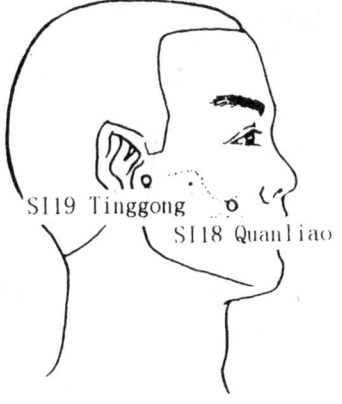

Fig. 9-25

【Method】 Puncture perpendicularly 0.5-0.8 cun.
【Acupoint Prescription】
　　Toothache: Quanliao (SI 18), Erjian (LI 2). (*A-B Classic of Acupuncture and Moxibustion*)
【Regional Anatomy】 Skin-subcutaneous tissue-zygomatic muscle-masseter muscle-temporal muscle. In the superficial layer, there are the branches of the infraorbital nerve from the maxillary nerve, the zygomatic and buccal branches of the facial nerve, and the branches or tributaries of the transverse facial artery and vein. In the deep layer, there are the branches of the mandibular nerve from the trigeminal nerve.
【Remark】 Puncturing Quanliao (SI 18) has an analgesic action and can treat trigeminal neuralgia. Its analgesic mechanism relates to the monosamine transmitters in the cerebrospninal fluid. For examples, needling Hegu (LI 4) and Quanliao (SI 18), or Neiguan (PC 6) and Quanliao (SI 18); or Hegu (LI 4), Neiguan (PC 6), Neiguan (LI 4) and Quanliao (SI 18), the content of Trp, 5-HT and 5-HIAA is increased, and that of Noradrenalin is decreased. The clinical acupuncture anesthesic effect is parallel to the changes caused by increasing the content of 5-HT system and decreasing that of Noradrenalin. Experiments also proved that stimulating the caudate nucleus and electropuncturing Hegu (LI 4), Neiguan (PC 6) and Quanliao (SI 18) have a coordinated analgesic effect.

SI 19 Tinggong (听宫)
(Listening Palace)

【Source】 *Miraculous Pivot*

【Name Explanation】 Ting (听), hearing; Gong (宫), place. Tinggong refers to the ear, the point is located in front of the ear and is indicated in otological diseases.

【Classification】The Crossing Point of the Hand Shaoyang, Foot Shaoyang and Hand Taiyang Meridians.

【Location】On the face, anterior to the tragus and posterior to the mandibular condyloid process, in the depression found when the mouth is open. (See Fig. 9-25)

【Localization】 Open the mouth slightly. The point is located in the depression between the anterior part of the tragus and the posterior margin of mandibular capitulum.

【Indications】

1) Diseases of the Head and Sense Organs: Tinnitus, deafness, tympanitis, earache, toothache.

2) Other Diseases: Lower back pain.

【Mechanism of Action】 It's the crossing point of Hand and Foot Shaoyang Meridian and Hand Taiyang Meridian. The Foot Shaoyang Meridian enters the ear from behind the ear, emerges and passes the anterior side of the ear. The branch of Hand Taiyang Meridian also "enters the ear". Deafness is one of the diseases of the Small Intestine Meridian. The meaning of Tinggong (SI 19) is palace of the hearing, so it is one of the commonly used points for treating otopathy, especially for deafness due to side effects of drugs. It is also effective for deafness caused by tympanitis.

【Method】 Puncture perpendicularly 0.1-0.3 cun. Moxibustion is applicable.

【Acupoint Prescriptions】

1) Psychic deafness: Tinggong (SI 19), Tinghui (GB 2), Yifeng (SJ 17). (*Great Compendium of Acupuncture and Moxibustion*)

2) Arthritis of the mandibular joint: Main points: Tinggong (SI 19), Tinghui (GB 2), Ermen (SJ 21); Supplementary points: Hegu (LI 4), Xiaguan (ST 7), Tianrong (SI 17). (*Abstract of Clinical Experience on Acupuncture and Moxibustion.*)

3) Acute pain (stuffy sensation) in the epigastrium: Tinggong (SI 19), Pishu (BL 20). (*Songs of Hundreds of Symptoms*)

【Regional Anatomy】 Skin-subcutaneous tissue-external meatal cartilage. There are the auriculotemporal nerve and the branches or tributaries of the anterior auricular branches of the superficial temporal artery and vein in this area.

【Remark】 Puncturing Tinggong (SI 19) can effectively treat neurosensorial deafness.

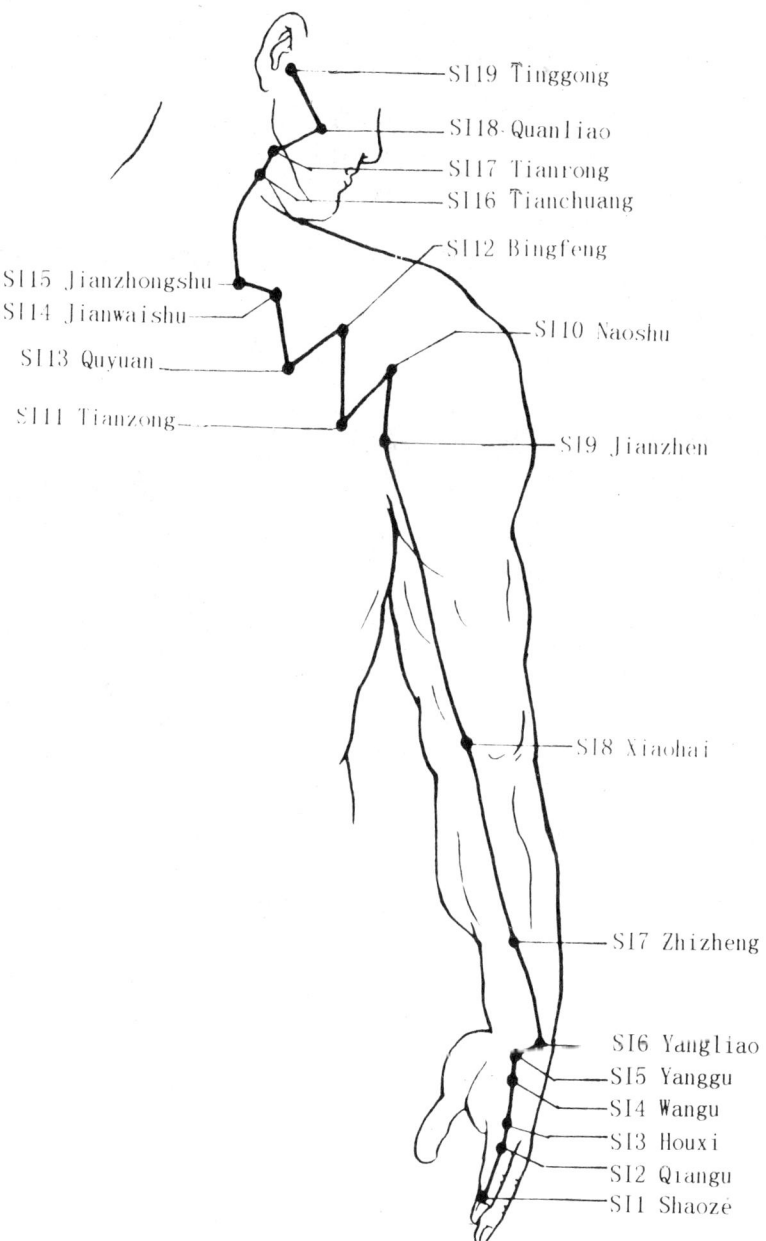

Fig 9-26 Acupoints of the Small Intestine Meridian of Hand Taiyang

Table 9-3
Indications and Actions of Acupoints of the Small Intestine Meridian of Hand Taiyang

Name of the points	Specific points	Common indications	Specific indications and functions
SI 1 Shaoze (少泽)	Jing-(Well) point		Clearing heat-fire and inducing resuscitation, eliminating heat and relieving sore-throat, dredging the collateral to promote lactation. Febrile disease, coma, syncope, precordial pain, dry mouth, stiffness of the neck, cataracts, sore throat, acute mastitis, lack of lactation
SI 2 Qiangu (前谷)	Ying-(Spring) point	Disorders of head, neck, ear, eye and throat: headache, neck rigidity with headache, eye pain, deafness, sore throat, conjunctival congestion, muscle contracture and pain of elbow, febrile disease	Dispersing wind and clearing away heat, dredging the collaterals to promote lactation. Headache, pain of eyes, tinnitus, sore throat, lack of lactation, febrile disease
SI 3 Houxi (后溪)	Shu-(Stream) point One of the eight influential points		Dredging the collaterals. Stiffness and pain of the neck, pain in the waist and back, muscle contracture and pain in the elbow and fingers, tinnitus, deafness, sore throat, epilepsy, manic-depression, malaria
SI 4 Wanggu (腕骨)	Yuan-(Source) point		Stiffness and pain in the neck, tinnitus, cataracts, jaundice, febrile disease, malaria, muscle contracture of finger, pain of wrist
SI 5 Yanggu (阳谷)	Jing-(River) point		Painful wrist
SI 6 Yanglao (养老)	Xi-(Cleft) point	Disorders of mind: coma, manic-depression.	Improving eyesight, dredging collaterals. Blurred vision, aching pain of shoulder, back, elbow and arm
SI 7 Zhizheng (支正)	Luo-(Connecting) point		Clearing heart-fire and relieving mental stress. Headache, dizziness, manic-depressive psychosis, terror and grief, febrile disease, aching pain of elbow and arm, stiffness in the neck
SI 8 Xiaohai (小海)	Confluent point		Pain of elbow and arm, manic-depression

Acupoints of Three Yang Meridians of Hand

Name of the points	Specific points	Common indications	Specific indications and functions
SI 9 Jianzhen (肩贞)			Dredging the collaterals, dispersing masses. Pain of shoulder and arm, tinnitus, scrofula
SI 10 Naoshu (臑俞)	Crossing point		Pain in the shoulder and arm
SI 11 Tianzong (天宗)			Relaxing muscles and tendons, activating collaterals, promoting flow of qi to soothe the chest. Pain in the shoulder blades, pain of ulnar side of the elbow and arm, fullness over the chest and hypochondria, dyspnea, cough, acute mastitis
SI 12 Bingfeng (秉风)	Crossing point		Relaxing muscles and tendons and activating collaterals. Pain of shoulder blade, aching and numbness of upper extremities, stiffness in the neck
SI 13 Quyuan (曲垣)			Pain in the shoulder blades
SI 14 Jianwaishu (肩外俞)			Pain in the shoulder and back, stiffness in the neck
SI 15 Jianzhongshu (肩中俞)			Promoting the dispersing function of the lung to expell superficial evils
SI 16 Tianchuang (天窗)		Disorders of ear and throat: deafness, tinnitus, sore throat	Expelling wind and clearing heat. Stiffness and pain in the neck, hemorrhoids
SI 17 Tianrong (天容)			Expelling wind and clearing heat, relieving sorethroat, soothing chest disorder. Chest pain, sensation of fullness over the chest, fever and chilliness, swelling and pain of neck
SI 18 Quanliao (颧髎)	Crossing point	Disorders of mouth, tooth and ear: distorted face, toothache, tinnitus, deafness	Dredging the meridian and collaterals, clearing away heat and expelling wind. Distorted face, fickering eyelid, toothache, puffy cheek
SI 19 Tinggong (听宫)	Crossing point		Improving hearing, inducing resuscitation. Tinnitus, deafness, toothache, epilepsy, manic-depressive psychosis

Chapter Ten

Acupoints of Three Yin Meridians of Foot

IX. Acupoints of the Spleen Meridian of Foot Taiyin

SP 1 Yinbai (隐白)
(Hidden White)

【Source】 *Miraculous Pivot and Plain Questions*
【Name Explanation】 Yin (隐), hidden; Bai (白), white. The point is in a hidden region, where the color is white.
【Classification】 Jing- (Well) Point of the Spleen Meridian of Foot Taiyin, pertaining to wood in the Five Element.
【Location】 On the medial side of the distal segment of the great toe, 0.1 cun from the corner of the toenail. (See Fig. 10-1).
【Localization】 In sitting position with the feet relaxed or in the supine position. Locatethe point at the intersection between the lines of the medial side of the 1st toenail and basal part.
【Indications】
    1) Diseases along the Course of the Meridian: Numbness in toes, paralysis of lower limbs with difficulty in walking due to coldness in the feet.
    2) Respiratory Diseases: Fullness sensation in the chest, cough, dyspnea.
    3) Digestive Diseases: Abdominal distention, diarrhea with sudden onset vomiting, poor

appetite, hematochezia, hematemesis.

4) Gynecopathy: Menorrhagia, metrorrhagia and leukorrhagia.

5) Angiocardiopathy: Chest pain, precordial pain.

6) Mental Diseases: Apoplexy, vexation, susceptibility to sorrow, chronic infantile convulsion, fainting spell, manic-depressive syndrome.

7) Other Diseases: Epistaxis, hemmaturia.

【Mechanism of Action】

1) Yangbai (SP 1) point can be used for arousing the patient from unconsciousness and also has an immediate effect on paralysis of the lower limbs due to sequela.

2) The point belongs to the Spleen Meridian and the spleen governs the blood. So it can be used to treat hematemesis, hematochezia, epistaxis, hematuria, metrorrhagia, metrostaxis by arresting bleeding. Positive results can be seen on metrorrhagia and metrostaxis with direct moxibustion.

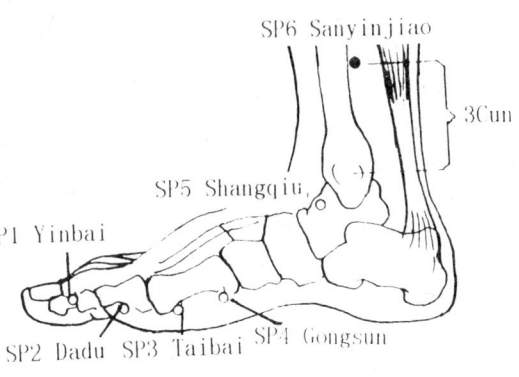

Fig. 10-1

3) The spleen is responsible for digestion and fluid transportation. So the point can be used to treat the diseases of alimentary system such as abdominal distention and diarrhea.

4) The point is a Jing-(well) point. All the Jing-(Well) points are used for restoring consciousness and inducing resuscitation. Therefore, it is used to treat fainting spell and other mental diseases.

【Method】 Puncture perpendicularly 0.1 cun or prick the point to cause bleeding. Moxibustion is applicable.

【Acupoint Prescriptions】

1) Corpse-like syncope: Yinbai (SP 1), Dadun (LR 1). (*Experience on Acupuncture and Moxibustion Therapy*)

2) Epistaxis: Yinbai (SP 1), Weizhong (BL 40). (*ibid*)

3) Syncope: Yinbai (SP 1), Yongquan (KI 1), Lidui (ST 45), Shaoshang (LU 11), Zhongchong (PC 9), Shenmen (HT 7). (*Guide Book for Saving Life.*)

【Regional Anatomy】 Skin-subcutaneous tissue-root of nail. There are the branches of themedial dorsal cutaneous nerve of the foot, the dorsal digital nerve and the dorsal digital artery and vein in this area.

【Remark】 It can be found that under X-ray puncutring Yinbai (SP 1) can make gastric peristalsis slow down.

SP 2 Dadu （大都）
(Big Capital)

【Source】 *Miraculous Pivot*

【Name Explanation】 Da （大）, big; Du （都）, assembling. The point is at the big toe, where the Qi of meridian gathers.

【Classification】 Ying-(Spring) Point of the Spleen Meridian of Foot Taiyin, pertaining to fire in the Five Element.

【Location】 On the medial surface of the foot, in the depression of the junction of the red and

white skin, anterior and inferior to the 1st metatarsophalangeal joint. (See Fig. 10-1).
【Localization】 In sitting position with the feet relaxed, or in the supine position. Locate the point at the medial surface of the 1st toe, at the depression which is anterior to the 1st metatarsophalangeal joint, at the junction of the red and white skin.
【Indications】
   1) Digestive Diseases: Abdominal distention, abdominal pain, epigastralgia, dyspepsia, hiccup, diarrhea, constipation, passing stool with pus and blood.
   2) Angiocardiopathy: Precordial pain with cold limbs, fullness sensation in the chest.
   3) Mental Diseases: Infantile convulsion.
   4) Other Diseases: Red and swollen toes, febrile disease without sweat, heavyness sensation and edema in the limbs.
【Mechanism of Action】 Dadu (SP 2) point is mainly used to strengthen the spleen and stomach, purge away the heat and alleviate pain. So it is used to treat diseases of alimentary system such as abdominal distention and epigastralgia.
【Method】 Puncture perpendicualrly 0.2-0.4 cun. Moxibustion is applicable.
【Acupoint Prescriptions】
   1) Precordial pain with cold limbs: Dadu (SP 2), Taibai (SP 3). (*Miraculous Pivot*)
   2) Diarrhea: Dadu (SP 2), Shangqiu (SP 5), Yinlingquan (SP 9), administered with moxibustion. (*The Classic of Sphygmology*)
   3) Epigastralgia: Dadu (SP 2), Yinbai (SP 1). (*A-B Classic of Acupuncture and Moxibustion*).
   4) Epigastralgia with diarrhea and abdominal distention: Dadu (SP 2), Taibai (SP 3). (*Thousand Golden Prescriptions*)
   5) Febrile disease without sweat: Dadu (SP 2), Jingqu (LU 8). (*Songs of Hundreds of Symptoms*)
【Regional Anatomy】 Skin-subcutaneous tissue-base of 1st phalanx. There are the proper digital plantar nerves of the medial plantar nerve, the superficial venous network and the branches or tributaries of the medial plantar artery and vein.
【Remark】 Observed under X-ray, puncturing Dadu (SP 2) point can reduce gastric peristalsis.

SP 3 Taibai (太白)
(Supreme Whiteness)

【Source】 *Miraculous Pivot*
【Name Explanation】 Tai (太), great; Bai (白), white. The point is on the great toe, where the white skin is widest.
【Classification】 Shu-(Stream) and Yuan-(Source) Point of the Spleen Meridian of Foot Taiyin.
【Location】 On the medial border of the foot, in the depression of the junction of the red and white skin, posterior and inferior to the 1st metatarsophalangeal joint. (See Fig. 10-1).
【Localization】 In sitting position with the feet relaxed. Locate the point at the medial side of the 1st toe, in the depression posterior to the 1st metatarsophalangeal joint.
【Indications】
   1) Diseases along the Course of the Meridian: Lumbago, soreness of thigh and knee, heavy sensation of the body, flaccidity syndrome.
   2) Digestive Diseases: Stomachache, abdominal distention, abdominal pain, borborygmus, vomiting, diarrhea, dysentery, constipation, anorexia, eructation, dyspepsia.

3) Angiocardiopathy: Precordial pain with moderate pulse, fullness and pain in chest and hypochondrium.

4) Other Diseases: Beriberi, feverish sensation accompanied with restlessness.

【Mechanism of Action】

1) Taibai (SP 3) is the Yuan-(Source) point of the Spleen Meridian, so it is usually used to treat the diseases of the alimentary system.

2) The point can be used to treat angiocardiopathy because the Spleen Meridian connects with the heart.

3) The Spleen Meridian and its Muscle Region distribute in the medial side of the leg and the spleen has the functions of resolving dampness, nourishing the blood and tendons. So the point can be used to treat both lumbago and flaccidity syndrome.

【Method】 Puncture perpendicularly 0.5-0.8 cun. Moxibustion is applicable.

【Acupoint Prescriptions】

1) Borborygmus: Taibai (SP 3), Gongsun (SP 4). (*Thousand Golden Prescriptions*)

2) Abdominal pain: Taibai (SP 3), Wenliu (LI 7), Zusanli (ST 36), Xiangu (ST 43). (*Experience on Acupuncture and Moxibustion Therapy*

3) Fever: Taibai (SP 3), Yanggang (BL 48). (*ibid*)

4) Acute appendicitis: Taibai (SP 3), Xiangu (ST 43), Dachangshu (BL 25). (*Great Compendium of Acupuncture and Moxibustion*)

【Regional Anatomy】 Skin-subcutaneous tissue-abductor muscle of the great toe-short flexor muscle of great the toe. In the superficial layer, there are the saphenous nerve and the superficial venous network. In the deep layer, there are the branchesor tributaries of the medial plantar artery and vein and the branches of the medial plantar nerve.

【Remark】 In clinical observation, acupuncture at Taibai (SP 3) can adjust the content of blood sugar. The effect varies with the manipulation of acupuncture. The content of blood sugar would ascend with the heat-producing manipulation and would descend with the way of cool-producing manipulation.

Puncturing at Taibai (SP 3) can relax oddi's sphincter and lower the pressure of the biliary duct.

SP 4 Gongsun (公孙) (Grandfather Grandson)

【Source】 *Miraculous Pivot*

【Name Explanation】 Gong (公), connection; Sun (孙), reficular collateral. Sun here refers to the collateral of the Spleen Meridian which connects with the Stomach Meridian and seperates from this point.

【Classification】 Luo-(Connecting) Point and the Yuan (source)-Point of the Spleen Meridian of Foot Taiyin, one of the Eight Confluent Points, Linking to the Chong Meridian.

【Location】 On the medial border of the foot, anterior and inferior to the proximal end of the 1st metatarsal bone. (See Fig. 10-1).

【Localization】 In sitting position with the feet relaxed or in the supine position, Locate the point at the posterior medial side of the 1st toe, anterior and inferior to the base of the 1st metatarsal bone, about 1 cun posterior to Taibai (SP 3).

【Indications】

1) Digestive Diseases: Stomachache, vomiting, diarrhea, dyspepsia, borborygmus, abdominal distention, abdominal pain, dysentery, hematochezia, excessive drinking.

2) Gynecopathy: Irregular menstruation, metrorrhagia and metrastaxis, leukohagia.

3) Mental Diseases: Mania, epilepsy, vexation, insomnia.

4) Other Diseases: Edema in face and head, general edema, drowsiness, jaundice, beriberi, malarial disease, hot sensation on the sole.

【Mechanism of Action】

1) Gongsun (SP 4) is the Luo-(connecting) point of the Spleen Meridian and connects with the stomach, thus, it is the commonly used point to regulate the functions of the stomach and spleen, and in the treatment of various diseases of these organs.

2) The spleen controls the blood circulation, so the point can be used to treat gynecopathy, such as irregular menstruation and leukorrhea. The spleen is also responsible for fluid transportation. So Gongsun(SP 4)can be used to treat edema and jaundice caused by dysfunction of the spleen in transportation and retention of water within the body.

3) The Spleen Meridian runs into the heart. Gongsun (SP 4) can be used to strengthen the spleen and nourish blood, resolve dampness and remove phlegm. That is why Gongsun (SP 4) is used to treat mental diseases.

4) Gongsun (SP 4) is one of the Eight Confluence Points. If it is used in conjunction with Neiguan (PC 6), the effect will be greater on the diseases mentioned above.

【Method】 Puncture perpendicularly 0.5-0.7 cun. Moxibustion is applicable.

【Acupoint Prescriptions】

1) Chronic malaria with anorexia: Gongsun (SP 4), Neiting (ST 44), Lidui (ST 45). (*Great Compendium of Acupuncture and Moxibustion*)

2) Flaccidity of lower limbs: Gongsun (SP 4), Zusanli (ST 36), Juegu (GB 39), Shenmai (BL 62). (*ibid*)

3) Abdominal pain: Gongsun(SP 4), Neiguan(PC 6). (*Songs on Point Selection of Miscellaneous Diseases*)

【Regional Anatomy】 Skin-subcutaneous tissue-abductor muscle of the great toe-short flexor muscle of the great toe-tendon of long flexor muscle of the great toe. In the superficial layer, there are the medial branches of the foot from saphenous nerve and the tributaries of the dorsal venous arch of the foot. In the deep layer, there are the branches or tributaries of the medial plantar artery and vein and the branches of the medial plantar nerve.

【Remark】 Acupuncture at Gongsun (SP 4) can inhibit the secretion of gastric acid but can also largely promote the secretion of intestinal fluid. The absorption rate of the small intestine to glucose may also increased. Puncturing other point will not have the same results. In most cases, manipulating Gongsun (SP 4) can regulate the movement of the small intestine and promote the peristalsis.

SP 5 Shangqiu (商丘)
(Shang Mound)

【Source】 *Miraculous Pivot*

【Name Explanation】 Shang (商), one of the Five Sounds which pertains to mind; Qiu (丘), hills. This is the Jing-(River) point of the Spleen Meridian and pertains to the mind. The point is below the medial malleolus, which resembles a hill.

【Classification】 Jing-(River)Point of the Spleen Meridian of Foot Taiyin, pertaining to metal in the Five Elements.

【Location】 On the depression anterior and inferior to the medial malleolus, at the midpoint of the line connecting the tuberosity of the navicular bone and the tip of the medial malleolus.

(See Fig. 10-1).

【Localization】In sitting position with the feet relaxed or in the supine position. Locate the point at the intersection between the straight line of the anterior side of the medial malleolus and the transverse line of the inferior side of the medial malleous.

【Indications】

1) Diseases along the Course of the Meridian: Pain on medial side of the thigh, red and swollen medial malleolus, weakness of the feet.

2) Respiratory Diseases: Cough, dyspnea.

3) Digestive Diseases: Abdominal distention, borborygmus, diarrhea, constipation, dyspepsia, jaundice, stomachache.

4) Gynecopathy: Sterility.

5) Mental Diseases: Manic-depressive syndrome, susceptibility to laugh, infantile clonic convulsion, melancholia, sighing, chronic infantile convulsion.

6) Other Diseases: Hemorrhoid, stiff tongue.

【Mechanism of Action】Shangqiu (SP 5) is effective in treating a stiff tongue and difficulty in swallowing because the Spleen Meridian reaches the root of the tongue and spreads over its lower surface. See also Dadu (SP 2), Taibai (SP 3), Gongsun (SP 4) for the rest.

【Method】Puncture perpendicularly 0.2-0.3 cun. Moxibustion is applicable.

【Acupoint Prescriptions】

1) Hemorrhoid: Shangqiu (SP 5), Fuliu (KI 7). (*Thousand Golden Prescriptions*).

2) Vomiting: Shangqiu (SP 5), Youmen (KI 21), Tonggu (KI 20). (*ibid*)

3) Susceptibility to sorrow and signing: Shangqiu (SP 5), Riyue (GB 24). (*Experience on Acupuncture and Moxibustion Therapy*)

4) Constipation due to insufficiency of the spleen: Shangqiu (SP 5), Sanyinjiao (SP 6). (*Great Compendium of Acupuncture and Moxibustion*).

5) Sterility: Shangqiu (SP 5), Zhongji (RN 3). (*ibid*)

6) Pain of foot: Shangqiu (SP 5), Jiexi (ST 41), Qiuxu (GB 40). (*Songs of Jade Dragon*)

【Regional Anatomy】Skin-subcutaneous tissue-medial (triangular) ligament-medial malleolus of tibia. In the superficial layer, there are the saphenous nerve and the great saphenous vein. In the deep layer, there are the branches or tributaries of the medial anterior malleolar artery and vein.

SP 6 Sanyinjiao (三阴交)
(Three Yin Meeting)

【Source】*A-B Classic of Acupuncture and Moxibustion*

【Name Explanation】Sanyin (三阴), three Yin meridians; Jiao (交), crossing. This is the interesecting point of the Spleen, Liver and Kidney Meridians.

【Classification】Crossing Point of the Meridians of Foot Taiyin, Shaoyin and Jueyin.

【Location】On the medial line of the leg, 3 cun above the tip of the medial malleolus, posterior to the medial border of the tibia. (See Fig. 10-1).

【Localization】In sitting or supine position. Locate the point at the posterior border of the medial tibia, four-fingers width (one "Fu") directly above the tip of the medial malleolus.

【Indications】

1) Diseases along the Course of the Meridian: Hemiplegia due to apoplexy, poliomyelitis, pain in medial side of the thigh.

2) Disorders of Head and Sense Organs: Inflammation of the throat, stiff tongue, epistaxis.

3) Respiratory Diseases: Cough, consumptive disease.

4) Digestive Diseases: Vomiting, hiccup, fullness and pain in chest and abdomen, epigastralgia, indigestion, anorexia, borborygmus, abdominal pain, diarrhea, dysentery, jaundice, edema, heaviness sensation in the body.

5) Urinary Diseases: Uroschesis, enuresis, five types of stranguria, gonorrhea.

6) Reproductive Diseases: Emission, impotence, premature ejaculation, pain in penis, seven types of hernia, irregular menstruation, dysmenorrhea, amenorrhea, leukorrhea with reddish discharge, prolapse of uterus, metrorrhagis and metrostaxis, dizziness due to deficiency of blood, retention of placenta, lochiostasis or lochiorrhea, sterility, mass in the abdomen.

7) Mental Diseases: Manic-depressive syndrome, epilepsy, insomnia, sorrow, dementia.

8) Other Diseases: Carbuncle, deep-rooted carbuncle, urticaria, exudative dermatitis, pain in the lower abdomen.

【Mechanism of Action】

1) Dysfunction of the spleen in transportation and failure of the liver in maintaining the normal flow of qi are the main causes of spleen and stomach diseases. Sanyinjiao(SP 6)point, where the Liver, Spleen and Kidney Meridians cross, can be used to soothe the liver and strenghthen the spleen. Therefore, Sanyinjiao (SP 6) is frequently used to treat diseases of the alimentary system.

2) The spleen dominates fluid transportation and transformation, the liver governs the dispersing and discharging, and the kidney controls water metabolism. The formation and excretion of urine is closely related to the functions of the kidney, spleen and liver. So the point is frequently used to treat enuresis, stranguria and other diseases of urinary system.

3) The spleen transports and transforms food essence and provides the material basis for the acquired constitution. The kidney is the foundation of the native constitution and has a close relationship with reproductive. The liver stores and regulates blood. Reproductive diseases mainly result from the dysfunction of the liver, spleen and kidney. For this reason, Sanyinjiao (SP 6) can be used to treat all kinds of reproductive diseases.

4) The Spleen Meridian goes along both sides of the throat, reaches the root of the tongue and spreads over its lower surface. The Kidney Meridian travels around the tongue root and the Liver Meridian circulates along the throat and terminates at the posterior aspect of the larynx. Therefore, Sanyinjiao (SP 6) can be used to treat painful throat and aphasia due to apoplexy. It is effective when treating chronic pharyngitis.

【Method】 Puncture perpendicularly 0.5-1 cun. Moxibustion is applicable.

【Acupoint Prescriptions】

1) Dystocia: Sanyinjiao (SP 6). (*Supplement to Thousand Golden Prescriptions*).

2) Watery distension: Sanyinjiao (SP 6), Shimen (RN 5). (*Experience on Acupuncture and Moxibustion Therapy*)

3) For artificial abortion: Reducing Sanjinjiao (SP 6) and reinforcing Hegu (LI 4). (*ibid*)

4) Pain in legs: Sanyinjiao (SP 6), Juegu (GB 39), Kunlun (BL 60). Apply moxibustion. (*Great Compendium of Acupuncture and Moxibustion*)

5) Dystocia: Sanyinjiao (SP 6), Hegu (LI 4), Taichong (LR 3), Kunlun (BL 60), Zhiyin (BL 67). (*New Acupuncture and Moxibustion*)

6) Retention of placenta: Sanyinjiao (SP 6), Zhongji (RN 3), Zhaohai (KI 6). (*ibid*)

7) Meteorism: Sanyinjiao (SP 6), Shuifen (RN 9), Zusanli (ST 36). (*Songs of Jade Dragon*)

8) Emission: Sanyinjiao (SP 6), Qihai (RN 6). (*Songs of Hundreds of Symptoms*)

【Regional Anatomy】 Skin-subcutaneous tissue-long flexor muscle of toes-posterior tibial muscle-long flexor muscle of the great toe. In the superficial layer, there are the medial cutaneous branches of the leg from the saphenous nerve and the tributaries of the great saphenous vein. In the deep layer, there are the tibial nerve and the posterior tibial artery and vein.

【Remark】 In the treatment of 47 cases of diabetes by puncturing Sanyinjiao (SP 6), the blood sugar levels decreased by 22.9% two hours after acupuncture, and decreased by 18.5% four hours later. But in the treatment of 30 cases of pancreatic diabetes, the blood sugar level increased by 19.3% and 16.4% respectively.

Acupuncture at Xuanzhong (GB 39), Yanglingquan (GB 34) and Sanyinjiao (SP 6) all have some effect on uterine contraction. Of them, Sanyinjiao (SP 6) is the most effective one. In the research on uterine contraction, distant acupuncture at Sanyinjiao (SP 6), Zusanli (ST 36) and Hegu (LI 4)) has a high effective rate, proximate acupuncture of Zhibian (BL 54), Qugu (RN 2), Henggu (KI 11)) may have an opposite result. Distant-proximate acupuncture has the highest effectual rate, making it the ideal way to apply clinically. Injecting small dose of oxytocin at parturient's Sanyinjiao (SP 6) or Hegu (LI 4) point will arouse or promote uterine contraction. But injecting the same dose of oxytocin in the buttock or at the Xuanzhong (GB 39) or Waiguan (SJ 5) points will rarely arouse uterine contraction or only bring about little change.

SP 7 Lougu (漏谷)
(Leaky Valley)

【Source】 *A-B Classic of Acupuncture and Moxibustion*

【Name Explanation】 Lou (漏), aparture; Gu (谷), valley. The point is located in the depression posterior to the tibia, like in a valley.

【Location】 On the medial side of the leg, on the line connecting the tip of the medial malleolus and Yinlingquan (SP 9), 6 cun from the tip of the medial malleolus, posterior to the medial border of the tibia. (See Fig. 10-2).

【Localization】 In sitting position or in the supine position. Locate the point 3 cun directly below Sanyinjiao (SP 6), the posterior border of the tibia.

【Indications】

1) Diseases along the Course of the Meridian: Damp arthralgia, beriberi, extreme cold and numbness of the knees and legs, painful swollen ankle.

2) Digestive Diseases: Abdominal distention, borborygmus, dyspepsia, emaciation.

3) Urinary Diseases: Dysuria.

4) Reproductive Diseases: Seminal emission.

【Mechanism of Action】 See also Dadu (SP 2), Taibai (SP 3) and Yinlingquan (SP 9) points.

【Method】 Puncture perpendicularly 0.5-1 cun. Moxibustion is applicable.

【Acupoint Prescriptions】

1) Qi stagnation of cold type: Lougu (SP 7), Huiyang (BL

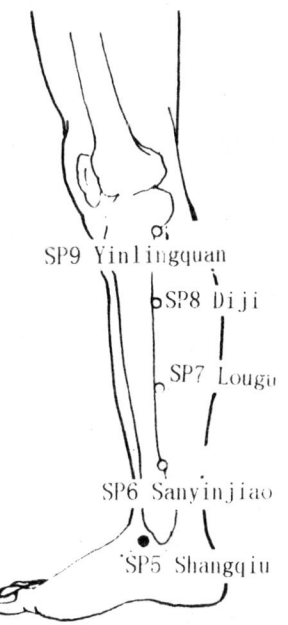

Fig. 10-2

35). (*Experience on Acupuncture and Moxibustion Therapy*).

2) Blood stasis: Lougu (SP 7), Ququan (LR 8). (*ibid*)

【Regional Anatomy】Skin-subcutaneous tissue-triceps muscle of calf-long flexor muscle of the toes-posterior tibial muscle. In the superficial layer, there are the medial cutaneous branches of the leg from the saphenous nerve and the great saphenous vein. In the deep layer, there are the tibia nerve and the posterior tibial artery and vein.

SP 8 Diji （地机）
（Earth Pivot）

【Source】*A-B Classic of Acupuncture and Moxibustion*

【Name Explanation】Di（地）, earth; Ji（机）, importance. Di, refers to the lower limbs where the point is located. The local muscle is very thick and is an important region of the leg movement.

【Classification】Xi-(Cleft) Point of the Spleen Meridian of Foot Taiyin

【Location】On the medial side of the leg and on the line connecting the tip of the medial malleolus and Yinglingquan (SP 9), 3 cun below Yinlingquan (SP 9). (See Fig. 10-2).

【Localization】In sitting position or in supine position. Locate Diji (SP 8) point 3 cun directly below Yinlingquan (SP 9), the posterior border of the medial tibia.

【Indications】

1) Diseases along the Course of the Meridian: Lumbago, pain in medial side of the thigh.

2) Digestive Diseases: Abdominal distention, borborygmus, vomiting, diarrhea, anorexia.

3) Reproductive Diseases: Pain in penis, seminal emission, irregular menstruation, prolapse of uterus, dysmenorrhea.

4) Urinary Diseases: Dysuria, incontinence of urine, edema.

5) Mental Diseases: Severe palpitation, insomnia.

【Mechanism of Action】Puncturing this point has a very good effect on dysmenorrhea. As for the treatment of diseases of alimentary system, see Dadu (SP 2) and Taibai (SP 3) for reference.

【Method】Puncture perpendicularly 0.5-1 cun. Moxibustion is applicable.

【Acupoint Prescriptions】

1) Anorexia: Diji (SP 8), Yinlingquan (SP 9), Shuifen (RN 9), Youmen (KI 21), Xiaochangshu (BL 27). (*Experience on Acupuncture and Moxibustion Therapy*)

2) Irregular menstruation: Diji (SP 8), Xuehai (SP 10). (*Songs of Hundreds of Symptoms*).

【Regional Anatomy】Skin-subcutaneous tissue-gastrocnemius muscle-soleus muscle. In the superficial layer, there are the medial cutaneous branches of the leg from the saphenous nerve and the great saphenous vein. In the deep layer, there are the tibial nerve and the posterior tibial artery and vein.

【Remark】Some experiments have shown that puncturing Diji (SP 8) may cause insulin production. However, puncturing Zusanli (ST 36) may not. It is indicated that acupuncture to Diji (SP 8) has a close relationship with the secretory function of islets of β-cell.

SP 9 Yinlingquan (阴陵泉)
(Yin Hill Fountain)

【Source】 *Miraculous Pivot*

【Name Explanation】 Yin (阴), Yin of Yin-Yang; Ling (陵), hill; Quan (泉), spring. The interior is Yin. The point is in the depression at the inferior border of the medial epicondyle of the tibia, like a spring at the foot of a hill.

【Classification】 He-(Sea) Point of the Spleen Meridian of Foot Taiyin, pertaining to water in the Five Element.

【Location】 On the medial side of the leg, in the depression posterior and inferior to the medial condyle of the tibia. (See Fig. 10-2).

【Localization】 In sitting position with the knees flexed or in the supine position. Locate the point at the medial genu, or the inferior side of the internal condyle of tibia, on the same level of the inferior side of the tuberosity of tibia.

【Indications】

   1) Diseases along the Course of the Meridian: Lumbago, hemiplegia, painful and swollen legs and knees.

   2) Digestive Diseases: Abdominal distention, pain in the abdomen, anorexia, vomiting, diarrhea, jaundice.

   3) Reproductive Diseases: Emission, pain in penis, leucorrhea, prolapse of uterus.

   4) Urinary Diseases: Dysuria, edema, incontinence of urine stranguria.

   5) Other Diseases: Consumptive disease, headache.

【Mechanism of Action】 Puncturing Yinlingquan (SP 9) has a function of strengthening spleen, benefiting vital energy, promoting diuresis to eliminate wetness-evil. So it can be used to treat edema, dysuria and other symptoms due to deficiency of the spleen. Compared with Sanyinjiao (SP 6) which is mainly used to treat diseases of mental, reproductive and urinary systems, Yinlingquan (SP 9) is good at treating abdominal distention, diarrhea, jaundice and edema.

【Method】 Puncture perpendicularly 0.5-1 cun. Moxibustion is applicable.

【Acupoint Prescriptions】

   1) Enuresis: Yinlingquan (SP 9), Yanglingquan (GB 34). (*Thousand Golden Prescriptions*).

   2) Dysentery: Yinlingquan (SP 9), Yinbai (SP 1). (*ibid*)

   3) Hernia: Yinlingquan (SP 9), Taixi (KI 3), Yinxi (HT 6). (*Experience on Acupuncture and Moxibustion Therapy*)

   4) Edema or edema leading to difficulty in lying flat: Moxibustion to Yinlingquan (SP 9). (*ibid*)

   5) Cholera morbus: Yinlingquan (SP 9), Chengshan (BL 57), Jiexi (ST 41), Taibai (SP 3). (*Great Compendium of Acupuncture and Moxibustion*)

   6) Dysuria: Yinlingquan (SP 9), Qihai (RN 6), Sanyinjiao (SP 6). (*ibid*)

   7) Acute bacillary dysentery: Yinlingquan (SP 9), Tianshu (ST 25), Zusanli (ST 36). (*Abstract of Clinical Experience on Acupuncture and Moxibustion*)

   8) Painful and swelling knees: Yinlingquan (SP 9), Yanglingquan (GB 34). (*Songs of Jade Dragon*)

   9) Edema: Yinlingquan (SP 9), Quchi (LI 11). (*Songs of Hundreds of Symptoms*)

   10) Pain of small intestine: Yinlingquan (SP 9), Yongquan (KI 1). (*Secret Songs of Changsangjun*)

11) Fullness sensation in the chest: Yinlingquan (SP 9), Chengshan (BL 57). (*Songs on Point Selection of Miscellaneous Diseases*)

12) Dysuria: Yinlingquan (SP 9), Zusanli (ST 36). (*ibid*)

【Regional Anatomy】 Skin-subcutaneous tissue-tendon of semitendinous muscle-medial head of gastrocnemius muscle. In the superficial layer, there are the medial cutaneous branches of the leg from the saphenous nerve, the great saphenous vein and the branches of descending genicular artery. In the deep layer, there are the medial inferior genicular artery and vein.

【Remark】 Acupuncture at Yinlingquan (SP 9) can regulate the tension of the urinary bladder making the relaxed bladder stronger and the ectatic bladder tense. Acupuncture at Yinlinquan (SP 9) can strengthen the peristalsis of the descending colon and rectum. Acupuncture at the point may also have some effect on function of the central nervous system. Some experiments have shown that strong stimulation to the point may result in an inhibition process in the cerebral corticalmotor area. But the inhibition process may be slow and weak in the comparatively healthy people. Slight stimulation to the patient may cause half the patients to show excitation process and the other half to show inhibition process. But slight stimulation to healthy people may arouse the excitation process in most people. These results indicate that the effects vary with functional conditions and degrees of acupuncture.

SP 10 Xuehai (血海)
(Blood Sea)

【Source】 *A-B Classic of Acupuncture and Moxibustion*

【Name Explanation】 Xue (血), blood; Hai (海), sea. This point is indicated in hematological diseases, in the sense of returning overflowed blood into the sea.

【Location】 With the knee flexed, on the medial side of the thigh, 2 cun above the superior medial corner of the patella, on the prominence of the medial head of the quadriceps muscle of the thigh. (See Fig. 10-3).

【Localization】
1) In sitting position with the knees flexed. Locate the point 2 cun above the medial superior border of patella, just at the center of the process of medial femoral muscle.
2) In sitting position with the knee flexed. The doctor uses the palm to press the patient's patella, with the palm facing the top of the patella and the thumb pointing to the medial side of the patella. The point is located at the tip of the thumb.

【Indications】
1) Digestive Diseases: Abdominal distention, adversed flow of qi.

2) Gynecopathy: Irregular menstruation, dysmenorrhea, amenorrhea, metrorrhagia and metrostaxis, leukorrhea, pruritus vulvae, swelling and pain of the vulva, lochiostesis.

3) Urinary Diseases: Stranguria.

4) Dermatosis: Eczema, urticaria, pruritis, erysipelas, all kinds of sores in medial side of thigh.

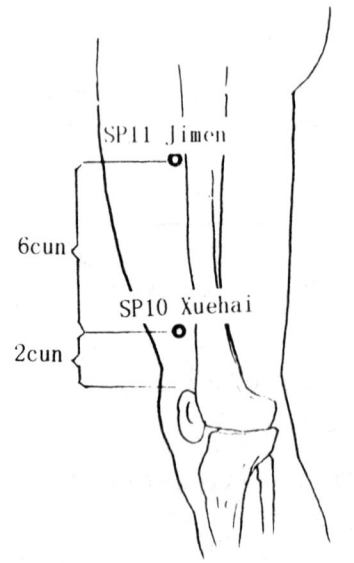

Fig. 10-3

5) Other Diseases: Anemia.

【Mechanism of Action】 Gynecopathy is mostly caused by dysfunction of the Chong and Ren Meridians and incoordination between qi and blood. Dermatosis mainly results from retention of damp heat, heat evil accumulated in blood and qi stagnation. Acupuncture to Xuehai (SP 10) has the functions of regulating the blood condition and menstruation, dispelling wind and removing dampness. So Xuehai (SP 10) is the point commonly used to treat gynecopathy and dermatosis.

【Method】 Puncture perpendicularly 0.7-1.2 cun. Moxibustion is applicable.

【Acupoint Prescription】

1) Irregular menstruation: Xuehai (SP 10), Daimai (GB 26). (*Experience on Acupuncture and Moxibustion Therapy*)

2) Rubella: Xuehai (SP 10), Sanyinjiao (SP 6), Quchi (LI 11), Hegu (LI 4). (*Essentials of Chinese Acupuncture*)

【Regional Anatomy】 Skin-subcutaneous tissue-medial vastus muscle of the thigh. In the superficial layer, there are the anterior cutaneous branches of the femoral nerve and tributaries of the great saphenous vein. In the deep layer, there are the muscular branches of the femoral artery and vein and the muscular branches of the femoral nerve.

【Remark】 Experimental research has shown that needling Xuehai (SP 10) has a relation with the functions of the hypophysitis-sexual gland, especially with the ovarian function. Needling Guilai (ST 29), Zhongji (RN 3) and Xuehai (SP 10) may cause hormone withdrawal bleeding in patients with secondary amenorrhea.

SP 11 Jimen (箕门)
(Squatting Gate)

【Source】 *A-B Classic of Acupuncture and Moxibustion*

【Name Explanation】 Ji (箕), dustpan; Men (门), door. With the patient sitting with legs stretched out in the shape of a dustpan, the point is at the medial aspect of either thigh, just like the opening side of the dustpan.

【Location】 On the medial side of the thigh and on the line connecting Xuehai (SP 10) and Chongmen (SP 12), 6 cun above Xuehai (SP 10). (See Fig. 10-3).

【Localization】 In sitting position with the knees flexed, both legs slightly streched out. Locate the point at the medial side of the sartorius muscle, about 6 cun above Xuehai (SP 10).

【Indications】

1) Urinary Diseases: Dysuria, enuresis, five kinds of stranguria.

2) Dermatosis and surgical diseases: Swelling and pain in groin, sore in two thighs, eczema of scrotum.

【Mechanism of Action】 Puncturing Jimen (SP 11) can strengthen the spleen, eliminate dampness, regulate blood condition and promote urination. Therefore, it is effective in dermatosis and urinary diseases.

【Method】 Puncture perpendicularly 0.8-1.2 cun.

【Acupoint Prescription】

Enuresis: Jimen (SP 11), Tongli (HT 5), Dadun (LR 1), Pangguangshu (BL 28), Taichong (KI 3), Weizhong (GB 40), Shenmen (HT 7). (*Experience on Acupuncture and Moxibustion Therapy*)

【Regional Anatomy】 Skin-subcutaneous tissue-medial vastus muscle of the thigh. In the superficial layer, there are the anterior cutaneous branches of the femoral nerve and the tributaries of the great saphenous vein. In the deep layer, there are the femoral artery and vein, the saphenous nerve and the muscular branches of the femoral nerve.

SP 12 Chongmen (冲门)
(Rushing Gate)

【Source】 *A-B Classic of Acupuncture and Moxibustion*

【Name Explanation】 Chong (冲), pass; Men (门), door. The point, in "Qi-Street", is an important door for the passage of the qi of the meridian.

【Classification】 The Crossing Point of the Meridians of Foot-Taiyin and Foot Jueyin.

【Location】 At the lateral end of the inguinal groove, 3.5 cun lateral to the midpoint of the upper border of the symphysis pubis, lateral to the pulsating external iliac artery. (See Fig. 10-4).

【Localization】 In the supine position, first locate Qugu (RN 2), and then locate the point at the 3.5 cun lateral to it.

【Indications】

1) Digestive Diseases: Abdominal distention, abdominal pain.

2) Gynecopathy: Upward flow of fetus-qi, edema during pregnancy, leukorrhea, postpartum hemorrhage.

3) Urinary Diseases: Dysuria.

4) Other Diseases: Hemorrhoid, hernia, abdominal mass and pain.

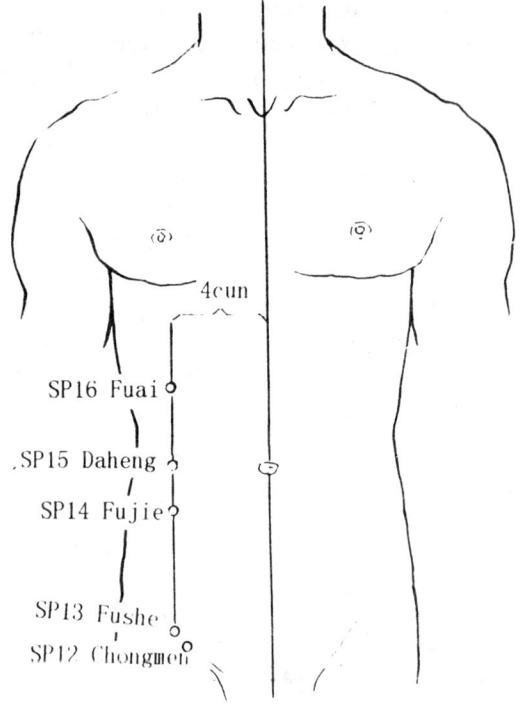

Fig. 10-4

【Mechanism of Action】 Pulse can be felt at Chongmen (SP 12) from where qi of the Spleen Meridian rushes upward into abdomen, so Chongmen (SP 12) can be used to treat diseases of the spleen and stomach. For instance, abdominal distention and upward flow of fetus-qi can be treated by pressing this point. The spleen dominates fluid transportation and controls the blood circulation. That is why Chongmen (SP 12) can be used to treat gynecopathy.

【Method】 Puncture perpendicularly 0.5-0.7 cun. Moxibustion is applicable.

【Acupoint Prescriptions】

1) Abdominal fullness: Chongmen (SP 12), Fushe (SP 13). (*Experience on Acupuncture and Moxibustion Therapy*)

2) Leukorrhea and metrorrhagia: Chongmen (SP 12), Qichong (ST 30). (*Songs of Hundreds of Symptoms*)

3) Mass beside umbilicus: Chongmen (SP 12), Qihai (RN 6). (*ibid*)

【Regional Anatomy】 Skin-subcutaneous tissue-aponeurosis of external oblique muscle of abdomen-internal oblique muscle of abdomen-transverse muscle of abdomen-iliopsoas muscle. In the superficial layer, there are the branches or tributaries of the superficial circumflex iliac artery and vein, the lateral cutaneous branches of the anterior branches of the 11th and 12th thoracic nerves and the 1st lumbar nerve. In the deep layer, there are the muscular branches of the anterior branches of the 11th and 12th thoracic nerves and the 1st lumbar nerve and their accompanying arteries and veins.

SP 13 Fushe (府舍)
(Mansion Room)

【Source】 *A-B Classic of Acupuncture and Moxibustion*
【Name Explanation】 Fu (府), Zang fu organs; She (舍), dwelling. The deep region of the point is the abdominal cavity, which is the dwelling place of the Zangfu organs.
【Location】 On the lower abdomen, 4 cun below the centre of the umbilicus, 0.7 cun above Chongmen (SP 12), and 4 cun lateral to the anterior midline. (See Fig. 10-4).
【Localization】 In the supine position, the point can be located 0.7 cun directly superior and 4 cun lateral to Qugu (RN 2).
【Indications】
1) Digestive Diseases: Vomiting and diarrhea due to cholera, constipation.
2) Other Diseases: Pain in abdomen due to mass, fullness sensation and pain in lower abdomen.
【Mechanism of Action】 Local reaction.
【Method】 Puncture perpendicularly 0.7-1 cun. Moxibustion is applicable.
【Acupoint Prescriptions】
Acute pancreatitis: Fushe (SP 13), Zhangmen (LR 13), Qimen (LR 14) and Zusanli (ST 36) which are used as main points; Shenque (RN 8), Xingjian (LR 2), Zhongwan (RN 12), Shangwan (RN 13) which are used as supplementary points. (*Abstract of Clinical Experience on Acupuncture and Moxibustion*)
【Regional Anatomy】 Skin-subcutaneous tissue-aponeurosis of external oblique muscle of abdomen-internal oblique muscle of abdomen-transversemuscle of abdomen. In the superficial layer, there are the branches or tributaries of the superficial circumflex iliac artery and vein, the lateral cutaneous branches of the anterior banches of the 11th and 12th thoracic nerves and 1st lumbar nerve. In the deep layer, there are the anterior branches of the 11th and 12th thoracic nerves and the 1st lumbar nerve and their accompanying arteries and veins.

SP 14 Fujie (腹结)
(Abdominal Convergence)

【Source】 *A-B Classic of Acupuncture and Moxibustion*
【Name Explanation】 Fu (腹), abdomen; Jie (结), stagnation. This point is indicated in abdominal stagnation.
【Location】 On the lower abdomen, 1.3 cun below Daheng (SP 15), and 4 cun lateral to the anterior midline. (See Fig. 10-4).
【Localization】 In the supine position, first locate Qihai (RN 6), and then locate the point 4 cun lateral and 0.2 cun superior to it.
【Indications】
1) Digestive Diseases: Diarrhea, dysentery, pain around the navel.
2) Other Diseases: Hernia.
【Mechanism of Action】 According to the location, this point is mainly used to treat intestinal dieases.

【Method】Puncture perpendicularly 0.7-1 cun. Moxibustion is applicable.
【Acupoint Prescriptions】
　　Precardial pain: Fujie (SP 14), Xingjian (LR 2). (*Experience on Acupuncture and Moxibustion Therapy*)
【Regional Anatomy】Skin-subcutaneous tissue-external oblique muscle of abdomen-internal oblique muscle of abdomen-transverse muscle of abdomen. In the superficial layer, there are the lateral cutaneous branches of the anterior branches of the 10th to 12th thoracic nerves and the tributaries of the thoracoepigastric vein. In the deep layer, there are the muscular branches of the anterior branches of the 9th to 11th thoracic nerves and their accompanying arteries and veins.
【Remark】In clinical treatment of acute gastroenteritis, symptoms can quickly disappear with one or two treatments of acupuncture and moxibustion to Zusanli (ST 36), Jiuwei (RN 15), Daheng (SP 15) and Fujie (SP 14) points.

SP 15 Daheng （大横）
（Big Cross）

【Source】*A-B Classic of Acupuncture and Moxibustion*
【Name Explanation】Da （大）, large; Heng （横）, horizontal. This point is on the large part of the abdomen, horizontal to the navel.
【Location】On the middle abdomen, 4 cun lateral to the centre of the umbilicus. (See Fig. 10-4).
【Localization】In the supine position, first locate Qizhong (RN 8), and then locate the point 4 cun lateral to it.
【Indications】
　　1) Digestive Diseases: Diarrhea, dysentery, constipation, abdominal pain, ascariasis, gastroptosia.
　　2) Other Diseases: Cold, spasm of four limbs, hyperhidrosis.
【Mechanism of Action】Daheng (SP 15) can be used to treat the diseases of the alimentary system. It is also used to treat cold, spasm, hyperhidrosis when accompanied by the disorders of the alimentary system such as cold of gastrointestinal type.
【Method】Puncture perpendicularly 0.7-1 cun. Moxibustion is applicable.
【Acupoint Prescriptions】
　　1) Gastroptosia: Daheng (SP 15) through Shenque (RN 8). (*The Science of Acupuncture and Moxibustion*)
　　2) Intestinal ascariasis: Daheng (SP 15), Zusanli (ST 36). (*Selection of Treatise of 30 Years*)
　　3) Acute ileus: Daheng (SP 15), Tianshu (ST 25), Zusanli (ST 36). (*ibid*)
【Regional Anatomy】Skin-subcutaneous tissue-external oblique muscle of abdomen-internal oblique muscle of abdomen-transverse muscle of abdomen. In the superficial layer, there are the lateral cutaneous branches of the anterior branches of the 9th to 11th thoracic nerves and the tributaries of the thoracoepigastric vein. In the deep layer, there are the muscular branches of the anterior branches of the 9th to 11th thoracic nerves and their accompanying arteries and veins.
【Remark】Acupuncture to Daheng (SP 15) can make the dysfunctional intestine become normal. Acupuncture at this point has a marked therapeutic effect on acute gastroenteritis. Clinical observation on treatment of infantile intestinal ascariasis by puncturing Daheng (SP 15) showed the same result.

SP 16 Fuai (腹哀)
(Abdomen Sob)

【Source】 *A-B Classic of Acupuncture and Moxibustion*
【Name Explanation】 Fu(腹), abdomen; Ai(哀), pain. This point is useful in treating abdominal pain.
【Location】 On the upper abdomen, 3 cun above the centre of the umbilicus, and 4 cun lateral to the anterior midline. (See Fig. 10-4).
【Localization】 In the supine position, first locate Daheng (SP 15), and then locate the point 3 cun directly superior to it.
【Indications】
　　Digestive Diseases: Stomachache, pain around navel, dyspepsia, dysentery.
【Mechanism of Action】 According to its location, this point can be used to treat diseases of the stomach and intestine.
【Method】 Puncture perpendicularly 0.7-1 cun. Moxibustion is applicable.
【Acupoint Prescription】 Dyspepsia: Fuai (SP 16), Taibai (SP 3). (*Experience on Acupuncture and Moxibustion Therapy*)
【Regional Anatomy】 Skin-subcutaneous tissue-external oblique muscle of abdomen-internal oblique muscle of abdomen-transverse muscle of abdomen. In the superficial layer, there are the lateral cutaneous branches of the anterior branches of the 7th to 9th thoracic nerves and tributaries of the thoracoepigastric vein. In the deep layer, there are the muscular branches of the anterior branches of the 7th to 9th thoracic nerves and their accompanying arteries and veins.

SP 17 Shidou (食窦)
(Feed Point)

【Source】 *A-B Classic of Acupuncture and Moxibustion*
【Name Explanation】 Shi (食), food; Dou (窦), sinus. This point, infero-lateral to the nipple, has a sinus for storing milk in its deep region. The point is useful in promoting absorption of food nutrients and for tonification.
【Location】 On the lateral side of the chest and in the 5th intercostal space, 6 cun lateral to the anterior midline. (See Fig. 10-5.)
【Localization】 In the supine position, first locate Ruzhong (ST 17), and then locate the point 2 cun lateral and a rib downward to it, the point is at the 5th intercostal space.
【Indications】
　　1) Respiratory Diseases: Fullness in chest and hypochondrium, edema, dyspnea.
　　2) Digestive Diseases: Abdominal dis-

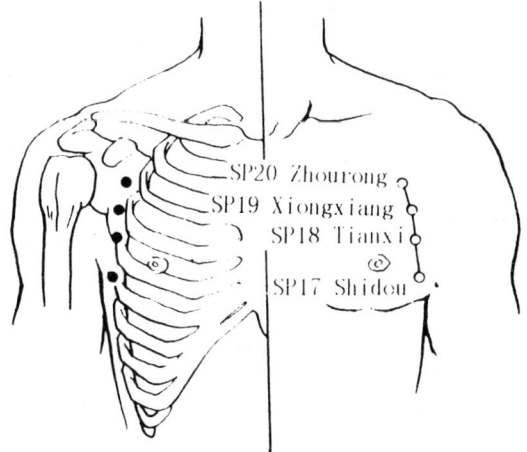

Fig. 10-5

tention, borborygmus, abdominal pain, frequent vomiting.
【Mechanism of Action】 This point is located near the stomach and lungs, so it is usually used to treat such disorders of the spleen and stomach as abdominal distention and borborygmus as well as dyspnea. Shidou (SP 17) on the right side can be used to treat dieseases of the liver and gallbladder like hypochondriac distention and pain.
【Method】 Puncture obliquely 0.3-0.5 cun. Moxibustion is applicable.
【Acupoint Prescriptions】
    1) Taiyin syndrome of febrile diseases: Moxibustion to Shidou (SP 17), Guanyuan (RN 4). (*Comprehension of Bianque's Medicine*)
    2) Intermittent dysentery: Shidou (SP 17), Guanyuan (RN 4) with moxibustion. (*ibid*).
    3) Senile fecal incontinence: Shidou (SP 17), Guanyuan (RN 4) with moxibustion. (*ibid*)
【Regional Anatomy】 Skin-subcutaneous tissue-anterior serratus muscle-external intercostal muscle. In the superfical layer, there are the lateral cutaneous branches of the 5th intercostal nerve and the thoracoepigastric vein. In the deep layer, there are the branches of the long thoracic nerve, the 5th intercostal nerve and the 5th posterior intercostal artery and vein.

SP 18 Tianxi (天溪)
(Heaven Stream)

【Source】 *A-B Classic of Acupuncture and Moxibustion*
【Name Explanation】 Tian (天), heaven; Xi (溪), valley. Tian refers to upper. The point is in the stream-like intercostal space.
【Location】 On the lateral side of the chest and in the 4th intercostal space, 6 cun lateral to the anterior midline. (See Fig. 10-5)
【Localization】 In the supine position, first locate Ruzhong (ST 17), this point is just located in the 4th intercostal space 2 cun lateral to Ruzhong (ST 17).
【Indications】
    1) Respiratory Diseases: Cough, dyspnea, excessive expectoration.
    2) Mastosis: Acute mastitis, hypogalactia.
【Mechanism of Action】 According to its location, this point is mainly used to treat diseases of the lungs and breast disorders.
【Method】 Puncture obliquely 0.3-0.5 cun. Moxibustion is applicable.
【Acupoint Prescriptions】
    1) Vomiting due to adverse rising of qi: Tianxi (SP 18), Zhongfu (LU 1). (*Experience on Acupuncture and Moxibustion Therapy*)
    2) Acute mastitis: Tianxi (SP 18), Xiaxi (GB 43). (*ibid*)
【Regional Anatomy】 Skin-subcutaneous tissue-greater pectoral muscle-smaller pectoral muscle. In the superficial layer, there are the lateral cutaneous branches of the 4th intercostal nerve and the tributaries of the thoracoepigastric vein. In the deep layer, there are the branches of the medial pectoral nerve and the lateral pectoral nerve, the pectoral branches of the thoracoacromial artery and vein and the branches or tributaries of the lateral thoracic artery and vein.

SP 19 Xiongxiang (胸乡) (Chest Village)

【Source】 *A-B Classic of Acupuncture and Moxibustion*
【Name Explanation】 Xiong (胸), chest; Xiang (乡), vast place. This point is located on the vast part of the upper chest.
【Location】 On the lateral side of the chest and in the 3rd intercostal space, 6 cun lateral to the anterior midline. (See Fig. 10-5).
【Localization】 In the supine position, first locate Ruzhong (ST 17), and then locate this point 2 cun lateral and a rib upward to it. The point is located in the 3th intercostal space.
【Indications】
　　1) Respiratory Diseases: Difficulty in lying and turning the body due to chest pain, cough.
　　2) Mastosis: Acute mastitis, hypogalactia.
【Mechanism of Action】 According to its location, this point is mainly used to treat diseases of the lungs and breasts.
【Method】 Puncture obliquely 0.3-0.5 cun. Moxibustion is applicable.
【Regional Anatomy】 Skin-subcutaneous tissue-greater pectoral muscle-smaller pectoral muscle. In the superficial layer, there are the lateral cutaneous branches of the 3rd intercostal nerve and the tributaries of the thoracoepigastric vein. In the deep layer, there are the branches of the medial pectoral nerve and the lateral perctoral nerve, the pectoral branches of the thoracoacromial artery, vein and the branches or tributaries of the lateral thoracic artery and vein.

SP 20 Zhourong (周荣) (Encircling Nourishment)

【Source】 *A-B Classic of Acupuncture and Moxibustion*
【Name Explanation】 Zhou (周), general; Rong (荣), nourishment. This point functions to harmonize nutrient qi and to nourish the whole body.
【Location】 On the lateral side of the chest and in the 2nd intercostal space, 6 cun lateral to the anterior midline. (See Fig. 10-5).
【Localization】 In the supine position, the point is located in the 2nd intercostal space, 2 cun lateral to the midclavicular line.
【Indications】
　　1) Respiratory Diseases: Cough, dyspnea, pain in the chest and hypochondrium.
　　2) Other Diseases: Poor appetite.
【Mechanism of Action】 According to its location, this point is mainly used to treat lung disorders.
【Method】 Puncture obliquely 0.3-0.5 cun. Moxibustion is applicable.
【Regional Anatomy】 Skin-subcutaneous tissue-great pectoral muscle-smaller pectoral muscle. In the superficial layer, there are the lateral cutaneous branches of the 2nd intercostal nerve and the superficial vein. In the deep layer, there are the medial pectoral nerve, the lateral pectoral nerve and the pectoral branches of the thoracoacromial artery and vein.

SP 21 Dabao (大包)
(General Control)

【Source】 *Miraculous Pivot*

【Name Explanation】 Da (大), large; Bao (包), containing. The point pertains to the Major Collateral of the Spleen Meridian. The spleen is in the center and is generally related to the Zangfu organs.

【Classification】 Luo-(connecting)point of the Spleen Meridian of Foot Taiyin.

【Location】 On the lateral side of the chest and the middle axillary line, in the 6th intercostal space. (See Fig. 10-6.)

【Localization】 In lateral position with the arm above the head, the point is located in the middle axillary line of the 6th intercostal space.

【Indications】

1) Respiratory Diseases: Dyspnea, oppressive feeling in the chest, pain in the chest and hypochondrium.

2) Other Diseases: General pain, myasthenia of the limbs.

【Action mechanism】 Dabao (SP 21) can be used to treat the diseases of respiratory system as it is close to the lung. Cupping at Dabao (SP 21) can treat intercostal neuralgia. This point is one of the Luo-(connecting) points, a major collateral of the spleen and has the function of connecting all the meridians. The spleen is responsible for both the activity of the limbs and the normality of the muscles. Therefore, applying moxibustion to Dabao (SP 21) can promote the recovery of arthralgia and flaccidity syndromes.

【Method】 Puncture obliquely 0.3-0.5 cun. Moxibustion is applicable.

【Regional Anatomy】 Skin-subcutaneous tissue-anterior serratus muscle.

In the superficial layer, there are the lateral cutaneous branches of the 6th intercostal nerve and the tributaries of the thoracoepigastric vein. In the deep layer, there are the branches of the long thoracic nerve and the branches or tributaries of the thoracodorsal artery and vein.

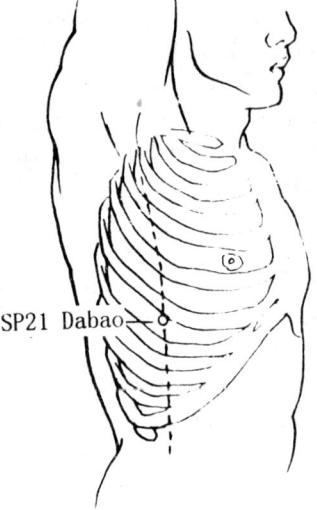

Fig. 10-6

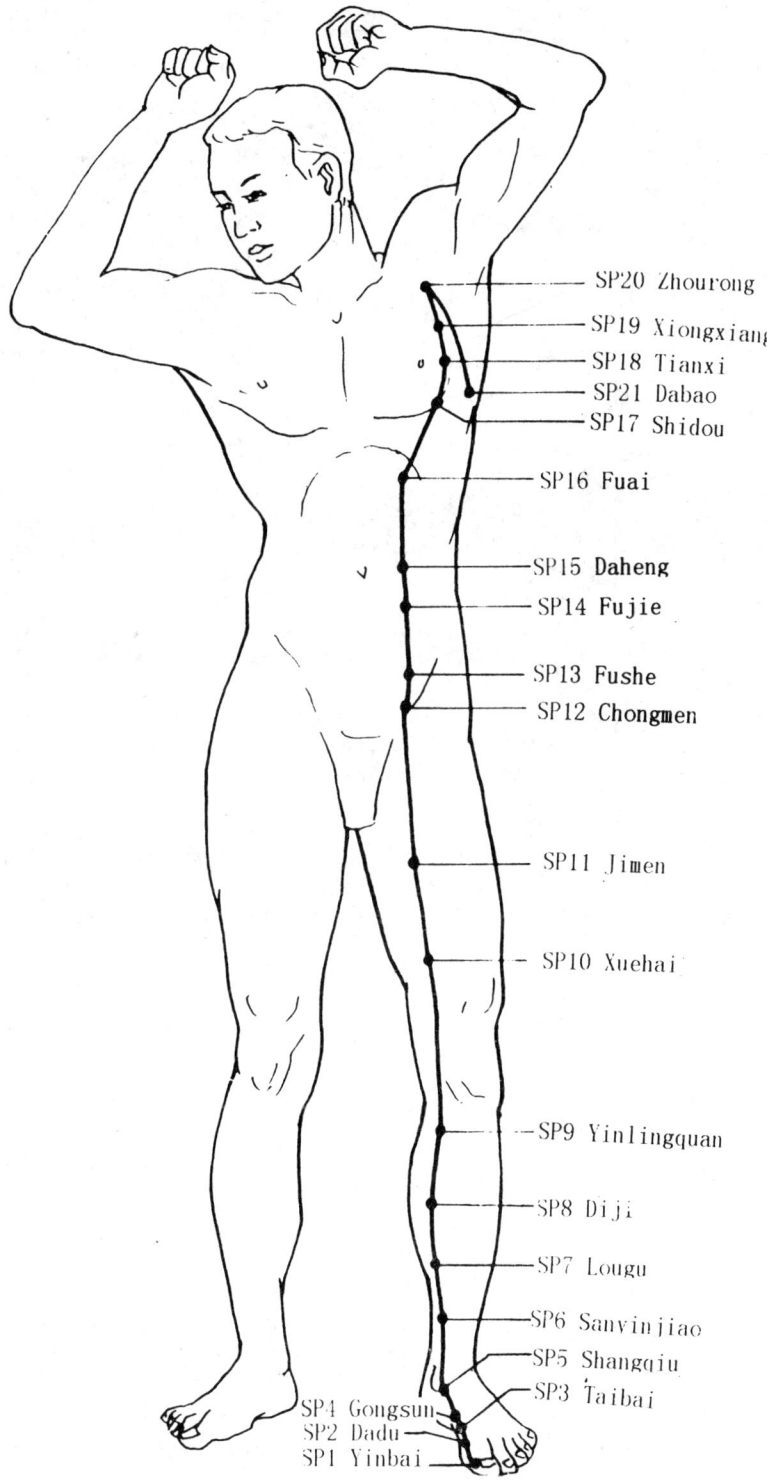

Fig. 10-7 Acupoints of the spleen Meridian of Foot Taiyin

Table 10-1 Indications and Actions of Acupoints of the Spleen Meridian of Foot Taiyin

Name of the points	Specific points	Common indications	Specific indications and functions
SP 1 Yinbai (隐白)	Jing-(Well) point	Disorders of the spleen and stomach: stomachache, abdominal pain and distention, vomiting, diarrhea Gynecopathy and disorders of external genitalia: menoxenia, dysmenorrhea, retention of urine, enuresis	Invigorating the spleen and stomach, benefiting vital energy to control blood, relieving mental stress, hematochezia, hematuria, menorrhagia, metrorrhagia, manic-depression, dreaminess, infantile convulsion, abdominal distention, vomiting, febrile disease
SP 2 Dadu (大都)	Ying-(Spring) point		Clearing heat, eliminating dampness evil, recuperating the depleted yang and rescuing the patient from danger. Febrile disease without sweat, feverish sensation accompanied with restlessness, abdominal distention, vomiting, diarrhea, infantile convulsion, cold hands and feet, stomachache
SP 3 Taibai (太白)	Shu-(Stream) point Yuan-(Source) point		Invigorating the spleen and stomach, regulating the flow of qi to eliminate the dampness evil. Stomachache, abdominal flatulence, constipation, diarrhea, hemorrhoids, beriberi
SP 4 Gongsun (公孙)	Luo-(Connecting)Point One of the eight confluence point		Coordinating the functions of spleen and stomach, regulating the function of the Chong meridian, stopping vomiting. Stomachache, vomiting, abdominal pain, diarrhea, restlessness, dysentery, insomnia It is also a commonly used point in acupuncture anaesthesia.
SP 5 Shanqiu (商丘)	Jing-(River) Point		Invigorating the spleen to eliminate dampness evil. Pain in the inguinal region, pain in the ankle, drowsiness, jaundice, chronic infantile convulsion
SP 6 Sanyinjiao (三阴交)	Crossing point		Invigorating the spleen to resolve dampness, soothing the liver and tonifying the kidney, regulating the function of the Lower Jiao. distention and pain in the abdomen, diarrhea, insomnia, irregular menstruation, leukorrhagia, vaginal hernia, sterility in female, dystocia, nocturnal emission, impotence, hernia, flaccidity of feet, beriberi
SP 7 Lougu (漏谷)			distention and pain in the abdomen, borborygmus, retention of urine, nocturnal emission, flaccidity of feet, numbness of knee and leg, pain and swelling of the ankle
SP 8 Diji (地机)	Xi-(Cleft) point		Regulating and invigorating the functions of the liver and kidney, regulating blood and restoring essence, invigorating the spleen to eliminate dampness. Irregular menstruation, dysmenorrhea, nocturnal emission, defective ejaculation, mass in the female abdomen, pain in the waist, pain of feet, edema
SP 9 Yinlingquan (阴陵泉)	Confluent point		Regulating blood and menstruation, expelling wind-evil and eliminating dampness. Irregular menstruation, dysmenorrhea, metrorrhagia, amenorrhea, leukorrhagia, urticaria, eczema, erysipelas, pruritus vulvae

Name of the points	Specific points	Common indications	Specific indications and functions
SP 10 Xuehai (血海)			Invigorating spleen to eliminate dampness, inducing diuresis for treating stranguria. Retention of urine, enuresis, five types of stranguria, pain and swelling in the inguinal region, eczema of scrotum
SP 11 Jimen (箕门)			Clearing heat and resolving dampness, inducing diuresis to alleviate edema, regulating and invigorating the functions of liver and kidney. Diarrhea, edema, cholera morbus, jaundice, enuresis, irregular menstruation, dysmenorrhea, nocturnal emission, pain in the penis, leukorrhagia, pain in the knee
SP 12 Chongmen (冲门)	Crossing point	Disorders of the stomach and intestine: abdominal pain, diarrhea, constipation, hernia	Dredging the meridian to promote the flow of qi, clearing heat and eliminating dampness. Abdominal pain, hernia, leukorrhagia, metrorrhagia, flaccidity and pain of feet
SP 13 Fushe (府舍)	Crossing point		Soothing the liver to stop pain, invigorating the spleen and regulating the flow of abdominal pain, hernia, mass in abdomen
SP 14 Fujie (腹结)			Expelling pathogenic cold from meridian, promoting the flow of qi and blood. Abdominal pain, pain around the navel, cough with dyspnea, diarrhea due to cold in abdomen
SP 15 Daheng (大横)	Crossing point		Pain around the navel, diarrhea, constipation, hysteria, dysentery
SP 16 Fuai (腹哀)	Crossing point		Dyspepsia, passing stool with blood and pus
SP 17 Shidou (食窦)		Disorders of chest and lung: pain and fullness over the chest and hypochondrium, cough	Soothing chest oppression, regulating qi and the middle Jiao. Swollen and painful chest and hypochondrium, eructation, frequent vomiting, distending abdomen, edema, pleurisy, hydrothorax
SP 18 Tianxi (天溪)			Soothing chest oppression and regulating the flow of qi, dredging the meridian to promote the flow of blood. Pain over the chest and hypochondrium, cough, hiccup, acute mastitis, lack of lactation
SP 19 Xiongxiang (胸乡)			Dredging the meridian. Swelling and pain of chest and hypochondrium, intercostal neuralgia
SP 20 Zhourong (周荣)			Promoting the dispersing function of the lung to resolve phlegm. Cough, adverse flow of qi, distention and fullness over the chest and hypochondrium, poor appetite
SP 21 Dabao (大包)	Major Luo-(Connecting) point		Soothing chest oppression and regulating the flow of qi, dredging the meridian, strengthening the bones and muscles. Asthma, pain over the chest and hypochondrium, pain all over the body, flaccidity of the limbs

X. Acupoints of the Liver Meridian of Foot Jueyin

LR 1 Dadun (大敦)
(Big Thick)

【Source】 *Miraculous Pivot and Plain Questions*
【Name Explanation】 Da (大), large; Dun (敦), thickness. Da, refers to the big toe. The point is at the medial aspect of the big toe, where the muscle is thick
【Classification】 Jing-(Well) Point of the Liver Meridian of Foot Jueyin, pertaining to wood in the Five Elements.
【Location】 On the lateral side of the distal segment of the great toe, 0.1 cun from the corner of the toe nail. (See Fig. 10-8)
【Localization】 Foot extended, locate the point at the intersection between the lines down from the lateral side of the great toe nail and its basal part.

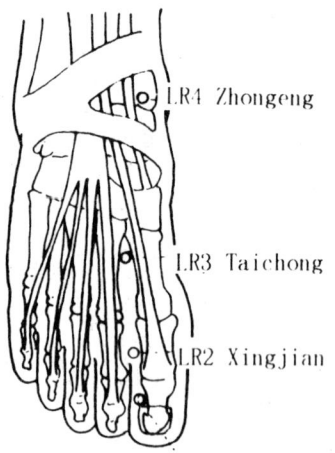

Fig. 10-8

【Indications】
1) Digestive Diseases: Epigastralgia, constipation, hematoquexia.
2) Reproductive Diseases: Prolapse of the uterus, perineal pain, pruritus vulvae, irregular menstruation, metrorrhagia and metrostaxis, amenorrhea, flaccid contraction of the penis, pain of the glans penis, painful and swollen testis.
3) Urinary Diseases: Hematuria, enuresis, stranguria, dysuria, frequent micturition.
4) Mental Diseases: Manic-depressive syndrome, epilepsy, apoplexy, drowsiness.
5) Other Diseases: Hernia, pain in the lower abdomen, blurring vision.

【Mechanism of Action】
1) Dadun (LR 1) is the Jing-(well) point of the Liver Meridian, which pertains to wood of the Five Elements. The hyperactive liver qi and failure of the liver in storing blood can cause many types of bleeding symptoms. Thus, this point is widely applied in clinic practice to treat metrorrhagia, metrostaxis, hematoquexia and hematuria.
2) The Liver Meridian circulates around the external genitalia, and is the only meridian connected directly with the vulva. So Dadun (LR 1) can be used to treat the diseases of the reproductive system such as hernia, prolapse of uterus and pruritus vulvae.
3) Liver has a close relation with "wind", so the point can be used to treat manic-depressive syndrome, epilepsy, apoplexy, etc.
4) The Liver Meridian flows around the stomach, smooths and regulates the flow of qi and blood, promotes digestion and absorption and has a close relation with the functions of the spleen and stomach. So Dadun (LR 1) can be used to treat diseases of the digestive system.

【Method】 Puncture obliquely 0.1-0.2 cun or prick the point to cause bleeding. Moxibustion is applicable.

【Acupoint Prescriptions】
   1) Hiccup: Dadun (LR 1), Shiguan (KI 8). (*Experience on Acupuncture and Moxibustion Therapy*)
   2) Infantile nocturia: Dadun (LR 1), Sanyinjiao (SP 6), Guanyuan (RN 4), Baihui (DU 20). (*Abstract of Clinical Experience on Acupuncture and Moxibustion*)
   3) Periumbilical colic due to cold-evil: Dadun (LR 1), Zhaohai (KI 6). (*Songs of Hundreds of Symptoms*)
   4) Seven kinds of hernia: Dadun (LR 1), Taichong (LR 3). (*Songs of Point Selection of Miscellaneous Diseases*)

【Regional Anatomy】 Skin-subcutaneous tissue-root of the nail. There are the lateral dorsal nerve of the great toe from the deep peroneal nerve and the dorsal digital artery and vein in this area.

【Remark】 Acupuncture at Dadun (LR 1) point can adjust the movement of the large intestine and can strengthen the peristalsis of the lower part of the descending colon and rectum. Acupuncture at this point can also strengthen the effect of Shenmen (HT 7) in lowering blood pressure.

LR 2 Xingjian (行间)
(Inter Column)

【Source】 *Miraculous Pivot*

【Name Explanation】 Xing (行), walking; Jian (间), middle. The point is in the depression anterior to the 1st and 2nd metatarsophalangeal joints. The qi of meridian runs between them.

【Classification】 Ying-(Spring) Point of the Liver Meridian of Foot Jueyin, pertaining to fire in the Five Elements.

【Location】 On the instep of the foot, between the 1st and 2nd toes, at the junction of the red and white skin proximal to the margin of the web. (See Fig. 10-8).

【Localization】 In sitting position with the feet relaxed, locate the point at the dorsum of the foot, in the depression between the 1st and 2nd toe, proximal to the margin of the web.

【Indications】
   1) Diseases along the Course of the Meridian: Pain in the medial side of the knee and thigh, hypochondriac pain, lumbago which causes difficulty in lying flat.
   2) Diseases of Head and Sense Organs: Headache, vertigo, red, painful and swollen eyes, optic atrophy, wry mouth, dry and painful throat, toothache.
   3) Respiratory Diseases: Cough, consumptive disease.
   4) Digestive Diseases: Epigastralgia, hiccup, hematemesis, abdominal distention, diarrhea, jaundice.
   5) Reproductive Diseases: Menorrhagia, dysmenorrhea, amenorrhea, leukorrhea, gonorrhea, pain of perineal area or penis.
   6) Urinary Diseases: Enuresis, stranguria.
   7) Mental Diseases: Apoplexy, epilepsy, clonic convulsion, hysteria infantile convulsion, depressive-syndrome, irritability, depressive-syndrome.
   8) Other Diseases: Hypertension, hernia, mammary abscess.

【Mechanism of Action】 It is one of the commonly-use points in clinic. See Taichong (LR 3) for further details.

【Method】 Puncture obliquely 0.5-0.8 cun. Moxibustion is applicable.

【Acupoint Prescriptions】

1) Precardial pain with cold limbs: Xingjian (LR 2), Taichong (LR 3). (*Thousand Golden Prescriptions*)

2) Dry sensation in pharynx: Xingjian (LR 2), Shenting (DU 24). (*Experience on Acupuncture and Moxibustion Therapy*)

3) Intercostal neuralgia: Xingjian (LR 2), Rugen (ST 18); The auxiliary points: Quchi (LI 11), Tanzhong (RN 17), Zhourong (SP 20). (*Science of Acupuncture and Moxibustion*)

4) Diabetes: Xingjian (LR 2), Yongquan (KI 1). (*Songs of Hundreds of Symptoms*).

【Regional Anatomy】Skin-subcutaneous tissue-between base of the proximal phalangeal bone of the great toe and the head of the 2nd metatarsal bone. There are the dorsal digital nerve of the deep peroneal nerve and the dorsal digital artery and vein in this area.

LR 3 Taichong (太冲)
(Supreme Rush)

【Source】*Miraculous Pivot*

【Name Explanation】Tai (太), big; Chong (冲), important pass. The point is on the foot, where the Qi of the meridian is abundant. It is an important pass of this meridian.

【Classification】Shu-(Stream) and Yuan-(Source) Point of the Liver Meridian of Foot Jueyin, pertaining to earth in the Five Elements.

【Location】On the instep of the foot, in the depression of posterior end of the 1st interosseous metatarsal space. (See Fig. 10-8).

【Localization】In sitting position with the feet relaxed, locate the point at the dorsum of the foot, between the 1st and 2nd metatarsal bones, in the depression anterior to the junction of the metatarsal plantares, On the lateral side of the tendon of the long extensor muscle of the great toe.

【Indications】

1) Diseases along the Course of the Meridian: Flaccidity and numbness of the lower limbs, hypochondriac pain.

2) Diseases of Head and Sense Organs: Headache, dizziness, red, painful and swollen eyes, optic atrophy, dry mouth, dry and painful throat.

3) Respiratory Diseases: Cough, oppressive sensation in the chest.

4) Digestive Diseases: Abdominal distention, borborygmus, epigastralgia, diarrhea, constipation, jaundice.

5) Reproductive Diseases: Irregular menstruation, amenorrhea, metrorrhagia and metrostaxis, dysmenorrhea, leukorrhea, persistent sweating after birth, pain of perineal area, shrinkage of the external genitals.

6) Urinary Diseases: Dysuria, enuresis, stranguria.

7) Mental Diseases: Manic-depressive syndrome, epilepsy, infantile convulsion, apoplexy, hysteria, irritability, depression.

8) Other Diseases: Hypertension, angina pectoris, hernia.

【Mechanism of Action】

1) Taichong (LR 3) is the Yuan-(source) point of the Liver Meridian. Liver Meridian runs around the inner surface of the lips, connects with the surrounding tissues of the eye, emerges from the forehead and finally meets the Du Meridian at the vertex. The liver dominates the interior and liver-wind stirring inside the body would result in headache, vertigo, dizziness, wry mouth, etc. Taichong (LR 3) can clear away heat-evil to stop the wind-syndrome, calm the liver and suppress the excessive Yang. Therefore, Taichong (LR 3) is an important point to treat all kinds of symptoms due to excessive liver Yang.

2) Liver controls the storage of blood and dominates dispersion and discharge. Failure of the liver in these actions may bring about imbalance of Chong and Ren Meridians, as a result, gynopathy may appear.

3) The Liver Meridian flows around the external genitalia. When there is a disorder of the liver meridian, the dampness and heat would go down to the lower Jiao along the Liver Meridian, which would result in diseases of the urinary system. So Taichong (LR 3) can treat the disease mentioned above through its function of clearing away heat-evil and promoting diuresis.

4) The liver is in charge of dispersing. If the liver-qi fails to disperse, the stagnated qi will turn to liver-fire which results in all kinds of mental diseases. Taichong (LR 3) is an important point to disperse the depressed liver qi, and is a commonly-used point to treat all kinds of mental diseases including irritability and depressive syndrome. Taichong (LR 3) is often used together with Hegu (LI 4) which is called "Siguan". The Liver Meridian passes by the stomach and has a close relation with the stomach and spleen. So this point is selected to treat disorders of incoordination between spleen and stomach due to stagnation of liver qi.

5) Liver Meridian is distributed at the hypochondrium. Taichong (LR 3) is one of the first important points to treat pain in the hypochondrium according to the principle: "Where meridian passes, where the indications are."

【Method】 Puncture perpendicularly 0.5-1 cun. Moxibustion is applicable.

【Acupoint Prescriptions】

1) Dysentery: Taichong (LR3), Ququan (LR 8). (*Thousand Golden Prescriptions*)

2) Defective ejaculation or oligospermatism: Taichong (LR 3), Zhongfeng (LR 4), Diji (SP 8). (*Experience on Acupuncture and Moxibustion Therapy*).

3) Red, painful and swelling eyes: Taichong (LR 3), Yanggu (SI 5), Kunlun (BL 60). (*ibid*)

4) Metrostaxis: Taichong (LR 3), Rangu (KI 2). (*ibid*)

5) Sartorial hernia: Taichong (LR 3), Dadun (LR 1). (*Great Compendium of Acupuncture and Moxibustion*)

6) Prolapse of the uterus: Taichong (LR 3), Shaofu (HT 8), Zhaohai (KI 6), Ququan (LR 8). (*ibid*)

7) Dystocia: Taichong (LR 3), Sanyinjiao (SP 6), Hegu (LI 4), Guanyuan (RN 4), Taixi (KI 3) to Kunlun (BL 60). (*Abstract of Clinical Experience on Acupuncture and Moxibustion*).

8) Enuresis in child: Taichong (LR 3), Taixi (KI 3), Guanyuan (RN 4), Zhongji (RN 3). (*ibid*)

9) Arthralgia due to stagnation of cold and heat: Taichong (LR 3), Hegu (LI 4). (*Songs of Secret on Acupuncture and Moxibustion*)

10) Difficulty in walking: Taichong (LR 3), Zusanli (ST 36), Zhongfeng (LR 4). (*Songs of Jade Dragon*)

【Regional Anatomy】 Skin-subcutaneous tissue-between tendons of long extensor muscle of great toe and long extensor muscle of toes-lateral side of short extensor muscle of great toe-1st dorsal interosseous muscle. In the superficial layer, there are the venous network of the dorsum of the foot and the medial dorsal cutaneous nerve of the foot. In the deep layer, there are the deep peroneal nerve and the 1st dorsal metatarsal artery and vein.

【Remark】 Acupuncture at Taichong (LR 3) alone can quickly lower the pressure of the biliary tract after morphine is injected.

LR 4 Zhongfeng (中封)
(Middle Seal)

【Source】 *Miraculous Pivot*
【Name Explanation】 Zhong (中), middle; Feng (封), earth heaped into a mound. The point is between the two malleoli as if between the mounds.
【Classification】 Jing-(River) Point of the Liver Meridian of Foot Jueyin, pertaining to metal in the Five Elements.
【Location】 On the instep of the foot, anterior to the medial malleolus, on the line connecting Shangqiu (SP 5) and Jiexi (ST 41), in the depression medial to the tendon of the anterior tibia muscle. (See Fig. 10-8).
【Localization】 On the dorsal foot inflexion, locate the point anterior and inferior to the medial malleolus, in the depression between the tendons of the anterior tibial muscle and the long extensor.
【Indications】
　1) Diseases along the Course of the Meridian: Flaccidity and numbness in the lower limbs, painful and swollen dorsum of the foot, hypochondriac pain.
　2) Disorders of Head and Sense Organs: Headache, dizziness, wry mouth, painful and swollen throat.
　3) Digestive Diseases: Tympanites, anorexia, jaundice.
　4) Urinary Diseases: Difficulty in urination, stranguria, pain in perineum, hernia, nocturnal emission.
【Mechanism of Action】 See Taichong (LR 3).
【Method】 Puncture perpendicularly 0.5-0.8 cun. Moxibustion is applicable.
【 Acupoint Prescriptions】
　1) Dysuria: Zhongfeng (LR 4), Xingjian (LR 2). (*Experience on Acupuncture and Moxibustion Therapy*)
　2) Distension of abdomen: Zhongfeng (LR 4), Siman (KI 14). (*ibid*)
　3) Pain around the umbilicus: Zhongfeng (LR 4), Shuifen (RN 9), Shenque (RN 8). (*ibid*)
　4) Jaundice: Zhongfeng (LR 4), Wuli (LI 13). (*ibid*)
　5) Acute infectious hepatitis: Main point: Zhongfeng (LR 4). Auxillary points: Houxi (SI 3), Hegu (LI 4), Zusanli (ST 36). (*Abstract of Clinical Experience on Acupuncture and Moxibustion*)
　6) Difficulty in walking: Zhongfeng (LR 4), Taichong (LR 3). (*Songs of Shengyu*)
【Regional Anatomy】 Skin-subcutaneous tissue-medial side of the tendon of the anterior tibial muscle-between talus and medial malleolus of tibia. There are the branches of the medial dorsal cutaneous nerve of the foot, the medial anterior malleolar artery and the superficial dorsal vein of the foot in this area.
【Remark】 Some experiments have shown that puncturing Zhongfeng (LR 4) can strengthen the function of Neiguan (PC 6) and Zusanli (ST 36) to reduce the heart rate.

LR 5 Ligou (蠡沟)
(Gourd Ditch)

【Source】 *Miraculous Pivot*
【Name Explanation】 Li (蠡), shell; Gou (沟), groove. The external shape of the gastrocnemius muscle looks like a shell and the point is in the groove medial and anterior to it.
【Classification】 Luo-(Connecting) Point of the Liver Meridian of Foot Jueyin.
【Location】 On the medial side of the leg, 5 cun above the tip of the medial malleolus, on the midline of the medial surface of the tibia. (See Fig. 10-9).
【Localization】 In sitting or supine position, 5 cun above the tip of the medial malleolus, locate the point at the intersection of the one-third distance between the posterior and the middle part of the medial side of the tibia.
【Indications】
 1) Diseases along the Course of the Meridian: Pain in the tibia, hypochondriac pain.
 2) Urinary Diseases: Dysuria, irregular menstruation, metrorrhagia and metrostaxis, leukorrhea with reddish discharge, prolapse of uterus, painful and swollen testis, fullness feeling and pain in lower abdomen.

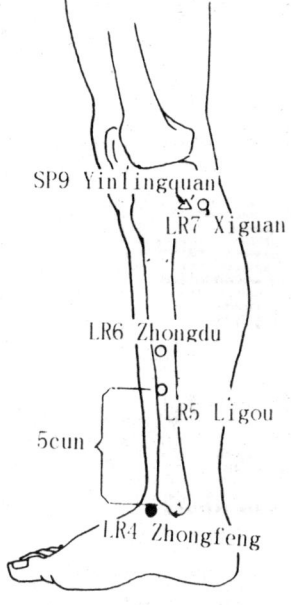

Fig. 10-9

【Mechanism of Action】 The liver dominates dispersion and discharge, controls the storage of blood and its meridian runs around the external genitalia. Stagnation of liver-qi which causes lower attack of dampness-heat can result in diseases of the reproductive and urinary systems. Ligou (LR 5) can remove the stagnation of liver qi, clear away heat and dampness-evils, thus it treats various diseases of urogenital system. Clinically, Ligou (LR 5) is usually used to treat stranguria, leukorrhagia with reddish and whitish discharge.
【Method】 Puncture subcutaneously 0.5-0.8 cun. Moxibustion is applicable.
【Regional Anatomy】 Skin-subcutaneous tissue-medial surface of tibia. There are the medial cutaneous branches of the leg from the saphenous nerve and the great saphenous vein in this area.

LR 6 Zhongdu (中都)
(Middle Capital)

【Source】 *A-B Classic of Acupuncture and Moxibustion*
【Name Explanation】 Zhong (中), middle; Du (都), confluence. The point is on the medial aspect of the leg and at midpoint of the leg. It is a confluence of the qi of the Liver Meridian.
【Location】 On the medial side of the leg, 7 cun above the tip of the medial malleolus, on the midline of the medial surface of the tibia. (See Fig. 10-9).
【Localization】 In sitting position or in supine position, 7 cun above the tip of the medial malleolus, locate the point at the intersection of the one-third distance between the superior

and middle parts of the medial side of the tibia.
【Indications】
1) Diseases along the Course of the Meridian: Flaccidity and numbness in lower limbs, hypochondriac pain.
2) Digestive Diseases: Diarrhea, dysentery, abdominal distention.
3) Reproductive Diseases: Hernia, pain in the lower abdomen, metrorrhagia and metrostaxis, leukorrhea with reddish discharge, retention of liquids, pain in perineum.
【Mechanism of Action】See Ligou (LR 5).
【Method】Puncture subcutaneously 0.5-0.8 cun. Moxibustion is applicable.
【Acupoint Prescription】Edema in the extremities: Zhongdu (LR 6), Hegu (LI 4), Quchi (LI 11), Zhongzhu (SJ 3), Yemen (SJ 2). (*Great Compendium of Acupuncture and Moxibustion*)
【Regional Anatomy】Skin-subcutaneous tissue-medial surface of tibia. There are the medial cutaneous branches of the leg from the saphenous nerve and vein in this area.

LR 7 Xiguan (膝关)
(Knee Pass)

【Source】*A-B Classic of Acupuncture and Moxibustion*
【Name Explanation】Xi (膝), knee; Guan (关), joint. The point is in the vicinity of the knee joint.
【Location】On the medial side of the leg, posterior and inferior to the medial epicondyle of the tibia, 1 cun posterior to Yinlingquan (SP 9), at the upper end of the medial head of the gastrocnemius muscle. (See Fig. 10-9).
【Localization】With the knee flexed, first locate Yinlingquan (SP 9) which is located at the inferior side of the medial condyle of the tibia, then locate the point 1 cun posterior to Yinlingquan (SP 9).
【Indications】Diseases along the Course of the Meridian: Flaccidity and numbness in lower limbs, painful and swollen knee.
【Mechanism of Action】According to its location, it is used to treat local diseases.
【Method】Puncture perpendicularly 1-0.5 cun. Moxibustion is applicable.
【Acupoint Prescription】
1) Swelling and pain of both knees: Xiguan (LR 7), Weizhong (BL 40), Zusanli (ST 36), Yinshi (ST 33) (*Experience on Acupuncture and Moxibustion Therapy*)
2) Aching knees: Xiguan (LR 7), Zusanli (ST 36) administered with moxibustion. (*ibid*)
【Regional Anatomy】Skin-subcutaneous tissue-medial surface of tibia. In the superficial layer, there are the medial cutaneous branches of the leg from the saphenous nerve and the tributaries of the great saphenous vein. In the deep layer, there are the popliteal artery and vein and the tibial nerve.

LR 8 Ququan (曲泉)
(Spring on Bend)

【Source】*Miraculous Pivot*
【Name Explanation】Qu (曲), crooked; Quan (泉), spring. The point is at the medial end

of the transverse crease of the popliteal fossa. With the knee flexed, the local depression is like a spring.

【Classification】 He-(Sea) Point of the Liver Meridian of Foot Jueyin, pertaining to water in the Five Elements.

【Location】 On the medial side of the knee, at the medial end of the popliteal crease when the knee is flexed, posterior to the medial epicondyle of the tibia, in the depression of the anterior border of the insertions of the semimenmbranous and semitendinous muscle. (See Fig. 10-10).

【Localization】 With the knees flexed, locate the point at the depression superior to the end of the cross striation in the medial side of the knee.

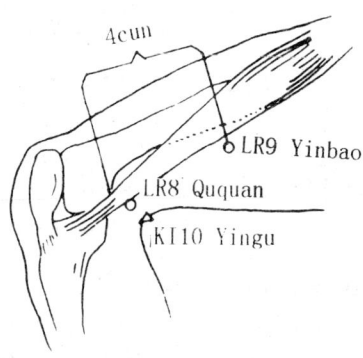

Fig. 10-10

【Indications】

1) Diseases along the Course of the Meridian: Flaccidity and numbness in lower limbs, painful and swollen knee joint.

2) Disorders of Head and Sense Organs: Headache, dizziness, painful eyes, epistaxis.

3) Digestive Diseases: Diarrhea, dysentery, fullness in the stomach, anorexia.

4) Reproductive Diseases: Irregular menstruation, dysmenorrhea, leukorrhagia, prolapse of uterus, pruritus and swelling of the perineal area, pain in abdomen after delivery, pain in the penis, impotence.

5) Urinary Diseases: Dysuria, stranguria, retention of urine.

6) Mental Diseases: Manic-depressive syndrome.

【Mechanism of Action】 Puncturing Ququan (LR 8) has the function of clearing away damp heat and regulating lower Jiao. So it is used to treat diseases of the urogenital system due to the attack of damp heat in the lower-jiao.

【Method】 Puncture perpendicularly 1-1.5 cun. Moxibustion is applicable.

【Acupoint Prescriptions】

1) Dysuria and pain in penis: Ququan (LR 8), Xingjian (LR 2). (*Experience on Acupuncture and Moxibustion Therapy*).

2) Swelling of the vulva: Ququan (LR 8), Dadun (LR 1), Qichong (ST 30). (*ibid*)

3) Enuresis: Ququan (LR 8), Yingu (KI 10), Yanglingquan (GB 34), Fuliu (KI 7). (*ibid*)

4) Clonic spasm of muscles around knee leading to inability to flex and walk: Ququan (LR 8), Liangqiu (ST 34), Xiyangguan (GB 33). (*ibid*)

5) Epistaxis: Ququan (LR 8), Yinbai (SP 1), Yixi (BL 45), Yinxi (HT 6), Yingxiang (LI 20). (*ibid*)

6) Wind-type consumptive disease: Ququan (LR 8), Pangguangshu (BL 28). (*ibid*)

7) Pain of the umbilicus: Ququan (LR 8), Zhongfeng (LR 4), Shuifen (RN 9). (*Great Compendium of Acupuncture and Moxibustion*).

8) Swelling of the scrotum: Ququan (LR 8), Zhongfeng (LR 4), Shangqiu (SP 5). (*ibid*)

9) Prolapse of uterus: Ququan (LR 8), Zhaohai (KI 6), Dadun (LR 1). (*ibid*)

【Regional Anatomy】 Skin-subcutaneous tissue-posterior border of sartorius muscle-posterior border of the tendon of graciles muscle-tendon of semimembranous muscle-medial head of gastrocnemius muscle. In the superficial layer, there are the saphenous nerve and the great saphenous vein. In the deep layer, there are the branches or tributaries of the medial superior genicular artery and vein.

LR 9 Yinbao（阴包）
（Yin Wrappage）

【Source】 *A-B Classic of Acupuncture and Moxibustion*
【Name Explanation】 Yin (阴), Yin of Yin-Yang; Bao (包), womb. The interior is Yin. Bao refers to the uterus. The point is at the medial aspect of the thigh and is indicated in disorders of the uterus.
【Location】 On the medial side of the thigh, 4 cun above the medial epicondyle of the femur, between the medial vastus muscle and sartorius muscle. (See Fig. 10-10).
【Localization】 With the knees flexed, locate the point 4 cun directly superior to Ququan (LR 8), between the medial vastus msculus and sartorius muscle.
【Indication】
　　Urogenital Diseases: Irregular menstruation, enuresis, dysuria.
【Mechanism of Action】 See Ququan (LR 8).
【Method】 Puncture perpendicularly 1-2 cun. Moxibustion is applicable.
【Acupoint Prescriptions】
　　1) Irregular menstruation: Yinbao (LR 9), Jiaoxin (KI 8). (*Experience on Acupuncture and Moxibustion Therapy*).
　　2) Dysuria: Yinbao (LR 9), Zhiyin (BL 67), Yinlingquan (SP 9), Diji (SP 8), Sanyinjiao (SP 6). (*ibid*)
【Regional Anatomy】 Skin-subcutaneous tissue-between sartorius muscle and graciles muscle-great adductor muscle. In the superficial layer, there are the cutaneous branches of the obturator nerve and the tributaries of the great saphenous vein. In the deep layer, there are the muscular branches of the femoral nerve, the saphenous nerve and the femoral artery and vein.

LR 10 Zuwuli（足五里）
（Foot Five Li）

【Source】 *A-B Classic of Acupuncture and Moxibustion.*
【Name Explanation】 Zu (足), lower limbs; Wu (五), five; Li (里), used as cun in ancient times. The point is in the lower limbs, 5 cun above Qi men.
【Location】 On the medial side of the thigh, 3 cun directly below Qichong (ST 30), at the proximal end of the thigh, below the pubic tubercle and on the lateral border of the long abductor muscle of the thigh. (See Fig. 10-11).
【Localization】 Supine position, first locate Qichong (ST 30) which lies 2 cun lateral to Qugu (RN 2), then locate the point 3 cun directly inferior to Qichong (ST 30).
【Indications】
　　1) Urogenital diseases: Dysuria, enuresis, pro-

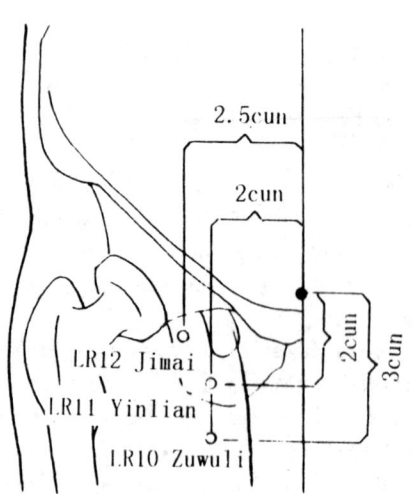

Fig. 10-11

lapse of uterus, leukorrhagia, painful and swollen testis, eczema and pruritus of scrotum.
【Mechanism of Action】Puncturing Zuwuli (LR 10) can clear damp heat and has a very good curative effect on leukorrhagia, eczema and pruritus of scrotum.
【Method】Puncture perpendicularly 1-2 cun. Moxibustion is applicable.
【Acupoint Prescription】Drowsiness: Zuwuli (LR 10), Taixi (KI 3), Dazhong (KI 4), Zhaohai (KI 6). (*Experience on Acupuncture and Moxibustion Therapy*)
【Regional Anatomy】Skin-subcutaneous tissue-long adductor muscle-short adductor muscle-great adductor muscle. In the superficial layer, there are the anterior cutaneous branches of the femoral nerve and the saphenous vein. In the deep layer, there are the anterior and posterior branches of the obturator nerve, the muscular branches of the deep femoral artery and vein, and the muscular branches of the medial femoral circumflex artery and vein.

LR 11 Yinlian (阴廉)
(Yin Side)

【Source】*A-B Classic of Acupuncture and Moxibustion.*
【Name Explanation】Yin (阴), Yin of Yin-Yang; Lian (廉), edge. The interior is Yin. The point is on the medial aspect of the thigh, near the genitalia.
【Location】On the medial side of the thigh, 2 cun directly below Qichong (ST 30), at the proximal end of the thigh, below the pubic tubercle and on the lateral border of the long abductor muscle of the thigh. (See Fig. 10-11.)
【Localization】Supine position, first locate Qichong (ST 30) which lies 2 cun lateral to Qugu (RN 2), then locate the point 2 cun directly inferior to Qichong (ST 30).
【Indications】
 1) Diseases along the Course of the Meridian: Pain in the medial side of thighs, spasm in lower limbs.
 2) Reproductive Diseases: Irregular menstruation, leukorrhea with reddish discharge.
【Mechanism of Action】See Zuwuli (LR 10).
【Method】Puncture perpendicularly 1-2 cun. Moxibustion is applicable.
【Acupoint Prescription】Pruritus vulvae: Yinlian (LR 11), Qugu (RN 2), Huiyin (LR 1). Apply twirling manipulation, with moderate stimulation, administered every day or every other day, four times constitutes one course. (*Abstract of Clinical Experience on Acupuncture and Moxibustion*)
【Regional Anatomy】Skin-subcutaneous tissue-long adductor muscle-short adductor muscle-small adductor muscle. In the superficial layer, there are the anterior cutaneous branches of the femoral nerve, the great saphenous vein and the superficial inguinal lymph nodes. In the deep layer, there are the anterior and posterior branches of the obturator nerve and the muscular branches of the medial femoral circumflex artery and vein.

LR 12 Jimai (急脉)
(Acute Pulse)

【Source】*Plain Questions*
【Name Explanation】Ji (急), urgent; Mai (脉), artery. The point is at the medial aspect of the thigh, where the artery is felt.
【Location】Lateral to the pubic tubercle, lateral and inferior to Qichong (ST 30), in the in-

guinal groove where the pulsation of the artery is palpable, 2.5 cun lateral to the anterior midline. (See Fig. 10-11)

【Localization】Supine position, locate the point 2.5 cun lateral to the inferior border of the pubic symphysis.

【Indications】
   1) Diseases along the Course of the Meridian: Pain in the medial side of the thigh.
   2) Reproductive Diseases: Hernia, pain in lower abdomen, prolapse of uterus, pain in penis.

【Mechanism of Action】See Zuwuli (LR 10).

【Method】Avoid puncturing the artery. Puncture perpendicularly 0.5-0.8 cun. Moxibustion is applicable.

【Regional Anatomy】Skin-subcutaneous tissue-pectineal muscle-lateral obturator muscle. In the superficial layer, there are the anterior cutaneous branches of the femoral nerve, the great saphenous vein and the superficial inguinal lymph nodes. In the deep layer, there are the external pudendal artery and vein, the branches or tributaries of the medial femoral circumflex artery and vein, and the anterior branches of the obturator nerve.

LR 13 Zhangmen (章门)
(Chapter Gate)

【Source】*A-B Classic of Acupuncture and Moxibustion*

【Name Explanation】Zhang (章), screen; Men (门), door. The point is below the hypochondrium, which is like a screen for the internal organs.

【Classification】Front-Mu point of the spleen. Influential Point of zang organs.

【Location】On the lateral side of the abdomen, below the free end of the 11th rib. (See Fig. 10-12).

【Localization】Supine position, locate the point in the mid-axillary line, at the place where the tip of the elbow touches when the elbow is flexed.

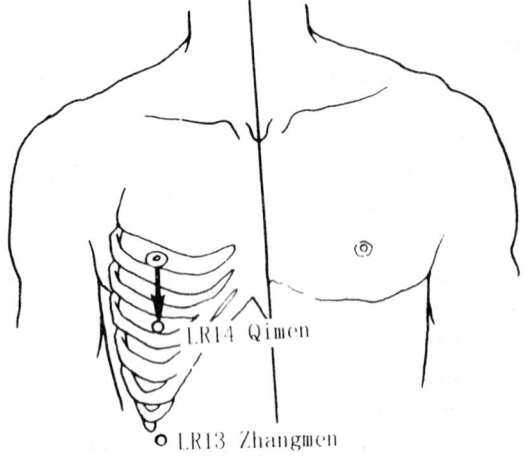

Fig. 10-12

【Indications】
   1) Respiratory Diseases: Cough, dyspnea, shortness of breath.
   2) Digestive Diseases: Abdominal pain, diarrhea, constipation, abdominal distention, borborygmus, stomachache, vomiting, anorexia, infantile malnutrition, jaundice.
   3) Urinary Diseases: Polyuria, gonorrhea, retention of urine.
   4) Other Diseases: Pain in the chest and hypochondrium, pain along the spinal column, lassitude, emaciation, abdominal masses.

【Mechanism of Action】
   1) Zhangmen (LR 13) is the Front-Mu point of the spleen. The spleen dominates the transportation and transformation of water and food, which are the main source of acquired nutrients for the body after birth. Therefore, it is used to treat diseases of the digestive sys-

tem, consumption diseases, lassitude and emaciation due to lack of acquired essence.

2) Earth generates metal. So it can also be used to treat diseases of the respiratory system.

3) The spleen controls blood circulation. Abdominal masses and hepatosplenomegaly due to stagnation of qi and blood can be treated by direct moxibustion to Zhangmen (LR 13) and Pigen (EX-B 4).

【Method】Puncture perpendicularly 0.8-1 cun. Moxibustion is applicable.

【Acupoint Prescriptions】

1) Stony edema: Administering moxibustion to Zhangmen (LR 13) and Rangu (KI 2). (*A-B Classic of Acupuncture and Moxibustion*)

2) Sensation of gas masses of ascending in the abdomen: Zhangmen (LR 13), Shimen (RN 5), Yinjiao (RN 7). (*Experience on Acupuncture and Moxibustion Therapy*)

3) Pain along spinal column: Zhangmen (LR 11), Ciliao (BL 33). (*ibid*)

4) Constipation: Zhangmen (LR 13), Taibai (SP 3), Zhaohai (KI 6). (*Great Compendium of Acupuncture and Moxibustion*)

5) Gastroptosis: Puncturing Zhangmen (LR 13) through Fujie (SP 11), Neiguan (PC 6) and Sanyinjiao (SP 6). (*ibid*)

【Regional Anatomy】Skin-subcutaneous tissue-external oblique muscle of abdomen-transverse muscle of abdomen. In the superficial layer, there are the lateral cutaneous branches of the anterior branches of the 10th and 11th thoracic nerves and the tributaries of the superficial thoracoepigastric of the 10th and 11th posterior intercostal arteries and veins.

LR 14 Qimen (期门)
(Cyclic Gate)

【Source】*Treatise on Exogenous Febrile Diseases*

【Name Explanation】Qi (期), cycle; Men (门), door. The flanks on both sides are like an open door, where the point is located. When the qi of meridian circulates here, it is considered as one cycle. The point is therefore named Qimen.

【Classification】Front-Mu Point of the liver.

【Location】On the chest, directly below the nipple, in the 6th intercostal space, 4 cun lateral to the anterior midline. (See Fig. 10-12).

【Localization】Supine position, first locate Ruzhong (ST 17) which is located in the 4th intercostal space, locate the point in the 2nd ribs directly inferior to Ruzhong (ST 17). For females, the point should be located in the 6th intercostal space on the midclavicular line.

【Indications】

1) Respiratory Diseases: Asthma, cough.

2) Digestive Diseases: Diarrhea, vomiting, hiccups, acid regurgitation, abdominal distention, stomachache, hunger without appetite.

3) Urinary Diseases: retention of urine, enuresis, dysuria.

4) Other Diseases: Fullness feeling in the chest and hypochondrium, malarial disease, sensation of gas masses ascending in the abdomen, evils passing the channels, heat-evil attacking the blood chamber.

【Mechanism of Action】Qimen (LR 14) is the Front-Mu point of the Liver Meridian and has the function of dispersing stagnant liver qi and invigorating the spleen. Therefore, the point is the first choice used to treat hepatitis, cholecystitis and other diseases of the digestive system due to hyperactive liver qi attacking the spleen.

2) Puncturing Qimen (LR 14) is effective to treat sudden cessation of menses, low fever,

chest fullness, anxiety and irritability, due to attacks of exopathogens during menstrual period.

【Method】 Puncture obliquely or subcutaneously 0.5-0.8 cun. Moxibustion is applicable.

【Acupoint Prescriptions】

　　1) Pain in the chest and hypochondrium: Qimen (LR 14), Quepen (ST 12). (*Thousand Golden Prescriptions*)

　　2) Precordial pain with shortness of breath: Qimen (LR 14), Changqiang (DU 1), Tiantu (RN 22), Jiabai (LU 4), Zhongchong (PC 9). (*ibid*)

　　3) Mania due to exogenous febrile disease: Qimen (LR 14), Qihai (RN 6), Quchi (LI 11). (*ibid*)

　　4) Optic atrophy: Qimen (LR 14), Tianquan (PC 2). (*ibid*)

　　5) Ileotyphus: Qimen (LR 14), Dazhui (DU 11), Zusanli (ST 36), Waiguan (SJ 5). (*Abstract of Clinical Experience on Acupuncture and Moxibustion*)

　　6) Gallstones: Qimen (LR 14), Riyue (GB 24). (*Selecton of Treatise of 30 Years*)

　　7) Mass in the hypochondrium and hernia: Qimen (LR 14), Dadun (LR 1). (*Songs of Jade Dragon*)

【Regional Anatomy】 Skin-subcutaneous tissue-inferior border of the greater pectoral muscle-external oblique muscle of abdomen-external intercostal muscle-internal intercostal muscle.

In the superficial layer, there are the lateral cutaneous branches of the 6th intercostal nerve and the tributaries of the thoracoepigastric vein. In the deep layer, there are the 6th intercostal nerve and the branches or tributaries of the 6th posterior intercostal artery and vein.

【Remark】 Puncturing Qimen (LR 14) has a certain effect in the treatment of chronic hepatitis and early cirrhosis. Puncturing Qimen (LR 14) can reduce hepatic blood flow and also increase the amount of white blood cells.

Puncturing Qimen (LR 14) can make the sphincter muscle of the bile duct contract, and become relaxed after withdrawing the needle, and promote the movement of the gallbladder.

Puncturing Qimen (LR 14) can also affect the movement of the urinary bladder. Twisting the needle can make the urinary bladder contract and the internal pressure increase, and when stop twisting, the urinary bladder becomes relaxed and the internal pressure goes down.

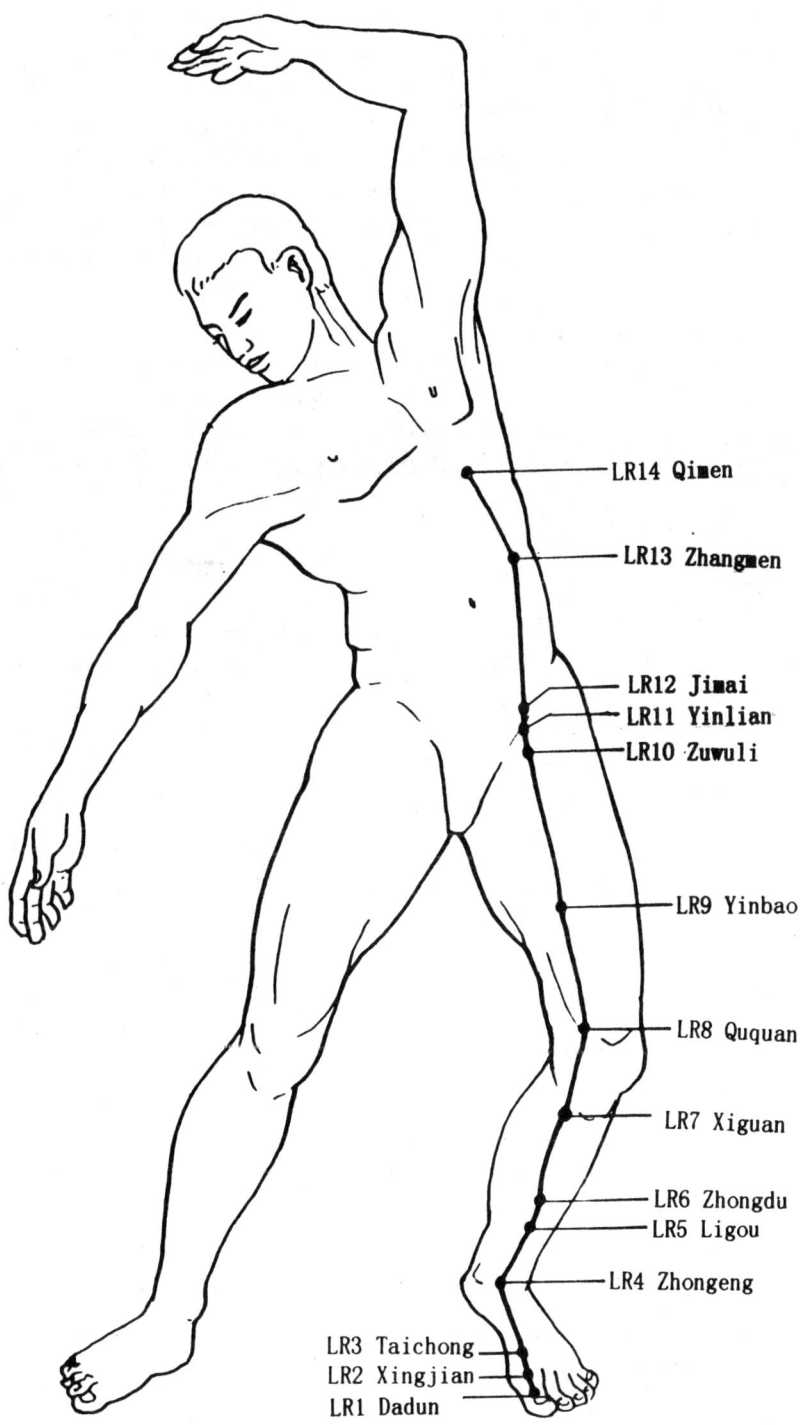

Fig. 10-13 Acupoints of the liver Meridian of Foot Jueyin

Table 10-2 Indications and Actions of Acupoints of the
Liver Meridian of Foot Jueyin

Name of the points	Specific points	Common indications	Specific indications and functions
LR 1 Dadun (大敦)	Jing-(Well) point	Disorders of external genitalia and gynecopathy: irregular menstruation, metrorrhagia, leukorrhagia, nocturnal emission, hernia, retention of urine, enuresis Disorders of the intestines	Soothing the liver, regulating blood, reviving the patient from unconsciousness, dredging the collaterals. Hernia, metrorrhagia, dysfunctional uterine bleeding, hernia, pain of external genitalia, pruritus vulvae, shrinkage of the external genitals, retention of urine, enuresis, manic-depression, stranguria
LR 2 Xingjian (行间)	Ying-(Spring) point		Clearing heat from the liver, soothing the stagnation of qi. Headache, dizziness, insomnia, bad temper, diabetes, cardialgia, hiccup, hematemesis, preapoplexy, wry mouth, manic-depression, swollen knee
LR 3 Taichong (太冲)	Shu-(Stream) point, Yuan-(Source) point		Calming the liver, regulating the flow of qi, dredging the collaterals. Pain of vertex, hypertension, insomnia, enuresis, metrorrhagia, thrombocytopenia, pain over the chest and hypochondrium, hernia, flaccidity of feet
LR 4 Zhongfeng (中封)	Jing-(River) point		Soothing the liver, dredging the collaterals. Hernia, distention of abdomen, coldness of feet, nocturnal emission, pain of waist, retention of urine
LR 5 Ligou (蠡沟)	Luo-(Connecting) point		Soothing the liver and regulating qi, regulating menstruation, promoting diuresis to eliminate dampness-evil. Irregular menstruation, leukorrhagia, pruritus of external genitals, pain of testicle, excessive sexual function, retention of urine, muscle contraction of muscles in the back and waist, aching pain in the tibia
LR 6 Zhongdu (中都)	Xi-(Cleft) point		Dredging the meridian and collaterals, regulating qi and blood, stopping pain. Pain of hypochondrium, abdominal flatulence, hernia, flaccidity of feet due to cold and pain, metrorrhagia, lochiorrhea

Name of the points	Specific points	Common indications	Specific indications and functions
LR 7 Xiguan (膝关)		The same as above.	Dispelling cold and removing dampness, easing joint movement. Pain in the knee, acute arthritis
LR 8 Ququan (曲泉)	Confluent point		Relaxing muscles and tendons, activating collaterals, clearing heat and dampness from the lower Jiao. Retention of urine, leukorrhagia, nocturnal emission, pruritus vulvae, hernia, dysmenorrhea, pain of knee
LR 9 Yinbao (阴包)			Soothing the liver to regulate menstruation, clearing heat and removing dampness. Enuresis, retention of urine, irregular menstruation, soreness in the thigh, pain in the lower abdomen due to lumbosacral pain
LR 10 Zuwuli (足五里)			Clearing away damp heat from lower Jiao. Distention and pain of the lower abdomen, retention of urine, enuresis, hernia, pruritus vulae swelling and pain of testicle, drowsiness
LR 11 Yinlian (阴廉)			Promoting menstruation to stop pain. Irregular menstruation, pain of lower abdomen, sterility in females, pain in the thigh
LR 12 Jimai (急脉)			Dredging the collaterals to stop pain, soothing the liver to regulate qi. Pain of lower abdomen, hernia, vaginal hernia, pain in the penis
LR 13 Zhangmen (章门)	Front—Mu point of the spleen One of the eight influential points (viscera point) Crossing point	Disorders of the stomach and intestine: abdominal distention, diarrhea, vomiting	Soothing the liver and invigorating the spleen, relieving distention and eliminating masses, activating blood circulation to dissipate blood stasis. Abdominal masses, pain over hypochondrium, flaccidity of extremities, jaundice, infantile malnutrition, hiccup, pain of back and waist, hepatosplenomegaly
LR 14 Qimen (期门)	Front-Mu point of the liver Crossing point	Gynecopathy	Dispersing the stagnated liver-qi, invigorating the spleen and stomach. Distension and fullness of the chest and hypochondrium, hiccup, acid regurgitation, hunger with disinclination to eat, heat—evil attacking the blood chamber, heat feeling over the chest, intercostal neuralgia, hepatitis

XI. Acupoints of the Kidney Meridian of Foot Shaoyin

KI 1 Yongquan (涌泉)
(Bubbling Fountain)

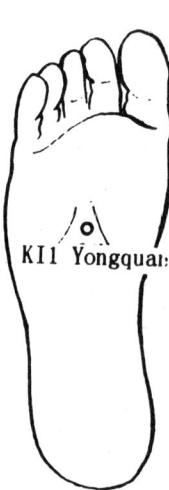

Fig. 10-14

【Source】 *Miraculous Pivot and Plain Questions*

【Name Explanation】 Yong (涌), to gush; Quan (泉), spring. Welled-up water is called gushing spring. The point is in the depression of the sole; the qi of the meridian flows upwards as a gushing spring.

【Classification】 Jing-(Well) Point of the Kidney Meridian of Foot Shaoyin, pertaining to wood in the Five Elements.

【Location】 On the sole, in the depression appearing on the anterior part of the sole when the foot is in the plantar flexion, approximately at the junction of the anterior third and posterior two-thirds of the line connecting the base of the 2nd and 3rd toes and the heel. (See Fig. 10-14).

【Localization】 In the supine position, with the foot in plantar flexion; locate the point in the depression anterior and middle to the sole, approximately one-third intersection from the anterior plantar line to the middle plantar line, slightly posterior to the 2nd and 3rd metatarsophalangeal joint.

【Indications】

1) Diseases along the Course of the Meridian: Cold and pain in feet and knees, pain in the lateral aspect of the femur, heat sensation over the center of the sole.

2) Diseases of Head and Sense Organs: Vertex pain, dizziness, vertigo, darkish complexion, blurring of vision, arcus senilis, inflammation of the throat, stiffness of the root of the tongue, aphonia, epistaxis.

3) Respiratory Diseases: Cough, shortness of breath, hemoptysis.

4) Digestive Diseases: Nausea, vomiting, epigastralgia, diarrhea, dyschesia.

5) Cardiovascular Diseases: Vexation, precordial pain, heart-heat.

6) Urogenital Diseases: Retention of urine, edema, sterility, impotence.

7) Mental Disorders: Coma, infantile convulsion, epilepsy, heat stroke, apoplexy, susceptibility to fright, amnesia and anger.

8) Other Diseases: Gastrointestinal neurosis, hernia, fever, jaundice, hypertension.

【Mechanism of Action】

1) The Kidney Meridian travels along the throat and terminates at the root of the tongue. According to the principles that "Points on the lower portion should be used for the diseases occurred on the upper portion of the body" and "where the meridian passes, where the indications are", Yongquan (KI 1) can be used to treat diseases of the head, face and sense organs. It can have an outstanding effect on headache and dizziness due to hyperactivity of the liver-Yang, sore throat, hysteria and aphasia due to Yin-deficiency.

2) According to the principle that "Jing-(Well) points are used to treat diseases of the Zang-organs," Yongquan (KI 1) is an important point for treating coma, shock, windstroke,

heatstroke and infantile convulsion.

3) The kidney stores the essence of life and is the foundation of the native constitution. So the point can be used to treat all kinds of diseases of viscera, especially those of the urogenital system. Applying moxibustion to this point can correct the position of fetus and reduce blood pressure.

【Method】 Puncture perpendicularly 0.3-0.5 cun. Moxibustion is applicable.

【Acupoint Prescriptions】

1) Cramp in cholera morbus: Yongquan (KI 1) (*A Handbook of Prescriptions for Emergencies*).

2) Sore throat with inability to swallow food: Yongquan (KI 1), Dazhong (KI 4) (*Thousand Golden Prescriptions*)

3) Beriberi marked by flaccidity or numbness and pain of lower limbs: Apply moxibustion to Yongquan (KI 1) (*Comprehension of Bianque's Medicine*)

4) Wind-type epilepsy: Yongquan (KI 1), Shencong (EX-HN 1), Qiangjian (DU 18). (*Experience on Acupuncture and Moxibustion Therapy*)

5) Ache and weakness in the tibia: Yongquan (KI 1), Taichong (LR 3). (*ibid*)

6) Rubella: Yongquan (KI 1), Huantiao (GB 30). (*ibid*)

7) Epilepsy: Yongquan (KI 1), Xinshu (BL 15), Zusanli (ST 36), Jiuwei (RN 15), Zhongwan (RN 12), Shaoshang (LU 1), Juque (RN 14) (*Great Compendium of Acupuncture and Moxibustion*)

8) Toxic shock: The Main points are Yongquan (KI 1), Zusanli (ST 36) and the supplementary points are Subcortex (AT 4), Arenal Gland (TG 29) and Endocrine (CO 18). At first, strong stimulation is used, if no obvious effect is gained, ear needling should be administered. For some patients, moxibustion to Baihui (DU 20) is added. (*Abstract of Clinical Experience on Acupuncture and Moxibustion*)

9) Tuberculosis: Yongquan (KI 1), Xinshu (BL 15), Fenglong (ST 40). (*Songs of Jade Dragon*)

【Regional Anatomy】 Skin-subcutaneous tissue-plantar aponeurosis-2nd common digital nerve of sole-2nd lumbrical muscle. In the superficial layer, there are the branches of the medial plantar nerve. In the deep layer, there are the 2nd common digital nerve of the sole and the 2nd common digital artery and vein of the sole.

【Remark】 Puncturing Yongquan (KI 1) is very useful for reducing blood pressure. Applying moxibustion to this point can adjust the position of fetus.

KI 2 Rangu （然谷）
（Blazing Valley）

【Source】 *Miraculous Pivot*

【Name Explanation】 Ran (然), tuberosity of the navicular bone; Gu (谷), valley. The point is in the depression below the tuberosity of the navicular bone, at the junction of the red and white skin.

【Classification】 Ying-(Spring) Point of the Kidney Meridian of Foot Shaoyin, pertaining to fire in the Five Elements.

【Location】 On the medial border of the foot, below the tubersity of the navicular bone, as in a valley. (See Fig. 10-15.)

【Localization】 In sitting or supine position, locate the point anterior and inferior to the medial malleolus, in the depression anterior and inferior to the tuberosity of the navicular bone.

【Indications】
1) Diseases along the Course of the Meridian: Pain and numbness of the legs, swelling on the dorsum of the foot, sprain, beriberi due to cold-damp evil.

2) Diseases of Head and Sense Organs: Painful throat, stiffness of the root of the tongue, aphonia.

3) Respiratory Diseases: Hemoptysis, shortness of breath.

4) Cardiovascular Diseases: Precordial pain, spontaneous perspiration, night sweating.

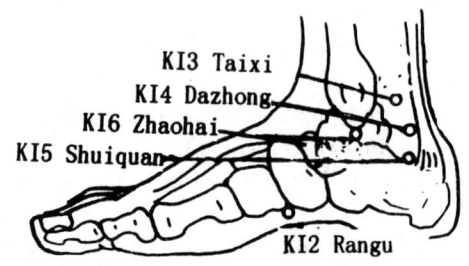

Fig. 10-15

5) Urogenital Diseases: Irregular menstruation, prolapse of the uterus, pruritus vulvae, impotence, emission, unclear urine, dysuria, retention of urine.

6) Digestive Diseases: Diarrhea, dysentery, anorexia.

7) Mental Disorders: Infantile convulsion, lockjaw, vulnerability to fright, manic depressive phychosis, tetanus.

8) Other Diseases: Diabetes, jaundice, fullness and pain in the lower abdomen.

【Mechanism of Action】 See Yongquan (KI 1).

【Method】 Puncture perpendicularly 0.8-1.2 cun. Moxibustion is applicable.

【Acupoint Prescriptions】
1) Precordial pain with cold limbs: Rangu (KI2), Taixi (KI3). (*Miraculous Pivot*)

2) Convulsive diseases: Rangu (KI 2), Yixi (BL 45). (*A-B Classic of Acupuncture and Moxibustion*)

3) Sterility: Moxibustion to Rangu (KI 2). (*Thousand Golden Prescriptions*)

4) Stony edema: Moxibustion to Rangu (KI 2), Qichong (ST 30), Siman (KI 14), Zhangmen (LR 13). (*ibid*)

5) Febrile disease with dysphoria, cold feet and hyporhidrosis: Rangu (KI 2), Taixi (KI 3). (*ibid*)

6) Profuse sweating due to malaria: Rangu (KI 2), Kunlun (BL 60) (*Experience on Acupuncture and Moxibustion Therapy*)

7) Slobbering: Rangu (KI 2), Fuliu (KI 7). (*ibid*)

【Regional Anatomy】 Skin-subcutaneous tissue-abductor muscle of great toe-tendon of long flexor muscle of toes. In the superficial layer, there are the medial cutaneous branches of the saphenous nerve to the leg, the cutaneous branches of the medial plantar nerve and the tributaries of the dorsal venous network of the foot. In the deep layer, there are the medial plantar nerve and the medial plantar artery and vein.

【Remark】 Rangu (KI 2) can be used for reducing blood pressure to primary hypertension. Puncturing this point has a certain influence on acidocyte and can also improve the endocrine function. For example, the comparison of the points which have the action of improving the endocrine system with the effect caused by injecting ACTH (25 unit) showed that Rangu (KI 2) had a stronger effect than that of the injection of ACTH.

KI 3 Taixi (太溪)
(Supreme Stream)

【Source】 *Miraculous Pivot*.
【Name Explanation】 Tai(太), great; Xi(溪), canyon. The point is in the depression between the medial malleolus and Achille's tendon, as in a vast canyon.
【Classification】 Shu-(Stream) Point and Yuan-(Source) Point of the Kidney Meridian of Foot Shaoyin, pertaining to earth in the Five Elements.
【Location】 On the medial side of the foot, posterior to the medial malleolus, in the depression between the tip of the medial malleolus and Achilles tendon. (See Fig. 10-15).
【Localization】 In sitting or supine position, locate the point between the posterior side of the medial malleolus and anterior side of the Achilles tendon, approximately at the level of the tip of the medial malleolus.
【Indications】
1) Diseases along the Course of the Meridian: Pain along spinal column, arthralgia, pain and extreme cold of the lower limbs, limited movement of the legs, painful and swollen heel and medial malleolus.
2) Diseases of Head and Sense Organs: Headache, dizziness, painful and swollen throat, toothache, tinnitus, deafness, epistaxis.
3) Respiratory Diseases: Cough, dyspnea, hemoptysis, chest pain, fullness in the chest and hypochondrium, sticky phlegm.
4) Digestive Diseases: Cholera morbus, diarrhea, constipation.
5) Cardiovascular Diseases: Palpitation, precordial pain.
6) Urogenital diseases: Irregular menstruation, mass in the abdomen, emission, impotence, whitish and turbid urine, frequent micturition, dark urine.
7) Mental Diseases: Insomnia, amnesia, vexation, irritability, susceptibility to fright.
8) Other Diseases: Diabetes, acute mastitis, hernia due to cold.
【Mechanism of Action】
1) The kidney is the foundation of the native constitution and stores the essence of life which is the material basis of reproduction. Taixi (KI 3) is the Yuan-(Source) point and has the function of replenishing essence and tonifying the kidney. Therefore, Taixi (KI 3) is applied to treat diseases of reproductive system due to the deficiency of kidney.
2) Taixi (KI 3) can be used to nourish Yin and suppress hyperactivity of Yang. That is why it is used for headache, dizziness, tinnitus, deafness due to the deficiency of the liver-yin, kidney-yin and hyperactivity of liver-yang.
3) Puncturing or pressing Taixi (KI 3) and Kunlun (BL 60) with the thumb has an immediate effect on painful throat, toothache and epistaxis due to deficiency of kidney-yin and flaring-up of fire of the deficient type.
4) The kidney stores essence and pertains to "water", the heart controls mental and emotional activities and pertains to "fire". The point can be used to treat mental diseases due to disharmony between the heart and the kidney.
5) The kidney dominates the storage and is in charge of discharge and retention. Diabetes and constipation result from the dysfunction of the kidney in controlling the discharge and retention.
6) Taixi (KI3) is an important point to invigorate primordial qi. Cholera morbus and diarrhea are easily to consume promordia qi, so the point is used to recuperate the depleted Yang and rescue the patient from danger.

【Method】 Puncture perpendicularly 0.5-1 cun. Moxibustion is applicable.
【Acupoint Prescriptions】
   1) Convulsion: Taixi (KI 3), Taibai (SP 3). (*A-B Classic of Acupuncture and Moxibustion*)
   2) Numbness in tibia: Taixi (KI 3), Ciliao (BL 32), Pangguangshu (BL 28). (*ibid*)
   3) Periumbilical colic due to invasion of cold: Taixi (KI 3), Xingjian (LR 2), Huangshu (KI 16), Ganshu (BL 18). (*Experience on Acupuncture and Moxibustion Therapy*)
   4) Epistaxis: Taixi (KI 3), Yinbai (SP 1), Fengmen (BL 12), Duiduan (DU 27), Naokong (GB 19). (*ibid*)
   5) Precardial pain: Moxibustion to Taixi (KI 3) and Kunlun (BL 60), then Fructus Tousendan Podwer is used orally. (*Plain Questions*)
   6) Spitting blood and shivering: Taixi (KI 3), Zusanli (ST 36), Lieque (LU 7), Taiyuan (LU 9). (*Great Compendium of Acupuncture and Moxibustion*)
   7) Painful penis: Taixi (KI 3), Yuji (LU 10), Zhongji (RN 3), Sanyinjiao (SP 6). (*ibid*)
   8) Painful and swollen teeth: Taixi (KI 3), Jiache (ST 6), Hegu (LI 4). (*ibid*)
   9) Pain in the upper part of the body: Taixi (KI 3), Taiyuan (LU 9), Shuigou (DU 26). (*ibid*)
   10) Swollen feet with difficulty in walking: Taixi (KI 3), Kunlun (BL 60), Shenmai (BL 61). (*Songs of Jade Dragon*)
   11) Aching and numbness of the feet: Taixi (KI 3), Pucan (BL 61), Neiting (ST 44). (*Songs on Point Selection of Miscellaneous Diseases*)
【Regional Anatomy】 Skin-subcutaneous tissue-between tendons of posterior tibial muscle and long flexor muscle of toes and tendon of plantar muscle and Achilles tendon-on flexor muscle of great toe. In the superficial layer, there are the medial cutaneous branches of the saphenous nerve to the leg and the tributaries of the great saphenous vein. In the deep layer, there are the tibial nerve and the posterior tibial artery and vein.
【Remark】 Puncturing Taixi (KI 3) can improve the respiratory function. For instance, puncturing at Ximen (PC 4), Taixi (KI 3), Yuji (LU 10) can reduce pendular movement of mediastinum due to thoracotomy. Acupuncture at Taixi (KI 3) can also improve renal function. It was reported that puncturing at Taixi (KI 3), Lieque (LU 7) could improve urinary function, increase output of phelnl red, reduce proteinuria, and lower the blood pressure. The effect could last for 2-3 hours or even as long as several days for individual case. It also has some effect on nephritic edema. Puncturing the point can influence acidocyte. It was reported that acidocyte reduced by 33.5% after retaining the needle at Taixi (KI 3) for 2 minutes and reduced by 44.2% after retaining the needle for 10 minutes.

KI 4 Dazhong (大钟)
(Big Bell)

【Source】 *Miraculous Pivot*.
【Name Explanation】 Da (大), large; Zhong (钟), heel. The point is at the heel. Since the calcaneous bone is large, it is called Dazhong.
【Classification】 Luo-(Connecting) Point of the Kidney Meridian of Foot-Shaoyin.
【Location】 On the medial side of the foot, posterior and inferior to the medial malleolus, in the depression medial to the attachment of the Achilles tendon. (See Fig. 10-15).
【Localization】 In sitting or supine position, locate the point posterior and inferior to the medial malleous, approximately anterior to the Achilles tendon, or first locate Taixi (KI 3) and

Qugu (KI 5), this point is located at the middle of these two points and approximately anterior to the Achilles tendon.

【Indications】

1) Diseases along the Course of the Meridian: Stiffness and pain along spinal column, pain of the heel.

2) Diseases of Head and Sense Organs: Pharyngodynia, tongue-bleeding.

3) Respiratory Diseases: Cough, dyspnea, fullness feeling of the chest.

4) Digestive Diseases: Dyschasia, constipation, abdominal fullness, vomiting, heat sensation in the mouth, dry tongue.

5) Urogenital Diseases: Dysuria, retention of urine, stranguria, irregular menstruation.

6) Mental Disorders: Dementia, timorousness, susceptibility to anger, insomnia, amnesia, dreaminess, hysteria.

【Method】 Puncture perpendicularly 0.3-0.5 cun. Moxibustion is applicable.

【Mechanism of Action】

1) The Kidney Meridian runs through the vertebral column and connects with gall bladder by its collaterals, so Dazhong (KI 4) is used for stiffness and pain along the spinal column and pain of the heel.

2) The kidney is reponsible for reproduction, controls water metabolism and connects with the urinary bladder. So it is used for diseases of urogenital system.

3) Refer to Yongquan (KI 1) and Taixi (KI 3) points for further details.

【Acupoint Prescriptions】

1) Terror and fear: Dazhong (KI 4), Ximen (PC 4). (*Supplement to Thousand Golden Prescriptions*)

2) Hemoptysis: Dazhong (KI 4), Rangu (KI 2), Xinshu (BL 15). (*Experience on Acupuncture and Moxibustion Therapy*)

3) Stridor serraticus: Dazhong (KI 4), Dabao (SP 21). (*ibid*)

【Regional Anatomy】 Skin-subcutaneous tissue-anterior side of tendon of plantar muscle and Archilles tendon. In the superficial layer, there are the medial cutaneous branches of the saphenous nerve to network formed by the medial malleous branches and the calcaneal branches of the posterior tibial artery.

KI 5 Shuiquan (水泉)
(Water Fountain)

【Source】 *A-B Classic of Acupuncture and Moxibustion.*

【Name Explanation】 Shui (水), water; Quan (泉), spring. The water spring means water source. The kidney dominates water clearance. This point is a Xi-(Cleft) point of the Kidney Meridian and is indicated in cases of dysuria.

【Classification】 Xi-(Cleft) Point of the Kidney Meridian of Foot Shaoyin.

【Location】 On the medial side of the foot, posterior and inferior to the medial malleolus, 1 cun directly below Taixi (KI 3), in the depression on the medial side of the tuberosity of the calcaneum. (See Fig. 10-15).

【Localization】 In sitting or supine position, first locate Taixi (KI 3), this point is located 1 cun directly inferior to Taixi (KI 3) on the calcaneus.

【Indications】

1) Obstetrical and Gynecological Diseases: Irregular menstruation, dysmenorrhea, amenorrhea, prolapse of uterus, metrorrhagia and metrostaxis.

2) Urinary Diseases: Dysuria, stranguria.

3) Other Diseases: Blurred vision, myopia, abdominal pain.
【Mechanism of Action】See Dazhong (KI 4).
【Method】Puncture perpendicularly 0.3-0.5 cun. Moxibustion is applicable.
【Regional Anatomy】Skin-subcutaneous tissue-medial side of calcaneus. In the superficial layer, there are the medial cutaneous branches of the saphenous nerve to the leg and the tributaries of the great saphenous vein. In the deep layer, there are the posterior tibial artery and vein, the medial and lateral plantar nerves and the medial calcaneal branches from the tibial nerve.

KI 6 Zhaohai (照海)
(Shining Sea)

【Source】 A-B Classic of Acupuncture and Moxibustion.
【Name Explanation】Zhao (照), to shine; Hai (海), sea. The point pertains to the Kidney Meridian and the qi is abundant as the sea. It means that the real Yang of the kidney may illuminate the whole body.
【Classification】 One of the Eight Confluent Points, connecting with the Yinqiao Meridian.
【Location】 On the medial side of the foot, in the depression below the tip of the medial malleolus. (See Fig. 10-15).
【Localization】 In sitting position with both soles face to face, select the point in the depression inferior to the medial malleolus, directly below the tip of the medial malleolus; or locate the point in the depression slightly inferior to the intersection between the vertical line of the medial malleolus and the transverse line inferior side of the medial malleolus.
【Indication】
  1) Diseases of Head and Sense Organs: Heaviness of the head, blurring of vision, dry and painful throat, lockjaw, conjunctival congestion, acute throat problems, darkish complexion.
  2) Respiratory Diseases: Cough, asthma, abundant expectoration, hemoptysis.
  3) Digestive Diseases: Anorexia, constipation.
  4) Gynecopathy: Irregular menstruation, leukorrhea with reddish discharge, prolapse of uterus, pruritus vulvae, dystocia, lochiostasis, postpartum abdominal pain.
  5) Urinary Diseases: Frequent micturition, yellow urine, stranguria.
  6) Mental Diseases: Night time epilepsy, terror, insomnia, depressive syndrome, susceptibility to sorrow.
  7) Other Diseases: Gastrointestinal neurosis, hernia, flaccidity in feet.
【Mechanism of Action】
  1) The Yinqiao Meridian travels from Zhaohai (KI 6) point, controlling the opening and closing of the eyelids as well as the motion of the lower limbs with the coordination of the Yangqiao Meridian. Yinqiao diseases are characterized by tension of Yin Merdians with relaxation of Yang Meridians. So Zhaohai (KI 6) is used to treat night time epilepsy, flaccidity in lower limbs with strephenopodia.
  2) The Kidney Meridian runs into the lung. Zhaohai (KI 6) is one of the Eight Confluent Points and often used together with Lieque (LU 7) to treat diseases of thoracic-diaphragmatic region and laryngopharynx. Therefore, the indications of Zhaohai includes diseases of respiratory system, such as cough, asthma and dyspnea, excessive phlegm, hemoptysis, sore throat, etc.
  3) For further applications, refer to Taixi (KI 3)
【Method】 Puncture perpendicularly 0.5-1 cun. Moxibustion is applicable.

【Acupoint Prescriptions】
1) Diseases of the foot: Zhaohai (KI 6), Shenmai (BL 62). (*Experience on Acupuncture and Moxibustion Therapy*)
2) Retention of placenta: Zhaohai (KI 6), Waiguan (SJ 5). (*Songs of Secret on Acupuncture and Moxibustion*)
3) Constipation: Zhaohai (KI 6), Zhigou (SJ 6). (*Songs of Jade Dragon*)
4) Seven kinds of hernia: Zhaohai (KI 6), Yinjiao (RN 7), Ququan (LR 8), Qihai (RN 6), Guanyuan (RN 4). (*Songs of Xihong*)
5) Removal of placenta: Zhaohai (KI 6), Neiguan (PC 6). (*Songs on Point Selection of Miscellaneous Diseases*)

【Regional Anatomy】Skin-subcutaneous tissue-tendon of posterior tibial muscle. In the superficial layer, there are the medial cutaneous branches of the saphenous nerve to the leg and the tributaries of the great saphenous vein. In the deep layer, there are the branches or tributaries of the medial tarsal artery and vein.

【Remark】Zhaohai (KI 6) point can be used to regulate the renal function. After a healthy person drinks 1.5 L of water on an empty stomach, this urinary function can be improved by puncturing Zhaohai (KI 6). Within 3 hours, the average micturition volume of the punctured group is 1.78 L while that of the control group is 1.48 L. Puncturing Zhaohai (KI 6), Lieque (LU 7), and Taixi (KI 3) on a patient with nephritis can obviously strengthen the urinary function, increase the output of phenolsal fonphthalein excretion and reduce both proteinouria and blood pressure levels.

KI 7 Fuliu (复溜)
(Returning Carrent)

【Source】*Miraculous Pivot and Plain Questions.*
【Name Explanation】Fu (复), continuing; Liu (溜), flowing. The point is above Zhaohai and refers to the qi of meridian flowing into the "sea", re-emerging and continuing to flow.
【Classification】Jing-(River) Point of the Kidney Meridian of Foot Shaoyin, pertaining to metal in the Five Elements.
【Location】On the medial side of the leg, 2 cun directly above Taixi (KI 3), anterior to the Achilles tendon. (See Fig. 10-16.)
【Localization】In sitting or supine position, first locate Taixi (KI 3), then locate the point 2 cun directly superior to Taixi (KI 3), anterior side to the Achilles tendon.
【Indications】
1) Diseases along the Course of the Meridian: Stiffness and pain along the spinal column, waekness of the feet, limited movement of the waist.
2) Diseases of Head and Sense Organs: Dry mouth, pain in nostrils.
3) Digestive Diseases: Diarrhea, borborygmus, abdominal pain, abdominal distention, constipation, dysentery, with pus and bloody stools, hemorrhoid.
4) Urinary Diseases: Retention of urine, five types of stranguria, emission, metrorrhagia and metrostaxis, gynecological diseases.

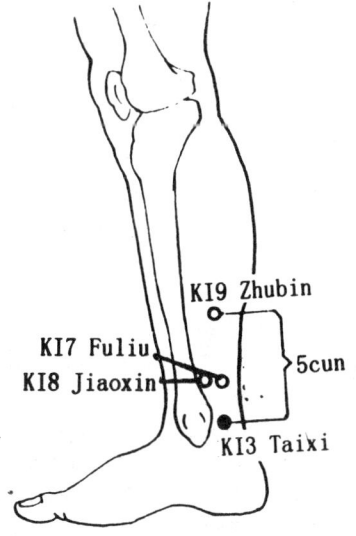

Fig. 10-16

5) Mental Disorders: Manic-depressive syndrome, susceptibility to anger.

6) Other Diseases: Edema, swollen limbs, weak and thready pulse, fever, lassitude, profuse sweating, night sweating, diabetes.

【Mechanism of Action】Fuliu (KI 7) pertains to "metal", corresponds to the lung and has the function of warming the kidney to promote diuresis and regulate Ying and Wei. So Fuliu (KI 7) is characterized by treating profuse sweating, anhidrosis, night sweat, edema. See Taixi (KI 3) for further applications.

【Method】Puncture perpendicularly 0.5-1 cun. Moxibustion is applicable.

【Acupoint Prescriptions】

1) Pain of lower abdomen: Fuliu (KI 7), Zhongfeng (LR 4), Shenshu (BL 23), Chengjin (BL 56), Yinbao (LR 9), Chengshan (BL 57), Dadun (LR 1). (*Thousand Golden Prescriptions*)

2) Dry sensation of pharynx: Fuliu (KI 7), Zhaohai (KI 6), Taichong (LR 3), Zhongfeng (LR 4). (*Experience on Acupuncture and Moxibustion Therapy*)

3) Dysentery: Fuliu (KI 7), Shugu (BL 65), Huiyang (BL 35). (*ibid*)

4) Susceptibility to anger: Fuliu (KI 7), Laogong (PC 8). (*ibid*)

5) Tympanites: Fuliu (KI 7), Zhongfeng (LR 4), Gongsun (SP 4), Taibai (SP 3), Shuifen (RN 9), Sanyinjiao (SP 6). (*A Great Compendium of Acupuncture and Moxibustion*).

6) Pulmonary tuberculosis: Fuliu (KI 7), Dazhu (BL 11), Dazhui (DU 14). (*Abstract of Clinical Experience on Acupuncture and Moxibustion*)

7) Infantile acute nephritis: Main points: Fuliu (KI 7), Feiyang (BL 58), Guanyuan (RN 4); Supplementary points: Sanyinjiao (SP 6), Zusanli (ST 36). (*ibid*)

8) Malaria with more chills than fever: Fuliu (KI 7); Malaria with more fever than chills: Jianshi (PC 5). (*Songs for Easy Acupoint Selection*)

【Regional Anatomy】Skin-subcutaneous tissue-anterior side of tendon of plantar muscle and Archilles tendon-long flexor of great toe. In the superficial layer, there are the medial cutaneous branches of the saphenous nerve to the leg and the tributaries of the great saphenous vein. In the deep layer, there are the tibial nerve and the posterior tibial artery and vein.

KI 8 Jiaoxin (交信)
(Meeting Spleen Meridian)

【Source】*A-B Classic of Acupuncture and Moxibustion*.

【Name Explanation】Jiao (交), crossing; Xin (信), belief. Xin is one of the Five Moralities (benevolence, loyalty, courtesy, intelligence and belief), pertaining to earth and referring to the Spleen. It is a crossing point with the Spleen Meridian.

【Classification】Xi-(Cleft) Point of the Yinqiao Meridian.

【Location】On the medial side of the leg, 2 cun above Taixi (KI 3), and 0.5 cun anterior to Fuliu (KI 7), posterior to the medial border of the tibia. (See Fig. 10-16.)

【Localization】In sitting or supine position, first locate Fuliu (KI 7), then locate the point 0.5 cun anterior to Fuliu (KI 7), or locate the point in the middle between Fuliu (KI 7) and the posterior side of the medial side of the tibia.

【Indications】

1) Diseases along the Course of the Meridian: Numbness and pain in medial side of legs, pain along spinal column.

2) Urogenital Diseases: Irregular menstruation, metrorrhagia and metrostaxis, amenorrhea, prolapse of uterus, pruritus vulvae, painful and swollen testicles, five types of stran-

guria, retention of urine.

　　3) Digestive Diseases: Diarrhea, constipation, dysentery.
【Mechanism of Action】See Taixi (KI 3).
【Method】Puncture perpendicularly 0.6-1.2 cun. Moxibustion is applicable.
【Acupoint Prescriptions】
　　1) Incarcerated hernia: Jiaoxin (KI 8), Zhongdu (LR 6), Daju (ST 27), Qugu (RN 2). (*Experience on Acupuncture and Moxibustion Therapy*)
　　2) Metrorrhagia: Jiaoxin (KI 8), Yingu (KI 10), Taichong (LR 3), Sanyinjiao (SP 6). (*ibid*)
　　3) Metrorrhagia due to deficiency of qi: Tianxin (KI 8), Heyang (BL 55). (*Songs of Hundreds of Symptoms*)
【Regional Anatomy】Skin-subcutaneous tissue-long flexor muscle of toes-posterior side of posterior tibial muscle-long flexor muscle of great toe. In the superficial layer, there are the medial cutaneous branches of the saphenous nerve of the leg and the tributaries of the great saphenous vein. In the deep layer, there are the tibial nerve and the posterior tibial artery and vein.

KI 9 Zhubin （筑宾）
（Guest Building）

【Source】*A-B Classic of Acupuncture and Moxibustion*.
【Name Explanation】Zhu (筑), strong; Bin (宾), knee and leg. The point is on the medial side of the leg. It has the function of strengthening the knee and leg.
【Classification】Xi-(Cleft) Point of the Yinwei Meridian.
【Location】On the medial side of the leg and on the line connecting Taixi (KI 3) and Yingu (KI 10), 5 cun above Taixi (KI 3), medial and inferior to the gastrocnemius muscle belly. (See Fig. 10-16).
【Localization】In sitting position or in the supine position, first locate Taixi (KI 3), then locate the point 5 cun directly superior to Taixi (KI 3), 2 cun posterior to medial side of the tibia.
【Indications】
　　1) Diseases along the Course of the Meridian: Pain in the medial aspect of the shank, weakness of the legs, systremma.
　　2) Mental Disorders: Manic-depressive syndrome, epilepsy, saliva regurgitation.
　　3) Other Diseases: Swollen and painful tongue, hernia, infantile umbilical hernia.
【Mechanism of Action】See Taixi (KI 3).
【Method】Puncture perpendicularly 1-1.5 cun. Moxibustion is applicable.
【Acupoint Prescription】
　　1) Vomiting and salivation: Zhubin (KI 9), Shaohai (HT 3). (*Experience on Acupuncture and Moxibustion Therapy*)
　　2) Wagging tongue: Zhubin (KI 9) and Taiyi (ST 23). (*ibid*)
【Regional Anatomy】Skin-subcutaneous tissue-triceps muscle of calf. In the superficial layer, there are the medial cutaneous branches of the saphenous nerve of the leg and the superficial veins. In the deep layer, there are the tibial nerve and the posterior tibial artery and vein.

KI 10 Yingu （阴谷）
（Yin Valley）

【Source】 *Miraculous Pivot*.
【Name Explanation】 Yin （阴）, Yin of Yin-Yang; Gu （谷）, valley. The interior is Yin. The point is at the medial side of the knee joint; the local depression is like a valley.
【Classification】 He-（Sea） Point of the Kidney Meridian of Foot Shaoyin, pertaining to water in the Five Elements.
【Location】 On the medial side of the popliteal fossa, between the tendons of the semitendinous and semimembranous mucles when the knee is flexed. (See Fig. 10-17.)
【Localization】 In sitting position with the knee flexed, locate the point on the medial side of the popliteal transverse line, between the tendons of m. semimembranous and semitendinous muscle. (See Fig. 10-18)
【Indications】

1)Diseases along the Course of the Meridian: Pain in the medial aspect of the thigh, pain in knee joint.

2) Digestive Diseases: Abdominal distention, epigastralgia.

3) Urogenital diseases: Irregular menstruation, metrorrhagia and metrostaxis, leukorrhea, pain in pudendum, impotence, eczema of scrotum, dysuria, pain in pudendum during urination.

4)Other Diseases: Hernia, protrusion of the tongue with salivation, manic-depressive syndrome.

【Mechanism of Action】

1) The kidney is in charge of reproduction and controls the water metabolism. Yingu(KI 10)can be used to strengthen the kidney, regulate menstruation and alleveate water retention. So it can be used to treat the diseases of urogenital system caused by the deficiency of kidney qi.

2) Because the Kidney Meridian terminates at the root of the tongue, the point can be used to treat persistent protrusion of the tongue with salivation.

3) Deficiency of kidney-yang may result in deficiency of spleen-yang. So the disorders of gastrointestinal system due to deficiency of both the spleen and the kidney can be treated by puncturing Yingu (KI10) point.

【Method】 Puncture perpendicularly 1-1.5 cun. Moxibustion is applicable.
【Acupoint Prescriptions】

1) Dysuria: Yingu (KI 10), Dadun (LR 1), Jimen (SP 11), Weizhong (BL 40), Weiyang (BL 39). (*Experience on Acupuncture and Moxibustion Therapy*)

2) Retention of urine: Yingu (KI 10), Yinlingquan (SP 9). (*Great Compendium of Acupuncture and Moxibustion*)

3) Phlegm retention: Yingu (KI 10), Rangu (KI 2), Fuliu (KI 7). (*ibid*)

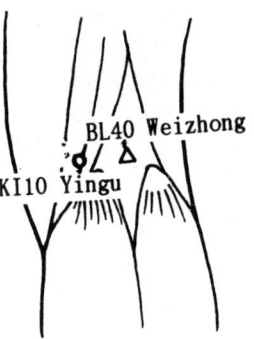

Fig. 10-17

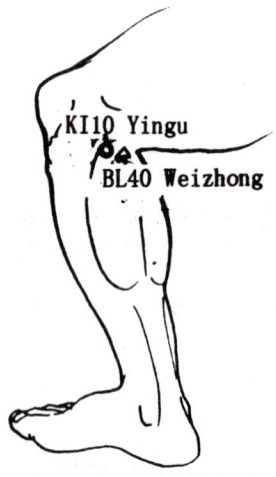

Fig. 10-18

4) Dark urine: Yingu (KI 10), Taixi (KI 3), Shenshu (BL 27), Qihai (RN 6), Pangguangshu (BL 28), Guanyuan (RN 4). (*ibid*)

【Regional Anatomy】 Skin-subcutaneous tissue-between tendons of semimembranous muscle and semitendinous muscle-medial head of gastrocnemius muscle. In the superficial layer, there are the posterior cutaneous nerves of the thigh and the subcutaneous veins. In the deep layer, there are the branches of the superior medial genicular artery and vein.

【Remark】 Puncturing Yingu (KI 10) can arouse the contraction of the bladder. It is also reported that puncturing at Yingu (KI 10), Gongsun (SP 4) and Zusanli (ST 36) can inhibit the secretion of intestinal juice. Puncturing Yingu (KI 10) point has some diuresis-inducing functions. Similar to Zhaohai (KI 6), Yingu (KI 10) can be used to increase the average output of urination for healthy people.

KI 11 Henggu （横骨）
（Transverse Bone）

【Source】 *A-B Classic of Acupuncture and Moxibustion*

【Name Explanation】 Henggu （横骨） is the ancient name of the pubis. The point is on the superior border of the pubis.

【Classification】 The Crossing Point of the Kidney Meridian of Foot-Shaoyin and the Chong Meridian.

【Location】 On the lower abdomen, 5 cun below the center of the umbilicus and 0.5 cun lateral to the anterior midline. (See Fig. 10-19.)

【Localization】 In the supine position, first locate Qugu (RN 2) which is located in the upper margin of symphysis pubis on the linea alba, then locate the point 0.5 cun lateral to Qugu (RN 2).

【Indications】
1) Urogenital Diseases: Pain in pudendum, amenorrhea, emission, impotence, enuresis, stranguria, retention of urine, pain in lower abdomen.

2) Other Diseases: Hernia, lumbago, red, swollen and painful eyes.

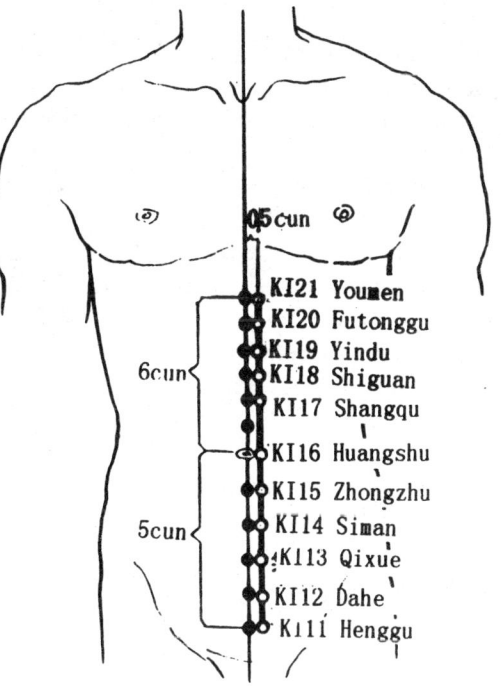

Fig. 10-19

【Mechanism of Action】 This point lies in the place where the organs of the urogenital system converge. Based on the principle that where the point locates, where the indications are, puncturing this point can treat the diseases mentioned above.

【Method】 Puncture perpendicularly 1-1.5 cun. Moxibustion is applicable.

【Acupoint Prescriptions】
1) Dysuria: Henggu (KI 11), Daju (ST 27), Qimen (LR 14). (*Thousand Golden Prescriptions and Experience on Acupuncture and Moxibustion Therapy*)

2) Abdominal pain due to stagnation of qi: Henggu (KI 11), Dadu (SP 2). (*Songs of*

Xihong)

【Regional Anatomy】Skin-subcutaneous tissue-anterior sheath of rectus muscle of abdomen-pryamidal muscle-rectus muscle of abdomen. In the superficial layer, there are the anterior cutaneous branches of the iliohypogastric nerve and the tributaries of the superficial epigastric vein. In the deep layer, there are the branches of the inferior epigastric artery and vein and the branches of the anterior branches of the 11th and 12th thoracic nerves.

【Remark】For stranuria due to occuit saoral vertihral fissare, puncturing Zhongji (RN 3), Henggu (KI 11) and Sanyinjiao (SP 6) can cause an obvious effect.

KI 12 Dahe （大赫）
（Big Glory）

【Source】*A-B Classic of Acupuncture and Moxibustion.*
【Name Explanation】Da（大）, great; He,（赫）plentiful. This point is the Confluent Point of the Kidney Meridian and Chongmai, where the Primary qi of the Lower Jiao is plentiful.
【Classification】The Crossing Point of the Kidney Meridian of Foot Shaoyin and the Chong Meridian.
【Location】On the lower abdomen, 4 cun below the center of the umbilicus and 0.5 cun lateral to the anterior midline. (See Fig. 10-19).
【Localization】In the supine position, first locate Zhongji (RN 3) which is located 1 cun directly superior to the upper margin of symphysis pubis on the linea alba, the point is located 0.5 cun lateral to Zhongji (RN 3).
【Indications】
    1) Digestive Diseases: Diarrhea, dysentery, pain in the lower abdomen.
    2) Urinary Diseases: Pain in pudendum, prolapse of uterus, irregular menstruation, dysmenorrhea, consumptive disease, emission, leucorrhea, pain in penis, enuresis, retention of urine, five types of stranguria.
    3) Other Diseases: Red swollen and painful eyes.
【Mechanism of Action】According to its location, this point is often used to treat urinary and digestive diseases.
【Method】Puncture perpendicularly 1-1.5 cun. Moxibustion is applicable.
【Acupoint Prescription】Spermatorrhea and flaccid construction of the penis: Dahe (KI 12), Rangu (KI 2). (*Experience on Acupuncture and Moxibustion Therapy*)
【Regional Anatomy】Skin-subcutaneous tissue-anterior sheath of rectus muscle of abdomen-superior and lateral border of pyramidal muscle-rectus muscle of abdomen. In the superficial layer, there are the branches of the superficial epigastric artery and vein, the anterior cutaneous branches of the anterior branches of the 11th and 12th thoracic and 1st lumbar nerves and the accompanying arteries and veins. In the deep layer, there are the branches of the inferior epigastric artery and vein, the muscular branches of the anterior branches of the 11th and 12th thoracic nerves and the related intercostal arteries and veins.
【Remark】Puncturing Dahe (KI 12) has some influence on the ovulation function of the ovaries. The experiment conducted by needling Dahe (KI 12), Zhongji (RN 3) and Guanyuan (RN 4) has shown that the sole acupuncture or acupuncture with luteinizing releasing hormone and follicular hormones may both cause changes of levels of plasm luteotropic hormone and follicular hormones, especially the combined method. It shows that acupuncture has an obvious effect on the endocrine system in women. If needle-imbedding method is used at these points, delayed ovulation or dysfunction of the corpus luteum can be rectified, indicating that needle-imbedding therapy may be used to treat dysfunction of ovulation.

KI 13 Qixue (气穴)
(Qi Point)

【Source】 *A-B Classic of Acupuncture and Moxibustion*
【Name Explanation】 Qi (气), vital energy; Xue (穴), cave.
【Classification】 Crossing Point of the Kidney Meridian of Foot Shaoyin and the Chong Meridian.
【Location】 On the lower abdomen, 3 cun below the centre of the umbilicus and 0.5 cun lateral to the anterior midline. (See Fig. 10-19).
【Localization】 In the supine position, first locate Guanyuan (RN 4) which is located 3 cun inferior to the umbilicus, then locate the point 0.5 cun lateral to Guanyuan (RN 4).
【Indications】
　　1) Digestive Diseases: Diarrhea, dysentery, intestinal colic.
　　2) Urogenital diseases: Irregular menstruation, leukorrhea, impotence, sterility, retention of urine, five types of stranguria.
　　3) Other Diseases: Pain along spinal column, gastrointestinal neurosis, red, painful and swollen eyes.
【Mechanism of Action】 See Dahe (KI 12).
【Method】 Puncture perpendicularly 1-1.5 cun. Moxibustion is applicable.
【Acupoint Prescription】 Irregular menstruation and pain along spinal column: Acupuncture and moxibustion to this point.
【Regional Anatomy】 Skin-subcutaneous tissue-anterior sheath of rectus muscle of abdomen. In the superficial layer, there are the branches or tributaries of the superficial epigastric artery and vein, the anterior cutaneous branches of the anterior branches of the 11th and 12th thoracic and 1st lumbar nerves and the accompanying arteries and veins. In the deep layer, there are the branches of the inferior epigastric artery and vein, the muscular branches of the anteior branches of the 11th and 12th thoracic nerves and the related intercostal arteries and veins.

KI 14 Siman (四满)
(Quadruple Fullness)

【Source】 *A-B Classic of Acupuncture and Moxibustion*
【Name Explanation】 Si (四), the fourth; Man (满), fullness. This is the fourth point of the Kidney Meridian on the abdomen, and is indicated in abdominal distension.
【Classification】 The Crossing Point of the Kidney Meridian of Foot Shaoyin and the Chong Meridian.
【Location】 On the lower abdomen, 2 cun below the centre of the umbilicus and 0.5 cun lateral to the anterior midline. (See Fig. 10-19).
【Localization】 In the supine position, first locate Shimen (RN 5) which is located in 2 cun directly inferior to the umbilicus, then locate this point 0.5 cun lateral to Shimen (RN 5).
【Indications】
　　1) Urogenital Diseases: Irregular menstruation, metrorrhagia and metrostaxis, leukorrhagia sterility, lochiorrhea, emission, gonorrhea, enuresis, edema, dysuria.
　　2) Digestive Diseases: Constipation, diarrhea, dysentery.

3) Other Diseases: Gastrointestinal neurosis, pain below the umbilicus, red, painful and swollen eyes.

【Mechanism of Action】See Dahe (KI 12).

【Method】Puncture perpendicularly 1-1.5 cun. Moxibustion is applicable.

【Acupoint Prescriptions】

1) Edema: Siman (KI 14), Rangu (KI 2). (*Thousand Golden Prescriptions*)

2) Hernia: Siman (KI 14), Zhongji (RN 3). (*Experience on Acupuncture and Moxibustion Therapy*)

3) Abdominal pain due to extravasated blood: Siman (KI 14), Shimen (RN 5). (*ibid*)

【Regional Anatomy】Skin-subcutaneous tissue-anterior sheath of rectus muscle of abdomen. In the superficial layer, there are the branches or tributaries of the superficial epigastric artery and vein, the anterior cutaneous branches of the anterior branches of the 10th to 12th thoracic nerves and the accompanying arteries and vein. In the deep layer, there are the branches of the inferior epigastric artery and vein, the muscle branches of the anterior branches of the 10th to 12th thoracic nerves and the related intercostal arteries and veins.

KI 15 Zhongzhu （中注）
（Centre Injection）

【Source】*A-B Classic of Acupuncture and Moxibustion*

【Name Explanation】Zhong (中), middle; Zhu (注), to pour. The qi of Kidney Meridian pours from this point into the middle Jiao.

【Classification】The Crossing Point of the Kidney Meridian of Foot Shaoyin and the Chong Meridian.

【Location】On the lower abdomen, 1 cun below the centre of the umbilicus and 0.5 cun lateral to the anterior midline. (See Fig. 10-19).

【Localization】In the supine position, first locate Yinjiao (RN 7) which is located 1 cun directly inferior to the umbilicus, then locate the point 0.5 cun lateral to Yinjiao (RN 7).

【Indications】

1) Digestive Diseases: Diarrhea, dysentery, constipation.

2) Urogenital diseases: Irregular menstruation, stranguria.

3) Other Diseases: Cold sensation, pain in the waist and abdomen, red, swollen and painful eyes.

【Mechanism of Action】See Dahe (KI 12).

【Method】Puncture perpendicularly 1-1.5 cun. Moxibustion is applicable.

【Acupoint Prescriptions】

1) Dyschesia constipation: Zhongzhu (KI 15), Taibai (SP 3). (*A-B Classic of Acupuncture and Moxibustion*)

2) Heart sensation in the lower abdomen, constipation: Zhongzhu (KI 15), Fuxi (BL 38). (*Experience on Acupuncture and Moxibustion Therapy*)

【Regional Anatomy】Skin-subcutaneous tissue-anterior sheath of rectus muscle of abdomen-straight muscle of abdomen. In the superficial layer, there are the periumbilical subcutaneous venous network, the anterior cutaneous branches of the anterior branches of the 10th to 12th thoracic nerves and the accompaning arteries and veins. In the deep layer, there are the branches of the inferior epigastric artery and vein, the muscular branches of the anterior branches of the 10th to 12th thoracic nerves and the related intercostal arteries and veins.

KI 16 Huangshu (肓俞)
(Vitals Shu)

【Source】 *A-B Classic of Acupuncture and Moxibustion*
【Name Explanation】 Huang (肓), Huang-membrane; Shu (俞), to transport. The qi of the Kidney infuses from this point into the Huang-membrane.
【Classification】 Crossing Point of the Kidney Meridian of Foot Shaoyin and the Chong Meridian.
【Location】 On the middle abdomen, 0.5 cun lateral to the centre of the umbilicus. (See Fig. 10-19).
【Localization】 In the supine position, locate the point 0.5 cun lateral to the umbilicus.
【Indications】
    1) Digestive Diseases: Vomiting, abdominal distention, pain around the umbilicus, heat sensation in lower abdomen, dysentery, diarrhea, constipation.
    2) Gynecopathy Diseases: Irregular menstruation.
    3) Other Diseases: Pain along the spinal column, hernia, painful and red eyes.
【Mechanism of Action】 According to its location, this point is mainly used to treat diseases of the intestine. Pain along the spinal column can be relieved when the pain just occurs opposite this point.
【Method】 Puncture perpendicularly 1-1.5 cun. Moxibustion is applicable.
【Acupoint Prescriptions】
    1) Epigastric fullness: Huangshu (KI 16), Qimen (LR 14), Zhongwan (RN 12). (*A-B Classic of Acupuncture and Moxibustion*)
    2) Five types of stranguria: Huangshu (KI 16), Henggu (KI 11). (*Songs of Hundreds of Symptoms*)
【Regional Anatomy】 Skin-subcutaneous tissue-anterior sheath of rectus muscle of abdomen-straight muscle of abdomen. In the superficial layer, there are the periumbilical subcutaneous venous network, the anterior cutaneous branches of the anterior branches of the 9th to 10th thoracic nerves and the accompanying arteries and veins. In the deep layer, there are the arterior venous network formed by the anastomosis of the superior epigastric arteries and veins with the inferior epigastric arteries and veins, the muscular branches of the anterior branches of the 9th to 11th thoracic nerves and the related intercostal arteries and veins.

KI 17 Shangqu (商曲)
(Shang Crook)

【Source】 *A-B Classic of Acupuncture and Moxibustion*
【Name Explanation】 Shang (商), one of the five sounds, pertaining to metal; Qu (曲), twist. Shang is a sound pertaining to metal and the large intestine also pertains to metal. This point corresponds to the twisting of intestines.
【Classification】 The Crossing Point of the Kidney Meridian of Foot-Shaoyin and the Chong Meridian.
【Location】 On the upper abdomen, 2 cun above the centre of the umbilicus and 0.5 cun lateral to the anterior midline. (See Fig. 10-19).
【Localization】 In supine position, first locate Xiawan (RN 10) which is located 2 cun directly

superior to the umbilicus, then locate the point 0.5 cun lateral to Xiawan (RN 10).
【Indications】
1) Digestive Diseases: Diarrhea, dysentery, abdominal pain, anorexia.
2) Other Diseases: Red and painful eyes.
【Mechanism of Action】 See Huangshu (KI 16).
【Method】 Puncture perpendicularly 1-1.5 cun. Moxibustion is applicable.
【Regional Anatomy】 Skin-subcutaneous tissue-anterior sheath of rectus muscle of abdomen-straight muscle of abdomen. In the superficial layer, there are the superficial epigastric vein, the anterior cutaneous branches of the anterior branches of 8th to 10th thoracic nerves and the accompanying arteries and veins. In the deep layer, there are the branches of the superior epigastric artery and vein, the muscular branches of the anterior branches of the anterior branches of the 8th to 10th thoracic nerves and the related intercostal arteries and veins.

KI 18 Shiguan (石关)
(Stone Pass)

【Source】 *A-B Classic of Acupuncture and Moxibustion*
【Name Explanation】 Shi (石), stone; Guan (关), importance. Shi here means hard in consistency. This is an important point in treating abdominal diseases of hard consistency.
【Classification】 Crossing Point of the Kidney Meridian of Foot-Shaoyin and the Chong Meridian.
【Location】 On the upper abdomen, 3 cun above the centre of the umbilicus and 0.5 cun lateral to the anterior midline. (See Fig. 10-19).
【Localization】 In the supine position, first locate Jianli (RN 11) which is located 3 cun directly superior to the umbilicus, then locate this point 0.5 cun lateral to Jianli (RN 11).
【Indications】
1) Digestive Diseases: Vomiting, hiccup, stomachache, epigastralgia, fullness and stiffness in the epigastrium, constipation.
2) Gynecopathy: Abdominal pain after childbirth, sterility, irregular menstruation, dysmenorrhea.
【Mechanism of Action】
1) Shiguan (KI 18) is used to treat diseases of the digestive system by means of the local reaction.
2) All points of the Kidney Meridian in the abdomen connect with the Chong Meridian which is named "the sea of blood", so most of these points can be used to treat gynecological diseases.
【Method】 Puncture perpendicularly 1-1.5 cun. Moxibustion is applicable.
【Acupoint Prescription】 Constipation and epigastric pain due to stagnation of qi: Moxibustion to Shiguan (KI 18), Dadu (SP 2) (*The Heart of Medical Prescriptions*)
【Regional Anatomy】 Skin-subcutaneous tissue-anterior sheath of rectus muscle of abdomen-straight muscle of abdomen. In the superficial layer, there are the superficial epigastric vein, the anterior branches of the 7th to 9th thoracic nerves and the accompanying arteries and veins. In the deep layer, there are the branches or tributaries of the superior epigastric artery and vein, the muscular branches of the anterior branches of the 7th to 9th thoracic nerves and the related intercostal arteries and veins.

KI 19 Yindu (阴都)
(Yin Capital)

【Source】 *A-B Classic of Acupuncture and Moxibustion*
【Name Explanation】 Yin (阴), Yin of Yin-Yang; Du (都), to gather. Yin refers to the abdomen and the Yin meridian. The point is in the abdomen where water and food meet.
【Classification】 Crossing Point of the Kidney Meridian of Foot-Shaoyin and the Chong Meridian.
【Location】 On the upper abdomen, 4 cun above the centre of the umbilicus and 0.5 cun lateral to the anterior midline. (See Fig. 10-19).
【Localization】 In the supine position, first locate Zhongwan (RN 12) which is located 4 cun directly superior to the umbilicus, then locate this point 0.5 cun lateral to Zhongwan (RN 12).
【Indications】
  1) Respiratory Diseases: Asthma, dyspnea.
  2) Digestive Diseases: Abdominal distention, borborygmus, stomachache, constipation, fullness of the upper abdomen, jaundice.
  3) Gynecopathy: Sterility.
  4) Other Diseases: Malaria, pain in the chest and hypochondrium, red and painful eyes.
【Mechanism of Action】 Yindu (KI19) is close to epigastrium, so it is used mainly for diseases of the digestive system. When this point is used to treat asthma, it not only has the action of invigorating the kidney but also the action of invigorating the spleen to eliminate phlegm.
【Method】 Puncture perpendicularly 1-1.5 cun. Moxibustion is applicable.
【Acupoint Prescriptions】
  1) Malaria with high fever: Yindu (KI 19), Shaohai (HT 3), Shangyang (LI 1), Sanjian (LI 3), Zhongzhu (SJ 3). (*Experience on Acupuncture and Moxibustion Therapy*)
  2) Vexation: Yindu (KI 19), Juque (RN 14). (*ibid*)
  3) Lung-distension: Moxibustion to Yindu (KI 19), Taiyuan (LU 9), Feishu (BL 13). (*Great Compendium of Acupuncture and Moxibustion*)
【Regional Anatomy】 Skin-subcutaneous tissue-anterior sheath of rectus muscle of abdomen-straight muscle of abdomen. In the superficial layer, there are the superficial epigastric vein, the anterior cutaneous branches of the anterior branches of the 7th to 9th thoracic nerves and the accompanying arteries and veins. In the deep layer, there are the branches of the superior epigastric artery and vein, the muscular branches of the anterior branches of the 7th to 9th thoracic nerves and the related intercostal arteries and veins.

KI 20 Futonggu (腹通谷)
(Passing Valley)

【Source】 *A-B Classic of Acupuncture and Moxibustion*
【Name Explanation】 Fu (腹), abdomen; Tong (通), passing; Gu (谷), water and food. The point is in the abdomen, where water and food pass.
【Classification】 Crossing Point of the Kidney Meridian of Foot Shaoyin and the Chong Meridian.
【Location】 On the upper abdomen, 5 cun above the centre of the umbilicus and 0.5 cun later-

al to the anterior midline. (See Fig. 10-19).

【Localization】 In the supine position, first locate Shangwan (RN 13) which is located 5 cun directly superior to the umbilicus, then locate this point 0.5 cun lateral to Shangwan (RN 13).

【Indications】
1) Respiratory Diseases: Cough, asthma.
2) Digestive Diseases: Abdominal pain, abdominal distention, vomiting.
3) Cardiovascular Diseases: Precordial pain, palpitation, pain in the chest and hypochondrium.
4) Mental Disorders: Epilepsy, palpitation due to fright.

【Mechanism of Action】
1) Futonggu (KI 20) point is close to epigastrium, so it is used to treat diseases of digestive system.
2) The Kidney Meridian runs into the lung, then exits from the lung and connects with the heart. There is a close relationship among the kidney, the lung and the heart. That is why Futonggu (KI20) is used for the diseases mentioned above.

【Method】 Puncture perpendicularly 0.5-1 cun. Moxibustion is applicable.

【Regional Anatomy】 Skin-subcutaneous tissue-anterioe sheath of rectus straight muscle of abdomen-straight muscle of abdomen. In the superficial layer, there are the superficial epigastric vein, the anterior cutaneous branches of the anterior branches of the 6th to 8th thoracic nerves and the accompanying arteries and veins. In the deep layer, there are the branches of the superior epigastric artery and vein, the muscular branches of the anterior branches of the 6th to 8th thoracic nerves and the related intercostal arteries and veins.

KI 21 Youmen (幽门)
(Hades Gate)

【Source】 *A-B Classic of Acupuncture and Moxibustion*

【Name Explanation】 You(幽), hiding; Men(门), door. The point pertains to Kidney Meridian and is located where the lower orifice of stomach is situated interiorly. It is hidden deep in the abdomen.

【Classification】 Crossing Point of the Kidney Meridian of Foot Shaoyin and the Chong Meridian.

【Location】 On the upper abdomen, 6 cun above the centre of the umbilicus and 0.5 cun lateral to the anterior midline. (See Fig. 10-19).

【Localization】 In the supine position, first locate Juque(RN 14) which is located 6 cun directly superior to the umbilicus, then locate this point 0.5 cun lateral to Juque (RN 14).

【Indications】
1) Digestive Diseases: Stomachache, abdominal distention, vomiting, diarrhea, dysentery.
2) Gynecopathy: Galactostasis, acute mastitis.
3) Other Diseases: Pain in the chest which involves the waist and the back, red and painful eyes.

【Action mechanism】
1) This point is close to epigastrium, so it is used to treat diseases of the spleen and stomach.
2) The spleen provides the material basis for the acquired constitution, benefits the flow of qi and blood and eliminates the dampness. So the point can be used to treat the diseases of gastrointestinal system and gynecological diseases due to qi deficiency of both the spleen and

stomach and retention of phlegm-dampness.

【Method】 Puncture perpendicularly 0.7-1 cun. In order to avoid puncturing the liver, deep insertion is not advisable. Moxibustion is applicable.

【Acupoint Prescription】 Restlessness and vomiting: Youmen (KI 21), Yutang (RN 18). (*Songs of Hundreds of Symptoms*)

【Regional Anatomy】 Skin-subcutaneous tissue-anterior sheath of rectus muscle of abdomen-straight muscle of abdomen. In the superficial layer, there are the anterior cutaneous branches of the anterior branches of the 6th to 8th thoracic nerves and the accompanying arteries and veins. In the deep layer, there are the branches of the superior epigastric artery and vein, the muscular branches of the anterior branches of the 6th to 8th thoracic nerves and the related intercostal arteries and veins.

【Remark】 Puncturing Youmen (KI21) slows the gastric peristalsis.

KI 22 Bulang (步廊)
(Walking Corridor)

【Source】 *A-B Classic of Acupuncture and Moxibustion*

【Name Explanation】 Bu (步), step; Lang (廊), corridor. The point lies along the Zhongting (CV, Ren 16) epigastric region. When the qi of meridian flows here, it is like stepping into a corridor on either side of a courtyard.

【Location】 On the chest, in the 5th intercostal space, 2 cun lateral to the anterior midline. (See Fig. 10-20).

【Localization】 In the supine position, locate the point in the middle of the mid-sternal line and the midclavecular line, in the 5th intercostal space.

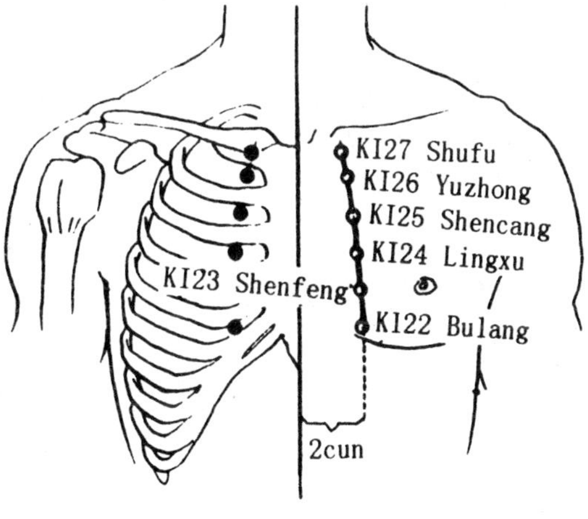

Fig. 10-20

【Indications】

1) Respiratory Diseases: Fullness sensation and pain in the chest and hypochondrium, cough, asthma, nasal obstruction.

2) Digestive Diseases: Vomiting, anorexia.

3) Other Diseases: Acute mastitis.

【Mechanism of Action】

1) Bulang (KI 22) point is located in the region of the lung and breast, so it is mainly used to treat cough, dyspnea, acute mastitis, etc.

2) Abnormal lung qi ascending will disturb the function of the spleen and stomach. Bulang (KI 22) is close to the lung, so it is used to treat vomiting and anorexia.

【Method】 Puncture perpendicularly or obliquely 0.5-0.8 cun. To avoid puncturing the heart and lung, deep insertion is not advisable. Moxibustion is applicable.

【Acupoint Prescription】 Dyspnea with chest distension: Bulang (KI 22), Yindu (KI 19). (*Experience on Acupuncture and Moxibustion Therapy*)

【Regional Anatomy】 Skin-subcutaneous tissue-greater pectoral muscle. In the superficial layer, there are the anterior cutaneous branches of the 5th intercostal nerve and the perforating branches of the internal thoracic artery and vein. In the deep layer, there are the branches of the medial and lateral pectoral nerves.

KI 23 Shenfeng (神封)
(Spirit Seal)

【Source】 *A-B Classic of Acupuncture and Moxibustion*
【Name Explanation】 Shen (神), heart; Feng (封), manor. The region where the point is located pertains to the heart.
【Location】 On the chest, in the 4th intercostal space, 2 cun lateral to the anterior midline. (See Fig. 10-20).
【Localization】 In the supine position, locate the point in the middle of the mid-sternal line and the midclavicular line, in the 4th intercostal space.
【Indications】
　　1) Respiratory Diseases: Cough, dyspnea, restlessness due to fullness in the chest.
　　2) Digestive Diseases: Vomiting, anorexia.
　　3) Other Diseases: Acute mastitis.
【Mechanism of Action】 See Bulang (KI 22).
【Method】 Puncture obliquely 0.5-0.8 cun; deep insertion is not advisable. Moxibustion is applicable.
【Acupoint Prescription】 Acute mastitis: Shenfeng (KI 23), Yingchuang (ST 16). (*Thousand Golden Prescriptions*)
【Regional Anatomy】 Skin-subcutaneous tissue-greater pectoral muscle. In the superficial layer, there are the anterior cutaneous branches of the 4th intercostal nerve and the perforating branches of the internal thoracic artery and vein. In the deep layer, there are the branches of the medial and lateral pectoral nerves.

KI 24 Lingxu (灵墟)
(Spirit Burial-ground)

【Source】 *A-B Classic of Acupuncture and Moxibustion*
【Name Explanation】 Ling (灵), heart; Xu (墟), mound. The point internally corresponds to the heart; externally it is on the muscle prominence, which looks like a mound.
【Location】 On the chest, in the 3rd intercostal space, 2 cun lateral to the anterior midline. (See Fig. 10-20).
【Localization】 In the supine position, locate the point in the middle of the mid-sternal line and the mid-clavicular line, in the 3rd intercostal space.
【Indications】
　　1) Respiratory Diseases: Cough, dyspnea, abundant expectoration.
　　2) Digestive Diseases: Vomiting, anorexia.
　　3) Other Diseases: Acute mastitis, fullness and pain in the chest and hypochondrium.
【Mechanism of Action】 See Bulang (KI 22).
【Method】 Puncture obliquely or subcutaneously 0.5-0.8 cun. Moxibustion is applicable.
【Regional Anatomy】 Skin-subcutaneous tissue-greater pectoral muscle. In the superficial layer, there are the anterior cutanious branches of the 3rd intercostal nerves and the perforating branches of the internal thoracic artery and vein. In the deep layer, there are the branches of the medial and lateral pectoral nerves.

KI 25 Shencang （神藏）
（Spirit Storage）

【Source】 *A-B Classic of Acupuncture and Moxibustion*
【Name Explanation】 Shen（神）, heart; Cang（藏）, concealment. The point is where the mind is concealed.
【Location】 On the chest, in the 2nd intercostal space, 2 cun lateral to the anterior midline. (See Fig. 10-20).
【Localization】 In the supine position, locate the point in the middle of the mid-sternal line and the midclavicular line, in the 2nd intercostal space.
【Indications】
　　1) Respiratory Diseases: Cough, asthma, profuse sputum, oppression and fullness feeling in the chest and hypochondrium.
　　2) Digestive Diseases: Vomiting, anorexia.
　　3) Other Diseases: Acute mastitis.
【Mechanism of Action】 See Bulang (KI 22).
【Method】 Puncture obliquely or subcutaneously 0.5-0.8 cun. Moxibustion is applicable.
【Acupoint Prescriptions】
　　1) Vomiting and fullness sensation in the chest: Shencang (KI 25), Lingxu (KI 24). (*Experience on Acupuncture and Moxibustion Therapy*)
　　2) Chest fullness and neck rigidity: Shencang (KI 25), Xuanji (RN 21). (*Songs of Hundreds of Symptoms*)
【Regional Anatomy】 Skin-subcutaneous tissue-greater pectoral muscle. In the superficial layer, there are the anterior cutaneous branches of the 2nd intercostal nerves and the perforating branches of the internal thoracic artery and vein. In the deep layer, there are the branches of the medial and lateral pectoral nerves.

KI 26 Yuzhong （彧中）
（In Literature）

【Source】 *A-B Classic of Acupuncture and Moxibustion*
【Name Explanation】 Yu（彧）, luxuriance; Zhong（中）, middle. The point is where the qi of Kidney is luxuriant when flowing into the chest.
【Location】 On the chest, in the 1st intercostal space, 2 cun lateral to the anterior midline. (See Fig. 10-20).
【Localization】 In the supine position, locate the point in the middle of the mid-sternal line and the midclavicular line, in the 1st intercostal space.
【Indications】
　　1) Respiratory Diseases: Cough, dyspnea, abundant expectoretion, fullness and pain in the chest and hypochondrium.
　　2) Digestive Diseases: Vomiting, anorexia.
　　3) Other Diseases: Acute mastitis.
【Mechanism of Action】 See Bulang (KI 22).
【Method】 Puncture obliquely or subcutaneously 0.5-0.8 cun. Deep puncture is not advisable. Moxibustion is applicable.

【Acupoint Prescriptions】
　　1) Cough with dyspnea: Yuzhong (KI 26), Shimen (RN 5). (*Thousand Golden Prescriptions*)
　　2) Cough, dyspnea and palpitation: Yuzhong (KI 26), Yunmen (LU 2). (*Experience on Acupuncture and Moxibustion Therapy*)

【Regional Anatomy】Skin-subcutaneous tissue-greater pectoral muscle. In the superficial layer, there are the anterior cutaneous branches of the 1st intercostal nerve and the perforating branches of the internal thoracic artery and vein. In the deep layer, there are the branches of the medial and lateral pectoral nerves.

KI 27 Shufu (俞府)
(Shu Mansion)

【Source】*A-B Classic of Acupuncture and Moxibustion*

【Name Explanation】Shu (俞), point; Fu (府), organ. The qi of Kidney infuses from this point into the Fu organs.

【Location】On the chest, below the lower border of the clavicle, 2 cun lateral to the midline. (See Fig. 10-20).

【Localization】In sitting position or in the supine position, locate the point in the middle of the mid-sternal line and the midclavicular line, in the lower margin of the clavicle.

【Indications】
　　1) Respiratory Diseases: Cough, dyspnea, pain in the chest, restlessness due to fullness in the chest.
　　2) Digestive Diseases: Abdominal distention, vomiting, anorexia.

【Mechanism of Action】See Bulang (KI 22).

【Method】Puncture obliquely or subcutaneously 0.5-0.8 cun, deep puncture is not advisable. Moxibustion is applicable.

【Acupoint Prescriptions】
　　1) Vomiting: Shufu (KI 27), Shencang (KI 25), Lingxu (KI 24), Juque (RN 14). (*Thousand Golden Prescriptions*)
　　2) Cough with dyspnea: Shufu (KI 27), Shencang (KI 25), Tianfu (LU 3). (*Experience on Acupuncture and Moxibustion Therapy*)

【Regional Anatomy】Skin-subcutaneous tissue-great pectoral muscle. In the superficial layer, there are the medial supraclavicular nerve. In the deep layer, there are the branches of the medial and lateral pectoral nerves.

【Remark】Shufu (KI 27) is frequently used to treat auricular fibrillation as one of its functions is to regulate the heart rate.

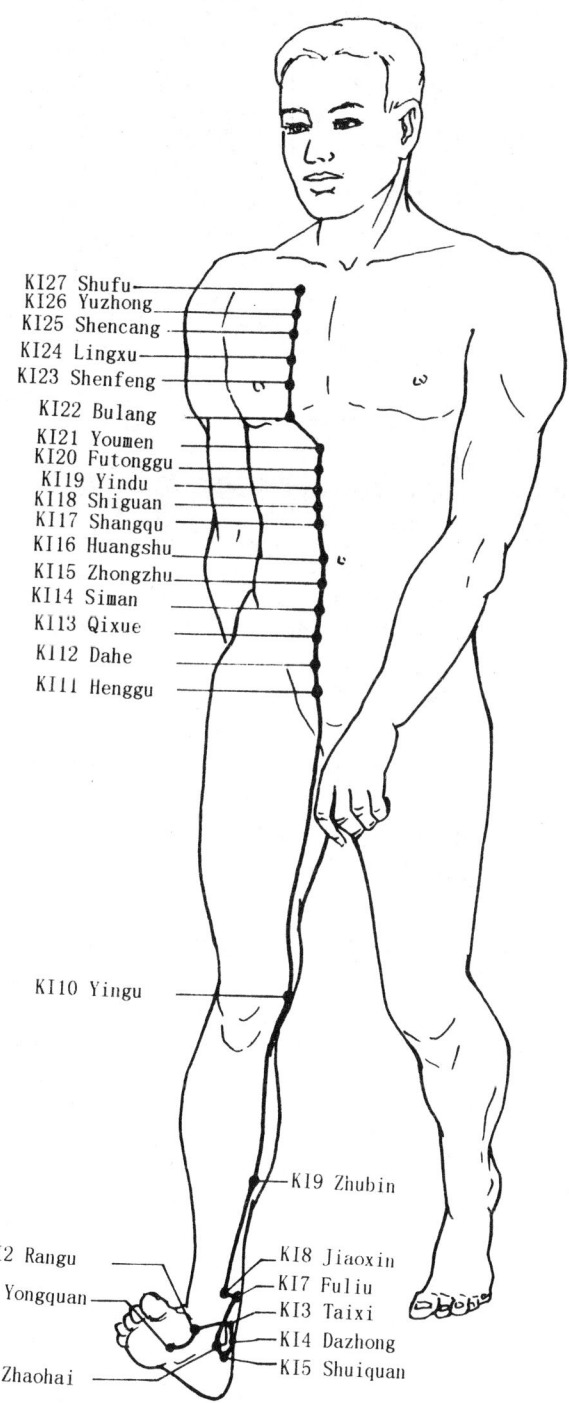

Fig. 10-21 **Acupoints of the Kidney Meridian of Foot Shaoyin**

Table 10-3 Indications and Actions of Acupoints of the Kidney Meridian of Foot Shaoyin

Name of the points	Specific points	Common indications	Specific indications and functions
KI 1 Yongquan (涌泉)	Jing-(Well) point	Gynecopathy and disorders of external genitalia, intestine, lung and throat: irregular menstruation, nocturnal emission, enuresis, retention of urine, constipation, sore throat, hemoptysis	Reviving the patient from unconsciousness, tranquilizing the mind. Headache, dizziness, insomnia, sore throat, dysphonia, constipation, retention of urine, infantile convulsion, manic-depression, syncope
KI 2 Rangu (然谷)	Ying-(Spring) point		Nourishing the kidney, clearing heat and removing dampness. Irregular menstruation, leukorrhagia, diabetes, diarrhea, neonatal tetanus, lockjaw, pruritus vulvae, flaccidity of feet
KI 3 Taixi (太溪)	Shu-(Stream) point Yuan-(Source) point		Nourishing the kidney, clearing the three Jiaos. Nocturnal emission, impotence, irregular menstruation, toothache, insomnia, diabetes, deafness, tinnitus, dyspnea, lumbago
KI 4 Dazhong (大钟)	Luo-(Connecting) point		Nourishing the kidney, clearing heat from the lung, benefiting the mind. Retention of urine, enuresis, hemoptysis, dyspnea, dementia, heel pain
KI 5 Shuiquan (水泉)	Xi-(Cleft) point		Regulating Chong and Ren meridians, clearing away heat and damp from the lower Jiao. Irregular menstruation, dysmenorrhea, amenorrhea, hernia, retention of urine
KI 6 Zhaohai (照海)	One of the eight confluence points		Clearing heat, tranquilizing the mind, relieving sore throat. Sore throat, nocturnal emission, manic-depression, insomnia, retention of urine, leukorrhagia, vaginal hernia, irregular menstruation

Acupoints of Three Yin Meridians of Foot

Name of the points	Specific points	Common indications	Specific indications and functions
KI 7 Fuliu (复溜)		Gynecopathy and disorders of external genitalia and intestine: irregular menstruation, vaginal hernia, metrorrhagia, abdominal flatulence, diarrhea.	Nourishing the kidney, removing dampness. Edema, abdominal distention, diarrhea, night sweat, febrile disease without sweat, flaccidity of lower extremities
KI 8 Jiaoxin (交信)	Xi- (Cleft) point of Yinqiao meridian		Regulating menstruation. Irregular menstruation, metrorrhagia
KI 9 Zhubin (筑宾)	Xi- (Cleft) point of Yinwei meridian		Nourishing the liver and kidney, dredging and activating the meridian. Manic-depression, epilepsy, vomiting, drooling, hernia, pain of leg
KI 10 Yingu (阴谷)	Confluent point		Nourishing the kidney, clearing away heat. Impotence, eczema of scrotum, hernia, metrorrhagia, retention of urine, aching pain of knee and poples.
KI 11 Henggu (横骨)	Crossing point	Gynecopathy and disorders of external genitalia and intestine: irregular menstruation, nocturnal emission, leukorrhagia, retention of urine, diarrhea, abdominal pain, constipation	Distention and pain of lower abdomen, retention of urine, enuresis, nocturnal emission, impotence, hernia
KI 12 Dahe (大赫)	Crossing point		Swelling and pain of vulva, hernia
KI 13 Qixue (气穴)	Crossing point		Regulating Chong and Ren meridians. Irregular menstruation, sterility in female
KI 14 Siman (四满)	Crossing point		Nourishing the liver and kidney, regulating menstruation, promoting diuresis, relieving fullness and dyspepsia. Lochiorrhea, leucorrhagia with reddish and whitish discharge

Name of the points	Specific points	Common indications	Specific indications and functions
KI 15 Zhongzhu (中注)	Crossing point	Disorders of stomach and intestine: abdominal distention and pain, vomiting, diarrhea, constipation	Irregular menstruation, constipation
KI 16 Huangshu (肓俞)	Crossing point		Nourishing the liver and kidney, regulating the function of intestine. Pain around umbilicus, hernia, five kinds of stranguria
KI 17 Shangqu (商曲)	crossing point		Coordinating the functions of spleen and stomach, relieving dyspepsia by purgation. Abdominal pain, diarrhea, constipation
KI 18 Shiguan (石关)	Crossing point		Regulating the Chong and Ren meridians. Puerperal abdominal pain, sterility in female
KI 19 Yindu (阴都)	Crossing point		Regulating Chong and Ren meridians. Sterility in females
KI 20 Futonggu (腹通谷)	Crossing point		Invigorating spleen and stomach, regulating the flow of qi and soothing the chest. Stomachache, sensation of fullness over the chest, dyspepsia
KI 21 Youmen (幽门)	Crossing point		Soothing the liver to stop pain
KI 22 Bulang (步廊)		Disorders of chest and lung: cough, dyspnea, pain and fullness over the chest and hypochondrium	Soothing chest disorders and regulating flow of qi. Pain and fullness in the chest and hypochondrium, intercostal neuralgia, pleurisy
KI 23 Shenfeng (神封)			
KI 24 Lingxu (灵墟)			
KI 25 Shencang (神藏)			
KI 26 Yuzhong (彧中)			
KI 27 Shufu (俞府)			

Chapter Eleven

Acupoints of Three Yang Meridians of Foot

XII. Acupoints of the Stomach Meridian of Foot Yangming

ST 1　Chengqi（承泣）
（Tear Receiver）

【Source】 *A-B Classic of Acupuncture and Moxibustion*
【Name Explanation】 Cheng (承), to recieve; Qi (泣), tears. The point is below the eye, a place for receiving tears.
【Classification】 The Crossing Point of the Yangjiao Meridian, the Ren Meridian and the Stomach Meridian of Foot Yangming.
【Location】 On the face, directly below the pupil, between the eyeball and the infraobital ridge. (See Fig. 11-1)
【Localization】 Sitting or in the supine position, look straight ahead, locate the point directly inferior to the pupil, between the eyeball and the infraorbital margin.
【Indications】
　　1) Diseases of the Head and Sense Organs: Eye lid tremors, conjunctival congestion with swelling and pain, epiphora induced by wind, nyctalopia, myopia, glaucoma, facial hemiparalysis, tinnitus, deafness.
　　2) Other Diseases: Hiccup, acute lumbar sprain, diabetes insipidus.
【Mechanism of Action】 This point has the function of improving eye sight, expelling wind and

can be used to treat eye diseases.

【Method】 Puncture perpendicularly 0.3-0.7 cun along the infraorbital ridge. It is not advisable to twist and rotate the needle with large amplitude. Moxibustion can not be applied.

【Acupoint Prescription】 Aphasia: Chenqi (ST 1), Dicang (ST 4), Daying (ST 5), Yuji (LU 10), Tongli (HT 5). (*Experience on Acupuncture and Moxibustion Therapy.*)

【Regional Anatomy】 Skin-subcutaneous tissue-the orbicular muscle of the eye-abipose body of the orbit-the inferior oblique muscle. In the superficial layer, there are the branches of the infraorbital nerve and the zygomatic branches of the facial nerve. In the deep layer, there are the branches of the oculomotor nerve and the branches or tributaries of the ophthalmic artery and vein.

【Remark】 It has been reported that puncturing Chengqi (ST 1) may slow down the heart rate.

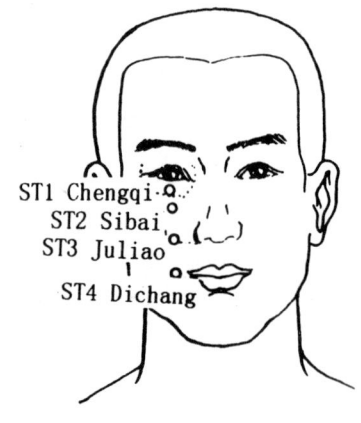

Fig. 11-1

ST 2 Sibai (四白)
(Four Whites)

【Source】 *A-B Classic of Acupuncture and Moxibustion*
【Name Explanation】 Si (四), four directions; Bai (白), brightness. This point is below the eye and is indicated in eye diseases. It is said to improve the vision and sharpen the eyesight in all four directions.
【Location】 On the face, directly below the pupil, in the depression of the infraobital foramen. (See Fig. 11-1)
【Localization】 Sitting or in the supine position, look straight ahead, the point is located directly inferior to the pupil, in the depression at the infraorbital foramen.
【Indications】
    1) Diseases of the Head and Sense Organs: Eye lid tremors, conjunctival congestion with swelling and pain, lacrimation induced by wind, facial hemiparalysis, nyctalopia, vertigo, headache and facial pain, trigeminal neuralgia.
    2) Other Diseases: Biliary ascariasis.
【Mechanism of Action】
    1) This point can be used for improving eye sight and expelling wind, so it is often used to treat eye diseases and facial hemiparalysis.
    2) It is reported that a remarkable curative effect has been achieved in treating biliary ascariasis and trigeminal neuralgia.
【Method】 Puncture perpendicularly 0.2-0.3 cun. Moxibustion can not be applied.
【Acupoint Prescription】 Headache and vertigo: Sibai (ST 2), Yongquan (KI 1), Dazhu (BL 11). (*Experience on Acupuncture and Moxibustion Therapy.*)
【Regional Anatomy】 Skin-subcutaneous tissue-the orbicular muscle of the eye, the levator muscle of the upper lip-the infraorbital foramen or the maxilla. In the superficial layer, there are the branches of the infraorbital nerve and the zygomatic branches of the facial nerve. In the deep layer, there are the infraorbital artery, vein and nerve which pass through the infraorbital foramen.

ST 3 Juliao (巨髎)
(Great Crevice)

【Source】 *A-B Classic of Acupuncture and Moxibustion*
【Name Explanation】 Ju (巨), huge; Liao (髎), foramen. The point is in the big foramen at the junction of the superior maxillary and zygomatic bones.
【Classification】 The Crossing Point of the Yangqiao Meridian and the Stomach Meridian of Foot Yangming.
【Location】 On the face, directly below the pupil, on the level of the lower border of ala masi, beside the nasolabial groove. (See Fig. 11-1)
【Localization】 Sitting or in the supine position, look straight ahead, the point is located at the intersection between the vertical line of pupil and horizontal line of inferior margin of the wing of the nose.
【Indications】
　1) Diseases of the Head and Sense Organs: Facial pain, facial hemiparalysis, eye lid tremors, clustered nebula, redness and pain of the eye, glucome conjunctival congestion and pain of lower orbit, stuffy nose, epistaxis, toothache, swelling lip and cheek, swelling jaw.
　2) Other Diseases: Beriberi, knee swelling, clonic convulsion.
【Mechanism of Action】
　1) This point can be used to treat the diseases of head, face and sense organs. Trigeminal neuralgia can be treated by inserting the needle deeply towards the canthus.
　2) Where the meridian passes, where the indications are, the point can be used to treat beriberi and knee swelling.
【Method】 Puncture perpendicularly 0.3-0.4 cun. Moxibustion is applied.
【Acupoint Prescription】 Swelling and painful cheek: Juliao (ST 3), Tianchuang (SI 16). (*Experience on Acupuncture and Moxibustion Therapy*.)
【Regional Anatomy】 Skin-subcutaneous tissue-the levator muscle of the upper lip-the levator muscle the angle of the mouth.
　There are the infraorbital nerve of the maxillary nerve, the buccal branches of the facial nerve, the anastomotic branches formed by the branches or tributaries of the facial artery and vein and the infraorbital artery and vein in this area.
【Remark】 It has been reported that puncturing Juliao (ST 3) point has a good effect on an anaesthestic during the operation on the thyroid gland. Its success rate is 99%, better rate is 92.5%, first-class rate is 62%. It is more effective than that by puncturing Hegu (LI 4) and Futu (LI 18) or Hegu (LI 4) and Neiguan (PC 6) points as an acupuncture anaesthestic during the operation of the thyroid gland.

ST 4 Dicang (地仓)
(Earth Granary)

【Source】 *A-B Classic of Acupuncture and Moxibustion*
【Name Explanation】 Di (地), earth; Cang (仓), granary. The five grains grow on the earth. The grain enters the stomach via the month, as entering a grainery. The point is at the corners of the mouth.
【Classification】 The Crossing Point of the Yangqiao Meridian, the Large Intestine Meridian of

Hand Yangming and the Stomach Meridian of Foot Yangming.
【Location】 On the face, directly below the pupil, beside the mouth angle. (See Fig. 11-1)
【Localization】 Sitting or in the supine position, look straight ahead, locate the point at the intersection between the vertical line of pupil and horizontal line of the angle of the mouth.
【Indications】
  Diseases of the Head and Sense Organs: Flaccid lip muscle with difficulty in closing the mouth, eye lid tremors, deviation of the mouth, toothache and cheek swelling, salivation.
【Mechanism of Action】 Facial hemiparalysis and salivation can be treated by puncturing Dicang (ST 4) through Jiache (ST 6).
【Method】 Puncture perpendicularly 0.2 cun or subcutaneously 0.5-1 cun towards Jiache (ST 6). Moxibustion is applied.
【Acupoint Prescriptions】
  1) Foot muscle atrophy: Dicang (ST 4), Shuiquan (KI 5). (*Thousand Golden Prescriptions.*)
  2) Migraine: Dicang (ST 4), Chengshan (UB 57), Shanglian (LI 9), Xialian (LI 9). (*Experience on Acupuncture and Moxibustion Therapy.*)
  3) Deviation of the mouth: Dicang (ST 4), Jiache (ST 6). (*Songs of Jade dragon.*)
【Regional Anatomy】 Skin-subcutaneous tissue-the orbicular muscle of the mouth-the depressor muscle of the angle. There are the buccal and infraobital branches of the trigeminal nerve and the branches or tributaries of the facial artery and vein in this area.

ST 5 Daying (大迎)
(Big Welcome)

【Source】 *Miraculous Pivot*
【Name Explanation】 Da (大), large; Ying (迎), to receive. The point lies beside the Daying artery.
【Location】 Anterior to the mandibular angle, on the anterior border of the masseter muscle, where the pulsation of the facial artery is palpable. (See Fig. 11-2)
【Localization】 Sitting or in the supinte position, close the mouth and bulge the cheeks, the point is located at the groove of mandibular margin, where the pulse can be felt.
【Indications】
  1) Diseases of the Head and Sense Organs: Trismus, deviation of the mouth, cheek swelling, facial swelling, dental luxation, lip tremors, scrofula, cervicodynia, stiff tongue with difficulty in speaking and chewing.
  2) Other Diseases: Fever with chills, apoplexy.
【Mechanism of Action】 This point has the function of expelling wind and dredging the meridian. It is one of the common points to treat diseases located in this area.

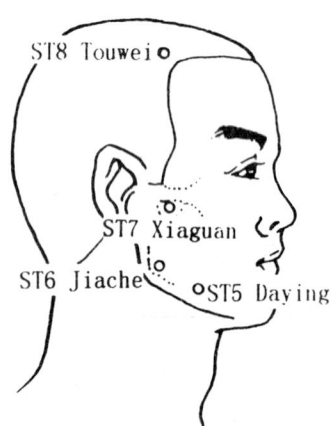

Fig. 11-2

【Method】 Puncture perpendicularly 0.3 cun. Moxibustion is applied.
【Acupoint Prescription】 Epileptic seizure, deviation of the mouth, asthma palpitation: Daying (ST 5), Meridians of Foot Yangming and Foot Taiyin. (*A-B Classic of Acupuncture and Moxibustion*)
【Regional Anatomy】 Skin-subcutaneous tissue-the depressor muscle of the mouth and playama muscle-the anterior border of the masseter muscle.

In the superficial layer, there are the buccal nerve of the mandibular branch of the trigeminal nerve and the marginal mandibular branch of the facial nerve. In the deep layer, there are the facial artery and vein.

ST 6 Jiache (颊车)
(Mandible Angle Chariot)

【Source】 *Miraculous Pivot*

【Name Explanation】 Jia (颊), cheek; Che (车), vehicle. Che refers to the mandible. This point is on the cheek, close to the angle of the mandible.

【Location】 On the cheek, one finger width anterior and superior to the mandibular angle, in the depression where the masseter muscle is prominent. (See Fig. 11-2)

【Localization】 Sitting or in the lateral position, the point is located at 0.4 cun directly superior to the angle of mandible and one finger breadth anterior. If the teeth are clenched, the masseter muscle is prominent; there is a depression with soreness and distending sensation by pressing the point when the mouth is open.

【Indications】

Diseases of the Head and Sense Organs: Toothache, facial hemiparalysis, apoplexy, lockjaw, aphonia, toothache with difficulty in chewing, neck pain, parotitis.

【Mechanism of Action】 Jiache (ST 6) is commonly used to treat deviations of the mouth by needling Jiache through Dicang (ST 4), or vice versa. This method of puncturing Jiache obliquely to the point anterior to the ear has the function of expelling wind and removing toxic substances. It can be used for treating parotitis. The Stomach Meridian goes into the upper teeth, the method of pressing this point with a finger is capable of alleviating toothache.

【Method】 Puncture perpendicularly 0.3-0.4 cun or obliquely towards Daying (ST 5) and Dicang (ST 4).

【Acupoint Prescriptions】

1) Pain in the cheek with difficulty in chewing and aversion to cold and wind: Jiache (ST 6), Quanliao (SI 18). (*Thousand Golden Prescriptions*)

2) Stiffness of the neck with difficulty in turning around: Jiache (ST 6), Dazhui (DU 14), Qishe (ST 11), Naokong (GB 19). (*Experience on Acupuncture and Moxibustion Therapy*)

3) Trismus: Jiache (ST 6), Baihui (DU 20), Chengjiang (RN 24), Hegu (LI 4). (*Great Compendium of Acupuncture and Moxibustion.*)

4) Pain in the upper teeth: Jiache (ST 6), Tianrong (SI 17), Xiaguan (ST 7), Taiyang (EX-HN 5), Hegu (LI 4). (*New Acupuncture and Moxibustion.*)

5) Parotitis: Jiache (ST 6), Hegu (LI 4), Daling (ST 5), Yifeng (SJ 17), Fengchi (GB 20), Zusanli (ST 36), Touwei (ST 8), Xiaguan (ST 7), Wangu (GB 12), Dashu (UB 11), Quyuan (SI 7). (*ibid*)

6) Deviation of mouth: Jiache (ST 6), Dicang (ST 4). (*Songs of Hundreds of Symptoms.*)

【Regional Anatomy】 Skin-subcutaneous tissue-masseter muscle. There are the branches of the great auricular nerve and the marginal mandibular branches of the facial nerve in this area.

【Remark】 Histopathologic examination showed that acupuncture to Jiache (ST 6) point caused hypothyrosis and also affected the pituitary-sexual gland functions. So it can be used to treat hyperthyroidism. Acupuncture applied to Sanyinjiao (ST 36), Xuanzhong (GB 39), and Jiache (ST 6) points may promote uterine contration. It has also been reported that puncturing this point may reduce salivary secretion.

ST 7 Xiaguan (下关)
(Lower Pass)

[Source] *Miraculous Pivot and Plain Questions*
[Name Explanation] Xia (下), lower; Guan (关), pass. Guan indicates the zygomatic arch; the point is below it.
[Classification] The Crossing Point of the Stomach Meridian of Foot Yangming and the Gallbladder Meridian of Foot Shaoyang.
[Location] On the face, anterior to the ear, in the depression between the zygomatic arch and mandibular notch. (See Fig. 11-2)
[Localization] Sitting or in the lateral position, close the mouth, locate the point at one finger breadth anterior to the tragus, in the depression inferior to the zagomatic arch. There is a depression when the mouth is closed. The depression will disappear when the mouth is open.
[Indications]
Diseases of the Head and Sense Organs: Facial pain, toothache, gingival swelling and pain, trismus with difficulty in opening and closing, facial hemiparalysis, deafness, tinnitus, pain of the ear, otitis media suppurativa, neck swelling, vertigo.
[Mechanism of Action] This point is commonly used to treat the diseases of the ear and the diseases of the mouth, for example, difficulty in opening and closing of the jaw.
[Method] Puncture perpendicularly 0.2-0.4 cun. Moxibustion is applied.
[Acupoint Prescriptions]
1) Tinnitus and deafness: Xiaguan (ST 7), Yangxi (LI 5), Guanchong (SJ 2), Yemen (SJ 2), Yangguan (DU 3). (*A-B Classic of Acupuncture and Moxibustion*.)
2) Pain due to dental caries: Xiaguan (ST 7), Daying (ST 6), Yifeng (SJ 17), Wangu (GB 12). (*Thousand Golden Prescriptions*.)
3) Inflammation in mandibular articulation: Selecting Xiaguan (ST 7) on the cpposite side, Shangguan (GB 3), Jiache (ST 6), Hegu (LI 4) on the opposite side and in combination with Tinghui (GB 2), Yifeng (SJ 17) when necessary, give treatment every other day, 10 times for a course of treatment. (*Abstract of Clinical Experience on Acupuncturn and Moxibustion*)
[Regional Anatomy] Skin-subcutaneous tissue-the parotid gland-between the masseter muscle and the zygomatic process of the temporal bone-the lateral pterygoid muscle. In the superficial layer, there are the branches of the auriculotemporal nerve, the zygomatic branches of the facial nerve and the transverse facial artery and vein. In the deep layer, there are the maxillary artery and vein, the lingual nerve, the inferior alveolar nerve, the middle meningeal artery and the pterygoid plexus.
[Remark] It has been reported that puncturing Xiaguan (ST 7) point may affect cerebral cortical motor area. Experiments showed that strong stimulation could develop an inhibitory process of the cerebral cortical motor area. But in the normal person, the inhibitory response develops very slowly. With slight stimulation, 50% of the patients exhibited an excitatory process of the cerebral cortical motor area, 50% of the patients exhibited inhibitory process. A few people exhibited inhibitory process in a normal population. This result indicated that different stimulation causes different reaction.

ST 8   Touwei (头维)
(Head Corner)

【Source】 *A-B Classic of Acupuncture and Moxibustion*
【Name Explanation】 Tou (头), head; Wei (维), corner or angle. The point is at the angle between two hairlines at the front.
【Classification】 The Crossing Point of the Gallbladder Meridian of Foot Shaoyang and the Yangwei Meridians.
【Location】 On the lateral side of the head, 0.5 cun above the anterior hairline at the corner of the forehead, and 4.5 cun lateral to the midline of the head. (See Fig. 11-2)
【Localization】 Sitting, first locate Toulinqi (GB 15), the point is located at the same distance from Toulinqi (GB 15) to Shenting (DU 24) lateral to Toulinqi (GB 15), 0.5 cun above the anterior hairline.
【Indications】
   Diseases of the Head and Sense Organs: Headache and migraine, vertigo, pain of eyes, lacrimation induced by wind, eyelid tremors.
【Mechanism of Action】 The stomache and the large intestine are linked together in the inner canthus, they go along the hair-line up about 5 fen and intersect at the point of Shenting (DU 24). This point is commonly used to treat migraine, headache, vertigo and eye diseases.
【Method】 Puncture subcutaneously 0.5-1 cun.
【Acupoint Prescriptions】
   1) Head diseases and eye pain: Touwei (ST 8), Daling (PC 7). (*Thousand Golden Prescriptions*.)
   2) Eyelid tremors: Touwei (ST 8), Cuanzhu (UB 2). (*Great Compendium of Acupuncture and Moxibustion*.)
   3) Epiphora induced by wind: Touwei (ST 8), Jingming (BL 1), Toulinqi (GB 15), Fengchi (GB 20). (*ibid*.)
【Regional Anatomy】 Skin-subcutaneous tissue-epicranial aponeurosis-subaponeurotic loose connective tissue-pericranium. There are the branches of the auriculotemporal nerve, the temporal branches of the facial nerve and the frontal branches of the superficial temporal artery and vein in this area.
【Remark】 Touwei (ST 8) point was used in the patients with gastro-duodenal ulcers. It inhibited gastric electric action, and increased WBCs. Therefore, it can be used to treat leukopenic patients resulting from hyperplenism.

ST 9   Renying (人迎)
(Man's Welcome)

【Source】 *Miraculous Pivot and Plain Questions*
【Name Explanation】 Ren (人), mankind; Ying (迎), to meet. The point lies beside the Renying artery.
【Location】 On the neck, beside the adams apple, and on the anterior border of the sternocleidomastoid muscle where the pulsation of the common carotid artery is palpable. (See Fig. 11-3)
【Localization】 Sitting with head rest, locate the point at 1.5 cun lateral to the Adam's apple

where there is arteriopalmus, be careful to avoid puncturing the artery.

【Indications】

1) Diseases of the Head and Sense Organs: Headache, vertigo, sore throat.

2) Respiratory Diseases: Fullness sensation in the chest, asthma.

3) Digestive Diseases: Cholera, vomiting, difficulty in swallowing.

4) Other Diseases: Hypertension.

【Mechanism of Action】

1) Its meridian goes along the hairline to the forehead so this point can be used to treat headache and vertigo caused by excessive heat in Yangming.

2) The Stomach Meridian belongs to the stomach, so this point can be used to treat cholera and vomiting.

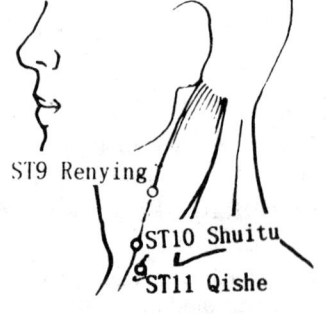

Fig. 11-3

3) On the basis of local indications of the acupoint, this point can be used to treat sore throat with difficult swallowing, and asthma. A remarkable curative effect has been produced in treating acute sore throat, as it can alleviate pain rapidly.

【Method】 Avoiding the artery, puncture perpendicularly 0.3-0.4 cun. Moxibustion is not advisable. (See Fig. 11-4)

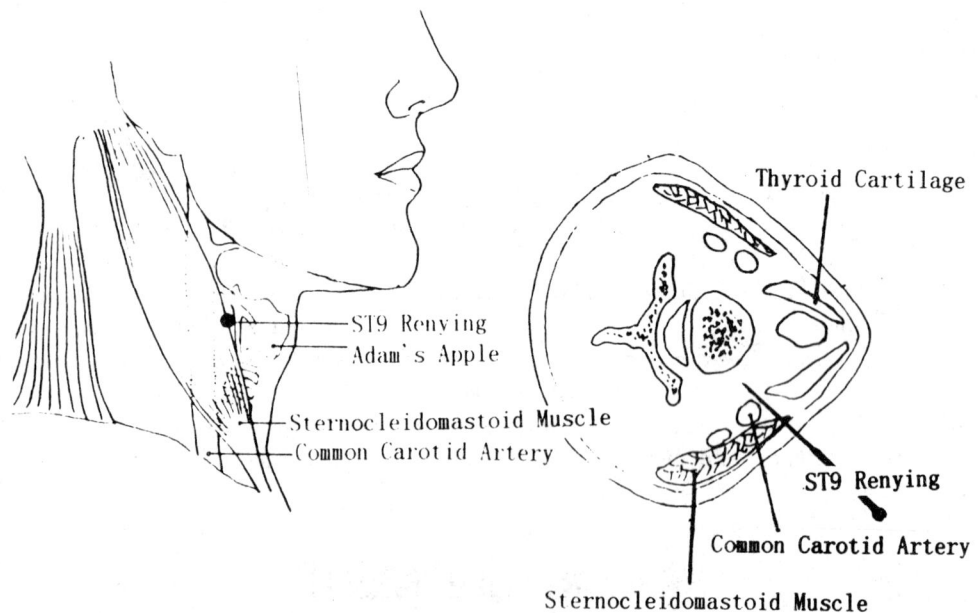

Fig. 11-4 Insetion of Needles of Renying point

【Acupoint Prescriptions】

1) Qi-mass in the chest: Reducing Renying (ST 9), Tiantu (RN 22), Houzhong (EX). (*A-B Classic of Acupuncture and Moxibustion*.)

2) Goiter: Main points: Penetrating Renying (ST 9) through Tiantu (RN 22). Supplementary points: Hegu (LI 14), Zusanli (ST 36), Zeqian (EX), Taixi (KI 3), Neiguan (PC 6), Sanyinjiao (SP 6). (*Science of Acupuncture and Moxibustion*.)

【Regional Anatomy】 Skin-subcutaneous tissue and the platysma muscle-the superficial layer of the cervical proper fascia and the anterior border of the sternocleidomastoid muscle-the deep layer of the cervical proper facia and the posterior border of the omohyoid muscle-the constrictor muscle of the pharynx. In the superficial layer, there are the transverse nerve of the neck and the cervical branches of the facial nerve. In the deep layer, there are the branches or tributaries of the superior thyroid artery and vein and the branches of the loop of the hypoglossal nerve.

【Remark】 Experiments showed that puncturing Renying (ST 9) increased pulmonary uentilation volume and function, slowed down heart rate and decreased blood pressure, such as hypertension caused by hypothyrosis or other reasons. It also has a theraputic effect on hypothyrosis.

ST 10　Shuitu（水突）
(Water Projection)

【Source】 *A-B Classic of Acupuncture and Moxibustion*
【Name Explanation】 Shui (水), water and food; Tu (突), passing through. The point is at the neck close to the esophagus, where water and food pass.
【Location】 On the neck and on the anterior border of the sternocleidomastoid muscle, at the midpoint of the line connecting Renying (ST 9) and qishe (ST 11). (See Fig. 11-3)
【Localization】 Sitting with head rest, the point is located directly inferior to Renying (ST 9), anterior border of sternocleidomastoid muscle, the same level with inferior margin of thyroid cartilage, at the midpoint of line joining Renying (ST 9) and Qishe (ST 11).
【Indications】
　1) Respiratory Diseases: Cough with dyspnea, shortness of breath with inability to fall sleep, sore throat.
　2) Other Diseases: Scrofula, goiter, hiccup, swelling shoulder.
【Mechanism of Action】 This point is located on the trachea of the throat where scrofula and goiter usually occur. On the basis of local indications of the acupoints, puncturing this point can ease the chest and regulate the flow of qi, resolve phlegm and relieve sore throat.
【Method】 Puncture perpendicularly 0.3-0.4 cun. Moxibustion is applied. (See Fig. 11-4)
【Acupoint Prescription】 Hoarseness: main points: Shuitu (ST 10), Renying (ST 9), Lianquan (RN 23), Tianding (LI 17), Futu (LI 18). Supplementery points: Jianshi (PC 5), Hegu (LI 4), Erjian (LI 2), Jiache (ST 6). (*Abstract of Clinical Experience on Acupuncture and Moxibustion.*)
【Regional Anatomy】 Skin subcutaneous tissue and the platysma muscle-the superficial layer of the cervical proper fascia and the sternocleidomastoid muscle-the deep layer of the cervical proper fascia, the omohyoid muscle and the sternothyroid muscle. In the superficial layer, there is the transverse nerve of the neck. In the deep layer, there is the thyroid gland.
【Remark】 Shuitu (ST 10) point is near the thyroid gland. So it affects the thyroid gland function and markedly decrease iodine intake.

ST 11　Qishe（气舍）
(Qi Room)

【Source】 *A-B Classic of Acupuncture and Moxibustion*
【Name Explanation】 Qi (气), vital energy; She (舍), residence. Qi refers to the vital energy of the Lung and Stomach. The point is beside the trachea and like a dwelling for qi.
【Location】 On the neck and on the upper border of the medial end of the clavicle, between the

sternal and clavicular heads of the sternocleidomastoid muscle. (See Fig. 11-3)
[Localization] Sitting with head rest, locate the point directly inferior to Renying (ST 9), which is located at the superior margin of the medial extremity of the clavicle. 1.5 cun lateral to Tiantu (RN 22).
[Indications]
  1) Respiratory Diseases: Cough with dyspnea, asthma, chocking sensation in the chest, sore throat.
  2) Other Diseases: Swollen shoulder, stiffness and pain of the neck and nape.
[Mechanism of Action] This point is near the lung with the function of regulating the flow of qi that alleviate pain and relieves asthma. It can be used to treat various respiratory diseases.
[Method] Puncture perpendicularly 0.3-0.5 cun. Moxibustion is applied.
[Regional Anatomy] Skin-subcutaneous tissue and the platysma muscle-between the sternal head and the clavicular head of the sternocleidomastoid muscle. In the superficial layer, there are the branches of the medial supraclavical nerve, the transverse nerve of the neck and the cervical branches of the facial nerve. In the deep layer, there are the arch connecting the bilateral anterior jugular veins and the brachiocephalicvein.
[Remark] It has been reported that puncturing Qishe (ST 11), Tianfu (RN 22), and Hegu (LI 4) points can treat endemic goiter. With an effective rate as high as 86.9%. After acupuncture, swelling of the neck and other symptoms were reduced or alleviated, iodine content in the urine was decreased and there was an increased iodine intake by the thyroid gland.

ST 12 Quepen (缺盆)
(Broken Basin)

[Source] *Plain Questions*
[Name Explanation] Que (缺), depression; Pen (盆), basin. Quepen refers to the supraclavicular fossa, where the point is located.
[Location] At the centre of the supraclavicular fossa, 4 cun lateral to the anterior midline. (See Fig. 11-5)
[Localization] Sitting with head rest, locate the point at middle of the supraclavivular fossa, just superior to the middle of clavicle, at the depression lateral to the clavicular head of sternocleidomastoid muscle.
[Indications]
  Respiratory Diseases: Cough, shortness of breath, hemoptysis, sore throat, choking sensation in the chest, feverish sensation in the chest.
[Mechanism of Action] Where the acupoint locates, where the indications are.
[Method] Puncture perpendicularly 0.3-0.5 cun. Moxibustion is applied. Deep puncture is prohibited.
[Acupoint Prescriptions]
  1) Lumbago with difficulty in bending forward and backward: Select Quepen (ST 12) first, then Changqiang (DU 1). (*A-B Classic of Acupuncture and Moxibustion*)

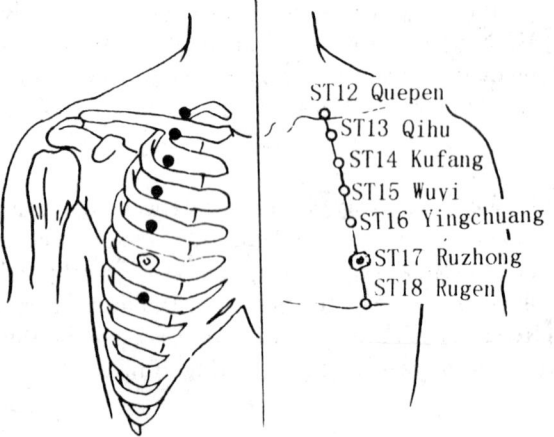

Fig. 11-5

2) Hemoptysis: Quepen (ST 12), Xinshu (BL 15), Ganshu (BL 18), Juque (RN 15). (*Thousand Golden Prescriptions*)

【Regional Anatomy】 Skin-subcutaneous tissue and the platysma muscle-between the clavicle and the trapezius muscle-between inferior belly of the omohyoid muscle and the subclavicular muscle-the brachial plexus. In the superficial layer, there is the intermediate supraclavicular nerve. In the deep layer, there are the transverse cervical artery and vein and the supraclavicular portion of the brachial plexus.

ST 13   Qihu (气户)
(Qi Door)

【Source】 *A-B Classic of Acupuncture and Moxibustion*

【Name Explanation】 Qi (气), vital energy; Hu (户), door. The point is on the upper chest and like a door for qi, the vital energy of the Lung and Stomach.

【Location】 On the chest, below the midpoint of the lower border of the clavicle, 4 cun lateral to the anterior midline. (See Fig. 11-5)

【Localization】 Sitting or in the supine position, locate the point at the middle of inferior margin of clavicle, 4 cun lateral to the mid-sternal line, directly superior to the nipple.

【Indications】
1) Respiratory Diseases: Dyspnea, cough, fullness sensation in the chest and hypochondrium, sore throat.
2) Digestive Diseases: Hiccup, dysphagia, hematemesis.

【Mechanism of Action】 On the basis of local indications of the acupoint Qihu (ST 13) can be used to treat respiratory diseases.

【Method】 Puncture obliquely 0.3-0.5 cun. Moxibustion is applied.

【Acupoint Prescriptions】
1) Pain of anterior thoracic nerves: Qihu (ST 13), Kufang (ST 14), Wuyi (ST 15), Yingchuang (ST 16). (*New Acupuncture and Moxibustion.*)
2) Pain in hypochondriac region: Qihu (ST 13), Huagai (RN 20). (*Songs of Hundreds of Symptoms.*)

【Regional Anatomy】 Skin-subcutaneous tissue-the pectoral muscle. In the superficial layer, there is the intermediate supraclavicular nerve. In the deep layer, there are the axillary artery and the thoracoacromial artery.

【Remark】 Puncturing Qihu (ST 13) can have a good therapeutic effect when treating bronchial asthma, and can also relieve bronchospasm and regulate bronchi function.

ST 14   Kufang (库房)
(Store House)

【Source】 *A-B Classic of Acupuncture and Moxibustion*

【Name Explanation】 Ku (库), storehouse; Fang (房), side room. Inhaled air is stored in the lung as if in a storehouse and descends as if through a door into a side room.

【Location】 On the chest, in the 1st intercostal space, 4 cun lateral to the anterior midline. (See Fig. 11-5)

【Localization】 Sitting or in the supine position, locate the point directly superior to the nipple,

at the middle of the 1st intercostal space.
【Indications】
　　Respiratory Diseases: Cough, dyspnea hemoptysis with pus, fullness sensation in the chest and hypochondrium.
【Mechanism of Action】 Kufang (ST 14) is in the dividing line of the lung, so it has the function of promoting circulation of qi to alleviate stagnation in the chest and relieving asthma.
【Method】 Puncture obliquely 0.3-0.5 cun. Moxibustion is applied.
【Acupoint Prescriptions】
　　1) Cough with dyspnea, or breath with frothy sputum, pus and blood: Kufang (ST 14), Zhongfu (LU 1), Zhourong (SP 20), Chize (LU 5). (*Experience on Acupuncture and Moxibustion Therapy*)
　　2) Cough with dyspnea: Kufang (ST 14), Wuyi (ST 15), Gaohuang (BL 46). (*ibid*)
【Regional Anatomy】 Skin-subcutaneous tissue-the greater pectoral muscle-the smaller pectoral muscle. In the superficial layer, there are the supraclavicular nerve and the cutaneous branches of the intercostal nerve. In the deep layer, there are the branches or tributaries of the thoracoacromial artery and vein and the branches of the medial pectoral and lateral pectoral nerve.

ST 15   Wuyi (屋翳)
(Chamber Root)

【Source】 *A-B Classic of Acupuncture and Moxibustion*
【Name Explanation】 Wu (屋), room; Yi (翳), concealment. The point is at the mid-chest. When the inhaled air reaches this point, it "conceals" itself in the underlying room.
【Location】 On the chest, in the 2nd intercostal space, 4 cun lateral to the anterior midline. (See Fig. 11-5)
【Localization】 In sitting or supine position, locate the point directly superior to the nipple, at the middle of the 2nd intercostal space.
【Indications】
　　1) Respiratory Diseases: Cough, asthma, hemoptysis with pus, fullness sensation in the chest and hypochondrium.
　　2) Other Diseases: pruritus on the whole body, pain of the skin with difficulty in touching (brushing) clothes, acute mastitis.
【Mechanism of Action】
　　1) This point is located in the chest and breast. So it is used to treat respiratory deseases and mastitis. Apply Hegu needling in clinical practice.
　　2) The Stomach Meridian is the meridian with more qi and blood. This point can be used to treat dermatosis by regulating Ying and Wei.
【Method】 Puncture obliquely 0.3-0.5 cun. Moxibustion is applied.
【Regional Anatomy】 Skin-subcutaneous tissue-the greater pectoral muscle-smaller pectoral muscle. In the superficial layer, there are the lateral cutaneous branches of the second intercostal nerve. In the deep layer, there are the branches or tributaries of the thoracoacromial artery and vein and the branches of the medial pectoral and lateral pectoral nerves.
【Remark】 A clinical report showed that puncturing Wuyi (ST 15) had a significant effect when compared with that of a control group taking testicular hormone in treating hyperplasia of mammary glands. The cellular immune function test indicated that it may increase immune function.

ST 16　Yingchuang (膺窗)
(Chest Window)

【Source】 *A-B Classic of Acupuncture and Moxibustion*
【Name Explanation】 Ying (膺), chest; Chuang (窗), window. The point is like a window in the chest.
【Location】 On the chest, in the 3rd intercostal space, 4 cun lateral to the anterior midline. (See Fig. 11-5)
【Localization】 Sitting or in the supine position, locate the point at directly superior to the nipple, at the middle of the 3rd intercostal space.
【Indications】
　　1) Respiratory Diseases: Cough, asthma, distension and pain in the chest and hypochondrium, shortness of breath.
　　2) Digestive Diseases: Diarrhea, borborygmus.
　　3) Other Diseases: Mastitis, swollen lips.
【Mechanism of Action】
　　1) The point can be used to treat respiratory diseases.
　　2) The Stomach Meridian belongs to the stomach, so it can be used to treat gastrointestinal diseases.
　　3) The point is in the breast, so it is used to treat mastitis by Hegu needling (puncturing perpedicularly and then obliquely right and left).
【Method】 Puncture obliquely 0.3-0.5 cun. Moxibustion is applied.
【Acupoint Prescriptions】
　　1) Swollen lips: Yingchuang (ST 16), Taichong (LR 3). (*Experience on Acupuncture and Moxibustion Therapy*)
　　2) Acute mastitis: Yingchuang (ST 16), Rugen (ST 18), Jianjing (GB 21), Quchi (LI 11), Shangjuxu (ST 37), Taichong (LR 3). (*Chinese Acupuncture and Moxibustion*)
【Regional Anatomy】 Skin-subcutaneous tissue-the greater pectoral muscle-the intercostal muscle. In the superficial layer, there are the lateral cutaneous branches of the intercostal nerve and the tributaries of the thoracoepigastic vein. In the deep layer, there are the medial and the lateral pectoral nerves, the branches or tributaries of the thoracoacromial artery and vein, the third intercostal nerve and the third posterior intercostal artery and vein.

ST 17　Ruzhong (乳中)
(Middle of Nipple)

【Source】 *A-B Classic of Acupuncture and Moxibustion*
【Name Explanation】 Ru (乳), breast; Zhong (中), center. The point is at the center of the nipple.
【Location】 On the chest, in the 4th intercostal space, at the centre of the nipple, 4 cun lateral to the anterior midline. (See Fig. 11-5)
【Localization】 Sitting or in the supine position, locate the point at directly superior to the nipple, and at the middle of the 4th intercostal space on males.
【Indications】 Acute epilepsy, epilepsy with sudden onset in children, heatstroke, retention of

placenta.

【Mechanism of Action】 This point is only used as the anatomical landmark at the chest region and is not used in the treatment of Acupuncture and Moxibustion.

【Regional Anatomy】 Skin of the mammary nipple-subcutaneous tissie-the greater pectoral muscle. In the superficial layer, there are the lateral cutaneous branches of the fourth intercostal nerve. In males, the subcutaneous tissue is mainly composed of the connective tissue and the trace, but not parenchyma, of the mammary gland. In the deep layer, there are the branches of the medial and lateral pectoral nerves and the branches or tributaries of the lateral pectoral artery and vein.

ST 18   Rugen (乳根)
(Breast Root)

【Source】 A-B Classic of Acupuncture and Moxibustion

【Name Explanation】 Ru (乳), breast; Gen (根), root or base. The point is at the base of the breast.

【Location】 On the chest, directly below the nipple, on the lower border of the breast, in the 5th intercostal space, 4 cun lateral to the anterior midline. (See Fig. 11-5)

【Localization】 Supine position, locate the point at directly superior to the nipple, at the middle of the 5th intercostal space.

【Indications】
 1) Respiratory Diseases: Cough with vomiting of bloody pus, oppressed feeling in the chest, swelling pain in chest.
 2) Digestive Diseases: Dysphagia, regurgitation with vomiting, acute abdominal distention, difficult breathing with qi ascending up to the heart and chest.
 3) Other Diseases: Mastitis, shortness of lactation.

【Mechanism of Action】 Today, this point is usually used to treat mastitis by means of Hegu needling.

【Method】 Puncture obliquely 0.3-0.5 cun. Moxibustion is applied.

【Acupoint Prescriptions】
 1) Cough due to disorder of qi and asthma due to stagnation of profuse phlegm: Rugen (ST 18), Shufu (KI 27). (Songs of Jade Dragon)
 2) Excessive lactation: Rugen (ST 18), Jianzhongshu (SI 15), Ganshu (BL 18), Xinshu (BL 15), Shaohai (HT 3), Tongli (HT 5). (New Acupuncture and Moxibustion)

【Regional Anatomy】 Skin-subcutaneous tissue-the greater pectoral muscle. In the superficial layer, there are the lateral cutaneous branches of the 5th intercostal nerve and the tributaries of the thoracoepigastric vein. In the deep layer, there are the branches or tributaries of the lateral pectoral artery and vein, the branches of the medial and lateral pectoral nerves, the 5th intercostal nerve and the 5th posterior intercostal artery and vein.

【Remark】 Clinical observation showed that puncturing Rugen (ST 18) may treat coronary heart disease, increase myocardial contractive power, slow down heart rate and improve abnormal electro-cardiogram.

ST 19 Burong (不容)
(No Admittance)

【Source】 A-B Classic of Acupuncture and Moxibustion

【Name Explanation】 Bu (不), not; Rong (容), contain. The point is on the upper abdomen and marks the upper limitation level for the stomach to recieve water and food.

【Location】 On the upper abdomen, 6 cun above the centre of the umbilicus and 2 cun lateral to the anterior midline. (See Fig. 11-6)

【Localization】 Supine position, locate the point at 6 cun superior to the umbilicus, 2 cun lateral to the mid-ventral line.

【Indications】
  1) Respiratory Diseases: Cough, hemoptysis, asthma.
  2) Digestive Diseases: Epigastralgia, vomiting, abdominal distention, borborygmus, hematemesis, dry mouth, poor appetite, infantile indigestion with food retention.
  3) Cardiovascular Diseases: Precordial pain, chest pain radiating to the back, pain in hypochondriac region.
  4) Other Diseases: Hernia, nyctalopia.

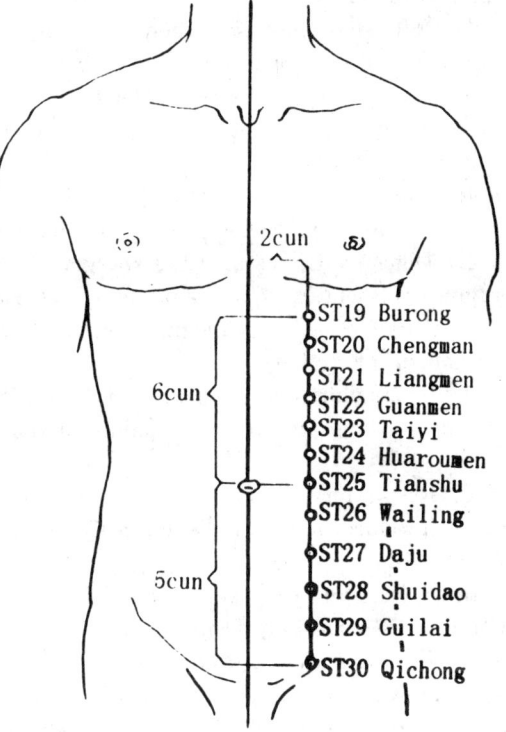

Fig. 11-6

【Mechanism of Action】 Patients suffering from precordial pain always have the symptom of epigastralgia. The Stomach Meridian is up to the heart, so this point can be used for patients who suffer from procordial pain affecting the stomach. (See also Liangmen (ST 21)).

【Method】 Puncture perpendicularly 0.5-1 cun. Moxibustion is applied.

【Acupoint Prescriptions】
  1) Terrible precordial pain with vomiting gastric acid: Burong (ST 19), Qimen (LR 14). (Experience on Acupuncture and Moxibustion Therapy)
  2) Hernia: Burong (ST 19), Zhongji (RN 3). (ibid)

【Regional Anatomy】 Skin-subcutaneous tissue-the anterior sheath of rectus muscle of the abdomen-the retus muscle of the abdomen. In the superficial layer, there are the lateral and anterior cutaneous branches of the anterior branches of the 6th to the 8th thoracic nerves and the superficial epigastic vein. In the deep layer, there are the branches or tributaries of the superior epigastic artery and vein and the muscular branches of the anterior branches of the 6th and the 7th thoracic nerves.

【Remark】 It has been reported that puncturing Burong (ST 19) affected the heart rate and treated paroxysmal tachyeardia.

ST 20 Chengman (承满)
(Fullness Receive)

【Source】 *A-B Classic of Acupuncture and Moxibustion*
【Name Explanation】 Cheng (承), receive; Man (满), full. The point is on the upper abdomen. The stomach is full when water and food reach this level.
【Location】 On the upper abdomen, 5 cun above the centre of the umbilicus and 2 cun lateral to the anterior midline. (See Fig. 11-6)
【Localization】 Supine position, locate the point at 5 cun superior to the umbilicus, 2 cun lateral to the mid-ventral line.
【Indications】
　　1) Respiratory Diseases: Asthma, tense pain in the hypochondrium.
　　2) Digestive Diseases: Epigastralgia, vomiting, hematemesis, abdominal distention, borborygmus, dysentery, poor appetite, undigested food, loose stool.
　　3) Other Diseases: Phlegm retention, body swelling, clonic convulsion.
【Mechanism of Action】
　　1) This point is near the stomach, so it is used to treat digestive diseases. Phlegm retention and body swelling are caused by failure of the spleen when transporting and transforming nutrients.
　　2) Respiratory diseases, such as asthma, are due to adverse rising of stomach qi, Earth does not produce Metal. Relieving asthma can be realized by regulating both the flow of qi and the stomach.
【Method】 Puncture perpendicularly 0.5-1 cun. Moxibustion is applied.
【Acupoint Prescription】 Diaphragm: Chengman (ST 20), Rugen (ST 18). (*Experience on Acupuncture and Moxibustion Therapy*.)
【Regional Anatomy】 Skin-subcutaneous tissue-the anterior sheath of rectus muscle of the abdomen-the retus muscle of the abdomen. In the superficial layer, there are the lateral and anterior cutaneous branches of the anterior branches of the 6th to the 8th thoracic nerves and the superficial epigastic vein. In the deep layer, there are the branches or tributaries of the superior epigastic artery and vein and the muscular branches of the anterior branches of the 6th and the 8th thoracic nerves.

ST 21 Liangmen (梁门)
(Beam Gate)

【Source】 *A-B Classic of Acupuncture and Moxibustion*
【Name Explanation】 Liang (梁), grain or food; Men (门), door. The point, on the upper epigastric region, is the door for passage of food to the stomach.
【Location】 On the upper abdomen, 4 cun above the centre of the umbilicus and 2 cun lateral to the anterior midline. (See Fig. 11-6)
【Localization】 Supine position, locate the point at 4 cun superior to the umbilicus, 2 cun lateral to the mid-ventral line.
【Indications】
　　1) Digestive Diseases: Epigastralgia, vomiting, poor appetite, loose stool, fullness in hypochondriac region and abdomen.

2) Other Diseases: Prolapse of anus, abdominal mass in women.

【Mechanism of Action】 This point is located in the stomach and mainly used to treat digestive diseases. The Yangming Meridian is a meridian which contains more qi and blood, masses in the abdomen can be treated by clearing and activating the meridians and collaterals, and promoting blood circulation to remove blood stasis.

【Method】 Puncture perpendicualrly 0.7-1 cun. Moxibustion is applied.

【Regional Anatomy】 Skin-subcutaneous tissue-the anterior sheath of rectus mescle of the abdomen-the retus muscle of the abdomen. In the superficial layer, there are the lateral and anterior cutaneous branches of the anterior branches of the 7th to the 9th thoracic nerves and the superficial epigastic vein. In the deep layer, there are the branches or tributaries of the superior epigastic artery and vein and the muscular branches of the anterior branches of the 7th and the 9th thoracic nerves.

【Remark】 It has been reported that puncturing Liangmen (ST 21) point may cause normalization of gastro-enteric function and inhibit gastric electiec action. Therefore, it can be used to treat ulcers of both the stomach and the duodeum along with intestinal dysfunctions.

ST 22 Guanmen (关门)
(Pivotal Gate)

【Source】 A-B Classic of Acupuncture and Moxibustion

【Name Explanation】 Guan (关), pass; Men (门), door. The point is close to the lower stomach and corresponds to the junction between the stomach and the intestines, opening and closing like a door.

【Location】 On the upper abdomen, 3 cun above the centre of the umbilicus and 2 cun lateral to the anterior midline. (See Fig. 11-6)

【Localization】 Supine position, locate the point at 3 cun superior to the umbilicus, 2 cun lateral to the mid-ventral line.

【Indications】

1) Digestive Diseases: Abdominal pain, abdominal distention, borborygmus and diarrhea, poor appetite.

2) Urinary Diseases: Enuresis, ascites, body swelling.

【Mechanism of Action】 The point is located near the intestines and stomach and is mainly used for treating digestive diseases. Ascites and body swelling can be treated by regulating the spleen's function of transporting and transforming nutrients.

【Method】 Puncture perependicularly 0.7-1 cun. Moxibustion is applied.

【Acupoint Prescriptions】

1) Enuresis: Guanmen (ST 22), Shenmen (HT 7), Weizhong (BL 40). (A-B Classic of Acupuncture and Moxibustion)

2) Enuresis: Guanmen (ST 22), Zhongfu (LU 1), Shenmen (HT 7). (Thousand Golden Prescriptions)

3) Sensation of gas rushing and distention feeling in the breast: Guanyuan (RN 4), Guanmen (ST 22), Shuidao (ST 28), Sanyinjiao (SP 6). (Great Compendium of Acupuncture and Moxibustion)

【Regional Anatomy】 Skin-subcutaneous tissue-the anterior sheath of rectus muscle of the abdomen-the retus muscle of the abdomen. In the superficial layer, there are the lateral and anterior cutaneous branches of the anterior branches of the 7th to the 9th thoracic nerves and the superficial epigastic vein. In the deep layer, there are the branches or tributaries of the superior ecpigastic artery and vein and the muscular branches of the anterior branches of the 7th and the 9th thoracic nerves.

ST 23　Taiyi (太乙)
(Supreme Yi)

【Source】 *A-B Classic of Acupuncture and Moxibustion*
【Name Explanation】 Tai (太), great; Yi (乙), one of ten Heavenly Stems. The center was considered as Taiyi in ancient times, Taiyi being the central Palace of Hetu (the eight diagrams). The Spleen is at the center, and the center of the abdomen is indentified with Taiyi. The point is on the lower stomach, corresponding to the center of the abdomen.
【Location】 On the upper abdomen, 2 cun above the centre of the umbilicus and 2 cun lateral to the anterior midline. (See Fig. 11-6)
【Localization】 Supine position, locate the point at 2 cun superior to the umbilicus, 2 cun lateral to the mid-ventral line.
【Indications】
　　1) Digestive Diseases: Epigastralgia, dysphagia.
　　2) Mental Diseases: Manic-depressive psychosis, wagging tongue, vexation.
　　3) Other Diseases: Hernia, beriberi, enuresis.
【Mechanism of Action】 This point is at the intestine and near the stomach. Digestive diseases can be treated by needling this point. Mental diseases are mainly caused by dysfunction of the spleen in transportation, retention of phlegm in the body and the heart disturbed by phlegm-fire. This point can be used for strengthening the spleen, eliminating dampness and resolving phlegm. Mental diseases can also be treated by clearing away the heat accumulated at Yangming Meridian.
【Method】 Puncture perpendicularly 0.7-1 cun. Moxibustion is applied.
【Acupoint Prescription】 Madness, wagging tongue: Taiyi (ST 23), Huaroumen (ST 24). (*A-B Classic of Acupuncture and Moxibustion*)
【Regional Anatomy】 Skin-subcutaneous tissue-the anterior sheath of rectus muscle of the abdomen-the retus muscle of the abdomen. In the superficial layer, there are the lateral and anterior cutaneous branches of the anterior branches of the 8th to the 10th thoracic nerves and the superficial epigastic vein. In the deep layer, there are the branches or tributaries of the superior epigastic artery and vein and the muscular branches of the anterior branches of the 8th and the 10th thoracic nerves.

ST 24　Huaroumen (滑肉门)
(Slippery Flesh Gate)

【Source】 *A-B Classic of Acupuncture and Moxibustion*
【Name Explanation】 Hua (滑), good; Rou (肉), muscle; Men (门), door. Huarou refers to the partially digested fine food. The point is at a level 1 cun above the navel where the food is separated into clear and turbid. It is also like a door where the fine food passes through.
【Location】 On the upper abdomen, 1 cun above the centre of the umbilicus and 2 cun lateral to the anterior midline. (See Fig. 11-6)
【Localization】 Supine position, locate the point at 1 cun superior to the umbilicus, 2 cun lateral to the mid-ventral line.
【Indications】
　　1) Digestive Diseases: Epigastralgia, vomiting, hematemesis, prolapse of anus.

2) Mental Diseases: Manic-depressive psychosis, epilepsy, wagging tongue, stiff tongue.
【Mechanism of Action】 See also Taiyi (ST 23).
【Method】 Puncture perpendicularly 0.7-1 cun. Moibustion is applied.
【Acupoint Prescription】 Wagging tongue: Huaroumen (ST 24), Shaohai (HT 3), Wenliu (LI 7). (*Experience on Acupuncture and Moxibustion Therapy*.)
【Regional Anatomy】 Skin-subcutaneous tissue-the anterior sheath of rectus muscle of the abdomen-the retus muscle of the abdomen. In the superficial layer, there are the lateral and anterior cutaneous branches of the anterior branches of the 8th to the 10th thoracic nerves and the periumbilical venous network. In the deep layer, there are the branches or tributaries of the superior epigastic artery and vein and the muscular branches of the anterior branches of the 8th and the 10th thoracic nerves.

ST 25　Tianshu (天枢)
(Heaven Pivot)

【Source】 *Miraculous Pivot*
【Name Explanation】 Tian (天), heaven; Shu (枢), pivot. The region above the navel is considered as heaven, pertaining to Yang, while the region below the navel is earth, pertaining to Yin. The point is on a level with the navel, like the pivot between heaven and earth.
【Classification】 Front-Mu Point of the Large Intestine.
【Location】 On the middle abdomen, 2 cun lateral to the centre of the umbilicus. (See Fig. 11-6)
【Localization】 Supine position, locate the point at 2 cun lateral to the umbilicus.
【Indications】
　　1) Digestive Diseases: Diarrhea, dysentery, abdominal distention, borborygmus, acute appendicitis, epigastralgia, vomiting, jaundice.
　　2) Gynecopathy: Irregular menstruation, incessant menstruation, mass in the abdomen, metrorrhagia and metrostaxis, dysmenorrhea, amenorrhea, leukorrhea, postpartum tormina, sterility.
　　3) Urinary Diseases: Difficult urination, edema, stranguria with turbid urine.
　　4) Mental Disease: Infantile convulsion, ravings, trance.
　　5) Other Diseases: Tympanites, umbilical hernia, pain around the navel, sensation of gas rushing, malaria, ravings due to intense heat, lumbago, vertigo, consumptive diseases.
【Mechanism of Action】
　　1) Tianshu (ST 25) is the Front Mu point of the large intestine and can be mainly used to treat the diseases in the large intestine, such as diarrhea, dysentery, constipation, acute appendicitis, enteroparelysis, pain around navel, and abdominal distention, etc.
　　2) The point (near the stomach) belongs to the Stomach Meridian and can be needled for stomachache and vomiting, etc. The diseases, such as jaundice, vertigo and consumption, can be treated by regulating the function of the stomach and intestine, restoring qi and removing dampness.
　　3) The point is near the lower abdomen, where the genitourinary system lies. The book Classic of Medical Problems states that one of the collaterals in Chong Meridian originates from Qichong (ST 30), and advances together with the Stomach Meridian. Chong Meridian, which originates from the uterus, is closely related with reproductive system and advances together with the Kidney Meridian. As the kidney is in charge of water, reproductive and urogenital diseases can be treated by needling this point.
　　4) According to the principle of corresponding treatment of points, if the location of lumber

pain is opposite to Tianshu (ST 25). This point can be used to relieve the pain. This method is called anterior-posterior point combination.

5) This point is needled for treating mental diseases due to dryness-heat in the stomach and intestine.

【Method】 Puncture perpendicularly 0.7-1 cun. Moxibustion is applied.

【Acupoint Prescriptions】

1) Pulse in Chi being tense, pain below the umbilical region: Moxibustion to Tianshu (ST 25), acupuncture to Guanyuan (RN 4) by reinforcing method. (*Classic of Meridians*)

2) Edema: Tianshu (ST 25), Fenglong (ST 40), Lidui (ST 45), Xiangu (ST 43), Chongyang (ST 42). (*Thousand Golden Prescriptions*)

3) Abdominal pain: Tianshu (ST 25), Wailing (ST 26). (*Experience on Acupuncture and Moxibustion Therapy*)

4) Ovaritis: Tianshu (ST 25), Daimai (GB 26), Sanyinjiao (SP 6); Acute bacillary dysentery: Tianshu (ST 25), Daju (ST 27), Qihai (RN 6), Zusanli (ST 36). (*Abstract of Clinical Experience on Acupuncture and Moxibustion*)

5) Acute Enterogastritis: Tianshu (ST 25), Zusanli (ST 36). (*ibid*)

6) Irregular Menstruation: Tianshu (ST 25), Shuiquan (KI 5). (*Songs of Hundreds of Symptoms*)

【Regional Anatomy】 Skin-subcutaneous tissue-the anterior sheath of rectus muscle of the abdomen-the retus muscle of the abdomen. In the superficial layer, there are the lateral and anterior cutaneous branches of the anterior branches of the 9th to the 11th thoracic nerves and the periumbilical venous network. In the deep layer, there are the branches or tributaries of the superior epigastic arteries and veins and the muscular branches of the anterior branches of the 9th and the 11th thoracic nerves.

【Remark】 Stimulation of needle on Tianshu (ST 25) caused normalizaion of intestinal function. Patients with acute bacillary dysentery received electro-acupuncture of Tianshu (ST 25), after 3 minutes intestinal gurgling sounds changed; some decreased and some increased. Upon 15-30 minutes intestinal gurgling sounds decreased greatly. After completion of treatment patients returned to pre-treatment level of intestinal gurgling. It has been reported that acupuncture of Tianshu (ST 25) eased the syndromes of acute and chronic enteritis, bacillary dysentery, diarrhea and constipation, and increased the survival rate and decreased recovery time.

ST 26 Wailing (外陵)
(Outer Hill)

【Source】 *A-B Classic of Acupuncture and Moxibustion*

【Name Explanation】 Wai (外), exterior; Lfing (陵), hill. The local prominence of the point is like a hill.

【Location】 On the lower abdomen, 1 cun below the centre of the umbilicus and 2 cun lateral to the anterior midline. (See Fig. 11-6)

【Localization】 Supine position, locate the point 1 cun inferior to the umbilicus, 2 cun lateral to the mid-ventral line.

【Indications】 Acute appendicitis, hernia, dysmenorrhea.

【Mechanism of Action】 This point is located near the genitals and intestine, and can be used to treat all the diseases mentioned above. Patients suffering from appendicitis always feel tenderness on this point, therefore it can also be used as a secondary means of diagnosis.

【Method】 Puncture perpendicularly 0.5-1 cun. Moxibustion is applicable.

【Regional Anatomy】 Skin-subcutaneous tissue-the anterior sheath of rectus muscle of the abdomen-the retus muscle of the abdomen. In the superficial layer, there are the lateral and anterior cutaneous branches of the anterior branches of the 10th to the 12th thoracic nerves and the superficial epigastic vein. In the deep layer, there are the branches or tributaries of the inferior epigastic artery and vein and the muscular branches of the anterior branches of the 10th and the 12th thoracic nerves.

【Remark】 It has been reported that puncturing Wailing (ST 26), and Qihai (RN 6) can relax a spastic colon and treat spastic colitis. Puncturing Wailing (ST 26) and Yinlingquan (SP 9) can treat acute bacillary dysentery. The result indicated that agglutinin average titer was higher in the acupuncture group than in the electro-acupuncture group. But both groups were superior to the drug group.

ST 27 Daju (大巨)
(Big Greatness)

【Source】 A-B Classic of Acupuncture and Moxibustion
【Name Explanation】 Da (大), large; Ju (巨), huge. The point is on the greatest prominence of the abdominal wall.
【Location】 On the lower abdomen, 2 cun below the centre of the umbilicus and 2 cun lateral to the anterior midline. (See Fig. 11-6.)
【Localization】 Supine position, locate the point 2 cun inferior to the umbilicus, 2 cun lateral to the mid-ventral line.
【Indications】
    1) Urogenital Diseases: Distention in the lower abdomen, difficult urination, emission, impotence, premature ejaculation.
    2) Mental Diseases: Palpitation due to fright with difficulty in falling sleep.
    3) Other Disease: Hemiplegia.
【Mechanism of Action】 This point is located near the organ of urogenital system and can be used to treat all the diseases mentioned above. It would be better to use this point to treat mental diseases such as palpitation due to fright with difficulty in falling sleep as it may be caused by the diseases mentioned above.
【Method】 Puncture perpendicularly 0.5-1 cun. Moxibustion is applicable.
【Acupoint Prescription】 Swelling of the scrotum: Daju (ST 27), Diji (SP 8), Zhongdu (LR 6). (A-B Classic of Acupuncture and Moxibustion)
【Regional Anatomy】 Skin-subcutaneous tissue-the anterior sheath of rectus muscle of the abdomen-the retus muscle of the abdomen. In the superficial layer, there are the lateral and anterior cutaneous branches of the anterior branches of the 10th to the 12th thoracic nerves and the superficial epigastic artery and vein. In the deep layer, there are the branches or tributaries of the inferior epigastic artery and vein and the muscular branches of the anterior branches of the 10th and the 12th thoracic nerves.

ST 28 Shuidao (水道)
(Water Path)

【Source】 A-B Classic of Acupuncture and Moxibustion
【Name Explanation】 Shui (水), water; Dao (道), pathway. The deep region of the point corresponds to the small intestine and is close to the urinary bladder. It pertains to the lower

Jiao, where the waterway passes.

【Location】 On the lower abdomen, 3 cun below the centre of the umbilicus and 2 cun lateral to the anterior midline. (See Fig. 11-6.)

【Localization】 Supine position, locate the point 3 cun inferior to the umbilicus, 2 cun lateral to the mid-ventral line.

【Indications】

1) Urogenital Diseases: Difficult urination, dysmenorrhea, pain radiating to the external genitals.

2) Other Diseases: Constipation, hernia, rigid pain in the spine and waist.

【Mechanism of Action】 This point is in the organ of urogenital system and near the rectum. So it can be used to treat urogenital diseases and constipation. Rigid pain in the spine and waist can be treated by anterior-posterior point association.

【Method】 Puncture perpendicularly 0.5-1 cun. Moxibustion is applicable.

【Acupoint Prescription】 Back rigidity: Shuidao (ST 28), Jinsuo (DU 8). (*Songs of Hundreds of Symptoms*)

【Regional Anatomy】 Skin-scbcutaneous tissue-the lateral border of the anterior sheath of rectus muscle of abdomen-the lateral border of the rectus muscle of the abdomen. In the superficial layer, there are the anterior and lateral cutaneous branches of the anterior branches of the 11th and 12th thoracic nerves and the 1st lumbar nerve, and the superficial epigastic artery and vein. In the deep layer, there are the muscular branches of the anterior branches of the 11th and 12th thuracic nerves.

【Remark】 Clinical observation indicated that puncturing Shuidao (ST 28), Shenshu (BL 23) and Ciliao (BL 32) eased pain caused by urinary lithiasis.

ST 29　Guilai（归来）
（Return）

【Source】 *A-B Classic of Acupuncture and Moxibustion*

【Name Explanation】 Gui (归), return; Lai (来), arrival. This point is indicated in prolapse of the uterus, and hernia, returning the organs to their original place.

【Location】 On the lower abdomen, 4 cun below the centre of the umbilicus and 2 cun lateral to the anterior midline. (See Fig. 11-6.)

【Localization】 Supine position, first locate Qugu (RN 2) which is located at the depression of the upper margin of pubic bone, and then 2 cun lateral and 1 cun superior to Qugu (RN 2).

【Indications】

Reproductive Diseases: Amenorrhea, leukorrhea, sterility, testis going up into the abdomen, pain in penis.

【Mechanism of Action】 Guilai (ST 29) is an important point of the Stomach Meridian in the lower abdomen. The stomach is the reservoir of food and the source of nutrient essence after birth. The Chong Meridian originates from Qijie (ST 30) and goes up along the navel with the Kidney Meridian. The Chong Meridian is the sea of blood, and belongs to the Yangming System and has close relationship with reproductive diseases, therefore, it is commonly used to treat reproductive diseases.

【Method】 Puncture perpendicularly 0.5-1 cun. Moxibustion is applicable.

【Acupoint Prescriptions】

1) Swelling with bearing-down pain of one testis and swollen painless testicles: Guilai (ST 29), Dadun (LR 1), Sanyinjiao (SP 6). (*Great Compendium of Acupuncture and Moxibus-*

tion)

2) Prostatitis: Guilai (ST 29), Zigong (RN 19), Guanyuan (RN 4), Zhubin (KI 9), Sanyinjiao (SP 6). (*Science of Acupuncture and Moxibustion*)

【Regional Anatomy】Skin-subcutaneous tissue-the lateral border of the anterior sheath of the rectus muscle of the abdomen-the lateral border of rectus muscle of the abdomen. In the superficial layer, there are the superficial epigastric artery and vein, the lateral and the anterior branches of the 11th and 12th thoracic nerves and the 1st lumbar nerve, and the branches or tricutaries of the superficial epigastric artery and vein. In the deep layer, there are the branches or tributaries of the inferior epigastric artery and vein, and the muscular branches of the anterior branches of the 11th and 12th thoracic nerves.

【Remark】Puncturing Guilai (ST 29), Zhongji (RN 3) and Xuehai (SP 10) points gave rise to hemorrhage caused by stopping hormonal therapy of the patients with secondary amenorrhea.

ST 30 Qichong (气冲)
(Qi Rush)

【Source】*A-B Classic of Acupuncture and Moxibustion*
【Name Explanationl】Qi (气), qi of meridian; Chong (冲), rushing. The point is located on qi "Street" and is a passage for the qi of the meridian to circulate.
【Location】Slightly above the inguinal groove, 5 cun below the centre of the umbilicus and 2 cun lateral to the anterior midline. (See Fig. 11-6.)
【Localization】Supine position, first locate Qugu (RN 2) which is located at the depression of the upper margin of the pubic bone, this point is located 2 cun lateral to Qugu (RN 2).
【Indications】

1) Reproductive Diseases: Painful swelling on the vulva, impotence, pain in the penis, testis pain, irregular menstruation, sterility, difficult labour, retention of placenta.

2) Other Diseases: Sensation of rushing gas, lumbago, prolapse of anus.

【Mechanism of Action】See also Guilai (ST 29).
【Method】Puncture perpendicularly 0.5-1 cun. Moxibustion is applicable.
【Acupoint Prescriptions】

1) Heat feeling in the stomach: Qichong (ST 30), Zusanli (ST 36), Shangjuxu (ST 37), Shanglian (LI 9), Xialian (LI 8). (*Plain Questions*)

2) Inability to lie flat: Qichong (ST 30), Zhangmen (LR 13).   (*Experience on Acupuncture and Moxibustion Therapy*)

【Regional Anatomy】Skin-subcutaneous tissue-the aponeurosis of the external oblique muscle of the abdomen-the internal oblique muscle of the abdomen-the transverse muscle of the abdomen. In the superficial layer, there are the superficial epigastric artery and vein, the lateral and anterior cutaneous branches of the anterior branches of the 12th thoracic nerve and the 1st lumbar nerve. In the deep layer, there are the spematic cord (or the round ligament of the uterus), the ilionguinal nerve, and the genital branch of the genitofemoral nerve in the inguinal canal at the inferior lateral side of this area.

【Remark】Acupuncture of Qichong (ST 30) relaxed the intestinal spasm caused by intractable vagotonia. It has been reported that effects contraception, which may be related to the sexual glands and ovarias function.

ST 31　Biguan（髀关）
（Femoral Pass）

【Source】 *Miraculous Pivot*
【Name Explanation】 Bi （髀）, thigh; Guan （关）, joint. The point is at the femoral junction.
【Location】 On the anterior side of the thigh and on the line connecting the anterior superior iliac spine and the superiolateral corner of the patella, on the level of the perineum when the thigh is flexed, in the depression lateral to the sartorius muscle. (See Fig. 11-7.)
【Localization】

    1) Supine position, locate the point at the intersection of the line joining the spine iliac anterior superior iliac spine and the lateral border of the base of patella and the extension line of gluteal cross striation.

    2) Using the midpoint of the 1st transverse crease of palm pressing ST 32, the palm extending forward, the point is located at the tip of middle finger.
【Indications】

    Diseases along the Course of the Meridian: Pain in the waist and lower extremities, muscular contracture, flaccidity of femur numbness in the lower extremities, coldness in the knee, radiating pain in the lower abdomen.
【Mechanism of Action】 Where the acupoint locates, where the indications are.
【Method】 Puncture perpendicularly 0.6-1 cun. Moxibustion is applicable.
【Regional Anatomy】 Skin-subcutaneous tissue-between the tensor muscle of the fascia lata and the asrtorius muscle-the rectus muscle of the thigh-the lateral vastus muscle of the thigh. In the superficial layer, there is the lateral cutaneous nerve of the thigh. In the deep layer, there are the ascending branches of the lateral curcumflex femoral artery and vein and the muscular branches of the femoral nerve.

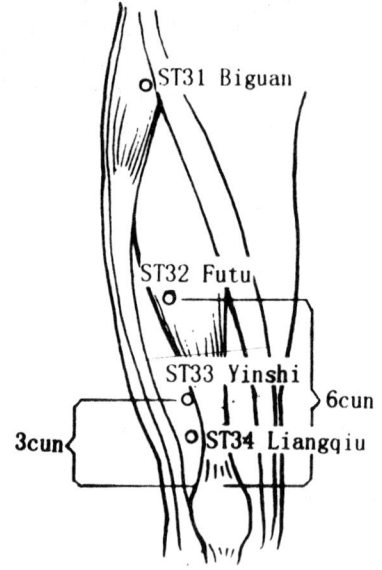

Fig. 11-7

ST 32　Futu（伏兔）
（Prostrate Rabbit）

【Source】 *Miraculous Pivot and Plain Questions*
【Name Explanation】 Fu （伏）, lying prostrate; Tu （兔）, rabbit. The prominence of the local muscle of the point looks like a rabbit in prostration.
【Location】 On the anterior side of the thigh and on the line connecting the anterior superior iliac spine and the superior lateral corner of the patella, 6 cun above this corner. (See Fig. 11-7.)
【Localization】 Sitting with the knees flexed, press the midpoint of the upper margin of patella with the midpoint of the 1st transverse crease of the palm, the point is located at the tip of middle finger.
【Indications】

1) Diseases along the Course of the Meridian: Pain in the waist and hip, coldness and pain in the legs and knees with numbness.

2) Other Diseases: Diabetes, periumbilical colic due to invasion of cold, beriberi, abdominal pain, edema.

【Mechanism of Action】 This point is mainly used to treat the diseases in the lower extremities. This point also has the function of strengthening the waist and legs, and regulating the flow of qi and blood.

【Method】 Puncture perpendicularly 1-1.5 cun. Moxibustion is applicable.

【Regional Anatomy】 Skin-subcutaneous tissue-the rectus muscle of the thigh-the intermediate vastus muscle of the thigh.

In the superficial layer, there are the lateral femoral vein, the anterior cutaneous branches of the femoral nerve and the lateral cutaneous nerve of the thigh. In the deep layer, there are the descending branches of the lateral curcumflex artery and vein and the muscular branches of the femoral nerve.

【Remark】 It has been reported that puncturing Futu (ST 32) has positive results when treating hematuria and capillary hemorrhage.

ST 33 Yinshi (阴市)
(Yin Market)

【Source】 A-B Classic of Acupuncture and Moxibustion

【Name Explanation】 Yin (阴), Yin of Yin-Yang; Shi (市), market. Yin refers to pathogenic cold, while shi means dispersion. The point is used to disperse pathogenic cold from the knee.

【Location】 On the anterior side of the thigh and on the line connecting the anterior superior iliac spine and superior lateral corner of the patella, 3 cun above this corner. (See Fig. 11-7.)

【Localization】 Sitting with the knees flexed, the point is located four fingers breadth directly superior to the lateral superior border of patella.

【Indications】

1) Diseases along the Course of the Meridian: Numbness and pain in the leg and knee with difficulty in bending and stretching, paraplegia, lumbago, beriberi, water distention of the lower extremities.

2) Digestive Diseases: Abdominal distention, abdominal pain, edema.

【Mechanism of Action】 See also Futu (ST 32) and Liangqiu (ST 34).

【Method】 Puncture perpendicularly 0.5-1 cun. Moxibustion is applicable.

【Acupoint Prescriptions】

1) Periumbilical colic due to invasion of cold: Yinshi (ST 33), Ganshu (BL 18). (*Experience on Acupuncture and Moxibustion Therapy*)

2) Periumbilical colic due to invasion of cold with abdominal pain: Yinshi (ST 33), Taixi (KI 3), Ganshu (BL 18). (*Great Compendium of Acupuncture and Moxibustion*)

【Regional Anatomy】 Skin-subcutaneous tissue-between the tendons of the rectus muscle and the lateral vastus muscle of the thigh-the intermediate vastus muscle of the thigh. In the superficial layer, there are the anterior cutaneous branches of the femoral nerve and the lateral cutaneous nerve of the thigh. In the deep layer, there are the descending branches of the lateral circumflex femoral artery and vein and the muscular branches of the femoral nerve.

ST 34 Liangqiu (梁丘)
(Beam Mound)

〖Source〗 *A-B Classic of Acupuncture and Moxibustion*
〖Name Explanation〗 Liang (梁), ridge; Qiu (丘), hills. The prominent muscle above the knee looks like a ridge in hills, This is where the point is located.
〖Classification〗 Xi-(Cleft) Point of the Stomach Meridian of the Foot Yangming.
〖Location〗 With the knee flexed, on the anterior side of the thigh and on the line connecting the anteriosuperior iliac spine and superior lateral corner of the patella, 2 cun above this corner. (See Fig. 11-7.)
〖Localization〗 Sitting with the knees flexed, the point is located 2 cun directly superior to the lateral superior border of patella.
〖Indications〗
   1) Diseases along the Course of the Meridian: Paraplegia, swollen knee, swelling pain in the waist and knee, cold limbs with difficulty in flexing and extending, mastitis.
   2) Digestive Disease: Stomachache.
〖Mechanism of Action〗
   1) On the basis of local indications of the acupoint, this point can be used to treat the diseases in the lower extremities and mastitis. The Stomach Meridian goes along the hypochondrium to the spine. This point, Yinshi (ST 33), and other points can be used to treat lumbago.
   2) This point is a Xi-(Cleft)point. Xi-(Cleft) points in the Yang Meridians are mainly used to treat sudden pain. In the clinic this point is commonly used for treating stomachache.
〖Method〗 Puncuture perpendicularly 0.5-1 cun. Moxibustion is applicable.
〖Acupoint Prescriptions〗
   1) Difficulty of the knee in bending and stretching: Liangqiu (ST 34), Ququan (LR 8), Yaoyangguan (DU 3). (*Thousand Golden Prescriptions*)
   2 Swelling of the breast: Liangqiu (ST 34), Diwuhui (GB 42).   (*Experience on Acupuncture and Moxibustion Therapy*)
〖Regional Anatomy〗 Skin-subcutaneous tissue-between the tendons of the rectus muscle of the thigh and the lateral vastus muscle of the thigh-the lateral side of the tendon of the intermediate vastus muscle of the thigh. In the superficial layer, there are the anterior cutaneous branches of the femoral nerve and the lateral cutaneous nerve of the thigh. In the deep layer, there are the descending branches of the lateral circumflex femoral artery and vein and the muscular branches of the femoral nerve.
〖Remark〗 Puncturing Liangqiu (ST 34) may cause normalization of gastric functions and inhibit gastric acid secretion.

ST 35 Dubi (犊鼻)
(Calf Nose)

〖Source〗 *Miraculous Pivot*
〖Name Explanation〗 Du (犊), calf; Bi (鼻), nose. The depressions below the kneecap are likened to the nostrils of a calf. The point is at the external foramen.
〖Location〗 With the knees flexed, the point is at the lower border of the patella, in the depres-

sion lateral to the patella ligament. (See Fig. 11-8.)

【Localization】 Sitting with the knees flexed, locate the point at the depression lateral to the patellar ligament, between the patella and tiba.

【Indications】
Cold-pain of the knee with difficulty in kneeling, flaccidity of the lower extremities.

【Mechanism of Action】 Dubi (ST 35) is a common point for treating pain of the knee joint.

【Method】 Puncture obliquely 0.7-1 cun with the tip of the needle slightly inwards. Moxibustion is applicable.

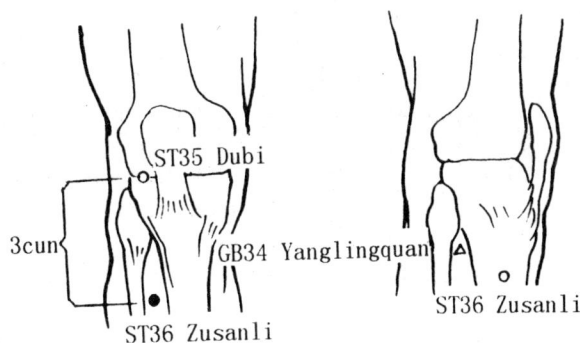

Fig. 11-8

【Acupoint Prescription】
Difficult movement of the knee joints: Dubi (ST 35), Biguan (ST 31), Yanglingquan (GB 34). (*Experience on Acupuncture and Moxibustion Therapy*)

【Regional Anatomy】 Skin-subcutaneous tissue-between the ligament of the patella and the lateral patellar retinaculum-the capsule of the knee joint and the alar folds. In the superficial layer, there are the lateral cutaneous nerve of the calf, the anterior cutanoeus branches of the femoral nerve, the infrapatellar branches of the saphenous nerve and the arteriovenous network of the knee joint. In the deep layer, there is the cavity of the knee joint.

ST 36   Zusanli (足三里)
(Foot Three Li)

【Source】 *Miraculous Pivot*

【Name Explanation】 Zu (足), lower limbs; San (三), there; Li (里), taken as cun in ancient times. The point is 3 cun below the knee.

【Classification】 He-(sea) Point of the Stomach Meridian, pertaining to wood in the Five Elements.

【Location】 On the anterior lateral side of the leg, 3 cun below Dubi (ST 35), one finger breadth from the anterior crest of the tibia. (See Fig. 11-8.)

【Localization】
1) Sitting with the knees flexed, locate the point 3 cun directly inferior to the medial Xiyan, one finger breadth from the anterior crest of the tibia.

2) Sitting with the knees flexed, the point is located at one cun directly inferior to the lower margin of tuberositas tibiae.

3) Sitting with the knees flexed, press the patella with the hand, then touch the tibia with the index finger, the point is located at the tip of the middle finger.

【Indications】
1) Diseases along the Course of the Meridian: Paraplegia, flaccidity, swelling pain in the foot and knee.

2) Diseases of the Head and Sense Organs: Blurred vision, dryness in the nose, stuffy nose, deafness, tinnitus, facial hemiparalysis, sore throat.

3) Digestive Diseases: Epigastralgia, fullness of abdomen, vomiting, hiccup, borboryg-

mus, diarrhea, abdominal pain, dysentery, dyspepsia, infantile indigestion with food retention, constipation.

4) Cardiovascular Diseases: Palpitation, oppressed feeling in the chest and shortness of breath, sudden precordial pain.

5) Respiratory Diseases: Cough, asthma, abundant expectoration, tuberculosis.

6) Urinary Diseases: Enuresis, difficult urination, edema.

7) Reproductive Diseases: Postpartum vertigo, abdominal pain after childbirth, leukorrhea, morning sickness, eclampsia graviderum.

8) Mental Diseases: Manic-depressive psychosis, wild laugh, hysteria, apoplexy.

9) Dermatosis: Furuncle, urticaria, acute appendicitis, mastitis, blood stasis in the chest.

10) Other Diseases: Insufficient vitality qi, excessive emaciation caused by five kinds of comsumptive diseases, weakness caused by seven kinds of impairments, summer-heat diseases, continuious fever of exgenous febrile diseases, fullness and rigidity sensation of the lower abdomen, febrile disease without sweating, high fever and even opisthotonos, jaundice, beriberi, hernia, swelling pain in the lower abdomen, distending pain in hypochondrium, hypertension.

【Mechanism of Action】

1) Zusanli (ST 36) is an important point which can be used to treat the diseases in the lower extremities, especiall flaccidity. *The Yellow Emperor's Internal Classic* says: "The Lung Meridian and Large Intestine Meridian can be used to treat the diseases above the waist, the Stomach Meridian and the Spleen Meridian can be used to treat the diseases below the waist", The Yangming Meridian which is the sea of the five zang-organs and six fu-organs can moisturize the tendon and muscle.

2) The tendons and muscles control bones to relieve rigidity of joints. The Chong Meridian is the sea of meridians, it oozes and irrigates intermuscular septum and intersects the Foot Yangming Meridian at urogenital region.

3) The Foot Yangming Meridian with the help of urogenital region meets at Qijie (ST 30), it belongs to the Dai Meridian and connects with the Du Meridian. Overactive sexual drive is caused by insufficiency of the Foot-Yangming Meridian.

4) Flaccidity of the foot is due to dysfunction of the Dai Meridian. "Canon on Internal Medicine" also says "Flaccidity to the lower limbs can be treated only by dealing with the Foot-Yangming Meridian." So Zusanli (ST 36) is used to treat arthritis, paralysis or flaccidity of lower limbs.

【Method】 Puncture perpendicularly 0.5-1 cun. Moxibustion is applicable.

【Acupoint Prescriptions】

1) Febrile diseases with vomiting and diarrhea, needling Zusanli (ST 36) firstly, Taibai (SP 3), Zhangmen (LR 13) secondly. (*Plain Questions*)

2) Lumbago with difficulty in turning around: Zusanli (ST 36), Yinshi (ST 33), Yangfu (GB 38), Ligou (LR 5). (*Thousand Golden Prescriptions*)

3) Food stagnancy: Zusanli (ST 36), Dachangshu (BL 25), Sanyinjiao (SP 6), Xiawan (RN 10), Sanjiaoshu (BL 22), Xuanshu (DU 5), Liangmen (ST 21). (*Experience on Acupuncture and Moxibustion Therapy*)

4) Intermittent fever due to phlegm: Zusanli (ST 36), Xiagu (ST 43), Xiaxi (GB 43), Feiyang (BL 58). (*ibid*)

5) Mass beside umbiliucs: Zusanli (ST 36), Taixi (KI 3). (*ibid*)

6) Abdominal distention: Zusanli (ST 36), Xingjian (LR 2), Ququan (LR 8). (*ibid*)

7) Foot flaccidity with difficulty in wearing shoes: Zusanli (ST 36), Chongyang (ST 42), Pucan (BL 61), Feiyang (BL 58), Fuliu (KI 7), Wangu (GB 12). (*ibid*)

8) Tonsillitis: Zusanli (ST 36), Wenliu (LI 7), Quchi (LI 11), Zhongzhu (SJ 3), Fenglong (ST 40). (*ibid*)

9) Chronic enteritis: Zusanli (ST 36), Tianshu (ST 25), Shangjuxu (ST 37), Guanyuan (RN 4), Xingjian (LR 2), Wailing (ST 26). (*New Acupuncture and Moxibustion*)

10) Appendicitis: Zusanli (ST 36), Huangshu (KI 16), Fushe (SP 13), Neiguan (PC 6), Quchi (LI 11), Qihaishu (BL 24), Dachangshu (BL 25). (*ibid*)

11) Vomiting of pregnancy: Zusanli (ST 36), Neiguan (PC 6), Chize (LU 5), Danshu (BL 19). (*ibid*)

12) Dysmenorrhea: Needling Zusanli (ST 36), moxibustion to Guanyuan (RN 4). (*ibid*)

13) Hypertension: Zusanli (ST 36), Neiguan (PC 6), Sanyinjiao (SP 6), Baihui (DU 20), Hegu (LI 4), Xingjian (LR 2). (*Science of Acupuncture and Moxibustion*)

14) Diarrhea and diseases in abdomen: Zusanli (ST 36), Neiting (ST 44). (*Songs on Point Selection of Miscellaneous Diseases*)

15) Expediting child delivery: Zusanli (ST 36), Zhiyin (BL 67). (*ibid*)

【Regional Anatomy】 Skin-subcutaneous tissue-the anterior tibial muscle-the interosseous membrane of the leg-posterior tibial muscle. In the superficial layer, there is the lateral cutaneous nerve of the calf. In the deep layer, there are the branches or tributaries of the anterior tibial artery and vein.

【Remark】 Effect of acupuncture at Zusanli (ST 34) on gastric peristalsis was observed in healthy people. The results showed that acupuncture at Zusanli (ST 36) regulated gastric peristalsis markedly and increased gastric emptying; note that, the effects were not obvious by acupuncture at non-gastric meridians or non-points.

Puncturing Zusanli (ST 36) alone, can treat duodenal ulcer, and regulate gastric acid secretion. Zusanli (ST 36) is a main point used to treat deficiency of both the spleen and the stomach. When there is a deficiency and coldness of the spleen and stomach, the deficiency of both the spleen and the kidneys are treated. Hepatic qi affects the stomach, Zusanli (ST 36) is still the main point, however, stimulation of this point must be combined with other points for an effective treatment.

Whether treating normal people or patients, acupuncture of Zusanli (ST 36) reduced the intestinal gurgling sound. However, acupuncture of Yanglingquan (GB 34) and control points were not effective. Acupunctures at 21 points of 50 people were used to observe the effect of Zusanli (ST 36) point. The result showed that acupuncture at Zusanli (ST 36) Xinshu (BL 15), Danshu (BL 19) points caused gallbladder contractions, but the effect of acupuncture of Zusanli (ST 36) was the best.

Acupuncture of Zusanli (ST 36) increased the content of glucose in the liver, decreased ketone bodies, free fatty acid and free cholesterol.

It also increased resting pulmonary ventilation volume (24.9%) and oxygen consumption. On the contrary, acupuncture at Tianshu (ST 25) or Liangmen (ST 34) points decreased ventilation volume and oxygen consumption.

Acupuncture of bilateral Zusanli (ST 36) of patients with algetic syndrome decreased blood pressure, especially systolic pressure. The effect was not significant by acupuncture at Hegu (LI 4) point.

Vertical puncturing at Zusanli (ST 36) point increased leukocytic and phagocytic function. Acupuncture at Zusanli (ST 36) and Neiguan (PC 6) eased pain in the upper abdomen, front of the neck.

ST 37 Shangjuxu (上巨虛)
(Upper Great Void)

【Source】 *Miraculous Pivot*

【Name Explanation】 Shang (上), upper; Ju (巨), great; Xu (虛), void. A large void is formed between the tibia and fibula. The point is in the upper part of the void.

【Classification】 Lower He-(Sea) Point of the Large Intestine

【Location】 On the anterior lateral side of the leg, 6 cun below Dubi (ST 35), one finger breadth from the anterior crest of the tibia. (See Fig. 11-9.)

【Localization】 Sitting with the knees flexed, the point is located 6 cun directly inferior to Dubi (ST 35), i.e: one finger breadth from the anterior crest of the tibia.

【Indications】
 1) Diseases along the Course of the Meridian: Paraplegia, flaccidity with pain and numbness, pains in the waist and knees with difficulty in bending and stretching, general edema of lower extremities.
 2) Digestive Diseases: Acute appendicitis, colic in abdomen, abdominal distension and borboryzmus, dysentery, stomachache, constipation, diarrhea, poor appetite.
 3) Other Diseases: Insufficient vitality-qi, tuberculosis, beriberi, retention of urine, adverse flow of gas to the chest, fullness in the chest and hypochondrium.

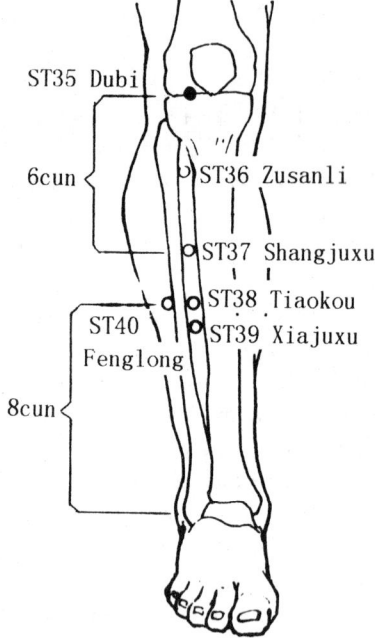

Fig. 11-9

【Mechanism of Action】
 1) The point is the He-(sea) Point of the large intestine, commonly used to treat the diseases in the intestines and is always used with Zusanli (ST 36). Refer to Zusanli (ST 36) or further mechanisms.
 2) The Stomach Meridian travels along the hypochondrium to the spine and spreads in the chest. Symptoms of upward adverse flow of gas to the chest or fullness in the chest and hypochondrium due to adverse rising of the stomach qi, can be treated with Shangjuxu (ST 37).

【Method】 Puncture perpendicularly 0.5-1 cun. Moxibustion is applicable.

【Acupoint Prescription】 Difficult urination and dark urine: Shangjuxu (ST 37), Xiajuxu (ST 39). (*Thousand Golden Prescriptions*)

【Regional Anatomy】 Skin-subcutaneous tissue-the anterior tibial muscle-interosseous membrane of the leg-the posterior tibial muscle. In the superficial layer, there is the lateral cutaneous nerve of the calf. In the deep layer, there are the anterior tibia artery and vein and the deep peroneal nerve. If the needle is inserted too deep, it may injure the posterior tibia artery and vein and the tibia nerve.

【Remark】 Puncturing Shangjuxu (ST 37) increased gastric peristalsis. Puncturing Shangjuxu (ST 37) and Zusanli (ST 36) increased intestinal peristalsis. However, puncturing Futu (ST 32) can decrease large intestinal peristalsis. After needling Shangjuxu (ST 37) twice (for 30 minutes to 3 hours) patients with acute bacillary dysentery, had blood sterilization and increased immunity. After puncturing this point on normal people for 12 days, both IgG and IgA in serum were increased, but IgM didn't change. After puncturing Shangjuxu (ST 37) and Tianshu (ST 25) (once a day for 3 days), β, γ globulin were increased. The sixth day after puncture, γ globulin was increased markedly. Specific antibodies and serum complements and serum lysozyme were increased markedly after the third day.

ST 38　Tiaokou (条口)
(Narrow Openning)

【Source】 *A-B Classic of Acupuncture and Moxibustion*
【Name Explanation】 Tiao (条), strip; Kou (口), space. The point is in the strip space between the fibula and tibia.
【Location】 On the anterior lateral side of the leg, 8 cun below Dubi (ST 35), one finger breadth from the anterior crest of the tibia. (See Fig. 11-9.)
【Localization】 Sitting with the knees flexed, locate the point directly inferior to Zusanli (ST 36), the same level with middle of the line joining Waixiyan (Extra 32) and tip of lateral melleolus.
【Indications】
　　1) Diseases along the Course of the Meridian: Pain of shoulders and arms, painful numbness of thighs and knees, spasm, flaccidity of feet, cold feet, heat and pain in sole.
　　2) Digestive Diseases: Stomachache and abdominal pain, dysentery.
　　3) Other Diseases: Beriberi, pain in enterocele, sore throat.
【Mechanism of Action】 At present this point is always used to treat pain in shoulders and arms, or pain and numbness in lower extremities, etc. The Stomach Meridian doesn't go up to shoulder, but the Large Intestine Meridian does, which links up with the Stomach Meridian. Tiaokou (ST 38) can be used to treat shoulder pain according to the principle that the point is used to treat diseases in the linked Meridians. In clinic, periarthritis of the shoulder is always treated by penetrating the needle from Tiaokou (ST 38) through Chengshan (BL 57). Practice proves that this point produces a positive effect on periarthritis of shoulder. Chengshan (BL 57) belongs to the Gallbladder Meridian which does not go up to the shoulder, and the two Meridians are linked up. So the point can be used for treating periarthritis of shoulder to the principle of point treating diseases in the linked meridians.
【Method】 Puncture perpendicularly 0.5-1.5 cun. Moxibustion is applicable.
【Acupoint Prescriptions】
　　1) Weakness of feet: Tiaokou (ST 38), Sanli (ST 36), Chengshan (BL 57), Chengjin (BL 56). (*Thousand Golden Prescriptions*)
　　2) Periarthritis of shoulder: Penetrating the needle from Tiaokou (ST 38) through Chengshan (BL 57). (*Abstract of Clinical Experience on Acupuncture and Moxibustion*)
【Regional Anatomy】 Skin-subcutaneous tissue-the anterior tibial muscle-interosseous membrane of the leg-the posterior tibial muscle. In the superficial layer, there is the lateral cutaneous nerve of the calf. In the deep layer, there are the anterior tibial artery and vein and the deep peroneal nerve. If the needle is inerted too deep, it may injure the posterior tibial artery and vein.
【Remark】 It has been reported that puncturing Tiaokou (ST 38) is effective on ventricular extra systole.

ST 39　Xiajuxu（下巨虚）
(Lower Great Void)

[Source] *Miraculous Pivot*
[Name Explanation] Xia（下）, lower; Ju（巨）, great; Xu（虚）, void. A large void is formed between the tibia and the fibula. The point is in the lower part of the void.
[Classification] Lower He-(Sea) point of the Small Intestine Meridian
[Location] On the anterior lateral side of the leg, 9 cun below Dubi (ST 35), one finger breadth from the anterior crest of the tibia. (See Fig. 11-9.)
[Localization] Sitting with the knees flexed, locate this point 6 cun directly inferior to Zusanli (ST 36).
[Indications]
　　1) Diseases along the Course of the Meridian: Hemiparalysis, flaccidity of lower extremities with difficulty in walking, painful heels or pain between toes, edema of lower extremities.
　　2) Digestive Diseases: Diarrhea, stool with pus and blood, dysentery, stomach heat, stomachache, poor appetite, emaciation.
　　3) Diseases of the Head and Sense Organs: Dry lips, salivation, inflammation of the throat.
　　4) Mental Diseases: Epilepsy, sudden terror, ravings.
　　5) Other Diseases: Pain in lower abdomen, pain in the waist and spine radiating to lower abdomen, pain in the chest and hypochondrium, breast pain.
[Mechanism of Action]
　　1) This point is the front-Mu point of the small intestine. Therefore, it is used to treat digestive diseases, such as, diarrhea and dysentery, etc.
　　2) Zusanli (ST 36) is the lower He-(sea) point of the stomach, Shangjuxu (ST 38) is the lower He-(sea) point of the large intestine, Xiajuxu (ST 39) is the lower He-(sea) point of the small intestine, the three points are always used together to treat various digestive diseases.
　　3) See Zusanli (ST 36).
[Method] Puncture perpendicularly 0.5-0.7 cun. Moxibustion is applicable.
[Acupoint Prescriptions]
　　1) Madness: Xiajuxu (ST 39), Qiuxu (GB 40). (*Thousand Golden Prescriptions*)
　　2) Diarrhea with pus and blood: Xiajuxu (ST 39), Youmen (KI 21), Taibai (SP 3). (*Experience on Acupuncture and Moxibustion Therapy*)
　　3) Stomach-heat with poor appetite: Xiajuxu (ST 39), Xuanzhong (GB 39). (*ibid*)
　　4) Wind syndrome of the head: Xiajuxu (ST 39), Wuchu (BL 5), Shenting (DU 24). (*ibid*)
[Regional Anatomy] Skin-subcutaneous tissue-the anterior tibial muscle-interosseous membrane of the leg-the posterior tibial muscle.
　　In the superficial layer, there is the lateral cutaneous nerve of the calf. In the deep layer, there are the anterior tibial artery and vein and the deep peroneal nerve.
[Remark] X-ray examinations showed that puncturing Xiajuxu (ST 39) on patients with gastritis, gastric ulcer and cancer increased both the basic electrical rhythm of the stomach and gastric peristalsis through X-ray examination.

ST 40 Fenglong (丰隆)
(Abundant Bulge)

【Source】 *Miraculous Pivot*
【Name Explanation】 Feng (丰), plentiful; Long (隆), abundance. At this point, the plentiful grain Qi of the Stomach Meridian overflows into its collateral.
【Classification】 Luo-(connecting) Point of the Stomach Meridian of Foot Yangming.
【Location】 On the anterior lateral side of the leg, 8 cun above the tip of the external malleolus, lateral to Tiaokou (ST 38), and two finger breadths from the anterior crest of the tibia. (See Fig. 11-9.)
【Localization】 Sitting with the knees flexed, locate the point at the same level with the midline joining Waixiyan (Extra 32) and tip of lateral malleolus, two finger breadth from the anterior crest of the tibia.
【Indications】
　　1) Diseases along the Course of the Meridian: Flaccidity of lower extremities with swelling and pain, flaccidity of the legs, difficulty in bending the feet.
　　2) Diseases of the Head and Sense Organs: Headache, vertigo, sore-throat, aphonia.
　　3) Digestive Diseases: Colic in abdomen, diarrhea, dysentery, constipation.
　　4) Respiratory Diseases: Cough, asthma, abundant expectoration.
　　5) Cardiovascular Diseases: Cardialgia, pain in the chest and hypochondrium.
　　6) Urinary Diseases: Retention of urine, edema of limbs, heaviness sensation in the limbs, edema of the face.
　　7) Gynecopathy: Amemia, metrorrhagia, gynecological disease.
　　8) Mental Diseases: Madness, epilepsy, susceptibility to laugh, dysphoria, apoplexy, insomnia.
　　9) Other Diseases: Beriberi.
【Mechanism of Action】
　　1) The Spleen has the function to transport and transform nutrients. The point is collateral point which belongs to the stomach and lies in spleen. Accumulation of phlegm is brought about by water retention due to hypofunction of the spleen. Cough with phlegm is caused by accumulation of phlegm-dampness in the lung; Many diseases, such as precordial pain, pain in the chest and hypochondrium, or mental diseases, such as madness, epilepsy, insomnia, and amnesia, are caused by stagnation of phlegm-dampness in heart-yang. Headache and vertigo are due to accumulation of phlegm-dampness in the upper meridians and collaterals, flaccidity and arthralgia-syndrome are caused by retention of phlegm-dampness in the lower meridians and collaterals. In a word, this point is commonly used to treat phlegm and fundamentally treating all the diseases mentioned above. The collaterals of the Stomach Meridian go up to the head, combine with other meridians' qi and then go down to the throat. The Stomach Meridian seperately goes up to the heart. All these provide meridian and collateral basis for treating the head, face, sense organs and cardiovascular diseases.
　　2) This point is effectively used for relaxing the bowels.
　　3) Periarthritis of the shoulder is commonly treated by putting the needle into Fenglong (ST 40) through Chengshan (BL 57).
【Method】 Puncture perpendicularly 0.5-1 cun. Moxibustion is applicable.
【Acupoint Prescriptions】
　　1) Stabbing pain in the chest: Fenglong (ST 40), Qiuxu (GB 40). (*Thousand Golden Prescriptions*)

2) Edema of limbs due to wind reversion: Fenglong (ST 40), Fuliu (KI 7). (*Experience on Acupuncture and Moxibustion Therapy*)

3) Difficulty of the limbs in bending: Fenglong (ST 40), Bishu (BL 20). (*ibid*)

4) Edema of the face: Fenglong (ST 40), Chengjiang (RN 24), Yangjiao (GB 35). (*ibid*)

【Regional Anatomy】 Skin-subcutaneous tissue-the long extensor muscle of toes-the long extensor muscle of the great toe-the interosseous membrane of the leg-the posterior tibial muscle.

In the superficial layer, there is the lateral cutaneous nerve of the calf. In the deep layer, there are the branches or tributaries of the anterior tibial artery and vein and the branches of the deep peroneal nerve.

【Remark】 Puncturing Fenglong (ST 40) point caused the blood vessels of small legs to contract. It has been reported that puncturing Fenglong (ST 40) and Quchi (LI 11) for weeks decreased blood pressure. The average level of systolic pressure was lowered 34.2 mm-Hg, while diastolic pressure 19.4 mm-Hg, average arterial pressure 23.6 mm-Hg. Treatment with acupuncture for 8 weeks resulted in decrease of blood pressure. 3-6 months of subsequent observation showed that in 80% of the patients, blood pressure did not elevate again. It also decreased both blood vessel spasms and pressure on the heart, with an improvement of left ventricle function. Although blood pressure decreased, cardiac output and blood volume increased.

ST 41　Jiexi（解溪）
（Dispersing Stream）

【Source】 *Miraculous Pivot*

【Name Explanation】 Jie (解), separation; Xi (溪), stream. Xi refers to a minor depression on the body surface. The point is in the anterior articular depression of the ankle joint.

【Classification】 Jing-(well) Point of the Stomach Meridian of Foot Yangming, pertaining to fire in the Five Elements.

【Location】 In the central depression of the crease between the instep of the foot and leg, between the tendons of the long extensor muscle of the great toe and the long extensor muscle of the toes. (See Fig. 11-10.)

【Localization】 In the supine position or sitting, locate the point from 2nd toe directly superior to the transverse crease of the ankle joint, between the tendon of long extensor muscle of great toe and tendon of long extensor muscle of toe.

【Indications】

1) Diseases along the Course of the Meridian: Flaccidity in lower extremities with swelling pain and heavy sensation.

2) Diseases of the Head and Sense Organs: Edema of head and face, flushed face, eye pain, nebula, headache, vertigo, pain in the supra-orbital bone.

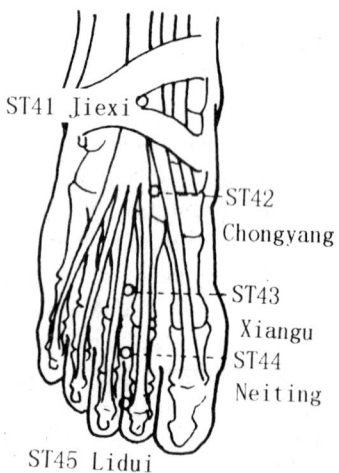

Fig. 11-10

3) Digestive Diseases: Abdominal distention, constipation, eructation, cholera morbus, stomachache.

4) Mental Diseases: Epilepsy, clonic convulsion, infantile convulsion, stomach-heat, delirium, palpitation and severe palpitation.

5) Other Diseases: Malaria, spasm, febrile disease with difficulty in sweating.

【Mechanism of Action】

1) Where the meridian passes, and where the indications are. So the point can be used to treat the diseases in the lower extremities, especially foot flaccidity.

2) This point has the function of clearing away the stomach-fire and resolving phlegm. It is commonly used for treating diseases of the head, face and sense organs, and mental diseases due to phlegm-fire stagnancy.

【Method】Puncuture perpendicularly 0.5-0.7 cun. Moxibustion is applicable.

【Acupoint Prescriptions】

1) The diseases of limbs: Jiexi (ST 41), Tiaokou (ST 38), Qiuxu (GB 40), Taibai (SP 3) are, needled to treat knee swelling and cramp. (*Thousand Golden Prescriptions*)

2) Retention of qi going up and down: Jiexi (ST 41), Xuanshu (DU 5). (*Experience on Acupuncture and Moxibustion Therapy*)

3) Abdominal distention: Jiexi (ST 41), Xuehai (SP 5). (*ibid*)

4) Pathogenic cold ascending to abdomen: Jiexi (ST 41), Tiantu (RN 22). (*Great Compendium of Acupuncture and Moxibustion*)

5) Vertigo due to wind syndrome of the head: Jiexi (ST 41), Fenglong (ST 40). (*ibid*)

【Regional Anatomy】Skin-subcutaneous tissue-between tendons of the long extensor muscle of the great toe and the long extensor muscle of the toes-talus. In the superficial layer, there are the medial dorsal cutaneous nerves and the subcutaneous veins. In the deep layer, there are the deep peroneal nerve and the anterior tibial artery and vein.

ST 42   Chongyang (冲阳)
(Rushing Yang)

【Source】*Miraculous Pivot*

【Name Explanation】Chong (冲), important; Yang (阳), Yang of Yin-Yang. The point is where the Chongyang Pulse is located.

【Classification】Yuan-(source) Point of the Stomach Meridian of Foot Yangming.

【Location】On the dome of the instep, between the tendons of the long extensor muscle of the great toe and the long extensor muscle of the toes, where the pulsation of the dorsal artery of the foot is palpable. (See Fig. 11-10.)

【Localization】In the supine position or sitting, locate the point at the top of dorsum of the foot, 3 cun from ST 43, at the place of arteriopalmus on the dorsum of the foot.

【Indications】

1) Diseases along the Course of the Meridian: Flaccidity of feet with weakness, red and swollen instep, paraplegia.

2) Diseases of the Head and Sense Organs: Headache, pain in forehead, edema of the face, facial hemiparalysis.

3) Digestive Diseases: Stomachache, abdominal distention, poor appetite.

4) Mental Diseases: Singing on the high, walking out without dressing, susceptibility to fright, clonic convulsion.

5) Other Diseases: Malaria, fever without sweating.

【Mechanism of Action】See Jiexi (ST 41).

【Method】Puncuture perpendicularly 0.3-0.5 cun just away from artery. Moxibustion can not be used.

【Acupoint Prescriptions】

1) Mania: Chongyang (ST 42), Fenglong (ST 40). (*Thousand Golden Prescriptions*)

2) Flaccidity of feet: Chongyang (ST 42), Sanli (ST 36), Pucan (BL 61), Feiyang

(BL 58), Fuliu (KI 7), Wangu (SJ 5). (*ibid*)

3) Migraine with thirst: Chongyang (ST 42), Dicang (ST 4). (*Experience on Acupuncture and Moxibustion Therapy*)

4) Pain in elbow: Chongyang (ST 42), Quchi (LI 11). (*ibid*)

【Regional Anatomy】 Skin-subcutaneous tissue-between tendons of the long extensor muscle of the great toe and the long extensor muscle of toes-the short extensor muscle of the great toe-the intermediate cuneiform bone. In the superficial layer, there are the medial dorsal cutaneous nerve and the dorsal venous network of the foot. In the deep layer, there are the dorsal pedal artery and vein and the deep peroneal nerve.

【Remark】 Through X-ray examination, it has been reported that puncturing Chongyang (ST 42) point may slow down gastric peristalsis. It may also slow down heart rate and increase myocardial cintractine power, P wave, R wave, Q-T period were prolonged.

ST 43 Xiangu (陷谷)
(Sinking Valley)

【Source】 *Miraculous Pivot*

【Name Explanation】 Xian (陷), depression; Gu (谷), valley. Gu impiles a depression on the body surface. The point is in the depression between the second and third metatarsal bones.

【Classification】 Shu-(Stream) point of the Stomach Meridian of Foot Yangming, pertaining to wood in the Five Elements.

【Location】 On the instep, in the depression distal to the commissure of the 2nd and 3rd metatarsal bones. (See Fig. 11-10)

【Localization】 In the supine position or sitting, locate the point at the depression anterior to the combining site of the 2nd and 3rd metatarsal bones.

【Indications】

1) Digestive Diseases: Epigastralgia, borborygmus, abdominal distention, abdominal pain, ascites, susceptibility to eructation.

2) Diseases of the Head and Sense Organs: Edema of face, conjunctival congestion with pain, weakness of upper eyelid.

3) Other Diseases: Swelling pain of instep, febrile disease without sweating, malaria, hysteria, night sweat, hypochondriac pain, hiccup, hernia.

【Mechanism of Action】 See Jiexi (ST 41). The spleen and the stomach are interior-exteriorly related, and the spleen has the function to nourish the muscles. So in clinic this point is commonly used for treating ptosis of the upper eyelid.

【Method】 Puncuture perpendicularly 0.3 cun or obliquely 0.5 cun. Moxibustion is applicable.

【Acupoint Prescriptions】

1) Borborygmus with pain: Xiangu (ST 43), Wenliu (LI 7), Fuliu (KI 7), Yanggang (BL 48). (*Thousand Golden Prescriptions*)

2) Edema: Xiangu (ST 43), Lieque (LU 7), (used for edema of the face). (*Experience on Acupuncture and Moxibustion Therapy*)

3) Susceptibility to eructation after childbirth: Xiangu (ST 43), Qimen (LR 14). (*ibid*)

4) Abdominal distention: Xiangu (ST 43), Xuanzhong (GB 39). (*ibid*)

5) Fullness in the chest and hypochondrium: Xiangu (ST 43), Shimen (RN 5). (*ibid*)

【Regional Anatomy】 Skin-subcutaneous tissue-tendons of the long extensor muscle of the toes-the medial side of the tendon of the short extensor muscle of the toes-the 2nd dorsal interosseous muscle-the oblique head of the abductor of the great toe. In the superficial layer, there are the medial dorsal cutaneous nerve and the dorsal venous network of the foot. In the deep layer, there are the 2nd dorsal metatarsal artery and vein.

ST 44 Neiting (内庭)
(Inner Court-Yard)

【Source】 *Miraculous Pivot*

【Name Explanation】 Nei (内), interior; Ting (庭), courtyard. This point is proximal to Lidui (ST 45), likened to its courtyard.

【Classification】 Ying-(Spring) point of the Stomach Meridian of Foot Yangming, pertaining to water in the Five Elements.

【Location】 On the instep, at the junction of the red and white skin proximal to the margin of the web between the 2nd and 3rd toes. (See Fig. 11-10)

【Localization】 In the supine position or sitting, locate the point at the gap junction between the 2nd and 3rd metatarsal bones.

【Indications】

1) Diseases along the Course of the Meridian: Pathogenic cold in limbs, pain in tibia with difficulty in bending.

2) Diseases of the Head and Sense Organs: Toothache, swollen gum, deviation of mouth, trismus, epistaxis, inflammation of the throat, edema of the face and deafness.

3) Digestive Diseases: Stomachache, abdominal pain, diarrhea, constipation, dysentery and acute appendicitis.

4) Other Diseases: Urticaria, hysteria, enterocele, bloody urine, fever with chills, malaria with poor appetite.

【Mechanism of Action】

1) The point belongs to the Stomach Meridian. Due to the principle that where the meridian passes, where the indications are, this point can be used to treat various digestive diseases.

2) The Stomach and the Large Intestine Meridians traverse the head and face, collaterals in the Stomach Meridian connect with the vertex, meet all kinds of meridian-qi and then connect down with throat. So this point together with auxilliary Hegu (LI 4) point is usually used for treating diseases of the head and face.

【Method】 Puncture perpendicularly 0.3-0.5 cun. Moxibustion is applicable.

【Acupoint Prescriptions】

1) Algial malaria with poor appetite: Neiting (ST 44), Lidui (ST 45), Gongsun (SP 4). (*Experience on Acupuncture and Moxibustion Therapy*)

2) Pain of Eyes: Neiting (ST 44), Shangxing (DU 23). (*Great Compendium of Acupuncture and Moxibustion*)

3) Fullness in lower abdomen: Neiting (ST 44), Sanli (ST 36), Sanyinjiao (SP 6). (*ibid*)

4) Dysentery: Neiting (ST 44), Tianshu (ST 25), Yinbai (SP 1), Qihai (RN 6), Zhaohai (KI 6), Neiguan (PC 6). (*ibid*)

5) Febrile disease with profuse sweating: Neiting (ST 44), Hegu (LI 4) (Reducing), Fuliu (KI 7) (Reinforcing), Bailao (EX). (*ibid*)

【Regional Anatomy】 Skin-subcutaneous tissue-between the tendons of the long and the short extensor muscle of the 2nd and 3rd toes-between the heads of the 2nd and 3rd metatarsal bones. In the superficial layer, there are the dorsal digital nerve of the medial dorsal pedal cutaneous nerve and the dorsal arteriovenous network of the foot. In the deep layer, there are the dorsal artery and vein.

ST 45   Lidui (厉兑)
(Sick Mouth)

【Source】 *Miraculous Pivot*
【Name Explanation】 Li (厉), stomach; Dui (兑), door. This point is at the end of the second toe, like a door of the Stomach Meridian.
【Classification】 Jing-(Well) point of the Stomach Meridian of Foot Yangming, pertaining to metal in the Five Elements.
【Location】 On the lateral side of the distal segment of the 2nd toe, 0.1 cun from the corner of the toenail. (See Fig. 11-10)
【Localization】 In the supine position or sitting, locate the point at the intersection of the lines between the lateral margin of 2nd toe nail and basal part.
【Indications】

1) Diseases along the Course of the Meridian: Swelling pain in front of the knee, cold in dorsum of the foot, pain in the breast.

2) Diseases of the Head and Sense Organs: Edema of the face, toothache, deviation of mouth, edema of the lips, edema of the neck, epistaxis, nasal obstruction, running nose.

3) Digestive Diseases: Fullness in the chest and abdomen, jaundice, polyorexia.

4) Mental Diseases: Madness, susceptibility to palpitation, corpse-like syncope with lockjaw.

5) Other Diseases: Febrile disease without sweating, edema, cold malaria, poor appetite, dark urine.

【Mechanism of Action】

1) The point is one of the Jing-(well)points. A Jing-(well) point has the function of inducing resuscitation, restoring conciousness, reducing fever and relieving convulsion. So this point is always used for treating mental diseases, such as clonic convulsion caused by febrile disease, etc.

2) This point in the Stomach Meridian is the furthest away from the head and face. Therefore it is usually used for treating the diseases of the head and face on the basis of distal-proximal point association.

【Method】 Puncuture perpendicularly 0.1 cun or prick the point to cause bleeding. Moxibustion is applicable.

【Acupoint Prescriptions】

1) Malaria with poor appetite and chill: Lidui (ST 45), Neiting (ST 44). (*Experience on Acupuncture and Moxibustion Therapy*)

2) Drowsiness: Lidui (ST 45), Dadun (LR 1). (*ibid*)

3) Fullness in the chest and abdomen: Lidui (ST 45). (*ibid*)

4) Febrile disease without sweating: Lidui (ST 45), Chongyang (ST 42), Jiexi (ST 41). (*ibid*)

5) Nightmare: Lidui (ST 45), Yinbai (SP 1). (*Songs of Hundreds of Symptoms*)

【Regional Anatomy】 Skin-subcutaneous tissue-root of the nail.

There are the dorsal digital nerve of the medial dorsal pedal cutaneous nerve and the dorsal digital arteriovenous network in this area.

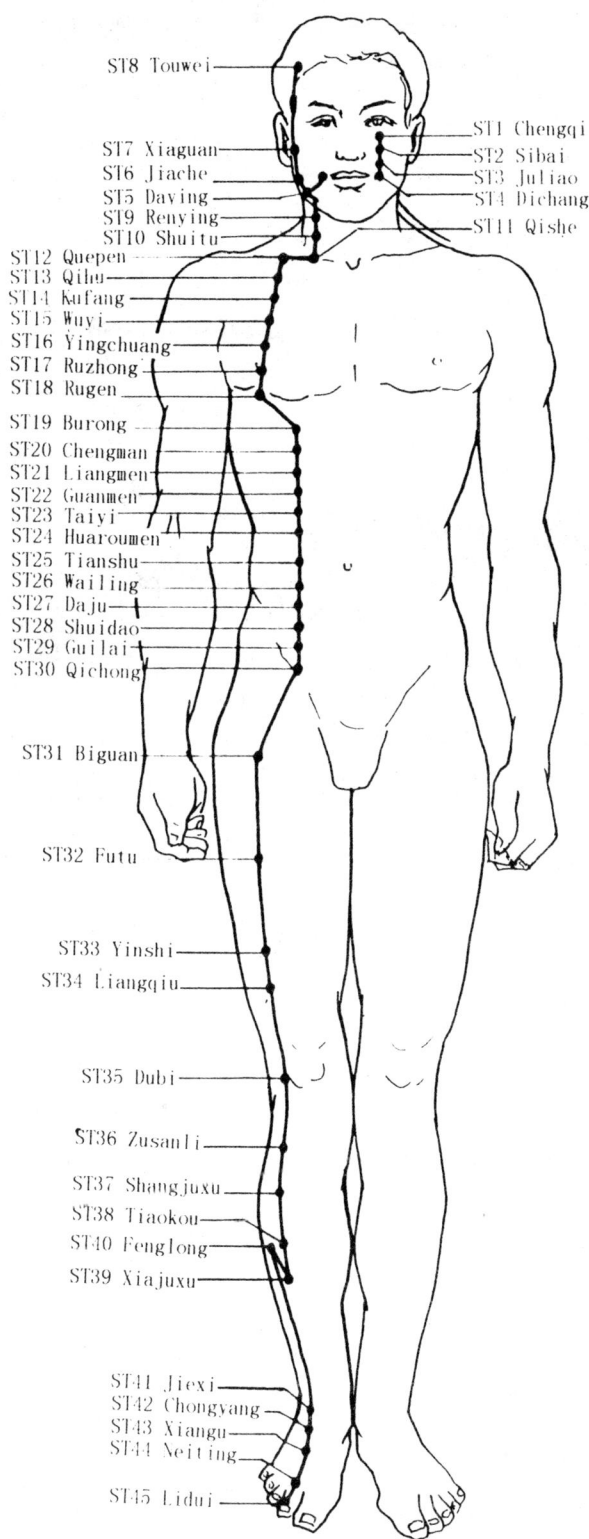

Fig. 11-11 **Acupoints of the Stomach Meridian of Foot Yangming**

Table 11-1
Indications and Actions of Acupoints of the Stomach Meridian of Foot Yangming

Name of the points	Specific points	Common indications	Specific indications and functions
ST 1 Chengqi (承泣)	Crossing point	Diseases of the head, face, eye, nose, mouth and tooth: conjunctival congestion, twitching of eye lids, distortion of mouth and eyes, epistaxis, toothache	Dispersing wind and dredging the meridian passage, clearing heat and improving eyesight. Conjunctival congestion, epiphora, night blindness, color blindness, myopia, hyperopia, optic atrophy
ST 2 Sibai (四白)			Facial spasm, rhinitis, nebula. One of the commonly used points in acupuncture anesthesia while operating on the ear, nose and laryngeal part of pharynx
ST 3 Juliao (巨髎)	Crossing point		One of the commonly used points in acupuncture anesthesia while operating on the ear, nose and laryngopharyngeal part of the body
ST 4 Dicang (地仓)	Crossing point		Dispersing wind and clearing the meridians, strengthening the body resistance and relieving pain. Distortion of the face, salivation, toothache, swelling of cheeks, numbness of the lips, facial spasm, prosopalgia, twitching of eyelids
ST 5 Daying (大迎)			Wry mouth, lockjaw, swelling of cheeks, toothache
ST 6 Jiache (颊车)			Dispersing wind and dredging the meridians, relieving tooth trouble and pain. Distortion of mouth and eyes, lockjaw, toothache, swelling of cheeks, stiffness of the neck
ST 7 Xiaguan (下关)	Crossing point		Dispersing wind and removing heat, activating meridians and relieving pain, causing resuscitation and inducing consciousness. Deafness, tinnitus, otitis media, distortion of mouth and eyes, toothache, prosopalgia, lockjaw
ST 8 Touwei (头维)	Crossing point		Clearing the head and improving acuity of vision. Dizziness, headache, eye pain, dacryorrhea, twitching of eyelids, blurred vision
ST 9 Renying (人迎)	Crossing point	The same as below	Regulating circulation of blood and qi, relieving sore throat, removing heat and preventing asthma. Asthma, scrofula, goiter, hypertension, hypotension
ST 10 Shuitu (水突)			Cough with dyspnea, shortness of breath, dyspnea which causes difficulty in lying on one's back

Acupoints of Three Yang Meridians of Foot

Name of the points	Specific points	Common indications	Specific indications and functions
ST 11 Qishe (气舍)			Sore throat, dyspnea, hiccup, goiter, scrofula, stiffness of neck
ST 12 Quepen (缺盆)			Regulating the circulation of qi and resolving phlegm, removing heat and resolving masses, clearing the meridians and activating collaterals. Heat and fullness sensation in the chest, pain in the supraclavicular fossa, numbness of the upper limbs, scrofula
ST 13 Qihu (气户)			Soothing the chest oppression and regulating the circulation of qi. Hiccup, fullness and discomfort in chest and hypochondrium, pain in the chest and back
ST 14 Kufang (库房)		Diseases of the throat, chest and lungs: sore throat, cough with dyspnea, distending pain in the chest and hypochondrium	Soothing chest oppression and regulating the circulation of qi, lowering the adverse flow of qi and resolving the phlegm. Distending pain in chest and hypochondrium, oppressive feeling in the chest, cough with turbid phlegm and purulent blood
ST 15 Wuyi (屋翳)			Clearing heat and resolving phlegm, dispersing wind and activating flow of blood. Cough with dyspnea or with purulent blood, acute mastitis, pain in chest, intercostal neuralgia, severe skin pain
ST 16 Yingchuang (膺窗)			Removing heat and alleviating mental depression, relieving pain and subduing smelling. Fullness in the chest, shortness of breath, acute mastitis with fever and chill, restlessness
ST 17 Ruzhong (乳中)	This point is only used as a sign of location.		
ST 18 Rugen (乳根)			Activating the collaterals and promoting lactation. Oppressive feeling in the chest, dysphagia, vomiting and regurgitation, lack of lactation, pain in the breast, acute mastitis
ST 19 Burong (不容)			Regulating the functions of the middle Jiao and stomach. Vomiting, stomachache, poor appetite, distention of abdomen, acid regurgitation
ST 20 Chengman (承满)		The same as below	Regulating the flow of qi and function of stomach, removing the distention and lowering the adverse flow of qi. Stomachache, vomiting of blood, poor appetite, vomiting, distension of abdomen, pain in the hypochondrium, borborygmus, diarrhea

Name of the points	Specific points	Common indications	Specific indications and functions
ST 21 Liangmen (梁门)		Gastrointestinal diseases: stomachache, abdominal pain and distention, borborygmus, vomiting, diarrhea Mental diseases: manic depression	Strengthening the spleen and stomach, promoting digestion. Stomachache, poor appetite, diarrhea, indigestion
ST 22 Guanmen (关门)			Regulating the flow of qi and resolving dampness, inducing diuresis and stopping diarrhea. Abdominal distention, abdominal pain, ascites, borborygmus, diarrhea, edema, enuresis
ST 23 Taiyi (太乙)			Regulating the function of the stomach and intestines, relieving mental stress and tranquilizing the mind. Manic-depression, restlessness, wagging tongue, stomachache, poor appetite, abdominal distenton and pain
ST 24 Huaroumen (滑肉门)			Manic depression, wagging tongue, stiffness of tongue, stomachache, vomiting
ST 25 Tianshu (天枢)	Front-Mu point of the large intestine		Strengthening the spleen and regulating the function of stomach, Promoting circulation of qi and activating the flow of blood. Abdominal distension, boryborygmus, pain around the umbilicus, intestinal Bi-syndrome, constipation, diarrhea, irregular menstruation, dysmenorrhea, leukorrhea, edema, abdominal masses
ST 26 Wailing (外陵)		Diseases of external genitalia: dysuria, hernia Gynecologial diseases: irregular menstruation	Regulating menstruation and relieving pain, regulating the functions of stomach and intestines, regulating the circulation of qi and promoting the flow of blood. Abdominal pain and distention, hernia, dysmenorrhea, irregular menstruation
ST 27 Daju (大巨)			Warming the kidney, invigorating qi and arresting spontaneous emission. Distension and fullness of lower abdomen, hernia, emission, premature ejaculation, palpitation due to fright, insomnia
ST 28 Shuidao (水道)			Clearing dampness and heat, regulating flow of qi and blood. Distension and fullness of lower abdomen, dysuria, nephritis, cystitis, edema, dysmenorrhea, sterility, hernia
ST 29 Guilai (归来)			Expelling cold from meridians, regulating flow of qi and blood, regulating and invigorating Chong and Ren meridians. Flaccid constriction of penis, penis pain, prolapse of uterus, polyuria at night, leukorrhea, amenorrhea, sterility

Name of the points	Specific points	Common indications	Specific indications and functions
ST 30 Qichong (气冲)	The origin of the Chong Meridian	The same as above	Borborygmus, abdominal pain, sensation of gas rushing from the lower abdomen, sterility, impotence, penis pain, diseases of the genital organs in woman
ST 31 Biguan (髀关)		Local diseases of the lower part of the body: flaccidity, numbness and pain of the lower limbs, knee pain	Promoting the flow of qi by warming the meridians, dispersing cold and eliminating dampness. Cold in loin and knee, flaccidity of lower limbs, pain of hip joint, abdominal pain
ST 32 Futu (伏兔)			Warming the meridians and clearing the collaterals, expelling wind and removing dampness, strengthening the loins and invigorating the kidney. Hernia, beriberi, coldness in loin and knee, numbness, wind-arthralgia, general urticaria, distention of abdomen
ST 33 Yinshi (阴市)			Coldness and pain in loin and knee, inability to extend the limbs, periumbilical colic due to invasion of cold, distension and pain in the abdomen
ST 34 Liangqiu (梁丘)	Xi- (Cleft) point		Clearing the meridian and collaterals, regulating the flow of qi and function of stomach. Stomachache, abdominal distention, distending pain of the breast, acute mastitis, swelling and pain of the knee, paralysis of lower limbs
ST 35 Dubi (犊鼻)			Relaxing the muscles, tendons and joints. Knee pain, numbness of lower extremities, difficulty in extending the limbs, beriberi
ST 36 Zusanli (足三里)	The lower He-(sea) point of the stomach He-(Sea) point	Enterogastric diseases: abdominal pain, diarrhea, constipation	Strengthening the spleen and stomach, removing stagnated food and relieving distention, regulating flow of qi and blood, clearing the meridians and collaterals. Stomachache, vomiting, hiccup, abdominal distention, diarrhea, dysentery, constipation, acute mastitis, edema, manic-depression, beriberi, arthralgia of lower limbs, emaciated body due to consumption. It is also an imporant point in preventative health care
ST 37 Shangjuxu (上巨虚)	The lower He-(Sea) point of the large intestine		Regulating the function of the stomach and intestine, removing dampness and heat, eliminating stagnation. Borborygmus, abdominal pain, acute appendicitis, diarrhea, constipation, edema of lower extremities, swelling and pain of keen, flaccidity and numbness of lower limbs, beriberi
ST 38 Tiaokou (条口)			Clearing the meridian and collaterals, dispelling wind and removing dampness. Epigastralgia, swelling of instep, spasm of calf, numbness of tibiocalcaneal part, omalgia

Name of the points	Specific points	Common indications	Specific indications and functions
ST 39 Xiajuxu (下巨虚)	The lower He-(Sea) point of the small intestine	The same as above	Regulating the function of intestines, dredging the meridians and collaterals. Acute mastitis, flaccidity and pain of lower extremities, pain along the spinal column which radiates to testicles, tibiocalcaneal pain
ST 40 Fenglong (丰隆)	Luo-(Connecting) point		Resolving phlegm and dampness, tranquilizing the mind. Headache, dizziness, vertigo, abundant expectoration, cough, vomiting, constipation, edema, manic-depression, flaccidity and pain of lower extremities
ST 41 Jiexi (解溪)	Jing- (River) Point	Diseases of the head, eye, nose, mouth, teeth and throat: distortion of mouth and eyes, conjunctival congestion, toothache, sore throat, epistaxis Gastrointestinal and mental diseases: manic-depression, dreaminess, febrile disease	Removing heat, tranquilizing the mind. Headache, dizziness, manic-depression, flaccidity and numbness of lower extremities, footdrop, red eyes, stomach heat, constipation
ST 42 Chongyang (冲阳)	Yuan- (Source) Point		Regulating the function of the stomach, tranquilizing mind, dredging meridians. Distortion of mouth and eyes, facial swelling, toothache, manic-depression, stomachache, weakness of lower limbs
ST 43 Xiangu (陷谷)	Shu- (Stream) Point		Removing heat, inducing diuresis and dredging collaterals. Edema of the face and body, con-junctival congestion, borborygmus, abdominal pain, febrile disease, pain in the dorsum of the foot
ST 44 Neiting (内庭)	Ying- (Spring) Point		Removing heat from the stomach, regulating flow of qi and relieving pain. Stomachache, acid regurgitation, dysentery, acute appendicitis, toothache, pharyngodynia, wry mouth, epistaxis, febrile disease, swelling and pain in the dorsum of the foot
ST 45 Lidui (厉兑)	Jing- (Well) Point		Eliminating heat, purging fire, tranquilizing the mind and inducing resuscitation. Lockjaw, syncope, febrile disease, manic-depression, dreaminess, epistaxis, toothache, sore throat, gastralgia, constipation, hemafecia

XIII. Acupoints of the Gallbladder Meridian of Foot Shaoyang

GB 1　Tongziliao（瞳子髎）
（Pupil Crevice）

【Source】 *A-B Classic of Acupuncture and Moxibustion*
【Name Explanation】 Tongzi（瞳子）, pupil; Liao（髎）, foramen. The point is in a foramen lateral to the outer canthus at the same level of the pupil.
【Classification】 The Crossing Point of Hand Taiyang Meridian, the Hand Shaoyang Meridian and the Foot Shaoyang Meridian.
【Location】 On the face, lateral to the outer canthus, on the lateral border of the orbit. (See Fig. 11-12)
【Localization】 Sitting position with the head resting and eyes closed, locate the point at the end of the stripe of the outer canthus.
【Indications】
　　Diseases of the Head and Sense Organs: Conjunctival congestion, conjunctivitis, ophthalmalgia, photophobia, epiphora induced by wind, myopia, cataract, blurred vision, facial paralysis, headache.
【Mechanism of Action】 This point is located around the eyes. On the basis of the principle that where the acupoint locates, where the indications are, this point is used to dispel wind and heat from the body, brighten the eyes and alleviate eye pain. It is commonly used to treat eye diseases. Intractable headache can be effectively treated by blood letting here and it is has the function of clearing and activating the meridians and collaterals.

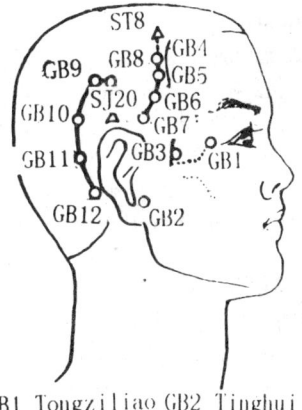

GB1 Tongziliao　GB2 Tinghui
GB4 Hanyan　　　GB5 Xuanlu
GB7 Qubin　　　　GB8 Shuaigu
GB10 Fubai　　　GB11 Touqiaoyin
ST8 Touwei　　　SJ20 Jiaosun
GB3 Shangguan　GB9 Tianchong
GB6 Xuanli　　　GB12 Wangu

Fig. 11-12

【Method】 Puncture 0.3-0.5 cun subcutaneously outwards. Moxibustion is applicable.
【Acupoint Prescriptions】
　　1) Cataracts: Tongziliao (GB 1), Hegu (LI 4), Toulinqi (GB 15), Jingming (BL 1). (*Great Compendium of Acupuncture and Moxibustion*)
　　2) Prosopalgia: main points: Tongziliao (GB 1), Hegu (LI 4), Taiyang; adjunct acupunture point: Yintang (EX-HN 2). (*Science of Acupuncture and Moxibustion*)
　　3) Monochromatism: main points: Tongziliao (GB 1), Shangguan (GB 3), Tianyou (SJ 16); supplementary points: Tinggong (SI 19), Jingming (BL 1), Sibai (ST 2), Juliao (ST 3). (*Abstract of Clinical Experience on Acupuncture and Moxibustion*)
【Regional Anatomy】 Skin-subcutaneous tissue-orbicular muscle of the eye-temporal fascia-temporal muscle. In the superficial layer, there are the zygomaticofacial and zygomaticotemporal branches of the zygomatic nerve. In the deep layer, there are the anterior and posterior deep temporal nerves and the branches of the anterior and posterior deep temporal arteries and veins.

GB 2 Tinghui (听会)
(Listening Convergence)

【Source】 A-B Classic of Acupuncture and Moxibustion
【Name Explanation】 Ting (听), hearing; Hui (会), gathering. The point is in front of the ear and functions in hearing; it is where the qi of the meridian gathers at the ear.
【Location】 On the face, anterior to the intertragic notch, in the depression posterior to the condyloid process of the mandible when the mouth is open. (See Fig. 11-12)
【Localization】 Sitting position with the head resting or in the lateral position, locate the point anterior to the intertragic notch and posterior to the Condyloid process of the mandible, on the is a depression occured when the mouth is opened.
【Indications】
    1) Diseases of the Head and Sense Organs: Headache, mumps, facial pain, tinnitus,, deaf-mutism, otitis media, earache, toothache, facial paralysis.
    2) Mental Diseases: Apoplexy, paralysis of the hands and feet, severe dizziness, salivation, running wildly due to mania, clonic convulsion.
    3) Other Disease: Mandibular luxation.
【Mechanism of Action】 Where the acupoint locates, where the indications are. It is used for inducing resuscitation, activating collaterals, opening auricular orifice and regulating collaterals to tranquilize the mind.
【Method】 Open the mouth, puncture perpendicularly 0.5-1 cun. Moxibustion is applicable.
【Acupoint Prescriptions】
    1) Tinnitus: Tinghui (GB 2), Tinggong (SI 19). (Experience on Acupuncture and Moxibustion Therapy)
    2) Pain and swelling of the ear: Tinghui (GB 2), Hegu (LI 4), Jiache (ST 6). (Great Compendium of Acupuncture and Moxibustion)
    3) Deafness: Tinghui (GB 2), Yangchi (SJ 4). (Secret Songs of Acupuncture and Moxibustion)
    4) Psychic deafness: Tinghui (GB 2), Yifeng (SJ 17). (Songs of Hundreds of Symptoms)
    5) Deafness: Tinghui (GB 2), Yingxiang (LI 20). (Songs of Xihong)
【Regional Anatomy】 Skin-subcutaneous tissue-capsule of the parotid gland-parotid gland. In the superficial layer, there are the auriculotemporal nerve and the great auricular nerve. In the deep layer, there are the superficial temporal artery and vein and the plexus of the facial nerve.

GB 3 Shangguan (上关)
(Upper Pass)

【Source】 Plain Questions
【Name Explanation】 Shang (上), upper; Guan (关), border or gate. Guan refers to the zygomatic arch. The point is at the upper margin of the zygomatic arch.
【Classification】 The Crossing Point of Hand-Shaoyang and Foot-Yangming Meridians.
【Location】 Anterior to the ear, directly above Xiaguan (ST 7), in the depression above the upper border of the zygomatic arch. (See Fig. 11-12)
【Localization】 Sitting position with the head resting or in the lateral position, locate the point on

the superior ridge of the preauricular zygomatic arch. The point is located with the mouth open.
【Indications】
　　1) Diseases of the Head and Sense Organs: Migraine, facial pain, tinnitus, deafness, otitis media, facial paralysis, lockjaw, toothache, optic atrophy, arcus senilis.
　　2) Mental Diseases: Manic-depressive psychosis, epilepsy, clonic convulsion.
【Mechanism of Action】 Where the acupoint locates, where the indications are. It is used for inducing resuscitation, refreshing, clearing and activating the meridians and collaterals.
【Method】 Puncture perpendicularly 0.5-1 cun, deep puncture can not be used. Moxibustion is applicable.
【Regional Anatomy】 Skin-subcutaneous tissue-superficial temporal fascia-deep temporal fascia-loose connective tissue-temporal muscle.
　　In the superficial layer, there are the auriculotemporal nerve, the temporal branch of the facial nerve and the superficial and deep anterior and posterior temporal nerves.

GB 4　Hanyan（颔厌）
(Jaw Detested)

【Source】 *A-B Classic of Acupuncture and Moxibustion*
【Name Explanation】 Han (颔), mandible; Yan (厌), obedience. The point is at the temple and moves along with the motion of the mandible when chewing.
【Classification】 The Crossing Point of the Hand and Foot Shaoyang and Foot Yangming Meridians.
【Location】 On the head, in the hair above the temples, at the junction of the upper one-fourth and lower three-fourths of the curved line connecting Touwei (ST 8) and Qubin (GB 7). (See Fig. 11-12)
【Localization】 Sitting position with the head resting or in the lateral position, first locate Touwei (ST 8) and Qubin (GB 7), drawing an arc line connecting the two points. Locate Xuanlu (GB 5) in the midpoint of this arc line. Hanyan (GB 4) is located in the midpoint of the arc line connecting Touwei (ST 8) and Xuanlu (GB 5). There is a slight movement when chewing.
【Indications】
　　1) Diseases of the Head and Sense Organs: Migraine, pain of the neck and outer canthus, toothache, tinnitus, facial paralysis, dizziness.
　　2) Mental Diseases: Epilepsy, clonic convulsion.
【Mechanism of Action】 Hanyan (GB 4) is located near the eyes. Its meridian goes into the ears, passes down through Jiache (ST 6) and intersects with the Foot-Yangming Meridian and the Hand-Yangming Meridian, which enters the teeth. This point is used for dispelling wind, removing heat and alleviating pain. The Gallbaldder Meridian and its collaterals spread over the face and eyes, therefore, the point is needled to treat the diseases of the head, face and sense organs.
【Method】 Puncture perpendicularly backwards 0.5-0.8 cun. Moxibustion is applicable.
【Regional Anatomy】 Skin-subcutaneous tissue-superior auricular muscle-temporal fascia-temporal muscle. In the superficial layer, there are the auriculotemporal nerve and the parietal branches of the superficial temporal artery and vein. In the deep layer, there are the branches of the anterior and posterior deep temporal nerves.

GB 5   Xuanlu (悬颅)
(Hanging Skull)

[Source] *Miraculous Pivot*
[Name Explanation] Xuan (悬), hang; Lu (颅), skull. The points are at the temples as if hanging on both sides of the skull.
[Classification] The Crossing Point of the Hand and Foot Shaoyang and Yangming Meridians.
[Location] On the head, in the hair above the temples, at the midpoint of the curved line connecting Touwei (ST 8) and Qubin (GB 7). (See Fig. 11-12)
[Localization] See Hanyan (GB 4).
[Indications]
　　Diseases of the Head and Sense Organs: Migraine, swelling of the face, outer canthus pain, toothache, epistaxis.
[Mechanism of Action] See Hanyan (GB 4).
[Method] Puncture perpendicularly backwards 0.5-0.8 cun. Moxibustion is applicable.
[Regional Anatomy] Same as Hanyan (GB 4).
[Remark] It has been reported that acupuncture at GB 5 on normal people for some minutes increase the myoelectric amplitude for 35 minutes. It also increases myoelectric amplitude of the patients with cerebrovascular occlusion.

GB 6   Xuanli (悬厘)
(Deviation From Hanging Skull)

[Source] *A-B Classic of Acupuncture and Moxibustion*
[Name Explanation] Xuan (悬), hanging; Li (厘), hair. The point is at the temple beneath long hair.
[Classification] The Crossing Point of the Hand and Foot Shaoyang and Yangming Meridians.
[Location] On the head, in the hair above the temples, at the junction of the upper three-fourths and lower one-fourth of the curved line connecting Touwei (ST 8) and Qubin (GB 7). (See Fig. 11-12.)
[Localization] Sitting position with the head resting or in the lateral position, locate the point at the intersection of the superior three-fourths and inferior one-fourth of the line connecting between Touwei (ST 8) and Qubin (GB 7).
[Indications]
　　1) Diseases of the Head and Sense Organs: Migraine, swelling of the face, outer canthus pain, tinnitus, toothache.
　　2) Digestive Diseases: Retching, anorexia, susceptibility to sneeze.
　　3) Mental Diseases: Clonic convulsion, irritability.
　　4) Other Disease: Febrile disease without sweating.
[Mechanism of Action] This point is the crossing point of its meridian, Hand Yangming and Foot Yangming Meridians. Hand Yangming and Foot Yangming Meridians have the function of regulating the stomach and spleen. According to the principle that a point can be used to treat diseases of the linked meridians, it can be needled to treat digestive and non-sweating febrile diseases. The acupoint is used for dispelling wind and removing heat, activating collaterals to relieve pain and punctured to treat the diseases of head, face, sense organs and convulsions. See

Hanyan (GB 4) for details.
【Method】 Puncture perpendicularly backwards 0.5-0.8 cun. Moxibustion is applicable.
【Acupoint Prescriptions】
   1) Migrain due to febrile disease: Xuanli (GB 6), Jiuwei (RN 15). (*Thousand Golden Prescriptions*)
   2) Depressive psychosis: Xuanli (GB 6), Shugu (GB 65). (*Experience on Acupuncture and Moxibustion Therapy*)
【Regional Anatomy】 Same as Hanyan (GB 4).

GB 7   Qubin (曲鬢)
(Twist Temple)

【Source】 A-B *Classic of Acupuncture and Moxibustion*
【Name Explanation】 Qu (曲), curve; Bin (鬢), hair at the temple. The point is in the hairline at the temple, superior to the ear.
【Classification】 The Crossing Point of the Foot Shaoyang and Foot Taiyang Meridians.
【Location】 On the head, at the crossing point of the vertical posterior line drawn from the border of the temples and the horizontal line through the ear apexes. (See Fig. 11-12)
【Localization】 Sitting or in the lateral position, the point is located 1 cun superior to the preauricula on the hairline, about 1 cun anterior to Jiaosun (SJ 20)
【Indications】
   Diseases of the Head and Sense Organs: Migraine, swelling of the submental region and cheek, conjunctival congestion with swelling pain, neck rigidity, facial paralysis, sudden loss of voice.
【Mechanism of Action】 This point is the crossing point of the Gallbladder and the Bladder Meridians. These two meridians spread over the head, neck and eyes. This point is used for dispelling wind and removing heat, activating collaterals to relieve pain and it is commonly used to treat the diseases of the head, face and sense organs.
【Method】 Puncture perpendicularly backwards 0.5-0.8 cun. Moxibustion is applicable.
【Acupoint Prescriptions】
   1) Headache, headache with toothache, intermittent attacks for many years: Using the Giant Typhonium Tuber Powder and moxibustion to Qubin (GB 7) moxibustion can treat diseases on the left side of the body by needling points on the right side and vice versa. (*Proof Sheet of the Complete Effective Prescriptions for Women*)
   2) Dental caries: Qubin (GB 7), Chongyang (ST 42). (*Thousand Golden Prescriptions*)
【Regional Anatomy】 Same as Hanyan (GB 4).

GB 8   Shuaigu (率谷)
(Leading Valley)

【Source】 A-B *Classic of Acupuncture and Moxibustion*
【Name Explanation】 Shuai (率), command; Gu (谷), valley. The point is above the ear and is the highest among all the points named gu, like a commander.
【Classification】 Crossing Point of Foot Shaoyang and Foot Taiyang Meridians.
【Location】 On the head, directly superior to the ear apex, 1.5 cun above the hairline, directly

over Jiaosun (SJ 20). (See Fig. 11-12)

【Localization】 Sitting or in the lateral position, press the posterior auricula forward, the point is located at 1.5 cun directly superior to the apex of the ear.

【Indications】

1) Diseases of the Head and Sense Organs: Migraine and headache, dizziness, conjunctival congestion with swelling and pain, tinnitus, deafness.

2) Digestive Diseases: Fullness feeling in the chest, restlessness and vomiting, anorexia.

3) Respiratory Diseases: Cough and expectoration.

4) Mental Diseases: Acute and chronic infantile convulsions.

【Mechanism of Action】 This point belongs to the Gallbladder Meridian. Fullness feeling in the chest and vomiting with anorexia are caused by stomach heat due to stagnated heat of Gallbladder Meridian. Cough and expectoration are due to deficiency of the spleen. The point is used for clearing heat, removing starg narcy, regulating the stomach, resolving phlegm, treating digestive and respiratory diseases, and acute or chronic infantile convulsions caused by phlegm-heat. The Gallbladder Meridian originates from side of the eye and goes into the ear. It is needled to treat the diseases of the head, face and sense organs.

【Method】 Puncture perpendicularly 0.5-0.8 cun. Moxibustion is applicable.

【Acupoint Prescription】 Cold phlegm in the stomach: Shuaigu (GB 8), Geshu (BL 17) (*Experience on Acupuncture and Moxibustion Therapy*)

【Regional Anatomy】 Skin-subcutaneous tissue-superior auricular muscle-temporal fascia-temporal muscle. There are the anastomotic branches of the auriculotemporal and the greater occipital nerves and the parietal branches of the superficial temporal artery and vein in this area.

GB 9   Tianchong (天冲)
(Heaven Rush)

【Source】 *A-B Classic of Acupuncture and Moxibustion*

【Name Explanation】 Tian (天), heaven; Chong (冲), gushing. Tian refers to the head, where the point is located. Qi and blood gush to the vertex of the head from this point.

【Classification】 The Crossing Point of the Foot Shaoyang and Foot Taiyang Meridians.

【Location】 On the head, directly above the posterior border of the ear root, 2 cun above the hairline and 0.5 cun posterior to Shuaigu (GB 8). (See Fig. 11-12)

【Localization】 Sitting or in the lateral position, the point is located 2 cun directly superior to the margin of the root of the ear, about 0.5 cun posterior to Shuaigu (GB 8).

【Indications】

1) Diseases of the Head and Sense Organs: Headache, gingivitis, goiter, tinnitus, deafness.

2) Mental Diseases: Depressive psychosis, epilepsy, palpitation due to fright.

【Mechanism of Action】 See Shuaigu (GB 8).

【Method】 Puncture perpendicularly 0.5-0.8 cun. Moxibustion is applicable.

【Regional Anatomy】 Skin-subcutaneous tissue-the superior auricular muscle-temporal fascia-temporal muscle. There are the anastomotic branches of the auriculotemporal nerve and the lesser and greater occipital nerves, the parietal branches of the superficial temporal artery and vein, and the posterior auricular artery and vein in this area.

GB 10　Fubai (浮白)
(Floating White)

【Source】 *Plain Questions*
【Name Explanation】 Fu (浮), floating; Bai (白), bright. The point is on the superficial portion of the body and its functions are to clear the mind and brighten the eyes.
【Classification】 The Crossing Point of the Foot Shaoyang and Foot Taiyang Meridians.
【Location】 On the head, posterior and superior to the mastoid process, at the junction of the middle one-third and upper one-third of the curved line connecting Tianchong (GB 9) and Wangu (GB 12). (See Fig. 11-12)
【Localization】 Sitting or in the lateral position, first locate Tianchong (GB 9) and Wangu (GB 12). Then locate this point at the intersection of the superior one-third and middle one-third of an arc line between Tianchong (GB 9) and Wangu (GB 12).
【Indications】
　　1) Diseases along the Course of the Meridian: Stiffness of the neck, carbuncle and swelling, difficult moving in the upper limbs, difficulty in walking, paralysis in the lower limbs.
　　2) Diseases of the Head and Sense Organs: Tinnitus, deafness, toothache, inflammation of the throat, ophthalmalgia.
　　3) Respiratory Diseases: Fullness in the chest, chest pain, syndrome characterized by dyspnea, cough with dyspnea, profuse sputum.
　　4) Other Diseases: Scrofula and goiter.
【Mechanism of Action】 Fubai (GB 10) is the crossing point of Foot Shaoyang and Foot Taiyang Meridians, these two meridians spread over the neck, shoulders and legs. According to the principle "if the diseases are in the lower part, the points in the upper can be used to treat them," this point can be needled to treat diseases in the shoulders, arms and lower limbs. See Shuaigu (GB 8) for further details.
【Method】 Puncture perpendicularly 0.5-0.8 cun. Moxibustion is applicable.
【Acupoint Prescription】
　　Dental caries: Fubai (GB 10), Wangu (GB 12). (*A-B Classic of Acupuncture and Moxibustion*)
【Regional Anatomy】 Skin-subcutaneous tissue-epicranial aponeurosis. There are the anastomotic branches of the lesser and the greater occipital nerves and the posterior auricular artery and vein in this area.

GB 11　Touqiaoyin (头窍阴)
(the Head Orifice Yin)

【Source】 *A-B Classic of Acupuncture and Moxibustion*
【Name Explanation】 Tou (头), head; Qiao (窍), opening; Yin (阴), Yin of Yin-Yang. The kidney and the liver pertain to Yin and are opened to the ear and eye. The point is on the head and is indicated in ear and eye diseases.
【Classification】 The Crossing Point of the Foot Shaoyang and Foot Taiyang Meridians.
【Location】 On the head, posterior and superior to the mastoid process, at the junction of the middle one-third and lower one-third of the curved line connecting Tianchong (GB 9) and Wangu (GB 12). (See Fig. 11-12).

【Localization】 Sitting or lateral position, first locate GB 9 and GB 12, then locate this point at the intersection of the inferior one-third and middle one-third of an arc line between Tianchong (GB 9) and Wangu (GB 12).

【Indications】

　　1) Diseases along the Course of the Meridian: Pain in the chest and hypochondrium, limb spasm, feverish sensation of feet and hands, stiffness of the neck, paralysis of lower limbs.

　　2) Diseases of the Head and Sense Organs: Deafness, tinnitus, earache, ophthalmalgia, inflammation of the throat, stiffness of the tongue, boils in the nose, vertigo, dizziness, headache, bitter taste.

【Mechanism of Action】 See Fubai (GB 10) and Wangu (GB 12).

【Method】 Puncture perpendicularly 0.5-0.8 cun. Moxibustion is applicable.

【Acupoint Prescription】

　　Headache: Touqiaoyin (GB 11), Qiangjian (DU 18). (*Thousand Golden Prescriptions*)

【Regional Anatomy】 Skin-subcutaneous tissue-epicranial aponeurosis. There are the lasser occipital nerve and the branches of the posterior auricular artery and vein in this area.

GB 12　Wangu (完骨)
(Whole bone)

【Source】 *Miraculous Pivot and Plain Questions*

【Name Explanation】 Wangu (完骨), mastoid process. The point is at the lower margin of the mastoid process of the temporal bone behind the ear.

【Classification】 The Crossing Point of the Foot Shaoyang and Foot Taiyang Meridians.

【Location】 On the head, in the depression posterior and inferior to the mastoid process. (See Fig. 11-12)

【Localization】 Sitting or in the lateral position, locate the point at the depression posterior and inferior to the mastoid process of the temporal bone.

【Indications】

　　1) Diseases along the Course of the Meridian: Foot flaccidity, limited movement of the lower limbs, stiffness of the neck.

　　2) Diseases of the Head and Sense Organs: Headache, edema of the head and face, toothache, facial paralysis, inflammation of the throat, lockjaw, swelling of the cheek, pain behind the ear.

　　3) Mental Diseases: Epilepsy, insomnia.

　　4) Other Disease: Malaria.

【Mechanism of Action】

　　1) The branch of the Foot Shaoyang Meridian goes up to the nasopharynx, comes out of the lower cheek and submental region, and spreads over the face. The points of the Gallbladder Meridian are generally used to treat inflammation of the throat, swelling and pain in the head and face.

　　2) Insomnia is commonly caused by disturbance of the mental activities due to the stagnant heat of the Gallbladder Meridian, this point is used for removing the heat and tranquilizing the mind.

　　3) Malaria is mainly caused by a pathogenic factor between the exterior and interior portions of the body, the disharmony between Ying and Wei, and the struggle between the vital energy and the pathogenic factor. And this disease is in the Shaoyang Meridian. So the point is needled to treat malaria and Shaoyang diseases by mediation.

【Method】 Puncture obliquely downwards 0.5-0.8 cun. Moxibustion is applicable.

【Acupoint Prescriptions】
1) Dark urine: Wangu (GB 12), Xiaochangshu (BL 27), Pangguangshu (BL 28). (*Experience on Acupuncture and Moxibustion Therapy*)
2) Neck pain: Wangu (GB 12), Hanyan (GB 4). (*ibid*)
3) Manic-depressive psychosis: Wangu (GB 12), Fengchi (GB 20). (*A-B Classic of Acupuncture and Moxibustion*)
4) Inflammation of the throat: Wangu (GB 12), Tianrong (SI 17), Qishe (ST 11). (*ibid*)

【Regional Anatomy】Skin-subcutaneous tissue-sternocleidomastoid muscle-splenius muscle of the head-longer muscle of the head. In the superficial layer, there are the lesser occipital nerve and the branches or tributaries of the posterior auricular artery and vein. In the deep layer, there is the deep cervical artery and vein. If the needle is inserted deeply, the vertebral artery may be injured.

GB 13   Benshen (本神)
(Spirit Source)

【Source】*A-B Classic of Acupuncture and Moxibustion*
【Name Explanation】Ben (本), essential; Shen (神), mind. The point is lateral to Shenting (DU 24) along the anterior hairline. The point is in the region where the brain is located and is considered as the residence and governor of the mind. It is therefore essential to the human body.
【Classification】The Crossing Point of the Foot Shaoyang and Yangwei Meridians.
【Location】On the head, 0.5 cun above the anterior hairline, 3 cun lateral to Shenting (DU 24), at the junction of the medial two-thirds and lateral one third of the line connecting Shenting (DU 24) and Touwei (ST 8). (See Fig. 11-13)
【Localization】Sitting position with the head resting, the point is located 3 cun lateral to the anterior midline, about 0.5 cun superior to the hair line.
【Indications】
1) Diseases along the Course of the Meridian: Hemiplegia, pain in the chest and hypochondrium, stiffness of the neck.
2) Diseases of the Head and Sense Organs: Headache, dizziness, conjunctival congestion, swelling and pain.
3) Mental Diseases: Depressive psychosis, epilepsy, infantile convulsion, coma due to stroke.

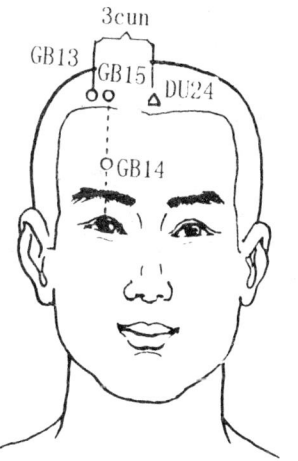

GB13 Benshen GB15 Toulinqi
GB14 Yangbai DU24 Shenting

Fig. 11-13

【Mechanism of Action】See Fubai (GB 10) and Wangu (GB 12).
【Method】Puncture subcutaneously backwards 0.5-0.8 cun. Moxibustion is applicable.
【Acupoint Prescriptions】
1) Epilepsy induced by terror: Benshen (GB 13), Qianding (DU 21), Xinhui (DU 22), Tianzhu (BL 10). (*Thousand Golden Prescriptions*)
2) Radiating pain in the chest and hypochondrium causing difficulty in moving: Benshen (GB 13), Luxi (SJ 19). (*ibid*)

【Regional Anatomy】Skin-subcutaneous tissue-the frontal belly of the occipitofrontal muscle.

There are the supraorbital artery and vein, supraorbital nerve and the frontal branches of the superficial temporal artery and vein in this area.

GB 14　Yangbai（阳白）
(Yang White)

【Source】 *A-B Classic of Acupuncture and Moxibustion*
【Name Explanation】 Yang（阳）, Yang of Yin-Yang; Bai（白）, brightness. The head is Yang. The point is at the head and its function is to brighten the eye.
【Classification】 The Crossing Point of the Foot Shaoyang and Yangwei Meridians.
【Location】 On the forehead, directly above the pupil, 1 cun above the eyebrow. (See Fig. 11-13)
【Localization】 Sitting with the head at rest, locate the point 1 cun directly superior to the midpoint of the eyebrow.
【Indications】
　　1) Diseases of the Head and Sense Organs: Headache, dizziness, eye pain, itching of the eye, myopia, nyctalopia, blepbarochalsis, flickering eyelids.
　　2) Other Diseases: vomiting, neck pain.
【Mechanism of Action】
　　Yangbai (GB 14) is in the forehead, and is commonly used to treat eyelid diseases. This point is subcutaneously needled downwards about 0.8 to 1 cun to treat difficulty in catacleisis, blepharoptosis and twitching of the eyelids.
【Method】 Puncture subcutaneously 0.5-0.8 cun. Moxibustion is applicable.
【Acupoint Prescription】 Electric ophthalmitis: Yangbai (GB 14), Yintang (EX-HN 3), Tongziliao (GB 1), Sibai (ST 2), Hegu (LI 4). (*Abstract of Clinical Experience on Acupuncture and Moxibustion*)
【Regional Anatomy】 Skin-subcutaneous tissue-frontal belly of the occipitofrontal muscle. There are the lateral branches of the supraorbital nerve and the lateral branches of the supraorbital artery and vein in this area.

GB 15　Toulinqi（头临泣）
(the Head Falling Tears)

【Source】 *Experience on Acupuncture and Moxibustion Therapy*
【Name Explanation】 Tou（头）, head; Lin（临）, regulation; Qi（泣）, tears. The point is on the head and is indicated for excessive lacrimation.
【Classification】 The Crossing Point of the Foot Shaoyang, Foot Taiyang and Yangwei Meridians.
【Location】 On the head, directly above the pupil and 0.5 cun above the anterior hairline, at the midpoint of the line connecting Shenting (DU 24) and Touwei (ST 8). (See Fig. 11-13)
【Localization】 Sitting with the head resting, locate the point 0.5 cun directly superior to the anterior hairline on the ocular median line, or locate the point on the midpoint of the line joining DU 24 and ST 8.
【Indications】
　　1) Diseases of the Head and Sense Organs: Headache, pain on the margins of the eyelids, outercanthus-ache, blurred vision, stuffy nose, rhinorrhea with turbid discharge, tinnitus,

deafness.

2) Cardiovascular Diseases: Obstruction of qi in the chest, precordial pain causing difficulty in turning the trunk.

3) Mental Diseases: Infantile convulsion, apoplexy, coma, epilepsy.

4) Other Diseases: Febrile disease, malaria, carbuncle of axilla.

【Mechanism of Action】 A branch of Foot-Shaoyang passes through the heart. The heart controls mental activities and blood circulation. So this point can be used to treat cardiovascular diseases and mental diseases.

【Method】 Puncture subcutaneously 0.5-0.8 cun. Moxibustion is applicable.

【Acupoint Prescriptions】

1) Lacrimation: Linqi (GB 15), Touwei (ST 8). (*Songs of Hundreds of Symptoms*)

2) Deafness: Linqi (GB 15), Jinmen (BL 63), Hegu (LI 4). (*Songs of Point Selection on Miscellaneous Diseases*)

【Regional Anatomy】 Skin-subcutaneous tissue-epicranial aponeurosis-loose connective tissue below aponeurosis. There are the supraorbital nerve and the supraorbital artery and vein in this area.

GB 16 Muchuang (目窗)
(Eye Window)

【Source】 *A-B Classic of Acupuncture and Moxibustion*

【Name Explanation】 Mu (目), eye; Chuang (窗), window. The point is above the eye and indicated in eye disorders, like a window for the eyes.

【Classification】 The Crossing Point of the Foot Shaoyang and Yangwei Meridians.

【Location】 On the head, 1.5 cun above the anterior hairline and 2.25 cun lateral to the midline of the head. (See Fig. 11-14)

【Localization】 Sitting with the head resting, locate the point 1.5 cun directly superior to the anterior hair line on the ocular median line, i.e., about 1 cun posterior to Toulinqi (GB 15).

【Indications】

1) Diseases of the Head and Sense Organs: Headache, vertigo, swelling of the face, conjunctival congestion and swelling pain, hypermetropia, myopia, optic atrophy, cataract, upper toothache, deafness, stuffy nose.

2) Mental Diseases: Child epilepsy induced by terror.

3) Other Diseases: Aversion to cold, fever without sweating.

【Mechanism of Action】 Muchuang (GB 16) is the crossing point of its own meridian and Yangwei Meridian. It can be punctured to treat aversion to cold, fever without sweating, and stuffy nose, etc. Mu, in Chinese, means "eyes", and Chuang, refers to "window". This meaning indicates that the point was used by ancient doctors to treat eye diseases.

【Method】 Puncture subcutaneously 0.5-0.8 cun. Moxibustion is applicable.

【Acupoint Prescriptions】

1) Conjunctival congestion: Muchuang (GB 16), Daling (PC 7). (*A-B Classic of Acupuncture and Moxibustion*)

2) Headache: Muchuang (GB 16), Tianchong (GB 9), Fengchi (GB 20). (*ibid*)

3) Vertigo: Muchuang (GB 16), Daling (PC 7), Hegu (LI 4), Yemen (SJ 2), Shangxing (DU 23), Cuanzhu (BL 2), Sizhukong (SJ 23). (*Great Compendium of Acupuncture and Moxibustion*)

【Regional Anatomy】 Skin-subcutaneous tissue-the galea aponeurosis-loose connective tissue below aponeurosis. There are the supraorbital nerve and the frontal branches of the superficial temporal artery and vein in this area.

GB 17   Zhengying (正营)
(Top Convergence)

【Source】 *A-B Classic of Acupuncture and Moxibustion*
【Name Explanation】 ZhengYing (正营), fright and fear. This point is indicated in treating mental states such as fright and fear.
【Classification】 The Crossing Point of the Foot Shaoyang and Yangwei Meridians.
【Location】 On the head, 2.5 cun above the anterior hairline and 2.25 cun lateral to the midline of the head. (See Fig. 11-14).
【Localization】 Sitting position with the head resting, first locate Toulinqi (GB 15) which islocated 0.5 cun directly superior to the hair line on the ocular median line, Zhengying (GB 17) located 2 cun directly superior to Toulinqi (GB 15).
【Indications】
   1) Diseases of the Head and Sense Organs: Headache, stiffness of the neck, vertigo, stiffness of lips, toothache.
   2) Other Diseases: Hemiplegia, aversion to cold.
【Mechanism of Action】 See Muchuang (GB 16).
【Method】 Puncture subcutaneously 0.5-0.8 cun. Moxibustion is applicable.
【Regional Anatomy】 Skin-subcutaneous tissue-epicranial aponeurosis-loose connective tissue below aponeurosis. There are the anastomotic branches of the supraorbital and greater occipital nerves and the parietal branches of the superficial temporal artery and vein in this area.
【Remark】 Puncturing Zhengying (GB 17) of normal people for 5 minutes may increase myoelectric amplitude. ($P<0.05$). It may also increase myoelectric amplitude of the patients with cerebrovascular occlusion.

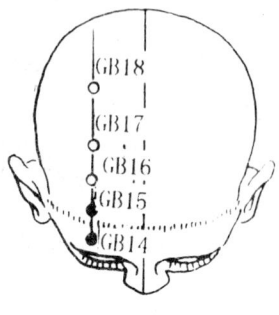

GB14 Yangbai
GB15 Toulinqi
GB16 Muchuang
GB17 Zhengying
GB18 Chengling

Fig. 11-14

GB 18   Chengling (承灵)
(Spirit Receiver)

【Source】 *A-B Classic of Acupuncture and Moxibustion*
【Name Explanation】 Cheng (承), support; Ling (灵), spirit. The brain dominates the mind, so the parietal bone is also called the Tianling bone and the point is just lateral and inferior to it.
【Classification】 The Crossing Point of the Foot Shaoyang and Yangwei Meridians.
【Location】 On the head, 4 cun above the anterior hairline and 2.25 cun lateral to the midline of the head. (See Fig. 11-14)
【Localization】 Sitting position with the head resting, the point is located 4 cun superior to the anterior hairline on the line joining Toulinqi (GB 15) and Fengchi (GB 20), on the same level with Tongtian (BL 7).
【Indications】
   1) Diseases of the Head and Sense Organs: Headache, ophthalmalgia, allergic rhinitis, stuffy nose, profuse nasal discharge.
   2) Respiratory Diseases: Cough, asthma, fever, aversion to cold.
【Mechanism of Action】 See Muchuang (GB 16) and Shuaigu (GB 8).

【Method】Puncture subcutaneously backwards 0.5-0.8 cun. Moxibustion is applicable.
【Regional Anatomy】Skin-subcutaneous tissue-epicranial aponeurosis-loose connective tissue below aponeurosis. There are the greater occipital nerve and the branches of the occipital artery and vein in this area.

GB 19   Naokong (脑空)
(Brain Hollow)

【Source】 *A-B Classic of Acupuncture and Moxibustion*
【Name Explanation】 Nao (脑), brain; Kong (空), cavity. The point is lateral to the occipital bone and internally related to the cranial cavity. It is indicated in treating neurological diseases.
【Classification】 The Crossing Point of the Foot Shaoyang and Yangwei Meridians
【Location】 On the head level with the upper border of the external occipital protuberance or Naohu (DU 17), 2.25 cun lateral to the midline of the head. (See Fig. 11-15)
【Localization】 Sitting or in the prone position, the point is located 1.5 cun directly superior to Fengchi (GB 20), on the same level with Naohu (DU 17) which is located at the upper margin of the external occipital protuterance.
【Indications】
   1) Diseases of the Head and Sense Organs: Headache, vertigo, conjunctival congestion and ophthalmalgia, epixtasis and nose pain, tinnitus, deafness, stiffness of the neck.
   2) Mental Diseases: Unconsciousness due to high fever, palpitation due to fright, depressive psychosis, mania, epilepsy.

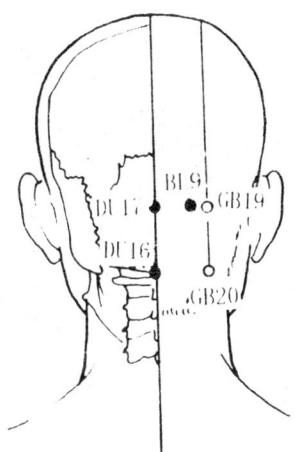

DU16 Fengfu
DU17 Naohu
GB19 Naokong
GB20 Fengchi
BL9 Yuzhen

Fig. 11-15

【Mechanism of Action】 See Muchuang (GB 16) and Shuaigu (GB 8).
【Method】 Puncture subcutaneously 0.5-0.8 cun. Moxibustion is applicable.
【Regional Anatomy】 Skin-subcutaneous tissue-occipital belly of the occipitofrontal muscle. There are the greater occipital nerve, the occipital artery and vein, and the posterior auricular branches of the facial nerve in this area.

GB 20   Fengchi (风池)
(Wind Pool)

【Source】 *Miraculous Pivot*
【Name Explanation】 Feng (风), pathogenic wind; Chi (池), depression, which is like a pool. It is an important point in eliminating pathogenic wind.
【Classification】 The Crossing Point of the Foot Shaoyang and Yangwei Meridians
【Location】 On the neck, below the occipital bone, on level with Fengfu(DU 16), in the depression between the upper ends of the sternocleidomastoid and trapezius muscle. (See Fig. 11-15)
【Localization】 Sitting or in the prone position, the point is located in the depression inferior to the occipital bone, between the upper region of trapezius muscle and upper extremity of the ster-

nocleidomastoid muscle.

[Indications]

1) Diseases along the Course of the Meridian: Neckache and backache, stiff neck, pain of shoulder and arms, pain in the back and loins, hemiplegia, flaccidity and arthralgia syndrome of lower limbs.

2) Diseases of the Head and Sense Organs: Migraine and headache, vertigo, conjunctival congestion, poor vision, lacrimation induced by wind, blepharoptosis, running nose, epistaxis, rhinorrhea with turbid discharge, tinnitus, deafness, toothache, swelling pain in the throat, facial paralysis, difficulty in swallowing.

3) Epidemic febrile diseases caused by exopathogen: Fever with chills, general arthralgia, summer heat diseases, epidemic fegrile diseases.

4) Mental Diseases: Apoplexy, coma, insomnia, clonic convulsion.

5) Other Diseases: Urticaria, erysipelas.

[Mechanism of Action]

1) Fengchi (GB 20) is used for both exogenous and endogenous wind. Many disease are caused by wind, as it brings cold, heat, dampness and phlegm together. Cold due to wind has the following symptoms; fever with chills, rigidity of the neck with headache, facial hemiparalysis, swelling pain in the throat and skin diseases. This point can be used to treat headache, vertigo and apoplexy caused by endogenous wind.

2) This point is often used to treat eye diseases, such as blepharoptosis, with good results. It can be used alone, however, if applied together with Yangbai (GB 14) and Xiangu (ST 43), it will be more effective.

3) It is very effective for treating swelling pain in the throat and difficult swallowing. Note that the tip of the needle should be aimed at the Adam's apple in these treatments.

[Method] Puncture obliquely 0.8-1.2 cun towards the inner canthus of the other side.

[Acupoint Prescriptions]

1) Ophthalmalgia with difficulty in vision: Fengchi (GB 20), Naohu (DU 17), Yuzhen (BL 9), Fengfu (DU 16), Shangxing (DU 23). (*Thousand Golden Prescriptions*)

2) Traumatic injury with cold and fever: Fengchi (GB 20), Tinghui (GB 2), Fuliu (KI 7). (*Experience on Acupuncture and Moxibustion Therapy*)

3) Epilepsy: Moxibustion to Fengchi (GB 20) and Baihui (DU 20). (*Great Compendium of Acupuncture and Moxibustion*)

4) Migraine and headache: Fengchi (GB 20), Hegu (LI 4), Sizhukong (SJ 23). (*ibid*)

5) Mumps: Fengchi (GB 20), Dazhu (BL 11), Quchi (LI 11), Tianjing (SJ 10), Waiguang (SJ 5), Hegu (LI 4), Yemen (SJ 2). (*Chinese Acupuncture and Moxibustion*)

6) Diffuse goiter: Fengchi (GB 20), Dazhui (DU 14), Dazhu (BL 11), Tiantu (RN 22), Shuitu (ST 10), Mingmen (DU 4), Zhongzhu (SJ 3). (*ibid*)

7) Acute laryngitis: Fengchi (GB 20), Yemen (SJ 2) and Yuji (LU 10) are selected as main points. Feishu (BL 13) and Shousanli (LI 10) can be added in severe cases. Prick Shaoshang (LU 11) to cause bleeding. (*ibid*)

8) Meniere's disease: Fengchi (GB 20), Baihui (DU 20), Taiyang (EX-HN 5), Shangxing (DU 23), Zusanli (ST 36), Taichong (LR 3). (*Selection of Theses*)

[Regional Anatomy] Skin-subcutaneous tissue-between the trapezius muscle and the sternocleidomastoid muscle-splenius muscle of the head-semispinal muscle of the head-between the large posterior straight muscle of the head and the superior oblique muscle of the head.

In the superficial layer, there are the lesser occipital nerve and the branches or tributaries of the occipital artery and vein. In the deep layer, there is the suboccipital nerve.

[Remark] Select Fengchi (GB 20), and Shangtianzhu (Extra: 0.5 cun above Tianzhu (BL 10)) as main points and puncture them with the method of conducting qi. Puncture Zusanli (ST 36) and Sanyinjiao (SP 6) points with rienforcing method can treat endocrine exophthalmos with certain therapeutic effect. It can improve blood stasis, microcirculation, blood rheology and hemodyanamics. It is reported that it has a due-regulating effect on gastric juice secretion in.

GB 21 Jianjing (肩井)
(Shoulder Well)

【Source】 *A-B Classic of Acupuncture and Moxibustion*
【Name Explanation】 Jian (肩), shoulder; Jing (井), well. The point is on the shoulder and the depression is like a well.
【Classification】 The Crossing Point of the Hand and Foot-Shaoyang, and Yangwei Meridians.
【Location】 On the shoulder, directly above the nipple, at the midpoint of the line connecting Dazhui (DU 14) and the acromion. (See fig. 11-16)
【Localization】
Sitting position, locate the point at the midpoint of the line joining the highest part of spinous process of the 7th cervical vertibra and the acromial extremity of the clavicle, directly superior to the nipple.

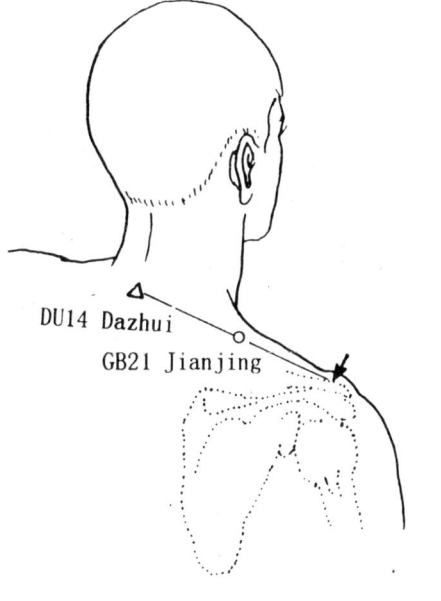

Fig. 11-16

【Indications】
1) Diseases along the Course of the Meridian: Stiffness of the neck, hemiplegia, hysterical paralysis, pain of the shoulder and back, stiff neck.
2) Obstetrical and gynecological diseases: Difficult labor, retention of placenta, uterine bleeding, cold limbs due to fetal abortion.
3) Other Diseases: Hypertension, scrfula, cough with dyspnea consumptive diseases, hernia, stomachache, acute mastitis, carbuncles, cellulitis, furuncles, boils.

【Mechanism of Action】
1) The point is the crossing point of the Hand Shaoyang and Foot Shaoyang and Yangwei meridians. It is commonly used to treat pain of the shoulder and back, stiff neck, and flaccidity of the lower limbs. *Songs of the Eight Points* says: "Jiangjing is mainly used to treat the diseases of the feet". It is quite effective to treat the flaccidity of the lower limbs. The tip of the needle should be pointed backwards.
2) The Muscle Regions of Foot-Shaoyang are connected with the pectoral muscle. This point has the function of regulating the flow of qi and promoting blood circulation by removing blood stasis. It is an effective point used to treat acute mastitis and other surgical diseases. The tip of the needle is pointed forwards, the therapeutic effect is the best.
3) Stomachache can be eased immediately by pressing the right thumb on Jiangjing of the left side and rubbing slightly on the abdomen with the left hand.
4) It is commonly used to treat stiffneck and shoulder-pain. The best way is to puncture obliquely and point the needle towards the affected part.
5) It is also commonly used to treat difficult labor, retention of placenta, metrorrhagia and metrostaxis.

【Method】 Puncture perpendicularly 0.3-0.5 cun, deep and forceful puncture can not be used.
【Acupoint Prescriptions】
　　1) Difficult labor: both the Jianjing (GB 21) points should be punctured 1 cun deep with reducing method. (*Thousand Golden Prescriptions*)
　　2) Migratory arthralgia and foot weakness: Jianjing (GB 21), Dazhui (DU 14), Fengchi (GB 20), Zusanli (ST 36). (*Experience on Acupuncture and Moxibustion Therapy*)
　　3) Galactostasis: Both the Jianjing (GB 21) points are used. (*Confucian's Duties to Their Parents*)
　　4) Impotence: Apply moxibustion to Jianjing (GB 21) and Guanyuan (RN 4) with 100 cones. (*Medical Ways*)
　　5) Consumptive diseases: Nocturnal emission: Jianjing (GB 21), Dazhui (DU 14), Gaohuang (BL 43), Pishu (BL 20), Weishu (BL 21), Xiawan (RN 10), Zusanli (ST 36). (*Great Compendium of Acupuncture and Moxibustion*)
　　6) Cellulitis, carbuncle: Jianjing (GB 21), Weizhong (BL 40). (*ibid*)
　　7) Scrofula: Jianjing (GB 21), Quchi (LI 11), Tianjing (SJ 10), Sanyangluo (SJ 8), Yinlingquan (SP 9). (*ibid*)
　　8) Acute mastitis: Jianjing (GB 21), Danzhong (RN 17), Zusanli (ST 36). (*Abstract of Clinical Experience on Acupuncture and Moxibustion*)
　　9) Aching of the arm: Jianjing (GB 21), Quchi (LI 11). (*Secret Songs on Acupuncture and Moxibustion*)
【Regional Anatomy】 Skin-subcutaneous tissue-the trapzius muscle-the levator muscle of the scapula. In the superficial layer, there are the supraclavicular nerve and the branches or tributaries of the superficial cervical artery and vein. In the deep layer, there are the branches or tributaries of the transverse cervical artery and vein and the branches of the dorsal scapular nerve.

GB 22　Yuanye（渊腋）
（Armpit Abyss）

【Source】 *Miraculous Pivot*
【Name Explanation】 Yuan (渊), deep pond; Ye (腋), axilla. The axilla is deep, like a pond, and the point is at the axilla.
【Location】 On the lateral side of the chest, on the midaxillary line when the arm is raised, 3 cun below the axilla, in the 4th intercostal space. (See Fig. 11-17)
【Localization】 Sitting position or in the lateral position, locate the point at the intersection of the superior one-fourth and inferior three-fourths of the line (12 cun long) between the midpoint of the axillary fossa and the end of the 11th rib.
【Indications】
　　1) Respiratory Diseases: Fullness sensation in the chest, cough, fever with chills.
　　2) Other Diseases: Hypochondriac pain, axilla swelling, inability to raise the arm.
【Mechanism of Action】 It is used for clearing heat, promoting the dispersing function of the lung and inducing menstruation to relieve dysmenorrhea.
【Method】 Puncture obliquely or subcutaneously 0.5-0.8 cun. Moxibustion is applicable.
【Acupoint Prescription】
　　Sabre and beadstring scrofula: Yuanye (GB 22), Zhangmen (LR 13), Zhigou (SJ 6). (*A-B Classic of Acupuncture and Moxibustion*)
【Regional Anatomy】 Skin-subcutaneous tissue-anterior serratus muscle-external intercostal muscle. In the superficial layer, there are the lateral cutaneous branches of the 3rd to 5th intercostal nerves, the long thoracic nerve and the lateral thoracic artery and vein. In the deep layer, there

are the 4th intercostal nerve and the 4th posterior intercostal artery and vein.

GB 23   Zhejin (辄筋)
(Flank Muscle)

【Source】 *A-B Classic of Acupuncture and Moxibustion*
【Name Explanation】 Zhe (辄), handles of a cart; Jin (筋), muscle. The muscle on both sides of the flanks is as prominent as the handles of the cart, the point is located here.
【Classification】 The Crossing Point of the Foot Taiyang and Foot Shaoyang Meridians
【Location】 On the lateral side of the chest, 1 cun anterior to Yuanye (GB 22), at the same level of the nipple, in the 4th intercostal space. (See Fig. 11-17)
【Localization】 Sitting position or in the lateral position, opening the axilla, 1 cun anterior to GB 22, about the same level with the nipple in males, the point is located at the depression between GB 22 and SP18.
【Indications】
    1) Respiratory Diseases: Asthma, fullness sensation in the chest leading to difficulty in lying flat, insomnia.
    2) Digestive Diseases: Vomiting, acid regurgitation, salivation, dysentery.
    3) Mental Diseases: Dysphasia, paralysis of the extremities.

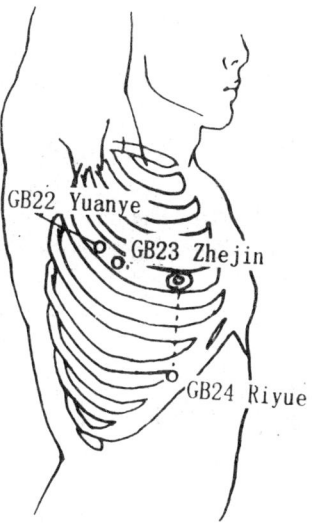

Fig. 11-17

【Mechanism of Action】
    1) Dysfunction of the spleen and stomach are caused by the stagnation of the liver qi and gallbladder qi. This point is used for regulating the flow of qi and soothing the liver and is punctured when treating the digestive diseases.
    2) This point is in the dividing line of the lung and it is needled to treat lung diseases.
【Method】 Puncture obliquely 0.5-0.8 cun. Moxibustion is applicable.
【Regional Anatomy】 Skin-subcutaneous tissue-the anterior serratus muscle-external intercostal muscle. In the superficial layer, there are the lateral cutaneous branches of the 3rd to 5th intercostal nerves and the branches or tributaries of the lateral thoracic artery and vein In the deep layer, there are the 4th intercostal nerve and the 4th posterior intercostal artery and vein.

GB 24   Riyue (日月)
(Sun and Moon)

【Source】 *The Classic of Sphygmology*
【Name Explanation】 Ri (日), sun; Yue (月), moon. Ri is Yang, indicating the gallbladder, while yue is Yin, indicated the liver. This is an important point in the treatment of liver and gallbladder diseases.
【Classification】 The Front-Mu Point of the gallbladder, the Crossing Point of the Foot Taiyin and Foot Shaoyang meridians.
【Location】 On the upper abdomen, directly below the nipple, in the 7th intercostal space, 4

cun lateral to the anterior midline. (See Fig. 11-17)

【Localization】 Sitting or in the supine position, locate the point at the 7th intercostal space on the midclavicular line.

【Indications】

1) Digestive Diseases: Stomachache, vomiting, acid regurgitation, hiccups, abdominal distention, salivation, jaundice.

2) Other Diseases: Pain in the chest and hypochondrium, sighing, susceptibility to sorrow.

【Mechanism of Action】

1) This point is the Front-Mu point of the gallbladder, where the vital essence and energy of the gallbladder are gathered. The liver and gallbladder are interiorly-exteriorly related. The dysfunction of the spleen and stomach is caused by the stagnation of the liver-qi and the gallbladder-qi. This point is used for soothing the liver, normalizing the secretion of the gallbladder, promoting the circulation of qi and relieving stagnation. It is used to treat diseases of the spleen and stomach due to stagnation of liver-qi. At present, Riyue (GB 24) on the right side is needled in clinic to treat diseases of the gallbladder, such as cholecystitis, gallstones, biliary ascariasis, gallbladder colic, acute and chronic hepatitis, etc.

2) This point has the function of soothing the liver and regulating the circulation of qi. It is one of the common points which are punctured to treat pain and distention in hypochondriac region, sighing and susceptibility to sorrow due to stagnation of liver qi.

【Method】 Puncture obliquely or subcutaneously 0.5-0.8 cun. Moxibustion is applicable.

【Acupoint Prescriptions】

1) Hot sensation in the lower abdomen, frequent sighing: Riyue (GB 24), Daheng (SP 15). (*Thousand Golden Prescriptions*)

2) Cholelithiasis: Riyue (GB 24) (right side), Qimen (LR 14) (right side). (*Abstract of Clinical Experience on Acupuncture and Moxibustion*)

3) severe pain in upper abdomen and gallbladder enlargement: Riyue (GB 24) (right side), Qimen (LR 14) (right side), penetrating right Juque (RN 14) to Fuai (SP 16), Danshu (BL 19). (*ibid*)

【Regional Anatomy】 Skin-subcutaneous tissue-external oblique muscle of abdomen-external intercostal muscle. In the superficial layer, there are the lateral cutaneous branches of the 6th to 8th intercostal nerves and the accompanying arteries and veins. In the deep layer, there are the 7th intercostal nerve and the 7th posterior intercostal artery and vein.

【Remark】 Electro-acupuncture or acupuncture at Riyue (GB 24) can promote secretion of bile and gallbladder contraction. So it has cholagogic and lithagogue effects. For example, puncturing Riyue (GB 24) patients during a choledochotomy with drainage for 30 minutes, showed that the common bile duct contracted regularly and contrast medium in the biliary system was eliminated to the duodenum through oddi's sphincter. Experiments conducted abroad showed that puncturing Riyue (GB 24) with intradermal needles contracted the gallbladder when seen through X-ray examination. It is reported that puncturing Qimen (LR 14) and Riyue (GB 24) has clinical effect on eliminating gallstones. Acupuncture, simultaneously with magnesiumsulfate can eliminate stones, the effective rate is 69% in the treated group, 20.5% in the control group. ($P < 0.01$).

GB 25　Jingmen（京门）
（Capital Gate）

【Source】 *The Classic of Sphygmology*

【Name Explanation】 Jing (京), primary; men (门), door. This is a Mu-Front point of the

Kidney Meridian which dominates the Primary Qi of the general body. The point is the door where the Qi of the Kidney enters and exits.

【Classification】 Front-Mu Point of the kidney

【Location】 On the lateral side of the waist, 1.8 cun posterior to Zhangmen (LR 13), below the free-end of the 12th rib. (See Fig. 11-18)

【Localization】 In the lateral or prone position, locate the point at the free end of the 12th rib on the lateral side of the lumbar region.

【Indications】

1) Digestive Diseases: Diarrhea, borborygmus, abdominal distention, vomiting.

2) Urinary Diseases: Dysuria, dark urine with face swelling.

3) Other Diseases: Fever with chills, back rigidity, shoulder pain, pain on the medial side of the scapula, hypochondriac pain.

【Mechanism of Action】 Jingmen (GB 25) is the Front-Mu point of the kidney, where the vital essence and energy of the kidney are gathered. It is used to treat urinary diseases, such as difficult urination and dark urine with swollen face. This point is in the hypochondrium, and the waist is the house of the kidney. Pain in the hypochondriac region can be treated by tonifying the kidney and promoting the circulation of the local qi. See Riyue (GB 24) and Zhejin (GB 23) for more details.

【Method】 Puncture perpendicularly 0.5-1 cun. Moxibustion is applicable.

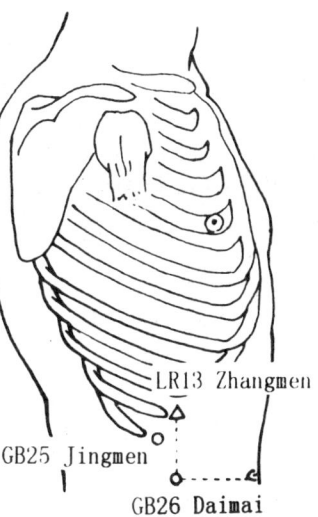

Fig. 11-18

【Acupoint Prescriptions】

1) Diarrhea: Jingmen (GB 25), Rangu (KI 2), Yinlingquan (SP 9). (*Thousand Golden Prescriptions*)

2) Lumbago leading to inability to stand and lie flat for long period: Jingmen (GB 25), Xingjian (LR 2). (*A-B Classic of Acupuncture and Moxibustion*)

3) Swelling in the lower abdomen: Jingmen (GB 25), Ligou (LR 5), Zhongfeng (LR 4). (*Experience on Acupuncture and Moxibustion Therapy*)

4) Dark urine, anuresis: Jingmen (GB 25), Zhaohai (KI 6). (*ibid*)

5) Dirrhea: Jingmen (GB 25), Kunlun (BL 60). (*ibid*)

6) Stiffness of the back: Jingmen (GB 25), Shiguan (KI 18). (*ibid*)

【Regional Anatomy】 Skin-subcutaneous tissue-external oblique muscle of abdomen-internal oblique muscle of abdomen-transverse muscle of abdomen. In the superficial layer, there are the lateral cutaneous branches of the anterior branches of the 11th and 12th thoracic nerves and the accompanying arteries and veins. In the deep layer, there are the muscular branches of the anterior branches of the 11th and 12th thoracic nerves and the related intercostal and subcostal arteries and veins.

【Remark】 Puncturing Jingmen (GB 25) point may cause a change in the acidotic state. It was reported that it was more effective than that in the ACTH injected group. Experiment of water diuresis indicated that puncturing Jingmen (GB 25) inhibited diuresis action. Micturition output was decreased 14.1-14.4% after 3 hours. Puncturing Jingmen (GB 25), together with other points can treat urinary lithiasis.

GB 26　Daimai（带脉）
（Belt Meridian）

【Source】 *Miraculous Pivot*

【Name Explanation】 Dai（带）, belt; Mai（脉）, meridian. The point pertains to the Gallbladder Meridian and meets at the Dai Mai.

【Classification】 Crossing Point of the Gallbladder Meridian of Foot-Shaoyang and the Dai Meridians.

【Location】 On the lateral side of the waist, 1.8 cun below Zhangmen (LR 13), at the crossing point of a vertical line through the free end of the 11th rib and a horizontal line through the umbilicus. (See Fig. 11-18)

【Localization】 Lateral position, locate the point at the intersection between the middle axillary line and transverse line which is lever with the umbilicus.

【Indications】

　　1) Gynaecological Diseases: Irregular menstruation, leukorrhea with reddish discharge, prolapse of uterus, pain in the lower abdomen.

　　2) Other Diseases: Lumbago, hernia, sorness and weakness of the waist, flaccidity of lower limbs.

【Mechanism of Action】

　　1) Dai Meridian comes out, connects with the 14th vertebra where the Mingmen (DU 14) lies, passes through the waist and the abdomen. The waist and the belly are the source of the meridian qi of the Chong, Ren and Du meridians (the three meridians originate from the uterus), so Dai Meridian is in close relation with them. Therefore, the point is commonly used for gynecopathy.

　　2) Dai Meridian runs around the waist like a belt, and has the function of restraining the channels going up and down. *The Yellow Emperor's Conon of Internal Medicine* says: "Flaccidity of the foot is caused by the dysfunction of the Belt Meridian due to the deficiency of Yangming Meridian." When the Belt Meridian is diseased, its symptoms may ensure the fullness in abdomen (feelings of sitting in water). The point is mainly used to treat the muscular relaxation and weakness of the waist, abdomen and lower limbs.

【Method】 Puncture perpendicularly 1-1.5 cun. Moxibustion is applicable.

【Acupoint Prescriptions】

　　1) Leukorrhea with reddish discharge: Moxibustion with 30 moxa-cones to Daimai (GB 26), Guanyuan (RN 4), Qihai (RN 6), Sanyinjiao (SP 6), Baihuanshu (BL 30), Jianshi (PC 5). (*Great Compendium of Acupuncture and Moxibustion*.)

　　2) Delivery without pain: Daimai (GB 26), Wushu (GB 27), Juliao (GB 29), Fushe (SP 13), Taichong (LR 3), with both sides of all points used. (*Abstract of Clinical Experience on Acupuncture and Moxibustion*)

　　3) Failure of Kidney function: Daimai (GB 26), Guanyuan (RN 4). (*Songs of jade Dragon*)

【Regional Anatomy】 Skin-subcutaneous tissue-the external oblique muscle of abdomen-the internal oblique muscle of abdomen-the transverse muscle of abdomen. In the superficial layer, there are the lateal cutaneous branches of the anterior branches of the 9th to 11th thoracic nerves and the accompanying arteries and veins. In the deep layer, there are the muscular branches of the anterior branches of the 9th to 11th thoracic nerves and the related arteries and veins.

GB 27　Wushu（五枢）
（Five Pivots）

【Source】*A-B Classic of Acupuncture and Moxibustion*

【Name Explanation】Wu（五）, five; Shu（枢）, pivot. The numeral 5 is a middle deficiency of the Yangming Meridian leading to the pubic region number and Shaoyang governs the pivot between the surface and the flaccid and incapacity of the Belt meridian, thus the feet lose function interior of the body. The point is in a vital place at the middle of them.

【Classification】The Crossing Point of the Foot Shaoyang and Dai Meridians.

【Location】On the lateral side of the abdomen, anterior to the lower anterior superior iliacspine, 3 cun below the level of the umbilicus. (See Fig. 11-19)

【Localization】Lateral position, locate the point at 0.5 cun anterior to the anterior superior iliac spine, and 3 cun anterior inferior to Daimai (GB 26).

【Indications】

1) Digestive Diseases: Constipation, tenesmus.

2) Reproductive Diseases: Prolapse of uterus, pain in the lower abdomen, leukorrhea with reddish discharge, irregular menstruation, hernia, shrinkage of the scrotum.

3) Other Diseases: Pain in the waist and hip, clonic convulsion.

【Mechanism of Action】Wushu (GB 27) on the left side is in the area of the decending colon. This point is commonly used to treat constipation and dysentery.

【Method】Puncture perpendicularly 1-1.5 cun. Moxibustion is applicable.

【Acupoint Prescription】Testis redux: Wushu (GB 27), Guilai (ST 29). (*Experience on Acupuncture and Moxibustion Therapy*)

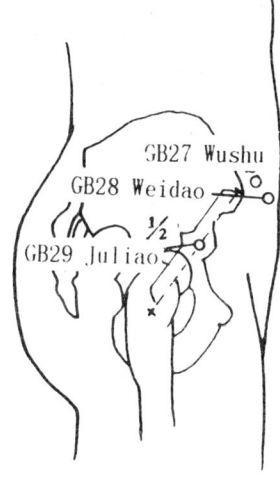

Fig. 11-19

【Regional Anatomy】Skin-subcutaneous tissue the external oblique muscle of abdomen-the internal oblique muscle of abdomen-the transverse muscle of abdomen. In the superficial layer, there are the lateral cutaneous branches of the anterior branches of the 11th and 12th thoracic and the 1st lumbar nerves and accompanying arteries and veins. In the deep layer, there are the deep circumflex iliac artery and vein, the muscular branches of the anterior branches of the 11th and 12th thoracic and the 1st lumbar nerves and the related arteries and veins.

【Remark】Puncturing Pishu (BL 20), Weishu (BL 21), Wushu (GB 27), Jingmen (GB 25) etc. has successfully been used as an anaesthetic during appendectomy, with the effective rate 69.49%. It is reported that puncturing GB 27, Weidao (GB 28), Qihaishu (BL 24), Yanglingquan (GB 34), etc also has a positive anaesthetic effect during a hysterectomy. It also enhances the activity of salivin.

GB 28 Weidao (维道) (Binding Path)

【Source】 *A-B Classic of Acupuncture and Moxibustion*
【Name Explanation】 Wei (维), maintain; Dao (道), passage. This point is the meeting point of the Gallbladder Meridian and Daimai, which maintains all the meridians.
【Classification】 The Crossing Point of the Foot Shaoyang and Dai Meridians.
【Location】 On the lateral side of the abdomen, anterior and inferior to the anterior superior iliac spine, 0.5 cun anterior and inferior to Wushu (GB 27). (See Fig. 11-19)
【Localization】 Lateral position, locate the point 0.5 cun anterior inferior to GB 27, near to groin region.
【Indications】
    1) Digestive Diseases: Acute appendicitis, vomitting and anorexia, constipation.
    2) Reproductive Diseases: Prolapse of uterus, irregular menstruation, pain in the lower abdomen, leukorrhea with reddish discharge.
    3) Other Diseases: Pain in the waist, abdomen and hip, edema, continuous cough with dyspnea, hernia.
【Mechanism of Action】 See Wushu (GB 27).
【Method】 Puncture perpendicularly 1-1.5 cun. Moxibustion is applicable.
【Regional Anatomy】 Skin-subcutaneous tissue-the external oblique muscle of abdomen-the internal oblique muscle of abdomen-the transverse muscle of abdomen-the iliopsoas muscle. In the superficial layer, there are the superficial circumflex iliac artery and vein, the lateral cutaneous branches of the anterior branches of the 11th and 12th thoracic and the 1st lumbar nerves and the accompanying arteris and veins. In the deep layer, there are the deep dircumflex iliac artery and vein, the lateral cutaneous nerve of the thigh, the muscular branches of the anterior branches of the 11th and 12th thoracic and the 1st lumbar nerves and the related arteries and veins.
【Remark】 Puncturing Ganshu (BL 18), Shenshu (BL 23), Henggu (KI 11) and Weidao (GB 28) of one side has a good effect as an anaesthesia during lower abdomen operation. It can block pain impulses of the ilioinguinal nerve. Especially, electro-acupuncture at Henggu (KI 11) and Weidao (GB 28) with high frequency stimulation can ease pain during a dermatotomy.

GB 29 Juliao (居髎) (Reside Crevice)

【Source】 *A-B Classic of Acupuncture and Moxibustion*
【Name Explanation】 Ju (居), reside; Liao (髎), foramen. The point is in the depression on the hip bone.
【Classification】 The Crossing Point of the Gallbladder Meridian of Foot Shaoyang and the Yangqiao Meridian.
【Location】 On the hip, at the midpoint of the line connecting the anterior superior iliac spine and the prominence of the great trochanter. (See Fig. 11-19)
【Localization】 Lateral position, the point is located at 3 cun posterior inferior to Weidao (GB 28), the depression of the midpoint of the line joining the anterior superior iliac spine and the highest of the greater trochanter.
【Indications】

1) Diseases along the course of the Meridians: Pain in the waist and leg, paralysis, flaccidity in feet.

2) Reproductive Diseases: Hernia, irregular menstruation, leukorrhea with reddish diacharge.

3) Digestive Disease: Dysentery.

【Mechanism of Action】

1) Juliao (GB 29) is the crossing point of the Gallbladder Meridian, Yangqiao Meridian and Yangwei Meridian. Where the meridian passes, where the indications are. It is mainly used to treat diseases in lower limbs. The pressure pain point around Juliao (GB 29) is used to treat shoulder pain, according to the corresponding principle of the acupoint treatment.

2) The Gallbladder Meridian intersects with the Dai Meridian. Thus, this point is used to treat the reproductive diseases.

【Method】 Puncture perpendicularly 1-1.5 cun. Moxibustion is applicable.

【Acupoint Prescriptions】 Leg pain due to pathogenic wind-dampness: Juliao (GB 29), Huantiao (GB 30), Weizhong (BL 40). (*Songs of Jade Dragon*)

【Regional Anatomy】 Skin-subcutaneous tissue-the fascia lata-the middle gluteal muscle-the least gluteal muscle. In the superficial layer, there are the superior clunial nerve and the lateral cutaneous branches of the iliohypogastric nerve. In the deep layer, there are the branches or tributaries of the superior gluteal artery and vein and the superior gluteal nerve.

GB 30　Huantiao（环跳）
（Jumping Circle）

【Source】 *A-B Classic of Acupuncture and Moxibustion*

【Name Explanation】 Huan（环）, a ring; Tiao（跳）, jump. The point is at the hip joint, which is the pivot for jumping.

【Classification】 The Crossing Point of the Foot Shaoyang and Foot Taiyang Meridians

【Location】 On the lateral side of the thigh, at the junction of the middle one-third and lateral one-third of the line connecting the prominence of the great trochanter and the sacral hiatus when the patient is in a lateral recumbent position with the thigh flexed. (See Fig. 11-20)

【Localization】

1) Lateral position, extending the lower leg and flexing the upper leg (at angle of 90), putting the transverse crease of the pollical joint on the head of the greater torchanter, the thumb pointed to the spine, the point is located at the tip of the thumb. (See Fig. 11-21)

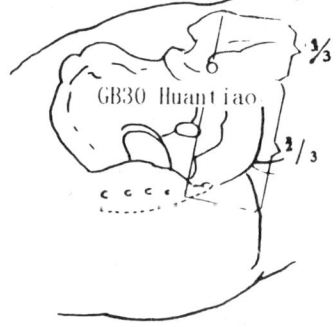

Fig. 11-20

2) Lateral position, locate the point at the depression posterior to greater torchanter, about the intersection of the lateral one-third and the middle one-third distance between the greater trochanter of the femur and the hiatus of the sacrum.

【Indications】

1) Diseases along the Course of the Meridian: Hemiplegia, flaccidity in lower limbs, pain in the waist and vertebrae, sprain and contusion.

2) Dermatosises: General rubella, urticaria.

3) Other Diseases: Edema, beriberi.

【Mechanism of Action】
1) This point is the crossing point of Foot Taiyang and Foot Shaoyang Meridians. The Gallbladder Meridian also intersects with the Yangwei Meridian and Yangqiao Meridian. Where the meridian passes, where the indications are. This point is commonly needled to treat the diseases in lower limbs, pain in the waist and spine, such as sciatica, arthralgia-syndrome, flaccidity-syndrome.

2) In clinic, pinpoint is needled backward a little, the needling response is conducted down along the back of lower limbs. Pinpoint is punctured forward a little, the needling response is conducted down along the front of the lower limbs. This point is needled with different acupuncture manipulations and has different needling responses depending on the position of the diseases and pain.

3) This point is one of the Four-yang and Nine-needle Points, and can be used to treat exhaustion of yang.

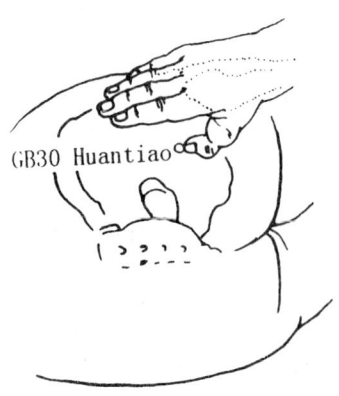

Fig. 11-21

【Method】 Puncture perpendicularly 2—3 cun. Moxibustion is applicable.

【Acupoint Prescriptions】
1) Pain in the hip joint with difficult moving: Huantiao (GB 30), Shugu (BL 65), Jiaoxin (KI 8), Yinjiao (RN 7), Yanggu (SI 5). (*Experience on Acupuncture and Moxibustion Therapy*)

2) Pain tibia with difficulty in moving: Huantiao (GB 30), Neiting (ST 44). (*ibid*)

3) Inability of feet to walk: Huantiao (GB 38), Yanglingquan (GB 34), Xiajuxu (ST 39), Yangfu (GB 38). (*ibid*)

4) Diseases up to the knee: Huantiao (GB 30), Fengshi (GB 31), applying moxibustion. (*Great Compendium of Acupuncture and Moxibustion*)

5) Difficult moving in the leg with spasm and aching: Huantiao (GB 30), Fengshi (GB 31), Yinshi (ST 33). (*Songs of Shengyu*)

6) Arthralgia due to cold-wind-dampness: Huantiao (GB 30), Yanglingquan (GB 34). (*Secret Songs of Chang Sang jun*)

7) Lumbago: Huantiao (GB 30), Weizhong (BL 40). (*Songs on Point Selection of Miscellaneous Disease*)

【Regional Anatomy】 Skin-subcutaneous tissue-the greatest gluteal muscle-sciatic nerve-the quadrate muscle of the thigh. In the superficial layer, there is the superior clunial nerve. In the deep layer, there are the sciatic nerve, the inferior gluteal nerve, the posterior cutaneous nerve of the thigh, and the inferior gluteal artery and vein.

【Remark】 Acupuncture at Huantiao (GB 30) may regulate gastric secretion in two ways.

GB 31　Fengshi (风市)
(Wind Market)

【Source】 *A Handbook of Prescriptions for Emergenceies*
【Name Explanation】 Feng (风), pathogenic wind; Shi (市), market. Market means gathering and dispersing. This is an important point for removing pathogenic wind.
【Location】 On the lateral side of the thigh, 7 cun above the popliteal crease, or at the place touching the tip of the middle finger when the patient stands erect with the arms relaxed. (See Fig. 11-22)

[Localization]

1) Standing up, with both arms relaxed at side, the point is located where the tip of the middle finger touches the leg.

2) Lateral position, locate the point 7 cun superior to the popliteal line on the lateral femoral median line.

[Indications]

1) Diseases along the Course of the Meridian: Paralysis of legs, pain in the waist and the leg.

2) Diseases of Head and Sense Organs: Headache, tinnitus, deafness, conjunctival congestion and pain.

3) Other Diseases: General pruritus, scrotitis, hernia, beriberi.

[Mechanism of Action] Fengshi (GB 31) in Chinese means "wind market". It is considered that this point has the function of dispelling the wind. General itching and flaccidity, pain and numbness in lower limbs are closely related with wind evil. This point can be punctured to treat the diseases in lower limbs, as it has the function of dispelling wind-dampness, regulating qi-blood and activating meridians and collaterals. It is reported that it is the most effective point for treating tinnitus and deafness. The Muscle Region of the Gallbladder Meridian is knotted in the buttock, thus needling Fengshi (Gb 31) is effective for treating acute lumbar sprain.

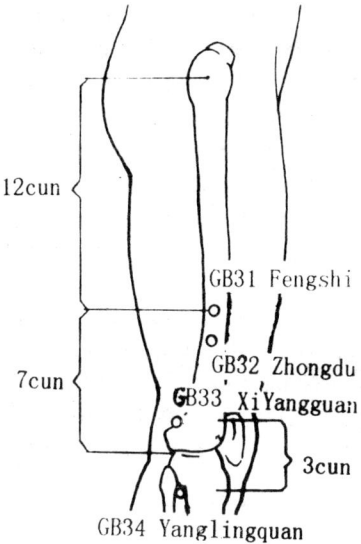

Fig. 11-22

[Method] Puncture perpendicularly 1-2 cun. Moxibustion is applicable.

[Acupoint Prescriptions]

1) Arthralgia syndrome: As soon as feeling weakness in feet, apply moxibustion on Fengshi (GB 31), Zusanli (ST 36), one to two hundred cones on each. (*Effective Prescriptions for Long Life*)

2) Weakness in feet: Fengshi (GB 31), Dubi (ST 35), Zusanli (ST 36), Juegu (GB 39). (*Experience on Acupuncture and Moxibustion Therapy*)

3) Pain and difficult moving in the waist: Fengshi (GB 31), Weizhong (BL 40), Xingjian (LR 2). (*Great Compendium of Acupuncture and Moxibustion*)

4) Pain in the leg: Fengshi (GB 31), Yinshi (ST 33). (*ibid*)

5) Urticaria: Fengshi (GB 31), Quchi (LI 11), Zusanli (ST 36) as main points, and Fengchi (GB 20), Yanglingquan (GB 34), Hegu (LI 4) as supplementary points. (*Abstract of Clinical Experience on Acupuncture and Moxibustion*)

6) Weakness in legs and feet: Fengshi (GB 31), Yinshi (ST 33). (*Songs of Jade Dragon*)

[Regional Anatomy] Skin-subcutaneous tissue-the iliotibial tract-the lateral muscle of the thigh-the intermediate vastus muscle of the thigh. In the superficial layer, there is the lateral cutaneous nerve of the thigh. In the deep layer, there are the muscular branches of the descending branches of the lateral circumflex femoral artery and the muscular branches of the femoral nerve.

GB 32 Zhongdu (中渎)
(Middle Canal)

[Source] *A-B Classic of Acupuncture and Moxibustion*

【Name Explanation】 Zhong (中), middle; Du (渎), small ditch. This point is between the tendons at the lateral aspect of the thigh, as if in a ditch.
【Location】 On the lateral side of the thigh, 2 cun below Fengshi(GB 31), or 5 cun above the popliteal crease, between the lateral vastus muscle and biceps muscle of the thigh. (See Fig. 11-22)
【Localization】 Lateral position, locate the point 5 cun superior to the popliteal line on the lateral femorral midian line.
【Indications】
　　Diseases along the Course of the Meridian: Flaccidity and arthralgia in legs, numbness, hemiplegia, pain in the waist involving the hip and the leg, beriberi.
【Mechanism of Action】
　　1) Where the meridian passes, where the indications are. This point can be used to dispel wind, resolve dampness and activate the meridians and collaterals.
　　2) It is reported that the pressure pain point between Zhongdu (GB 32) and Liangqiu (ST 34) can produce a good therapeutic effect on cystic colic.
【Method】 Puncture perpendicularly 1-2 cun. Moxibustion is applicable.
【Regional Anatomy】 Skin-subcutaneous tissue-the iliotibial tract-the lateral vastus muscle of the thigh-the intermediate vastus muscle of the thigh. In the superficial layer, there is the lateral cutaneous nerve of the thigh. In the deep layer, there are the muscular branches of the descending branches of the lateral circumflex femoral artery and vein and the muscular branches of the femoral nerve.

GB 33　Xiyangguan (膝阳关)
(Knee Yang Pass)

【Source】 *A-B Classic of Acupuncture and Moxibustion*
【Name Explanation】 Xi (膝), knee; Yang (阳), Yang of Yin-Yang; Guan (关), joint. The exterior is Yang. The point is at the lateral aspect of the knee joint.
【Location】 On the lateral side of the knee, 3 cun above Yanglingquan (GB 34), in the depression above the external epicondyle of the femur. (See Fig. 11-22)
【Localization】 Flex the knees, locate the point posterior to the external epicondyle of the femur, the depression between the iliotibialtrace, and the tendon of the musculus biceps femoris or 3 cun directly superior to Yanglingquan (GB 34) on the lateral femoral median line.
【Indications】
　　1) Diseases along the Course of the Meridian: Hemiplegia, swelling pain in the knee and knee-cap, contracture or subjective sensation of contraction in the regions nearby, numbness in the shank, beriberi.
　　2) Other Diseases: Continuiously vomiting, salivation.
【Mechanism of Action】 The disturbance in ascending and descending of the spleen and stomach are caused by the stagnant heat in the Gallbladder Meridian. This point can be used to treat vomiting and ptyalism in accordance with its function of soothing the liver, normalizing the gallbladder function, invigorating the spleen, and resolving dampness.
【Method】 Puncture perpendicularly 1-1.5 cun. Moxibustion is applicable.
【Acupoint Prescription】 Numbness in the shank: Xiyangguan (GB 33), Huantiao (GB 30), Chengjin (BL 56). (*Experience on Acupuncture and Moxibustion Therapy*)
【Regional Anatomy】 Skin-subcutaneous tissue-iliotibial tract-the lateral vastus muscle of the thigh-the intermediate vastus muscle of the thigh. In the superficial layer, there is the lateral cutaneous nerve of the thigh. In the deep layer, there are the lateral superior genicular artery and vein.

GB 34　Yanglingquan（阳陵泉）
（Yang Hill Fountain）

【Source】 *Miraculous Pivot*

【Name Explanation】 Yang（阳），Yang of Yin-Yang；Ling（陵），mound；Quan（泉），spring. The exterior is Yang. The head of the fibula in the lateral aspect of the knee is prominent as a mound, below which there is a depression where the point is located, like a spring.

【Classification】 He-(Sea) Point of the Gallbladder Meridian of Foot Shaoyang pertaining to earth in the Five Elements. The Inflential Point of tendons

【Location】 On the lateral side of the leg, in the depression anterior and inferior to the head of the fibula. (See Fig. 11-22)

【Localization】 Sitting with the knees flexed and the foot relaxed, the point is located at the anterior and inferior to the little head of the fibula.

【Indications】

1) Diseases along the Course of the Meridian: Pain in the waist and sacrum, hemiplegia, flaccidity and arthralgia, numbness in the leg, pain in hypochondriac region, shoulder pain.

2) Diseases of the Head and Sense Organs: Headache, sore-throat, swelling pain and congestion in eyes, tinnitus, deafness.

3) Digestive Diseases: Stomachache, abdominal distention, borborygmus, jaundice, constipation.

4) Respiratory Diseases: Cough due to consumption.

5) Urinary Diseases: Enuresis, edema.

6) Mental Diseases: Infantile convulsion, tetanus, epilepsy, convulsion.

【Mechanism of Action】

1) As the lower He-(Sea) point of the Gallbladder Meridian, the point is used to treat cholecystitis and other digestive diseases due to cholecystopathy, such as abdominal distention, borborygmus and jaundice, etc. The point has the function of soothing the liver, normalizing the secretion of the gallbladder, promoting the flow of qi and relieving stagnation.

2) As the Influential Point of the tendons, the point can be needled to treat weakness, flaccidity, arthralgia, pain and numbness of the lower limbs and hemiplegia. As the Foot Shaoyang Meridian connects with the Hand-Shaoyang Meridian which spreads over the shoulder, this point can be used to treat shoulder pain.

3) The Gallbladder Meridian is distributed over the side of the head, chest and the hypochondrium. It is mainly used to treat the diseases of the head, face and sense organs, and the pain in the chest and hypochondrium. All kinds of hypochondriac pain can be treated by penetrating Yanglingquan (GB 34) through Zusanli (ST 36). This is the most effective way to treat hypochrondiac pain aggravated by cough.

【Method】 Puncture prependicularly 1-1.5 cun. Moxibustion is applicable.

【Acupoint Prescriptions】

1) Sperm urine due to consumption: Applying moxa-cones to Yanglingquan (GB 34) or Yinlingquan (SP 9) with the cone number being same as the patient's age, or 30 cones at the 10th or 19th vertebra. (*Experience on Acupuncture and Moxibustion Therapy*)

2) Hemihidrosis, hemiplegia: Yanglingquan (GB 34), Huantiao (GB 30), Quchi (LI 11). (*ibid*)

3) Wheezing in the throat: Yanglingquan (GB 34), Tianchi (PC 1), Danzhong (RN 17). (*ibid*)

4) Fullness sensation in the chest and hypochondrium: Yanglingquan (GB 34), Zusanli

(ST 36), Shangjuxu (ST 37). (*Great Compendium of Acupuncture and Moxibustion*).

5) Foot flaccidity: Yanglingquan (GB 34), Chongyang (ST 42), Taichong (LR 3), Qiuxu (GB 40). (*ibid*)

6) Acute infectious hepatitis: Yanglingquan (GB 34), Zusanli (ST 36). (*Abstract of Clinical Experience on Acupuncture and Moxibustion*)

【Regional Anatomy】Skin-subcutaneous tissue-long peroneal muscle-long extensor muscle of the toes. In the superficial layer, there is the lateral sural cutaneous nerve. In the deep layer, there are the anterior recurrent tibial artery and vein, the branches tributaries of the lateral inferior genicular artery and vein, and the branches of the common peroneal nerve.

【Remark】Puncturing GB 34 resulted in 45 people (73.7%) whose gallbladder image showed contraction from a total of 65 normal people. But there was no change in the gallbladder image in the 24 non-punctured people. (Puncturing GB 34 on 37 people, there were 28 people whose gallbladder image showed contraction (75.7%). Gallbladder contraction was not obvious in 4 experiments while puncturing Xiabai (LU 4), Chize (LU 5), Taiyuan (LU 9) points, etc. (non-Gallbladder Meridian points or non-point), while screening 21 points of 50 people, such as Yanglingquan (GB 34), Zusanli (ST 36) points, etc. It was found that puncturing Zusanli (ST 36), Xinshu (BL 15) and Danshu (BL 19) points caused gallbladder contraction, especially Zusanli (ST 36) with an especially strong effect.

GB 35　Yangjiao (阳交)
(Yang Crossing)

【Source】*A-B Classic of Acupuncture and Moxibustion*

【Name Explanation】Yang (阳), Yang of Yin-Yang; Jiao (交), crossing. The exterior is Yang. The point is on the lateral aspect of the leg, where it crosses the Bladder Meridian.

【Classification】Xi-(Cleft) Point of the Yangwei Meridian.

【Location】On the lateral side of the leg, 7 cun above the tip of the exteral malleolus, on the posterior border of the fibula. (See Fig. 11-23)

【Localization】Sitting or in the lateral position, locate the point 7 cun superior to the tip of the lateral malleolus, in the posterior margin of the fibula on the lateral shank.

【Indications】

1) Diseases along the Course of the Meridian: Flaccidity and arthralgia in legs, hemiplegia, pain in the chest and hypochondrium, etc.

2) Respiratory Diseases: Dyspnea with fever and chills, inflammation of the throat, aphasia.

3) Mental Diseases: Terror and mania, depressive psychosis.

【Mechanism of Action】

1) This point can be needled to treat flaccidity in the lower limbs and hemiplegia by activating the meridians and collaterals.

2) Since the Gallbladder Divergent Meridian goes up to the throat. This point can be used to treat inflammation of

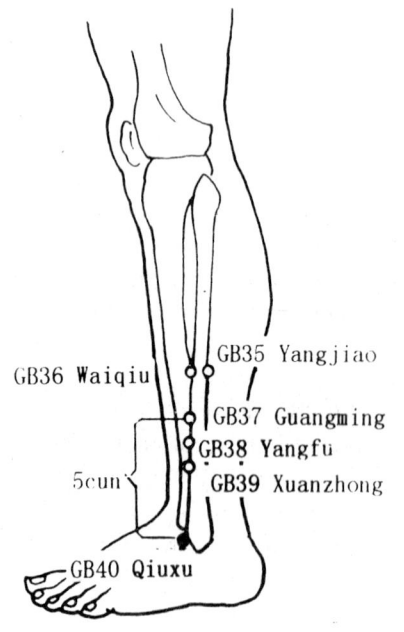

Fig. 11-23

the throat and aphonia.

3) This point is used for soothing the liver, normalizing the gallbladder function, relieving convulsion and tranquilizing the mind in mental diseases.

【Method】 Puncture perpendicularly 1-1.5 cun. Moxibustion is applicable.

【Acupoint Prescriptions】

1) Fullness feeling in the chest: Yangjiao (GB 35), Zulinqi (GB 41). (*Experience on Acupuncture and Moxibustion Therapy*)

2) Palpitation due to fright: Yangjiao (GB 35), Jiexi (SI 41). (*Songs of Hundreds of Symptoms*)

【Regional Anatomy】 Skin-subcutaneous tissue-triceps muscle of the calf-long peroneal muscle-posterior intermuscular septum-long flexor muscle of the great toe. In the superficial layer, there is the lateral sural cutaneous nerve. In the deep layer, there are the peroneal artery and vein, the posterior tibial artery and vein and the tibial nerve.

GB 36 Waiqiu (外丘)
(Outer Mound)

【Source】 *A-B Classic of Acupuncture and Moxibustion*

【Name Explanation】 Wai (外), lateral; Qiu (丘), mound. The point is above the lateral malleolus and the local muscle is prominent as a mound.

【Classification】 Xi-(Cleft) Point of the Gallbladder Meridian of Foot Shaoyang.

【Location】 On the lateral side of the leg, 7 cun above the tip of the external malleolus, on the anterior border of the fibula at the same level of Yangjiao (GB 35). (See Fig. 11-23)

【Localization】 Sitting or in the lateral position, locate the point 7 cun superior to the tip of the lateral malleolus, at the anterior margin of the fibula on the lateral shank.

【Indications】

1) Diseases along the Course of the Meridian: Headache, stiffness of the neck, flaccidity and numbness of the lower limbs, feeling of fullness in the chest and hypochondrium.

2) Mental Disease: Depressive psychosis.

3) Other Diseases: Infantile pigeon breast and xifosis, chills and fever due to rabies virus.

【Mechanism of Action】 See Yangjiao (GB 35).

【Method】 Puncture perpendicularly 1-1.5 cun. Moxibustion is applicable.

【Regional Anatomy】 Skin-subcutaneous tissue-the long and short peroneal muscles-the anterior intermuscular septum-the long extensor muscle of the toes-the long extensor muscle of the great toe. In the superficial layer, there is the lateral sural cutaneous nerve. In the deep layer, there are the superficial and deep peroneal nerves and the anterior tibial artery and vein.

GB 37 Guangming (光明)
(Brightness)

【Source】 *Miraculous Pivot*

【Name Explanation】 Guangming (光明), brightness. This is a Luo-Connecting Point of the Gallbladder Meridian and is indicated in eyes diseases to regain brightness.

【Classification】 Luo-(Connecting) Point of the Gallbladder Meridian of Foot Shaoyang.

【Location】 On the lateral side of the leg, 5 cun above the tip of the extenal malleolus, on the anterior border of the fibula. (See Fig. 11-23)

【Localization】 Sitting or in the lateral position, locate the point at 5 cun superior to the tip of the lateral malleolus, on the anterior border of the fibula.

【Indications】

1) Diseases along the Course of the Meridian: Flaccidity and numbness of the lower limbs, hemiplegia, distending pain of the breast.

2) Diseases of Head and Sense Organs: Itch of the eyes, pain of the eyes, cataract, night blindness, optic atrophy.

3) Other Diseases: Infantile pigeon breast and xifosis, migraine, rabies.

【Mechanism of Action】

1) Guangming (GB 37) point is the Luo-(Connecting) point of the Gallbladder Meridian, which connects with the Liver Meridian. The Gallbladder Meridian starts from the outer canthus of the eyes, and connects with the Liver Meridian and opens into the eyes. It is effective to treat night blindness, catarct and juvenile myopia. Needling response in some patients can directly go up to the eyes.

2) The Gallbladder Muscle Region spreads over the breast. The Gallbladder Meridian is distributed over the hypochondrium. This point is used for soothing the liver and regulating the circulation of qi, and is commonly used to treat distending pain of the breast, and fullness sensation in the chest and hypochondrium.

【Method】 Puncture perpendicularly 1-1.5 cun. Moxibustion is applicable.

【Acupoint Prescription】 Itch and pain of eyes: Guangming (GB 37), Diwuhui (GB 42). (*Secret Songs of Acupuncture and Moxibustion*)

【Regional Anatomy】 Skin-subcutaneous tissue-the short peroneal muscle-the anterior intermuscular septum-the long extensor muscle of the toes-the long extensor muscle of the great toe-the interosseous membrane of the leg-the posterior tibial muscle. In the superficial layer, there are the superficial peroneal nerve and the lateral sural cutaneous nerve. In the deep layer, there are the deep peroneal nerve and the anterior tibial artery and vein.

【Remark】 Acupuncture at this point and Taichong (LR 3) is effective for juvenile myopia. 38. 2 percent of the patients felt the needling response reached the eyes. If matching with Taichong (LR 3) and Waiguan (SJ 5) points, alternately every other day can improvevision.

GB 38　Yangfu（阳辅）
(Yang Aid)

【Source】 *Miraculous Pivot*

【Name Explanation】 Yang (阳), Yang of Yin-Yang; Fu (辅), auxillary. The exterior is Yang and Fu is the fibula. The point is anterior to the fibula on the lateral aspect of the leg.

【Classification】 Jing-(River) Point of the Gallbladder Meridian of Foot shaoyang pertaining to fire in the Five Elements.

【Location】 On the lateral side of the leg, 4 cun above the tip of the external malleolus, slightly anterior to the anterior border of the fibula. (See Fig. 11-23)

【Localization】 Sitting or in the lateral position, locate the point 4 cun superior to the tip of the lateral malleolus, anterior margin of the fibula on the lateral shank.

【Indications】

1) Diseases along the Course of the Meridian: Hemiplegia, distending pain in the chest and hypochondrium, pain in the lateral part of the lower limbs, lumbago, edema in the lower limbs and skin lesions similar to beriberi on the limbs.

2) Diseases of the Head and Sense Organs: Aversion to cold and fever, migraine, pain in the outer canthus, inflammation of the throat.

3) Other Diseases: Scrofula, malaria, hypochodriac pain.
【Mechanism of Action】 See Xuanzhong (GB 39), Toulinqi (GB 41).
【Method】 Puncture perpendicularly 1-1.5 cun. Moxibustion is applicable.
【Acupoint Prescriptions】
　　1) Arthralgia due to wind-evil: Yangfu (GB 38), Xiyangguan (GB 33). (*Expeience on Acupuncture and Moxibustion Therapy*)
　　2) Cold limbs: Yangfu (GB 38), Zulinqi (GB 41), Zhangmen (LR 13). (*Great Compendium of Acupuncture and Moxibustion*)
　　3) Armpit swelling: Yangfu (GB 38), Qiuxu (GB 39), Zulinqi (GB 41). (*ibid*)
　　4) Axillar and neck scrofulae: Yangfu (GB 38), Taichong (LR 3). (*ibid*)
　　5) Numbness of the feet: Yangfu (GB 38), Yangjiao (GB 35), Juegu (GB 39), Xingjian (LR 2). (*ibid*)
【Regional Anatomy】 Skin-subcutaneous tissue-the long extensor muscle of the toes-long extensor muscle of the great toe-interosseous membrane of the leg-posterior tibial muscle. In the superficial layer, there are the lateral sural cutaneous nerve and the superficial peroneal nerve. In the deep layer, there are the peroneal artery and vein.

GB 39　Xuanzhong (悬钟)
(Hanging Bell)

【Source】 *A-B Classic of Acupuncture and Moxibustion*
【Name Explanation】 Xuan (悬), hanging; Zhong (钟), bell. The point is above the lateral malleolus, where the children in ancient times used to hang a bell.
【Classification】 Influential Point of the marrow.
【Location】 On the lateral side of the leg, 3 cun above the tip of the exteral malleolus, on the anterior border of the fibula. (See Fig. 11-23)
【Localization】 Sitting or in the lateral position, locate the point 3 cun superior to the tip of the lateral malleolus, the anterior margin of the fibula.
【Indications】
　　1) Diseases along the Course of the Meridian: Pain in the chest and hypochondrium, hemiplegia, stiffness of the neck, lumbosacral pain, pain in the lateral side of lower the Limbs.
　　2) Diseases of Head and Sense Organs: Inflammation of the throat, migraine, epistaxis, pain and dryness of nasal cavity.
　　3) Digestive Diseases: Stomach heat, poor appetite, constipation.
　　4) Urinary Diseases: Dysuria, stranguria.
　　5) Respiratory Diseases: Cough, hyperthermia in febrile disease.
【Mechanism of Action】
　　1) The Divergent Meridians of the Gallbladder Meridians pass along the throat. Gallbladder-heat attacking the head will result in nasosinusitis. Puncturing Xuanzhong (GB 39) can remove heat to expel wind. It is also the influential point of marrow, so it is frequently selected to treat nasosinusitis, epistaxis and painful swollen throat, etc.
　　2) The muscle region of the Gallbladder runs posteriorly and knots at the sacrum, and the straight branch ascends across the ribs, dispersing around and anterior to the axilla, connecting first at the breast region and then knotting at Quepen (ST 12). According to the principle that "Where the meridian passes, where the indications are." Xuanzhong (GB 39) and the other points in the meridian can be used to treat pain in the chest and hypochondrium, pain in the supraclavicular fossa and lumbosacral pain.

【Method】 Puncture perpendicularly 1-1.5 cun. Moxibustion is applicable.
【Acupoint Prescriptions】
　1) Scrofula: Xuanzhong (GB 39). (*Thousand Golden Prescriptions*)
　2) Infantile abdominal fullness: Xuanzhong (GB 39). (*ibid*)
　3) Distension and fullness in the chest and abdomen: Xuanzhong (GB 39), Neiting (SI 44). (*Great Compendium of Acupuncture and Moxibustion*)
　4) Malarial disease: Xuanzhong (GB 39), Baihui (UD 20), Gaohuang (BL 43), Hegu (LI 4). (*ibid*)
　5) Hypertension: Xuanzhong (GB 39), Sanyinjiao (SP 6). (*Abstract of Clinical Experience on Acupuncture and Moxibustion*)
　6) Difficulty in walking: Xuanzhong (GB 39), Huantiao (GB 30). (*Secret Songs of Acupuncture and Moxibustion*)
　7) Foot drop: Xuanzhong (GB 39), Tiaokou (SI 38), Chongyang (SI 42) (*Secret Songs of Chang Sangjun*)
　8) Difficulty in walking: Xuanzhong (GB 39), Tiaokou (SI 38). (*Songs of Point Selection on Miscellaneous Diseases*)
【Regional Anatomy】 Skin-subcutaneous tissue-the long extensor muscle of toes-the interosseous membrane of the leg. In the superficial layer, there is the lateral sural cutaneous nerve. In the deep layer, there are the branches of the deep peroneal nerve. If the needle penetrates through the interosseous membrane of the leg, the peroneal artery and vein may be injured.
【Remark】 Xuanzhong (GB 39) is commonly used to treat anemia and some people belive this point has a relation to the formation of RBC. Acidocphiles are sensitive to Xuanzhong (GB 39) and have the specificity for them. Xuanzhong (GB 39) can also be used to reduce blood pressure in hypertension, especially for terciary hypertension. Experiments have proved that acupuncture at this point can elevate the patient's myoelectricity, which can last for 30 minutes after 5 minutes of acupuncture. It is reported that puncturing GB 39, combined with Sanyinjiao (SP 6), causes the uteri of pregnant women to contract.

GB 40　Qiuxu（丘墟）
（Big Mound）

【Source】 *Miraculous Pivot*
【Name Explanation】 Qiu (丘), mound; Xu (墟), large mound. The point is between the lateral malleolus and the peroneal trochlea of the calcaneus (like a large mound).
【Classification】 Yuan-(Source) Point of the Gallbladder Meridian of Foot Shaoyang.
【Location】 Anterior and inferior to the external malleolus, in the depression lateral to the tendon of the long extensor muscle of the toes. (See Fig. 11-24)

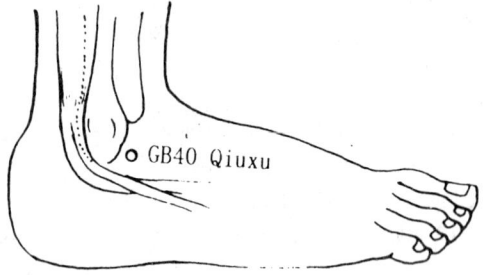

Fig. 11-24

【Localization】 Sitting with the foot relaxed or lateral position, locate the point at the anterior and inferior to the lateral malleolus, on the lateral side of the tendon of the long extensor muscle of the toe, in the depression at the talocalcaneal articulation.
【Indications】
　1) Diseases along the Course of the Meridian: Pain in the neck, pain and fullness in the

chest and the hypochondrium, pain in the waist and lower extremities, hemiplegia, spasm, periankle injury, flaccidity of the lower limbs.

2) Diseases of the Head and Sense Organs: Migraine (hemicraneal), red swollen and painful eyes, blurring of vision.

3) Other Diseases: Malaria diseases, cough with dyspnea, susceptibility to sighing.

【Mechanism of Action】
1) Qiuxu (GB 40) is the source point of the Gallbladder Meridian. According to the principles that "where the meridian passes, where the indications are" and "points on the lower portion could be selected for the upper disorders" Qiuxu (GB 40) is frequently used to treat migraine (hemicraneal), pain and fullness in the chest and the hypochondrium.

2) *The Internal Classic* says "The disorders of the five solid organs and six hollow organs will involve the lung and cough ensues." The Gallbladder Meridian travels along the inside of the hypochondrium and connects with the lung. In addition, Qiuxu (GB 40) can clear away the gallbladder heat and disperse the stagnated liver-energy. So this point can be used to treat cough and other respiratory diseases due to liver-fire attacking the lung and heat retention in the liver and the gallbladder.

3) Qiuxu (GB 40) is one of the most important points to activate vital energy and relieve stagnation. So it can be used to treat the patients who suffer from stagnation of liver-qi.

【Method】 Puncture perpendicularly 0.5-0.8 cun. Moxibustion is applicable.

【Acupoint Prescriptions】
1) Edema: Qiuxu (GB 40). (*Thousand Golden Prescriptions*)
2) Cataract: Qiuxu (GB 40), Tongziliao (GB 1). (*Experience on Acupuncture and Moxibustion Therapy*)
3) Abrupt pain and swelling of the testicles: Qiuxu (GB 40), Dadun (LR 1), Yinshi (SI 33), Zhaohai (KI 6). (*Great Compendium of Acupuncture and Moxibustion*)
4) Difficulty in walking: Qiuxu (GB 40), Xingjian (LR 2), Kunlun (BL 60), Taichong (LR 3). (*ibid*)

【Regional Anatomy】 Skin-subcutaneous tissue-short extensor muscle of toes-lateral talocalcaneal ligament-tarsal sinus. There are the superficial vein of the dorsum of the foot, the lateral dorsal cutaneous nerve of the foot, the intermediate dorsal cutaneous nerve of the foot, and the lateral anterior malleolar artery and vein in this area.

【Remark】 Acupuncture at Qiuxu (GB 40) can strengthen the contraction of gallbladder and common bile duct. It has a good effect in treating of chronic cholecystitis.

GB 41　Zulinqi（足临泣）
(Foot Falling Tears)

【Source】 *Miraculous Pivot*

【Name Explanation】 Zu (足), foot; Lin (临), treatment; Qi (泣), to cry. The point is at the foot and is indicated in lacrimation and other eye disorders.

【Classification】 Shu-(Stream) Point of the Gallbladder Meridian of Foot Shaoyang, pertaining to wood in the Five Element.

【Location】 On the lateral side of the instep of the foot, posterior to the 4th metatarsophalangeal joint, in the depression lateral to the tendon of the extensor muscle of the little toe. (See Fig. 11-25)

【Localization】 Sitting with the foot relaxed to the ground, locate the point at the anterior to the 4th and 5th planta pedis, in the depression at the lateral side of the 5th tendon of the muscle extensor digitorum pedis longi.

【Indications】

1) Diseases of the Head and Sense Organs: Hemicranial migraine, pain in the outer canthus, dizziness, feeling of dryness in eyes, deafness, tinnitus.

2) Other Diseases: Hemiplegia, irregular menstruation, acute mastitis.

【Mechanism of Action】 See Qiuxu (GB 40) and Xuanzhong (GB 39).

【Method】 Puncture perpendicularly 0.3-0.5 cun. Moxibustion is applicable.

【Acupoint Prescriptions】

1) Fullness feeling in the chest: Zulinqi (GB 41), Tianchi (PC 1), Xuanji (RN 21), Shufu (KI 27). (*Experience on Acupuncture and Moxibustion Therapy*)

2) Dizziness: Zulinqi (GB 41), Zhongzhu (SJ 3). (*ibid*)

3) Stuffy nose: Zulinqi (GB 41), Tongtian (BL 27). (*ibid*)

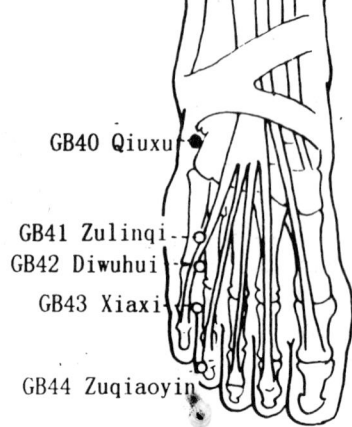

Fig. 11-25

4) Dizziness due to wind pathogen: Zulinqi (GB 41), Yanggu (SI 5), Wangu (SI 4), Shenmai (BL 62). (*Great Compendium of Acupuncture and Moxibustion*)

5) Irregular menstruation: Zulinqi (GB 41), Sanyinjiao (SP 6), Zhongji (RN 3). (*ibid*)

【Regional Anatomy】 Skin-subcutaneous tissue-the 4th dorsal interosseous muscle and the 3rd plantar interosseous muscle.

There are the venous network of the dorsum of the foot, the intermediate dorsal cutaneous nerve of the foot, the 4th dorsal metatarsal artery and vein and the branches of the lateral plantar nerve in this area.

【Remark】 Acupuncture at Zulinqi (GB 41) can strenghthen the peristalsis, but with less effect than punctruing Zusanli (ST 36) or Shangjuxu (ST 37).

GB 42   Diwuhui (地五会)
(Five Convergences)

【Source】 *A-B Classic of Acupuncture and Moxibustion*

【Name Explanation】 Di (地), ground; Wu (五), five; Hui (会), confluence. The ground is inferior, indicating the foot. There are five points of the Gallbladder Meridian on the foot. This point is among them and is a confluence of upper and lower qi of the meridian.

【Location】 On the lateral side of the instep of the foot, posterior to the 4th metatarsophalangeal joint, between the 4th and 5th metatarsal bones, medial to the tendon of the extensor muscle of the little toe. (See Fig. 11-25).

【Localization】 Sitting with the foot relaxed to the ground locate the point between the 4th and the 5th phalanges on the dorsum of the foot, in the depression on the medial side of the 5th tendon of the muscle èxtensoris digitorum pedis longi.

【Indications】

1) Diseases along the Course of the Meridian: Swollen and painful dorsum of the foot, fullness and pain in the chest and the hypochondrium, acute mastitis, lumbago, pain in the lower limbs.

2) Diseases of the Head and Sense Organs: Hemicranial migraine, red swollen and painful eyes, deafness, tinnitus.

3) Other Diseases: Hemoptysis due to visceral injury.

【Mechanism of Action】 See Qiuxu (GB 40), and Xuanzhong (GB 39).

【Method】 Puncture perpendicularly 0.3-0.5 cun. Moxibustion is applicable.

【Acupoint Prescription】 Swelling in the axilla: Diwuhui (GB 42), Yangfu (GB 38), Shenmai (BL 62), Weiyang (BL 39), Tianchi (PC 1), Zulinqi (GB 41). (*Thousand Golden Prescriptions*)

【Regional Anatomy】 Skin-subcutaneous tissue-tendon of the long extensor muscle of the toes-lateral side of the tendon of the short extensor muscle of the toes-the 4th interosseous muscle-the 3rd plantar interosseous muscle. In the superficial layer, there are the intermediate dorsal cutaneous nerve of the foot, the venous network of the dorsum of the foot and the dorsal metatarsal artery and vein. In the deep layer, there are the common digital plantar nerve and the common digital plantar artery and vein.

GB 43 Xiaxi (侠溪)
(Stream Insertion)

【Source】 *Miraculous Pivot*

【Name Explanation】 Xia (侠), to press from both sides; Xi (溪), stream. The point is in the space between the 4th and 5th toes. The space is like a stream.

【Classification】 Ying-(Spring) Point of the Gallbladder Meridian of Foot Shaoyang, pertaining to water in the Five Element

【Location】 On the lateral side of the instep of the foot, between the 4th and 5th toes, at the junction of the red and white skin, proximal to the margin of the web. (See Fig. 11-25)

【Localization】 Sitting with the foot relaxed to the ground, locate the point between the 4th and the 5th toes, proximal to the margin of the web.

【Indications】

1) Diseases along the Course of the Meridian: Pain in the chest and hypochondrium, hemiplegia, pain in the lower limbs, acute mastitis, edema of the dorsum of the foot.

2) Diseases of the Head and Sense Organs: Hemicrania, dizziness, deafness, swollen cheek, tinnitus, red and painful outer canthus, dacryorrhea.

3) Other Diseases: Amenorrhea, malaria, exterior syndrome of febrile disease.

【Mechanism of Action】

1) Xiaxi (GB 43) belongs to the Meridian of Foot Shaoyang and has the functions of eliminating the evil in Shaoyang and clearing heat-evil. So it is selected for diseases of Shaoyang, such as malaria disease and exterior syndrome of febrile disease.

2) The liver has the function of smoothing and regulating the flow of vital energy and blood. And the liver has an exterior-interior relationship with the gallbladder. So the points of the Gallbladder Meridian also have the function of dispelling the stagnated liver-energy. It is why Xiaxi (GB 43) is used to treat amenorrhea, dyamenorrhea and other gynecopathies due to stagnation of liver-energy.

【Method】 Puncture perpendicularly 0.3-0.5 cun. Moxibustion is applicable.

【Acupoint Prescriptions】

1) Malaria disease: Xiaxi (GB 43), Qiuxu (GB 40), Guangming (GB 37). (*A-B Classic of Acupuncture and Moxibustion*)

2) Scrofula: Xiaxi (GB 43), Yangfu (GB 38), Taichong (LR 3). (*Thousand Golden Prescriptions*)

3) Pain in the lateral side of the knee: Xiaxi (GB 43), Xiyangguan (GB 33). (*ibid*)
　　4) Swollen submental region and cheek: Xiaxi (GB 43), Heliao (SJ 22), Jiache (SI 6). (*Experience on Acupuncture and Moxibustion Therapy*)
【Regional Anatomy】Skin-subcutaneous tissue-between the tendons of the 4th long and short extensor muscles of the toe and the tendons of the 5th long and the short extensor muscle of the toe-between bases of the 4th and the 5th proximal phalangeal bones. There are the dorsal digital nerve of the intermediate dorsal cutaneous nerve of the foot and the dorsal digital artery and vein in this area.

GB 44　Zuqiaoyin (足窍阴)
(Foot Orifice Yin)

【Source】*Miraculous Pivot*
【Name Explanation】Zu (足), foot; Qiao (窍), opening; Yin (阴), Yin of Yin-Yang. The kidney and the liver pertain to Yin are opened into the ear and the eye. The point is on the foot and is indicated to treat ear and eye disorders.
【Classification】Jing-(Well) Point of the Gallbladder Meridian of Foot Shaoyang, pertaining to metal in the Five Element.
【Location】On the lateral side of the distal segment of the 4th toe, 0.1 cun from the corner of the toe nail. (See Fig. 11-25)
【Localization】Sitting with the foot relaxed to the ground, locate the point at the intersection of the line drawn from the lateral side of the 4th toe nail and its basal part.
【Indications】
　　1) Diseases along the Course of the Meridian: Hemiplegia, distension and fullness feeling in the chest and the hypochondrium.
　　2) Diseases of Head and Sense Organs: Hemicranial migraine, dizziness, red swollen and painful eyes, tinnitus, deafness, inflammation of the throat, stiffness of the tongue.
　　3) Respiratory Diseases: Cough, asthma.
　　4) Gynecopathies: Irregular menstruation, amenorrhea.
　　5) Surgical Diseases: Carbuncle, acute mastitis.
　　6) Mental Diseases: Insomnia and dreamful sleep.
【Mechanism of Action】See Xuanzhong (GB 39), Qiuxu (GB 40), Xiaxi (GB 43).
【Method】Puncture subcutaneously 0.1 cun. Moxibustion is applicable.
【Acupoint Prescriptions】
　　1) Contracture of arm and elbow: Zuqiaoyin (GB 44), Shousanli (LI 10). (*Experience on Acupuncture and Moxibustion Therapy*)
　　2) Headache: Zuqiaoyin (GB 44), Qiangjian (DU 18). (*ibid*)
【Regional Anatomy】Skin-subcutaneous tissue-the root of the nail.
　　There are the dorsal digital nerve of the intermediate dorsal cutaneous nerve of the foot, and the arteriovenous network formed by the dorsal digital arteries and veins of the foot with the proper plantar arteries and veins in this area.
【Remark】Acupuncture at Zuqiaoyin (GB 44) can change the subjective colour sensation and enhance the reflection in the temporal retina.

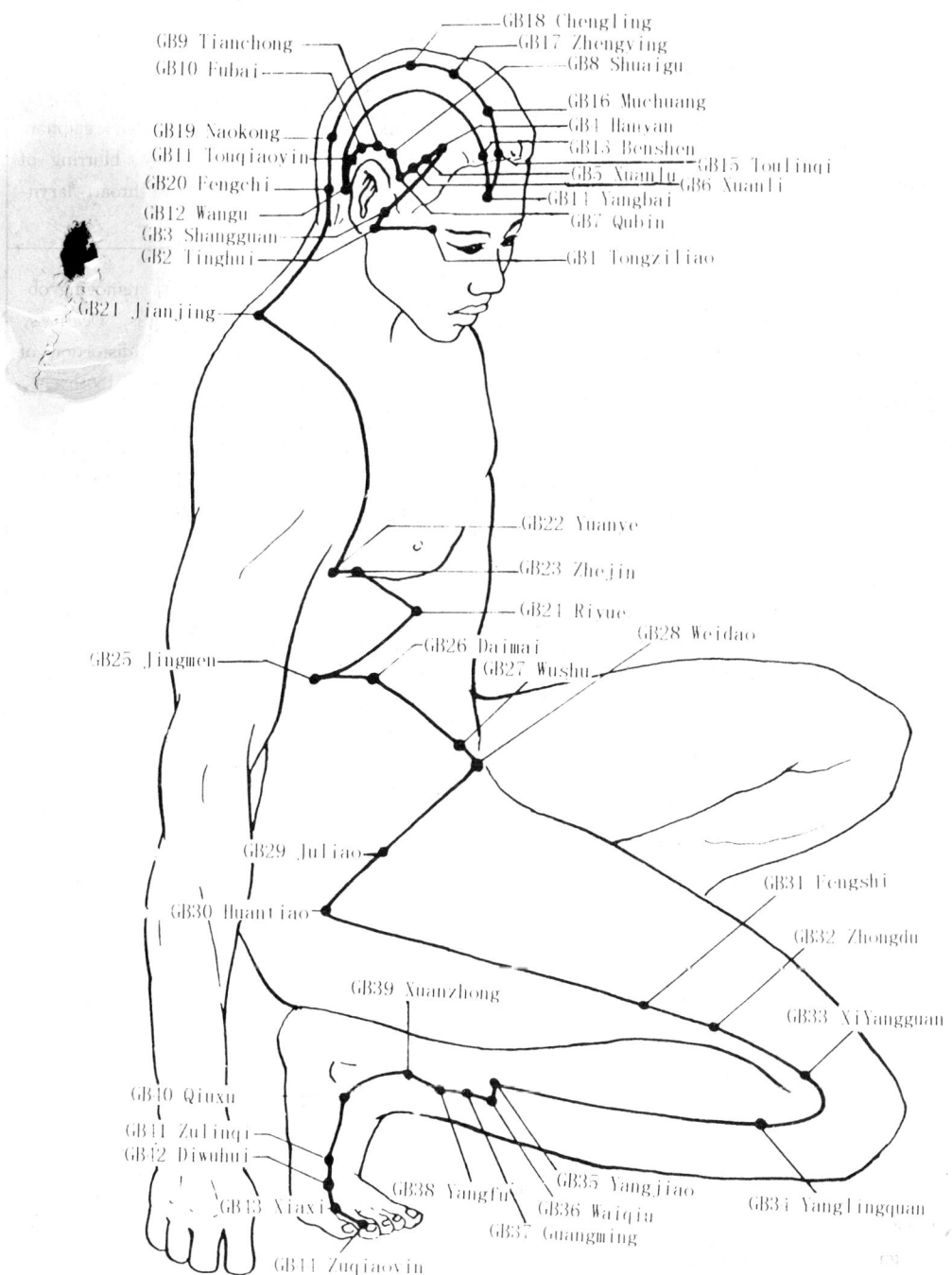

Fig. 11-26 **Acupoints of the Gallbladder Meridian of Foot Shanyang**

Table 11-2
Indications and Actions of Acupoints of the Gallbladder Meridian of Foot Shaoyang

Name of the points	Specific points	Common indications	Specific indications and functions
GB 1 Tongziliao (瞳子髎)	Crossing point	Diseases of the head, neck and five sense organs: headache, stiffness and pain of the neck, conjunctival congestion, deafness, tinnitus, toothache, stuffy nose, dizziness, hemicrania	Dispelling wind and removing heat, improving acuity of vision. Headache, conjunctival congestion, epiphora induced by wind, nebula, itching eyes, blurring of sight, distortion of mouth and eyes, sore throat, laryngitis
GB 2 Tinghui (听会)			Dispelling wind and clearing away heat, removing obstruction from the external auditory meatus. Deafness, tinnitus, otitis media, deaf and mute, distortion of mouth and eyes, arthritis of lower jaw, toothache, swelling of cheek
GB 3 Shangguan (上关)	Crossing point		Clearing the meridian and activating collaterals, inducing resuscitation and clearing the brain. Hemicrania, tinnitus, deafness, distortion of mouth and eyes, toothache, lockjaw, clonic convulsion
GB 4 Hanyan (颔厌)	Crossing point		Dispelling wind, dredging the collaterals and relieving pain. Hemicrania, dizziness, vertigo, pain in the eyelids, tinnitus, toothache
GB 5 Xuanlu (悬颅)			Dispelling wind and dredging the collaterals, relieving swelling and stopping pain. Hemicrania, pain in the eyelids, conjunctival congestion, edema of face, epistaxis
GB 6 Xuanli (悬厘)	Crossing point		Hemicrania, red, swelling and painful eyes
GB 7 Qubin (曲鬓)	Crossing point		Calming the endogenous wind and relieving convulsion and spasm, removing heat and subduing swelling. Hemicrania, lockjaw, sudden loss of voice, infantile convulsion, distortion of mouth and eyes
GB 8 Shuaigu (率谷)	Crossing point		Calming the endogenous wind and relieving convulsion and spasm, clearing the diaphragm and regulating the stomach. Dizziness, acute and chronic convulsion in children, restlessness, cold-syndrome of stomach, hypochondriac pain, vomiting

Name of the points	Specific points	Common indications	Specific indications and functions
GB 9 Tianchong (天冲)	Crossing point	The same as above	Relieving mental stress and tranquilizing the mind, arresting convulsion and stopping pain. Headache, epilepsy, fright, swelling and pain in the gums
GB 10 Fubai (浮白)	Crossing point		Dispelling wind and removing heat, dredging meridian and collaterals. Headache, stiffness and pain of neck, tinnitus, deafness, toothache, inability to raise the arms due to pain in shoulder joint, flaccidity of feet and legs
GB 11 Touqiaoyin (头窍阴)	Crossing point		Clearing the ear. Deafness, tinnitus, earache and other ear diseases
GB 12 Wangu (完骨)	Crossing point		Dredging and activating meridian and collaterals. Stiffness and pain of neck, distortion of mouth and eyes, flaccidity of leg and foot, pain behind the ear, dizziness
GB 13 Benshen (本神)	Crossing point		Calming the endogenous wind and arresting convulsion and spasm, removing heat and relieving convulsion. Headache, dizziness, epilepsy, infantile convulsion, distortion of mouth and eyes, hemiplegia, pain in the chest and hypochondrium
GB 14 Yangbai (阳白)	Crossing point		Improving acuity of vision. Dizziness, pain of eyes, blurred vision, nyctalopia, drooping eyelids and other eye diseases, headache
GB 15 Toulinqi (头临泣)	Crossing point		Clearing the head and improving acuity of vision, clearing the nasal passage. Pain of the outer canthus, dacryorrhea, nebula, red, swelling and painful eyes, stuffy nose, rhinorrhea with turbid discharge, epilepsy, headache
GB 16 Muchuang (目窗)	Crossing point		Clearing the head and improving acuity of vision, calming wind and dredging the collaterals. Conjunctival congestion, blurring vision, optic atrophy, stuffy nose, edema of face, headache, infantile convulsion

Name of the points	Specific points	Common indications	Specific indications and functions
GB 17 Zhengying (正营)	Crossing point	The same as above	Headache, pain in the neck, toothache, dizziness, vomiting
GB 18 Chengling (承灵)	Crossing point		Clearing the nasal passage. Stuffy nose, rhinorrhea with turbid discharge, epistaxis
GB 19 Naokong (脑空)	Crossing point		Clearing the head and clearing the passages, dredging the meridian and collaterals. Severe headache, vertigo, stiffness and pain in the neck, febrile disease, palpitation with fright, epilepsy
GB 20 Fengchi (风池)	Crossing point	Diseases of the head, neck and shoulder: Headache, stiffness and pain in the occiput, pain in the shoulder and back	Dispelling wind and removing heat, restoring consciousness and inducing resuscitation, improving hearing and acuity of vision, clearing meridians and activating collaterals. Headache, common cold, eye diseases, rhinorrhea with turbid discharge, stiffness and pain of the neck, epilepsy, stroke
GB 21 Jianjing (肩井)	Crossing point		Dredging meridians and activating collaterals, regulating circulation of qi and eliminating phlegm. Stiffness and pain of the neck, pain in the shoulder and back, dystocia, acute mastitis, galactostasis, scrofula, dysfunctional uterine bleeding, accumulation of phlegm, cough with dyspnea
GB 22 Yuanye (渊腋)		Diseases in the hypochondrium: fullness in the chest, hypochondriac pain, asthma	Soothing the chest oppression and regulating the circulation of qi. Fullness sensation in the chest, hypochondriac pain, cough, scrofula, inability to raise arms
GB 23 Zhejin (辄筋)			Soothing the liver and regulating function of the stomach. Vomiting, acid regurgitation, fullness of chest, hypochondriac pain, asthma
GB 24 Riyue (日月)	Front Mu point of the gallbladder Crossing point.		Soothing the liver and normalizing the functioning of the gall bladder, lowering the adverse flow of qi and regulating the middle-jiao. Hypochondrial pain, vomiting, acid regurgitation, dyspnea, jaundice, abdominal pain

Name of the points	Specific points	Common indications	Specific indications and functions
GB 25 Jingmen (京门)	Mu – Front point of the gall bladder.	Gynecopathies and other diseases of external genitalia and intestines: Irregular menstruation, leukorrhea, prolapse of uterus, hernia, abdominal pain, distension of abdomen	Warming the kidney and strengthening the spleen, clearing the water passage. Dysuria, edema, borborygmus, abdominal distention, diarrhea, cold pain in loins and knees, hypochondrial pain, stiffness of spinal cord
GB 26 Daimai (带脉)	Crossing point		Regulating menstruation and arresting leukorrhea, removing dampness and heat. Irregular menstruation, amenorrhea, abdominal pain, leukorrhea, prolapse of uterus, annexitis, pelvic inflammation, cold sensation in loin
GB 27 Wushu (五枢)	Crossing point		Regulating menstruation and arresting leukorrhea, strengthening the waist and invigorating the kidney. Abdominal pain, leukorrhea, hernia, irregular menstruation, pain in loin and buttock, flaccid constriction of penis, endometrial inflammation
GB 28 Weidao (维道)	Crossing point		Regulating menstruation, warming and invigorating the lower Jiao, inducing diuresis and clearing collaterals. Flaccid constriction and abdominal pain, leukorrhea with reddish discharge, prolapse of uterus, edema, ascites, pelvic inflammation, pain in loin and legs
GB 29 Juliao (居髎)	Crossing point	Diseases of loins and legs: lumbago, flaccidity and arthralgia of lower extremities	Relaxing muscles and tendons, activating the flow of qi and blood in the meridians and collaterals, strengthening the waist and legs. Lumbago, flaccidity and arthralgia of the lower limbs, hernia
GB 30 Huantiao (环跳)	Crossing point		Clearing meridians and activating collaterals, dispelling wind and expelling cold, strengthening the waist and legs. Hemiplegia, rubella, urticaria, cold, neurosism, beriberi, sciatica
GB 31 Fengshi (风市)			Removing wind, dampness and heat, relieving itching and pain, strengthening the muscles and tendons. General pruritis, neurodermatitis, urticaria, beriberi, numbness, coldness and arthralgia of the lower extremities, flaccidity and weakness of legs and knees

Name of the points	Specific points	Common indications	Specific indications and functions
GB 32 Zhongdu (中渎)			Dispelling wind and removing dampness, dredging meridians and clearing collaterals. Flaccidity and arthralgia of lower extremities, numbness, beriberi, pain in the waist and buttocks, hemiplegia
GB 33 Xiyangguan (膝阳关)			Dispelling wind and eliminating dampness, relaxing muscles, tendons and joints. Swelling, pain and spasm of the knees, numbness of the leg
GB 34 Yanglingquan (阳陵泉)	He- (sea) point One of eight influential points (influential point of tendons)	The same as below.	Soothing the liver and regulating the functioning of gall bladder, removing heat and dampness, strengthening the waist and legs. Bitter taste in the mouth, vomiting, angitis, jaundice, hepatitis, cholecystitis, beriberi, intercostal neuralgia, red, swelling and pain of the knee
GB 35 Yangjiao (阳交)	Xi- (Cleft) point of Yangwei meridian		Soothing the liver and relieving mental stress. Distension, fullness and pain in the chest and hypochondrium, syncope, clonic convulsion, manic-depression, pain in the buttocks and knees, flaccidity and arthralgia of lower extremities, edema of face
GB 36 Waiqiu (外丘)	Xi- (Cleft) point		Soothing the liver and regulating the flow of qi, clearing the meridian and collaterals. Distending pain in the chest and hypochondrium, stiffness and pain of the neck, flaccidity and arthralgia of lower limbs, beriberi, manic-depression
GB 37 Guangming (光明)	Luo- (Connecting) point		Regulating the function of liver and improving the acuity of vision. Eye pain, night blindness, blurred vision and other eye diseases, acute mastitis with distending pain, aching pain of knees and calf, cheek swelling
GB 38 Yangfu (阳辅)	Jing- (Well) point		Migraine, outer canthus pain, flaccidity and arthralgia of lower limbs

Name of the points	Specific points	Common indications	Specific indications and functions
GB 39 Xuanzhong (悬钟)	One of the eight influential points (Influential point of marrow)	Diseases of the head, eyes, ear, throat and hypochondrium: Headache, migraine, eye disease, tinnitus, deafness, sore throat, hypochondriac pain, mental illnesses and febrile disease	Soothing the liver and regulating the flow of qi, dredging the meridian and activating the collaterals. Stiffness and pain of the neck, distension and fullness of gastric cavity and abdomen, hypochondrial pain, flaccidity and arthralgia of lower extremities, beriberi, stiffneck, acute appendicitis, hemorrhoids
GB 40 Qiuxu (丘墟)	Yuan- (source) point		Soothing the liver and regulating the functioning of the gall bladder, clearing the collaterals and resolving the stagnation. Fullness and pain sensation in the chest and hypochondrium with shortness of breath, subaxillary swelling, flaccidity and arthralgia of lower extremities, swelling pain of external malleolus, spasm, cholecystitis, pain in loins and buttock
GB 41 Zulinqi (足临泣)	Shu- (Stream) point; One of the eight confluence points		Relieving the depressed liver and regulating the functioning of gall bladder, clearing the head and improving the acuity of vision. Headache, eye disease, hypochondrial pain, acute mastitis, irregular menstruation, spasm of toes, enuresis
GB 42 Diwuhui (地五会)			Acute mastitis, swelling pain of dorsum of foot, conjunctival congestion
GB 43 Xiaxi (侠溪)	Ying- (Spring) point		Removing heat and calming endogenous wind, inducing resuscitation, arresting pain. Headache, dizziness, eye disease, acute mastitis, febrile disease, mobile pain all over the body, intercostal neuralgia, swelling pain of dorsum of foot, hypertension
GB 44 Zuqiaoyin (足窍阴)	Jing- (Well) point		Calming the liver to stop the endogenous wind, removing heat and inducing resuscitation. Migraine, vexation, hiccup, insomnia, heat sensation in the center of hand and foot, inflammation of the throat, stiffness of tongue, sudden deafness, dreaminess, hypertension, swelling and pain of dorsum of foot

XIV. Acupoints of the Bladder Meridian of Foot Taiyang

BL 1 Jingming (睛明)
(Eye Brightness)

【Source】 *A-B Classic of Acupuncture and Moxibustion*
【Name Explanation】 Jing (睛), eye; Ming (明), brightness. The point is located near the eye; its function is to clear the eyes.
【Classification】 The Crossing Point of the Hand and Foot Taiyang, Foot Yangming, Yinqiao and Yangqiao Meridians.
【Location】 On the face, in the depression closely above the inner canthus. (See Fig. 11-27)
【Localization】 In sitting or supine position, the point is located 0.1 cun medial to the inner canthus, and 0.1 cun upward, near the medial margin of the orbit.
【Indications】
  1) Ophthalmopathy: Conjunctival congestion, dizziness, epiphora, itching pain in the inner canthus, pterygium, nebula, blurred vision, myopia, night blindness, color blindness, eye disorders in children due to malnutrition.
  2) Other Diseases: Aversion to cold, headache, lumbago.

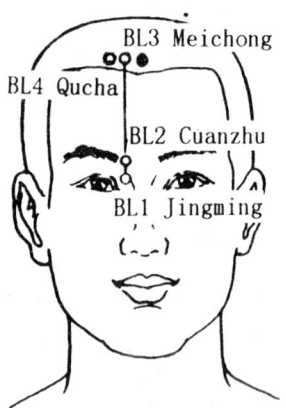

Fig. 11-27

【Mechanism of Action】
  1) The point lies near the eye, and since all points have local indications, many eye diseases can be treated by puncturing this point.
  2) The Urinary Bladder Meridian of Foot Taiyang circulates through the lumbar region. According to the principle that where the meridian passes, where the indications are, this point can be used to treat lumbago and with good results.
【Method】 Puncture perpendicularly 0.3 cun along the infraorbital ridge. It is not advisable to twist or manipulate the needle with large amplitude.
【Acupoint Prescriptions】
  1) Conjunctival congestion: Jingming (BL 1), Houxi (SI 3), Muchuang (GB 16), Tongziliao (GB 1). (*Experience on Acupuncture and Moxibustion Therapy*)
  2) Cold tears: Jingming (BL 1), Linqi (GB 15), Fengchi (GB 20), Wangu (SI 4). (*Great Compendium of Acupuncture and Moxibustion*)
  3) Conjunctivitis: Jingming (BL 1), Hegu (LI 4), Sibai (ST 2). (*ibid*)
  4) Fluxion of tears: Jingming (BL 1), Yingxiang (LI 20) (The needle is inserted quickly, twisted and twirled lightly without retention.) (*Abstract of Clinical Experience on Acupuncture and Moxibustion*)
  5) Acute conjunctivitis: Jingming (BL 1), Yuyao (EX-HN 4), Chengqi (ST 1), Cuanzhu (BL 2), Sizhukong (SJ 23), Tongziliao (GB 1). (*New Acupuncture and Moxibustion*)

6) Night blindness: Jingming (BL 1), Tongziliao (GB 1), Cuanzhu (BL 2), Sizhukong (SJ 23), Yuyao (EX-HN 4), Sibai (ST 2), Shangxing (DU 23), Yangbai (GB 14). (*ibid*)

7) Ocular diseases: Jingming (BL 1), Taiyang (EX-HN 5), Yuwei (EX-HN). (*Songs of Jade Dragon*)

8) Nyctalopia due to liver dysfunction: Jingming (BL 1), Xingjian (LR 2). (*Song of Hundreds of Symptoms*)

[Regional Anatomy] Skin-subcutaneous tissue-orbicular muscle of the eye-upper side of superior lacrimal duct-between internal muscle of the eye and orbital lamina of ethmoid bone. In the superficial layer, there are the supratrochlear nerve of the ophthalmic branches of the trigeminal nerve and the branches or tributaries of the angular artery and vein. In the deep layer, there are the branches or tributaries of the ophthalmic artery and vein, the branches of the ophthalmic nerve and the branches of the oculomotor nerve.

[Remark] Experiments have shown that puncturing Jingming (BL 1) can slow down the heart rate.

BL 2 Cuanzhu (攒竹)
(Gathering Eyebrows)

[Source] *A-B Classic of Acupuncture and Moxibustion*
[Name Explanation] Cuan (攒), to assemble; Zhu (竹), bamboo. The point is at the end of the eyebrow, which appears like a luxuriant bamboo plant.
[Location] On the face, in the depression of the medial end of the eyebrow, in the supraorbital notch. (See Fig. 11-27)
[Localization] Head resting or supine position, locate the point at the medial portion of the eyebrow, about 0.1 cun lateral to the tip of the eyebrow.
[Indications]

1) Diseases of the Head and Sense Organs: Headache, pain in the supra-orbital bone, facial paralysis, flushed face, swollen cheeks, epistaxis, dizziness, conjunctivits, blurred vision, conjunctival congestion, epiphora, itching and pain of the eyes, myopia, night blindness, fickering eyelids.

2) Mental Diseases: Coma, manic-depressive psychosis, epilepsy, clonic convulsion, infantile convulsion.

3) Other Diseases: Hemorrhoids, aversion to wind and cold, neck stiffness, sciatica.

[Mechanism of Action]

1) The point is located at the supra-orbital bone of the face, thus, it can be used to treat diseases of the face and eyes.

2) The Bladder Meridian is connected with the brain by its collaterals, thus, it is mainly used to treat mental diseases.

3) The Bladder Meridian circulates in the lower limbs along which line sciatica often occurs. Puncturing this point may straighten the leg and relieve the pain.

[Method] Puncture subcutaneously 0.3-0.5 cun downwards or against the ophryon.

[Acupoint Prescriptions]

1) Facial diseases: Cuanzhu (BL 2), Yinjiao (BL 2), Yuzhen (BL 9) which are mainly for flushed face, red and swelling cheek. (*Thousand Golden Prescriptions*)

2) Coma: Cuanzhu (BL 2), Heliao (LI 19) (*Experience on Acupuncture and Moxibustion Therapy*)

3) Sudden onset of blindness: Cuanzhu (BL 2), Qianding (DU 21). (*Great Compendium of Acupuncture and Moxibustion*)

4) Manic-depressive psychosis due to the heart causes: Cuanzhu (BL 2), Chize (LU 5), Jianshi (PC 5), Yangxi (LI 5). (*ibid*)

5) Wind-syndrome of head: Cuanzhu (BL 2), Yintang (EX-HN 3), Sanli (ST 36). (*ibid*)

6) Electric ophthalmitis: Cuanzhu (BL 2), Jingming (BL 1), Hegu (LI 4). If the pain becomes unbearable, Yangbai and Fengchi (GB 20) should be added. (The needle is inserted by twisting and twirling with a medium stimulation and retained for ten minutes). (*Abstract of Clinical Experience on Acupuncture and Moxibustion*)

7) Ophthalmalgia and headache: Cuanzhu (BL 2), Touwei (ST 8). (*Songs of Jade Dragon*)

8) Blurred vision: Cuanzhu (BL 2), Sanjian (LI 3). (*Song of Hundreds of Symptoms*)

【Regional Anatomy】 Skin-subcutaneous tissue-orbicular muscle of the eye.

In the superficial layer, there are the supratrochlear nerve of the frontal nerve, and the branches or tributaries of the superior orbital artery and vein. In the deep layer, there are the temporal and zygomatic branches of the facial nerve.

【Remark】 Puncturing this point can slow down the heart rate. It has a good anaesthetic effect for operations on the eyes and viscera. For example, when this point is punctured through to Jingming (BL 1) to give anaesthesia to patients operated for strabismus, the effective rate is 85.86%. Hemilateral acupuncture is better than contralateral acupuncture. Painthreshold and two-point discrimination tests favour the concept that hemilateral effect is superior to the contralateral one. For partial gastrectomy, puncturing this point deeply to Jingming (BL 1) and Tinghui (GB 2) has a better anaesthetic effect with a slight visceral pulling reaction, than points on the abdomen.

BL 3 Meichong (眉冲)
(Eyebrow Rush)

【Source】 *Classic of the Pulse*

【Name Explanation】 Mei (眉), eyebrow; Chong (冲), upward. The point is at the anterior hairline directly above the eyebrow.

【Location】 On the head, directly above Cuanzhu (BL2), 0.5 cun superior to the anterior hairline, on the line connecting Shenting (DU 24) and Quchai (BL 4). (See Fig. 11-27)

【Localization】 In sitting position with the head at rest or supine position, locate the point at the intersection between the horizontal line from Shenting (DU 24) and the vertical line from Cuanzhu (BL 2).

【Indications】

1) Diseases of Head and Sense Organs: Conjunctival congestion, blurred vision, stuffy nose, headache, dizziness, vertigo.

2) Other Disease: Epilepsy.

【Mechanism of Action】 This point lies in the head. Its meridian originates in the inner canthus and its muscle region is linked with the nose. Based on the local and adjacent action of acupoints and because the meridian runs through it, this point can be used to treat diseases of the face and the head.

【Method】 Puncture perpendicularly 0.3-0.5 cun.

【Acupoint Prescription】 Exogenous diseases (headache and pantalgia): Meichong (BL 3), Nieru (EX-HN). (*Classic of the Pulse*)

【Regional Anatomy】 Skin-subcutaneous tissue-frontal belly of occipit of rontal muscle. In the superficial layer, there are the supratrochlear nerve and the supratrochlear artery and vein. In the deep layer, there are the subaponeurotic loose connective tissue and the pericranium.

BL 4 Qucha (Quchai) (曲差)
(Crooked Branch)

【Source】 *A-B Classic of Acupuncture and Moxibustion*
【Name Explanation】 Qu (曲), crooked or curved; Chai (差), unevenness. This meridian curves laterally from Meichong (BL3) and then runs posteriorly from this point.
【Location】 On the head, 0.5 cun directly above the midpoint of the anterior hairline and 1.5 cun lateral to the midline, at the junction of the medial third and middle third of the line connecting Shenting (DU 24) and Touwei (ST 8). (See Fig. 11-27)
【Localization】 Sit with the head resting on, locate the point at the intersection of the middle one-third and interior one-third distance of the arc line joining Shenting (DU 24) and Touwei (ST 8).
【Indications】 Diseases of Head and Sense Organs: Headache, dizziness, blurred vision, ophthalmalgia, stuffy nose, epistaxis.
【Mechanism of Action】 See also Meichong (BL 3).
【Method】 Puncture subcutaneously 0.3-0.5 cun.
【Acupoint Prescriptions】
　　1) Nasal diseases: Quchai (BL 4), Shangxing (DU 13), Yingxiang (LI 20) Suliao (DU 25), Shuigou (DU 26), Yinjiao (RN 7), Tongtian (BL 7), Heliao (LI 19), Fengfu (DU 16). (*Thousand Golden Prescriptions*)
　　2) Rhinorrhea with turbid discharge, runny nose with offensive odor: Quchai (BL 4), Shangxing (DU 23). (*Great Compendium of Acupuncture and Moxibustion*)
【Regional Anatomy】 Skin-subcutaneous tissue-frontal belly of occipitofrontal muscle. In the superficial layer, there are the supratrochlear nerve and the supratrochlear artery and vein. In the deep layer, there are the subaponeurotic loose connective tissue and the pericranium.

BL 5 Wuchu (五处)
(Five Stops)

【Source】 *A-B Classic of Acupuncture and Moxibustion*
【Name Explanation】 Wu (五), fifth; Chu (处), place. This is the fifth point of the Bladder Meridian of Foot-Taiyang.
【Location】 On the head, 1 cun directly above the midpoint of the anterior hairline and 1.5 cun lateral to the midline. (See Fig. 11-28)
【Localization】 In sitting position with the head resting, first locate Quchai (BL 4). The point is located 0.5 cun directly superior to Quchai (BL 4).
【Indications】
　　1) Diseases of Head and Sense Organs: Headache, dizziness.
　　2) Mental Diseases: Infantile convulsion, epilepsy.
【Mechanism of Action】 See also Meichong (BL 3) and Cuanzhu (BL 2).
【Method】 Puncture subcutaneously 0.3-0.5 cun.
【Acupoint Prescriptions】

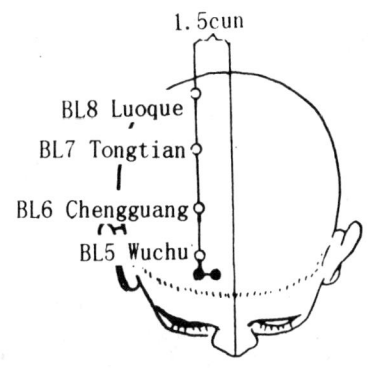

Fig. 11-28

1) Febrile diseases (sweating, fever and chill): Wuchu (BL 5), Cuanzhu (BL 2), Zhengying (GB 17), Shangguan (GB 3), Quepen (ST 12), Zhongfu (LU 1). (*Thousand Golden Prescriptions*)

2) Back rigidity, clonic convulsion, epilepsy, heaviness sensation of the head: Wuchu (BL 5), Shenzhu (DU 12), Weizhong (BL 40), Weiyang (BL 39), Kunlun (BL 60). (*Experience on Acupuncture and Moxibustion Therapy*)

3) Exogenous febrile diseases (with sweating, fever and chill): Wuchu (BL 5), Cuanzhu (BL 2), Shangwan (RN 13). (*Essentials of Acupuncture and Moxibustion*)

【Regional Anatomy】 Skin-subcutaneous tissue-frontal belly of occipitofrontal muscle. In the superficial layer, there are the supratrochlear nerve and the supratrochlear artery and vein. In the deep layer, there are the subaponeurotic loose connective tissue and the pericranium.

BL 6   Chengguang (承光)
(Receiving Light)

【Source】 *A-B Classic of Acupuncture and Moxibustion*
【Name Explanation】 Cheng (承), to receive; Guang (光), brightness. The point is at the vertex of the head, where brightness is easily received.
【Location】 On the head, 2.5 cun directly above the midpoint of the anterior hairline and 1.5 cun lateral to the midline. (See Fig. 11-28)
【Localization】 In sitting position with the head at rest, first locate Quchai (BL 4). The point is located 2 cun directly superior to Quchai (BL 4).
【Indications】
1) Diseases of Head and Sense Organs: Headache, dizziness, stuffy nose, running nose.
2) Other Diseases: Febrile disease without sweating, vomiting, dysphoria.
【Mechanism of Action】 See Meichong (BL 3) and Tianzhu (BL 10).
【Method】 Puncture subcutaneously 0.3-0.5 cun. Moxibustion is applicable.
【Acupoint Prescription】 Vomiting: Chengguang (BL 6), Dadu (SP 2). (*Experience on Acupuncture and Moxibustion Therapy*)
【Regional Anatomy】 Skin-subcutaneous tissue-epicranial aponeurosis. In the superficial layer, there are the supraorbital nerve and the supraorbital artery and vein. In the deep layer, there are the subaponeurotic loose connective tissue and the pericranium.

BL 7   Tongtian (通天)
(Reaching Heaven)

【Source】 *A-B Classic of Acupuncture and Moxibustion*
【Name Explanation】 Tong (通), reaching; Tian (天), heaven. The upper part of the head is considered as heaven. The point is at the head and connects upward with the vertex.
【Location】 On the head, 4 cun directly above the midpoint of the anterior hairline and 1.5 cun lateral to the midline. (See Fig. 11-28)
【Localization】 In sitting position with the head resting, first locate Quchai (BL 4). The point is located 4 cun posterior to Quchai (BL 4). Or first locate Baihui (DU 20), this point is located 1.5 cun lateral to Baihui (DU 20) and then 1 cun anterior.
【Indications】
1) Diseases of Head and Sense Organs: Headache, heaviness in the head, dizziness, verti-

go, deviation of the mouth and face, stuffy nose with watery discharge, epitaxis, pyogenic infection of nose, stuffy nose, neck pain which causes difficulty in turning the head.

2) Other Disease: Goiter.

【Mechanism of Action】 The Muscle Region of the Bladder Meridian of Foot Taiyang connects upwards with the face and head and downwards with the lower part of the zygoma, thus this point and other points in this meridian have the function to treat distortion of face.

【Method】 Puncture subcutaneously 0.3-0.5 cun. Moxibustion is applicable.

【Acupoint Prescriptions】

1) Goiter: Moxibustion to Tongtian (BL 7), Xiongtang (EX), Yangtian (EX) with 100 moxa cones. (*Thousand Golden Prescriptions*)

2) Corpse-like syncope: Tongtian (BL 7), Luoque (BL 8). (*Experience on Acupuncture and Moxibustion Therapy*)

3) Facial paralysis: Tongtian (BL 7), Chengguang (BL 6). (*ibid*)

【Regional Anatomy】 Skin-subcutaneous tissue-epicranial aponeurosis. In the superficial layer, there are the supraorbital nerve and the supraorbital artery and vein, the interneural and intervascular anastomotic network of the greater occipital nerve, the occipital artery and vein, the auriculotemporal nerve and the superficial temporal artery and vein. In the deep layer, there are the subaponeurotic loose connective tissue and the pericranium.

【Remark】 It has been reported that puncturing this point can normalize the electroencephalogram in patients with grand mal epilepsy.

BL 8 Luoque (络却)
(Return Collateral)

【Source】 *A-B Classic of Acupuncture and Moxibustion*

【Name Explanation】 Luo (络), linking; Que (却), return. The collateral of the Bladder Meridian returns to the body surface from this point after linked with the brain.

【Location】 On the head, 5.5 cun directly above the midpoint of the anterior hairline and 1.5 cun lateral to the midline. (See Fig. 11-28)

【Localization】 In sitting position with the head at rest, first locate Baihui (DU 20). This point is located 1.5 cun lateral to it, and then 0.5 cun posterior.

【Indications】

1) Diseases of Head and Sense Organs: Dizziness, vertigo, tinnitus, stuffy nose, deviation of the mouth and face, blurred vision, swelling in the neck.

2) Other Diseases: Goiter, manic-depressive psychosis, epilepsy.

【Mechanism of Action】 The collateral of the Urinary Bladder of Foot Taiyang originates in vertex and ends in the upper part of the ear. The kidney is related interiorly-exteriorly with the urinary bladder and its related orifice is the ear, thus, it can be used to treat ear diseases. Since it is at this point that the Bladder Collateral of Foot Taiyang is connected with the brain, the organ concerned with mentality, this point as well as many other points on this meridian can be used to treat such mental diseases as manic depression and epilepsy. For others, refer to Cuanzhu (BL 2) and Meichong (BL 3).

【Method】 Puncture subcutaneously 0.3-0.5 cun. Moxibustion is applicable.

【Acupoint Prescription】 Manic-depressive psychosis: Luoque (BL 8), Tinghui (GB 2), Shenzhu (DU 12). (*Thousand Golden Prescriptions*)

【Regional Anatomy】 Skin-subcutaneous tissue-epicranial aponeurosis. In the superficial layer, there are the greater occipital nerve and the occipital artery and vein. In the deep layer, there are the subaponeurotic loose connective tissue and the pericranium.

BL 9 Yuzhen (玉枕)
(Jade Occiput)

【Source】 *A-B Classic of Acupuncture and Moxibustion*
【Name Explanation】 Yu (玉), jade; Zhen (枕), pillow. The antient name of the occipital bone is Yuzhengu (jade pillow bone). This point is on it.
【Location】 On the head, 2.5 cun directly above the midpoint of the posterior hairline and 1.3 cun lateral to the midline, in the depression at the level of the upper border of the external occipital protuberance. (See Fig. 11-29)
【Localization】 Sit with the head straight or bowed, first locate Naohu (DU 17) which is located in the upper margin of the external occipital protuberance. This point is located 1.3 cun lateral to it.
【Indications】
  1) Diseases of Head and Sense Organs: Headache, myopia, opthalamalgia, stuffy nose.

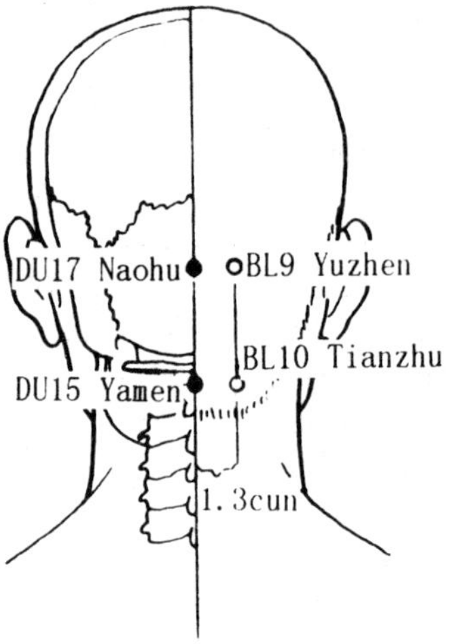

Fig. 11-29

  2) Other Diseases: Aversion to cold and wind, vomiting.
【Mechanism of Action】 Refer to Meichong (BL 3) and Tianzhu (BL 10).
【Method】 Puncture subcutaneously 0.3-0.5 cun. Moxibustion is applicable.
【Acupoint Prescriptions】
  1) Febrile disease (with no sweating and aversion to cold): Yuzhen (BL 9), Dazhu (BL 11), Ganshu (BL 18), Xinshu (BL 15), Geshu (BL 17) and Taodao (DU 13). (*Thousand Golden Prescriptions*)
  2) Stuffy nose: Yuzhen (BL 9), Baihui (DU 20), Mingtang (EX), Taiyang (EX-HN 5) and Linqi (GB 15). (*Experience on Acupuncture and Moxibustion Therapy*)
  3) Neck pain: Yuzhen (BL 9), Wanggu (GB 12). (*ibid*)
  4) Exogenous febrile disease with no sweat and aversion to cold: Yuzhen (BL 9), Ganshu (BL 18), Geshu (BL 17), Taodao (DU 13). (*Essentials of Acupuncture and Moxibustion*)
【Regional Anatomy】 Skin-subcutaneous tissue-epicranal aponeurosis. In the superficial layer, there are the greater occipital nerve and the occipital artery and vein. In the deep layer, there are the subaponeurotic loose connective tissue and the pericranium.

BL 10 Tianzhu (天柱)
(Celestial Pillar)

【Source】 *Miraculous Pivot*
【Name Explanation】 Tian (天), heaven; Zhu (柱), pillar. Upper is considered to be heaven. The cervical spine was called Zhugu (Pillar bone) in ancient times; the point is lateral to it.
【Location】 On the neck, in the depression of the lateral border of the trapezius muscle 1.3 cun lateral to the midpoint of the posterior hairline. (See Fig. 11-29)
【Localization】 In sitting position with the head bowed slightly forward, first locate Yemen (DU 15). This point is located 1.3 cun lateral to it, at the lateral side of the trapezius muscle.

【Indications】
1) Diseases of Head and Sense Organs: Headache, stiffness of the nape and the neck, vertigo, stuffy nose, anosmia, sore throat, conjunctival congestion.
2) Other Diseases: Torticollis and pain in shoulder and back.

【Mechanism of Action】
1) The nape of the neck is the place where the Bladder Meridian of Foot Taiyang branches off as it distributes on the back. The Foot Taiyang Meridian dominates muscular diseases, thus, it is useful for stiffness and pain of the neck, torticollis, occipital headache and lumbago. This point can be used to expell pathogenic wind from the body surface and dredge the meridians and collaterals.

2) The Foot Taiyang Meridian dominates the superficial and is regarded as the fence of the body. It is often the first meridian to be affected by exogenous factors, thus, this point can effectively used for headache and sore throat in exogenous diseases. Puncturing perpedicularly 1 cun and retaining the needle for 20-30 minutes, good results can be gained in acute tonsillitis and pharyngitis.

【Method】 Puncture perpendicularly 0.4-0.6 cun. Moxibustion is applicable.

【Acupoint Prescriptions】
1) Febrile disease without sweating: Tianzhu (BL 10), Fengchi (GB 20), Shangyang (LI 1), Guanchong (SJ 1), Yemen (SJ 2). (*A-B Classic on Acupuncture and Moxibustion*)

2) Vertigo, blurred vision, proptosis of the eyes: Tianzhu (BL 10), Taodao (DU 13), Kunlun (BL 60) (*Thousand Golden Prescriptions*)

3) Headache: Tianzhu (BL 10), Taodao (DU 13), Dazhu (BL 11), Kongzui (LU 6), Houxi (SI 3). (*ibid*)

4) Neck rigidity: Tianzhu (BL 10), Qiangjian (DU 18). (*Chinese Acupuncture and Moxibustion*)

5) Gastroptosis: Tianzhu (BL 10), Dazhu (BL 11), Geshu (BL 17), Ganshu (BL 18), Sanjiaoshu (BL 22), Chengman (ST 20), Liangmen (ST 21) (administered once a day with warming needle, moxa cones may be added). (*ibid*)

6) Thyroid enlargement: Tianzhu (BL 10), Fengmen (BL 12), Lianquan (RN 23), Renying (ST 9), Yaoyangguan (DU 3), Daimai (GB 26), Shenzhu (DU 12) (punctured moderately.) (*ibid*)

7) Headache: Tianzhu (BL 10), Fengchi (GB 20), Jianjing (GB 21), Qiangjian (DU 18), Dazhu (DU 14), Baihui (DU 20), Fengfu (DU 16), Touwei (ST 8), Tongziliao (GB 1), Taiyang (EX-HN 5). (*New Acupuncture and Moxibustion*)

8) Exophthalmus: Tianzhu (BL 10), Fengchi (GB 20), Dazhu (BL 11), Dazhui (DU 14), Shenzhu (DU 12), Tiantu (RN 22), Shuitu (ST 10), Renying (ST 9), Lianquan (RN 23), Zhongzhu (KI 15), Daimai (GB 26), Wailing (ST 26), Tongziliao (GB 1), Sibai (ST 2). (*ibid*)

9) Eclampsia (during the period of attack): Tianzhu (BL 10), Fengfu (DU 16), Fengchi (GB 20), Shuigou (DU 26). (*ibid*)

【Regional Anatomy】 Skin-subcutaneous tissue-trapezius muscle-medial border of splenius muscle of the head-semispinal muscle of the head. In the superficial layer, there are the medial branches of the posterior branches of the 3rd cervical nerve and the subcutaneous vein. In the deep layer, there is the greater occipital nerve.

【Remark】 By means of stimulating the ulnar nerve with surface electrode to induce hypothenar activity, observation was made on the myoelectric amplitude of the patients who were in the convalescence stage of cerebral thrombosis. The result showed that puncturing Futu (LI 18) and Tianzhu (BL 10) on the affected side for 5 minutes could increase the myoelectric amplitude ($P < 0.05$) and this state lasted for 45 minutes.

BL 11   Dazhu (大杼)
(Great Axle)

【Source】 *Miraculous Pivot*

【Name Explanation】 Da (大), large; Zhu (杼), shuttle. The first thoracic vertebra is bigger than the others; the spinous process is like a shuttle, and the point is lateral to it.

【Classification】 Influential Point of Bones. Crossing Point of the Hand- and Foot-Taiyang Meridians.

【Location】 On the back, below the spinous process of the 1st thoracic vertebra, 1.5 cun lateral to the posterior midline. (See Fig. 11-30)

【Localization】 In sitting position with the head bowed, locate the point below the spinous process of the 1st thoracic vertebrae, about 1.5 cun lateral to Taodao (DU 13).

【Indications】

1) Diseases along the Course of Meridian: Scapular pain, pain and stiffness in the neck, pain in the back and waist, pain of the knees with inability to flex.

2) Diseases of the Head and Sense Organs: Splitting headache, dizziness, inflammation of the throat.

3) Respiratory Diseases: Cough, asthma, exogenous febrile disease without sweating.

4) Mental Diseases: Oppressive feeling in the chest, epilepsy, stroke.

【Mechanism of Action】 Refer to Tianzhu (BL 10) and Luoque (BL 8).

【Method】 Puncture obliquely 0.5 cun. Moxibustion is applicable.

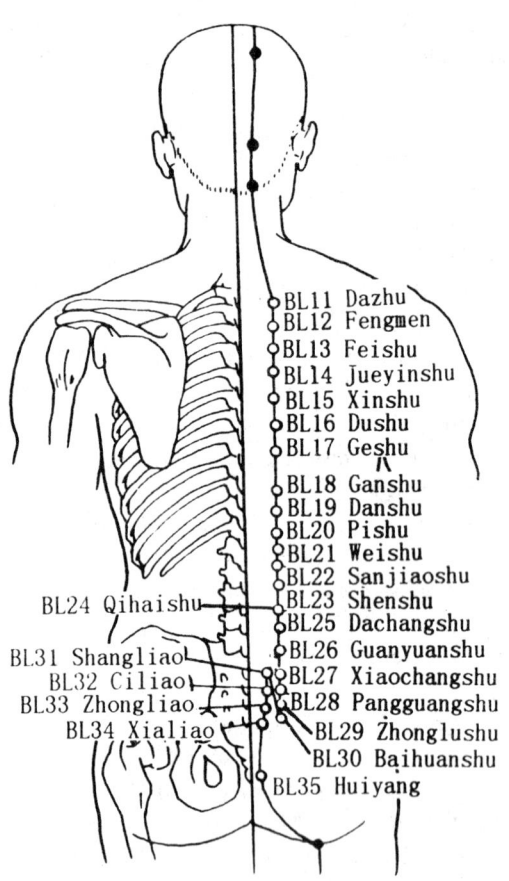

Fig. 11-30

【Acupoint Prescriptions】

1) Febrile disease (feeling of heat in the chest): Dazhu (BL 11), Zhongfu (LU 1), Quepen (ST 12), Fengmen (BL 12). (*Plain Questions*)

2) Restlessness: Dazhu (BL 11), Xinshu (BL 15). (*Thousand Golden Prescriptions*)

3) Bronchitis: Dazhu (BL 11), Feishu (BL 13), Tiantu (RN 22), Chize (LU 5), Waiguan (SJ 5), Jingqu (LU 8), Sanyinjiao (SP 6) (puncture daily) (*Chinese Acupuncture and Moxibustion*)

4) Wind arthralgia, flaccidity with cold limbs: Dazhu (BL 11), Ququan (LR 8). (*A Handbook of Prescriptions for Emergencies*)

5) Hernia: Dazhu (BL 11), Changqiang (DU 1). (*Songs of Xihong*)

【Regional Anatomy】 Skin-subcutaneous tissue-trapezius muscle-rhomboid muscle-superior posterior seratus muscle-splenius muscle of the neck-erector spinal muscle. In the superficial layer, there are the medial cutaneous branches of the posterior branches of the 1st and 2nd thoracic nerves and the medial cutaneous branches of the accompanying posterior intercostal arteries and veins. In the deep layer, there are the muscular branches of the posterior branches of the 1st and 2nd thoracic nerves and the branches of the dorsal branches of the related posterior intercostal arteries and veins.

【Remark】 Acupuncture or electric-acupuncture on this point can regulate pulmonary function and increase unilateral pulmonary ventilation volume during operations of the chest under acupuncture anesthesia. Experiments have shown that puncturing this point is related to calcium metabolism. For example, puncturing this point with Feiyang (BL 58), Zusanli (ST 36) and retaining the needles for 7 minutes can make the calcium content in the blood increase by 1 mg%; retained for 15 minutes can increase it by 3 mg%. However, if retaining the needle was further prolonged, no further corresponding changes of the calcium in the blood occurre.

BL 12　Fengmen (风门)
(Windy Gate)

【Source】 *A-B Classic of Acupuncture and Moxibustion*
【Name Explanation】 Feng (风), pathogenic wind; Men (门), door. The point is located where it is easily invaded by pathogenic wind and so is useful in treating diseases caused by pathogenic wind. This point is therefore considered as the door of pathogenic wind.
【Classification】 Crossing Point of the Foot Taiyang and Du Meridians.
【Location】 On the back, below the spinous process of the 2nd thoracic vertebra, 1.5 cun lateral to the posterior midline. (See Fig. 11-30)
【Localization】 In sitting position with the head bowed, locate the point below the spinous process of the 2nd thoracic vertebrae, about 1.5 cun lateral to the posterior midline.
【Indications】
　　1) Respiratory Diseases: Cough due to attack by pathogenic cold factors, asthma, stuffy nose, abundant discharge from the nose, fever, headache, neck stiffness and various febrile diseases.
　　2) Mental Diseases: Windstroke, unconsciousness, epilepsy, convulsion.
　　3) Other Diseases: Arthralgia-syndrome, carbuncle, cellulitis, urticaria, dizziness.
【Mechanism of Action】
　　1) This point is also named Refu which means that this place is the door for pathogenic wind, thus, it can be used to treat aversion to cold, fever, headache, cough and asthma which are caused by pathogenic factors and also arthralgia and urticaria caused by pathogenic wind.
　　2) Pathogenic wind is the main cause of various diseases, and windstroke, and epilepsy are both related to it. The Bladder Meridian of Foot Taiyang is also connected to the brain which is the organ concerned with mental function. The function of this point is to expel wind, thus, it is often used to treat stroke and epilepsy.
【Method】 Puncture obliquely 0.5 cun. Moxibustion is applicable.
【Acupoint Prescriptions】
　　1) Sneezing: Fengmen (BL 12) and Wuchu (BL 5). (*Thousand Golden Prescriptions*)
　　2) Pain in the shoulder and back: Fengmen (BL 12), Jianjing (GB 21), Zhongzhu (SJ 3), Zhigou (SJ 6), Houxi (SI 3), Wangu (GB 12), Weizhong (BL 40). (*Great Compendium of Acupuncture and Moxibustion*)
　　3) Febrile disease after the fever subsides: Fengmen (BL 12), Hegu (LI 4), Xingjian (LR 2), Juegu (GB 34). (*ibid*)
　　4) Intercostal neuralgia: Fengmen (BL 12), Feishu (BL 13), Jueyinshu (BL 14), Xinshu (BL 15), Geshu (BL 17), Ganshu (BL 18), Danshu (BL 19), Yuzhong (KI 26),

Shencang (KI 25), Lingxu (KI 24), Bulang (KI 22). (*New Acupuncture and Moxibustion*)

【Regional Anatomy】 Skin-subcutaneous tissue-trapezius muscle-rhomboid muscle-superior posterior seratus muscle-splenius muscle of the neck-erector spinae muscle. In the superficial layer, there are the medial cutaneous branches of the posterior branches of the 2nd and 3rd thoracic nerves and the medial cutaneous branches of the dorsal branches of the accompanying posterior intercostal arteries and veins. In the deep layer, there are the muscular branches of the posterior branches of the 2nd and 3rd thoracic nerves and the branches of the dorsal branches of the related posterior intercostal arteries and veins.

【Remark】 Puncturing this point can regulate pulmonary ventilation, but the effect is relatively slow. It does not occur after until a week of daily needling. However, if the effect is obtained, it can last for a peroid, even after the needling has been ended.

BL 13 Feishu (肺俞)
(Lung Shu)

【Source】 *Miraculous Pivot*
【Name Explanation】 Fei (肺), lung; Shu (俞), point. This point is where the qi of Lung infuses in the back.
【Classification】 Back-Shu point of the Lung.
【Location】 On the back, below the spinous process of the 3rd thoracic vertebra, 1.5 cun lateral to the posterior midline. (See Fig. 11-30)
【Localization】 In sitting position with the head bowed, locate the point below the spinous process of the 3rd thoracic vertebrae, about 1.5 cun lateral to Fengmen (DU 12).
【Indications】
　　1) Respiratory Diseases: Cough, fullness of the chest, abundent expectoration, asthma, consumptive lung disease, high fever, night sweating, hematemesis and inflammation of the throat.
　　2) Digestive Diseases: Epigastralgia, vomiting, diarrhea, hiccup, loss of appetite, involuntary drooling, dysentery and infantile malnutrition.
　　3) Mental Diseases: Manic-depression, epilepsy and clonic convulsion.
　　4) Other Diseases: Cutaneous pruritis, urticaria, deafness, diabetes, jaundice, goiter, pain in the back and loin, kyphosis in children.
【Mechanism of Action】
　　1) This point lies in the area of the lung and is the place where lung-qi converges, so it can be used to treat lung diseases caused by internal and external evils. The lung is in charge of skin, thus, various skin diseases can be treated by treating the lung.
　　2) The Lung Meridian originates in the gastric cavity in the middle-jiao, so it can be used to treat diseases of the digestive system, especially the cases complicated with lung diseases.
　　3) Diabetes is divided into three types involving upper, middle or lower Jiao. Diabetes involving the upper Jiao is mainly due to deficiency of lung yin, so this point is often used to treat it.
【Method】 Puncture obliquely 0.5 cun. Moxibustion is applicable.
【Acupoint Prescriptions】
　　1) Lung-distension: Feishu (BL 13) and for Taiyuan (LU 9). (*A-B Classic on Acupuncture and Moxibustion*)
　　2) Night sweating, alternating chills and fever, aversion to cold: Feishu (BL 13), Yindu (KI 19). (*Experience on Acupuncture and Moxibustion Therapy*)

3) Kyphosis in children: Feishu (BL 13), Xinshu (BL 15), Geshu (BL 17) (administering moxibustion respectively with three wheat-sized ignited moxa cones on them). (*The Yellow Emperor's Mingtang Classic on Moxibustion*)

4) Cough due to obstruction of lung qi: Feishu (BL 13), Danzhong (RN 17), Zhigou (SJ 6), Daling (PC 7). (*Great Compendium of Acupuncture and Moxibustion*)

5) Whooping cough: Feishu (BL 13), Lieque (LU 7) (punctured daily) (*Science of Acupuncture and Moxibustion*)

6) Bronchiectasis: Feishu (BL 13), Dushu (BL 16), Pishu (BL 20), Fenglong (ST 40), Zhongwan (RN 12), Qihai (RN 6), Zhusanli (ST 36). (*Chinese Acupuncture and Moxibustion*)

7) Infiltrative pulmonary tuberculosis: main points: Feishu (BL 13), Gaohuang (BL 38) (moxibustion with 3 to 5 cones twice a week, three months constituting one course). (*Abstract of Clinical Experience on Acupuncture and Moxibustion*)

8) Continuous cough: Feishu (BL 13), Tiantu (RN 22). (*Songs of Hundreds of Symptoms*)

9) Cough: Feishu (BL 13), Fengmen (BL 12). (*Guide to Acupuncture*)

[Regional Anatomy] Skin-subcutaneous tissue-trapezius muscle-rhomboid muscle-superior posterior seratus muscle-erector spinal muscle.

In the superficial layer, there are the medial cutaneous branches of the posterior branches of the 3rd and 4th thoracic nerves and the medial cutaneous branches of the dorsal branches of the accompanying posterior intercostal arteries and veins. In the deep layer, there are the muscular branches of the posterior branches of the 3rd and 4th thoracic nerves and the branches or tributaries of the dorsal branches of the related posterior intercostal arteries and veins.

BL 14　Jueyinshu（厥阴俞）
（Jueyin Shu）

[Source] *Thousand Golden Prescriptions*
[Name Explanation] Jueyin（厥阴）, the end of the two Yin meridian, here refers to the pericardium; Shu（俞）, point. This point is where the qi of the pericardium infuses in the back.
[Classification] Back-Shu point of the Pericardium.
[Location] On the back, below the spinous process of the 4th thoracic vertebra, 1.5 cun lateral to the posterior midline. (See Fig. 11-30)
[Localization] In sitting with the head bowed, locate the point below the spinous process of the 4th thoracic vertebrae, about 1.5 cun lateral to the posterior midline.
[Indications]

1) Cardiovascular Diseases: Cardialgia, palpitation, chest pain radiating to the back, fullness and oppressive feeling in the chest.

2) Respiratory Diseases: Cough, asthma.

3) Digestive Diseases: Gastralgia, vomiting.

4) Other Diseases: Toothache, costalgia.

[Mechanism of Action]

1) This point is the Back-Shu point of pericardium, thus, it can be used to treat diseases of the cardiovascular system. Flaring up of heart-fire may cause toothache, so it is often used to treat toothache.

2) This point lies in the area of the lung. Although it is not a lung point, it can be used to treat lung diseases. Since the Lung Meridian originates in the middle-jiao, it can be used to treat diseases of the digestive system as well as lung diseases.

3) The costal region is adjacent to the back. So it can be used to treat pain in the hypochondrium.
【Method】 Puncture obliquely 0.5 cun. Moxibustion is applicable.
【Acupoint Prescriptions】
   1) Cardiolgia: Jueyinshu (BL 14), Shenmen (HT 7), Toulinqi (GB 15). (*Experience on Acupuncture and Moxibustion Therapy*)
   2) Rheumatic heart diseases: Jueyinshu (BL 14), Jianshi (PC 5), Sanyinjiao (SP 6). (*Abstract of Clinical Experience on Acupuncture and Moxibustion*)
【Regional Anatomy】 Skin-subcutaneous tissue-trapezius muscle-rhomboid muscle-erector spinal muscle. In the superficial layer, there are the medial cutaneous branches of the posterior branches of the 4th and 5th thoracic nerves and the medial cutaneous branches of the dorsal branches of the accompanying posterior intercostal arteries and veins. In the deep layer, there are the muscular branches of the posterior branches of the 4th and 5th thoracic nerves and the branches or tributaries of the dorsal branches of the related posterior intercostal arteries and veins.
【Remark】 Puncturing this point can inhibit the formation of coronary atherosclerosis.

BL 15 Xinshu (心俞)
(Heart Shu)

【Source】 *Miraculous Pivot*
【Name Explanation】 Xin (心), heart; Shu (俞), point. This point is where the qi of Heart infuses in the back.
【Classification】 Back-Shu point of the Heart.
【Location】 On the back, below the spinous process of the 5th thoracic vertebra, 1.5 cun lateral to the posterior midline. (See Fig. 11-30)
【Localization】 Locate the point below the spinous process of the 5th thoracic veratebrae, 1.5 cun lateral to the posterior midline.
【Indications】
   1) Cardiovascular Diseases: Cardiolgia, palpitation, backache due to pain in the chest, fullness and oppression feeling in the chest.
   2) Respiratory Diseases: Cough, asthma, hemoptysis.
   3) Digestive Diseases: Vomiting, lack of appetite.
   4) Mental Diseases: Manic-depressive psychosis, epilepsy, schizophrenia, palpitation due to fright, insomnia, amnesia.
   5) Other Diseases: Stroke, hemiplegia, nocturnal emission, white and turbid urine, jaundice, pain in the shoulders and back.
【Mechanism of Action】
   1) This point is one of the back-shu points closely related to the heart, and the place where heart-qi converges. Since the heart is in charge of blood circulation and controls mental activities, it can be used to treat cardiovascular diseases and mental illnesses.
   2) This point lies in the area of the lungs, thus, it can be used to treat lung diseases.
   3) This point lies near the area of the esophagus, so when diseases of the digestive system such as vomiting and loss of appetite are complicated with lung diseases or heart diseases, it is advisable to select this point. In the case caused by dysphagia, this point has the function to clear up the local disorder of qi, promote the circulation of blood and dredge the meridian.
   4) For the symptoms of seminal emission and cloudy urine due to disharmony between the heart and kidney and overabundance of heart-fire, this point is selected to clear heart-fire.
【Method】 Puncture obliquely 0.5 cun. Moxibustion is applicable.

【Acupoint Prescriptions】
  1) Distension related to the heart: Xinshu (BL 15), Lieque (Lu 7). (*A-B Classic on Acupuncture and Moxibustion*)
  2) Trance due to grief: Xinshu (BL 15), Tianjing (SJ 7), Shendao (DU 11). (*Experience on Acupuncture and Moxibustion Therapy*)
  3) Weeping due to overjoy or sorrow: Xinshu (BL 15), Shenmen (HT 7), Jiexi (ST 41), Daling (PC 7). (*ibid*)
  4) Nocturnal emission, cloudy urine: Xinshu (BL 15), Shenshu (BL 23), Guanyuan (RN 4), Sanyinjiao (SP 6). (*Great Compendium of Acupuncture and Moxibustion*)
  5) Seminal emission: Xinshu (BL 15), Shenshu (BL 23), Yaoyangguan (DU 3), Guanyuan (RN 4), Huiyin (RN 1), Sanyinjiao (SP 6) (punctured once a day or every other day). (*Chinese Acupuncture and Moxibustion*)
  6) Arrhythmia: Xinshu (BL 15), Jueyinshu (BL 14), Shenzhu (DU 12), Shendao (DU 11), Zhiyang (DU 9). (*Abstract of Clinical Experience on Acupuncture and Moxibustion*)
  7) Rheumatic heart disease: Xinshu (BL 15), Neiguan (PC 6), Zusanli (ST 36). (*ibid*)
  8) Nocturnal emission: Xinshu (BL 15), Shenshu (BL 23). (*Songs of Jade Dragon*)

【Regional Anatomy】 Skin-subcutaneous tissue-trapezius muscle-inferior border of the rhomboid muscle-erector spinal muscle. In the superficial layer, there are the medial cutaneous branches of the posterior branches of the 5th and 6th thoracic nerves and the medial cutaneous branches of the dorsal branches of the accompanying arteries and veins. In the deep layer, there are the muscular branches of the posterior branches of the 5th and 6th thoracic nerves and the branches or tributaries of the dorsal branches of the related posterior intercostal arteries and veins.

【Remark】 Clinical observation has shown that puncturing this point could treat atrial fibrillation which indicats that it can regulate heart rate. Needling this point and Danzhong (RN 17) can substantially increase the contraction amplitude of the left ventricle wall and cardiac output, strengthen the myocardium contraction. Experimental observation with electrocardiogram showed that puncturing this point can cause all precordial leading to change, especially in patients with heart disease. By observing EKG, it was found that needling this point and Shimen (RN 5) might prolong the P-P interval, narrow the QRS complex, shorten the Q-T interval and elevate and widen the T-wave. It was reported that after needling Xinshu (BL 15), Feishu (BL 13) and Jueyinshu (BL 14) for 12 weeks, there were significantly fewer coronary atherosclerotic lesions than that in the control group. The atherosclerosis lesions occuring in the arterioles of both the panmyocardium and the myocardium of the left ventricle were fewer than those of the control group.

Additional information has showen that needling this point could relieve bronchospasm, stop attacks of bronchial asthma or ease the symptoms. It can also regulate heart rate.

BL 16 Dushu (督俞)
(Du Shu)

【Source】 *The Peaceful Holy Benevolent Prescriptions*
【Name Explanation】 Du (督), governor vessel meridian; Shu (俞), point. This point is where the qi of Du Meridian infuses in the back.
【Location】 On the back, below the spinous process of the 6th thoracic vertebra, 1.5 cun lateral to the posterior midline. (See Fig. 11-30)
【Localization】 Locate the point below the spinous process of the 6th thoracic vertebrae, about

1.5 cun lateral to Lingtai (DU 10).

【Indications】
　　1) Digestive Diseases: Epigastric and abdominal pain, distension of the abdomen, borborygmus, hiccup.
　　2) Cardiovascular Diseases: Percardial pain, palpitation.
　　3) Other Diseases: Fever and aversion to cold.

【Mechanism of Action】 As this point lies in the area of the heart and lungs and near the epigastrium, it can be used to treat various diseases of the heart, lungs, spleen and stomach.

【Method】 Puncture obliquely 0.5 cun. Moxibustion is applicable.

【Regional Anatomy】 Skin-subcutaneous tissue-trapezius muscle-erector spinal muscle. In the superficial layer, there are the medial cutaneous branches of the posterior branches of the 6th and 7th thoracic nerves and the medial cutaneous branches of the dorsal branches of the accompanying arteries and veins. In the deep layer, there are the muscular branches of the posterior branches of the 6th and 7th thoracic nerves and the branches or tributaries of the dorsal branches of the related posterior intercostal arteries and veins.

BL 17　Geshu（膈俞）
（Diaphragm Shu）

【Source】 *Miraculous Pivot*

【Name Explanation】 Ge（膈）, diaphragm; Shu（俞）, point. This point is where the qi of the diaphragm infuses in the back.

【Classification】 Influential Point of the Blood.

【Location】 On the back, below the spinous process of the 7th thoracic vertebra, 1.5 cun lateral to the posterior midline. (See Fig. 11-30)

【Localization】 In prone position, locate the point below the spinous process of the 7th thoracic vertebrae, about 1.5 cun lateral to Zhiyang (DU 9), at the same level of the inferior angle of the scapula.

【Indications】
　　1) Digestive Diseases: Distending pain over the epigastrium, hiccups, vomiting, hematemesis, hematochezia, loss of appetite, distension of the abdomen, solid mass in the abdomen, jaundice, dysphagia.
　　2) Respiratory Diseases: Asthma, cough, hemoptysis, inflammation of the throat, high fever, spontaneous sweating, night sweating.
　　3) Cardiovascular Diseases: Precardial pain, sensation of fullness in the chest and hypochondriac pain.
　　4) Other Diseases: Anemia, urticaria, pruritus, metrorrhagia, pantalgia, febrile disease without sweating, lassitude feeling of the limbs.

【Mechanism of Action】
　　1) This point is the influential point of blood, so it can be used to treat various bleeding disorders such as anemia and leukopenia. There is a saying in TCM that "wind syndrome should be treated via blood, and by normalizing blood circulation the pathogenic wind will be eliminated". Thus, it is a common point used for urticaria and other skin diseases.
　　2) This point is located in the diaphragm between the heart and lungs which are located in the upper-jiao and the spleen and stomach which are in the lower-jiao, so it can be used to treat hiccup and many disorders of the heart, lungs, spleen and stomach.

【Method】 Puncture obliquely 0.5 cun. Moxibustion is applicable.

【Acupoint Prescriptions】

1) Diseases of the Head and Sense Organs: Geshu (BL 17), Ganshu (BL 18). (*A-B Classic on Acupuncture and Moxibustion*)

2) Febrile disease: Geshu (BL 17), Zhongfu (LU 1) which are mainly for alternating chills and fever, muscular and bone pain, inability to lie flat due to dyspnea, chest distress. (*Thousand Golden Prescriptions*)

3) Consumptive diseases: Geshu (BL 17), Mingmen (DU 4), Taixi (KI 3). (*Experience on Acupuncture and Moxibustion Therapy*)

4) Chronic fluid-retention: Geshu (BL 17), Tonggu (KI 20). (*Great Compendium of Acupuncture and Moxibustion*)

5) Acute peritonitis: Geshu (BL 17), Xiaochangshu (BL 27), Sanyinjiao (SP 6), Xingjian (LR 2), Yinlian (LR 11). (*New Acupuncture and Moxibustion*)

6) Anemia: Geshu (BL 17), Pishu (BL 20), Sanjiaoshu (BL 22), Dachangshu (BL 25), Guanyuan (RN 4), Zusanli (ST 36) (small moxa cones on all points 5 times daily). (*Chinese Acupuncture and Moxibustion*)

7) Leukemia: Geshu (BL 17), Ganshu (BL 18), Pishu (BL 20), Sanjiaoshu (BL 22), Mingmen (DU 4), Guanyuan (RN 4), Zusanli (ST 36), (moxibustion with medicine-contained in rolls or cones every or every other day). (*ibid*)

8) Epigastralgia: Geshu (BL 17), Pishu (BL 20), Weishu (BL 21), Neiguan (PC 6), Yangfu (GB 38), Shangqiu (SP 5) (all with moxibustion). (*Science of Acupuncture and Moxibustion*)

9) Infiltrative pulmonary tuberculosis: The main points are Geshu (BL 17), Danshu (BL 19) (moxibustion with 3 to 5 moxa cones for each point twice a week, three months constituting one course). (*Abstract of Clinical Experience on Acupuncture and Moxibustion*)

[Regional Anatomy] Skin-subcutaneous tissue-trapezius muscle-latissimus muscle of the back-erector spinal muscle.

In the superficial layer, there are the medial cutaneous branches of the posterior branches of the 7th and 8th thoracic nerves and the medial cutaneous branches of the dorsal branches of the accompanying arteries and veins. In the deep layer, there are the muscular branches of the posterior branches of the 7th and 8th thoracic nerves and the branches or tributaries of the dorsal branches of the related posterior intercostal arteries and veins.

[Remark] Puncturing this point can regulate pulmonary function. When there is unilateral respiratory dysfunction due to exudative pleurisy or lobectomy of the lung, puncturing this point can strengthen the restricted respiratory function of the affected side, and decrease the increased respiratory function of the healthy side, thus, keep the normal respiration in balance.

Needling this point can also decrease blood pressure. It has a good effect on treating hypertension in the primary and secondary stages.

Puncturing this point has a regulating action on blood sugar. Needling this point can cause of blood sugar levels to decrease after eating too much sugar or cause it to increase if the person's blood sugur is too low. In addition, it has some curative effect on diabetes, esp. for type 2 diabetic patients who maintain good health without relying on insulin; For the patients who mainly depend on insulin, it has a poor therapeutic effect.

BL 18 Ganshu (肝俞)
(Liver Shu)

[Source] *Miraculous Pivot*

[Name Explanation] Gan (肝), liver; Shu (俞), point. This point is where the qi of Liver infuses in the back.

【Classification】 Back-Shu point of the Liver.
【Location】 On the back, below the spinous process of the 9th thoracic vertebra, 1.5 cun lateral to the posterior midline. (See Fig. 11-30)
【Localization】 In prone position, locate the point below the spinous process of the 9th thoracic vertebrae, about 1.5 cun lateral to Jinsuo (DU 8).
【Indications】
　　1) Diseases along the Course of the Meridian: Hypochondriac pain.
　　2) Diseases of Head and Sense Organs: Headache, dizziness, conjunctival congestion, blurred vision, night blindness, optic atrophy, nebula, pterygium and epiphora.
　　3) Digestive Diseases: Dysfunctions of the liver, jaundice, epigastralgia, anorexia, abdominal pain, diarrhea.
　　4) Mental Diseases: Epilepsy, mania.
　　5) Other Diseases: Windstroke, insufficient lactation, flaccidity-syndrome, pain along the spinal column.
【Mechanism of Action】 This point is one of the back-shu points related closely with the liver and the place where the liver-qi converges, so it can be used to treat acute and chronic hepatitis and cholecystitis. Since the Liver Meridian distributes through the hypochondriac region, and the Bladder Meridian of Foot Taiyang runs along the lumbar spine, it can be used to treat hypochondriac and spinal pain. The eye is the window of the liver and the Liver Meridian runs upwards to the vertex, thus, disorders of the face and head can be treated by puncturing this point. Stroke is mostly caused by hyperactivity of yang and deficiency of yin, so this point is commonly used to treat and prevent stroke. The liver and gallbladder have a close relation with the spleen and stomach and stagnation of liver-qi is the main cause of diseases of the spleen and stomach. Thus, for diseases of the spleen and stomach due to non-cooperation of the liver and gallbladder, this point is often used to soothe the liver and regulate the circulation of qi.
【Method】 Puncture obliquely 0.5 cun. Moxibustion is applicable.
【Acupoint Prescriptions】
　　1) Pain in the lower abdomen: Ganshu (BL 18), Xiaochangshu (BL 27), Ligou (LR 5), Zhaohai (KI 3), Xialian (LR 8), Qiuxu (GB 40), Zhongdu (LR 6). (*Experience on Acupuncture and Moxibustion Therapy*)
　　2) Spitting of blood: Ganshu (BL 18), Chengman (ST 20), Jianzhongshu (SI 15). (*ibid*)
　　3) Cataract: Ganshu (BL 18), Jiexi (ST 41). (*ibid*)
　　4) Optic atrophy: Ganshu (BL 18), Shangyang (LI 1). (*Great Compendium of Acupuncture and Moxibustion*)
　　5) Abdominal distention: Ganshu (BL 18), Pishu (BL 20), Sanjiaoshu (BL 22), Shuifen (RN 9), Gongsun (SP 4), Dadun (LR 1) (moxibustion is applicable). (*Illustrated Supplementary to Systematic Complation of the Intevnal Classic*))
　　6) Liver mass: Ganshu (BL 18), Zhangmen (LR 13), Xingjian (LR 2). (*ibid*)
　　7) Infectious hepatitis: Ganshu (BL 18), Zhiyang (DU 9), Zusanli (ST 36) (For acute cases, 10 days constitutes one course, and for chronic cases, 14 days constitutes one course). (*Acupuncture and Moxibustion*)
　　8) Acute infectious hepatitis: Ganshu (BL 18), Danshu (BL 19), Zusanli (ST 36), Taichong (LR 3) (with complex reduction technique, i. e. manipulating the needle in backward direction along the meridian, inserting the needle slowly once and withdrawing it quickly three times, retaining the needle for 20 to 30 minutes.) (*Abstract of Clinical Experience on Acupuncture and Moxibustion*)
【Regional Anatomy】 Skin-subcutaneous tissue-trapezius muscle-latissimus muscle of the back-inferior posterior serratus muscle-erector spinal muscle.
　　In the superficial layer, there are the cutaneous branches of the posterior branches of the 9th

and 10th thoracic nerves and the medial cutaneous branches of the dorsal branches of the accompanying arteries and veins. In the deep layer, there are the muscular branches of the posterior branches of the 9th and 10th thoracic nerves and the branches or tributaries of the related posterior intercostal arteries and veins.

【Remark】 Puncturing this point can affect the function of the digestive tract. For example, in patients with intestinal dysfunction, puncturing this point can make the function of intestines normal. Needling this point, Pishu (BL 20), Weishu (BL 21), Waiguan (SJ 5) and Zusanli (ST 36), can treat gastric acidity with the total gastric acid and free acid secreted more normally. Puncturing this point can substantially decrease hepatic blood flow. It can also affect the blood constituents. For example, needling this point can improve the symptoms of patients with both purpura due to thrombocytopenia and splenic panhematopenia. In addition, needling Ganshu (BL 18) has a regulating action on blood sugar. It enables the high glucose tolerance curve to go down and the low curve to rise. Ganshu (BL 18) can markedly decrease high cholesterol levels but has no effect on normal cholesterol levels.

BL 19   Danshu (胆俞)
(Gallbladder Shu)

【Source】 *Plain Questions*
【Name Explanation】 Dan (胆), gallbladder; Shu (俞), point. This point is where the qi of the Gallbladder infuses in the back.
【Classification】 Back-Shu point of the Gallbladder.
【Location】 On the back, below the spinous process of the 10th thoracic vertebra, 1.5 cun lateral to the posterior midline. (See Fig. 11-30)
【Localization】 In prone position, locate the point below the spinous process of the 10th thoracic vertebrae, about 1.5 cun lateral to Zhongshu (DU 7).
【Indications】
　　1) Diseases along the Course of the Meridian: Hypochondriac pain, subaxillary swelling.
　　2) Diseases of Head and Sense Organs: Headache, sore throat.
　　3) Digestive Diseases: Jaundice, bitter taste, dry tongue, vomiting, loss of appetite, distension and pain in the stomach and abdomen.
【Mechanism of Action】 The Gallbladder Meridian runs along the costal region and passes through the hypochondriac region. Incoordination between the liver and gallbladder often brings about disorders of the spleen and stomach, thus, this point can be used to treat cholecystitis, cholelithiasis, jaundice, hypochondriac pain and diseases of the digestive system. Upward attack of gallbladder-heat may result in headache and sore throat which can be treated with this point by clearing away the heat and normalizing the function of the gallbladder.
【Method】 Puncture obliquely 0.5 cun. Moxibustion is applicable.
【Acupoint Prescriptions】
　　1) Dry mouth: Danshu (BL 19), Shangyang (LR 1), Xiaochangshu (BL 27). (*Thousand Golden Prescriptions*)
　　2) Infectious hepatitis: Danshu (BL 19), Taichong (LR 3), Yanglingquan (GB 34) (punctured once a day. For acute cases, 10 days constitute one course; for chronic cases, 14 days constitute one course). (*Science of Acupuncture and Moxibustion*)
【Regional Anatomy】 Skin-subcutaneous tissue-trapezius muscle-latissimus muscle of the back-inferior posterior serratus muscle-erector spinal muscle.

　　In the superficial layer, there are the cutaneous branches of the posterior branches of the

10th and 11th thoracic nerves and the medial cutaneous branches of the dorsal branches of the accompanying arteries and veins. In the deep layer, there are the muscular branches of the posterior branches of the 10th and 11th thoracic nerves and the branches or tributaries of the related posterior intercostal arteries and veins.

【Remark】 Puncturing this point in patients with intestinal dysfunction can normalize the intestine function. It also has a regulating action on gastric juice in cases with gastric or duodenal ulcer, and the function to make the total gastric acid and free acid normalize.

Needling this point may enhance both the immulogic function and the phagocytic function of the macrophages.

Puncturing Zusanli (ST 36), Ganshu (BL 18) and Danshu (BL 19) can increase the pituitary-adrenal function.

For chronic hepatitis without jaundice, regardless whether it is of hepatitis A or B, it has a positive therapeutic effect and is a commonly used point to treat this disease.

BL 20　Pishu（脾俞）
(Spleen Shu)

【Source】 *Miraculous Pivot*
【Name Explanation】 Pi（脾）, spleen; Shu（俞）, point. This is where the qi of the spleen infuses in the back.
【Classification】 Back-Shu point of the Spleen.
【Location】 On the back, below the spinous process of the 11th thoracic vertebra, 1.5 cun lateral to the posterior midline. (See Fig. 11-30)
【Localization】 In prone position, locate the point below the spinous process of the 11th thoracic vertebrae, about 1.5 cun lateral to Jizhong (DU 6).
【Indications】

　　1) Digestive Diseases: Stomachache, distension and pain in the abdomen, vomiting, diarrhea, dysentery, jaundice, dysphagia, tympanites, lassitude, drowsiness, polyphagia with emaciated body or loss of appetite, chronic infantile convulsion due to dysfunction of the spleen.

　　2) Respiratory Diseases: Cough, abundant expectoration.

　　3) Other Diseases: Stiffness of the back and loin, distension and feeling of fullness in the chest and hypochondrium, abdominal masses.
【Mechanism of Action】 This point is one of the back-shu points, and is closely related with the spleen and the place where the spleen-qi converges. The spleen has the function of transportation and tranformation of nutrients, nourishing the muscles and the four limbs, so this point can be used to treat various diseases of the spleen and stomach. If the spleen fails to transport and transform the nutrients, it can cause retention of water in the body, abundant expectoration and edema. For these cases, this point is used to invigorate the spleen.
【Method】 Puncture obliquely 0.5 cun. Moxibustion is applicable.
【Acupoint Prescriptions】

　　1) Convulsion due to heat: Pishu (BL 20), Shenshu (BL 23).　(*A-B Classic on Acupuncture and Moxibustion*)

　　2) Polyphagia with emaciated body: Pishu (BL 20), Dachangshu (BL 25). (*Experience on Acupuncture and Moxibustion Therapy*)

　　3) Stiffness of the waist and spine: Pishu (BL 25), Xiaochangshu (BL 27), Pangguangshu (BL 28), Yaoshu (DU 2), Shendao (DU 11), Jizhong (DU 6), Changqiang (DU 1). (*ibid*)

　　4) Infectious hepatitis: Pishu (BL 20), Qimen (LR 14), Tianzhu (BL 10) (punctured

with medium and heavy manipulations once a day. For acute cases, 10 days constitute one course; for chronic cases, 14 days make one course). (*Science of Acupuncture and Moxibustion*)

5) Pulmonary tuberculosis: (deficiency syndrome of the spleen and stomach) Pishu (BL 20), Zhongwan (RN 12), Tianshu (ST 25), Zusanli (ST 36). (*Abstract of Clinical Experience on Acupuncture and Moxibustion*)

6) Indigestion due to hypofunction of the spleen: Pishu (BL 20), Pangguangshu (BL 28). (*Song of Hundreds of Symptoms*)

[Regional Anatomy] Skin-subcutaneous tissue-latissimus muscle of the back-inferior posterior serratus muscle-erector spinal muscle. In the superficial layer, there are the cutaneous branches of the posterior branches of the 11th and 12th thoracic nerves and the medial cutaneous branches of the dorsal branches of accompanying arteries and veins. In the deep layer, there are the muscular branches of the posterior branches of the 11th and 12th thoracic nerves and the branches or tributaries of the related posterior intercostal arteries and veins.

[Remark] Gastric peristalsis in the human body was observed through the method of air-pocket recording. The result indicated that puncturing this point could cause gastric contraction, however, puncturing Quchi (LI 11) could decrease gastric peristalsis.

BL 21   Weishu (胃俞)
(Stomach Shu)

[Source] *A-B Classic of Acupuncture and Moxibustion*
[Name Explanation] Wei (胃), stomach; Shu (俞), point. This is where the qi of Stomach infuses in the back.
[Classification] Back-Shu point of the Stomach.
[Location] On the back, below the spinous process of the 12th thoracic vertebra, 1.5 cun lateral to the posterior midline. (See Fig. 11-30)
[Localization] In prone position, locate the point below the spinous process of the 12th thoracic vertebrae, about 1.5 cun lateral to the posterior midline.
[Indications]
1) Digestive Diseases: Cold feeling in the stomach, vomiting of watery fluid, pain in the epigastrium, regurgitation, vomiting, loss of appetite, dysphagia, polyphagia with emaciated body, vomiting of milk in children, abdominal pain, borborygmus, diarrhea, dysentery, indigestion, infantile malnutrition, convulsion due to dysfunction of the spleen, prolapse of the rectum.
2) Respiratory Diseases: Cough, consumptive disease.
3) Other Diseases: Pain in the chest and hypochondrim, spinal pain, flaccidity-syndrome, amenorrhea, edema, tympanites, abdominal mass.
[Mechanism of Action] This point is the back-shu point of the stomach and at the place where stomach-qi converges. Thus, it can be used to treat various diseases of the spleen and stomach. For more details, see Pishu (BL 20).
[Method] Puncture obliquely 0.5 cun. Moxibustion is applicable.
[Acupoint Prescriptions]
1) Vomiting: Weishu (BL 21), Shenshu (BL 23), Shimen (RN 5), Zhongting (RN 16). (*Experience on Acupuncture and Moxibustion Therapy*)
2) Cold and distension in the stomach, Polyphagia with emaciated body: Weishu (BL 21), Shenshu (BL 23). (*ibid*)
3) Pulmonary tuberculosis: (poor appetite): Moxibustion to Weishu (BL 21), Zusanli

(ST 36) and Zhongwan (RN 12) (*Abstract of Clinical Experience on Acupuncture and Moxibustion*)

【Regional Anatomy】 Skin-subcutaneous tissue-superficial layer of thoracolumbar fascia and aponeurosis of the latissimus muscle of the back-inferior posterior serratus muscle-erector spinal muscle.

In the superficial layer, there are the cutaneous branches of the posterior branches of the 12th thoracic and 1st lumbar nerves and the medial cutaneous branches of the dorsal branches of the accompanying arteries and veins. In the deep layer, there are the muscular branches of the posterior branches of the 12th thoracic and 1st lumbar nerves and the branches or tributaries of the related posterior intercostal arteries and veins.

【Remark】 Acupuncture at this point can regulate gastro-intestinal peristalsis. When gastric peristalsis is weak, puncturing this point can increase it.

BL 22 Sanjiaoshu (三焦俞)
(Triple Warmer Shu)

【Source】 *A-B Classic of Acupuncture and Moxibustion*
【Name Explanation】 Sanjiao (三焦), three regions of the body cavity; Shu (俞), point. This is where the qi of the Sanjiao infuses in the back.
【Classification】 Back-Shu point of the Sanjiao.
【Location】 On the lower back, below the spinous process of the 1st lumbar vertebra, 1.5 cun lateral to the posterior midline. (See Fig. 11-30)
【Localization】 In prone position, locate the point below the spinous process of the 1st lumbar vertebrae, about 1.5 cun lateral to the posterior midline.
【Indications】
1) Digestive Diseases: Abdominal distension, borborygmus, indigestion, vomiting, abdominal pain, diarrhea, dysentery, infantile malnutrition.
2) Urinary Diseases: Dysuria, edema.
3) Other Diseases: Muscular spasm of the shoulder and back, stiffness and pain of spine, headache, dizziness, fever without sweating, jaundice, abdominal mass in women.

【Mechanism of Action】 This point lies in the regional area of the spleen and stomach in the middle-jiao, thus, it is mainly used to treat various diseases of the spleen and stomach. Sanjiao has the function of controlling the fluid metabolism and dredging the water pathway, so edema, dysuria and jaundice are often treated with this point.
【Method】 Puncture obliquely 0.5 cun. Moxibustion is applicable.
【Acupoint Prescriptions】
1) Borborygmus, distension of the abdomen with tendency towards diarrhea: Sanjiaoshu (BL 22), Xiaochangshu (BL 27), Xialiao (BL 34,) Yishe (BL 44), Zhangmen (LR 13). (*Experience on Acupuncture and Moxibustion Therapy*)
2) Cholelithiasis: Sanjiaoshu (BL 22), Shenshu (BL 23), Qihaishu (BL 24), Dachangshu (BL 25), Shangwan (RN 13), Jiuwei (RN 15), Waiguan (SJ 5), Zusanli (ST 36), Right-Zhangmen (LR 13), Right-Jingmen (GB 24). (*New Acupuncture and Moxibustion*)
3) Chronic pyelonephritis: Sanjiaoshu (BL 22), Dushu (BL 16), Ciliao (BL 32) (stimulate mildly, then use moxa cones on Zusanli (ST 36) and Weizhong (BL 40) punctured only). (*Science of Acupuncture and Moxibustion*)

【Regional Anatomy】 Skin-subcutaneous tissue-aponeurosis of latissimus muscle of the back and superficial layer of thoracolumbar fascia-erector spinal muscle. In the superficial layer, there are the cutaneous branches of the posterior branches of the 1st and 2nd lumbar nerves and the medial cutaneous branches of the dorsal branches of the accompanying arteries and veins. In the deep layer, there are the muscular branches of the posterior branches of the 1st and 2nd lumbar nerves and the branches or tributaries of the dorsal branches of the related lumbar arteries and veins.

【Remark】 Shenshu (BL 23), Sanjiaoshu (BL 22), Jingmen (GB 25), Tianshu (ST 25) and Qihai (RN 6) are the main points in treating calculi in the urinary system.

Most of them are also effective for treating urinary calculi and in half of the patients the calculi can be eliminated.

BL 23   Shenshu (肾俞)
(Kidney Shu)

【Source】 *Miraculous Pivot*
【Name Explanation】 Shen (肾), kidney; Shu (俞), point. This is where the qi of kidney infuses in the back.
【Classification】 Back-Shu point of the Kidney.
【Location】 On the lower back, below the spinous process of the 2nd lumbar vertebra, 1.5 cun lateral to the posterior midline. (See Fig. 11-30)
【Localization】 In prone position, first locate Mingmen (DU 4) which is located opposite to the umbilicus. The point is located 1.5 cun lateral to Mingmen (DU 4).
【Indications】
   1) Diseases of Head and Sense Organs: Vertigo, dizziness, deafness, tinnitus, blurred vision, night blindness, aphonia.
   2) Urogenital Diseases: Enuresis, frequent micturition, dysuria, dribbling urination, hematuria, edema, impotence, seminal emission, painful and swollen testis, leukorrhagia, irregular menstruation, dysmenorrhea.
   3) Respiratory Diseases: Cough with shortness of breath, asthma which is exacerbated with movement.
   4) Digestive Diseases: Stomachache, abdominal distension, borborygmus, diarrhea, indigestion.
   5) Mental Diseases: Epilepsy.
   6) Other Diseases: Soreness and pain in lower back and knees, cold sensation in the back, five kinds of strain and seven kinds of impairments, diabetes, pain in the lower abdomen due to fullness and distension in the hypochondrium.
【Mechanism of Action】
   1) This point is the back-shu point of the kidney and the place where kidney-qi converges. The kidney dominates reproduction and controls water metabolism. This point is one of the main points to treat the disorders of the reproductive and urinary systems.
   2) The lung is in charge of respiration and the kidney controls and promotes inspiration, so this point can chiefly be used to treat disorders of the respiratory system caused by failure of the kidney in promoting inspiration.
   3) The lumbar area is the place where the kidney is located, and deficiency of the kidney easily results in lumbago; For this disease, this point is the first choice.
   4) Deficiency of kidney-yang which fails to nourish the spleen may bring about insufficiency of spleen-yang. This point is applicable to the disorders of the digestive system which are caused by yang-insufficiency of both the spleen and the kidney.
【Method】 Puncture perpendicularly 1-1.5 cun. Moxibustion is applicable.
【Acupoint Prescriptions】

1) Lumbago: Shenshu (BL 23), Qihaishu (BL 24) and Zhonglushu (BL 29). (*Experience on Acupuncture and Moxibustion Therapy*)

2) Pudendal pain: Shenshu (BL 23), Zhishi (BL 47), Yingu (KI 10) and Taichong (LR 3). (*ibid*)

3) Severe cardialgia: Shenshu (BL 23), Fuliu (KI 7), Daling (PC 7) and Yunmen (LU 2). (*ibid*)

4) Edema due to various diseases: Shenshu (BL 23) and Weicang (BL 45). (*ibid*)

5) Seminal emission with cloudy urine: Shenshu (BL 23), Guanyuan (RN 4) and Sanyinjiao (SP 6). (*Great Compendium of Acupuncture and Moxibustion*)

6) Tinnitus: Shenshu (BL 23), Zusanli (ST 36) and Hegu (LI 4). (*ibid*)

7) Diabetes: group one: Shenshu (BL 23), Guanyuan (RN 4) and Zusanli (ST 36); group two: Shenshu (BL 23), Shuidao (ST 28), Zhongwan (RN 12) and Sanyinjiao (SP 6) (puncturing heavily once a day with the two groups of points administered alternately, 10 days constituteing one course). (*Science of Acupuncture and Moxibustion*)

8) Infection of urinary tract: Shenshu (BL 23), Zhubin (KI 19), Fuliu (KI 17), Guilai (ST 29), Feiyang (BL 58) and Zhongji (RN 3) (with only two or three points punctured heavily each day). (*ibid*)

9) Acute pyelonephritis: Shenshu (BL 23), Dachangshu (BL 25), Weizhong (BL 40), Xuehai (SP 10), Dazhong (KI 4), Zusanli (ST 36) and Sanyinjiao (SP 6) (with strong stimulation). (*ibid*)

10) Enuresis: Shenshu (BL 23), Guanyuan (RN 4), Zhongji (RN 3) (with moxibustion) and Sanyinjiao (SP 6) (with acupuncture). (*Abstract of Clinical Experience on Acupuncture and Moxibustion*)

11) Male infertility: Shenshu (BL 23), Jinggong (EX), Guanyuan (RN 4), Qihai (RN 5), Zhongji (RN 3), Zusanli (ST 36), Sanyinjiao (SP 6), Xuehai (SP 10). (*ibid*)

12) Ureterolithiasis: Shenshu (BL 23), Kunlun (BL 60), Jiaoxin (KI 18), Fujie (SP 14), Yinjiao (RN 7), Guanyuan (RN 4) and Ashi-points. (*ibid*)

【Regional Anatomy】 Skin-subcutaneous tissue-aponeurosis of latissimus muscle of the back and superficial layer of thoracolumbar fascia-erector spinal muscle. In the superficial layer, there are the cutaneous branches of the posterior branches of the 2nd and 3rd lumbar nerves and the medial cutaneous branches of the dorsal branches of the accompanying arteries and veins. In the deep layer, there are the muscular branches of the posterior branches of the 2nd and 3rd lumbar nerves and the branches or tributaries of the dorsal branches of the related lumbar arteries and veins.

【Remark】 Needling this point can regulate renal function. Puncturing this point and Qihai (RN 6) in patients with nephritis can strongly enhance urinary function, make the phenolsulfonphthalein excretion rate higher, and the protein content in urine decrease. In addition, blood pressure can be reduced and edema alleviated or even removed. Generally these effects may last 2-3 hours, and in some cases can even last several days.

In addition, puncturing this point in patients with intestinal dysfuncion can normalize the intestinal function.

BL 24 Qihaishu (气海俞)
(Energy sea Shu)

【Source】 *The Peaceful Holy Benevolent Prescriptions*

【Name Explanation】 Qihai (气海), sea of primary qi; Shu (俞), point. This point is opposite Qihai (RN 6), where primary qi infuses in the back.

【Location】 On the lower back, below the spinous process of the 3rd lumbar vertebra, 1.5 cun

lateral to the posterior midline. (See Fig. 11-30)
【Localization】 In prone position, first locate Mingmen (DU 4). The point is located one spinous process inferior to it, and then 1.5 cun lateral.
【Indications】
 1) Urogenital Diseases: Irregular menstruation, dysmenorrhea, metrorrhagia and metrostaxis, leukorrhea, seminal emission, impotence, premature ejaculation, cloudy urine, stranguria, dysuria, incontinence of urine.
 2) Anal Diseases: Hemorrhoid and hematochezia.
 3) Other Diseases: Pain along the spinal column, flaccidity and numbness of the lower limbs.
【Mechanism of Action】
 1) This point is at the same level as Qihai (RN 6) of the Ren Meridian. Qihai is the place where the primordial qi converges. The primordial qi originates in the kidney which dominates reproduction and water metabolism. Below this point is the reproductive and urinary systems, thus, this point is one of the commonly-used points for treating diseases of these two systems.
 2) In treating diseases of lower limbs, this point should be punctured deeply to make the needling sensation go to the affected part.
【Method】 Puncture perpendicularly 1-1.5 cun. Moxibustion is applicable.
【Acupoint Prescription】 Vesical calculus: Qihaishu (BL 24), Dachangshu (BL 25), Xiaochangshu (BL 27), Pangguangshu (BL 28), Shangliao (BL 31), Zhongliao (BL 33), Zusanli (ST 36) and Sanyinjiao (SP 6). (*New Acupuncture and Moxibustion*)
【Regional Anatomy】 Skin-subcutaneous tissue-aponeurosis of latissimus muscle of the back and superficial layer of thoracolumbar fascia-erector spinal muscle. In the superficial layer, there are the cutaneous branches of the posterior branches of the 3rd and 4th lumbar nerves and the medial cutaneous branches of the dorsal branches of the accompanying arteries and veins. In the deep layer, there are the muscular branches of the posterior branches of the 3rd and 4th lumbar nerves and the branches or tributaries of the related lumbar arteries and veins.

BL 25 Dachangshu (大肠俞)
(Large Intestine Shu)

【Source】 *A-B Classic of Acupuncture and Moxibustion*
【Name Explanation】 Dachang (大肠), large intestine; Shu (俞), point. This point is where the qi of Large Intestine infuses in the back.
【Classification】 Back-Shu point of the Large Intestine.
【Location】 On the lower back, below the spinous process of the 4th lumbar vertebra, 1.5 cun lateral to the posterior midline. (See Fig. 11-30)
【Localization】 In prone position, first locate the middle part of a line joining both side of the highest point of the iliac crests. This point corresponds with the lower border of the spinous process of the 4th lumar vertebrae (DU 3), then locate the point 1.5 cun lateral to Yaoyangguan (DU 3).
【Indications】
 1) Digestive Diseases: Abdominal pain, severe pain around the umbilicus, abdominal distension, borborygmus, diarrhea, indigestion, constipation, dysentery, periappendicular abscess, polyphagia with emaciated body, prolapse of rectum.
 2) Urogenital Diseases: Enuresis, difficulty in micturition, menorrhagia.
 3) Other Diseases: Pain in the loins and knees, spinal rigidity with difficulty in lying flat.
【Mechanism of Action】

1) This point is the Back-shu point of the large intestine and the place where qi of the large intestine converges, thus, it can be used to treat diarrhea, abdominal pain and other diseases of large intestine.

2) This point lies in the lower Jiao where the organs of the reproductive and urinary systems converge. According to the acupuncture principle that where the point is located, where the indications are, this point can be used to treat diseases of the reproductive and urinary systems.

【Method】 Puncture perpendicularly 1-1.5 cun. Moxibustion is applicable.

【Acupoint Prescriptions】

1) Diarrhea, dyspepsia: Dachangshu (BL 25) and Shenshu (BL 23). (*Experience on Acupuncture and Moxibustion Therapy*)

2) Lack of appetite with desire for drinking: Dachangshu (BL 25) and Zhourong (SP 20). (*ibid*)

3) Cystitis: Dachangshu (BL 25), Pangguangshu (BL 28), Shenshu (BL 23), Chengfu (BL 50), Yinmen (BL 51), Huiyang (BL 35), Guanyuan (RN 4), Daheng (SP 15) and Sanyinjiao (SP 6). (*New Acupuncture and Moxibustion*)

4) Diseases of the Excretory and Urinary Systems: Dachangshu (BL 25) and Xiaochangshu (BL 27). (*Songs of Miraculous Light*)

【Regional Anatomy】 Skin-subcutaneous tissue-aponeurosis of the latissimus muscle of the back and superficial layer of thoracolumbar fascia-erector spinal muscle. In the superficial layer, there are the cutaneous branches of the posterior branches of the 4th and 5th lumbar nerves and the medial cutaneous branches of the dorsal branches of accompanying arteries and veins. In the deep layer, there are the muscular branches of the posterior branches of the 4th and 5th lumbar nerves and the branches or tributaries of the related lumbar arteries and veins.

BL 26 Guanyuanshu (关元俞)
(Guan Yuan Shu)

【Source】 *The Peaceful Holy Benevolent Prescriptions*

【Name Explanation】 Guan (关), storage; Yuan (元), primary qi; Shu (俞), point. This point is opposite to Guanyuan (RN 4), where the stored qi of the primary Yin and primary Yang infuses in the back.

【Location】 On the lower back, below the spinous process of the 5th lumbar vertebra, 1.5 cun lateral to the posterior midline. (See Fig. 11-30)

【Localization】 In prone position, first locate the spinous process of the 4th lumbar vertebrae, then locate the lower border of the spinous process just inferior to it (5th lumbar vertebrae) then locate the point 1.5 cun lateral to it.

【Indications】

1) Digestive Diseases: Abdominal distention, diarrhea.

2) Urogenital Diseases: Dysuria, enuresis, anuria, frequent micturition, menorrhagia, irregular menstruation, abdominal mass.

3) Other Diseases: Lumbago due to wind, cold and overstrain, diabetes.

【Mechanism of Action】 This point lies in the lower-jiao where qi of the large and small intestines, urinary bladder and the organs of the reproductive system converge. Thus, it can be used to treat diseases of the digestive, urinary and reproductive systems. This point connects with Guanyuan (RN 4) which is the pathway of the primordial qi, thus, it can be used to treat kidney-type diabetes.

【Method】 Puncture perpendicularly 0.7-1 cun. Moxibustion is applicable.

【Acupoint Prescription】 Lumbago due to wind and overstrain: Guanyuanshu (BL 26) and

Pangguangshu (BL 28). (*Experience on Acupuncture and Moxibustion Therapy*)
【Regional Anatomy】 Skin-subcutaneous tissue-superficial layer of thoracolumbar fascia-erector spinal muscle. In the superficial layer, there are the cutaneous branches of the posterior branches of the 5th lumbar and 1st sacral nerves and the accompanying arteries and veins. In the deep layer, there are the muscular branches of the posterior branches of the 5th lumbar nerves.

BL 27   Xiaochangshu （小肠俞）
(Small Intestine Shu)

【Source】 *A-B Classic of Acupuncture and Moxibustion*
【Name Explanation】 Xiaochang （小肠）, small intestine; Shu （俞）, point. This is where the qi of the Small Intestine infuses in the back.
【Classification】 Back-Shu point of the Small Intestine.
【Location】 On the sacrum at the level of the 1st posterior sacral foramen, 1.5 cun lateral to the medial sacral crest. (See Fig. 11-30)
【Localization】 In prone position, locate the point below the 1st sacral vertebrae, 1.5 cun lateral to the posterior midline.
【Indications】
   1) Digestive Diseases: Diarrhea, dysentery, stool with purulent and bloody discharge, hemorrhoids, constipation, anorexia.
   2) Urogenital Diseases: Seminal emission, leukorrhea, enuresis, hematuria, dysuria with dark urine, stranguria, anuria.
   3) Other Diseases: Numbness and pain in the waist and legs, hernia, diabetes.
【Mechanism of Action】
   1) This point is the back-shu point of the small intestine and the place where qi of the small intestine converges, so it can be used to treat diseases of the digestive system.
   2) This point lies in the place where the organs of the reproductive and urinary systems converge, thus, it can be used to treat diseases of the reproductive and urinary systems.
【Method】 Puncture perpendicularly 0.5-1 cun. Moxibustion is applicable.
【Acupoint Prescriptions】
   1) Pain along the spinal column: Xiaochangshu (BL 27), Zhonglushu (BL 29) and Baihuanshu (BL 30). (*Thousand Golden Prescriptions*)
   2) Shortness of breath: Xiaochangshu (BL 27), Yuji (LU 10), Daling (PC 7) and Ganshu (BL 18). (*Experience on Acupuncture and Moxibustion Therapy*)
【Regional Anatomy】 Skin-subcutaneous tissue-medial border of the greatest gluteal muscle the erector spinal muscle tendon. In the superficial layer, there are the middle gluteal nerves. In the deep layer, there are the branches of the inferior gluteal nerve and the muscular branches of the posterior branches of the related spinal nerves.

BL 28   Pangguangshu （膀胱俞）
(Bladder Shu)

【Source】 *A-B Classic of Acupuncture and Moxibustion*
【Name Explanation】 Pangguang （膀胱）, bladder; Shu （俞）, point. This point is where the qi of the bladder infuses in the back.
【Classification】 Back-Shu point of the Bladder.

【Location】 On the sacrum at the level of the 2nd posterior sacral foramen, 1.5 cun lateral to the medial sacral crest. (See Fig. 11-30)
【Localization】 In prone position, locate the point below the 2nd sacral vertebrae, 1.5 cun lateral to the posterior midline.
【Indications】
　　1) Digestive Diseases: Abdominal pain, flatulence and fullness sensation of the abdomen, constipation, dyspepsia.
　　2) Urogenital Diseases: Seminal emission, abdominal mass in women, swelling, pain and sores in the pudendal area, dampness and pruritus vulvae, dysuria with dark urine, enuresis, dysuria, stranguria.
　　3) Other Diseases: Rigidity and pain of the spine, coldness and weakness of the knees and feet accompanied by spasms.
【Mechanism of Action】 This point is Back-Shu point of the urinary bladder and the place where the urinary bladder-qi converges. It also lies in the place where the large and small intestines and the organs of the reproductive system converge. Based on the principle in acupuncture "where the point is located, where the indications are", it can be used to treat the diseases mentioned above.
【Method】 Puncture perpendicularly 0.5-1 cun. Moxibustion is applicable.
【Regional Anatomy】 Skin-subcutaneous tissue-the greatest gluteal muscle-erector spinal muscle. In the superficial layer, there are the middle gluteal nerves. In the deep layer, there are the branches of the inferior gluteal nerve and the muscular branches of the posterior branches of the related spinal nerves.
【Remark】 Puncturing the point can regulate vesical function. When acupuncture is administered at this point, twirling the needle can cause bladder contraction and increase internal pressure; However, when the twirling is stopped, the bladder relaxes and the internal pressure decreases.

BL 29　Zhonglushu（中膂俞）
(Intro-back Muscle Shu)

【Source】 *A-B Classic of Acupuncture and Moxibustion*
【Name Explanation】 Zhong (中), center; Lu (膂), muscles on both sides of the spine; Shu (俞), point. This point is in the center of the body, where the qi of the muscles on both sides of the spine is infused into the back.
【Location】 On the sacrum at the level of the 3rd posterior sacral foramen, 1.5 cun lateral to the medial sacral crest. (See Fig. 11-30)
【Localization】 In the prone position, locate the point below the 3rd sacral vertebrae, 1.5 cun lateral to the posterior midline.
【Indications】
　　1) Digestive Diseases: Diarrhea, abdominal distention.
　　2) Other Diseases: Stiffness and pain along the spinal column with difficulty in lying flat, hernia.
【Mechanism of Action】 This point lies in the lumbosacral part of the body and is also the place where qi of the large and small intestines converges, thus, their respective diseases can be treated by using this point.
【Method】 Puncture perpendicularly 0.5-1 cun. Moxibustion is applicable.
【Acupoint Prescriptions】
　　1) Convulsive diseases: Zhonglushu (BL 29), Changqiang (DU 1) and Shenshu (BL 23). (*Thousand Golden Prescriptions*)
　　2) Abdominal distension: Zhonglushu (BL 29), Yixi (BL 40) and Geshu (BL 19).

(*Experience on Acupuncture and Moxibustion Therapy*)
【Regional Anatomy】 Skin-subcutaneous tissue-greater gluteal muscle-sacrotuberous ligament. In the superficial layer, there are the middle gluteal nerves. In the deep layer, there are the branches or tributaries of the superior and inferior gluteal arteries and veins and the branches of the inferior gluteal nerve.

BL 30　Baihuanshu（白环俞）
（White Ring Shu）

【Source】 *A-B Classic of Acupuncture and Moxibustion*
【Name Explanation】 Bai（白）, white; Huan（环）, ring; Shu（俞）, point. This point is indicated in leukorrhea.
【Location】 On the sacrum at the level of the 4th posterior sacral foramen, 1.5 cun lateral to the medial sacral crest. (See Fig. 11-30)
【Localization】 In the prone position, locate the point below the 4th sacral vertebrae, 1.5 cun lateral to the posterior midline.
【Indications】
　　1) Urogenital Diseases: Leukorrhea, irregular menstruation, metrorrhagia and metrostaxis, seminal emission, cloudy urine, dysuria, dark urine.
　　2) Other Diseases: Pain in the lower back and legs, flaccidity and numbness in the lower limbs, hernia.
【Mechanism of Action】 Below the point is the place where the organs of the reproductive and urinary systems converge, thus, it can be used to treat diseases of the reproductive and urinary systems and is especially suitable for seminal emission and clear and turbid urine.
【Method】 Puncture perpendicularly 0.5-1 cun. Moxibustion is applicable.
【Acupoint Prescriptions】
　　1) Difficulty in bowel movement and in micturition: Baihuanshu (BL 30), Chengfu (BL 50), Dachangshu (BL 25). (*Experience on Acupuncture and Moxibustion Therapy*)
　　2) Lumbago and backache: Baihuanshu (BL 30), Weizhon (BL 40). (*Songs of Hundreds of Symptoms*)
【Regional Anatomy】 Skin-subcutaneous tissue-the greatest gluteal muscle-sacrotuberous ligament-piriform muscle. In the superficial layer, there are the middle and inferior gluteal nerves. In the deep layer, there are the branches or tributaries of the superior and inferior gluteal arteries and veins and the sacral nervous and venous plexus.

BL 31　Shangliao（上髎）
（Upper Crevice）

【Source】 *Plain Questions*
【Name Explanation】 Shang（上）, upper; Liao（髎）, foramen. The point is at the first dorsal sacral foramen.
【Location】 On the sacrum, at the midpoint between the superior iliac spine and the posterior midline, at the 1st posterior sacral foramen. (See Fig. 11-30)
【Localization】 In the prone position, put the tip of the index finger on the middle between Xiaochangshu (BL 27) and the spinal column, and the little finger on the upper side of the coccyx, which have a round process like a small soybean (sacral horn), the middle and the ring fin-

gers must be separated by the same distance. So Shangliao (BL 31) is located at the tip of the index finger, Ciliao (BL 32) is located at the tip of the middle finger, Zhongliao (BL 33) is located at the tip of the ring finger, and Xialiao (BL 34) is located at the tip of the little finger.
【Indications】
　　1) Urogenital Diseases: Irregular menstruation, hysteroptosis, leukorrhagia with reddish and whitish discharge, vulva pruritus, dysmenorrhea, sterility, seminal emission, impotence, dysuria, stranguria with turbid urine.
　　2) Other Diseases: Lumbosacral rigidity and pain, flaccidity and pain of the knees and legs.
【Mechanism of Action】 This point lies in the place where the organs of the reproductive and urinary systems converge. Based on the principle in acupuncture "where the point is located, where the indications are", it has the function to strengthen the lumbus, tonify the kidney, remove the dampness and promote diuresis.
【Method】 Puncture perpendicularly 0.7-1 cun. Moxibustion is applicable.
【Acupoint Prescriptions】
　　1) Febrile disease without sweating: Shangliao (BL 31) and Kongzui (LU 6). (*A-B Classic of Acupuncture and Moxibustion*)
　　2) Fever and chill syndrome: Shangliao (BL 31) and Pianli (LI 6). (*Experience on Acupuncture and Moxibustion Therapy*)
　　3) Epistaxis: Shangliao (BL 31), Houxi (SI 3) and Fengfu (DU 16). (*ibid*)
【Regional Anatomy】 Skin-subcutaneous tissue-superficial layer of the thoracolumbar fascia-erector spinal muscle-1st posterior sacral foramen. In the superficial layer, there is the middle gluteal nerve. In the deep layer, there are the posterior branches of the 1st sacral nerve and the lateral sacral artery and vein.
【Remark】 Puncturing this point and Sanyinjiao (SP 6) and Guanyuan (RN 4) has a therapeutic effect on impotence. It was reported that puncturing the points of Shangliao (BL 31), Xialiao (BL 34) and Ciliao (BL 32) were effective when treating gynecological diseases. For example, inserting a long needle at the subcutaneous part close to the sacrum through Xialiao (BL 34), Zhongliao (BL 33), Ciliao (BL 32) and Shangliao (BL 31) points respectively, using strong stimulation and non-retaining method, then needling Zusanli (ST 36) and Quchi (LI 11) for 3 to 7 successive days could gradually improve the patients condition.

BL 32　Ciliao（次髎）
(Secondary Crevice)

【Source】 *Plain Questions*
【Name Explanation】 Ci （次）, second; Liao （髎）, foramen. The point is at the second posterior sacral foramen.
【Location】 On the sacrum, medial and inferior to the posterior-superior iliac spine, at the 2nd posterior sacral foramen. (See Fig. 11-30)
【Localization】 Refer to Shangliao (BL 31).
【Indications】
　　1) Urogenital Diseases: Irregular menstruation, leukorrhagia with reddish and whitish discharge, dysmenorrhea, pudendal pain, impotence, dysuria with deep-colored urine, stranguria with turbid urine.
　　2) Digestive Diseases: Borborygmus, diarrhea.
　　3) Other Diseases: Pain along the spinal column with the inability to turn the body around, lumbar numbness radiating down to the feet.
【Mechanism of Action】 This point lies in the place where the large and small intestines and the

organs of the reproductive and urinary systems converge. Based on the acupuncture principle: "where the point locates, where the indications are", it can be used to treat the diseases in this region. Among the Eight-Liao Points, this point is the most commonly-used. It has the function of regulating the lower jiao, strengthening both the lumbar area and the knees and dredging the meridians.

【Method】 Puncture perpendicularly 0.7-1 cun. Moxibustion is applicable.

【Acupoint Prescriptions】

1) Pain along the spinal column, aversion to cold: Ciliao (BL 32), Baohuang (BL 48) and Chengjin (BL 56). (*Thousand Golden Prescriptions*)

2) Sterility: Ciliao (BL 32) and Shangqiu (SP 5). (*Experience on Acupuncture and Moxibustion Therapy*)

【Regional Anatomy】 Skin subcutaneous tissue-erector spinal muscle-2nd posterior sacral foramen. In the superficial layer, there is the middle gluteal nerve. In the deep layer, there are the posterior branches of the 2nd sacral nerve and the lateral sacral artery and vein.

【Remark】 Puncturing this point can affect the vesical functions and cause bladder contraction. For cases accompanied by mild paralysis of the lower limbs, needling this point may greatly decrease the residual urine in the bladder. Strong acupuncture response can be made by using different manipulations. However, if the point is punctured many times, or the twirling range is wide, with a long period of needle retention, the needling response may abate. It was reported that puncturing this point reduced pain during labour. If the pregnant women had abdominal pain accompanied by both soreness and pain in the sacral part, Ciliao (BL 32) and Fujie (SP 14) could be punctured towards Qichong (ST 30). If the acupuncture was given at the time when the uterine cervix was dialated 3-4 cm for primipara and 2 cm for multiparas the effective anaesthetic rate could reach 90%. It proved that puncturing this point had the function of enhancing the uterine contraction and shortening the stages of labour, but could not reduce difficult labour. It also caused bladder contractions and decreased residual urine in patients with lower limbs paresis. Stronger stimulation can cause stronger effect.

BL 33   Zhongliao (中髎)
(Middle Crevice)

【Source】 *Plain Questions*.

【Name Explanation】 Zhong (中), center; Liao (髎), foramen. The point is at the third posterior sacral foramen, approximately at the middle part.

【Location】 On the sacrum, medial and inferior to Ciliao (BL 32), at the 3rd posterior sacral foramen. (See Fig. 11-30)

【Localization】 Refer to Shangliao (BL 31).

【Indications】

1) Urogenital Diseases: Irregular menstruation, leukorrhagia with reddish and whitish discharge, sterility, dysuria, stranguria with turbid urine.

2) Digestive Diseases: Constipation, abdominal pain, dysentery, diarrhea.

3) Other Diseases: Lumbosacral pain.

【Mechanism of Action】 See Ciliao (BL 32) for more details.

【Method】 Puncture perpendicularly 0.7-1 cun. Moxibustion is applicable.

【Acupoint Prescription】 Constipation: Zhongliao (BL 33), Shimen (RN 5), Chengshan (BL 57), Taichong (LR 3), Zhongwan (RN 12), Dazhong (KI 4), Taixi (KI 3) and Chengjin (BL 56). (*Thousand Golden Prescriptions*)

【Regional Anatomy】 Skin-subcutaneous tissue-greater gluteal muscle-erector spinal muscle. In the superficial layer, there is the middle gluteal nerve. In the deep layer, there are the posterior branches of the 3rd sacral nerve and the lateral sacral artery and vein.

BL 34　Xialiao（下髎）
(Lower Crevice)

【Source】*Plain Questions*
【Name Explanation】Xia（下）, lower; Liao（髎）, foramen. The point is at the lowest posterior sacral foramen.
【Classification】The point where Foot Taiyin (Yang), Foot Jueyin and Foot Shaoyin Meridians knot.
【Location】On the sacrum, medial and inferior to Zhongliao (BL 33), just at the 4th posterior sacral foramen. (See Fig. 11-30)
【Localization】Refer to Shangliao (BL 31).
【Indications】
　　1) Urogenital Diseases: Dysuria, leukorrhagia, dysmenorrhea.
　　2) Digestive Diseases: Borborygmus, diarrhea, constipation, hematochezia, acute pain in the lower abdomen.
　　3) Other Diseases: Lumbago with difficulty in turning the body.
【Mechanism of Action】Same as Ciliao (BL 32).
【Method】Puncture perpendicularly 0.7-1 cun. Moxibustion is applicable.
【Regional Anatomy】Skin-subcutaneous tissue-the greatest gluteal muscle-erector spinal muscle. In the superficial layer, there is the middle gluteal nerve. In the deep layer, there are the branches or tributaries of the superior and inferior gluteal arteries and veins, the inferior gluteal nerve of the 4th sacral nerve and the posterior branches of the lateral sacral artery and vein.

BL 35　Huiyang（会阳）
(Converging Yang)

【Source】*A-B Classic of Acupuncture and Moxibustion*
【Name Explanation】Hui（会）, crossing; Yang（阳）, Yang of Yin-Yang. This point pertains to Yang meridian and is crossed with the Du Meridian which is considered as the sea of the Yang meridians.
【Location】On the sacrum, 0.5 cun lateral to the tip of the coccyx. (See Fig. 11-30)
【Localization】Kneeling, locate the point 0.5 cun lateral to the coccygeal end.
【Indications】
　　1) Urogenital Diseases: Leukorrhagia with reddish and whitish discharge, menstrual lumbago, impotence, sweating, dampness and pruritus in the vulvar area.
　　2) Digestive Diseases: Dysentery, diarrhea, hematochezia, hemorrhoidal disease, coldness and pain in the abdomen.
　　3) Other Disease: Lumbago.
【Mechanism of Action】See Ciliao (BL 32) for more details.
【Method】Puncture perpendicularly 0.5-1 cun. Moxibustion is applicable.
【Regional Anatomy】Skin-subcutaneous tissue-greater gluteal muscle-tendon of the elvator of the anus. In the superficial layer, there is the middle gluteal nerve. In the deep layer, there are the branches or tributaries of the inferior gluteal artery and vein and the inferior gluteal nerve.

BL 36　Chengfu (承扶)
(Supporting by Hand)

【Source】 *A-B Classic of Acupuncture and Moxibustion*
【Name Explanation】 Cheng (承), supstaining; Fu (扶), support. This point is on the upper part of the femur at the midpoint of the gluteofemoral crease. Its function is to support the lower limbs and sustain the body weigh.
【Location】 On the posterior side of the thigh, at the midpoint of the inferior gluteal crease. (See Fig. 11-31)
【Localization】 In the prone position, locate the point at the midpoint where the medial line of the posterior aspect of the thigh meets the transverse gluteal crease.
【Indications】
　　1) Diseases along Course of the Meridian: Pain in the lumbosacral region, pain along the spinal column, coldness and pain in the lower back, swelling pain in the perineum.
　　2) Urinary Disease: Dysuria.
　　3) Anal Diseases: Hemorrhoidal disease, difficult bowel movement.

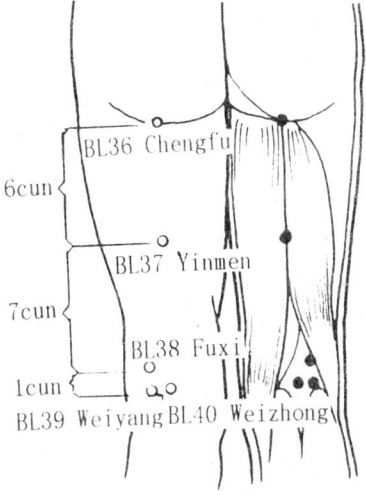

Fig. 11-31

【Mechanism of Action】 This point belongs to Urinary Bladder Meridian and is close to the anus and genitals, thus, it can be used to treat urinary and anal diseases. The treatment of other diseases is based on the rule: where the meridian passes, where the indications are.
【Method】 Puncture perpendicularly 0.5-1.5 cun. Moxibustion is applicable.
【Regional Anatomy】 Skin-subcutaneous tissue-greater gluteal muscle-the long head of the biceps muscle of the thigh and semitendinous muscle. In the superficial layer, there are the branches of the posterior femoral cutaneous nerve and the inferior gluteal nerve. In the deep layer, there are the trunk of the posterior femoral cutaneous nerve, the sciatic nerve and the accompanying arteries and veins.

BL 37　Yinmen (殷门)
(Big Red Gate)

【Source】 *A-B Classic of Acupuncture and Moxibustion*
【Name Explanation】 Yin (殷), thickness; Men (门), door. The local muscle of the point is thick, and the point is a door where the qi of Bladder Meridian passes.
【Location】 On the posterior side of the thigh and on the line connecting Chengfu (BL 36) and Weizhong (BL 40), 6 cun below Chengfu (BL 36), Weizhong (BL 36). (See Fig. 11-31)
【Localization】 In the prone position, first locate BL 36 and BL 40, the point is located at the intersection of the superior three-sevenths and inferior four-sevenths of the distance between BL 36 and BL 40.
【Indications】 Rigidity and pain of the spinal column with difficulty in lying on the back, pain in the legs and in lateral side of the thigh.
【Mechanism of Action】 This point is commonly used when treating flaccidity, numbness, pain and paralysis of the lower limbs. It can be used to relieve rigidity of muscles, activate collaterals

and alleviate numbness and pain.
【Method】 Puncture perpendicularly 0.7-1.5 cun. Moxibustion is applicable.
【Regional Anatomy】 Skin-subcutaneous tissue-the long head of biceps femoris muscle of thigh and semitendinous muscle. In the superficial layer, there is the posterior femoral cutaneous nerve. In the deep layer, there are the sciatic nerve and the accompanying artery and vein and the perforating branches of the deep femoral artery.
【Remark】 Puncturing this point and Feishu (BL 13) may alleviate bronchial asthma within 3 to 45 minutes.

BL 38   Fuxi (浮郄)
(Superficial Crevice)

【Source】 A-B Classic of Acupuncture and Moxibustion
【Name Explanation】 Fu (浮), floating; Xi (郄), seam. This point is on the upper borders of the poplital fossa.
【Location】 At the lateral end of the popliteal crease, 1 cun above Weiyang (BL 39), medial to the tendon of the biceps femoris muscle of the thigh. (See Fig. 11-31)
【Localization】 In the prone position, first locate Weiyang (BL 39) which located at 1 cun lateral to the middle of the popliteal fossa, Fuxi (BL 38) is located 1 cun directly superior to the Weiyang (BL 39), on the medial aspect of the tendon biceps femoris.
【Indications】 Numbness of gluteal area and thigh, muscular stiffness of upper arms.
【Mechanism of Action】 Based on the acupuncture principle where the meridian passes and the point locates, where the indications are, it can be used to relax muscles and tendons and activate the flow of qi in the meridians and collaterals.
【Method】 Puncture perpendicularly 0.5-1 cun. Moxibustion is applicable.
【Regional Anatomy】 Skin-subcutaneous tissue-medial border of the tendon of biceps femoris muscle of thigh-lateral head of gastrocnemius muscle. In the superficial layer, there is the posterior femoral cutaneous nerve. In the deep layer, there are the common peroneal nerve, the lateral cutaneous nerve of the calf and the lateral superior genicular artery and vein.

BL 39   Weiyang (委阳)
(Popliteal Yang)

【Source】 Miraculous Pivot and Plain Questions
【Name Explanation】 Wei(委), crooked; Yang(阳), Yang of Yin-Yang. The exterior pertains to Yang. The point is lateral to Weizhong(BL 40)on the transverse crease of the popliteal fossa.
【Classification】 Lower He-(Sea) point of Sanjiao Meridian.
【Location】 At the lateral end of the popliteal crease, medial to the tendon of the biceps femoris muscle of the thigh. (See Fig. 11-31)
【Localization】 In the prone position, the point is located 1 cun lateral to Weizhong (BL 40), which is located in the middle point of the transverse crease of the popliteal fossa.
【Indications】
   1) Diseases along the Course of the Meridian: Rigidity and pain of the loins and spine, pain and muscular contracture of the legs and feet, flaccidity and numbness of the limbs.
   2) Urinary Diseases: Dysuria, retention of urine, enuresis, stranguria, distending pain in the lower abdomen.

3) Other Diseases: Epilepsy, febrile diseases. hemorrhoid, constipation.

【Mechanism of Action】 This point is the He (sea) -point of the lower jiao. The Sanjiao dominates the dredging of the water pathway and controls the function of the organs in this region. It can be used to treat dysuria and retention of urine.

【Method】 Puncture perpendicularly 0.5-1 cun. Moxibustion is applicable.

【Acupoint Prescriptions】

1) Lumbago with difficulty in lying on the back: Weiyang (BL 39), Yinmen (BL 51), Taibai (SP 3), Yinlingquan (SP 9) and Xingjian (LR 2). (*Thousand Golden Prescriptions*)

2) Stranguria: Weiyang (BL 39), Zhishi (BL 47) and Zhongliao (BL 33). (*Experience on Acupuncture and Moxibustion Therapy*)

3) Axilla swelling: Weiyang (BL 39) and Tianchi (PC 1). (*Songs of Hundreds of Symptoms*)

【Regional Anatomy】 Skin-subcutaneous tissue-biceps femoris muscle of thigh-lateral head of the gastrocnemius muscle-origin of the popliteal muscle and plantar muscle. In the superficial layer, there is the posterior femoral cutaneous nerve. In the deep layer, there are the common peroneal nerve and the lateral cutaneous nerve of the calf.

BL 40 Weizhong (委中)
(Popliteal Center)

【Source】 *Miraculous Pivot*

【Name Explanation】 Wei (委), crooked; Zhong (中), center. The point is at the midpoint of the transverse crease of the popliteal fossa.

【Classification】 He-(Sea) point of the Bladder Meridian of Foot Taiyang.

【Location】 At the midpoint of the popliteal crease, between the tendons of the biceps femoris muscle of the thigh and the semitendinous muscle. (See Fig. 11-31)

【Localization】 In the prone position, locate the point at the midpoint of the transverse crease of the poplital fossa, between the two tendons mentioned above.

【Indications】

1) Diseases along the Course of the Meridian: Pain in the loins and back, heaviness and pain in the lumbasacral region, flaccidity and numbness due to wind and dampness, paralysis of the lower limbs, muscular contracture of the upper arms, knee pain with limited movement.

2) Digestive Diseases: Cholera morbus, epigastric pain, vomiting, diarrhea.

3) Mental Diseases: Windstroke, coma, epilepsy, clonic convulsion.

4) Dermatosis: Lumbodorsal cellulitis, erysipelas, eczema, breast abscess, vulvar pruritus, leprosy.

5) Other Diseases: Febrile disease without sweating, summer-heat disease, malaria, intretable, epistaxis, sore throat, spontaneous sweating, night sweating.

【Mechanism of Action】

1) Based on the acupuncture principle where the meridian passes, where the indications are, this point is the most commonly used to treat rigidity and pain of the spinal column and hemiparalysis.

2) This point is also named Xuexi (blood leak). Blood letting at this point has some effect in restoring consciousness, clearing heat and toxic materials, relaxing the muscles and tendons and to activate the flow of blood. It is often used for stroke, coma, heat-stroke, acute vomiting, sore throat, skin eruptions and surgical diseases.

3) This point belongs to the Bladder Meridian and the urinary bladder is the place where body fluid is stored, thus, it can be used to treat dysuria.

【Method】 Puncture perpendicularly 0.5-1 cun or prick the point with a three-edged needle to cause bleeding. Moxibustion is applicable.

【Acupoint Prescriptions】

1) Stubborn epistaxis: Weizhong (BL 40), Yinbai (SP 1) and (*Thousand Golden Prescriptions*)

2) Muscular contracture and fever: Weizhong (BL 40) and Weiyang (BL 39) (*ibid*)

3) Arthralgia due to wind-dampness: Weizhong (BL 40) and Xialian (LI 8). (*Experience on Acupuncture and Moxibustion Therapy*)

4) Multicolored urine: Weizhong (BL 40) and Qiangu (SI 2). (*Great Compendium of Acupuncture and Moxibustion*)

5) Severe pain over the loins and back: Weizhong (BL 40) and Fuliu (KI 7). (*ibid*)

【Regional Anatomy】 Skin-subcutaneous tissue-between lateral and medial heads of the gastrocnemius muscle. In the superficial layer, there are the posterior femoral cutaneous nerve and the small saphenous vein. In the deep layer, there are the tibial nerve, the popliteal artery and vein, and the peroneal artery.

【Remark】 Puncturing this point can adjust vesical pressure. In general, it can make the intravesical pressure descend, but in patients with a relaxed bladder or urinary retention it makes it ascend.

BL 41　Fufen（附分）
(Lateral Separation)

【Source】 *A-B Classic of Acupuncture and Moxibustion*

【Name Explanation】 Fu (附), attached; Fen (分), separation. The Bladder Meridian runsdownward bilaterally from the neck. This point is at the beginning of the second line attached to the first line.

【Clessification】 Crossing Point of Foot Taiyang and Hand Taiyang Meridians

【Location】 On the back, below the spinous process of the 2nd thoracic vertebrae, 3 cun lateral to the posterior midline. (See Fig. 11-32)

【Localization】 In the prone position, locate the point below the spinous process of the 2nd thoracic vertebrae, 3 cun lateral to the posterior midline.

【Indications】 Muscular spasm of shoulder and back, rigidity and pain of the neck with difficulty in turning the head, numbness of the upper arm.

【Mechanism of Action】 It has the function of promoting the flow of qi and blood in the local region.

【Method】 Puncture obliquely 0.3-0.5 cun. Moxibustion is applicable.

【Regional Anatomy】 Skin-subcutaneous tis-

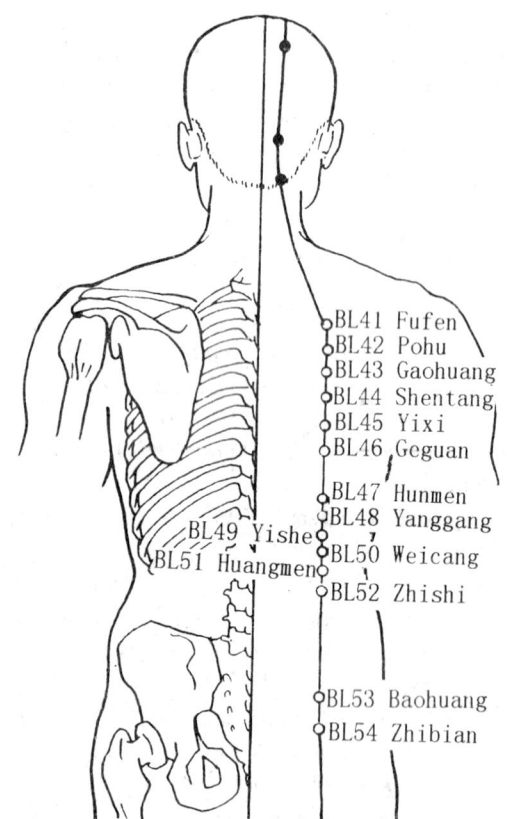

Fig. 11-32

sue-trapezius muscle-rhomboid muscle-superior posterior serratus muscle-erector spinal muscle. In the superficial layer, there are the cutaneous branches of the posterior branches of the 2nd and 3rd thoracic nerves and the accompanying arteries and veins. In the deep layer, there are the dorsal scapular nerve, the dorsal scapular artery and vein, the muscular branches of the posterior branches of the 2nd and 3rd thoracic nerves and the branches or tributaries of the dorsal branches of the related posterior intercostal arteries and veins.

BL 42   Pohu (魄户)
(Soul Shelter)

【Source】 A-B Classic of Acupuncture and Moxibustion
【Name Explanation】 Po (魄), spirit; Hu (户), door. The lungs store the spirit. The point is at the level of Feishu (BL 13), like a door for the qi of the Lungs.
【Location】 On the back, below the spinous process of the 3rd thoracic vertebrae, 3 cun lateral to the posterior midline. (See Fig. 11-32)
【Localization】 In sitting position with the head bowed, locate the point below the spinous process of the 3rd thoracic vertebrae, 3 cun lateral to Shenzhu (DU 12).
【Indications】
　　1) Respiratory Diseases: Cough, asthma, impairment of the lung due to overstrain, consumptive lung diseases, pulmonary tuberculosis, hectic fever due to yin-deficiency.
　　2) Digestive Diseases: Cholera, vomiting, choking sensation in the chest.
　　3) Other Diseases: Neck rigidity causing difficulty in turning the head, pain in the waist and back, brachialgia.
【Mechanism of Action】 This point is beside Feishu (BL 13). For more details, see Feishu (BL 13).
【Method】 Puncture obliquely 0.5 cun. Moxibustion is applicable.
【Acupoint Prescriptions】
　　1) Cough with dyspnea: Pohu (BL 42), Qishe (ST 11) and Yixi (BL 45). (*A-B Classic of Acupuncture and Moxibustion*)
　　2) Cough with asthma: Pohu (BL 42) and Zhongfu (LU 1). (*Thousand Golden Prescriptions*)
　　3) Nape stiffness sith difficulty in turning the head: Pohu (BL 42) and Jianjing (GB 21). (*Experience on Acupuncture and Moxibustion Therapy*)
　　4) Cough with dyspnea: Pohu (BL 42), Qishe (ST 11), Yixi (BL 45) and Qimen (LR 14). (*ibid*)
　　5) Consumptive disease: Pohu (BL 42), Gaohuang (BL 38). (*Songs of Hundreds of Symptoms*)
【Regional Anatomy】 Skin-subcutaneous tissue-trapezius muscle-rhomboid muscle-superior posterior serratus muscle-erector spinal muscle. In the superficial layer, there are the cutaneous branches of the posterior branches of the 3rd and 4th thoracic nerves and the accompanying arteries and veins. In the deep layer, there are the dorsal scapular nerve, the dorsal scapular artery and vein, the muscular branches of the posterior branches of the 3rd and 4th thoracic nerves and the branches or tributaries of the dorsal branches of the related posterior intercostal arteries and veins.

BL 43　Gaohuang（膏肓）
（Vital Organs）

[Source] *Miraculous Pivot*

[Name Explanation] Gao（膏），fat；Huang（肓），membrane. Gaohuang refers to the fat tissue and the membrane below the heart and above the diaphragm. Because this part is close to the pericardium, these are taken as the component of the pericardium. The point is at the same level of Jueyinshu（BL 14）point.

[Location] On the back, below the spinous process of the 4th thoracic vertebrae, 3 cun lateral to the posterior midline. （See Fig. 11-32）

[Localization] In sitting position with the head bowed, locate the point below the spinous process of the 4th thoracic vertebrae, 3 cun lateral to the posterior midline.

[Indications]

1) Respiratory Diseases: Hemoptysis due to consumptive lung disease, hemoptysis, lassitude of the four limbs, hectic fever, night sweating, cough, dyspnea.

2) Digestive Diseases: Weakness of the spleen and stomach, indigestion, dysphagia, vomiting, consumptive disease, five kinds of strains and seven kinds of impairments.

3) Reproductive Diseases: Noctural emission.

4) Mental Diseases: Amnesia, sleeplessness, vertigo, dizziness.

5) Other Diseases: Pain in the shoulders and back, carbuncle, cellulitis, breast abscess.

[Mechanism of Action]

1) In ancient times people had realized that this point is effective when treating consumptive diseases, such as: hemoptysis due to consumptive lung disease, hectic fever, night sweating, lassitude of the limbs, spontaneous sweating, amnesia, sleeplessness, noctural emission and emaciation due to prolonged illness. Moxibustion is often used on this point.

2) This point lies in the scapular area and is close to the extra point Jiafeng（EX）. Therefore, it is a commonly used point for scapular pain disorders. Particularly if the patient has a painful sensation when this point is pressed.

3) This point is corresponding to the breast and has a corresponding therapeutic effect. Therefore, it is often used to treat mammary carbuncles together with the ones on the back.

[Method] Puncture obliquely 0.3-0.5 cun downwards to the scapula. Moxibustion is applicable.

[Acupoint Prescriptions]

1) Miscellaneous disease: Gaohuang（BL 43）, Zusanli（ST 36）and Yongquan（KI 1）. （*Experience on Acupuncture and Moxibustion Therapy*）

2) Protracted cough: Moxibustion to Gaohuang（BL 43）and Feishu（BL 13）. （*ibid*）

3) Pain in the shoulder and back: Gaohuang（BL 43）and Jianjing（GB 21）. （*ibid*）

4) Tuberculosis, hectic fever due to yin-deficiency: Gaohuang（BL 43）, Feishu（BL 13）, Sihuaxue（EX）. （*Four Canons on Acupuncture and Moxibustion*）

5) Consumptive diseases: Gaohuang（BL 43）, Bailao（EX）. （*Guide to Acupuncture*）

[Regional Anatomy] Skin-subcutaneous tissue-trapezius muscle-rhomboid muscle-erector spinal muscle. In the superficial layer, there are the cutaneous branches of the posterior branches of the 4th and 5th thoracic nerves and the accompanying arteries and veins. In the deep layer, there are the dorsal scapular nerve, the dorsal scapular artery and vein, the muscular branches of the posterior branches of the 4th and 5th thoracic nerves and the branches or tributaries of the dorsal branches of the related posterior intercostal arteries and veins.

[Remark] This point is commonly used for hemorrhagic diseases. It is reported that erythrocyte increase from $100,000/mm^3$ to $337,000/mm^3$ after 5 days of puncturing this point when treating pernicious anemia.

BL 44 Shentang (神堂)
(Spiritual House)

【Source】 *A-B Classic of Acupuncture and Moxibustion*
【Name Explanation】 Shen (神), mind; Tang (堂), hall. The heart houses the mind. The point is at the same level of Xinshu (BL15), like a hall where the mind is housed.
【Location】 On the back, below the spinous process of the 5th thoracic vertebrae, 3 cun lateral to the posterior midline. (See Fig. 11-32)
【Localization】 In sitting position with the head bowed, locate the point below the spinous process of the 5th thoracic vertebrae, 3 cun lateral to DU 11.
【Indications】
　　1) Angiocardiopathies: Severe palpitation, cardialgia, fullness and oppression sensation on the chest, shortness of breath.
　　2) Respiratory Diseases: Cough with dyspnea due to adverse ascending of qi, fever, aversion to cold.
　　3) Mental Diseases: Vexation, insomnia.
　　4) Other Diseases: Pain in the shoulder and back, rigidity of the spinal column which causes difficulty in lying on the back.
【Mechanism of Action】 This point is beside Xinshu (BL 15). See Xinshu (BL 15) for more detials.
【Method】 Puncture obliquely 0.5 cun. Moxibustion is applicable.
【Acupoint Prescription】 Dysphagia: Shentang (BL 44), Zhongfu (LU 1). (*Experience on Acupuncture and Moxibustion Therapy*)
【Regional Anatomy】 Skin-subcutaneous tissue-trapezius muscle-rhomboid muscle-erector spinal muscle. In the superficial layer, there are the cutaneous branches of the posterior branches of the 5th and 6th thoracic nerves and the accompanying arteries and veins. In the deep layer, there are the dorsal scapular nerve, the dorsal scapular artery and vein, the muscular branches of the posterior branches of the 5th and 6th thoracic nerves and the branches or tributaries of the dorsal branches of the related posterior intercostal arteries and veins.

BL 45 Yixi (譩譆)
(Yi Xi)

【Source】 *Plain Questions*
【Name Explanation】 Yixi (譩譆), the sighing sound. If the patient is asked to say "Yixi" when the point is being located, the doctor's fingers may feel the vocal fremitus.
【Location】 On the back, below the spinous process of the 6th thoracic vertebrae, 3 cun lateral to the posterior midline. (See Fig. 11-32)
【Localization】 In sitting position with the head bowed, locate the point below the spinous process of the 6th thoracic vertebrae, 3 cun lateral to Lingtai (DU 10).
【Indications】
　　1) Respiratory Diseases: Cough with dyspnea, ches͏͏͏͏͏͏͏͏͏͏͏͏͏͏͏͏͏͏͏͏͏͏͏͏͏͏͏͏͏͏ack.
　　2) Other Diseases: Febrile disease without swea͏͏͏͏͏͏͏͏͏͏͏͏͏͏͏͏͏͏͏͏͏͏d restlessness due to deficiency of Yin, dizziness, ophthalmalgia,

【Mechanism of Action】 This point lies in the distributed area of the heart and lung, so it is used for diseases of the heart and lung. The occurance of febrile disease without sweating and epistaxis is associated with the failure of the lung in keeping the lung-qi pure and descendant. It also has the function of treating sleeplessness due to the feeling of oppression in the chest.
【Method】 Puncture obliquely 0.5 cun. Moxibustion is applicable.
【Acupoint Prescriptions】
　　1) Warm-type malaria: Yixi (BL 45), Zhongwan (RN 12), Baihuanshu (BL 30). (*Experience on Acupuncture and Moxibustion Therapy*)
　　2) Wind-type malaria: Yixi (BL 45), Zhizheng (SI 7), Xiaohai (SI 8). (*ibid*)
　　3) fullness sensation in the abdomen: Yixi (BL 45), Zusanli (ST 36). (*ibid*)
【Regional Anatomy】 Skin-subcutaneous tissue-trapezius muscle-rhomboid muscle-erector spinal muscle. In the superficial layer, there are the cutaneous branches of the posterior branches of the 6th and 7th thoracic nerves and the accompanying arteries and veins. In the deep layer, there are the dorsal scapular nerve, the dorsal scapular artery and vein, the muscular branches of the posterior branches of the 6th thoracic nerve and the branches or tributaries of the dorsal branches of the related posterior intercostal arteries and veins.

BL 46　Geguan （膈关）
（Diaphragm Pass）

【Source】 *A-B Classic of Acupuncture and Moxibustion*
【Name Explanation】 Ge (膈), diaphragm; Guan (关), pass. The point is at the same level of Geshu (BL 17).
【Location】 On the back, below the spinous process of the 7th thoracic vertebrae, 3 cun lateral to the posterior midline. (See Fig. 11-32)
【Localization】 In sitting position with the head bowed, locate the point below the spinous process of the 7th thoracic vertebrae, 3 cun lateral to Zhiyang (DU 9), at the same level with the inferior angle of the scapula.
【Indications】
　　1) Digestive Diseases: Loss of appetite, feeling of choking and oppression in the chest, vomiting, hiccup, eructation, ptyalism.
　　2) Other Diseases: Pain along the spinal column, yellowish urine, various blood disorders.
【Mechanism of Action】 This point is near the stomach in the middle jiao, so it is mainly used to treat the diseases of the spleen and stomach. However, because it lies beside Geshu (BL 17), it can also be used to treat various hemorrhagic diseasce. See Geshu (BL 17) for more details.
【Method】 Puncture obliquely 0.5 cun. Moxibustion is applicable.
【Acupoint Prescription】 Backache, aversion to cold of the back, rigidity of the spine which causes inability to lie flat: Geguan (BL 46), Zhibian (BL 49), Jinggu (BL 64). (*Experience on Acupuncture and Moxibustion Therapy*)
【Regional Anatomy】 Skin-subcutaneous tissue-trapezius muscle-rhomboid muscle-erector spinal muscle. In the superficial layer, there are the cutaneous branches of the posterior branches of the 7th and 8th thoracic nerves and the accompanying arteries and veins. In the deep layer, there are the dorsal scapular nerve, the dorsal scapular artery and vein, the muscular branches of the posterior branches of the 7th and 8th thoracic nerves and the branches or tributaries of the dorsal branches of the related posterior intercostal arteries and veins.

BL 47 Hunmen (魂门)
(Soul Gate)

【Source】 *A-B Classic of Acupuncture and Moxibustion*
【Name Explanation】 Hun (魂), soul, Men (门), door. The liver stores the soul. The point is at the same level of Ganshu (BL18), like a door for the qi of Liver.
【Location】 On the back, below the spinous process of the 9th thoracic vertebrae, 3 cun lateral to the posterior midline. (See Fig. 11-32)
【Localization】 In the prone position with the head bowed, locate the point below the spinous process of the 9th thoracic vertebrae, 3 cun lateral to Jinsuo (DU 8).
【Indications】
    1) Disorders of Head and Sense Organs: Headache, dizziness.
    2) Digestive Diseases: Loss of appetite, vomiting, borborygmus, diarrhea.
    3) Other Diseases: Distending pain in the chest and hypochondrium, pain in the back and loins, corspe-like syncope, epigastric pain radiated to the back, muscular contracture with arthralgia, reddish urine.
【Mechanism of Action】 The liver stores mood; and the point lies beside Ganshu (BL 18). See Ganshu (BL 18) for more details.
【Method】 Puncture obliquely 0.5 cun. Moxibustion is applicable.
【Acupoint Prescriptions】
    1) Vomiting: Hunmen (BL 47), Yangguan (EX). (*Thousand Golden Prescriptions*)
    2) Indigestion due to coldness in the stomach: Pomen (BL 47) Weishu (BL 21). (*Songs of Hundreds of Symptoms*)
【Regional Anatomy】 Skin-subcutaneous tissue-latissimus muscle of the back-inferior posterior serratus muscle-erector spinal muscle. In the superficial layer, there are the lateral cutaneous branches of the posterior branches of the 9th and 10th thoracic nerves and the accompanying arteries and veins. In the deep layer, there are the muscular branches of the posterior branches of the 9th and 10th thoracic nerves and the branches of the dorsal branches of the related posterior intercostal arteries and veins.

BL 48 Yanggang (阳纲)
(Yang Principles)

【Source】 *A-B Classic of Acupuncture and Moxibustion*
【Name Explanation】 Yang (阳), Yang of Yin-Yang; Gang (纲), key link. The Gallbladder pertains to Yang, the point is at the same level of Danshu (BL 19) and is important in treating gallbladder diseases.
【Location】 On the back, below the spinous process of the 10th thoracic vertebrae, 3 cun lateral to the posterior midline. (See Fig. 11-32)
【Localization】 In sitting position with the head bowed, locate the point below the spinous process of the 10th thoracic vertebrae, 3 cun lateral to Zhongshu (DU 7).
【Indications】
    1) Digestive Diseases: Abdominal pain, borborygmus, diarrhea, fullness feeling and distension in the abdomen, loss of appetite.
    2) Other Diseases: Distension and pain over the chest and hypochondrium, jaundice,

fever, diabetes.

【Mechanism of Action】 This point lies beside Danshu (BL 19). See Danshu (BL 19) for more details.

【Method】 Puncture obliquely 0.5 cun. Moxibustion is applicable.

【Acupoint Prescriptions】

1) Loss of appetite: Yanggang (BL 48), Qimen (LR 14), Shaoshang (LU 11) and Laogong (PC 8). (*Experience on Acupuncture and Moxibustion Therapy*)

2) Icteric aclera: Yanggang (BL 48) and Danshu (BL 19). (*Songs of Hundreds of Symptoms*)

【Regional Anatomy】 Skin-subcutaneous tissue-latissimus muscle of the back-inferior posterior serratus muscle-erector spinal muscle. In the superficial layer, there are the lateral cutaneous branches of the posterior branches of the 10th and 11th thoracic nerves and the accompanying arteries and veins. In the deep layer, there are the muscular branches of the posterior branches of the 10th and 11th thoracic nerves and the branches or tributaries of the dorsal branches of the related posterior intercostal arteries and veins.

BL 49 Yishe (意舍)
(Thought Refuge)

【Source】 *A-B Classic of Acupuncture and Moxibustion*

【Name Explanation】 Yi (意), ideas; She (舍), residence. The spleen stores ideas. The point is at the level of Pishu (BL 20), like a residence of the qi of the spleen.

【Location】 On the back, below the spinous process of the 11th thoracic vertebrae, 3 cun lateral to the posterior midline. (See Fig. 11-32)

【Localization】 In the prone position with the head bowed, locate the point below the spinous process of the 11th thoracic vertebrae, 3 cun lateral to Jizhong (DU 6).

【Indications】

1) Digestive Diseases: Fullness feeling and distention in the abdomen, borborygmus, diarrhea, vomiting, loss of appetite.

2) Other Diseases: Diabetes, fever with jaundice, urine with reddish and yellowish colour, spinal pain, aversion to cold and wind.

【Mechanism of Action】 The spleen stores idea and this point lies beside Pishu (BL 20) and has similar functions. See Pishu (BL 20) for more details.

【Method】 Puncture obliquely 0.5 cun. Moxibustion is applicable.

【Acupoint Prescription】 Kidney deficiency, diabetes, hypohidrosis: Yishe (BL 49) and Zhonglushu (BL 29). (*Experience on Acupuncture and Moxibustion Therapy*)

【Regional Anatomy】 Skin-subcutaneous tissue-latissimus muscle of the back-inferior posterior serratus muscle-erector spinal muscle. In the superficial layer, there are the lateral cutaneous branches of the posterior branches of the 11th and 12th thoracic nerves and the accompanying arteries and veins. In the deep layer, there are the muscular branches of the posterior branches of the 11th and 12th thoracic nerves and the branches or tributaries of the dorsal branches of the related posterior intercostal arteries and veins.

BL 50 Weicang (胃仓)
(Stomach Granary)

【Source】 *A-B Classic of Acupuncture and Moxibustion*

【Name Explanation】 Wei (胃), stomach; Cang (仓), storehouse. The point is at the level of Weishu (BL 21). The stomach receives food, acting like a storehouse.
【Location】 On the back, below the spinous process of the 12th thoracic vertebrae, 3 cun lateral to the posterior midline. (See Fig. 11-32)
【Localization】 In the prone position, locate the point below the spinous process of the 12th thoracic vertebrae, 3 cun lateral to the posterior midline.
【Indications】
    1) Digestive Diseases: Abdominal pain, stomachache, infantile dyspepsia, constipation.
    2) Other Diseases: Edema, pain along the spinal column which causes difficulty in lying flat.
【Mechanism of Action】 This point is located beside and has the similar functions to Weishu (BL 21). See Weishu (BL 21) for more details.
【Method】 Puncture obliquely 0.5 cun. Moxibustion is applicable.
【Acupoint Prescription】 Loss of appetite: Weicang (BL 50), Yishe (BL 44) and Geguan (BL 41). (*Experience on Acupuncture and Moxibustion Therapy*)
【Regional Anatomy】 Skin-subcutaneous tissue-latissimus muscle of the back-inferior posterior serratus muscle-erector spinal muscle-lumbar quadrate muscle. In the superficial layer, there are the lateral cutaneous branches of the posterior branches of the 10th thoracic and the 1st lumbar nerves and the accompanying arteries and veins. In the deep layer, there are the muscular branches of the posterior branches of the 12th thoracic and the 1st lumbar nerves and the branches or tributaries of the dorsal branches of the related posterior intercostal arteries and veins.

BL 51　Huangmen (肓门)
(Huang Gate)

【Source】 *A-B Classic of Acupuncture and Moxibustion*
【Name Explanation】 Huang (肓), membrance; Men (门), door. The point is at the level of Sanjiaoshu (BL 22), like a door for the qi of Sanjiao.
【Location】 On the back, below the spinous process of the 1st lumbar vertebrae, 3 cun lateral to the posterior midline. (See Fig. 11-32)
【Localization】 In the prone position with the head bowed, locate the point below the spinous process of the 1st lumbar vertebrae, 3 cun lateral to Xuanshu (DU 5).
【Indications】
    1) Digestive Diseases: Abdominal pain, stomachache, abdominal mass, constipation.
    2) Postpartum Diseases.
【Mechanism of Action】 This point is located beside and has similar functions to Sanjiaoshu (BL 32). See Sanjiaoshu (BL 32) for more details.
【Method】 Puncture perpendicularly 0.5-1 cun. Moxibustion is applicable.
【Regional Anatomy】 Skin-subcutaneous tissue-aponeurosis of latissimus muscle of the back-erector spinal muscle. In the superficial layer, there are the lateral cutaneous branches of the posterior branches of the 1st and 2nd lumbar nerves and the accompanying arteries and veins. In the deep layer, there are the muscular branches of the posterior branches of the 1st and 2nd lumbar nerves and the branches or tributaries of the dorsal branches of the 1st lumbar artery and vein.

BL 52　Zhishi（志室）
(Will Cabinet)

[Source] *A-B Classic of Acupuncture and Moxibustion*

[Name Explanation] Zhi（志）, will; Shi（室）, chamber. The Kidney stores the will. The point is at the level of Shenshu (BL 23), like a chamber where the qi of kidney gathers.

[Location] On the back, below the spinous process of the 2nd lumbar vertebrae, 3 cun lateral to the posterior midline. (See Fig. 11-32)

[Localization] In the prone position, first locate Mingmen (DU 4) (opposite to the umbilicus). Zhishi (BL 52) is located 3 cun lateral to Mingmen (DU 4).

[Indications]

　　1) Urogenital Diseases: Seminal emission, impotence, swelling and pain in pudendal area, stranguria, edema.

　　2) Digestive Diseases: Dyspepsia, abdominal distension, vomiting.

　　3) Mental Diseases: Insomnia, amnesia, dreaminess.

　　4) Other Diseases: Backache, rigidity and pain of spinal column which causes difficulty in lying flat, acute pain in the hypochondrium.

[Mechanism of Action] The kidney stores the will. This point lies beside Shenshu (BL 23), both are important points for tonifying the kidney. See Shenshu (BL 23) for more details.

[Method] Puncture perpendicularly 0.7-1 cun. Moxibustion is applicable.

[Acupoint Prescriptions]

　　1) Lumbago and back rigidity: Zhishi (BL 52) and Jingmen (GB 25). (*Thousand Golden Prescriptions*)

　　2) Pudendal pain and swelling: Zhishi (BL 52) and Baohuang (BL 53), (*Experience on Acupuncture and Moxibustion Therapy*)

　　3) Pain along the spinal column, dyspepsia, abdominal mass and distension: Zhishi (BL 52) and Baohuang (BL 53). (*ibid*)

　　4) Painless delivery: Zhishi (BL 52), and the point which is two fingers width level to Qihaishu (BL 24), Shangliao (BL 31), Ciliao (BL 32) and Taichong (LR 3) (all double-punctured). (*Abstract of Clinical Experience on Acupuncture and Moxibustion*)

[Regional Anatomy] Skin-subcutaneous tissue-apponeurosis of latissimus muscle of the back-erector spinal muscle. In the superficial layer, there are the lateral cutaneous branches of the posterior branches of the 1st and 2nd lumbar nerves and the accompanying arteries and veins. In the deep layer, there are the muscular branches of the posterior branches of the 1st and 2nd lumbar nerves and the branches or tributaries of the dorsal branches of the related posterior intercostal arteries and veins.

[Remark] Puncturing this point may cause some changes in the composition of the urine. After needling Fuliu (KI 17) and Zhishi (BL 52) in normal people, in most of the cases the amount of cyclic adenosine monophosphate (C-AMP) and creatinine increased.

BL 53　Baohuang（胞肓）
(Bladder Vitals)

[Source] *A-B Classic of Acupuncture and Moxibustion*

[Name Explanation] Bao（胞）, cystic; Huang（肓）, membrane. Bao refers to the bladder.

Acupoints of Three Yang Meridians of Foot

The point is at the level of Pangguangshu (BL 28).

【Location】 On the gluteal at the level of the 2nd posterior sacral foramen, 3 cun lateral to the medial sacral crest. (See Fig. 11-32)

【Localization】 In the prone position, locate the point below the 2nd sacral vertebrae, 3 cun lateral to the posterior midline.

【Indications】

1) Urogenital Diseases: Dysuria, stranguria, distension of lower abdomen, uroschesis, swelling vulva.

2) Digestive Diseases: Borborygmus, abdominal distension, constipation.

3) Other Disease: Pain along the spinal column.

【Mechanism of Action】 Baohuang in fact refers to the urinary bladder. This point lies beside and has similar functions to Pangguangshu (BL 28).

【Method】 Puncture perpendicularly 0.7-1.3 cun. Moxibustion is applicable.

【Acupoint Prescriptions】

1) Uroschesis: Baohuang (BL 53) and Zhibian (BL 54). (*Experience on Acupuncture and Moxibustion Therapy*)

2) Dysuria: Baohuang (BL 53), Shimen (RN 5), Guanyuan (RN 4), Yinjiao (RN 7), Zhongji (RN 3), Qugu (RN 2). (*ibid*)

【Regional Anatomy】 Skin-subcutaneous tissue-greater gluteal muscle-the middle gluteal muscle. In the superficial layer, there are the superior and middle gluteal nerves. In the deep layer, there are the superior gluteal artery and vein and the superior gluteal nerve.

BL 54　Zhibian (秩边)
(Lowermost in Order)

【Source】 *A-B Classic of Acupuncture and Moxibustion*

【Name Explanation】 Zhi (秩), order; Bian (边), edge. The Back-Shu points of the Bladder Meridian are arranged in order. This point is the lowest among them.

【Location】 On the gluteal area at the level of the 4th posterior sacral foramen, 3 cun lateral to the medial sacral crest. (See Fig. 11-32)

【Localization】 In the prone position, locate the point level with the 4th posterior sacral foramen, 3 cun lateral to the posterior midline.

【Indications】

1) Diseases along the course of the Meridian: Lumbosacral area pain which causes difficulty in lying flat, heaviness sensation in the lumbosacral region with limited movement, flaccidity and numbness of the lower limbs.

2) Diseases of the Two Lower Orifices: Dysuria, reddish urine, pudendal pain, dyschesia, hemorrhoid.

【Mechanism of Action】

1) Where the meridian passes, where the indications are. It can be used to treat the above mentioned diseases along the course.

2) Different needling depths and angle of insertion in this point indicate different diseases. Inserting the needle vertically can be used to treat the lower extremities; inserting the needle obliquely upward and deeply can be used to treat anal and external genital diseases. If the needle is punctured more deeply upward and obliquely, then, prostatitis and other urinary diseases can be treated. When acupuncture is administered, it is necessary that the needling sensation reach the affected area. That is, needling sensation to the lower limbs can be used to treat numbness and pain of the lower extremities; needling sensation to the external genitalia can be used to treat

genital and anal diseases; while needling sensation to the lower abdomen can be used to treat prostatitis and gynecological diseases.

【Method】 Puncture perpendicularly or obliquely upwards 1-1.5 cun. Moxibustion is applicable.

【Regional Anatomy】 Skin-subcutaneous tissue-greater gluteal muscle-the middle gluteal muscle-lesser gluteal muscle. In the superficial layer, there are the middle and inferior gluteal nerves. In the deep layer, there are the superior and inferior gluteal arteries and veins, and the superior and inferior gluteal nerves.

【Remark】 Puncturing this point can instantly enhance the uterine contraction of a pregnant woman, but the effect will disappear after removing the needle. The duration of the uterine contraction caused by puncturing this point is similar to that caused by intravenous oxytocin. It is considered that puncturing this point is related to the secretion of alphahypophamine. It was reported that puncturing Baihui (DU 20), Shendao (DU 11), Mingmen (DU 4), and this point has a certain effect on dysuria caused by an occult sacral fissure.

BL 55　Heyang（合阳）
(Combining Yang)

【Source】 *A-B Classic of Acupuncture and Moxibustion*

【Name Explanation】 He (合), confluence; Yang (阳), Yang of Yin-Yang. The meridian runs downward from the neck, from where it branches out into two lines. After meeting at Weizhong (BL 40), it travels downward and gradually ascends along the muscle. The highest point is considered as Yang.

【Location】 On the posterior side of the leg and on the line connecting Weizhong (BL 40) and Chengshan (BL 57), 2 cun below Weizhong (BL 40). (See Fig. 11-33)

【Localization】 In the prone or sitting position with feet in plantar flexion, locate the point 2 cun directly inferior to Weizhong (BL 40).

【Indications】

1) Diseases along the Course of the Meridian: Pain along the spinal column which radiates to the lower abdomen, pain and numbness of lower extremities, heaviness, swelling and pain of the knees and calves.

2) Reproductive Diseases: Metrorrhagia and metrostaxis, leukorrhea, pudendal pain, testitis, impotence.

3) Mental Diseases: Epilepsy, muscular spasm, clonic convulsion.

4) Other Diseases: Hernia, pain in the upper and lower abdomen.

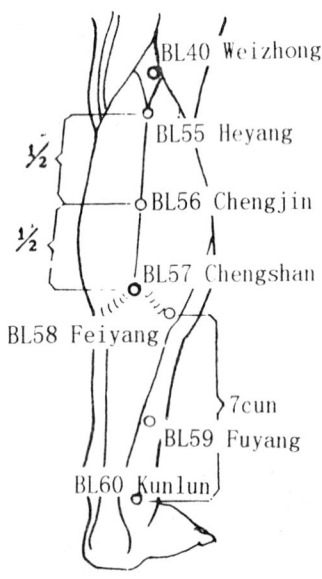

Fig. 11-33

【Mechanism of Action】

1) Where the meridian passes, where the indications are, thus, it can be used to treat illnesses of the spinal column and lower limbs.

2) The Bladder Meridian of Foot Taiyang is connected with the brain, spine, back and gluteal area by its collaterals, so it can be used to treat disorders of the head, epilepsy and clonic convulsion.

3) The Bladder Meridian of Foot Taiyang and Kidney Meridian of Foot Shaoyin are interiorty-exteriorly related with the kidney dominating reproduction, thus, this point also can be

used to treat disorders of the reproductive system.
【Method】 Puncture perpendicularly 0.7-1 cun. Moxibustion is applicable.
【Regional Anatomy】 Skin-subcutaneous tissue-gastrocnemius muscle-the plantar muscle. In the superficial layer, there are the small saphenous vein, the posterior cutaneous nerve of the thigh and the medial cutaneous nerve of the calf. In the deep layer, there are the popliteal artery and vein and the tibial nerve.

BL 56　Chengjin (承筋)
(Supporting Tenden)

【Source】 *A-B Classic of Acupuncture and Moxibustion*
【Name Explanation】 Cheng (承), sustain; Jin (筋), tendon and muscle. The point is on the gastrocnemius, an important muscle of the leg which supports the upper part of the body.
【Location】 On the posterior side of the leg. On the line connecting Weizhong (BL 40) and Chengshan (BL 57), at the center of the gastrocnemius muscle belly, 5 cun inferior to Weizhong (BL 40). (See Fig. 11-33)
【Localization】 In the prone or sitting position with the foot in plantar flexion, locate the point at the centre of the gastrocnemius muscle, midpoint between Heyang (BL 55) and Chengshan (BL 57).
【Indications】
　1) Diseases along the Course of the Meridian: Spasm and pain along spinal column, soreness, heaviness, pain or numbness of knees and calves, cramp in cholera morbus, pain and contracture of the feet with edema of the dorsum.
　2) Diseases of Head and Sense Organs: Dizziness and headache, epistaxis.
　3) Digestive Diseases: Vomiting, diarrhea, constipation, hemorrhoid.
【Mechanism of Action】 The collaterals of the Bladder Meridian of Foot Taiyang are linked with the anus and have the functions of regulating qi and keep the functional activities of the intestines in order, thus, it can be used to treat digestive diseases, particularly anal diseases. See also Chengshan (BL 57).
【Method】 Puncture perpendicularly 0.5-1.5 cun. Moxibustion is applicable.
【Acupoint Prescriptions】
　1) Hemorrhoid: Chengjin (BL 56), Chengfu (BL 50), Weizhong (BL 40) and Yanggu (SI 5). (*Thousand Golden Prescriptions*)
　2) Muscular cramp due to cholera morbus: Chengjin (BL 56), Yongquan (KI 1), and the spot of dorso-ventral boundary of the heel. (*The Medical Secrets of an Official*)
　3) Cholera: Chengjin (BL 56), Pucan (Pushen) (BL 61), Yinlingquan (SP 9). (*Experience on Acupuncture and Moxibustion Therapy*)
【Regional Anatomy】 Skin-subcutaneous tissue-gastrocnemius muscle-plantar muscle. In the superficial layer, there are the small saphenous vein and the medial cutaneous nerve of the calf. In the deep layer, there are the posterior tibial artery and vein, the peroneal artery and vein and the tibial nerve.

BL 57　Chengshan (承山)
(Supporting Hill)

【Source】 *A-B Classic of Acupuncture and Moxibustion*

[Name Explanation] Cheng (承), sustain; Shan (山), mountain. The two bellies of the gastrocnemius muscle are as prominent as mountains. The point is below them, as if holding up mountains.

[Location] On the posterior midline of the leg, between Weizhong (BL 40) and Kunlun (BL 60), in the depression formed below the gastrocnemius muscle belly when the leg is stretched or the heel is lifted. (See Fig. 11-33)

[Localization]

1) In the prone position, straighten the leg with the dorsum of the foot extended upwards, locate the point below the tip of the "人" shape of the gastrocnemius muscle.

2) Standing on tip toes, locate the point below the tip of the "人" shape of the gastrocnemius muscle.

[Indications]

1) Diseases along the Course of the Meridian: Pain of the waist and back, pain and spasm of the legs, pain in heel, contracture of the foot which brings about pain in the lower abdomen, beriberi.

2) Diseases of Head and Sense Organs: Epistaxis, running nose, sore throat.

3) Digestive Diseases: Hemorrhoid, constipation, vomiting, diarrhea.

4) Mental Diseases: Epilepsy, infantile convulsion.

5) Other Diseases: Hernia.

[Mechanism of Action]

1) This point belongs to the Bladder Meridian whose collaterals distribute in the head, neck, back and lower limbs, thus, it can be used to treat limb diseases, infantile convulsion and epilepsy with muscular cramps.

2) The Taiyang meridians are the most superficial of the three yang meridians, playing a role in protecting the body like a fence. They are often the first ones to be affected by external pathogenic factors. Thus, most of the points of the Taiyang meridians may be used to treat sore throat due to exopathic factors and epistaxis due to heat resulting from the attack of exogenous evils.

3) The Bladder Muscle Region of the Foot Taiyang is related to the nose. Symptoms of disorders of the Bladder Collaterals of Foot Taiyang include a stuffy nose due to a excess syndrome and epistaxis due to a deficiency syndrome. The Foot Shaoyin Meridian and Foot Taiyang Meridian are interiorly-exteriorly related and the Kidney Meridian of Foot Shaoyin passes through the throat, thus, all these mentioned above provide a theoretical basis to the meridian doctrine for this point and the points of Foot Taiyang Meridian in treating sore throat and epistaxis.

[Method] Puncture perpendicularly 0.5-1 cun. Moxibustion is applicable.

[Acupoint Prescriptions]

1) Early stage of beriberi, spasms: Chengshan (BL 57) and Chengjin (BL 56). (*The Medical Secrets of an Official*)

2) Tenesmus: Chengshan (BL 57), Jiexi (ST 41), Taibai (SP 3) and Daimai (GB 26). (*Great Compendium of Acupuncture and Moxibustion*)

3) Hemorrhoid with blood, abdominal pain: Chengshan (BL 57) and Fuliu (KI 7). (*ibid*)

4) Edema in lower limbs: Chengshan (BL 57) and Kunlun (BL 60). (*ibid*)

5) Visceral intoxication: Chengshan (BL 57), Pishu (BL 20), Jinggong (EX) and Changqiang (DU 1). (*ibid*)

6) Cramp in cholera morbus: Chengshan (BL 57) and Zhongfeng (BL 57). (*ibid*)

7) Spasm, dizziness: Chengshan (BL 57) and Kunlun (BL 60). (*Songs of Xihong*)

[Regional Anatomy] Skin-subcutaneous tissue-gastrocnemius muscle-plantar muscle. In the superficial layer, there are the small saphenous vein and the medial cutaneous nerve of the calf. In the deep layer, there are the tibial nerve and the posterior tibial artery and vein.

[Remark] Puncturing this point has an effect in treating early ventricular contraction. Children of 6-12 years old were treated with Zhiyin (BL 67) and Chengshan (BL 57) being stimulated with a low frenquency electric pulse. It was found that the urine volume, Na^+, K^+ and cyclic AMP content in the urine of 11 children was elevated in the first two hours after the needling sensation appeared There was a smaller increase in 14 children who did not feel the needling sensation. 24 hours after acupuncture, the urine volume and the total content of Na^+ and K^+ in the urine of the sensation positive group was 20% higher than those of the non-sensation group, but the cylic AMP content in the urine had decreased.

BL 58 Feiyang (飞扬)
(Flying up)

[Source] *Miraculous Pivot*
[Name Explanation] Fei (飞) to fly; Yang (扬), lifting. The exterior is Yang. The point is the Luo-connecting point of the Urinary Bladder Meridian and is located on the lateral aspect of the leg, and the collateral of this meridian flies out from this point to the Kidney Meridian.
[Classification] Luo-(Connecting) Point of the Bladder Meridian of Foot Taiyang.
[Location] On the posterior side of the leg, 7 cun directly above Kunlun (BL 60) and 1 cun lateral and inferior to Chengshan (BL 57). (See Fig. 11-33)
[Localization] Sitting position with the foot in plantar flexion, locate the point 1 cun obliquely inferior to Chengshan (BL 57), directly superior to Kunlun (BL 60).
[Indications]
  1) Diseases along the Course of the Meridian: Pain in the back and loins, lassitude and weakness of the legs, contracture of the muscles and tendons which causes difficulty in flexing, leprosy.
  2) Diseases of Head and Sense Organs: Headache, dizziness, stuffy nose, epistaxis.
  3) Mental Disease: Epilepsy.
  4) Other Diseases: Hemorrhoidal diseases, fever without sweating.
[Mechanism of Action] Refer to the Chengshan (BL 57) and Chengjin (BL 56).
[Method] Puncture perpendicularly 0.7-1 cun. Moxibustion is applicable.
[Acupoint Prescriptions]
  1) Neck pain, leprosy, perspiration: Feiyang (BL 58), Yongquan (KI 1), Hanyan (GB 4) and Houding (DU 19). (*Thousand Golden Prescriptions*)
  2) Protrusion of the tongue due to manic-depressive psychosis: Feiyang (BL 58), Taiyi (ST 23) and Huaroumen (ST 24). (*Experience on Acupuncture and Moxibustion Therapy*)
  3) Vertigo: Feiyang (BL 58) and Feishu (BL 13). (*ibid*)
[Regional Anatomy] Skin-subcutaneous tissue-triceps muscle of the calf-the long flexor muscle of the great toe. In the superficial layer, there is the lateral cutaneous nerve of the calf. In the deep layer, there are the tibial nerve and the posterior tibial artery and vein.
[Remark] Puncturing this point can enhance urinary function. It was reported that needling Dazhu (BL 11), Zusanli (ST 36) and retaining the needle for ten minutes could make calcium content in the blood increase by 1 mg%, and retaining the needle for 15 minutes, by 3 mg%.

BL 59 Fuyang (跗阳)
(Yang of Foot Dorsum)

[Source] *A-B Classic of Acupuncture and Moxibustion*
[Name Explanation] Fu(跗), tarsus; Yang(阳), Yang of Yin-Yang. The exterior and superior

are Yang, the point is at the superior aspect of the tarsus and at the lateral aspect of the leg.

〖Classification〗 Xi-(Cleft) point of the Yangqiao Meridian.

〖Location〗 On the posterior side of the leg, posterior to the lateral malleolus, 3 cun directly above Kunlun (BL 60). (See Fig. 11-33)

〖Localization〗 Sitting position with the foot in plantar flexion, the point is located 3 cun directly superior to BL 60 which is located at the midpoint of the the line joining the lateral malleous and the Achilles tendon.

〖Indications〗

1) Diseases along the Course of the Meridian: Shoulder pain, torticollis, lumbago, flaccidity and numbness of the lower extremities, semiparalysis, beriberi, calf spasm.

2) Diseases of Head and Sense Organs: Headache, heaviness sensation in the head, vertigo.

3) Other Diseases: Epilepsy, clonic convulsion.

〖Mechanism of Action〗

1) This point is one of the sixteen Xi-(Cleft) points of the Yangqiao Meridian, which are mainly used to treat acute pain. The Yangqiao Meridian distributes to the lateral side of the lower limbs, shoulders and head where the meridians of Foot Taiyang, Foot Shaoyang, Hand-Shaoyang and Foot Yangming converge. The Qiao meridians of Yin and Yang are respectively in charge of the activity and inertia, of which Yangqiao Meridian governs Yang-qi while Yinqiao Meridian controls Yin-qi, and have the dominating and regulating actions on the meridians of Yin and Yang that are distributed respectively in the lateral and medial sides of the lower limbs. Thus, for acute pain in shoulder, torticollis, hemiparalysis, flaccidity and numbness of lower limbs, this point is often used.

2) The Yangqiao Meridian links many Yang meridians which converge in the head, this point is often used to treat headache, heaviness of the head and vertigo.

〖Method〗 Puncture perpendicularly 0.5-1 cun. Moxibustion is applicable.

〖Acupoint Prescription〗 Clonic convulsion: Fuyang (BL 59) and Tianjing (SJ 10); Pain and heaviness sensation in the head: Fuyang (BL 59) and Naohu (DU 17). (*Experience on Acupuncture and Moxibustion Therapy*)

〖Regional Anatomy〗 Skin-subcutaneous tissue-the short peroneal muscle-the long flexor muscle of the great toe. In the superficial layer, there are the sural nerve and the small saphenous vein. In the deep layer, there are the branches of the tibial nerve and the muscular branches of the posterior tibial artery and vein.

BL 60   Kunlun（昆仑）
(Big and high)

〖Source〗 *Miraculous Pivot*

〖Name Explanation〗 Kunlun（昆仑）, the name of some mountains in the West of China. The lateral malleolus is shaped like a mountain, and the point is located next to it.

〖Classification〗 Jing-(River) point of the Bladder Meridian of Foot Taiyang, pertainig to fire in the Five Elements.

〖Location〗 Posterior to the lateral malleolus, in the depression between the tip of the external malleolus and Achilles tendon. (See Fig. 11-34)

〖Localization〗 Sitting position with the foot in plantar flexion or the prone position, select the point at the midpoint between the apex of the lateral malleolus and the Achilles tendon.

〖Indications〗

1) Diseases along the Course of the Meridian: Neck rigidity, cramping of the shoulder and back, lumbosacral pain, pain in the heel, swelling of feet causing inability to stand up.

2) Diseases of Head and Sense Organs: Headache, dizziness, unbearable pain in eye, epistaxis.

3) Gynecopathies: Dystocia, retention of placenta, swelling and pain in vulva.

4) Digestive Diseases: Abdominal pain, diarrhea, dyschesis.

5) Mental Diseases: Epilepsy, clonic convulsion, infantile epilepsy.

6) Other Diseases: Malaria, epigastric pain radiating to back, fullness sensation in the chest with sudden asthma.

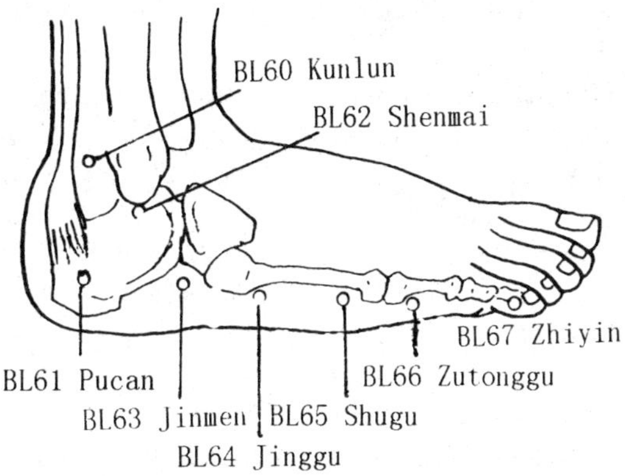

Fig. 11-34

【Mechanism of Action】

1) This point has an important effect when used to treat occipital headache and pain in the back and neck and is often used together with Houxi (SI 3).

2) The kidney dominates the reproductive function. The Urinary Bladder and Kidney Meridians are interior-exteriorly related, so the points of these two meridians can both treat the visceral diseases. Therefore, this point is commonly used for dystocia and retention of placenta.

【Method】 Puncture perpendicularly 0.5 cun. Moxibustion is applicable.

【Acupoint Prescriptions】

1) Blindness: Kunlun (BL 60) and Yangxi (LI 5). (*Experience on Acupuncture and Moxibustion*)

2) Severe lumbago: Kunlun (BL 60) and Weizhong (BL 54). (*Plain Questions*)

3) Pedal eczema: Kunlun (BL 60), Qiuxu (GB 40), Shangqiu (SP 5) and Zhaohai (KI 3). (*Great Compendium of Acupuncture and Moxibustion*)

4) Carbuncle, cellulitis: Kunlun (BL 60), Chengjiang (RN 24) and Sanyinjiao (SP 6). (*ibid*)

5) Hysterical attack: Kunlun (BL 60) and Houxi (SI 3). (*Science of Acupuncture and Moxibustion*)

6) Pain in ankle bone: Kunlun (BL 60), Juegu (GB 39) and Qiuxu (GB 40). (*The Peaceful Holy Benevolent Prescriptions*)

7) Pain in knees and feet: Kunlun (BL 60) and Taixi (KI 3). (*A Handbook of Prescriptions for Emergencies*)

【Regional Anatomy】 Skin-subcutaneous tissue-loose connective tissue anterior to Archilles tendon. In the superficial layer, there are the sural nerve and the small saphenous vein. In the deep layer, there are the branches or tributaries of the peroneal artery and vein.

【Remark】 Puncturing this point may enhance the peristalsis of the lower part of the descending colon and rectum, bringing about the desire to defecate. With reducing manipulation, it has the action of lowering high blood pressure in primary hypertension.

BL 61 Pucan (仆参)
(Worship on Bended Kness)

【Source】 *A-B Classic of Acupuncture and Moxibustion*

【Name Explanation】 Pu (仆), servant; Can (参), paying respects. The point is at the lateral aspect of the heel and therefore is exposed when a servant would pay respect.

【Location】 On the lateral side of the foot, posterior and inferior to the external malleolus, directly below Kunlun (BL 60), lateral to the calcaneum, at the junction of the red and white skin. (See Fig. 11-34)

〖Localization〗 Sitting position with the foot in plantar flexion or in the prone position, locate the point directly inferior to Kunlun (BL 60), in the depression at the junction of the red and white skin.

〖Indications〗

　　1) Diseases along the Course of the Meridian: Heel pain, lumbago, cramps due to cholera morbus, beriberi, pain in the knees, flaccidity and weakness of the lower limbs.

　　2) Mental Diseases: Manic-depressive psychosis, epilepsy, corpse-like syncope.

　　3) Other Diseases: Vomiting, regurgitation, stranguria with turbid urine.

〖Mechanism of Action〗 This point is mainly used to treat heel pain and lumbago.

〖Method〗 Puncture perpendicularly 0.2-0.3 cun. Moxibustion is applicable.

〖Acupoint Prescriptions〗

　　1) Infantile epilepsy: Pucan (BL 61) and Jinmen (BL 63). (*A-B Classic of Acupuncture and Moxibustion*)

　　2) Calf spasm: Pucan (BL 61), Qiaoyin (GB 44), Zhiyin (BL 67), Jiexi (ST 41) and Qiuxu (GB 40). (*Experience on Acupuncture and Moxibustion Therapy*)

〖Regional Anatomy〗 Skin-subcutaneous tissue-calcaneus.

　　There are the tributaries of the small saphenous vein, the lateral calcaneal branches of the sural nerve and the calcaneal branches of the peroneal artery and vein in this area.

BL 62　Shenmai（申脉）
(Stretching Channel)

〖Source〗 *A-B Classic of Acupuncture and Moxibustion*

〖Name Explanation〗 Shen（申）, to extend; Mai（脉）, meridian. The point pertains to the Bladder Meridian, from where the meridian extends to the Yangqiao Meridian.

〖Classification〗 One of the Eight Confluent Points.

〖Location〗 On the lateral side of the foot, in the depression directly below the external malleolus. (See Fig. 11-34)

〖Localization〗 Sitting position with the foot in plantar flexion or in the supine position, locate the point 0.5 cun directly inferior to the lateral malleolus, between the malleolus and the cartilage.

〖Indications〗

　　1) Diseases along the Course of the Meridian: Cold-pain in the lower back and coccyx, pain in the waist and legs, foot and calf pain, swelling of external ankle, paralysis of the lower limbs.

　　2) Disorders of Head and Sense Organs: Headache, dizziness, tinnitus, conjunctival congestion, epistaxis, distortion of the face.

　　3) Mental Diseases: Manic-deppressive psychosis, daily epilepsy, aphasia during apoplexy, opistotonos.

　　4) Other Diseases: Aversion to cold, fever.

〖Mechanism of Action〗

　　1) This point is one of the Eight-confluent Points and connects with Yangqiao Meridian. It is the place where Yangqiao Meridian originates. Yinqiao and Yangqiao Meridians distribute in the medial and lateral sides of the lower limbs, run upward and end in the inner canthus. Qiao meridians have a regulating function to keep the activities of Yin and Yang in balance. The signs of disorders of the Yangqiao Meridian are acuteness in Yang and mildness in Yin and that of Yin-

qiao Meridianare acuteness in Yin and mildness in yang. Because this point is the confluent point with the Yangqiao Meridian, it can be used to treat foot drop with inversion due to paralysis of the lower limbs and epilepsy that attacks only during the day.

2) The Bladder Meridian of Foot Taiyang distributes in the eyes, head and neck, thus, it can be used to treat diseases of the face and head.

【Method】 Puncture perpendicularly 0.2-0.3 cun. Moxibustion is applicable.

【Acupoint Prescriptions】

1) Lumbago which cause limitation of movement: Shenmai (BL 62), Taichong (LR 3) and Yangqiao (GB 35). (*Thousand Golden Prescriptions*)

2) Epilepsy: Shenmai (BL 62), Houxi (SI 3) and Qiangu (SI 2). (*Experience on Acupuncture and Moxibustion*)

3) Conjunctival congestion: Shenmai (BL 62), Taichong (LR 3), Ququan (LR 8) and Yangxi (LI 5). (*ibid*)

4) Headache due to attack of wind-evil on the head: Shenmai (BL 62), Jinmen (BL 63). (*Secret Songs on Acupuncture and Moxibustion*)

5) Chronic intermittent headache, dizziness, neck rigidity: Shenmai (BL 62), Jinmen (BL 63), Shousanli (LI 10). (*Songs on Point Selection of Miscellaneous Diseases*)

【Regional Anatomy】 Skin-subcutaneous tissue-tendon of the long peroneal muscle-the tendon of the short peroneal muscle-lateral talocalcaneal ligament.

There are the branches of the small saphenous vein, the sural nerve and the lateral anterior malleolus artery and vein in this area.

BL 63   Jinmen (金门)
(Golden Gate)

【Source】 *A-B Classic of Acupuncture and Moxibustion*

【Name Explanation】 Jin (金), gold; Men (门), door. The point pertains to the Bladder Meridian of Foot Taiyang and is the starting point of Yangweimai (Yangwei Meridian), as a door to enter the Yangweimai.

【Classification】 Xi-(Cleft) point of the Bladder Meridian of Foot Taiyang.

【Location】 On the lateral side of the foot, directly below the anterior border of the external malleolus, on the lower border of the cuboid bone. (See Fig. 11-34)

【Localization】 Sitting position with the foot in plantar flexion or in the supine position, locate the point 0.5 cun anterior and inferior to Shenmai (BL 62), in the depression at the lateral side of the cuboid bone.

【Indications】

1) Diseases along the Course of the Meridian: Lumbago, flaccidity or numbness of lower limbs, soreness and pain in knees and calves, cramping due to cholera morbus, swelling and pain in the external ankle.

2) Diseases of Head and Sense Organs: Headache, tinnitus, deafness.

3) Mental Diseases: Epilepsy, coma, corpse-like syncope, infantile convulsion.

4) Other Diseases: Sudden hernia, pain in the lower abdomen.

【Mechanism of Action】 This point is the Xi-(Cleft) point of the Bladder Meridian of Foot Taiyang, and also the point of origin of the Yangwei Meridian. Thus, it can be used to treat headache, acute pain in the loins and cramps due to cholera morbus.

【Method】 Puncture perpendicularly 0.3-0.5 cun. Moxibustion is applicable.

【Acupoint Prescriptions】

1) Cramp due to cholera morbus: Jinmen (BL 63), Pucan (BL 61), Chengshan (BL

57) and Chengjin (BL 56). (*A-B Classic of Acupuncture and Moxibustion*)

2) Pain due to sudden hernia: Jinmen (BL 63) and Qiuxu (GB 40). (*Experience on Acupuncture and Moxibustion*)

3) Epilepsy: Jinmen (BL 63) and Pucan (BL 61). (ibid.)

4) Cramps: Jinmen (BL 63) and Qiuxu (GB 40). (*Songs of Hundreds of Symptoms*)

5) Deafness due to exogenous febrile disease: Jinmen (BL 63) and Tinghui (GB 2). (*Songs of Xihong*)

【Regional Anatomy】 Skin-subcutaneous tissue-the tendon of the long peroneal muscle and abductor muscle of the little toe.

There are the lateral dorsal cutaneous nerve of the foot and the lateral vein of the foot (the small saphenous vein) in this area.

BL 64 Jinggu (京骨)
(Jing Bone)

【Source】 *Miraculous Pivot*

【Name Explanation】 Jinggu (京骨) is an ancient name for the tuberosity of the 5th meatatarsus. The point is in the lateral aspect of this tuberosity.

【Classification】 Yuan-(Source) point of the Bladder Meridian of Foot Taiyang.

【Location】 On the lateral side of the foot, below the tuberosity of the 5th metatarsal bone, at the junction of the red and white skin. (See Fig. 11-34)

【Localization】 Sitting position with the foot in plantar flexion or in the supine position, locate the point at the junction of the red and white skin in the lateral margin of the foot, anterior and inferior to the margin of the 5th metatarsal tuberosity.

【Indications】

1) Diseases along the Course of the Meridian: Neck rigidity, acute pain in the waist which causes difficulty in lying flat, pain in lower back and legs, knee pain with contracture of the feet.

2) Diseases of Head and Sense Organs: Headache, dizziness, erosion in the inner canthus, nebula, epistaxis.

3) Digestive Diseases: Diarrhea, fullness sensation in the abdomen, loss of appetite.

4) Cardiovascular Diseases: Precordial pain, palpitation.

5) Mental Diseases: Manic-depressive psychosis, epilepsy, infantile convulsion, spasm, convulsion.

6) Other Diseases: Malaria, headache due to alternate spells of fever and chill.

【Mechanism of Action】 Refer to Jinmen (BL 63) and Pucan (BL 61).

【Method】 Puncture perpendicularly 0.3-0.5 cun. Moxibustion is applicable.

【Acupoint Prescriptions】

1) Precordial pain accompanied by backache: Jinggu (BL 64) and Kunlun (BL 60). (*Miraculous Pivot*)

2) Pathogenic Fright: Jinggu (BL 64), Dazhong (KI 4) and Daling (PC 7). (*Experience on Acupuncture and Moxibustion Therapy*)

【Regional Anatomy】 Skin-subcutaneous tissue-abductor muscle of the little toe. There are the lateral dorsal cutaneous nerve of the foot and the lateral vein of the foot (the small saphenous vein) in this area.

BL 65　Shugu (束骨)
(Shu Bone)

【Source】 *Miraculous Pivot*
【Name Explanation】 Shu (束), bundle up; Gu (骨), bone. Shugu is an ancient name for the head of the 5th metatarsus. The point is at the lateral and inferior aspect of the head of the 5th metatarsus.
【Classification】 Shu-(Stream) point of the Bladder Meridian of Foot Taiyang.
【Location】 On the lateral side of the foot, posterior to the 5th metatarsophalangeal joint, at the junction of the red and white skin. (See Fig. 11-34)
【Localization】 Sitting position with the foot in plantar flexion or in the supine position, locate the point at the junction of the red and white skin in the lateral margin of the foot, on the posterior side of the head of the 5th metatarsal bone.
【Indications】
　　1) Diseases along the Course of the Meridian: Neck rigidity causing difficulty in turning the head, acute pain of the back and lower back with difficulty while lying flat, pain in legs and loins, pain in the posterior side of the lower limbs.
　　2) Diseases of Head and Sense Organs: Headache, dizziness, erosion in the inner canthus, hyperdacryosis, deafness.
　　3) Digestive Diseases: Diarrhea, dysentery, inferic sclera.
　　4) Gynecopathies: Metrorrhagia and metrostaxis.
　　5) External Diseases: Hemorrhoid, carbuncle, cellulitis and carbuncle of back, furuncle.
　　6) Mental Diseases: Manic-depressive psychosis.
　　7) Other Diseases: Fever, aversion to cold.
【Mechanism of Action】 Refer to Jinmen (BL 63) and Pucan (BL 61).
【Method】 Puncture perpendicularly 0.3 cun. Moxibustion is applicable.
【Acupoint Prescriptions】 Unbearable lumbago: Shugu (BL 65), Feiyang (BL 58) and Chengjin (BL 56). (*Thousand Golden Prescriptions*)
【Regional Anatomy】 Skin-subcutaneous tissue-abductor muscle of the little toe-tendon of opponens muscle of the little toe-short flexor muscle of the little toe. In the superficial layer, there are the lateral dorsal cutaneous nerve of the foot and the tributaries of the arch of the dorsal venous arch of the foot. In the deep layer, there are the proper digital plantar nerve and the proper digital plantar arteries and veins.

BL 66　Zutonggu (足通谷)
(Passing Valley)

【Source】 *Miraculous Pivot*
【Name Explanation】 Zu (足), foot; Tong (通), passing; Gu (谷), valley. The point is in the depression of the foot, which is compared to a valley through which the qi of meridian passes.
【Classification】 Ying-(Spring) point of the Bladder Meridian of Foot Taiyang, pertaining to water in the Five Elements.
【Location】 On the lateral side of the foot, anterior to the 5th metatarsophalangeal joint, at the junction of the red and white skin. (See Fig. 11-34)
【Localization】 Sitting position with the foot in plantar flexion, locate the point at the junction of

the red and white skin in the lateral side of the foot, in the anterior margin of the 5th metatarsophalangeal joint.

【Indications】
　　1) Diseases along the Course of the Meridian: Heaviness and pain sensation in the head, neck rigidity, vertigo, stuffy nose.
　　2) Diseases of Head and Sense Organs: Dizziness and epistaxis.
　　3) Respiratory Diseases: Cough due to fullness in the chest.
　　4) Gynecopathies: Metrorrhagia and metrostaxis.
　　5) Mental Diseases: Manic-depressive psychosis, susceptibity to fright.

【Mechanism of Action】 Refer to Jinmen (BL 63) and Pucan (BL 61).

【Method】 Puncture perpendicularly 0.2-0.3 cun. Moxibustion is applicable.

【Acupoint Prescriptions】
　　1) Fullness feeling and discomfort in the chest and hypochondrium: Tonggu (BL 66), Zhangmen (LR 13), Ququan (LR 8), Geshu (BL 17), Qimen (LR 14), Shidou (SP 17), Xiangu (ST 43) and Shimen (RN 5). (*Thousand Golden Prescriptions*)
　　2) Precordial pain: Tonggu (BL 66), Juque (RN 14), Taicang (EX), Xinshu (BL 15), Danzhong (RN 17) and Shenfu (EX). (*ibid*)
　　3) Susceptibility to fright: Tonggu (BL 66) and Zhangmen (LR 13). (*Experience on Acupuncture and Moxibustion Therapy*)

【Regional Anatomy】 Skin-subcutaneous tissue-plantar surface of the proximal end of the little toe. There are the lateral dorsal cutaneous nerve of the foot, the tributaries of the arch of the dorsal veins of the foot, and the proper digital plantar arteries and veins in this area.

BL 67　Zhiyin（至阴）
(Reaching Yin)

【Source】 *Miraculous Pivot*

【Name Explanation】 Zhi (至), reaching; Yin (阴), Yin of Yin-Yang. Yin refers to the Foot-Shaoyin Meridian. This is the last point of the Bladder Meridian of the Foot Taiyang, from where it reaches the Foot Shaoyin Meridian.

【Classification】 Jing-(Well) point of the Bladder Meridian of Foot Taiyang, pertaining to metal in the Five Elements.

【Location】 On the lateral side of the distal segment of the little toe, 0.1 cun from the corner of the toenail. (See Fig. 11-34)

【Localization】 Sitting position with foot in plantar flexion or in the the supine position, the point is located at the intersection of the lines drawn from the lateral margin of the little toe nail and its basal part.

【Indications】
　　1) Diseases along the Course of the Meridian: Swelling knees and feet, spasm and clonic convulsion, hot sensation on the sole.
　　2) Diseases of Head and Sense Organs: Headache, rigidity and pain in the neck, ophthalmalgia, plerygium, stuffy nose, epistaxis.
　　3) Urogenital Diseases: Dysuria, seminal emission, abnormal fetal position, dystocia, retention of placenta.
　　4) Other Diseases: Hernia, generalized pruritus, nonsweating, dysphoria.

【Mechanism of Action】
　　1) The Bladder Meridian of Foot Taiyang originates in the eye, distributes in the head, neck, lumbar region, the back, and its muscle region connects with the nose. The Foot-

Taiyang Meridian plays a body protecting role and is regarded as a fence of the body. According to the principle in acupuncture that to treat disorders in the upper part of the body, we must manipulate the lower part, and also according to the clinical experiences, this point can be used to treat diseases of the face and head, especially headache with difficulty in opening the eyes.

2) The kidney and urinary bladder are inferior-exteriorly related. The kidney dominates the reproductive function, thus, Kunlun (BL 60) and Zhiyin (BL 67) have the function of correcting the position of the fetus. Zhiyin (BL 67) is the point which is used most often. Administering moxa on the point or kneading this point directly may correct the position of fetus and promote delivery.

[Method] Puncture obliquely 0.1 cun. Moxibustion is applicable for difficult labor.

[Acupoint Prescriptions]

1) Seminal emission: Zhiyin (BL 67), Ququan (LR 8) and Zhongji (RN 3). (*Experience on Acupuncture and Moxibustion Therapy*)

2) Non-sweating: Zhiyin (BL 67), Yuji (LU 10), Ququan (LR 8), Xiaxi (GB 43), Zhonglushu (BL 29). (*ibid*)

3) Carbuncle and sores on the back: Zhiyin (BL 67), Tonggu (BL 66), shugu (BL 65), Kunlun (BL 60) and Weizhong (BL 40). (*A Collection for Preserving Life and the Mechanism of Diseases from Plain Questions*)

4) Exopathic disease characterized by stroke, anhidrosis and aversion to cold: Taiyang (EX-HN 5), Zhiyin (BL 67) (punctured till bleeding), Kunlun (BL 60) and Yangqiao (EX). (*ibid*)

[Regional Anatomy] Skin-subcutaneous tissue-the root of the nail. There are the dorsal digital nerve of the lateral dorsal cutaneous nerve of the foot and the arteriovenous network of the dorsal digital arteries and veins in this area.

[Remark] Manipulating this point with moxibustion and laser can correct the position of the fetus. The effective rate is 70-80%. There was a report on the mechanism of moxibustion to this point in correcting the position of fetus. There were 2096 women who accepted the moxibustion therapy. Their pregnancy stages ranged from 29-40 weeks and the positions of the fetus were all abnormal. Moxa the Zhiyin (BL 67) on both sides using moxa sticks until hot but not buring pain. The results showed that the corrective rate on the position of the fetus was 90.3%; of which 86% of the cases gained success within 1-4 treatment and 14% of the cases obtained success within 5-10 treatments. Of the 2096 cases, 2041 cases the fetus was in the breech position (1840 cases were corrected successfully) and 28 cases whose fetus were in the transverse position (all cases were corrected successfully) and there was no obvious difference in the therapeutic effect between the premiparace and pluriparae with 6 children or more. Experimental observation was conducted on the successfully-treated cases. The test on the functional activity of hormones of 33 cases of pregnant women showed that before moxibustion, the numerical value of 17-hydroxycorticosteroid and 17-ketosteroid in the urine of the pregnant women was higher than that of the non-pregnant women; after moxibustion, hormone values increased further. Similar results were obtained when the test was conducted on the plasma free cortisol before and after moxibustion. The results indicated that moxibustion could activate the pituitary-adrenal cortex system and strengthen uterine contraction. At the same time, it could also enhance fetal movement (making the fetal heartbeat increase), thereby assist the fetus to correct the position by itself.

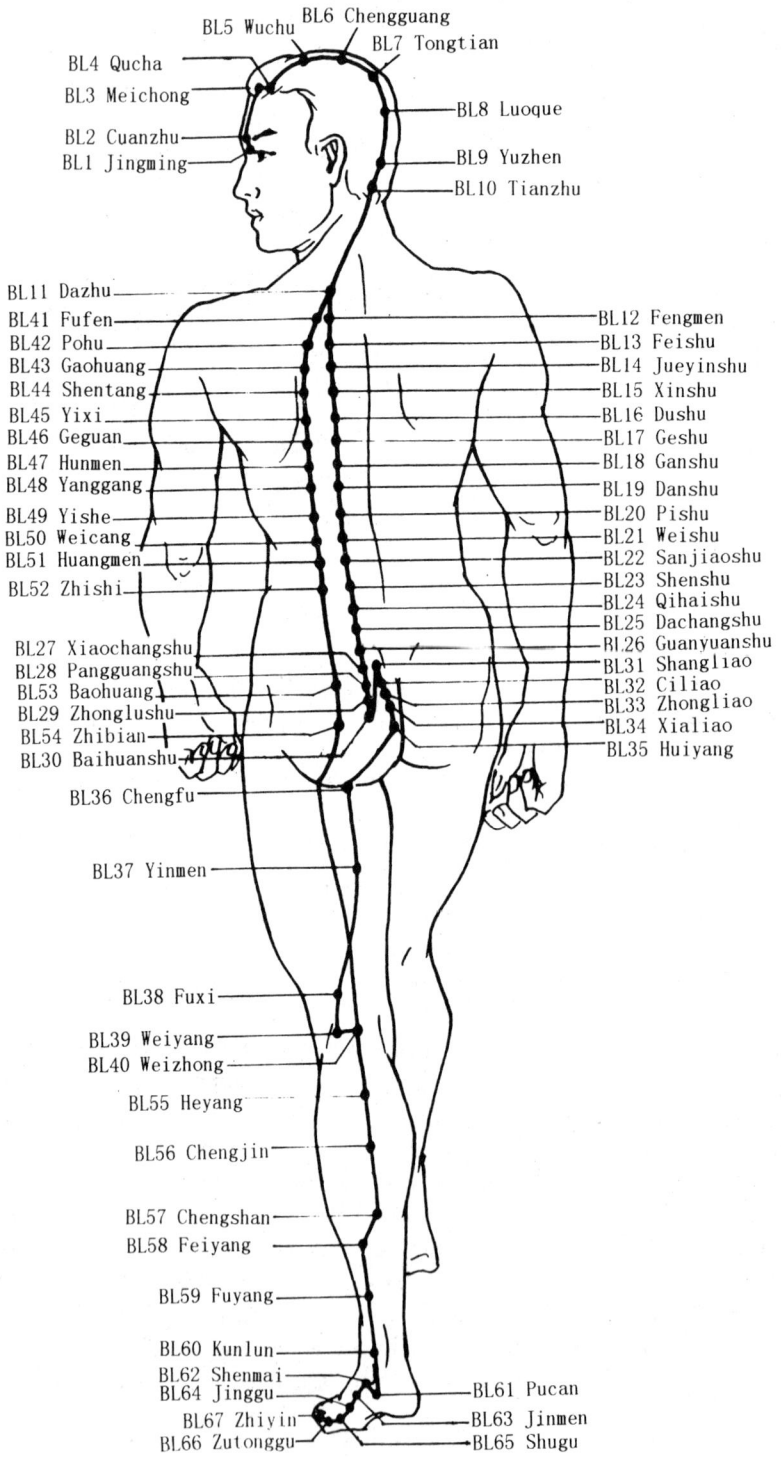

Fig. 11-35 Acupoints of the Bladder Meridian of Foot Taiyang

Table 11-3
Indications and Actions of Acupoints of the Bladder Meridian of Foot Taiyang

Name of the points	Specific points	Common indications	Specific indications and functions
BL 1 Jingming (睛明)	Crossing point	Diseases of the head, neck, eyes and nose: headache, nape pain, dizziness, vertigo, eye pain, stuffy nose, epistaxis Mental disease: manic-depression	Dispelling wind and removing heat, clearing collaterals and improving acuity of vision. Conjunctival congestion, epiphora, twitching of eyelids, blurring vision, dizziness, myopia, night blindness, colour blindness
BL 2 Cuanzhu (Zanzhu) (攒竹)			Eliminating wind and improving acuity of vision. Headache, distortion of mouth and eyes, pain in the supra-orbital bone, dropping of eye lid, blurring vision, epiphora, conjunctival congestion
BL 3 Meichong (眉冲)			Headache, dizziness, stuffy nose, epilepsy
BL 4 Qucha (曲差)			Removing heat and inducing resuscitation, clearing head and improving acuity of vision. Headache, stuffy nose, epistaxis, blurred vision, vexation
BL 5 Wuchu (五处)			Headache, dizziness, epilepsy
BL 6 Chengguang (承光)			Dispelling wind and improving eyesight. Dizziness, nebula, blurred vision, stuffy and runny nose, dry mouth, headache, febrile disease
BL 7 Tongtian (通天)			Expelling wind and clearing head, clearing the nasal passage. Headache, heaviness in the head, vertigo, insomnia, stuffy nose, epistaxis, pyogenic infection of nose, distortion of mouth and eyes
BL 8 Luoque (络却)			Dizziness, blurring vision, tinnitus, manic-depressive psychosis
BL 9 Yuzhen (玉枕)			Clearing the nasal passage and improving the eyesight. Pain of head and neck, eye pain, stuffy nose

Name of the points	Specific points	Common indications	Specific indications and functions
BL 10 Tianzhu (天柱)		The same as above	Expelling wind and clearing head, dredging the meridian and activating collaterals. Headache, neck stiffness, pain of the shoulder and back, stuffy nose, manic-depression, febrile disease
BL 11 Dazhu (大杼)	Confluential Points of bone Crossing point		Eliminating wind and relieving exterior syndrome, ventilating the lung and lowering the adverse flow of qi, relaxing muscles and tendons. Cough, fever without sweat, splitting headache, fullness in the chest with dyspnea, neck stiffness, pain of the shoulder and back, stiffness and pain along the spinal column
BL 12 Fengmen (风门)	Crossing point		Ventilating the lung, dispelling wind and removing heat. Common cold, cough, fever, headache, neck stiffness, pain in the chest and back
BL 13 Feishu (肺俞)	Back-shu point of the lung	Diseases of the heart and lung: precardial pain, cough, chest oppression	Regulating the flow of lung-qi, nourishing yin and removing heat. Cough, asthma, hematemesis, hectic fever, night sweats, stuffy nose
BL 14 Jueyinshu (厥阴俞)	Back-shu point of the pericardium		Dredging the heart meridian, soothing the chest oppression and regulating the flow of qi. Precardial pain, oppression in the chest, cough, vomiting
BL 15 Xinshu (心俞)	Back-shu point of the heart		Relieving mental stress and tranquilizing mind, regulating the flow of both blood and qi. Palpitation, precardial pain, oppression in the chest, vexation, insomnia, amnesia, cough, hematemesis, night sweats, nocturnal emission, epilepsy
BL 16 Dushu (督俞)			Regulating the flow of qi and soothing the chest oppression. Precardial pain, oppression in chest, abdominal pain, fever and chills, asthma

Name of the points	Specific points	Common indications	Specific indications and functions
BL 17 Geshu (膈俞)	Confluential Points of blood		Relieving stuffiness of the chest and lowering adverse flow of qi, regulating circulation of blood and resolving stasis, regulating flow of qi and invigorating the body resistance. Vomiting, hiccup, asthma, cough, hemitemesis, epistaxis, hemafecia, hectic fever, night sweat, syncope due to consumption
BL 18 Ganshu (肝俞)	Back-shu point of the liver		Soothing the liver and regulating functioning of the gall bladder, dispelling heat and regulating flow of qi, clearing head and improving eye sight. Jaundice, hypochondrial pain, hematemesis, red eyes, dizziness, optic atraphy, manic-depression, pain along the spinal column
BL 19 Danshu (胆俞)	Back-shu point of the gall bladder	Gastrointestinal diseases: gastralgia, abdominal distension, diarrhea, vomiting, borborygmus Diseases of chest and lung	Clearing away pathogenic heat from the liver and gall bladder, normalizing function of the stomach and soothing the diaphragm by regulating the flow of qi. Jaundice, bitter taste, pain in the hypochondrium, fullness and distension in the gastric cavity and abdomen, vomiting, consumptive disease, hectic fever
BL 20 Pishu (脾俞)	Back-shu point of the spleen		Regulating spleen-qi, aids in transporting and transforming nutrients, clearing dampness and regulating the nutrients and blood. Abdominal distension, jaundice, vomiting, diarrhea, dysentery, hemafecia, edema, pain in the loins, back and shoulder, chronic convulsion in children
BL 21 Weishu (胃俞)	Back-shu point of the stomach		Regulating stomach-qi, inducing diuresis and removing stagnation. Pain in the chest and hypochondrium, epigastralgia, vomiting, abdominal pain, boryborygium, anorexia, indigestion
BL 22 Sanjiaoshu (三焦俞)	Back-shu point of the Sanjiao		Regulating flow of qi, inducing diuresis. Boryborygmus, abdominal distension, vomiting, diarrhea, dysentery, edema, stiffness and pain of loins and back

Name of the points	Specific points	Common indications	Specific indications and functions
BL 23 Shenshu (肾俞)	Back-shu point of the kidney	Diseases of intestines, external genitalia and gynecopathy: abdominal pain and distension, boryborygmus, diarrhea, constipation, hemorrhoidal disease, irregular menstruation, leukorrhea, dysmenorrhea, emission, impotence	Invigorating the kidney, strengthening the waist and nourishing the auditory functions. Dysuria, enuresis, seminal emission, impotence, irregular menstruation, leukorrhea, edema, deafness, tinnitus, lumbago
BL 24 Qihaishu (气海俞)			Regulating and invigorating blood and qi, strengthening the waist and knees. Boryborygmus, abdominal distention, hemorrhoid complicated by anal fistula, dysmenorrhea, metropathia, hemorrhagica, lumbago, flaccidity and arthralgia of lower limbs
BL 25 Dachangshu (大肠俞)	Back-shu point of the large intestine		Regulating the function of stomach and intestines, relieving the trouble of loins and knees. Pain and distension in abdomen, boryborygmus, diarrhea, constipation, appendicitis, lumbago, flaccidity and arthralgia of lower extremities
BL 26 Guanyuanshu (关元俞)			Regulating the function of lower Jiao, resolving stagnation of dampness. Abdominal distension, diarrhea, frequent urination or dysuria, enuresis, lumbago
BL 27 Xiaochangshu (小肠俞)	Back-shu point of the small intestine		Clearing the intestine and regulating the function of Fu-organs, removing heat and inducing diuresis. Abdominal pain, diarrhea, dysentery, enuresis, hematuria, emission, leukorrhea, hemorrhoidal disease, lumbago
BL 28 Pangguangshu (膀胱俞)	Back-shu point of the bladder		Regulating the function of the urinary bladder, relieving the troubles of loins and spine. Dysuria, enuresis, diarrhea, constipation, stiffness and pain of loins and spine
BL 29 Zhonglüshu (中膂俞)			Diarrhea, hernia, stiffness and pain in loins and spine
BL 30 Baihuanshu (白环俞)			Warming and invigorating qi in the lower part of the body, regulating the flow of blood and qi. Enuresis, hernia, emission, irregular menstruation, leukorrhea, pain in the sacrum

Acupoints of Three Yang Meridians of Foot

Name of the points	Specific points	Common indications	Specific indications and functions
BL 31 Shangliao (上髎)			Strengthening the waist and invigorating the kidney, clearing the meridians and activating the flow of blood. Sacralgia, impotence, emission, prolapse of uterus, irregular menstruation, leukorrhea, difficulty in bowel movement and urination
BL 32 Ciliao (次髎)			Hernia, irregular menstruation, dysmenorrhea, leukorrhea, dysuria, emission, lumbago, flaccidity and arthralgia of lower extremities
BL 33 Zhongliao (中髎)			Constipation, diarrhea, dysuria, irregular menstruation, leukorrhea, lumbago
BL 34 Xialiao (下髎)			Abdominal pain, constipation, dysuria, leukorrhea, lumbago
BL 35 Huiyang (会阳)			Strengthening the waist and invigorating the kidney, removing heat and inducing diuresis. Diarrhea, hemafecia, hemorrhoid, impotence, leukorrhea
BL 36 Chengfu (承扶)		Local diseases: lumbago, flaccidity and arthralgia of the lower extremities	Pain in loins, sacrum and buttock, hemorrhoidal disease
BL 37 Yinmen (殷门)			Lumbago, flaccidity and arthralgia of lower extremities
BL 38 Fuxi (浮郄)			Constipation, pain and numbness in the thigh
BL 39 Weiyang (委阳)	The lower Confluent Point of the bladder		Relaxing the muscles and tendons, activating the movement of joints, clearing the water passage. Fullness of the abdomen, dysuria, stiffness and pain of the loins and spinal column, spasm of the leg and feet
BL 40 Weizhong (委中)	Confluent point		Relaxing the muscles and tendons, clearing the collaterals, strengthening the waist and legs, expelling summer-heat, arresting vomiting and diarrhea. Lumbago, flaccidity and arthralgia of lower extremities, heatstroke, vomiting with diarrhea, abdominal pain, dysuria, erysipelas, enuresis

Name of the points	Specific points	Common indications	Specific indications and functions
BL 41 Fufen (附分)	Crossing point	Diseases of the chest and lung: cough, asthma, oppression in the chest, pain of the shoulder and back	Relaxing muscles and tendons, activating collaterals. Stiffness and pain of the neck, spasm of shoulder and back, numbness of elbows and arms
BL 42 Pohu (魄户)			Ventilating the lung, relieving the asthma and arresting cough. Cough, asthma, consumptive disease, neck stiffness, pain of the shoulder and back
BL 43 Gaohuang (膏肓)			Regulating the flow of lung-qi, tonifying the lung by restoring qi. Cough, asthma, tuberculosis, amnesia, emission, indigestion
BL 44 Shentang (神堂)			Relieving stuffiness of the chest and regulating the flow of qi. Cough, asthma, oppression in the chest, stiffness and pain of spine and back
BL 45 Yixi (譩譆)			Cough, asthma, malaria, febrile disease, pain of shoulder and back
BL 46 Geguan (膈关)			Regulating the function of the stomach and lowering the adverse flow of qi, soothing the oppression in the chest and hypochondrium. Chest oppression, eructation, vomiting, stiffness and pain of the spine
BL 47 Hunmen (魂门)		Gastrointestinal diseases: abdominal pain and distension, boryborygmus, diarrhea, constipation, vomiting, pain along the spine	Relieving the depressed liver and regulating the circulation of qi, invigorating the spleen and regulating the stomach. Pain in the chest and hypochondrium, vomiting, diarrhea, backache
BL 48 Yanggang (阳纲)			Removing damp-heat from the liver and gall bladder. Boryborygmus, abdominal pain, diarrhea, jaundice, diabetes
BL 49 Yishe (意舍)			Abdominal distention, boryborygmus, vomiting, diarrhea

Name of the points	Specific points	Common indications	Specific indications and functions
BL 50 Weicang (胃仓)		The same as above.	Normalizing function of the stomach and removing dampness, regulating the flow of qi and clearing the middle-jiao. Gastralgia, abdominal distension, infantile indigestion with food retention, edema, pain along the spine
BL 51 Huangmen (肓门)			Relieving distension and fullness in the chest, promoting lactation. Mass in the abdomen, mammary disease, abdominal pain, constipation
BL 52 Zhishi (志室)		Diseases of intestines, external genitalia and gynecology: Boryborygmus, abdominal distension, constipation, dysuria, emission, impotence, stiffness and pain along spinal column	Invigorating the kidney, tonifying the essence and removing dampness by inducing diuresis. Impotence, emission, dyuresis, edema, stiffness and pain of the loins and spine
BL 53 Baohuang (胞肓)			Dredging the lower Jiao. Boryborygmus, abdominal distension, constipation, retention of urine, stiffness and pain along the spinal column
BL 54 Zhibian (秩边)			Dredging the lower Jiao, strengthening the waist and knee. Dysuria, constipation, hemorrhoidal disease, lumbosacral pain, flaccidity and numbness of lower extremities
BL 55 Heyang (合阳)			Relaxing muscles and tendons, clearing the collaterals, dispelling wind and eliminating dampness. Stiffness and pain along the spinal column, flaccidity and arthralgia of lower extremities, hernia, metrorrhagia and metrostaxis
BL 56 Chengjin (承筋)			Hemorrhoidal disease, spasm and pain of waist and leg
BL 57 Chengshan (承山)			Relaxing muscles and tendons, clearing the collaterals and regulating the functions of intestines. Hemorrhoidal disease, beriberi, constipation, pain and spasm of waist and legs

Name of the point	Specific points	Common Indications	Specific Indications and Functions
BL 58 Feiyang (飞扬)	Luo- (Connecting) point	Diseases of the head, neck, eyes and nose: Headache, stiffness of neck, eye pain, dizziness, insomnia, stuffy nose, epistaxis	Dispelling pathogenic factors from Taiyang meridians, removing wind and dampness from meridians and collaterals. Headache, dizziness, epistaxis, pain in loins and legs, hemorrhoidal disease
BL 59 Fuyang (跗阳)	Xi- (Cleft) point of the Yangqiao, meridian		Headache, lumbosacral pain, flaccidity and arthralgia of lower extremities, swelling and pain of lateral malleolus
BL 60 Kunlun (昆仑)	Jing- (River) point		Headache, stiffness of neck, dizzinese, epistaxis, epilepsy, dystocia, lumbosacral pain, swelling and pain of heels
BL 61 Pucan (仆参)			Flaccidity and arthralgia of lower extremities, pain in heels, epilepsy
BL 62 Shenmai (申脉)	One of the Eight Confluential Points		Inducing resuscitation, restoring consciousness and relaxing muscles and tendons. Headache, dizziness, manic-depression, red and painful eyes, insomnia, soreness, pain, numbness and lassitude of waist and lower extremities
BL 63 Jinmen (金门)	Xi- (Cleft) point		Inducing resuscitation and relieving mental stress by removing endogenous wind. Headache, neck stiffness, nebula, epistaxis, epilepsy, lumbago

Name of the point	Specific points	Common Indications	Specific Indications and Functions
BL 64 Jinggu (京骨)	Yuan- (Source) point	Mental illnesses: manic-depression and epilepsy

Diseases of back, waist and bacterior side of lower extremities: pain in the lumbasacral part and legs, flaccidity and arthralgia of lower extremities, pain in heels, hemorrhoidal diseases | Dispelling wind and removing heat, relieving mental stress and clearing head. Headache, neck stiffness, nebula, epistaxis, epilepsy, lumbago |
BL 65 Shugu (束骨)	Shu- (Stream) point		Refreshing head. Headache, stiffness of neck, dizziness, manic-depression, pain of the waist and lower extremities
BL 66 Zutonggu (足通谷)	Ying- (Spring) point		Dispelling wind and removing heat. Headache, stiffness of head, dizziness, epistaxis, manic-depressive psychosis
BL 67 Zhiyin (至阴)	Jing- (Well) point		Dispelling wind, eliminating heat, correcting the abnormal position of fetus. Headache, eye pain, stuffy nose, epistaxis, dystocia

Chapter Twelve

Extraordinary Points

Ⅰ. Points of Head and Neck, EX-HN

EX-HN 1 Sishencong (四神聪)
(Wisdom Spirit)

【Source】 *A Supplement to Thousand Gololen Prescriptions*
【Location】 On the vertex of the head, 1 cun anterior, posterior and lateral to Baihui (DU 20), four points in total. (See Fig. 12-1)
【Localization】 In sitting or supine position, first locate Baihui (DU 20) the point is located 1 cun anterior, posterior, left and right to DU 20, 4 points in total.
【Indications】 Wind-stroke, headache, blurred vision, epilepsy, manic-depressive disorders, poor memory, dreaminess, insomnia, tinnitus, hydrocephadus and cerebral dysgenesis.
【Method】 Puncture horizontally 0.5-0.8 cun with the tip of needle pointing towards Baihui (DU 20). Moxibustion is applicable.
【Regional Anatomy】 Skin − subcutaneous tissue − epicranial aponeurosis − subaponeurotic loose connective tissue. The local area is supplied by the occipital artery and vein, the parietal branches of the greater occipital, auriculotemporal and supraorbital nerves.

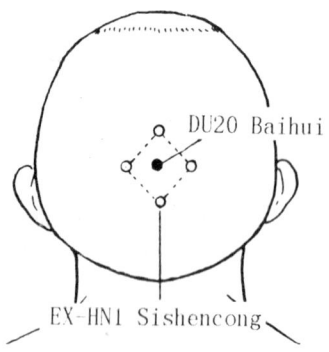

Fig. 12-1

EX-HN 2　Dangyang（当阳）
(Just above Yangbai)

【Source】 *Thousand Golden Prescriptions for Emergency*
【Location】 At the frontal part of the head, directly above the pupil and 1 cun above the anterior hairline. (See Fig. 12-2)
【Localization】 In sitting position, when the patient looks straight ahead, the point is located 1 cun superior to the anterior hair line, directly superior to the pupil. Or the point can be located at the midpoint between Toulinqi (GB 15) and Muchuang (GB 16), about 0.5 cun to GB 15 and GB 16.
【Indications】 Dizziness, stuffy nose, headache, coma, acute pain in the eyes, acute conjunctivitis, acute Keratitis and dacryocystitis.
【Method】 Puncture horizontally with the tip of needle pointing upward to downward 0.5-0.8 cun. Moxibustion is applicable.
【Regional Anatomy】 Skin-subcutaneous tissue-procerus muscle. There are the supratrochlear branch of the frontal nerve and the frontal artery from the ophthalmic artery and the accompanying vein in this area.

EX-HN 3　Yintang（印堂）
(Front Hall)

【Source】 *Great Compendium of Acupuncture and Moxibustion*
【Location】 On the forehead, on the midpoint between the bilateral eyebrows. (See Fig. 12-2)
【Localization】 Sit with head at rest. The point is located at the ophryon between the two eyebrows, directly superior to the apex of the nose.
【Indications】 Infantile convulsion, headache, conjunctival congestion with swelling pain, maternal dizziness due to excessive bleeding, eclamptia, dizziness, rhinorrhea, epistaxis, insomnia, facial furuncle and trigeminal neuralgia.
【Method】 Puncture horizontally with the tip of needle pointing toward downward or upward 0.3-0.5 cun, or prick to cause bleeding. Moxibustion is applicable.
【Regional Anatomy】 Skin-subcutaneous tissue-procerus muscle. There are the supratrochlear branch of the frontal nerve, the frontal artery from the ophthalmic artery, and local veins in this area.

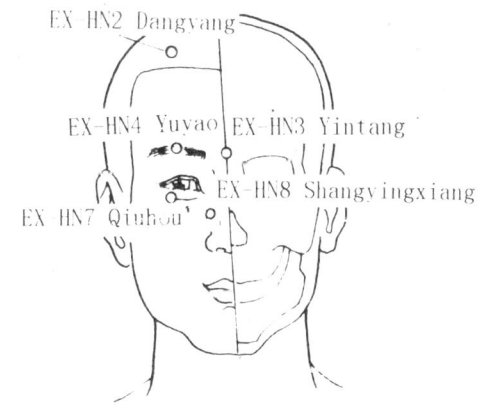

Fig. 12-2

EX-HN 4 Yuyao (鱼腰)
(Fish Lumbar)

[Source] *Great Compendium of Acupuncture and Moxibustion*
[Location] On the forehead, directly above the pupil, and within the eyebrow. (See Fig. 12-2)
[Localization] When the patient looks straight ahead, the point is located at the middle of the eyebrow, directly superior to the pupil.
[Indications] Redness, swelling and pain of the eyes, blurred vision, twitching of eyelid, ptosis, deviation of the eyes and mouth, supraorbital neuralgia, acute conjunctivitis, Keratitis with Guangming (GB 37), facial nerve spasm or paralysis, and ocular paralysis.
[Method] Puncture the points of both sides subcutaneously 0.5 cun. Moxibustion is prohibited.
[Regional Anatomy] Skin-subcutaneous tissue-orbicular muscle of eye-frontal belly of occipitofrontal muscle. There are the lateral branches of the supraorbital nerve, the branches of the facial nerve and the lateral branches of the supraorbital artery and vein in this area.

EX-HN 5 Taiyang (太阳)
(Large Yang)

[Source] *Thousand Golden Prescriptions for Emergency*
[Location] Located on the temples, in the depression one finger-breath posterior to the midpoint between the lateral end of the eyebrow and the outer canthus. (See Fig. 12-3)
[Localizations] Face looking upward, the point is located at the midpoint of the line joining the tip of the eyebrow and outer canthus 1 cun posterior, in the depression.
[Indications] Migraine, redness, swelling and pain of the eyes, dizziness, blurred vision, dryness of the eyes, toothache, deviation of the eyes and mouth, trigeminal neuralgia, neurosis, angioneurotic headache, optic atrophy, retinal hemorrhage and acute conjunctivitis.
[Method] Puncture perpendicularly or obliquely 0.3-0.5 cun, or prick to cause bleeding or use cupping therapy. Moxibustion is prohibited.
[Regional Anatomy] Skin-subcutaneous tissue-orbicular muscle of the eye-temporal fascia-temporal muscle. There

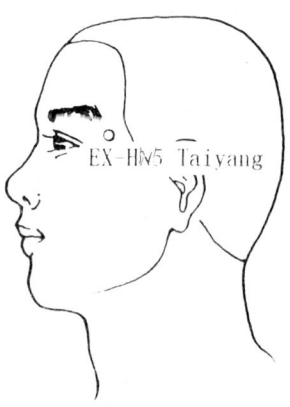

Fig. 12-3

are the zygomaticofacial branch of the zygomatic nerve, the temporal and zygomatic branches of the facial nerve, the temporal nerve of the mandibular nerve and the branches or tributaries of the superficial temporal artery and vein in this area.

EX-HN 6 Erjian (耳尖) (Ear Tip)

[Source] *Great Compendium of Acupuncture and Moxibustion*

[Location] On the apex of the ear, formed by the tip of the auricle when the ear is folded forward. (See Fig. 12-4)

[Localization] In sitting position, locate the point at the apex of the auriculae when the auriculae is pressed forward, it is located at the highest point in the margin of the auriculae.

[Indications] Conjunctivitis, redness, swelling and pain of eyes, migraine, inflammation of the throat, stye and keratitis.

[Method] Puncture perpendicularly 0.1-0.2 cun, or prick to cause bleeding. Apply moxibustion with moxa 3-5 cones, or "Sparrow-Pecking" moxibustion.

[Regional Anatomy] Skin-subcutaneous tissue-auricualr cartilage. There are the anterior auricular branches of the superficial temporal artery and vein, the posterior auricular branches of the posterior auricular artery and vein, the anterior auricular branches of the auriculotemporal nerve, the posterior auricular branches of the lesser occipital nerce, and the auricular branches of the facial nerve in this area.

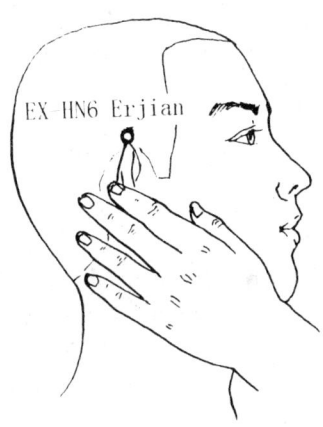

Fig. 12-4

EX-HN 7 Qiuhou (球后) (Behind Eyeball)

[Source] *Chinese Acupuncture and Moribustion*

[Location] On the face, at the junction of the lateral one fourth and medial three fourths of the infraorbital margin. (See Fig. 12-2)

[Localization] Sit with the head rest and the eyes slightly closed. Locate the point at the lateral one-fourth of the eye, on the lower margin of the orbit.

[Indications] Glaucoma, cataracts, optic neuritis, optic atrophy, retinetis pigmentosa, central retinitis and myopia.

[Method] Puncture slowly perpendicularly 1-1.5 cun from external downward to internal upward along the infraorbital margin, towards optic foramen. It's not advisable to twirl or lift and thrust the needle. Moxibustion is prohibited.

[Regional Anatomy] Skin-subcutaneous tissue-orbicular muscle of the eye-adipose body of orbit between inferior oblique muscle and inferior wall of orbit. In the superficial layer, there are the branches of the infraorbital and facial nerves and the branches or tributaries of the infraorbital artery and vein. In the deep layer, there are the inferiorbranches of the oculomotor nerve, the branches or tributaries of the ophthalmic artery and vein, and the infraorbital artery and vein.

EX-HN 8 Shangyingxian（上迎香）
(Upper Yingxiang)

【Source】 *Concise Book of Acupuncture and Moxibustion*
【Location】 On the face, at the junction of the alar cartilage of the nose and the nasal concha, near the upper end of the nasolabial groove. (See Fig. 12-2)
【Localization】 Sit with the head rest. The point is located at the intersection between the alar cartilage and bone in the back of the nose.
【Indications】 Headache, stuffy nose, nasal polyps, epidemic hemorrhagic conjunctivitis, epiphora induced by wind.
【Method】 Puncture obliquely with the tip of needle pointing internally upwards 0.3-0.5 cun. Moxibustion is applicable.
【Regional Anatomy】 Skin-subcutaneous tissue-levator muscle of upper lip and nasal ala. There are the branches of the infraorbital and infratrochlear nerves, the buccal branches of the facial nerve, and the angular artery and vein in this area.

EX-HN 9 Neiyingxiang（内迎香）
(Inner Yingxiang)

【Source】 *Great Compendium of Acupuncture and Moxibustion*
【Location】 In the nostril, at the junction between the mucosa of the alar cartilage of the nose and the nasal concha. (See Fig. 12-5)
【Localization】 The point is located at the upper extremity of the intranasial mucosa, or in the mucosa of the middle and lateral aspects of the nostril.
【Indications】 Burning pain in the eyes, severe headache, sunstroke, febrile disease, nasal diseases, inflammation of the throat and vertigo.
【Method】 Prick to cause bleeding, Moxibustion cannot be applicable.
【Regional Anatomy】 Tongue mucosa-submucous loose connective tissue. There are the arteriovenous network of the dorsal nasal branches of the facial atery and vein and the lateral branches of the anterior ethmoidal nerve in this area.

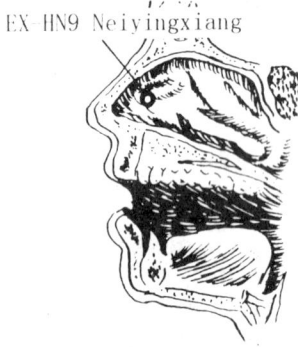

Fig. 12-5

EX-HN 10 Juquan（聚泉）
(Convergence Spring)

【Source】 *Great Compendium of Acupuncture and Moxibustion*
【Location】 In the mouth, at the midpoint of the dorsal midline of the tongue. (See Fig. 12-6)

【Localization】 Open the mouth with the tongue extending out. The point is located at the centre of the median raphe on the dorsum of the tongue.
【Indications】 Stiff tongue, flaccid tongue with aphasia, slurred speech, difficulty discriminating tastes, diabetes and asthma.
【Method】 Puncture perpendicularly 0.1-0.2 cun or prick to cause bleeding. Moxibustion is prohibited.
【Regional Anatomy】 Mucosa-submucous loose connective tissue-lingual muscle. There are the lingual nerve from the mandibular nerve, the hypoglossal nerve, the nervous fibers of the tympanic cord, and the arteriovenous network of the lingual artery and vein in this area.

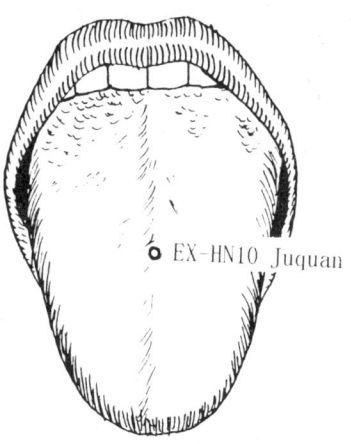

Fig. 12-6

EX-HN 11　Haiquan（海泉）
（Sea Spring）

【Source】 *Great Compendium of Acupuncture and Moxibustion*
【Location】 In the mouth, at the midpoint of the frenulum of the tongue. (See Fig. 12-7)
【Localization】 Curling the tongue, the point is located slightly posterior to the midpoint between Jinjin (EX-HN 12) and Yuye (EX-HN 13) which are located at the veins on both sides of the frenulum of the tongue.
【Indications】 Hiccups, diabetes, congenital deformity of the tongue, tonsillitis, inflammation of the throat adding Hegu (LI 4) and Shaoshang (LI 11), vomiting, diarrhea, diaphragmatic spasm, and acute gastroenteritis adding Zusanli (ST 36).
【Method】 Puncture perpendicularly 0.1-0.3 cun, or prick to cause bleeding.

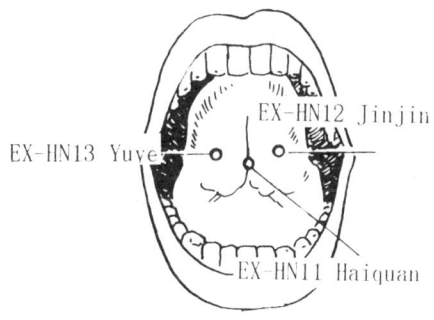

Fig. 12-7

【Regional Anatomy】 Mucosa-submucous tissue-lingual muscle. There are the lingual nerve from the mandibular nerve, the hypoglossal nerve, the nervous fibres of the tympanic cord from the facial nerve, the deep lingual artery from the lingual artery, and the deep lingual veins to the lingual nein in this area.

EX-HN 12　Jinjin（金津）
（Gold Fluid）

【Source】 *Great Compendium of Acupuncture and Moxibustion*
【Location】 In the mouth, on the vein on the left and right side of the frenulum of the tongue.
【Localization】 See Yuye (EX-HN 13).
【Indication】 See Yuye (EX-HN 13).

【Method】 See Yuye (EX-HN 13).

【Regional Anatomy】 Mucosa-submucous tissue-genioglossus muscle. There are the gnathic nerve from the mandibular nerve, the hypoglossal nerve, the nerve fibres of the tympanic cord from the facial nerve, the deep lingual artery of the lingual artery and the deep lingual veins to the lingual vein in this area.

EX-HN 13　Yuye (玉液)
(Jade Fluid)

【Source】 *Great Compendium of Acupuncture and Moxibustion*

【Location】 In the mouth, on the vein on the right side of the frenulum of the tongue. (See Fig. 12-7)

【Localization】 Curling the tongue, the points are located on the veins on both sides of the frenulum of the tongue, the left is Jinjin (EX-HN 12), the right is Yuye (EX-HN 13).

【Indications】 Aphthous, swelling of the tongue, inflammation of the throat, diabetes, jaundice, vomiting, diarrhea, acute throat problems, tonsillitis and aphasia. It is recorded in "Great Compendium of Acupuncture and Moxibustion" that Lianquan (RN 23) is used for swelling of the tongue, and slurred speech, Chengjiang (RN 24) for diabetes, Lianquan (RN 23) and Fengfu (DU 16) for stiff tongue." Now these two points are often used for stuttering, glossopharyngeal nerve paralysis and laryngitis.

【Method】 Prick to cause bleeding, Moxibustion is prohibited.

【Regional Anatomy】 Same as Jinjin (EX-HN 12).

EX-HN 14　Yiming (翳明)
(Brightness Screen)

【Source】 *Chinese Medical Journal*

【Location】 On the nape, 1 cun posterior to Yifeng (SJ 17). (See Fig. 12-8)

【Localization】 Sit or sit with the head bent, locate the point at the inferior portion of the mastoid process at the same level with ear lobe.

【Indications】 Myopia, hyperopia, night blindness, optic atrophy, early stage of cataract, headache, dizziness, tinnitus, insomnia and mental disease.

【Method】 Puncture perpendicularly 0.5-1.5 cun, Moxibustion is applicable.

【Regional Anatomy】 Skin-subcutaneous tissue-sternocleidomastoid muscle-splenius muscle of head-the longest muscle of the head. In the superficial layer, there are the branches of the great auricular nerve. In the deep layer, there are the deep cervical artery and vein.

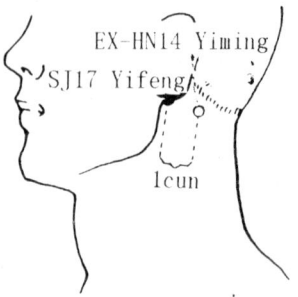

Fig. 12-8

EX-HN 15 Jingbailao (颈百劳)
(Neck Labours)

【Source】 *Great Secret of Acupuncture and Moxibustion*
【Location】 On the nape, 2 cun above Dazhui (DU 14) and 1 cun lateral to the posterior midline. (See Fig. 12-9)
【Localization】 On the nape of the neck, the point is located 2 cun directly superior to Dazhui (DU 14), 1 cun lateral to the posterior median line.
【Indications】 Tuberculosis, profuse sweating, scrofula, cough and neck pain. The point is often used for occipital neuralgia, chronic bronchitis, whooping cough and tuberculosis of lung.
【Method】 Puncture perpendicularly 0.5-1 cun. Moxibustion is applicable.
【Regional Anatomy】 Skin-subcutaneous tissue-trapezius muscle-superior posterior serratus muscle-splenius muscles of the head and neck-semispinalis muslce of the head-multifidus muscle. In the superficial layer, there are the cutaneous branches of the posterior branches of the 4th and 5th cervical nerves. In the deep layer, there are the branches of the posterior branches of the 4th and 5th cervical nerves.

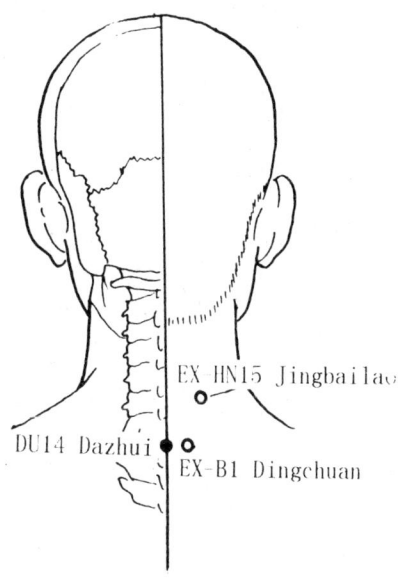

Fig. 12-9

II. Points of Chest and Abdomen, EX-CA

EX-CA 1 Zigong (子宫)
(Uterus)

【Source】 *Illustration of Acupoints*
【Location】 On the lower abdomen, 4 cun below the center of the umbilicus and 3 cun lateral to Zhongji (RN 3). (See Fig. 12-10)
【Localization】 In supine position, the point is located 3 cun lateral to Zhongji (RN 3).
【Indications】 Prolapse of uterus, infertility, metrorrhagia and metrostaxis, irregular menstruation, dysmenorrhea, hernia and lumbago.
【Method】 Puncture perpendicularly 0.8-1.2 cun. Moxibustion is applicable.
【Regional Anatomy】 Skin-subcutaneous tissue-aponeurosis of external oblique muscle of abdomen-internal oblique muscle of abdomen-transversemuscle of abdomen-transverse fascia of ab-

domen. In the superficial layer, there are the lateral cutaneous branches of the iliohypogastric nerve and the superficial epigastric vein. In the deep layer, there are the branches of the iliohypogastric nerve and the branches or tributaries of the inferior epigastric artery and vein.

III. Points of back, EX-B

EX-B 1   Dingchuan (定喘)
(Relief Asthma)

【Source】 *Chinese Acupuncture and Moxibustion*
【Location】 On the back, below the spinous process of the 7th cervical vertebra and 0.5 cun lateral to the posterior midline. (See Fig. 12-9)
【Localization】 In prone position, locate the point below the spinous process of the 7th cervical vertebrae, 0.5 cun lateral to the posterior median line, i. e. 0.5 cun lateral to Dazhui (DU 14).
【Indications】 Asthma, cough, urticaria, stiffness of the neck, shoulder, back pain and upper limb pain.
【Method】 Puncture perpendicularly or obliquely 0.5 – 1 cun towards the spinal column. Moxibustion is applicable.
【Regional Anatomy】 Skin-subcutaneous tissue-trapezius muscle-rhomboid muscle-superior posterior serratus muscle-splenius muscle of neck-erector spinae muscles. In the superficial layer, there are the medial cutaneous branches of the posterior branch of the 8th cervical nerve. In the deep layer, there are the branches or tributaries of the deep cervical artery and vein and the transverse cervical artery and vein and the muscular branches of the posterior branches of the 8th cervical and 1st thoracicnerves.

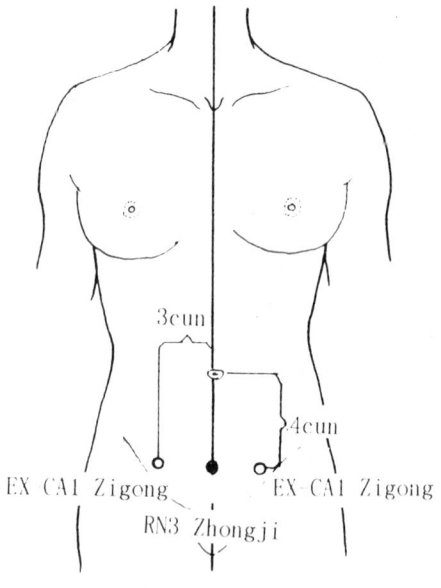

Fig. 12-10

EX-B 2   Jiaji (夹脊)
(Side of Spine)

【Source】 *A Handbook of Prescriptions for Emergencies*
【Location】 On the upper and lower back, a total of 34 points on both sides, below the spinous processess from the 1st thoracic vertebra to the 5th lumbar vertebar, and 0.5 cun lateral to the posterior midline. (See Fig. 12-11)

【Localization】 Sit with the head bent or in prone position, the points are located 0.5 cun lateral to each spinous process, from the 1st thoracic vertebra to the 5th lumbur vertebra. Each side of the spinal column has 17 points, for a total of 34 points.

【Indications】 Weakness, fever of deficiency type, night sweat, tuberculosis, asthma, cough and other chronic diseases. Upper thoracic points are for the heart, lung and upper limbs diseases; lower thoracic points for gastro-intestinal diseases; the points of the lumbar region for the loins. abdomen and lower limbs diseases.

These points can also be used for neuroises, tuberculosis of the lung, bronchitis and infantile chronic malnutrition, rickets, chronic indigestion and bronchial asthma.

【Method】 Puncture perpendicularly 0.3-0.5 cun, or prick with a plum blossom needle. Moxibustion is applicable.

【Regional Anatomy】 The related muscles, blood vessels and nerves are not totally alike because the location of each point is different. The layer structures are usually: Skin-subcutaneous tissue-superficial muscles

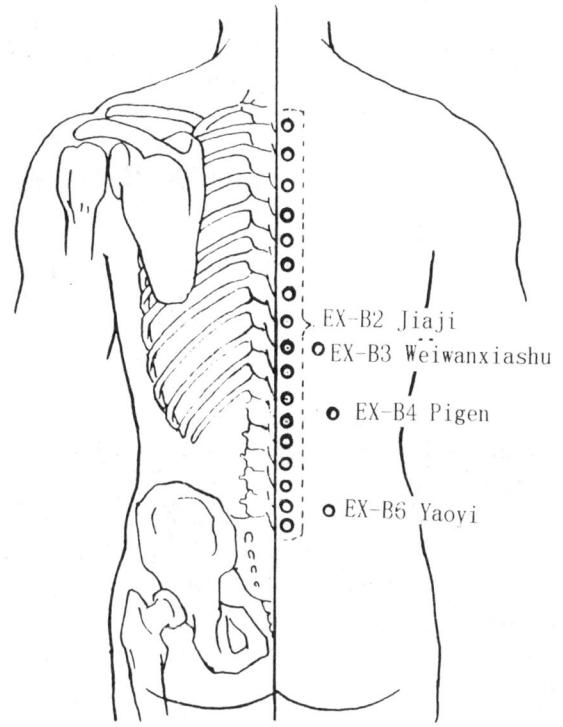

Fig. 12-11

(trapezius muscle, latissimus muscle of back, rhomboid muscle, superior posterior serratus muscle, inferior posterior serratus muscle) -deep muscles (erector spinal muscle, transversospinal muscle.) In the superficial layer, there are the medial cutaneous branches of the posterior branches of the 1st thoracic nerve to the 5th lumbar nerve and the accompanying arteries and veins. In the deep layer, there are the muscular branches of the posterior branches of the 1st thoracic nerve to the 5th lumbar nerve, the branches or tributaries of the dorsal branches of the posterior intercostal arteries and veins or lumbar arteries and veins respectively.

EX-B 3　Weiwanxiashu（胃脘下俞）
（Below Stomach）

【Source】 *Thousand Golden Prescriptions for Emergency*
【Location】 On the back, below the spinous process of the 8th thoracic vertebra and 1.5 cun lateral to the posterior midline. (See Fig. 12-11)
【Localization】 In prone position, the point is located 1.5 cun lateral to the spinous process of the 8th thoracic vertebrae.
【Indications】 Stomachache, pancreatitis, diabetes, cough, dry throat, pain in the chest and hypochondrac region, abdominal pain and vomiting.
【Method】 Puncture obliquely 0.3－0.5cun antorior and inferior. Moxibustion is applicable.
【Regional Anatomy】 Skin-subcutaneous tissue-trapezius muscle-latissimus muscle of back-erector spinal muscle. In the superficial layer, there are the cutaneous branches of the posterior branch

of the 8th thoracic nerve and the accompanying artery and vein. In the deep layer, there are the muscular branches of the posterior branch of the 8th thracic nerve and the branches or tributaries of the dorsal branches of the 8th posterior intercostal artery and vein.

EX-B 4   Pigen (痞根)
(Mass Root)

【Source】 *An Introduction to Medicine*
【Location】 On the lower back, below the spinous process of the 1st lumbar vertebra and 3.5 cun lateral to the posterior midline. (See Fig. 12-11)
【Localization】 In prone positioin, the point is located 3.5 cun lateral to the middle of the lower margin of the spinous process of the 1st lumbar vertebrae, or 0.5 cun lateral to Huangmen (BL 51).
【Indications】 Mass in the abdomen, distending pain in the epigastrium, lumbago, nausea, gastrospasm, gastric dilatation, enteritis, enterocele, lumbar neuralgia and infantile chronic malnutrition adding Tianshu (ST 25).
【Method】 Puncture perpendicularly 0.5-1 cun. Moxibustion is applicable.
【Regional Anatomy】 Skin-subcutaneous tissue-latissimus muscle of back-inferior posterior serratus muscle-iliocostal muscle. In the superficial layer, there are the lateral cutaneous branches of the posterior branch of the 12th thoracic nerve and the accompanying artery and vein. In the deep layer, there are the muscular branches of the posterior branch of the 12th thoracic nerve.

EX-B 5   Xiajishu (下极俞)
(Lower Extremity)

【Source】 *A Supplement to Thousand Golden Prescriptions*
【Location】 On the midline of the low back, below the third lumbar spinous process. (See Fig. 12-12)
【Localization】 In prone position, the point is located below the spinous process of the 3rd lumbar vertebrae.
【Indications】 Abdominal pain, diarrhea, lumbago, dysfunction of the urinary bladder, dysuria, enuresis and soreness and pain in the lower limbs.
【Method】 Puncture perpendicularly 0.5-1 cun. Moxibustion is applicable.
【Regional Anatomy】 Skin-subcutaneous tissuesupraspinal ligament-interspinal ligament.
   In the superficial layer, there are the medial branches of the posterior branch of the fourth lumbar nerve and the accompanying artery and vein. In the deep layer, there are the external (posterior) vertebral venous plexus of the spinous process, the posterior branch of the 4th lumbar nerve and the branch of the dorsal branch of the 4th lumbar artery and vein.

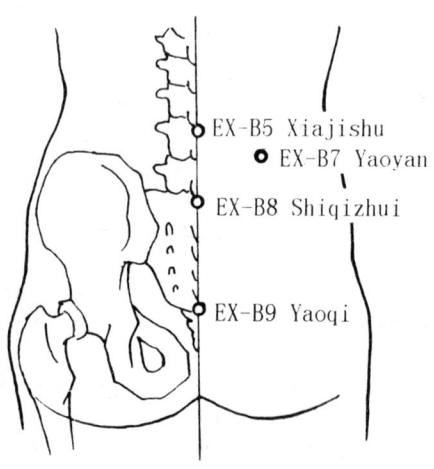

Fig. 12-12

EX-B 6　Yaoyi（腰宜）
（Lumbar Benefit）

【Source】 *Guide to Acupoints and Acupuncture Therapeutics*
【Location】 On the lower back, below the spinous process of the 4th lumbar vertebra and 3cun lateral to the posterior midline. (See Fig. 12-11)
【Localization】 In prone position, the point is located below the spinous process of the 4th lumbar vertebrae, 4 finger breadth lateral to the posterior midline.
【Indications】 Uterine bleeding and lumbago.
【Method】 Puncture perpendicularly 0.5-1 cun. Moxibustion is applicable.
【Regional Anatomy】 Skin-subcutaneous tissue-superficial layer of thoracolumbar fascia-erector spinal muscle (or medial and superior border of the greatest gluteal muscle). In the superficial layer, there is the superior clunail nerve. In the deep layer, there are the muscular branches of the posterior branch of the 4th lumbar nerve and the branches or tributaries of the dorsal branches of the 4th lumbar artery and vein.

EX-B 7　Yaoyan（腰眼）
（Lumbar Eyes）

【Source】 *Supplement to Thousand Golden Prescriptions*
【Location】 On the low back, below the spinous process of the 4th lumbar vertebra, and in the depression 3.5 cun lateral to the posterior midline. (See Fig. 12-12)
【Localization】 Prone position with foot extended, both palms pressing the forehead, the point is located below the spinous process of the 4th lumbar vertebrae, 3.5 cun lateral to the posterior median line.
【Indications】 Tuberculosis, lumbago, diabetes, lower abdominal diseases, gynecological diseases, frequent urination. The point also can be used for tuberculosis, bronchitis, weakness, lumbar neuralgia and inflammation of the testes.
【Method】 Puncture perpendicularly 0.5-1 cun, moxibustion can be used.
【Regional Anatomy】 Skin-subcutaneous tissue-superficial layer of thoracolumbar fascia and aponeurosis of latissimus muscle of back-iliocostal muscle-deep layer of thoracolumbar fascia-quadrate muscle of loins. In the superficial layer, there are the superiro clunial nerve and the cutaneous branches of the posterior branch of the 4th lumbar nerve. In the deep layer, there are the muscular branches of the posterior branch of the 4th lumbar nerve and the branches or tributaries of the 4th lumbar artery and vein.

EX-B 8　Shiqizhui（十七椎）
（Seventeenth Vetebrea）

【Source】 *Thousand Golden Prescriptions for Emergency*
【Location】 On the low back, on the posterior midline, at the spinous process of the 5th lumbar vertebra. (See Fig. 12-12)
【Localization】 In prone position, the point is located below the spinous process of the 5th lum-

bar vertebrae (the spinous process of the 3rd lumbar vertebrae is located at the intersectioin between the lines joining both sides of the anterior superior iliac spine and spinal column. The spinous process of the 4th lumbar vertebrae is located at the intersection betweeen the line joining both sides of the iliac crest and spinal column.)

【Indications】 Lumbosacral pain, enuresis, gynecological diseases, dysmenorrhea, metrorrhagia and metrostaxis and pain along the spinal column. The point also can be used for chronic uterine inflammation, cervicitis cervical erosion and chronic pelvic inflammation.

【Method】 Puncture perpendicularly 0.5-1 cun. Moxibustion is applicable.

【Regional Anatomy】 Skin-subcutaneous tissue-supraspinal ligament-interspinal ligament. In the superficial layer, there are the cutaneous branches of the posterior branch of the 5th lumbar nerve and the accompanying artery and vein. In the deep layer, there are the branches of the posterior branch of the 5th lumbar nerve and the external (posterior) vertebral venous plexus between the adjacent spinous processes.

EX-B 9   Yaoqi (腰奇)
(Lumbar Marvel)

【Source】 *Journal of Traditional Chinese Medicine*

【Location】 On the low back, 2 cun directly above the tip of the coccyx, in the depression between the sacral horns. (See Fig. 12-12)

【Localization】 In prone position, locate the point 2 cun directly superior to the sacral apex.

【Indications】 Epilepsy, headache, insomnia and constipation.

【Method】 Puncture upwards horizontally 1-1.5 cun. or perpendicularly 0.3 cun. Moxibustion is applicable.

【Regional Anatomy】 Skin-subcutaneous tissue-supraspinal ligament. There are the branches of the posterior branches of the 2nd and 3rd sacral nerves and the accompanying artery and vein in this area.

Ⅳ. Points of Upper Extremities, EX-UE

EX-UE 1   Zhoujian (肘尖)
(Elbow Tip)

【Source】 *A Supplement to Thousand Golden Prescriptions*

【Location】 On the posterior side of the elbow, at the tip of the olecranon when the patient's elbow is flexed. (See Fig. 12-13)

【Localization】 The point is located at the apex of the the elbow.

【Indications】 Large carbuncles, periappendicular abscesses, scrofula and cholera.

【Method】 Apply moxibustion with 7-15 moxacomes

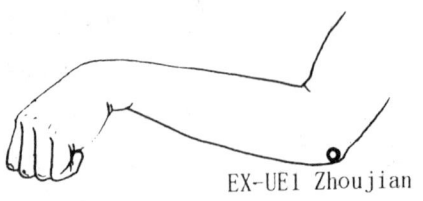

Fig. 12-13

for 10-30 minutes.
【Regional Anatomy】 Skin-subcutaneous tissue-subcutaneous bursa of olecranon-tendon of the brachial triceps muscle. There are the posterior cutaneous nerve of the forearm and the arteriovenous network around the elbow joint in this area.

EX-UE 2　Erbai （二白） （Two White）

【Source】 *Essential of Acupuncture and Moxibustion*
【Location】 On the palmar side of each forearm, 4 cun proximal to the crease of the wrist, and on each side of the tendon of the radial flexor muscle of the wrist. (See Fig. 12-14)
【Localization】 The point is located 4 cun directly superior to the transverse crease of the wrist, between the two tendons; and 0.5 cun lateral to the tendon of the carpal flexor.
【Indications】 Hemorrhoid with bleeding, pain and itching, prolapse of rectum, pain in forearm, chest and hypochondrium.
【Method】 Puncture perpendicularly 0.5-0.8 cun. Moxibustion is applicable.
【Regional Anatomy】 Skin-subcutaneous tissue-between tendons of long palmar muscle and radial flexor muscle of wrist-superficial digital flexor muscle-median nerve-long flexor muscle of the thumb-interosseousmembrane of forearm. In the superficial layer, there are the lateral cutaneous nerve of the forearm and the tributaries of the median brachial vein. In the deep layer, there are the median nerve and the median artery.

The lateral point: Skin-subcutaneous tissue-between radial flexor muscle of the wrist and tendon of brachioradial muscle-superficial flexor muscle of fingers-long flexor muscle of the thumb. In the superficial layer, there are the lateral cutaneous nerve of the forearm and the tributries of the cephalic vein. In the deep layer, there are the radial artery and vein.

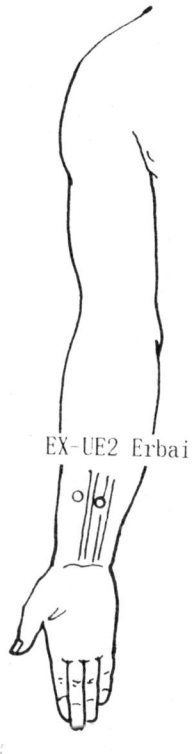

Fig. 12-14

EX-UE 3　Zhongquan （中泉） （Middle Spring）

【Source】 *Supplementary to Illustrated to the Classified Canon*
【Location】 On the dorsal crease of the wrist, in the depression on the radial side of the tendon of the common extensor muscle of the fingers. (See Fig. 12-15)
【Localization】 Bend the elbow with the palm facing downwards, locate the point at the midpoint of the line joining Yangchi (SJ 4) and Yangxi (LI 5).
【Indications】 Cataract, fullness sensation in chest, inability of forearm to supinate, adverse rising of the stomach qi, hemoptysis, pain in the chest and abdomen, feverish sensation in palms,

lung distention, distending pain in the warist.

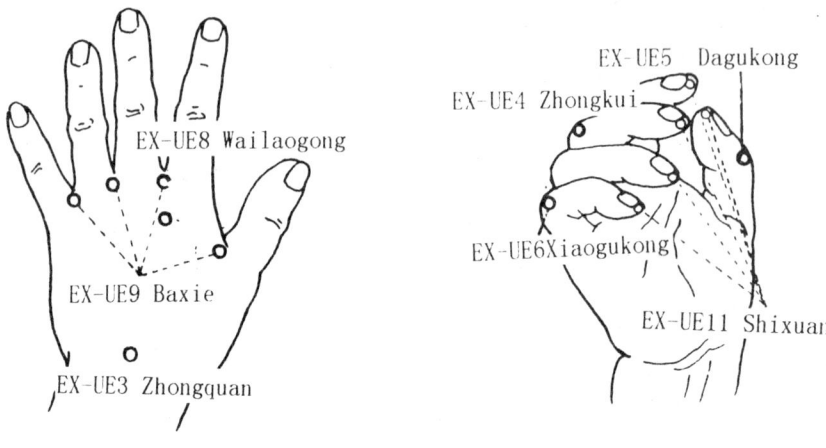

Fig. 12-15   Fig. 12-16

【Method】 Puncture perpendicularly 0.3-0.5 cun. Moxibustion is applicable.
【Regional Anatomy】 Skin-subcutaneous tissue-between tendons of extensor muscle and short radial extensor muslce of wrist.

EX-UE 4   Zhongkui (中魁)
(Middle Chief)

【Source】 *A Supplement to Thousand Golden Prescriptions*
【Location】 On the dorsal side of the middle finger, at the centre of the proximal interphalangeal joint. (See Fig. 12-16)
【Localization】 When the fingers are flexed, locate the point at the apex of the interphalangeal articulations of the middle finger.
【Indications】 Dysphagia, nausea, vomiting, epistaxis, vitiligo, toothache, esophagostenosis, poor appetite and gastric dilatation.
【Method】 Apply moxibustion with 3-7 moxa cones for 5-15 minutes.
【Regional Anatomy】 Skin-subcutaneous tissue-dorsal digitl aponeurosis. There is the dorsal digital nerve in this area. Its radial branch originates from the radial nerve, and its ulnar branch originates form the ulnar nerve. There are the dorsal digital artery from the dorsal palmar artery and the dorsal digital vein to the dorsal venous network of the palm.

EX-UE 5   Dagukong (大骨空)
(Large Bone Hole)

【Source】 *Illustrated Supplementary to the Classified Canon*
【Location】 On the dorsal aspect of the thumb, at the centre of the interphalangeal joint. (See Fig. 12-16)

【Localization】 Make the palm face downward, or make a fist. Locate the point at the middle of interphalangeal articulations on the dorsum of the thumb, or on the apex of the interphalangeal articulations on the dorsum of the thumb.
【Indication】 Diarrhea, opthalmopathy and vomiting.
【Method】 Apply moxibustion with 3-5 moxa cones for 5-15 minutes.
【Regional Anatomy】 Skin-subcutaneous tissue-tendon of long extensor muscle of the thumb.

EX-UE 6   Xiaogukong (小骨空)
(Small Bone Hole)

【Source】 *Great Compendium of Acupuncture and Moxibustion*
【Location】 On the dorsal side of the little finger, at the center of the proximal interphalangeal joint. (See Fig. 12-16)
【Localizations】 Make the palm facing downward or make a fist. Locate the point at the apex of the interphalangeal articulations on the dorsum of the little finger.
【Indications】 Ophthalmopathy, marginal blepharitis, cataract, deafness, finger joint pain and sore throat.
【Method】 Apply moxibustion with 3-9 moxa cones for 10-30 minutes.
【Regional Anatomy】 Skin-subcutaneous tissue-dorsal digital aponeurosis. There are the branches or tributaries of the dorsal digital artery and vein and the branches of the dorsal digital nerve of the ulnar nerve in this area.

EX-UE 7   Yaotongdian (腰痛点)
(Lumbago Point)

【Source】 *Concise Book of Acupuncture and Moxibustion*
【Location】 On the dorsum of each hand, between the 1st and 2nd and between the 3rd and 4th metacarpal bones, at the midpoint between the dorsal crease of the wrist and the metacarpophalangeal joint. (See Fig. 12-17)
【Localization】 Make the Palm face downward, or make a loose fist. The point is located between the 2nd and 3rd metacarpal bones and the 4th and 5th metacarpal bones at the midpoint between the transverse crease of the wrist and metacarpophalangeal articulation.
【Indication】 Acute lumbar sprain.
【Method】 Puncture obliquely 0.5 - 0.8 cun towards the centre of palm on both sides 0.5-0.8 cun.
【Regional Anatomy】 One of the points: Skin-subcutaneous tissue-tendons of digital extensor muscle and short radial extensor muscle of the wrist. Another point: Skin-subcutaneous tissue-between tendons of extensor muscle of the little finger and extensor muscle of the 4th finger.

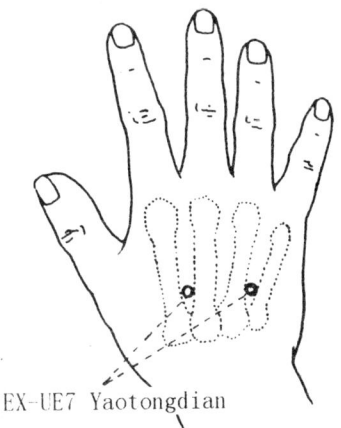

EX-UE7 Yaotongdian

Fig. 12-17

There are the dorsal venous network of the hand, the dorssal palmar artery, the superficial branches of the radial nerve and the dorsal branches of the hand from the ulnar nerve in the area of these two points.

EX-UE 8　Wailaogong（外劳宫）
（Outer Laogong）

【Source】 *Thousand Golden Prescriptions for Emergency*
【Location】 On the dorsum of the hand, between the 2nd and 3rd metacarpal bones, 0.5 cun proximal to the metacarpophalangeal joint. (See Fig. 12-15)
【Localization】 Make the palm face downward. Locate the point at the centre of the dorsum of the hand.
【Indications】 Inability of extention-flexion movement of fingers, numbness, itching, pain, redness and swelling of dorsum of hand, diarrhea and cervical spondylosis.
【Method】 Puncture perpendicularly 0.5-0.8 cun. Moxibustion is applicable.
【Regional Anatomy】 Skin-subcutaneous tissue-the 2nd dorsal interosseous muscle-the 1st palmar interosseous muscle. There are the dorsal digital nerve from the superficial branch of the radial nerve, the dorsal venous network of the hand, and the dordalpalmar artery in this area.

EX-UE 9　Baxie（八邪）
（Eight Evils）

【Source】 *Great Compendium of Acupuncture and Moxibustion*
【Location】 On the dorsum of each hand, at the junction of the red and white skin proximal to the margin of the webs between each two fingers of the hand. (See Fig. 12-15)
【Localization】 Make a loose fist. The points are located on the webs between the fingers of the hands 8 points in total.
【Indications】 Wind syndrome of head, sore throat, toothache, high fever, ophthalmalgia, swelling and pain in the dorsum of hand, numbness of fingers, tinea unguimum, malaria and snakebites.
【Method】 Puncture obliquely upwards 0.5-0.8 cun, or prick to cause bleeding. Moxibustion is applicable.
【Regional Anatomy】 Skin-subcutaneous tissue-dorsal interosseous muscle-palmar interosseous muscle-lumbrical muscle. In the superficial layer, there are the dorsal metacarpal artery and vein or the dorsal digital artery and vein and the dorsal digital nerve. In the deep layer, there are the common digital palmar artery and vein or the proper palmar digital artery and vein and the proper palmar digital nerve.

EX-UE 10　Sifeng（四缝）
（Four Seams）

【Source】 *Great Compendium of Acupuncture and Moxibustion*
【Location】 On the palmar side of the 2nd to the 5th finger, and at the centre of the proximal interphalangeal joint. (See Fig. 12-18)
【Localization】 Make the palm face upward. The points are located at the midpoint of the transverse crease of the proximal interphalangeal joints of the index, middle, ring and little fingers.
【Indications】 Infantile malnutrition, weakness (adding Zusanli (ST 36)), asthma, tuberculosis, infantile diarrhea, ascariasis and whooping-cough.
【Method】 Prick 0.1-0.2 cun to cause or let out small amount of yellow-white transparent mucus or bleeding.
【Regional Anatomy】 Skin-subcutaneous tissue-the tendon of the deep digital flexor muscle. The blood vessels in the area of each point are the branches or tributaries of the proper palmar digital artery and vein and the subcutaneous digital vein. The nerve in the area of the point between the thumb and index or between the index and the middle fingers is the proper palmar digital nerve from the median nerve; between the middle and ring fingers is the proper palmar digital nerve from the median nerve for the radial side and from the ulnar nerve for the ulnar side; between the index and the little fingers is the proper palmar digital nerve from the ulnar nerve.

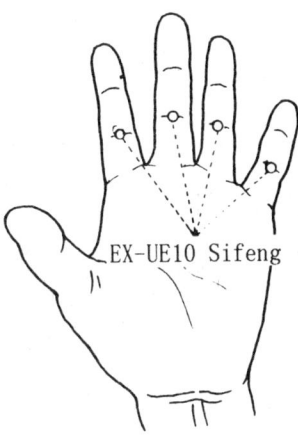

Fig. 12-18

EX-UE 11　Shixuan（十宣）
（Ten Drains）

【Source】 *Thousand Golden Prescriptions for Emergency*
【Location】 At the tips of the ten fingers and 0.1 cun from the free margin of the nails. (See Fig. 12-16)
【Localization】 The points are located at the tips of the ten fingers, about 0.1 cun distal to the nails, 10 points in total.
【Indications】 This point is often used for emergency case, such as coma, fulminating disease, syncope due to summer heat, sunstroke, febrile disease, manic-depressive disorders, infantile convulsion, vomiting, diarrhea, sore-throat, tonsillitis and numbness of the tip of fingers.
【Method】 Puncture perpendicularly 0.1-0.2 cun, or prick to cause bleeding.
【Regional Anatomy】 Skin-subcutaneous tissue. The nerves innervating the areas of the points on the thumb, index and middle fingers are from the median nerve; on the ring finger is from both the median and ulnar nerves; on the little finger is from the ulnar nerve.

V. Points of Lower Extremities, EX−LE

EX-LE 1   Kuangu (髋骨)
(Hip Bone)

【Source】 *Illustrated Supplementary to the Classified Canon*
【Location】 In the lower part of the surface of the thigh 1.5 cun lateral and medial to Liangqiu (ST 34). (See Fig. 12-19)
【Localization】 select the point 1.5 cun lateral to either side of Liangqiu (ST 34) which is located 2 cun lateral to the upper margin of the patella.
【Indications】 Leg pain, arthritis in the knee, foot pain, limited movement of leg and thigh.
【Method】 Puncture perpendicularly 0.5-0.8 cun. Moxibustion is applicable.
【Regional Anatomy】 Lateral side point: Skin-subcutaneous tissue-lateral muscle of the thigh. In the superficial layer, there are the anterior cutaneous branches of the femoral nerve and the lateral cutaneous nerve of the thigh. In the deep layer, there are the branches or tributaries of the descending branches of the lateral circumflex femoral artery and vein.

   Medial side point: Skin-subcutaneous tissue-medial of the thigh. In the superficial layer, there are the anterior cutaneous branches of the femoral nerve. In the deep layer, there are the muscular branches of the deep femoral artery and vein.

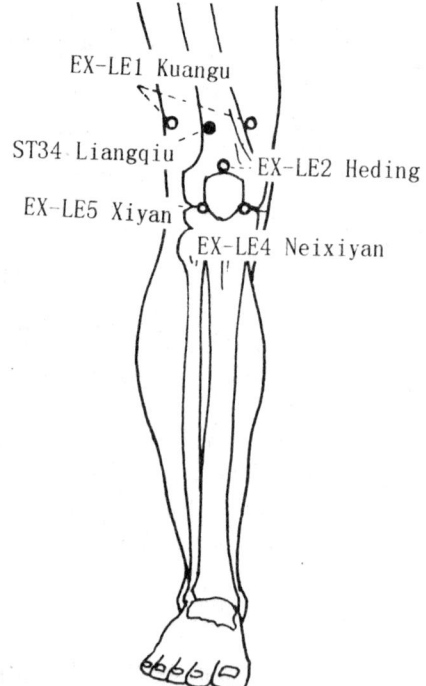

Fig. 12-19

EX-LE 2   Heding (鹤顶)
(Crane Crown)

【Source】 *An Outline of Medicine*
【Location】 Above the knee, in the depression at the midpoint of the upper border of the patella. (See Fig. 12-19)
【Localization】 Locate the point in the depression superior to the midpoint of the upper margin of the patella.
【Indications】 Weakness of feet and knee, swelling and pain in knee, arthrosis of knee and beriberi.
【Method】 Puncture perpendicularly 0.5-0.8 cun. Moxibustion is applicable.
【Regional Anatomy】 Skin-subcutaneous tissue-the tendon of quadriceps muscle of the thigh. In

the superficial layer, there are the anterior cutaneous branches of the frmoral nerve and the tributaries of the great saphenous vein. In the deep layer, there is the arteriovenous network of the knee joint.

EX-LE 3   Baichongwo (百虫窝)
(Worm Nest)

【Source】 *Great Compendium of Acupuncture and Moxibustion*
【Location】 2 cun above the medial side of the knee, 1 cun away from Baichongwo (EX-LE 3). It is therefore not the same point. (See Fig. 12-20)
【Localization】 Locate the point 1 cun superior to Xuehai (SP 10).
【Indications】 Malnutrition due to parasitic infestation, eczema, soreness in lower parts of the body, urticaria.
【Method】 Puncture perpendicularly 1-1.5 cun. Moxibustion is applicable.
【Regional Anatomy】 Skin-subcutaneous tissue-medial intermuscle of thigh. In the superficial layer, there are the anterior branch of the femoral nerve and great saphenous vein. In the deep layer, there are the muscular branch of the femoral artery and vein and the femoral nerve.

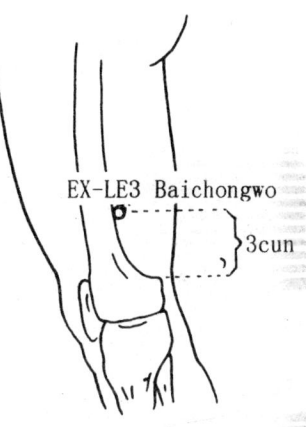

Fig. 12-20

EX-LE 4   Neixiyan (內膝眼)
(Inner Knee Eyes)

【Source】 *Thousand Golden Prescriptions for Emergency*
【Location】 In the depression on both sides of the patellar ligament when the patient's knee is flexed, the medial and lateral points being named "Neixiyan" and "Waixiyan" respectively. (See Fig. 12-19)
【Localization】 The points are located at the depressions below both sides of the patella, 4 points in total.
【Indications】 Soreness and pain in knee joint, arthritis in the knees, leg pain adding Kuangu (EX-LE 1) and beriberi.
【Method】 Puncture obliquely 0.5-1 cun towards the knee, or apply penetrating needing. Moxibustion is applicable.
【Regional Anatomy】 Skin-subcutaneous tissue-between patellar ligament and medial patellar retinaculum-articular capsule of the knee joint and alar folds.

EX-LE 5   Xiyan (膝眼)
(Knee Eyes)

【Source】 *Thousand Golden Prescriptions for Emergency*

[Location] In the depression on both sides of the patellar ligament when the patient's knee is flexed, the medial and lateral points being named "Neixiyan" and "Waixiyan" respectively. (See Fig. 12-19)

[Localization] The points are located at the depressions below both sides of the patella, 4 points in total.

[Indications] Soreness and pain in knee joint, arthritis in the knees, leg pain adding Kuangu (EX-LE 1) and beriberi.

[Method] Puncture obliquely 0.5 – 1 cun towards the knee, or apply penetrating needing. Moxibustion is applicable.

[Regional Anatomy] For the lateral point: refer to Dubi (ST 35).

EX-LE 6　Dannang（胆囊）
（Gallbladder）

[Source] *Testbook of Acupuncture and Moxibustion*

[Location] At the upper part of the lateral surface of the leg, 2 cun directly below the depression anterior and inferior to the head of the fibula. (See Fig. 12-21)

[Localization] The point is located 1-2 cun inferior to Yanglingquan (GB 34), where there is tenderness.

[Indications] Biliary disease. (stomachache, jaundice, biliary colic, cholecystitis, biliary ascariasis, etc) deviation of the eyes and mouth, lower limb paralysis and hypochondrac pain.

[Method] Puncture perpendicularly 1-1.5 cun. Moxibustion is applicable.

[Regional Anatomy] Skin-subcutaneous tissue-long peroneal muscle. In the superficial layer, there is the lateral sural cutaneous nerve. In the deep layer, there are the superficial peroneal nerve, the deep peroneal nerve and the anterior tibial artery and vein.

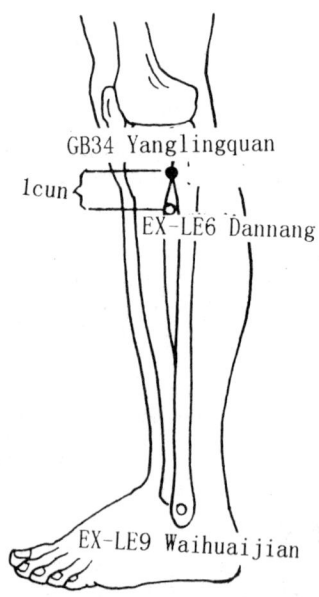

Fig. 12-21

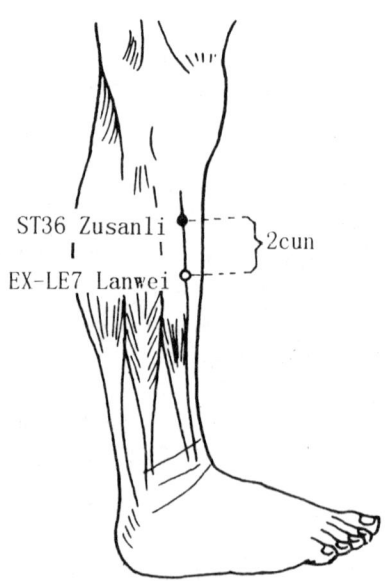

Fig. 12-22

EX-LE 7 Lanwei (阑尾) (Appendix)

【Source】 *Common Acupoints in Clinic*
【Location】 At the upper part of the anterior surface of the leg, 5 cun below Dubi (ST 35) and one finger-breadth lateral to the anterior crest of the tibia. (See Fig. 12-22)
【Localization】 In supine position with the knee flexed, locate the point 5 cun inferior to Xigan (EX-LE 5) (or 2 cun inferior to Zusanli (ST 36), 1 cun lateral to the tibia, where there is soreness, numbness and distending sensation when it is pressed.
【Indications】 Periappendicular abscess acute simple appendicitis, stomachache, acute abdominal pain, indigestion and lower limb paralysis.
【Method】 Puncture perpendicularly 0.5-1 cun, Moxibustion is applicable.
【Regional Anatomy】 Skin-subcutaneous tissue-the anterior tibial muscle-interosseous membrane of the leg-posteior tibial muscle.

In the superficial layer, there are the lateral sural cutaneous nerve and the superficial veins. In the deep layer, there are the deep peroneal nerve and the anterior tibial artery and vein.

EX-LE 8 Neihuaijian (内踝尖) (Inner Ankle Tip)

【Source】 *Thousand Golden Prescriptions for Emergency*
【Location】 On the medial side of the foot, at the tip of the medial malleolus. (See Fig. 12-23)
【Localization】 When the Legs are extended, the point is located at the apex of the medial mallelus, 2 points in total.
【Indications】 Upper jaw toothache, sorethroat, tonsillitis, foot spasm, infantile aphasia.
【Method】 Puncture perpendicularly 0.1 cun. Moxibustion is applicable.
【Regional Anatomy】 Skin-subcutaneous tissue-medial melleolus. There are the branches of the medial cutaneous branch of the leg from the saphenous nerve, the medial mellolar network of the anteruior tibial artery, the branches of the medial anterior malleolar artery and the medial malleolar branches of the posterior tibial artery in this area.

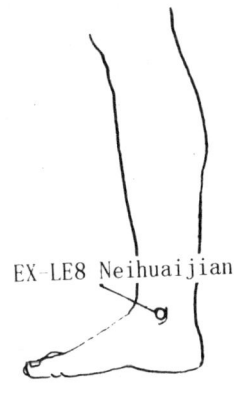

Fig. 12-23

EX-LE 9 Waihuaijian (外踝尖) (Outer Ankle Tip)

【Source】 *Chinese Acupuncture and Moxibustion*
【Location】 On the lateral side of the foot, at the tip of the lateral malleolus. (See Fig. 12-21)
【Localization】 The point is located at the apex of the lateral malleolus, 2 points in total.

【Indications】 Toothache, sore-throat and aphthae.
【Method】 Apply moxibustion with 7 moxa cones for each point. Acupuncture is not applicable.
【Regional Anatomy】 Skin-subcutaneous tissue-the lateral malleolus.

There are the lateral malleolar network of the anterior tibial artery, the lateral malleolar branches of the peroneal artery, the branches of the sural nerve and the superficial peroneal nerve in this area.

EX-LE 10　Bafeng（八风）
（Eight Winds）

【Source】 *Thousand Golden Prescriptions for Emergency*
【Location】 On the instep of both feet, at the junction of the red and white skin, proximal to the margin of the webs between each toe. (See Fig. 12-24)
【Localization】 The point is located at the margins on the webs between the five toes, 8 points in total.
【Indications】 Beriberi, swelling and pain in feet, redness and swelling in the dorsum of feet, irregular menstruation, tinea versicolor, malaria, headache, toothache, purplish toes and snake-bite.
【Method】 Puncture obliquely 0.1 cun, or prick to cause bleeding. Moxibustion is applicable.
【Regional Anatomy】 The anatomy of the one between the great and 2nd toes is the same as that in Xingjian (LR 2). The anatomy of the one between the 2nd and 3rd toes is the same as Neiting (ST 44). The anatomy of the one between the 4th and little toes is the same as Xiaxi (GB 43). The anatomy of the one between the 3rd and 4th toes is: skin-sucutaneous tissue-between tendons of the long and short extensor muscles of the 3rd and 4th toes-between heads of the 3rd and 4th metatarsal bones.

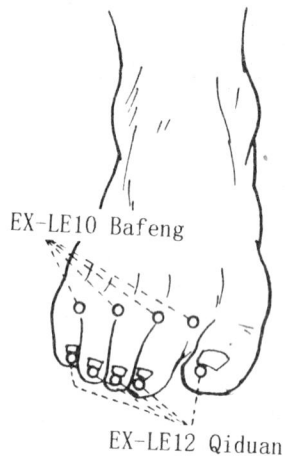

Fig. 12-24

In the superficial layer, there are the dorsal digital nerve of the intermediate dorsal cutaneous nerve of the foot and the superficial venous network of the foot. In the deep layer, there are the dorsal digital artery from the dorsal metatarsal artery, and the dorsal digital veins to the dorsal metatarsal vein.

EX-LE 11　Duyin（独阴）
（Extremity Yin）

【Source】 *Great Compendium of Acupuncture and Moxibustion*
【Location】 On the plantar side of the 2nd toe, at the centre of the distal interphalangeal joint. (See Fig. 12-25)
【Localization】 The point is located in the middle of the 2nd transverse crease of the 2nd toe.
【Indications】 Difficult labour, retention of dead fetus, retention of placenta, irregular menstruation, nausea, vomiting, hematemesis, chest pain, acute epigastric pain, acid regurgitation, hernia and infantile convulsion.
【Method】 Puncture obliquely 0.1-0.2 cun with the tip of needle pointing posteriorly and anteri-

orly. Moxibustion is applicable.
【Regional Anatomy】 Skin-subcutaneous tissue-tendons of the short and long flexor muscles of toes. There are the prope digital plantar nerve and the branches or tributaries of the proper digital plantar artery and vein in this area.

EX-LE 12 Qiduan (气端)
(Qi Termination)

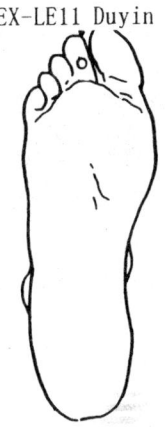

Fig. 12-25

【Source】 *Thousand Golden Prescriptions for Emergency*
【Location】 At the tips of the ten toes of both feet, 0.1 cun from the free margin of each toenail. (See Fig. 12-24)
【Localization】 The points are located at the apex of the ten toes, 10 points in total.
【Indications】 Beriberi, redness, swelling and pain in the dorsum of the feet, acute abdominal pain, wind stroke for emergency and numbness of toes.
【Method】 Puncture perpendicularly 0.1-0.2 cun. It's better to prick to cause bleeding.
【Regional Anatomy】 Skin-subcutaneous tissue.

Innervation: The point on the great and 2nd toes is innervated by the dorsal digital nerves from the superficial peroneal and deep peroneal nerves, and the proper digital plantar nerve from the tibial nerve. The point on the 3rd and 4th toes is innervated by the dorsal digital nerve from the superficial peroneal nerve and the proper digital plantar nerve from the tibial nerve. The point on the little toe is innervated by the dorsal digital nerve from the sural nerve and from the superficial peroneal nerve, and the proper digital plantar nerve from the tiibal nerve.

Vasculature: The points are supplied by the proper digital plantar artery from the medial and lateral plantar arteries of the foot and thedorsal digital artery from the dorsal artery of the foot.

图书在版编目(CIP)数据

经络腧穴学:英文/刘公望主编.—北京:华夏出版社,1997.12
ISBN 7—5080—1429—4

Ⅰ.经… Ⅱ.刘… Ⅲ.①经络学－英文②腧穴学－英文 Ⅳ.R224

中国版本图书馆 CIP 数据核字(97)第 25701 号

华 夏 出 版 社 出 版 发 行
(北京东直门外香河园北里4号 邮编:100028)
新 华 书 店 经 销
北 京 房 山 先 锋 印 刷 厂 印 刷
787×1092 1/16开本 33印张 1031千字
1997年12月北京第1版 1998年1月北京第1次印刷
印数1—3000册
定价:140.00元
本版图书凡印刷、装订错误,可及时向我社发行部调换